ALL ABOUT

ROASTING

BUTTERFLYING PORK TENDERLOIN
(PAGE 180)

Also by Molly Stevens

ALL ABOUT BRAISING

SEASONING ONE-HOUR ROSEMARY RIB ROAST (PAGE 93)

ALL ABOUT
ROASTING

A New Approach to a Classic Art

Molly Stevens

photographs by Quentin Bacon

wine pairings by Tim Gaiser

W. W. NORTON & COMPANY

NEW YORK | LONDON

In memory of my father,
E. W. Dann Stevens,
who loved to gather around the table.

CONTENTS

INTRODUCTION
THE **PRINCIPLES**
of **ROASTING**

1

BEEF & **LAMB**

2

PORK

3

QUICK GO-WITHS FOR ROASTED FOODS

A S YOU MASTER THE TECHNIQUE OF ROASTING, YOU WILL DISCOVER THAT A PERFECTLY COOKED ROAST NEEDS NO EMBELLISHMENT. IN FACT, A PER-fectly cooked roast often *deserves* no embellishment. It's almost a matter of respect, especially if you make the effort to buy top-quality, humanely raised meat and poultry. I realize, however, that there are times when we all crave a little something extra—a little piz-zazz on the plate. For these instances, you have two options. The first is to make a pan-sauce or gravy from the drippings left in the roasting pan. You'll find examples of these throughout the book and an explanation of how to improvise on page 31. Your second option is to make what I call *go-withs*—a variety of boldly flavored relishes, pestos, flavored butters, vinai-grettes, seasoned salts, and dips that complement the savory taste of roasted foods. *Go-withs* are made separately from whatever you're roasting and have the advantage of being hugely versatile. The following charts list all the *go-withs* in the book, along with suggestions for alternate pairings.

Salsas, Pestos, Relishes, and Condiments

	GOES WITH . . .	ALSO GOOD WITH . . .
Arugula-Pistachio Pesto, *page 412*	Salmon	Other fish, pork, poultry, steak
Blue Cheese Dip, *page 326*	Chicken wings	Steak, hamburgers, oven fries
Celery Leaf Salsa Verde, *page 429*	Striped bass	Other fish, pork, poultry
Charmoula, *page 131*	Lamb chops	Other lamb, beef, pork
Chimichurri, *page 66*	Tri-tip steak	Other beef, lamb, poultry, fish
Coriander-Fennel Salt, *page 503*	Oven fries	Other roasted vegetables
Dukkah, *page 508*	Roasted roots	Other roasted vegetables
Fig, Mint, and Pine Nut Relish, *page 118*	Rack of lamb	Chicken, pork
Garlic-Chile Mayonnaise, *page 503*	Oven fries	Burgers, steaks, tuna

Homemade Steak Sauce, *page 107*	Steak	Burgers
Hot-and-Sweet Soy-Cilantro Sauce, *page 430*	Striped bass	Other fish, shellfish, chicken
Roasted Applesauce with Thyme, *page 524*	Pork	Chicken
Roasted Corn, Tomato, and Black Bean Salad/Salsa, *page 456*	Burgers	Chicken
Roasted Lemon Chutney, *page 536*	Fish	Chicken, pork
Romesco Sauce, *page 291*	Roast chicken	Other poultry, potatoes
Sweet-and-Sour Golden Raisin Relish, *page 425*	Swordfish	Other fish, poultry
Tomato-Orange Relish, *page 434*	Trout	Other fish, poultry
Tunisian-Style Harissa, *page 158*	Goat	Poultry, beef, lamb, pork
Wasabi-Ginger Mayonnaise, *page 422*	Tuna	Other fish, oven fries

Vinaigrettes

	GOES WITH . . .	ALSO GOOD WITH . . .
Black Olive, Orange, and Mint Vinaigrette, *page 317*	Chicken thighs	Other poultry, salmon, lamb
Cumin-Mint Vinaigrette, *page 515*	Beets	Other vegetables, chicken
Green Olive Vinaigrette, *page 423*	Tuna	Chicken, lamb, beef
Kalamata Vinaigrette, *page 462*	Broccoli	Chicken, lamb
Tomato-Fennel Vinaigrette, *page 144*	Lamb	Seafood, chicken, pork

Sauces

	GOES WITH . . .	ALSO GOOD WITH . . .
Béarnaise Sauce, *page 82*	Chateaubriand	Other beef, fish
Creamy Mustard Sauce, *page 77*	Tenderloin	Other beef, pork
Horseradish Cream Sauce, *page 69*	Roast beef	Other beef, burgers, pork
Shallot and Port Wine Sauce, *page 73*	Tenderloin	Other beef, lamb

Flavored Butters

	GOES WITH . . .	ALSO GOOD WITH . . .
Blue Cheese and Chive Butter, *page 111*	Steak	Other beef, chicken
Chive-Shallot Butter, *page 413*	Salmon	Other fish, shellfish, steak

CONVERSION TABLES

MOST AMERICAN COOKS USE A STANDARD SYSTEM OF MEASURING LIQUID BY TEASPOONS, TABLESPOONS, CUPS, AND QUARTS. WHEN IT comes to dry measure, the customary U.S. system is again one of spoons and cups, but since weight is the most reliable measure for dry measure, many cooks (especially bakers) choose to measure dry ingredients by weight. For instance, 1 cup of flour can weigh between 3½ and 5 ounces, depending on the climate and method of filling the cup measure, whereas 4 ounces of flour will always be the same.

When converting a recipe from U.S. measure to imperial or metric, it's important to use a little basic kitchen sense. For example, the exact equivalent of 1 cup of water is 236.5 milliliters. In all but the most exacting kitchen laboratories, this amount can be interpreted as 250 milliliters. Likewise, if a recipe calls for 1 pound of peaches, and the market sells them in ½ kilo (500 gram) sacks, there's no need to fuss around trying to weigh out 453 grams of peaches. The key is to be consistent and follow the spirit of the recipe.

The Standard Gradated System of U.S. Measures

1 teaspoon	1 cup
1 tablespoon = 3 teaspoons	1 pint = 2 cups
¼ cup = 4 tablespoons	1 quart = 4 cups
½ cup = 8 tablespoons	1 gallon = 4 quarts

Liquid Measures

EXACT CONVERSION: *1 fluid ounce = 29.57 milliliters*

U.S. STANDARD	UK IMPERIAL	FLUID OUNCES	PRACTICAL METRIC EQUIVALENT	EXACT METRIC EQUIVALENT
1 teaspoon	1 teaspoon		5 ml	
2 teaspoons	2 teaspoons	¼ fl oz	10 ml	7 ml
1 tablespoon	1 tablespoon	½ fl oz	15 ml	14.8 ml
1½ tablespoons	1½ tablespoons	¾ fl oz	22.5 ml	22.2 ml
2 tablespoons	2 tablespoons	1 fl oz	30 ml	29.57 ml
3 tablespoons	3 tablespoons	1½ fl oz	45 ml	44.4 ml
¼ cup	4 tablespoons	2 fl oz	60 ml	59 ml
⅓ cup		2½ fl oz	75 ml	73.9 ml
½ cup		4 fl oz	125 ml	118 ml
⅔ cup	¼ pint or 1 gill	5 fl oz	150 ml	148 ml
¾ cup		6 fl oz	185 ml	177 ml
1 cup		8 fl oz	250 ml	237 ml
1¼ cups	½ pint	10 fl oz	300 ml	296 ml
1½ cups		12 fl oz	375 ml	355 ml
2 cups		16 fl oz	500 ml	473 ml
2½ cups	1 pint	20 fl oz	600 ml	591 ml
1 quart (4 cups)	1⅔ pints	32 fl oz	1 liter	946 ml
2 quarts (8 cups)		64 fl oz	2 liters	1.9 liters
1 gallon (4 qts)		128 fl oz	4 liters	3.78 liters

Weight Equivalents
EXACT CONVERSION: *1 ounce = 28.35 grams*

U.S. STANDARD (AVOIRDUPOIS) IN OUNCES	U.S. STANDARD (AVOIRDUPOIS) IN POUNDS	PRACTICAL METRIC EQUIVALENT	EXACT METRIC EQUIVALENT
½ oz		15 g	14 g
1 oz		25 g	28 g
2 oz		50 g	56 g
4 oz	¼ lb	125 g	113 g
5¼ oz	⅓ lb	150 g	149 g
8 oz	½ lb	225 g	226 g
12 oz	¾ lb	350 g	342 g
16 oz	1 lb	450–500 g	453 g
24 oz	1½ lb	750 g	680 g
32 oz	2 lb	1 kg	907 g

Oven Temperatures
To convert temperature from Fahrenheit to Celsius: subtract 32, multiply by 5, and divide by 9. To convert from Celsius to Fahrenheit: multiply by 9, divide by 5, and add 32.

FAHRENHEIT	CELSIUS	GAS MARK	DESCRIPTION
250	120	½	very low
275	140	1	very low
300	150	2	low
325	160	3	low/moderate
350	175	4	moderate
375	190	5	moderately hot
400	200	6	hot
425	220	7	very hot
450	230	8	very hot

Length

EXACT CONVERSION: *1 inch = 2.54 cm*

IMPERIAL	METRIC
¼ inch	0.5 cm
½ inch	1 cm
1 inch	2.5 cm
6 inches	15 cm
1 foot (12 inches)	30 cm

Butter

American cooks often measure butter in sticks; use the following table to convert.

U.S. STANDARD	IMPERIAL WEIGHT	METRIC
1 tablespoon	½ oz	15 g
2 tablespoons	1 oz	30 g
½ stick (4 tablespoons)	2 oz	60 g
1 stick (8 tablespoons)	4 oz	120 g

Some Useful Dry Volume Measure Equivalents

INGREDIENT	U.S. STANDARD	IMPERIAL WEIGHT	METRIC
Kosher salt	1 teaspoon	⅒ oz	3–4 g
	1½ teaspoons	⅕ oz	5 g
	1 tablespoon	⅓ oz	10 g
Grated cheese	1 tablespoon	⅙ oz	5 g
	¼ cup	1 scant oz	20–25 g
Bread crumbs	1 tablespoon	⅛ oz	4 g
	¼ cup	½ oz	16 g
All-purpose flour	1 tablespoon	¼ oz	8 g
	¼ cup	1 oz	30g
	½ cup	2½ oz	70 g
Granulated sugar	1 tablespoon	½ oz	15 g

Useful Equivalents

All-purpose flour = plain flour
Kosher salt = coarse salt
Cornstarch = corn flour
Superfine sugar = caster sugar
Heavy cream = double cream
Light cream = single cream
Cheesecloth = muslin
Parchment paper = greaseproof paper

SEASONING PORK PICNIC SHOULDER FOR PERNIL AL HORNO (PAGE 231)

PREFACE

W HEN I FIRST SET OUT TO WRITE A COOKBOOK ON THE TIME-HONORED TECHNIQUE OF ROASTING, I THOUGHT I HAD A PRETTY GOOD HANDLE on how to go about it. I would start by researching the history of roasting (the old English major in me never tires of the term-paper approach to learning), next I would establish an outline, and then I would head to the kitchen to develop and test the recipes. It was there, in the kitchen, that I began to lose my way. You see, it's not that my recipes weren't turning out well—they were. The dishes and meals that came out of my kitchen were as good as ever—my roast chicken was plump, with a glistening bronzed skin; the pork was tender and delicious; the beef meaty and luxurious; the fish exquisite; the vegetables caramelized and downright addictive; and so on—but I wasn't satisfied.

For months (actually years) I filled notebooks with shorthand recipes tracking my results for roasting all manner of meat, poultry, fish, and even fruit, but I still felt as though there were some elusive key, some template that I needed to discover. I kept fiddling with variables, trying different oven temperatures and different techniques. And then, one afternoon as I was reaching into the oven to pour vermouth over a sizzling leg of lamb, it struck me: There is no single path to perfect roasting. It's a process, a conversation between you the cook, the oven heat, and the food you're roasting. The variables are endless, and there are very few strict rules. Once this dawned on me, I realized that my job was not to offer an ironclad prescription for the single best way to roast, but to teach why we should embrace the various approaches to roasting (high heat, low heat, basting, trussing, and so forth) and to guide you in choosing which works best when.

The upside of my quest for singular perfection is that I did learn quite a lot about what really goes on when you roast and how the variables affect the outcomes, all of which you will find in The Principles of Roasting, starting on page 3. Here I outline everything from choosing oven temperature and what type of pan to use to handling the roast before and after cooking. The intention of this chapter is to help you become better at roasting and to provide you with the knowledge you need to roast without recipes. You do not, however, *need* to read this introduction in order to cook your way through the recipes in this book. Indeed, you can simply open to a recipe that appeals to you, and get cooking. All of the recipes reflect what I've learned about various roasting methods, and in each case I use the best approach to produce the desired results consistently.

If you do read the book in a more orderly fashion, you may notice that within each chapter I often start with the most basic rendition of a roast (usually seasoned with just salt and pepper). You'll then find a number of variations on the basic method, which include options like spice rubs, glazes, and sauces. I chose this setup for two reasons. Roasting makes foods so delicious that a well-seasoned yet otherwise unadorned piece of beef, chicken, pork, lamb, or even fish is something to be celebrated and relished, which is what these basic recipes do. But once you know and appreciate that, it can be exciting to embellish a roast with even more layers of flavor; learning the basic recipe gives you the freedom either to follow my options or to come up with your own.

In addition to the recipes in this book, you will find numerous asides on shopping for various kinds of meat, chicken, fish, and vegetables. I've included these because roasting, perhaps more than any other cooking method, concentrates the intrinsic flavors in foods; it only makes sense that starting with the best ingredients you can find will lead to better-tasting results.

Happy roasting.

ALL ABOUT

ROASTING

PRESALTING CHICKEN (PAGE 26)

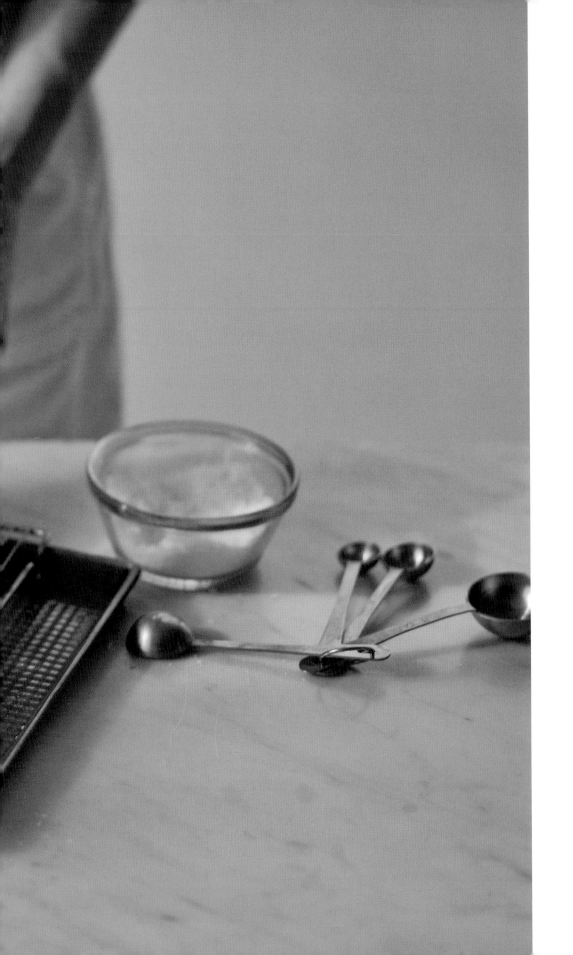

INTRODUCTION

THE **PRINCIPLES**
of **ROASTING**

ASSEMBLING PORCHETTA ROAST (PAGE 213)

A cook may be taught, but a man who can roast is born with the faculty.
—Jean Anthelme Brillat-Savarin, 1755–1826

I do not say with Brillat-Savarin that a good roaster is born and not made; I merely state that one may become a good roaster with application, observation, care, and a little aptitude.
—Auguste Escoffier, 1846–1935

T HE WORD *ROAST* CARRIES A LOT OF SIGNIFICANCE. THE MERE SUGGESTION OF SERVING *A ROAST* FOR DINNER CONJURES IMAGES OF JUICY, WELL-seared meats, caramelized drippings, crispy nubbins of goodness, concentrated flavors, and gustatory pleasure. Whether it's roasted pork loin or roasted asparagus spears, we expect a depth of taste and a certain succulence, whether from tender meat drizzled with lip-smackingly good pan drippings or a vegetable's inherent sweetness intensified and paired with a light touch of extra-virgin olive oil. We anticipate a handsome exterior, like the deep-hued crust of a majestic standing rib roast or the crispy brown edges of herb-roasted potatoes. Few foods whet our appetites more.

Successful chefs have long understood the universal, almost primordial appeal of roasted foods. The New York restaurateur Danny Meyer, who knows a thing or two about popular appetites, once said, "The best way to get people to try something new is to let them know it is roasted." Every accomplished home cook has a repertoire of roasted dishes, from a plump roast chicken for Sunday supper to an impressive rack of lamb for the most special occasions. Yet in researching the topic for this book, I learned early on that knowing how to produce a good roast dinner doesn't necessarily mean understanding the technique involved, and this can lead to trouble. To my mind, the finest cooks are the ones who understand the "why" behind the "how," so in writing this book I have set out to explain the principles behind this magnificent, popular cooking technique and to provide plenty of reliably delicious recipes. If you're just looking for a great dinner, be it quick sear-roasted salmon fillets or a more impressive pork rib roast, you may want to flip directly to the recipe chapters. If you're interested in understanding what's really going on in your oven and how best to control the results, I invite you to read this entire chapter. In the end, this knowledge will make you a better cook, one who is well equipped to improvise and problem solve when you set out to roast—with or without recipes.

What Is Roasting?

As a cooking teacher, I often begin my lessons with a definition, but to my mind, and for the purposes of this book, the standard definition of roasting that appears in dictionaries and culinary reference books—*to roast is to cook food, uncovered, by exposure to dry heat, especially in an oven*—falls short. When I scrutinize this paltry explanation, I am reminded of a quote by Michael Field, a legendary cookbook editor, author, and cooking teacher working in the 1960s and 1970s:

> *The linguistics of cookery are fascinating but at the same time so often confusing that I have sometimes wondered how a cook facing a stove for the first time coped with the language. It is, indeed, a language all its own.*

When I think of roasting, my mind travels beyond the technicalities of the inadequate textbook definition to imagine the goodness of the results. I agree that roasting involves cooking by direct exposure to dry heat, but I add that roasting produces a well-done exterior and a perfectly cooked interior. The role of roasting is to elevate already delicious ingredients by giving them a savory crust and maintaining their own juices and tenderness. Roasting implies more than a generalized technique; it expresses nuance and sensibility. Roasting denotes a direct, honest approach to cooking, as it leaves the inherent characteristics of ingredients intact while enhancing the intrinsic flavors and transforming them into the best expressions of themselves.

Roasting also carries cultural implications in the significant role it has played in festive meals and family gatherings from ancient times to the present. From cozy family suppers to lavish dinner parties to full-on traditional holiday celebrations, a big roast is often the most appropriate and appreciated focal point of the meal. Consider the Thanksgiving turkey, the Christmas roast beef, the springtime lamb, and so on. Hugh Fearnley-Whittingstall, the brilliant British chef and cookbook author, sums up the social significance of roasting like this in *The River Cottage Meat Book*: "Serving a roast has long been the most inclusive, magnanimous, and welcoming gesture a host can make to friends and family gathered round a table." I couldn't agree more, and in the chapters of this book I have attempted to include roasts for all occasions, from the most humble to the most lavish—and I invite you to gather friends and family around your table to share in this long-standing tradition.

AN ABRIDGED HISTORY OF ROASTING
(AND HOW IT RELATES TO BAKING)

THE WORD *ROASTING* ORIGINALLY referred to cooking in front of a live fire—a challenging and often inefficient technique that cooks throughout history have worked to simplify and control. According to culinary historians, the earliest roasting involved placing meat, game, or poultry in front of the hearth, on the floor or suspended from an iron hook, where the radiant heat from the fire would cook the food and heat the room in the process. The problem was that only the side of the meat facing the fire would cook, so someone would have to stand by to turn the food and regulate its distance from the fire. By the 1500s, resourceful cooks in the Western world began designing spits to rotate the meat or fowl so that it would cook evenly. That meant some unlucky soul (in wealthier homes, typically a servant, a "cook-boy," or a young apprentice) had the task of standing dangerously close to the fire, breathing in hot clouds of smoke, and turning the spit at intervals so the meat would cook evenly. Any inattention on the part of the turner would result in a poorly cooked roast. Advancements in kitchen technology led to mechanical spits and jacks that relied on springs or pulleys and weights wound like clock mechanisms and made the cook's job slightly less grueling. Even so, spit-roasting remained an all-consuming, labor-intensive, and dirty enterprise, requiring close scrutiny and a lot of stooping, turning, lifting, and sweating.

The precursor of the kind of oven roasting we recognize today began during the late eighteenth century in England and the American colonies with the invention of the free-standing iron stove, an innovation that initially had little to do with cooking. Instead, the stove was created in reaction to the increasing cost and scarcity of fuel. Benjamin Franklin, who counted an iron stove (the famous Franklin stove) among one of his many inventions, wrote, "Wood, our common fewel [*sic*], which within these 100 years might be had at every man's door, must now be fetch'd near 100 miles to some towns, and makes a very considerable article in the expence [*sic*] of families." (Proof that an energy crisis is not a modern phenomenon.) Since open fireplaces required prodigious amounts of wood and created formidable cold drafts, they were uneconomical. A closed stove, in contrast, could heat a room better and burned far less fuel in the process. Cooking in (or on) these newfangled "closed hearths," as they were first called, was secondary to their primary purpose of heating a home, but it was often impractical to have two heat sources in an ordinary home. The whole point of the new stove was to economize, so homemakers learned a new way to cook. As with most changes in domestic habit, not everyone welcomed the development. During the first half of the nineteenth century, there was a great deal of debate and hand-wringing over the loss of the open hearth in favor of the cookstove. Writings during the period reflected a lively cultural and gastronomical discussion on the merits of each. Some scholars and artists of the time decried the demise of the open hearth as a sign of moral decline and a threat to family unity. Cooks complained that the new ovens were small and cramped (merely a box inside the heated stove chamber) and therefore caused meats to steam in their own moisture and drippings. The British food historian Dorothy Hartley writes of this time, "Undeniably, much good English cooking, perhaps the best of English cooking, was lost when the oven door shut on the English roast and turned it into a funeral feast of *baked* meats." (The emphasis on the word *baked* is mine.)

Before the arrival of the cookstove, birds and beasts were always roasted in front of an open fire, while assembled dishes (what we would call casseroles), breads, and cakes were baked in a brick oven or under domed "bake pans" (basically an inverted bowl set near the hearth or covered in embers). To put it simply, baking, defined as an indirect cooking method by which food was surrounded by hot, dry air, mainly applied to casseroles, breads, and cakes. Meat and poultry were roasted; in other words, they were directly exposed to the radiant heat from a live fire. Early cooks were as clear about the difference between the techniques as they were about which produced superior results for meats and poultry. In *The American Kitchen Directory and Housewife*, written in 1867, the author states that "meat is better roasted than baked, but in these days of cooking stoves, the latter mode of cooking is generally the most convenient."

By the 1850s, the practicality of the cookstove prevailed, and roasting in front of an open fire had become the exception to the rule. And as people transferred their hearth cooking to the cookstove oven, they transferred the term *roasting* along with it. While the original technique of roasting effectively disappeared from everyday cooking, the term endured, but it acquired a new meaning along the way.

Over time, the words *roasting* and *baking* became interchangeable for describing the technique of cooking food, uncovered, in an oven. Yet some quirky semantic distinctions and persistent confusion remained. For instance, as early as 1872 *The Appledore Cook Book* explained how to roast beef, lamb, pork, veal, and whole fowl in an oven, while fish, ham, and vegetables were said to bake—same technique, simply different ingredients. This way of distinguishing between the two techniques based on the food being cooked remains. From *Fannie Farmer* to *The Silver Palate*, we are instructed to roast beef, whole chicken, pork, veal, lamb, and game, but we're directed to bake ham, fish, cut-up poultry, vegetables, and of course breads and sweets. Even the *Oxford English Dictionary* states that "baking is not sharply separated from roasting." Indeed, I once came across a recipe in *Gourmet* for Roasted Halibut with Garlic Sauce that instructed readers to "*bake* [emphasis mine], uncovered, until fish is just cooked through." I daresay no one following the recipe would have noticed that the direction did not correspond to the title. In light of the similarity of these two techniques, it's tempting to conclude that there is no real difference between roasting and baking, but I know in my heart (and in my gut) that roasting does set itself apart, in terms of both technique and nuance. Even the phonetics of the word influence its meaning, as *roast* ends with a seductive *st* that we make by releasing a little sigh of air with a flick of the tongue. As such, it carries the aesthetic of seared surfaces, caramelized pan drippings, and crispy end bits. *Bake*, in contrast, is a quieter, less provocative word, which brings to mind homemade breads, delicate cakes, and sweet cookies.

How Roasting Works: The Science Behind the Technique

The first step in learning how to roast involves a quick look at the science behind the technique. Here's how it works: roasting involves all three methods of heat transfer: radiation, convection, and conduction. First, heat radiates from the heated oven walls to cook the surface of the food. Second, whenever air is heated, it swirls, or convects, so that the hot, dry air inside a closed oven swirls around and transfers heat to the food through convection (even in a conventional, nonconvection oven). And finally, once the outside of the food heats up through radiation and hot-air convection, the heat then transfers to the interior of the food by means of conduction (a bit of conduction also occurs where the food meets the hot pan or roasting rack).

Understanding how to manage the first two methods of heat transfer is relatively simple: the hotter the oven, the stronger the radiation and the more aggressive the convection, so the surface of the food will cook more quickly. It's the final stage—the conduction of heat within the food—that gets a little tricky. To begin with, solid pieces of food are poor conductors of heat. Explaining the way heat moves through a piece of food, Harold McGee, the authoritative food scientist, notes that "foods behave more like insulators." In fact, the cellular structures of raw meat, poultry, and seafood actually *obstruct* the transfer of heat. What this means for the cook is that no matter how hot your oven is, the rate at which the food will cook is largely determined by how quickly (or slowly) the heat transfers through the food itself.

The greatest determining factor for how long it takes for anything to cook through is the shape and size of the food being cooked: the larger, thicker, taller, and/or rounder the roast, the longer it takes to cook through. The oven temperature and the temperature of the food before it goes into the oven will, perhaps obviously, also affect overall cooking time. Another factor to consider is the presence or absence of fat and bones. Intramuscular fat (the fat laced throughout a piece of meat) acts as an insulator, which means that a fatty roast will cook more slowly than a similar-sized lean roast. This explains why cooks used to thread strips of fat through the interior of lean roasts (a process called larding) in order to slow down the cooking and add succulence (for more on this, see The Role of Fat in Roasting, page 23). How bones affect roasting is not as straightforward, as some bones effectively conduct heat while others actually further insulate the meat (the difference has to do with the bones' configuration and composition). Also, the conductivity of food changes as the food cooks, so that a raw piece of meat takes a long time to heat through, but as the meat cooks, the heat transfer speeds up. This helps explain why a roast can go from perfectly done to overdone in a matter of minutes.

The challenge when roasting meats, poultry, fish, and even vegetables is that we want the outside nicely browned, which means it can reach temperatures as high as 400 degrees (the temperature at which significant browning occurs), but we want the inside to remain juicy and not overcooked, which means anywhere from 120 degrees for rare meat to 170 degrees for most poultry. That's a difference of more than 200 degrees between the outside and the inside. If we blast food in a hot oven, we'll succeed at getting an appealing browned crust, but it's more difficult to cook the inside perfectly. But, if we keep the oven heat consistently low, so the heat penetrates more slowly, allowing us to control its progress better, we may be left with a pallid roast.

So what's a cook to do? Fortunately, we're not limited to one single approach to roasting, and once you understand the basic methods, you can effectively control the outcomes.

DRY HEAT VS. MOIST HEAT

ALL COOKING METHODS CAN be categorized as either dry heat or moist heat, and roasting is definitively dry-heat cooking. (Other dry-heat methods are grilling, sautéing, and baking; moist-heat methods include stewing, simmering, and braising.) The most dramatic distinction between dry- and moist-heat cooking is that foods will brown with one and not the other. Compare a roasted chicken to a poached one or a baked biscuit to a simmered dumpling; the dry-heat one browns, the moist-heat one doesn't. This has to do with the temperature at which foods begin to brown (above 220 degrees) and the fact that foods cooked with moist heat can never reach temperatures above 212 degrees (the temperature at which moisture evaporates and thus becomes "dry"). It is therefore the dry heat of a closed oven that is responsible for all those lovely browned surfaces. As heat radiates off the heated oven walls and as hot air convects around the food, moisture is pulled toward the surface of the food, where it vaporizes, creating a dry surface and immediately allowing browning to occur (see The Science Behind Browning, page 12). The higher the heat and the longer the roasting time, the greater the drying effects. The benefit of dry heat is that it produces the handsomely browned surfaces we expect on roasted food; the challenge is that this drying effect can lead to . . . well, dryness, if the roasting time goes too long.

How to Roast

Today there are four or five favorite attacks on the roasting of beef. Each is successful in its own way, and it remains for the cook to compare results.
—*James Beard, 1972*

When it comes to roasting, James Beard got it right. You can "attack" it in any number of ways, and each has its own merits. Back when I first tried my hand at cooking in my mother's kitchen, ovens were not much more than insulated boxes with basic temperature dials. A good cook would strive to purchase the right cut of meat, select an oven temperature, season the meat, and slide it into the heated oven, and remove it when it was done. Today, developments in equipment and ingredients have given us ever more choices when it comes to roasting. Modern ovens offer various settings, often including convection, and most have a larger capacity than ovens used to, requiring the cook to decide whether to roast in the upper, lower, or center portion of the oven. Our understanding of the basic technique has broadened as well, and there is no single approach to roasting. What follows is an outline of the methods and their advantages and suitability for various foods. As you cook your way through this book, you'll find recipes that utilize all these methods to turn out beautifully roasted dishes.

Basic Roasting Methods
Roasting can happen quickly, with a blast of heat, or slowly, in a gentle oven. The decision of which method to use depends on the food being roasted, the desired outcome, and even your schedule.

High heat (400 degrees and up; or 375 degrees and up convection)

BEST FOR: *the most tender cuts, especially smaller roasts or those with narrow diameters, such as tenderloin. Good for small pieces of seafood. Also good for most vegetables and fruits.* The most straightforward approach to roasting entails cranking up the oven temperature to 400 degrees or higher, placing seasoned meat, seafood, or vegetables on a roasting pan, and sliding the pan into the oven. The greatest benefit of high-heat roasting is that foods develop a well-seared exterior with an appealing meaty savor and maintain a juicy, rare or medium-rare interior. That is, of course, if you don't overcook them. This one caveat points to the greatest challenge of high-heat roasting: It requires almost split-second timing. I compare the technique to driving a car really fast; you might get to your destination faster if you're going 80 mph, but you can't stop as quickly (and therefore might miss your turnoff). The same holds true for roasting at high heat. If you're hoping to cook a piece of meat to an exact internal temperature—say, 125 for medium-rare roast beef—it's very easy to zoom right past this in a super-heated oven.

High-heat roasting therefore is an aggressive approach, ideal for quick-cooking smaller cuts of naturally tender meats that are best appreciated rare or medium-rare, with centers that are juicy and pink. Many vegetables turn unbelievably sweet and tender in a super-hot oven as well. The major limitation of high-heat roasting is that it does not work well for larger roasts. With something like a bone-in leg of lamb or a whole turkey, by the time the center of the roast reaches the desired degree of doneness, the outer layer has become overcooked, dried out, and even charred. High-heat roasting can also create a lot of smoke, the result of the juices being drawn from the food and then splattering onto the roasting pan and the oven surfaces. (Frequently cleaning your oven should become a habit for anyone who does a lot of high-heat roasting.)

THE SCIENCE BEHIND BROWNING: THE MAILLARD REACTION

MOST PEOPLE UNDERSTAND THE term *caramelize* to describe how the surfaces of foods turn wonderfully brown and fragrant when cooked to a certain degree. To be scientifically correct, however, caramelization refers only to the way sugars (sucrose, glucose, and fructose) brown. It does not explain the browning of other components, including the proteins, fats, and nonsugar carbohydrates found in meat, poultry, fish, and vegetables. For everything that is not sugar, the browning can be explained by the less catchy term *the Maillard reaction*. Named after a French scientist in the early twentieth century, Louis Camille Maillard, the Maillard reaction explains how all foods (besides sugar) turn toasty, roasty, and brown when cooked to temperatures of 220 degrees and beyond. On a molecular level, as food cooks, moisture evaporates. As the moisture disappears, the fats, proteins, and starches begin a series of reactions that form large, dark-colored, savory, and aromatic molecules. Not only do these reactions change the appearance of food, but, more importantly, they create flavor—and tons of it. We don't need a scientist to tell us that these Maillard-produced flavors are deeper, richer, and more intense than any in the pre–Maillard reaction molecules. In fact, scientists do tell us that the Maillard reaction actually produces hundreds of new flavor compounds that can be described as everything from savory to meaty to earthy and even floral.

In cookbooks and food magazines, you will often see the term *caramelize* used to describe the browning of the surface of a chicken or a well-seared roast. While it may not be scientifically accurate, it is surely evocative. For the purposes of this book, I have tried not to overuse the word *caramelize*, but I draw the line at describing anything as handsomely "Maillardized." If on occasion I have evoked caramel to describe something nicely browned, fragrant, and appetizing, my intended meaning refers to the color and aroma and not the scientific explanation for how it occurred.

Low heat (225 to 300 degrees or 200 to 275 degrees convection)

BEST FOR: *tougher cuts like shoulder, round, and leg, and for a variety of pork roasts. Also good for certain vegetables with high moisture content, including onions and tomatoes.*

Low-heat roasting is slow roasting and therefore requires a certain time commitment—anywhere from a couple hours for sweet onions to all day for a pork shoulder. But the results are well worth the wait. Slow roasting is very much like traditional barbecue, albeit without the smoke. And as they say in barbecue parlance, "Slow and low is the way to go." With slow roasting, you won't hear the sizzle or smell the sear that you would when high-heat roasting. Instead, whatever you're roasting will slowly and gently cook to utter tenderness and succulence.

With slow roasting, there is less moisture loss, and foods cook more evenly. For instance, imagine a large top round of beef. If you were to cook this cut in a hot oven until the center was medium-rare, you would quickly end up with a very small eye of pink at the center of the roast surrounded by increasingly brown-gray meat as you moved toward the beautifully browned, crisp exterior. But cook that same cut in a low-temperature oven until medium-rare, and the "eye" of juicy pink would extend evenly almost all the way to the exterior of the roast. (That exterior, however, would lack the handsomely browned, crusty surface that high heat creates.) If you weighed the two roasts before and after roasting, you would notice that the high-heat roast lost a good deal more moisture than the low-heat one. The amount of moisture forced from food during cooking relates directly to how aggressively it is heated; therefore hotter ovens increase moisture loss, while lower-temperature ovens help foods retain their natural juices. Another advantage of low heat is a bigger window for doneness, which translates to less stress and more flexibility for the cook.

Perhaps the most miraculous aspect of low-heat roasting is how it can transform tougher, so-called lesser cuts like pork shoulder into tender, succulent roasts. These heartier cuts contain varying amounts of collagen (connective tissue), which remains chewy and unpalatable unless carefully—and slowly—cooked. A collagen-rich cut of meat will melt into tenderness when gently cooked to an internal temperature in the range of 160 degrees or above—well beyond the medium and medium-rare we're after when we high-heat roast. Also, when any piece of meat or poultry is slow-cooked over the course of several hours, it actually releases its own tenderizing enzymes, which further relax the meat as it cooks. And because these slow-cooked roasts lose much less moisture than their high-heat-roasted counterparts, they turn out delectably tender, succulent, and flavorful.

The disadvantage of slow roasting is that food doesn't brown well in a low oven. Even at oven temperatures above 220 degrees, which is the temperature when meats and poultry begin to brown (see The Science Behind Browning, page 12), the surface temperature of the meat or poultry stays much lower because of the cooling effects of the evaporation of moisture from the food. (The moisture loss may be less than it is under high heat, but it's enough to keep the surface too cool to brown.) In a hotter oven, although there's a greater moisture release and thus greater evaporation, the strong heat is aggressive enough to compensate and drive the surface temperature well above 220 degrees, allowing the food to brown up nicely. The hotter the oven, the greater the rate of browning. You can slightly increase the chances of browning foods when slow roasting by turning on the convection fan (if your oven has one). The drying effects of the fan will speed the evaporation so it doesn't cool the surface of the meat as much; it will also cause a slight increase in moisture loss, but not enough to worry about.

Moderate heat (325 to 395 degrees or 300 to 370 degrees convection)

BEST FOR: *larger cuts, such as whole turkey and pork loin roasts.*

Moderate-heat roasting offers a compromise between the extremes of high-heat and low-heat roasting, and, not surprisingly, you end up with some of the benefits and pitfalls of both. What I like best about moderate-heat roasting is that larger roasts and poultry have time to cook through without overcooking near the surface. Also, meats and poultry lose less moisture than they do in a super-hot oven but don't require the prolonged time commitment of slow roasting. Moderate-heat roasting is especially useful for lean cuts that risk drying out when cooked at high heat. One drawback of this method is that foods, especially those cooked in under an hour, don't brown as dramatically as they do in a super-hot oven.

High to low (or moderate) heat, or sear roasting

BEST FOR: *anytime you use low- to moderate-heat roasting and want significant browning.* A dual heat method of roasting can offer the best of both worlds: an initial blast of high heat (either in a 450- to 500-degree oven or on top of the stove in a skillet) to effectively brown the surface of the meat or poultry, and then gentle and even roasting to doneness in a moderate or low oven. Especially beneficial for larger roasts that would burn on the outside before the interior reached proper doneness if left at high heat, the two-step process is also useful for lean, smaller cuts, such as a pork rib roast, that are best nicely browned but that risk drying out if cooked at high heat.

For large, unwieldy roasts like a leg of lamb, it's easiest to use the oven for both stages, but for something smaller—say, rack of lamb—it's quicker and more direct to sear the meat in a skillet on top of the stove and then transfer it to a preheated oven. Depending on the size of the roast and whether it gets seared in a skillet or blasted in an oven, the initial high-heat step takes anywhere from 8 to 30 minutes.

Other roasting methods

• **Grill roasting** refers to cooking foods on a covered grill heated by charcoal, gas, wood, or a combination. Once covered, the grill acts like an outdoor oven, with heat radiating off the heated surfaces and hot air circulating around—plus you get the bonus of your roasts picking up that smoke-kissed appeal of grilled foods. The only special equipment you need to grill-roast (besides a working grill, of course) is a reliable oven thermometer. Place the oven thermometer on the grill near where you plan to set the roast and proceed as if you were roasting in an oven. Grill roasting works best at moderate (around 350 degrees) to low temperatures (closer to 250 degrees), but you can also build a two-part fire (or adjust the gas burners) to provide a hot side and a cool side of the grill, which gives you the possibility of sear roasting in your outdoor "oven." (Most recipes in this book that use sear roasting, moderate-heat roasting, or low-heat roasting can be adapted to work on a covered grill.) The one downside of grill roasting for those who like to make gravies and pan sauces is that this method doesn't easily yield any drippings on which to base these. (Some cooks will place a heatproof pan under the meat or poultry to catch drippings when grill-roasting, but the flavor tends to be mostly smoky.)

• **Spit roasting** describes the technique of impaling food on a skewer, or spit, and turning it in front of a live fire or other heat source, including gas or infrared. This primal roasting method hearkens back to the days before modern ovens, and it still has its advocates. Also described as rotisserie (from the French word *rotir*, to roast) cooking, it is used by many restaurants and full-service supermarkets, which attract patrons with the sight and aroma of plump chickens turning before gas flames. Some well-equipped home kitchens (indoors and out) boast rotisseries or spits, but since this is the exception and not the norm, I have not included recipes for spit roasting in these pages. If you are interested in experimenting with spit roasting, keep in mind that the food should be evenly impaled and trussed as necessary so it turns smoothly. Beyond that, this type of cooking is akin to grilling over a live fire, in that it requires a watchful eye and a willingness to learn by trial and error.

• **Wet roasting** is a phrase that appears in some cookbooks, especially Italian ones, to describe a method whereby a small amount of aromatic liquid (often tomatoes, wine, and/or lemon juice) is added to the roasting pan and used to baste the meat. To me, this doesn't constitute a separate roasting method, since nearly every roast releases a certain amount of juices, so the presence of a bit of moisture in the roasting pan doesn't dramatically alter any formula or recipe. (For more on basting, turn to page 23.) In many of my recipes, I use this technique to enrich the pan juices. Keep in mind, however, that you want to add only enough liquid to moisten the bottom of the roasting dish and not enough to cause the meat to steam. This means anywhere from a few tablespoons to a cup, depending on the size of the roast and the pan.

• **Pan roasting** is a term I see bandied about a lot, especially on restaurant menus. While I admit the term has a certain sex appeal, the trouble is, there's little consensus over what it means. For instance, the much-celebrated oyster pan roast served at the Grand Central Oyster Bar in New York City is a luxurious dish made of oysters quickly stewed in butter with a healthy dose of cream. Nothing roasted about it. On other menus, I've seen *pan-roasted* used to mean something cooked over moderately high heat in a skillet and frequently basted with butter (or another tasty fat). Another interpretation refers to searing the food in a skillet on top of the stove and then transferring it to the oven to roast—the one usage that involves actual roasting. In my recipes, I refer to this last technique as sear roasting, and I avoid the term pan roast altogether.

HOW ROASTING RELATES TO GRILLING
(AND WHERE BROILING FITS IN)

THE ORIGINAL DISTINCTION BETWEEN grilling and roasting is that the former referred to cooking directly on a grill suspended over a fire or bed of coals, while the latter indicated rotating the food beside the fire so it cooked evenly by indirect exposure to the radiant heat.

(The word *grill* relates to *gridiron*, a flat framework of metal bars.) In the advancement of cooking techniques, grilling has remained largely unchanged (aside from the development of more efficient fuel and more sophisticated equipment), and much of its persistent appeal comes from the primitive satisfaction of cooking over live fire. Roasting, however, has moved well beyond the realm of hearth cooking with real fire to become one of the most prevalent cooking methods in modern kitchens.

Broiling is a term that gets less play than *grilling*, but it is by definition nearly identical. Broiling means cooking by exposure to direct, intense heat (the root of the word comes from the French *brûler*, to burn). Many culinary dictionaries suggest that the only distinction between grilling and broiling is the direction of the heat source: To grill, we place the food over the fire; to broil, the food goes below the broiler. More general dictionaries, however, contend that foods can be broiled under or over direct heat, and make the distinction that broiling always implies an intensity of heat. For example, the powerful gas jets of a professional commercial broiler (known as a salamander) well illustrate the quintessential broiler. Either way, grilling and broiling both refer to cooking food, one side at a time, by putting it close to the heat source. (The meats best suited to these one-sided cooking techniques are quick-cooking and relatively thin cuts, like steaks and chops.) Roasting, however, refers to surrounding the food with heat—either the old-fashioned way, by rotating the food, or, as we do today, by placing the food in the center of a hot oven—and as such is a far more versatile and useful cooking method for everything from chunks of vegetables to the Thanksgiving turkey.

Roasting Times and Doneness Tests for Meat and Poultry

The act of roasting is simple; it's knowing when to stop roasting that presents problems. If you've ever overcooked a pricey beef tenderloin (I have) or started to carve the Thanksgiving turkey only to find that the thigh meat is undercooked (done that too), you know first-hand the distress caused by misjudging the cooking time. And while it's easier to remedy an undercooked roast than an overdone one, the best approach is to get it right the first time. But how?

Any honest cook will admit that there are no surefire formulas for determining how long a particular roast will take to reach perfection. Prescriptions of minutes per pound or minutes per inch can be helpful in getting you into the ballpark (for instance, will the turkey take 2 hours or 6?), but there really is no accurate or simple way to calculate the precise cooking time. The actual roasting time will be affected by everything from the shape of the roast to the efficiency and size of your oven to the temperature of the refrigerator where you stored the roast before cooking. The only way to truly know if a roast is done is by empirical evidence. Does it look done? Does it feel done (when you press on the breast meat or wiggle the leg on a chicken, for instance)? Does it smell done (a test all too often underrated)? And finally, what is the temperature of the center?

To appreciate the importance of proper doneness (and how it contributes to pleasurable eating), it helps to understand what happens to protein (meat, poultry, and seafood) as it cooks. Raw animal proteins consist of about 75 percent water, and cooking is all about managing how much of this water the protein will hold on to or release. Heat causes the network of protein fibers first to unravel gently (to denature) and then, with increasing energy, to tighten (*coagulate* is the technical term), and then ultimately to release the water the fibers once contained. When meat is cooked to rare or medium-rare, the fibers firm up enough to be pleasantly chewable (as opposed to raw meat, which is mostly unpleasant to chew unless it is chopped into tartare or thinly sliced into carpaccio) but still contain enough water to be juicy. As heat is continually applied and meat moves past medium into the well-done range, the fibers continue to squeeze tight and eventually eliminate a maximum of water, leaving the meat tough and dry.

This progression from juicy and rare to dry and well-done is most relevant when we are talking about red meat, namely beef and lamb. When we get into the realm of pork and poultry, we need to consider other factors. Because of the texture and protein structure of pork and poultry, few eaters enjoy rare or (in most cases) medium-rare pork and poultry the way they do beef and lamb (the exception being duck breast, which behaves more like red meat and can be enjoyed very rare). The temperature range for pork and poultry therefore is narrower than that for red meat, and because that temperature range is higher, it becomes even trickier to manage. (Remember, the internal temperature rises more quickly as the protein gets hotter, so it's actually easier to gauge a rare steak successfully than a fully cooked chicken breast.)

This doesn't mean, however, that pork and poultry should be cooked until completely well-done. Many of us older cooks first learned to cook all pork to maximum doneness to guard against trichinosis. Happily, the threat of this parasite has all but disappeared, and we now have a growing appreciation for pork, especially loin cuts, served with a trace of pink at the center. The same holds true for chicken and turkey; certainly we don't want to serve it rare, but that's not an excuse to overcook it either. Ideally, the juices of turkey and chicken breast meat should run clear, with just the faintest whisper of pink.

In the recipes in this book, I have offered doneness temperatures for meats, poultry, and some seafood (with seafood, it's often easiest just to cut into it and look). I have also provided suggested cooking times, but please keep in mind the wide range of factors that affect cooking times, which may explain why your rack of lamb roasts more quickly than mine—and vice versa. Below I have provided a list of recommended doneness temperatures for meat and poultry, and as much as I encourage you to use a thermometer to judge doneness. I think it's a mistake to become a slave to any doneness chart, including mine. Roasting is not an exact science, and doneness temperatures and descriptions are not irrefutable. There are no calibrated notches as we move from rare to medium-rare, and I expect a certain degree of subjectivity when it comes to judging doneness.

DONENESS TEMPERATURES FOR ROASTS

As roasted meats and poultry progress from rare to medium to well-done, their interiors change in color, texture, juiciness, and temperature. Below find my definitions of how these various stages look and feel. The chart then provides the corresponding internal temperatures.

Truly rare: Often referred to as *bleu* or blue, indicating a deep red, almost purple color, cold and slippery.

Rare: Deep red, cool and wet-looking at the very center.

Medium-rare: Deep pink and with red juices, meat beginning to firm up.

Medium: Rosy pink, firm, mostly clear juices.

Medium-well: Gray, few juices, quite firm.

		Out of the oven	*After resting*
BEEF AND LAMB	Truly rare	115°	120°
	Rare	120°	125°
	Medium-rare	125° to 130°	130° to 135°
	Medium	135° to 140°	140° to 145°
	Medium-well	145°	150° to 155°
PORK	Loin, rib, and tenderloin roasts		
	Medium-rare	130°	135°
	Medium	135° to 140°	140° to 145°
	Medium-well	145°	150°
	Shoulder roasts	175° to 180°	185° to 195°
POULTRY	Whole birds and breasts	165° to 170°	170° to 175°
	Legs and thighs	180° to 190°	185° to 195°

LESSONS IN DETERMINING DONENESS

SUCCESSFUL ROASTING DEMANDS THAT you pay attention to what is happening in your oven. If you're new to roasting and interested in getting better at judging cooking times, consider investing in a continuous-read or probe thermometer (the kind you leave in the roast with a display that sits on the counter) and use it to monitor the internal temperature of meat and poultry during roasting. Normally we wait to check the internal temperature until we sense a roast is close to ready (or until the recipe suggests it's done). As a learning experience, place the thermometer in the roast even before you place it in the oven and then monitor the temperature over time. You'll see that the temperature rises slowly at first, but as the meat or poultry cooks, the temperature increase quickens. Getting comfortable with this rate of increase can help you better judge a roast's progress. (For more on probe thermometers, see page 36.)

The next lesson is to learn to judge doneness by feel. If you've ever seen a professional cook poking a piece of meat, poultry, or fish as it cooks and wondered why, here's your answer. Raw meat and poultry feels soft and squishy when pressed or prodded. As it cooks, the proteins coagulate and water is forced from the meat, resulting in a firmer texture. At the far end of the spectrum, an overdone piece of meat or poultry will be stiff and unyielding to your touch. With experience, it's possible to identify the feeling of rare versus medium versus well-done, and the best way to do this is to press on the meat or poultry as it hits the corresponding temperatures on the probe thermometer.

Factors that affect roasting times

• **The starting temperature of the food.** Ingredients directly out of the refrigerator will take longer to cook than ones that have sat at room temperature for any length of time. Cooking is all about energy transfer, so simply taking the edge off the chill of a roast means it will begin roasting more readily and will roast more evenly. Unless you live in the tropics, there is no worry of meat, poultry, or even seafood spoiling when left at room temperature for a time (anywhere from 30 minutes to a couple of hours). Indeed, the internal temperature of a 3-pound pork roast left on a kitchen counter in a 70-degree kitchen for 1 hour will rise from about 40 degrees (refrigeration temperature) to 45 degrees—nowhere near the temperature at which foods spoil. The bigger the roast is, the longer it can sit out. For instance, a simple fish fillet shouldn't sit for longer than 30 minutes, while an enormous pork shoulder can easily sit for 2 hours to lose its chill.

• **The actual oven temperature and the oven's ability to maintain an even temperature.** Every oven heats a little differently, and very few run true to what the gauge on the outside reads. Positioning a reliable oven thermometer (see Thermometers, page 35) in your oven is an important first step in getting to know how it heats. Factors that are more difficult to assess include how well insulated your oven walls are, how often your oven cycles on and off (gas-heated ovens tend to fluctuate more than electric), and how often you open the oven door to check the roast's progress.

- **The size and shape of a given roast.** Even two roasts of the same weight will have slightly different conformation and composition. These affect their cooking time and make it impossible to predict cooking time precisely.

- **Your choice of roasting pans.** Deep-sided pans shield the meat from the heat radiating off the oven walls and thus slow the cooking time. Glass pans act as insulators and also slow the cooking time (see page 39 for more on roasting pans).

The Importance of Rest and Carry-over Cooking

It would be impossible to overstate the importance of letting meat and poultry rest after roasting and before carving. No matter how perfectly you manage to roast something, failing to let it sit undisturbed before cutting into it can instantly undo all your good work. During roasting (especially in a super-hot oven), the juices in the meat or poultry continually migrate toward the surface of the roast. Once roasting stops, the juices eventually stop moving and redistribute themselves evenly throughout the roast. The juices also thicken some (which, according to the modern food technologist Nathan Myhrvold, is because they dissolve the degraded proteins in the meat). But this takes some time (anywhere from 5 minutes to 40 minutes, depending on the size of the roast). If you slice into a roast immediately after taking it from the oven, the juices will still be on the move and will in essence drain from the meat, causing it to be dry, no matter what the internal temperature. In addition to giving the juices a chance to resettle and thicken, the period of rest also gives the internal temperature a chance to even out and stabilize. During roasting, the internal temperature continually increases. Once out of the oven, the insulating qualities of the meat cause it to continue to cook some (this is called carry-over cooking) before it begins to level off. The rest period ensures that the temperature has stabilized and you aren't serving a roast while it's still cooking. In addition, the rest period can ameliorate a slightly underdone or overdone roast. Even if the meat's a bit overcooked, it will be juicier once rested, and if the center was underdone, it will be somewhat less so after resting.

The ideal environment to rest meat is a spot that is slightly warmer than room temperature. I often leave the meat right near the oven, as long as there are no fans blowing hot or cold air. Whatever the spot, take care that it is neither cool nor drafty. In most instances,

I prefer not to cover the meat as it rests, since this can soften any crispness you've worked to create on the surface (or skin, in the case of poultry). If you do need to cover the roast, either because the kitchen is chilly or because you need to let it sit for longer than the recommended time, then cover it loosely with a tent of foil. This will minimize the heat loss and not make the outside too soggy.

The amount of time needed to rest and the expected amount of carry-over cooking relate directly to the size of the roast and the temperature of the oven. A very large roast—say, a full prime rib—possesses a significant thermal mass and will therefore continue to cook as much as 10 or even 15 additional degrees once out of the oven. The larger the roast, the longer it needs to rest. The internal temperature of a smaller roast, such as a rack of lamb, can be expected to rise only about 3 to 5 degrees once out of the oven. The rate of cooking also affects the amount of carry-over cooking: roasts cooked in a super-hot oven will continue to cook out of the oven longer than similar-size roasts cooked in a low-temperature oven. I have also noticed that the juicier the roast is to begin with, the more it needs to rest. In other words, large, rich cuts like prime rib or a belly-wrapped pork loin seem to suffer more when deprived of adequate resting time than leaner pork tenderloin or chicken breast. Having said that, I urge you not to underestimate the importance of rest, no matter the cut.

QUICK TIPS TO SUCCESSFUL ROASTING

- **Buy the best ingredients you can afford.** Roasting concentrates the intrinsic flavors and characters of a piece of meat, fowl, or fish. The better the raw product, the better the results.
- **Avoid deep-sided roasting pans for all but the heftiest, tallest roasts.** The goal when roasting is to allow the hot air of the oven to circulate freely around the food.
- **Heat the oven fully.** Don't trust the little chime that tells you the oven is up to temperature. Most ovens take at least 25 to 35 minutes to heat entirely. The only real way to know is to use an oven thermometer.
- **Use an instant-read meat thermometer for meats, poultry, and fish.** Cooking times vary widely based on the oven, the size and shape of the roast, and even the pan material. The surest way to test for doneness is by internal temperature (see Doneness Temperatures for Roasts, page 19).
- **Let the food rest after roasting.** During roasting, the juices are driven toward the center of the roast. When you let it rest, the juices redistribute and thicken and you get a juicier roast (see The Importance of Rest, page 21).

The Role of Fat in Roasting

As you read (and hopefully cook) through the recipes in this book, you will notice that many begin by instructing you to smear whatever you're about to roast (be it animal or vegetable) with some sort of fat. The main reason for this is that fat conducts heat much better than air. For instance, you can easily (and painlessly) put your hand into an oven heated to 350 degrees, but if you were even so much as to splatter your hand with 350-degree oil (the temperature of many deep-fryers), it would hurt—a lot. For this reason, a thin coating of fat helps transfer the dry oven heat to the surface of the food evenly, thus making the cooking process more efficient and promoting the wonderfully browned surfaces we crave; your roasts would look splotchy and dried out without it. The more fat there is on the food, the more the surface will, in a sense, fry, turning crispy and brown. This is why, for instance, smearing a little butter or olive oil on a chicken before roasting gives you crisper skin. Fat also adds a lot of flavor to food, and during roasting it lubricates and enriches as it melts and trickles down whatever you're cooking. A thin coating of fat also helps seasonings to adhere to the surface of foods.

Fat is often already present on meats—as in the fat cap protecting a meaty pork rib or a rack of lamb—but in other instances, notably vegetables and lean seafood, it must be added. The choice of fat and the amount depends on what you're roasting and what flavors you're after. Some of the fats I use in roasting are extra-virgin olive oil, butter, goose fat, duck fat, and lard or bacon drippings.

The Effects of Basting

I am not terribly strict about basting—that is, spooning fat, liquid, or pan juices over food as they roast. Sometimes I do, sometimes I don't, and the reasons relate both to what I'm roasting and to the more capricious elements of my mood and my schedule. Let's start with the practical side of things: Not all roasts produce enough juices to warrant basting. Since the goal when roasting is to preserve much of the natural moisture of the food (this is especially true with meats and poultry), good technique can translate into few juices in the bottom of the pan available to spoon over the top of the food. In this case, opening the oven to capture a teaspoonful of drippings to dribble over the roast hardly seems worth it. Also, if the food is well lubricated, either by its natural fat coating or by fat you've added, the fat will melt over the surface and keep it moist and glistening.

Before I start to sound too cavalier, let's look at the advantages—and disadvantages—of basting. The best argument I've heard in favor of the technique is that it cools the surface of the meat, preventing it from drying out. Basting liquid (as long as it contains some meat juices, broth, or other watery liquid and not just fat) will be cooler than the oven air (remember that liquid can't be hotter than 212 degrees without vaporizing). This cooler liquid evaporates on the surface of the meat and thereby brings down its temperature. It's similar to running through a sprinkler on a hot day, and as such is only temporary. In my experience, the better practice is to control the cooking of the surface of the meat by using combination cooking methods, such as sear-roasting.

However, I do like to baste when I'm planning on making a pan sauce and I want to enrich the pan drippings. In this case, I often add a bit of flavorful liquid (broth or wine) to the roasting pan to give some volume to the pan juices. Each time these get spooned over the roast (or poultry), they pick up some toasty, caramelized flavors from the surface. The flavor difference is subtle but noticeable. As a side benefit, basting with a flavorful liquid can result in more even browning on the outside of your roast.

Less scientifically, I sometimes baste simply because I'm hovering and like to play with my food as it cooks. Other times I neglect to baste simply because I have a zillion other things to do around the house. You certainly won't hurt a roast by basting it, nor will you ruin it by letting it be. You may alter the roasting time, though, since each time you open the oven door to baste, you let out a blast of hot air and cool the oven. Depending on your oven, you can expect to add 3 to 5 minutes cooking time for every time you baste.

FROTHING: AN OLD-FASHIONED WAY TO FINISH A ROAST

IN RESEARCHING THIS BOOK, I came across a reference to a technique that I'd never heard of called *frothing*. In his tremendous book, *The River Cottage Meat Book*, Hugh Fearnley-Whittingstall explains that frothing refers to sprinkling meat, game, and poultry with flour during the last 10 minutes of roasting and then basting every 2 to 3 minutes until the roast is done and topped with a crisp, brown crust. Curious about the origins of the term—and the technique—I did a little more digging. According to Dorothy Hartley in *Food in England*, spit-roasted meats were often dredged with seasoned flour, oatmeal, or bread crumbs and then basted toward the end of roasting, and this combination technique (dredging and basting) was indeed known as frothing. Liquids used for frothing included everything from boiling water to wine and fruit juice to beer. In a recipe for roast mutton, Hartley explains that mint tea "makes a good frothing." Over time, the term frothing seems to have fallen out of use, but the technique of dredging roast meats with flour (but not so much oatmeal and only occasionally bread crumbs) and basting continued. In the original Fannie Farmer cookbook (published in 1896) all recipes for roast meat and poultry included instructions to dredge with flour before and during roasting and baste frequently. Over time, however, this dredging and basting seems to have fallen out of favor. By the late 1970s, when the Fannie Farmer cookbook was thoroughly updated, there was little dredging and far less basting. I do know some cooks who will rub a fatty rib roast (or other rich cut) with flour before roasting to help it brown, but I find this can make it brown too much, and, more importantly, I generally prefer the purer flavor of meat and poultry without a flour coating. As for the last-minute frothing, I found getting the timing right can be tricky—if you start too early, the crust risks burning, and if you start too late, you will need to overcook the roast to brown the crust.

Positioning Oven Racks for Roasting

Ideally, you want the center of the food you're roasting to be as near the center of the oven as possible; this is where it will heat the most evenly. For low-profile foods like vegetable chunks and pork tenderloin, this means setting the oven rack near the middle of the oven. For something larger, like a turkey or prime rib, you'll need to set the oven rack down low so the roast will be centered. For something in between—say, a whole chicken—the best position is in the bottom third of the oven. In every case, I urge you to use your own good sense, basing your decision on the overall dimensions of your oven and, most importantly, your experience. For instance, the oven at my grandmother's summer cottage tends to get very hot near the bottom and less so up top; obviously, when I'm roasting (or baking) at the cottage, I need to adjust accordingly.

Although all the recipes in this book suggest an ideal oven rack position, I realize that most home ovens are designed to accommodate more than one rack of food at a time, and quite often we need to multitask our ovens. It would be inefficient—and misleading—to suggest otherwise. When you're sharing an oven and have to make room, it's a good idea to check on the food and turn it or rotate the pans (from low to high) if you notice that things are cooking unevenly. In many ovens, when you have two (or more) racks of food, the food on the lower rack cooks more slowly than the one on top. This is largely due to the fact that the pan on top shields the food on the bottom rack from the oven heat. If you can rotate to solve this, do so. If, for whatever reason, you cannot rotate the pans, expect the food on the bottom to take a bit longer and not brown as well. A good convection fan can help alleviate this problem. Also, if one pan of food is smaller than the other, put the smaller pan on the higher rack: it will be less of a shield. Finally, while using two (or three, if you have a commercial-size oven) racks at a time may be efficient, keep in mind that overcrowding the oven is never a good idea; always leave some space between the oven walls and whatever you're cooking. Roasting relies on circulating oven air, so you need to allow room for that to happen.

The one instance when I would counsel against sharing the oven would be when you are cooking something in a water bath, such as custard or cheesecake. Water baths are designed to moderate the oven heat so that delicate custards don't cook too quickly and curdle. When it comes to roasting, a steamy oven would slow down the cooking, but, much more importantly, it would interfere with the roast's ability to brown. Remember, moist foods don't brown well.

The Wonder of Salting Poultry and Meat Before Roasting

I learned about the importance of presalting protein when I spent a little time in the kitchen of Judy Rodger's Zuni Café in San Francisco. In Judy's kitchen, every piece of meat and poultry is presalted, often several days in advance of cooking. At the time I didn't question the approach—the food served was superb, after all—but I didn't fully understand it. Once back home in my own kitchen, I began to experiment and research the technique of presalting protein, and I soon became a convert to the practice, especially before roasting. To this day, I am still amazed at how significantly this simple step can improve the flavor and texture of poultry and meat.

Presalting relies on two facts: animal protein contains about 75 percent water, and salt is hydroscopic (in other words, salt attracts and absorbs moisture). These two facts mean that when used in the right amounts and at the right time, salt can actually help roasted meats and poultry stay moist. The practice does require a little forethought, but the improvement in flavor and texture is undeniable. Throughout the book, I encourage you to presalt in many recipes, but you can always skip this step if time doesn't allow or if you, or someone you cook for, is on a sodium-restricted diet. In my experience, the proteins that benefit most from presalting are the leaner ones (like poultry and pork) and anything cooked past medium-rare (again, poultry and pork). For this reason, I emphasize this technique more in the poultry and pork chapters than in the red meat chapter.

Dry salting

You can presalt food in either of two ways, dry or wet. After many years and many cooking experiments, I have developed a preference for dry salting over wet salting (also known as brining), so I'll start with an explanation of how this works. Imagine that you're getting ready to grill a big fat steak. Believing that the coals are ready, you season the steak generously with salt, but at the last minute you realize that the coals are in fact still too hot (this happens to me all the time). So you leave the steak on the counter, open a cold beer, and wait.

What happens to the steak? Within a matter of minutes, beads of moisture appear on the surface as the salt draws moisture out of the meat. This is why many cooks and cookbooks tell us never to salt a piece of meat in advance, admonishing that doing so will dry out the meat. But wait. Leave that salted steak for another hour or more and a remarkable thing occurs: The salt and beads of moisture disappear altogether, leaving the surface perfectly dry and the color a deeper red, so the steak looks not unlike a piece of dry-aged beef.

The scientific explanation for what happens to the salted meat involves the principles of osmosis and diffusion. In case you don't remember your high school biology, osmosis is the movement of liquid across semipermeable cell membranes. The salt on the surface, being hydroscopic, draws moisture from the meat. The surface moisture then dissolves the salt, so that the steak is—at first—wet with salty steak juices. Now the principle of diffusion takes over, whereby particles from an area of greater concentration move to the area with lesser concentration. In other words, to correct the fact that the surface is saltier than the interior, the salty particles move to the unsalted interior, dispersing throughout the meat. The steak reabsorbs the salty surface moisture, leaving the surface dry and the interior salted. The magic of presalting doesn't end there, however. Once the salt has been absorbed into the steak, it begins to transform the meat proteins on a molecular level, causing them to begin to unravel, weaken, and push away from one another, a process known as denaturing. The unraveling of the proteins makes the meat more tender, while the presence of the water-hugging sodium helps the meat to stay juicy even during cooking.

In addition to enhancing the texture of meat and poultry, presalting intensifies the flavor in a way that no amount of last-minute seasoning can. In what seems at first to be a contradiction, dry-salted meats lose a small amount of moisture to evaporation before roasting. This slight moisture loss is more than compensated for by the fact that a presalted piece of meat actually loses less moisture *during* cooking than its non-presalted counter-part. More importantly, this slight moisture loss actually serves to deepen the flavor of the meat or poultry, in much the way a side of beef loses moisture during dry aging.

A final benefit of dry salting is unique to poultry: crispier skin. As the salt gets drawn into the flesh of the bird, the surface—the skin—transforms from moist and flabby to taut and dry. During roasting, this drier skin browns and crisps more readily than it would otherwise.

Wet salting, or brining

Wet salting, better known as brining, is probably best known as an ingenious way to guar-antee a moist, tender Thanksgiving turkey, but it's also widely used for chicken and pork. This technique involves dissolving a measure of salt (and often sugar and other flavorings) in water and submerging poultry or meat in this solution for a day or two. As the poultry or meat soaks in the salty bath, it absorbs water and sodium, which makes it plumper, more tender, and seasoned throughout. Brining works on the same principles of osmosis and diffusion described earlier, with one important difference: The muscle fibers of brined meats swell up to absorb 10 percent of their original weight in water and salt. This ensures that the meat will remain juicy even when cooked to well-done.

My preference for dry salting relates to the added water weight that you get when you brine. While the water absorption does make the meat juicier, almost bouncy, brined meats can taste a little watered-down, sacrificing some amount of flavor to remain moist. With dry salting, the moisture trapped inside the muscle fibers by the sodium is the natural juice of the meat, giving us a deeper flavor. The juices may not gush from a piece of dry-salted meat the way they can from brined meat, but that's a small sacrifice for the enhanced flavor.

This slight advantage of dry salting over brining doesn't mean that I never brine. Brining remains useful for certain cuts of pork and for when I have less time (brining works more quickly than dry salting). Pork responds especially well to brining, which adds moisture and juiciness to what too often can be a dry eating experience. In order to counter the bland taste of added water, I take care to add plenty of seasoning to the brine.

QUICK TIPS FOR SUCCESSFUL PRESALTING

• **Presalt large roasts and whole poultry a day or two in advance (at least 8 hours ahead of time).** For smaller roasts, 8 hours will do, but longer won't hurt. The salt needs enough time to penetrate the meat (or poultry) fully and distribute evenly. Less time will leave the surface salty and the interior unaffected.

• **Cold slows everything down.** If you're short on time and trying to cut short the salting time, pull the roast from the refrigerator 2 to 3 hours before roasting. The salt penetrates faster at room temperature.

• **Trim meats and poultry before salting.** Protein and muscle fibers firm up after salting, making them more difficult to trim.

• **Use ½ to ¾ teaspoon kosher salt per pound of meat or poultry.** Use the lesser amount for poultry and boneless roasts and the greater amount for bone-in beef, lamb, and pork. If you regularly salt raw meat by eye, this may appear to be more salt than you're accustomed to, but I encourage you to trust the process. The salt will disperse as it penetrates the entire roast and leave you with perfectly seasoned—and moist—meat. I base these recommendations on using Diamond Crystal brand kosher salt. If you use Morton kosher salt, use slightly less. (For more on salt brands, see page 29.) If you prefer to use less salt than called for, by all means, do. You will still gain some benefits from presalting, although the difference will not be as dramatic.

- **Do not rinse after presalting.** The surface of meat and poultry will be dry with no evident salt after proper presalting (all the salt will have been absorbed), leaving no salt to rinse or brush away.

- **Add other seasonings at the same time.** Take advantage of salt's ability to penetrate the cells to further enhance the flavor of a roast by adding other seasonings. In Ginger Roast Chicken and Elbow Macaroni with Tomatoes and Pan Sauce (page 283), for example, I combine the salt with fresh ginger and ground black pepper. As the salt makes its quiet journey into the cell structure of the chicken, it carries along with it the flavors of the ginger and black pepper. The other reason to season now is that a presalted roast emerges from the refrigerator dry, almost parched, which makes it difficult for any dry seasoning (spices and herbs, for instance) to adhere, so it's simply easier to add them early, along with the salt. You can, however, easily smear a presalted roast with any sort of seasoned fat, spice paste, or flavorful spread.

- **Set presalted roasts on a wire rack over a tray or baking sheet.** This is not essential, but it helps salt disperse more evenly and allows better air circulation.

- **Leave salted meats and poultry uncovered or loosely covered in the refrigerator.** This helps dry the surface for better browning during roasting and is most important with poultry to promote crisp skin. If you prefer not to leave raw foods uncovered in your refrigerator (or if you've used a pungent spice rub), cover the roast loosely with plastic wrap.

WHY DIAMOND CRYSTAL?

OF THE TWO MAJOR brands of kosher salt readily available in most supermarkets (Diamond Crystal and Morton's), I prefer Diamond Crystal for its texture. As the name suggests, the actual grains of Diamond Crystal are flakier and larger than those of Morton's. In other words, a teaspoon of Diamond Crystal salt weighs less than one of Morton's. I find the larger crystals easier to pick up and control when salting by hand, meaning I'm less apt to oversalt, and the flakier crystals tend to dissolve better. In terms of taste, Morton's contains an anticaking additive that can leave a slight metallic edge. If you live in a very humid environment, you may still prefer Morton's because it doesn't clump as much (or perhaps it's simply what you're used to). In this case, I suggest you reduce the amount of salt called for in my recipes by 25 to 30 percent. If you're a salt fanatic, by all means substitute any favorite medium-grain salt. For instance, I often use medium-grain sea salt, or sometimes *sel gris*.

Pan Drippings, Gravies, and *Jus*

No discussion of roasting is complete without talking about the drippings left in the pan and what to do with them. Many of the recipes in this book give specific instructions for turning the pan drippings into a sauce or gravy, but for the most part, the best way to deal with the drippings is extemporaneously. In other words, evaluate what you have in the pan, decide what you have a hankering for, and wing it. Sometimes after roasting a chicken I do nothing more than drag a crust of bread through the gooey, savory, concentrated drippings to snack on; other times I drizzle them—as is—over the carved chicken; other times I use them as a base for a full-on sauce; and yes, sometimes, I admit, I ignore them altogether and just enjoy the chicken.

One of the most surprising things I've learned from all the roasting I've done in working on this book is how varied pan drippings can be—even when you follow the same recipe. Every piece of meat and poultry is unique and will, for any number of reasons, produce different amounts of drippings. The type of oven and type of heat will also affect the drippings. For instance, a roast cooked at low heat will produce fewer drippings than one roasted at high temperature. A convection fan will evaporate more drippings, and at the same time leave them more caramelized. Presalting meat and poultry (because it traps moisture) also leads to fewer drippings. These variables are one more reason that making a sauce, gravy, or *jus* works best on a case-by-case basis.

A LEXICON FOR PAN DRIPPINGS, GRAVIES, AND *JUS*

JUST AS THE STEPS to making a sauce from pan drippings are open to interpretation, so are the terms used to define these sauces. Here is a quick look at the terms I use (and some that I don't):

DRIPPINGS. This term comes from the days of spit roasting, when the juices that dripped from a roast as it turned before an open fire were called, not surprisingly, drippings. In the modern kitchen, drippings include the combination of fat and meat (or poultry) juices that are released during roasting. Some texts will refer to *clarifying the drippings* to indicate the process of skimming or pouring the fat from the meaty, savory drippings.

SUCS OR *FONDS*. These two French words are often used in professional cooking circles to refer to the meaty part of drippings that remain *after* any fat has been poured off. Unfortunately, neither of these terms translates easily (the word *sucs* means sap or juice, while *fond* means base or bottom), and as such, I prefer not to use them. Instead, I refer to the drippings as drippings, and leave it to you to decide how much of the clear fat to decant or to keep.

JUS. At its most basic, the term *jus*, the French word for juice, refers to the natural juices of meat and (to a lesser extent) poultry. The best example of a true *jus* is the pinkish liquid that collects around roast beef as you carve. The trouble is, you'd have to really wring out a roast to get enough *jus* to go around, so many times we enhance the natural *jus* with a compatible broth. In the kitchen (and on the table) a *jus* is an unthickened sauce made from a combination of pan drippings and any juices released from the meat or poultry during resting and carving.

GRAVY. Gravy commonly refers to a flour-thickened sauce made from pan drippings and enhanced with broth and, quite often, another flavorful liquid such as wine and/or spirits.

Basic steps for making a pan sauce

No matter what you call it, or whether you are making a thick gravy or a thin *jus*, the first few steps to making a tasty sauce are always the same.

- **Remove the roast** to a carving board to rest—preferably a carving board with a trough, so you can capture any juices that seep from the roast and add them to the sauce.
- **Evaluate the drippings.** Are there enough drippings to fuss with? Tilt the pan to determine how much fat is floating on the surface. Take a taste. Are the drippings salty, savory, caramelized, concentrated? If they taste bitter, scorched, or unpleasant in any way, it's not worth bothering. If they taste good, you might want to capture every last drop.
- **Pour off any excess fat—or not.** This is entirely a matter of personal choice. Depending on what you've roasted and what you're serving it with, you may welcome a few extra tablespoons of fat. Also, if you're planning to thicken the sauce with flour or any other starch, you can get away with leaving a little extra fat. Alternatively, if you're after a cleaner, lighter-flavored sauce, pour off most of the fat, being careful not to pour off any of the flavorful drippings. When you do remove fat, consider saving it for another use. (See Gleaning Fat from Drippings, page 33, for ideas.)

Once you have your drippings you can be as straightforward or as complicated as you like, and most of what follows builds from one step to the next.

- **Use the drippings straight up.** There's no law that says you have to amend the pan drippings; they are often delicious as is, and I frequently just scrape what little bit of drippings there are right onto the meat or poultry and happily call it dinner. Another excellent way to use pure drippings is to return the carved meat and any carving juices to the roasting pan. Turn the slices over in the drippings to bathe them and serve directly from the roasting pan. For a more formal presentation, coat the carved meat in the pan drippings and then transfer them to a serving platter.

- **Deglaze to add a little volume.** If you want to add a little more volume to your drippings and if there are lots of nice browned bits cooked onto the pan, you'll want to deglaze the roasting pan. Set the pan over a burner set to medium-low and add a measure of water, wine, broth, or even spirits (anywhere from ¼ to 1 cup, depending on the size of the pan and the number of guests at your table). Heat to a simmer, scraping with a wooden spoon to dissolve all the cooked-on bits. You can stop now or simmer to reduce a little, taste for salt and pepper, add any carving juices, and pour this over the carved meat.

- **Thicken deglazed juices directly in the roasting pan with a little flour.** The simplest way to make a gravy is to thicken the sauce with flour, sprinkling a tablespoon or so over the deglazing liquid as it simmers, and whisking vigorously so it dissolves without lumping. You can also avoid lumps by using a special, finely ground flour, sometimes called instant-flour or gravy-flour, such as Wondra. Alternatively, whisk the flour into a little water (this is called a slurry) and pour this into the simmering liquid. The dry method requires a little more finesse, but both work. Either way, be sure to simmer the gravy long enough to eliminate any floury taste and to enable the flour to thicken up the liquid. If it is too thin, add a bit more flour; too thick, a bit more broth. Taste for salt and pepper, add the carving juices, and spoon the gravy over the carved meat.

- **Or transfer deglazed juices to a saucepan to reduce and enrich.** For a more refined sauce, pour (or scrape) the unthickened drippings into a small saucepan (straining them if you like) and use them as a base for your sauce. Add more broth and/or wine, heat over medium heat, and simmer to reduce and concentrate the flavors. At this point, you can use any number of finishes—whisk in a few pats of butter, add some heavy cream or crème fraîche, thicken with a little cornstarch dissolved in water. (Unlike flour, which leaves a pasty taste unless simmered for about 10 minutes, cornstarch is tasteless. It does, however, add a certain sheen to the sauce and, unlike flour, won't hold up to extended simmering.) If the sauce seems watery even after reducing, this is the perfect place to use a little dab of meat glaze (see Shopping for Demi-Glace, page 75) if you have some on hand. If the sauce tastes flat, consider adding a few drops of lemon juice or a splash of vinegar. Fresh herbs are always good, too.

GLEANING FAT FROM DRIPPINGS

THE NEXT TIME YOU find yourself skimming or pouring the fat off a roasting pan full of drippings, I urge you to remember a favorite kitchen axiom: "fat is flavor." While you may not want that extra bit of fat in the pan sauce you're making or even just spooned over the carved roast, that doesn't mean you should discard it. Instead, consider transferring the fat to a little container and saving it until the next time you need a bit of flavorful richness. For instance, use a spoonful of roasting pan fat in place of butter when making a roux for sauce, or toss some into a skillet with olive oil next time you're sautéing vegetables. You can also combine the saved fat with olive oil to coat vegetables before roasting, or try warming the saved fat (it will solidify as it cools) to make a warm vinaigrette for a salad, or drizzle the warm fat over mashed potatoes, rice, pasta, or other grains (much as you would butter or olive oil). However you use it, it will add a welcome savory flavor to your dishes. I also like to use saved roasting pan fat to rub onto the next roast I make, for instance, a few teaspoons of fat saved from roasting a pork shoulder adds a nice meaty edge to my next roast chicken. The best way to store gleaned fat is covered and labeled in your refrigerator for up to 2 weeks. You can also freeze it, where it will last for a month or two.

Carving

A favorite book in my culinary library is a slim volume entitled *The Art of Carving,* published in 1959 by the editors of *House & Garden.* The pages are filled with black-and-white photographs of food celebrities of the day, including James Beard, Dione Lucas, and maître d's and chefs from classic restaurants such as Lutèce, the Four Seasons, and Prunier's in London, demonstrating their carving skills. The book is wonderfully old-fashioned—for instance, it assumes that every bride and groom *must* receive a "handsome carving set" for a wedding gift—but its message remains relevant: Knowing how to carve a roast may be as useful as knowing how to prepare it. Throughout the chapters in this book, I offer explanations on how to carve individual roasts, but there are a few guiding principles.

- **Have the proper tools.** Although you don't need an actual carving set, your job will be much easier if you have a sturdy meat fork (a two-pronged one) for stabilizing the roast as you carve and a sharp knife with a long, thin blade (at least 9 inches long). A smaller, thin-bladed boning knife can also be useful for dejointing poultry. Whatever knife you use, make sure it's sharp; a dull knife will actually toughen the meat, as the blunt blade tears at the fibers instead of cutting them, thus causing juices to run out. It is also very helpful to have a wooden carving board with a trough around the edges that is deep enough to catch the juices so you can spoon these over the meat or add them back to any sauce you're making. If you don't have a board with a trough, or if the trough is simply too shallow, consider setting the carving board inside a rimmed baking sheet to catch any juices (see page 65 for an example).

CARVING BOARDS (WITH TROUGHS)　　**ANTIQUE CARVING BOARD (WITH TROUGH)**

• **Carve across the grain.** Meat is made up of muscle fibers, and the direction of these fibers determines the grain of the meat. For instance, in tenderloin (pork or beef), the grain, or the fibers, runs the length of the roast. When you slice the tenderloin into medallions, you are neatly cutting across the grain. In other roasts—a pork shoulder, for instance—it may take a little while to figure out which way the grain runs (and this may change as you work your way through the various muscles that make up the roast), but carving across the grain can make all the difference between a tough and a tender slice of roast. Meat sliced with the grain will be tough to chew, no matter how carefully roasted. In instances when it is awkward to cut across the grain, angle your knife so you are at least cutting on a bias and not directly with the grain.

- **Make slices thick or thin.** Both have their advantages. Thicker slices are best for naturally tender roasts (such as tenderloin and prime rib), when there's no worry about the meat being dry or tough. Plus there's a certain visceral pleasure in digging into a generous slab of juicy meat. But if you're carving something less tender—say, top round or leg of lamb—aim for thinner slices for more tender eating.
- **Remove any kitchen string as you go.** If the roast has been tied, and especially if it's been stuffed, removing the string as you go helps it hold its shape.
- **Carve only as much as you will serve immediately.** Leftover roasted meat keeps moist if left unsliced. If people ask for seconds, pick up the knife and carve off a little more.
- **Take advantage of the pan drippings.** One of my favorite ways to serve a roast is to carve the meat and set the slices back in the roasting pan so they can soak up all those good pan drippings. I know it's not a very formal presentation to serve directly from a roasting pan, but it's a wonderful way to keep the meat moist and capture any tasty drippings. Of course, spoon any carving juices over the sliced meat as well.
- **Don't worry.** My final bit of advice is to relax and enjoy yourself. Don't feel pressure to carve in front of your guests, but don't be afraid to, either. Carving, especially at the table, is more about gracious hospitality than about perfection. If you appear to be at ease, your guests will be too. My little carving book offers the best carving advice, quoting an 1887 manual on household etiquette: "Avoid all scowling or contortion of the mouth if a difficult spot is touched." It offers sage advice for your guests as well: "Never stare at the carver. Remember you are invited to dine, not to take a lesson in carving."

Roasting Equipment

Thermometers

A well-equipped kitchen needs two thermometers, one for the roasts and one for the oven.

MEAT THERMOMETER. Forget the roasting pans and carving forks—the single most important piece of kitchen equipment for roasting (beyond an oven) is a reliable meat thermometer. A meat thermometer allows you to gauge the progress and determine the doneness of all manner of meat, poultry, and even fish. When I started cooking in my mother's kitchen, her meat thermometer was a sturdy affair sporting a square, glass-encased face and a blunt, ½-inch-thick stem that you inserted into the meat before roasting. You could watch the temperature needle climb as the internal temperature of the meat rose. The problem with these primitive models was that they lacked accuracy; many didn't even list actual temperatures but simply offered ranges for beef, poultry, and pork (most of them too high). They also left a large hole in your roast. Fortunately, a whole slew of more accurate meat thermometers that are much less damaging to your food are now available.

You'll see that in this book I refer to a meat thermometer as an *instant-read thermometer*. The term *meat thermometer* is a little outdated, because today's cooks use thermometers to check everything from meat and poultry to breads and custards. *Instant-read* refers to the fact that our modern thermometers provide a reading very quickly after they come in direct contact with the food. Unlike my mother's old meat thermometer, instant-read thermometers are not meant to be left in the roast—a very important detail to remember, as many have plastic parts that would melt very quickly in a hot oven.

When shopping for an instant-read thermometer, you will find everything from a simple pocket-size model for less than $10 to a commercial type that costs upward of $100. Here I have listed the various types of thermometers along with their advantages and disadvantages.

- The most basic instant-read thermometer is a small **dial thermometer** that houses a coil of wires that contract and expand according to the temperature of whatever is in contact with the metal tip. The advantage of dial thermometers is that they require no batteries to operate and they are inexpensive. The downside is that they take longer than other kinds to get a reading—as long as 15 seconds—which means leaving the oven door open longer. They also tend to be rather fragile and easily go out of whack if you drop them on the floor.
- The next step up is a **digital thermometer** that has an electronic sensor in the tip of the probe which sends a reading to the face. These can be simple pocket-size thermometers or the more complicated continuous-read, or probe, thermometers.
- **Probe thermometers** are two-part thermometers with a heatproof cable that connects the probe (the part that gets inserted in the food) to the digital display. The idea is that you leave the display on the countertop, so you can keep an eye on the progress of your roast without opening the oven to check. Many cooks find these handy and like the reassurance of being able to watch the internal temperature of the roast climb. Many models even come with alarms that you can set to alert you when the roast reaches your desired temperature. If you do decide to use a probe thermometer, I recommend that you set the alarm 10 degrees lower than your target temperature. When it sounds, remove the probe (using an oven mitt) and test a few other spots to be sure you're getting an accurate reading.
- Many newer ovens come equipped with **built-in probe thermometers.** The probe is

attached to a cable that you plug into a socket on the oven wall and the temperature readout appears with the oven controls. While I like these in theory, many force you to set a target temperature, and the oven turns itself off as soon as the meat reaches that target temperature. Call me a Luddite, but I find this enormously frustrating—especially when I'm cooking more than one thing at a time in the oven. My solution is simply to set the target temperature too high, but this somewhat defeats the purpose, because you need to monitor the display carefully.

• Of all the thermometers I've used (and I still keep several around), I reach most often for my **Thermapen**. This is a folding digital thermometer that provides a super-fast readout, and I mean fast—in less than 4 seconds. I also like the fact that the probe is thinner than most, making it useful for thin steaks and delicate fish. Finally, this thermometer seems to stand up better than any others to heavy-duty usage, which is important in my kitchen. The only drawback I've found is the price tag—in the $90 range. Something for your holiday wish list, perhaps!

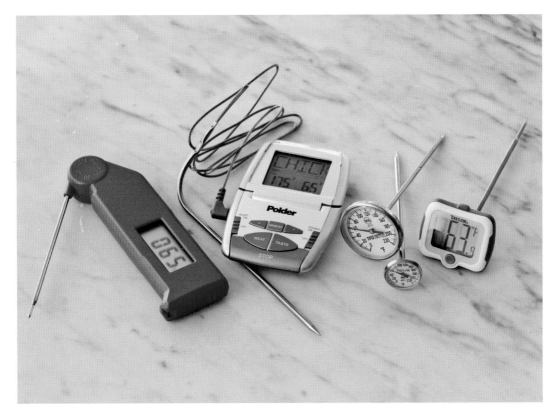

INSTANT-READ THERMOMETERS: (FROM LEFT TO RIGHT) THERMAPEN, PROBE THERMOMETER, DIAL THERMOMETERS, DIGITAL THERMOMETER

TIPS FOR USING AN INSTANT-READ THERMOMETER

REGARDLESS OF WHAT KIND of thermometer you use, here are a few tips for doing so.

- Verify the accuracy of the thermometer occasionally. This is especially important for the less expensive dial models and for any thermometers that bang around in a utensil drawer. To check the accuracy, bring a small pot of water to a strong boil and test the temperature. Depending on your altitude, it should be close to 212 degrees. Some models can be recalibrated (the simple dial ones have a hex nut at the top of the stem that you turn with a wrench). It may also be time for a new thermometer.
- Check the temperature of the roast *before* the suggested cooking time is up. Every oven cooks a little differently, and it's good practice to check on the progress of your roast as it cooks.
- Check the temperature when you think the roast may be close to done, but don't check it incessantly. Every time you open the oven door to check the temperature, you lose a good deal of heat and slow the cooking. Plus, each time you poke the roast with the thermometer juices run out. Excessive probing can dry out the roast.
- It's often most efficient to check the temperature of the roast *without* removing it from the oven. This does, however, mean leaving the oven door open, reaching into a hot oven, maneuvering around a sizzling roast, and, in the case of a floor-mounted oven, stooping to get an accurate read. If you prefer to remove the roast from the oven and set it on the counter (closing the oven door as you do so) to determine the internal temperature, by all means, do so. Just keep in mind that every minute the roast sits out of the oven will add several minutes to the roasting time.
- Measure food temperature in a few spots. There are vagaries in the composition of every piece of meat (and fowl), so you do well to test in a few spots.
- Wash the probe of the thermometer thoroughly with soapy water after checking underdone meat and poultry before rechecking. Since underdone animal proteins can contain harmful bacteria, you don't want to spread them by using a contaminated thermometer.

OVEN THERMOMETER. No matter what kind of oven you have (or how new or fancy it is), there's a very good possibility that it runs cooler or hotter than the temperature displayed, and this can affect your roasting time. The best practice is to set an oven thermometer on the rack to help you monitor the actual oven temperature. This is also helpful in determining when the oven is fully preheated. Using an oven thermometer helps you get to know your oven better. When using an oven thermometer, if you find a great disparity (25 degrees or more) between the temperature setting and the actual temperature, then you have two choices: Call to have someone come and recalibrate the oven thermostat, or make your own adjustments by setting the oven either higher or lower as needed. This second solution can be tricky, because chances are the oven thermostat will get worse, so be sure to check the oven thermometer regularly.

You can shop for oven thermometers in the equipment section of most well-stocked supermarkets. If you roast a lot, you may find that eventually the glass face of the thermometer gets as too dirty to see through. Try scrubbing it with scouring powder, being careful not to get water in the works. Leaving it in the oven during a self-cleaning cycle can burn out most regular models, so I don't recommend it. Thankfully, most are inexpensive, so you may just elect to replace them regularly.

Roasting pans

When I set out to write this book, I imagined myself investing in a slew of new roasting pans—I even worried about how much that might set me back and where I might store them all. As I dug into the rigorous recipe development and testing, however, I found that I really only needed a few pans, many of which most cooks will have in the cupboard. In addition to the specifics outlined below, the best pans for roasting have flat bottoms with no raised patterns or ridges (these can make it hard to deglaze when making pan sauces, and they can interfere when turning delicate foods). Also, I discourage the use of nonstick surfaces for any roast where you want to capture the drippings for a sauce. For vegetables and other recipes in which I suggest lining the pan with parchment paper, nonstick pans are a fine choice. Here are the pans I use most:

HEAVY-DUTY RIMMED BAKING SHEETS. No other pans get as much action in my kitchen as my set of rimmed baking sheets. Also known as sheet pans (or half- and quarter-sheet pans and jelly-roll pans), these look like an average cookie sheet with one notable exception: a sturdy 1-inch rim that prevents food from sliding off. They are ideal for roasting because their low sides expose the food to as much hot oven air as possible, shy of roasting directly on the oven rack. I use them mainly for vegetables and small cuts of meat, poultry, and fish. For really large, heavy roasts, and when I plan to make a sauce from the drippings, I generally use a roasting pan. Baking sheets tend to buckle and scorch if you try to heat the drippings on top of the stove after roasting. It's not impossible to start a pan sauce on a baking sheet, just not ideal.

Not long ago, the only place to buy heavy-duty rimmed baking sheets was restaurant supply stores (these durable pans are a mainstay of most restaurant kitchens). These days you can find them at any good kitchenware store and on-line (see Sources & Resources, page 539). Avoid insulated baking sheets or those coated with any sort of nonstick surface. Look for the words *commercial quality* or *heavy-duty*; anything less will warp in the oven. The standard size is 18 by 12 inches. It's worth looking for a nesting set of three that includes two smaller pans (16 by 11 inches and 13 by 9 inches). Don't fret over exact measurements; every manufacturer differs slightly. Reliable brands are Norpro and Chicago Metallic. If you don't have a heavy-duty baking sheet, the bottom part of a standard enameled-steel broiler pan works well.

HEAVY-DUTY RIMMED BAKING SHEETS

ROASTING PANS. Even though my baking sheet pans get a workout (and yours will too if you cook your way though this book), I would be lost without one, preferably two, serious roasting pans. For any of the larger roasts (such as whole turkey, prime rib, leg of lamb, pork shoulder), you will have much better results if you use the proper pan—and you'll be safer too. If you've ever had to roast the Thanksgiving turkey in one of those disposable aluminum "roasting pans" sold at the supermarket, you know how tricky it can be to maneuver a steaming-hot 13-pound bird around the kitchen in a flimsy pan. Plus a sturdy roasting pan is essential for making pan gravy on top of the stove.

ROASTING PANS

When choosing a roasting pan, be sure to find one that has heft, so it will support the weight of the roast, so it will not warp or buckle when exposed to high heat, and so you'll get an even distribution of heat, which reduces hot spots and scorched drippings. If you're shopping at a bricks-and-mortar store, it's easy to tell the difference between something with substance and something flimsy. If you're shopping on-line, you'll have to read the product details to find out how much it weighs. If it's only a pound or two, keep looking. However, if it weighs in at 13 pounds (and trust me, some do), then you'll have to ask yourself if you can manage a 13-pound pan plus a 15-pound roast. My favorite pans are somewhere in between—in the 6- to 8-pound range. Bottom line: Buy the heaviest pan you can lift (and afford).

The heftiest roasting pans are made from stainless steel, and I like this material for its bright surface, which enables me to evaluate the drippings well. (I find that the darker anodized aluminum pans make it hard to determine whether the drippings are nicely browned or scorched.) Stainless steel is a poor conductor of heat, and to counteract this, many of the better manufacturers sandwich a layer of a more conductive metal (aluminum or copper) between the layers of stainless steel to make their pans. You will pay more for these, but they do perform better. Many manufacturers offer nonstick roasting pans, and while these do facilitate cleanup, your pan sauces and gravies will be lacking, because it's the fact that the drippings stick (and caramelize) that gives sauces their character and flavor.

When it comes to shape, look for a pan with sides that are about 3 inches high; any higher and they will shield the food too much, lower and they won't protect you enough from sloshing pan juices. The pan should also have sturdy handles, which to my mind means fixed, riveted handles, not thinner, wire-bale handles that flop down when not in use. Keep in mind, however, that fixed handles add width and height to the overall dimensions, so you might want to measure the inside of your oven (and perhaps your kitchen cabinet) to make sure the pan will fit. If storage is at a premium, fold-down handles may make more sense.

Lately I've seen more and more oval lidded roasters, but I don't have much use for these. First off, cooking with a lid on is no longer roasting. Second, I find the oval shape less useful than the standard rectangular.

The overall dimensions depend on how you cook. For instance, if you plan never to host Thanksgiving or other really big gatherings, I suggest you consider starting with a pan in the 14-by-10- or 12-inch range. This will accommodate all but the biggest roasts and be quite versatile. If, however, you do want to be able to roast a whole turkey, leg of lamb, and such, then I would steer you toward something closer to 16 to 18 by 13 inches. Thankfully, a roasting pan (of any size) is a good investment. A good one—or two—will last a lifetime.

GRATIN OR BAKING DISHES. Low-sided oval gratin or baking dishes work perfectly for holding a whole chicken, a rack of lamb, and other modest-sized roasts. The low sides of the traditional gratin dish (most are 1½ to 2 inches) expose the food to the hot oven air better than the serious roasting pans discussed above. Plus the pans tend to be lighter to maneuver. Just keep in mind that if you're planning to make a pan sauce (which may mean putting the pan on top of the stove), you'll need to use a flameproof pan, such as the enamel-coated cast-iron ones made by Le Creuset and Staub.

Baking dishes (often referred to as brownie pans) also make a fine choice for smaller roasts, with the one drawback that few are flameproof. If you do use a baking dish, keep in mind that food will cook (and brown) more quickly in glass and dark metal pans than in shiny metal ones.

OVENPROOF SKILLETS. A skillet works especially well when roasting smaller foods, such as salmon fillets or chicken breasts, that need to be seared on top of the stove and then finished in the oven. Good skillets are valued for their even, steady heat, a trait that makes them ideal for roasting. I especially love to roast in my old cast-iron skillets, choosing the size depending on what I'm planning to roast. I don't generally use nonstick skillets for sear-roasting, because most manufacturers recommend that they not be used at super-high heat—plus nonstick results in less flavorful drippings.

GRATIN AND BAKING DISHES **OVENPROOF SKILLETS**

A NOTE ON CHOOSING THE RIGHT SIZE ROASTING PAN

THE FIRST THING TO consider when selecting a pan for roasting is the size. Ideally, you want a pan that will accommodate the food neatly without crowding and without too much exposed space. Leaving a lot of empty space in the pan puts any pan drippings at risk of burning in the hot dry oven air. If the only pan you have is much too large for whatever you are roasting, it's good practice to cut up some vegetables (onions, carrots, and potatoes, for instance), toss them with a light coating of oil, season them, and scatter them around the roast. The vegetables will prevent the exposed surfaces of the pan from scorching and, as a bonus, you'll get a built-in side dish. Just be sure to gauge the size of the vegetable chunks to the estimated cooking time for the roast.

Parchment paper

When you turn to the vegetable and fish chapters, you will notice that I often recommend lining the roasting pan (often a heavy-duty rimmed baking sheet) with parchment paper before roasting. I make this optional (with a few exceptions), because I know that some cooks don't always have parchment paper on hand, but I encourage you to try it and see if you're not convinced. A liner of parchment helps keep the delicate, high-moisture vegetables and fish fillets from sticking to the pan. Instead, any yummy browned, crispy surfaces stick to the vegetables (or fish) themselves. Also, the parchment leads to much less scrubbing to remove the caramelized sugars after roasting. The only trick to using parchment is that it can sometimes get ruffled and in the way when you stir or flip the food during roasting. I solve this by grabbing hold of the edge of the parchment (using an oven mitt or towel, of course) when I slide the pan out to get access. I skip the parchment whenever I'm adding any amount of liquid to the pan or hoping to create any kind of pan sauce.

Roasting racks

A roasting rack can be any kind of ovenproof rack that holds food off the surface of the roasting pan, and while it's handy to have one on hand for the Thanksgiving turkey and a few other roasts, I tend to roast without a rack more often than not. The argument for using a roasting rack explains that lifting the food off the surface of the pan allows the hot oven air to circulate freely around the bottom of the roast, and since roasting, by definition, is all about surrounding food with hot air, this makes good sense. The trouble is, a roasting rack can also present a number of obstacles. My biggest complaint is that it can greatly decrease the amount of tasty drippings left in the roasting pan. When the roast sits up above the pan, as opposed to on it, the juices that drip out of the meat during cooking drop down onto the hot pan and immediately evaporate or, worse, burn. High-heat roasting magnifies this problem, since the pan will be as hot as the oven (upward of 400 degrees), and in addition to a pan full of burned drippings you'll end up with a smoke-filled oven and kitchen. Using a roasting rack also prevents the commingling of flavors and juices that you get anytime you add vegetables or aromatics to the roasting pan. Having a rack in the pan can make it very hard (if not impossible) to stir the vegetables surrounding the roast during cooking as well. In my experience, a more effective way to promote even cooking is to use low-sided roasting pans that won't shield the lower part of the roast. Yes, the bottom may not be as dry or crusty as the top, but a pan full of nicely caramelized drippings is well worth it.

There are, however, times when I do find a roasting rack useful, most notably with very large roasts that produce a lot of fat, such as goose or certain cuts of pork. If a roast sits in its own drippings (especially when they are prodigious), the bottom can get somewhat greasy, almost like a confit. One easy assurance when using a roasting rack is to add some

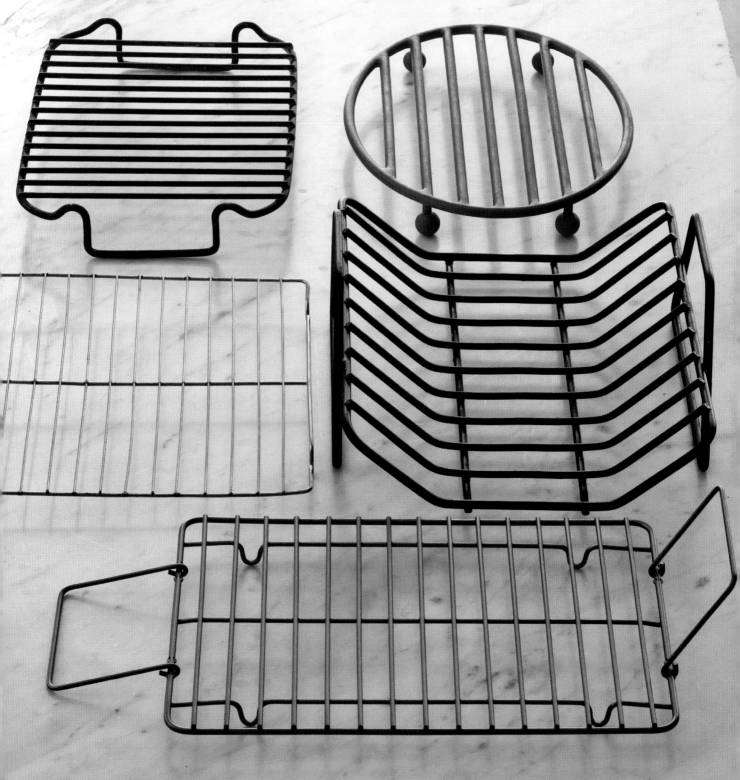

amount of liquid (wine, broth, or water) to the roasting pan. This prevents the drippings from burning and gives you a head start on any gravy or pan sauce you might make. I also find a rack helpful for a few smaller, fatty cuts, such as roasted hamburgers and lamb loin chops. Because these both roast at relatively high temperatures and release a fair amount of fat during roasting, I found that they can "fry" a little on the bottom if not lifted off the pan. To avoid the smoke that would result (and because I have no plans to use the drippings for a sauce), I line the roasting pan with a thin layer of salt to absorb the drippings and avoid the clouds of smoke that would otherwise ensue.

Cooks who favor the use of a roasting rack for poultry suggest that a rack can keep the skin from sticking to the bottom of the pan. My trick for avoiding this is to set the chicken on a few slices of onions and/or lemons. This prevents it from sticking to the pan, but at the same time it keeps the chicken close enough to the pan's surface to protect the drippings from burning—plus the onions and/or lemons add their own flavors to the drippings.

For the occasions when a roasting rack is useful, there are several types to choose from—adjustable, nonadjustable, V-shaped, U-shaped, basket-shaped, flat, and even vertical—but the most important criteria are that the rack is sturdy and easy to clean (simple construction without any intricate gridwork or hard-to-reach places). For this reason, I am not a big fan of adjustable racks, as they tend to be flimsy. Also, I don't have much use for vertical roasters (the idea is to stand the chicken upright), since I tend to shy away from single-purpose tools and I don't often use a rack to roast chicken. In terms of materials, stainless steel is always a good choice, as it's durable and sturdy. Many racks come with a nonstick coating that can make cleaning easier.

In my kitchen (and for all the recipes in this book), I use three roasting racks. The one I reach for most often is a flat 12-by-8-inch oval rack that sits about 1 inch above the roasting pan. It fits in a variety of roasting pans and handles all but the largest roasts. Next, I use the U-shaped rack (nonadjustable) that came with my largest roasting pan and comfortably holds a turkey or a goose. And finally, I sometimes use a metal cake cooling rack when I want to hold a number of small items, such as oven-roasted chicken wings or strips of Chinese-style roast pork. A large flat roasting rack would work just as well.

AN IMPROVISED ROASTING RACK

YOU CAN ALSO EASILY create a makeshift roasting rack using a trick I learned from the test kitchen at *Saveur* magazine when I wrote an article on roasting for them in 2007. Take 2 to 3 feet of aluminum foil (depending on the size of your roast) and scrunch it into a thick rope. Bend or spiral the rope to create a "rack" to set the roast on.

Ovens

The most essential piece of cooking equipment for roasting is, obviously, your oven. Its size, strength, and design will have a greater effect on your roasting results than any other equipment or variable. The trouble is, there are so many kinds of ovens that it is nearly impossible to catalogue all the features and characteristics of each. In testing the recipes for this book, I made it a point to send them to cooks in a variety of kitchens with different types of ovens, and in the end, I designed the recipes to work no matter what kind of oven you have. That said, however, all ovens—even the same model installed in different kitchens—behave a little differently, and I can't stress enough the importance of getting to know your own oven. Here I provide a few general guidelines that may help you.

Gas vs. electric

The most fundamental characteristic of any oven is the type of heat: gas or electric. Many equipment reviews claim that electric provides a more even heat than gas, especially at very low temperatures, but in my experience the difference is minor. It's more a question of the overall quality and construction of the oven. In other words, the thickness of the walls will have more to do with evenness of heat than the fuel type. On the low end, yes, a low-quality electric oven will probably heat more evenly than a gas oven of similar quality (which will cycle on and off dramatically during cooking), but once you hit the mid and high range, there is little difference.

The real difference is that you can get true convection (as described below) only in an electric range. Fortunately for cooks like myself who prefer gas burners and a true convection oven, most manufacturers make dual-fuel ranges, with gas for the stove, electricity for the oven.

Convection ovens

Fifty years ago, about the only cooks who knew what convection meant or had access to convection ovens were professionals. Today, more and more home ovens offer convection, but there's still some confusion about what this means and how to use it. First, let's examine how a nonconvection oven (also called a conventional oven, a radiant oven, or a thermal oven) works. Most conventional ovens have two heating elements, one top and one bottom, that heat the oven air and oven walls (some rudimentary ovens, like tiny apartment ovens, come with only one element). A convection oven includes a fan (usually on the back wall) to blow air around the oven, following the principle that moving air transfers heat (and cold) more quickly than still air. (For more on the principle of convection, turn to How Roasting Works: The Science Behind the Technique, page 9). The problem is that not all convection ovens are created equal. In order for the fan to be truly effective, it needs to have a third, dedicated heating element that heats the air as it circulates. Ovens that include this third element are referred to as true convection (also European convection, pure convection, and third-element convection) and are superior at cooking food evenly and quickly. Many of the early convection ovens (and some of the lower-end models today) merely had a fan but no heating element, and blowing unheated air around the inside of the oven actually reduces the effectiveness of the top and bottom elements, making the oven heat unevenly. If you have a convection oven at home but have never been impressed with its efficiency, you may very well have faux convection. If you determine that your oven's convection is not true convection, you are better off leaving the fan turned off.

When it comes to roasting, convection is a real boon, because moving air helps to dry the surfaces of the food, thus promoting browning. The natural sugars in vegetables caramelize more deeply and the exteriors of poultry and meats turn a bit crisper and browner. True convection also provides a more even heat than a conventional oven, so the browning is more even, more picture-perfect. Finally, the blowing hot air helps a true convection oven recover its temperature more quickly anytime you open the oven door to check on the roast, making it that much more efficient.

The standard formula for accommodating the accelerated action of a convection oven is to lower the set temperature 25 degrees below what you would normally use *and* to reduce the cooking time (some say by as much as 25 percent). In my experience, the 25-degree temperature reduction is accurate, but for roasting, I find that there are too many other variables (the shape of the roast, the size of the oven) to make a similarly formulaic reduction in cooking time. For the recipes in this book, I provide oven temperatures for conventional ovens and true convection, and I encourage you to use true convection if you have it. As with all recipes, the suggested cooking times in my recipes are just that—suggested. More importantly, I urge you to use the doneness test (including appearance, texture, and internal temperature).

Many true convection ovens offer a number of features that can be confusing. For instance, several offer "convection roast," "convection bake," and even "convection broil," and unfortunately their meaning is not universal. You will have to check the manual or contact the manufacturer's customer service department to be certain, but in most cases these various settings have to do with the fan speed and which heating elements are in use. For instance, "convection roast" can mean a faster fan and the use of the top and bottom elements, while "convection bake" indicates a moderately fast fan and use of only the third element (the one dedicated to the fan). "Convection broil" suggests that simply the top element is used along with the fan. Obviously, all of these will affect the rate at which foods cook, so it may take a little experimentation to find the one that works best for you. When selecting an oven setting, keep in mind that true convection means that the element dedicated to heating the circulating air is turned on. Also, most true convection ovens offer the option of cooking without the fan; these settings will be listed simply as "bake," "roast," and so on.

I've also seen convection ovens that automatically convert the temperature for you. In other words, they assume that you are following a recipe written for a conventional oven, so when you set the oven to, say, 350 degrees convection, the oven makes a calculation and sets itself to 325 degrees. This aggravates me, as I've never liked machines to do my thinking for me, but as long as you know what's going on, I'm confident you can out-think your oven.

ONE-HOUR ROSEMARY RIB ROAST IN PAN (PAGE 93)

BEEF & LAMB

BEEF & LAMB
RECIPES

CARVING A ROASTED RACK OF LAMB (PAGE 116)

M Y EUREKA MOMENT FOR WRITING THIS BOOK CAME DURING A DINNER PARTY, WHEN I STOOD AT THE HEAD OF OUR DINING ROOM TABLE carving a whole leg of lamb to serve to a gathering of friends. The lamb was handsomely browned on the outside, with the shank bone protruding from the end evoking the intrinsic carnivorous appeal of meat cooked on the bone. Slicing into the meat with a long carving knife revealed the inside, which was rosy pink, juicy, and mouthwatering. Conversation paused for a moment as plates were passed. Now *this*, I thought, is what roasting is all about. There's something about roasting red meat that resonates deep within, awakening our appetites with the primal appeal of meat and fire. For that reason, it seems only fitting to start a book on roasting by talking about beef and lamb.

In describing the taste of beef and even of that leg of lamb, we often use the word *meaty* to convey flavor and aroma. According to food scientists, the notion of meaty flavor derives from an actual chemical reaction that produces hundreds of flavor compounds and aromas when we cook red meat—especially when we sear the exterior, as we usually do in roasting. During roasting, the dry oven heat concentrates these meaty flavor compounds, making them more pronounced, more savory, and more delicious. From a cook's perspective, this means that beef and lamb offer enough robust flavor on their own—which is why I often stick to flavoring them with just salt and pepper—but also hold up to a world of seasonings, from subtle to bold.

The recipes in this chapter focus on the naturally tender cuts of beef and lamb—mainly those from the pricier rib and loin sections. The best way to enjoy these is by cooking them just enough to firm the texture but not so much as to dry them out. In other words, roast them no further than medium (around 135 degrees) or, better still, medium-rare (125 to 130 degrees) or even rare (115 degrees). It's at these temperatures that you can fully taste all the goodness that comes from a high-quality piece of red meat. Unlike pork and chicken, where the roasted meat is mainly the same color throughout, red meat can have an intensely dark exterior that gives way to a pink or even red interior filled with meaty juices. To achieve this, I often use a combination roasting method, searing the outside of the roast to yield the delicious crust and bits of crispy fat that we love, and then roasting at a more moderate temperature to coax the meat to doneness without going too far.

In the beef recipes that follow, you will find a combination of big and small roasts and something for almost every occasion. In addition to well-loved cuts like tenderloin and standing rib roast, I encourage you to try some of the lesser-known roasts, like flank steak, which is delicious when stuffed with an intriguing rajas filling (page 97), or top round, slow-roasted to make an exceptional roast beef (page 68) that's even better when served with horseradish cream sauce (page 69). Then there are familiar cuts you might not think about roasting, such as strip steak (page 105) with homemade steak sauce (page 107) and even hamburgers (page 112), which turn out amazingly juicy when cooked in the oven.

While lamb is less popular than beef (at least in America), people who love it do so intensely. If you (or someone you cook for) are on the fence about lamb, I encourage you to try it again—perhaps the simple rack of lamb on page 116 or the roasted lamb loin chops on page 130. Be careful not to overcook it. You may be surprised. Many times people think they don't like lamb only because they've never tasted anything but well-done lamb, which tends to be overly musky, almost gamy, and not nearly the sweet, tender morsel you get when you roast lamb to no more than medium-rare.

Whether you are cooking lamb or beef, I urge you to buy the best quality you can afford, and please pay attention to the instructions for allowing the roasts to rest after cooking. I explain the science behind this step in The Principles of Roasting (page 21), and while every roast benefits from a period of rest before carving, nowhere is this more important than with large hunks of red meat. I know it's hard to wait when that gorgeous tenderloin or plump rolled leg of lamb is filling the kitchen with its irresistible aroma, but slice into it too soon and no matter how perfectly cooked it is, the meat will be dry. Maybe it's because red meat can be so pricey, or maybe it's because these roasts are often part of a special occasion, but the dryness you encounter when you carve into an underrested roast beef or lamb seems much more dramatic and disappointing than if you make the same mistake with poultry or pork. Fortunately, for tender and juicy results, all you need to do is follow the suggested resting times.

Buying good-quality beef

As with all things, the best roast beef starts with good-quality meat, but deciphering the various labels and options can be a little confusing. For instance, I've seen beef labeled "certified," but I've yet to hear a good explanation of what this means. You might also see "natural" stamped on a label, which sounds great, but according to the United States Department of Agriculture, this only means that the beef has been minimally processed and contains no preservatives or artificial ingredients. Since virtually all fresh beef conforms to these standards, the label has no real significance. There are, however, a few terms and phrases that can make a big difference in the flavor of your roast.

PRIME, CHOICE, AND SELECT. The USDA has a grading system for beef that's based on the steer's age and conformation and on the amount of marbling, the visible fat that's streaked throughout the muscle tissue. It's this marbling that matters most to the cook, as it makes beef more tender, richer-tasting, and juicy. The highest grade is assigned to meat with the most marbling. Simply put, beef that's labeled "prime" is considered superior; "choice" is a runner-up, and "select" is third. (There are lower ratings, but these are not generally sold at the retail level.) Only a small percentage of all beef earns the prime rating, and most of it is sold to to high-end restaurants and hotels. If you'd like to splurge and treat yourself to a prime cut, you'll need to shop at a specialty butcher or mail-order source. The best grade you'll find in most supermarkets is choice, but this is actually the broadest category, and can vary quite a bit in quality and flavor. Some is nearly as good as prime, while some is much closer to select. Unfortunately, to the untrained eye, it can be difficult to differentiate between top-choice and low-choice. If you don't see a grade label on the meat, that usually means that it hasn't been graded. Unlike inspection (which is mandatory), grading is a voluntary (and expensive) process that meat producers undergo in order to be able to advertise their products as being of high quality. For this reason, some smaller, independent producers do not bother with the expense of having their beef graded. Instead they rely on their brand name and reputation to promote their products. As a shopper, I rely more and more on brand names, buying meat from producers whose names I recognize and trust to sell good-tasting meat.

GRASS-FED. Though cows naturally are inclined to eat grass and hay, most factory farms feed their cattle grain in order to fatten them quickly. Healthwise, grass-fed beef has more nutrients (especially vitamins A and E) and less saturated fat, and has less risk of carrying the dangerous *E. coli* bacteria, than grain-fed beef. I love grass-fed beef for all of these reasons and more. What I also like about it is that it generally comes from smaller farms, which are likely to have happier and healthier cows. I also enjoy the flavor of grass-fed beef, which may be different from what you are used to if you have been eating grain-fed beef all your life. To me, grass-fed beef tastes . . . well, beefier. But purely grass-fed beef can be lean, which means it will have less intramuscular fat and will be less forgiving than grain-fed beef if overcooked. If you're concerned that grass-fed beef is too lean or too strong tasting, you might look for beef that comes from cows that spent most of their lives grazing but were finished on all-vegetarian grain, such as the products sold by Niman Ranch in California; this beef seems to offer the best of both choices. When shopping for grass-fed beef, keep in mind that the term does not *guarantee* that the animal didn't spend some time in a feedlot, and it's also not an indication of quality. Again, your best strategy is to find a farm or brand that you like and trust and cultivate your own relationship and knowledge.

DRY-AGED BEEF. If you have seen dry-aged beef for sale at the butcher, you know it's expensive. If you have tasted it, you know it's exquisite. But what exactly is dry-aged beef?

All beef must age for a period of time after slaughter to become tender and palatable. Traditionally, this means leaving entire sides of steer hanging in a temperature- and humidity-controlled meat locker, uncovered and exposed to the air for anywhere from 10 days to 12 weeks—a process known as dry aging. As the sides hang, a chemical change occurs, rendering the meat more tender and flavorful—the longer the beef hangs, the more intense the flavor. The side also shrinks significantly in weight (as much as 20 percent), due to moisture loss and the fact that the surface dries out so much that the outermost bits need to be carved off and discarded. In the end, the sides are cut into dense, deep red roasts and steaks that cost a good deal more per pound than the original steer (due to the weight loss and expense of maintaining the meat locker). These days, most modern producers shortcut the aging process by quickly breaking down the steer after slaughter into roasts and steaks and packaging these in heavy-duty plastic, vacuum-sealed pouches, a process often referred to as Cryovac. The individual cuts then "age" for as few as 3 or 4 days, sometimes only as long as it takes to ship the beef to the market. In contrast to dry aging, this modern method is known as wet aging, indicating that the vacuum seal traps all the moisture, leaving the surface wet. The financial advantage to the producer is that meat sealed in a vacuum pack will not lose any weight due to evaporation. Since meat is all sold by the pound, this means obvious savings. While there is nothing inherently wrong with wet-aged meat, you'll never get the same intensity of flavor you get from a properly dry-aged steak. Fortunately, some specialty producers are still willing to take the time and care to dry-age beef for the optimum 4 to 5 weeks. (Though some ambitious DIY home cooks tout methods for dry aging at home, I prefer to leave it to the pros, who can be meticulous about temperature and humidity.) Be aware, however, that you will pay a *lot* of money for a dry-aged beef roast, which almost always begins with prime grade beef.

ORGANIC. The label "organic" does little to inform you about what flavor the beef will have. Beef that carries the USDA organic logo has met the department's standards, which prohibit the use of growth hormones, antibiotics, genetically modified feed, and animal byproducts, among other things. The standards do not require a grass-only diet; the animal may be fed organic grain for its whole life. When it comes to flavor or texture, the label has little bearing.

HERITAGE. Heritage beef is usually not something you will find at the supermarket, because "heritage" breeds are not as efficient as the cattle breeds found on industrial farms. Heritage breeds come from pure and crossbred livestock and from rare and endangered breeds. Because of the way they are raised, they are generally grass-fed, but that is not a part of the definition.

FREE-RANGE OR FREE-ROAMING. These terms suggest that the animal had access to the outdoors, but for cattle there are no standards that producers need to follow. In terms of flavor, the term has little effect on the cuts used typically for roasting, which are not from the part of the animal that gets exercised very much anyway.

STEAK LOVER'S ROAST BEEF (ROAST STRIP LOIN)

When it comes to putting on an impressive roast beef dinner with minimal effort, in terms of both prep and carving, you can't go wrong with a strip loin roast. For added flavor and succulence, I smear the strip roast with butter. During the initial sizzle, the buttery drippings caramelize on the bottom of the roasting pan, the start of a very flavorful *jus*. To keep the juices from burning, I pour a small glass of water into the pan when I lower the oven temperature and leave the meat to finish roasting gently and evenly. While you could use dry white wine in place of water, the *jus* tastes lighter and purer when made with water. In the end, you have a simple, beefy *jus* and a perfectly cooked roast.

If you're serving more than 8 people, order a larger strip loin roast (figure 6 ounces per person for generous meatcentric servings). The roasting time will increase only incrementally, as a larger roast will merely be longer and not thicker. For each added pound, expect to add only a few minutes' roasting time. This recipe also works for boneless rib roast. For a steak-and-potato dinner, serve this with Oven Fries (page 501) or Herb-Roasted Potatoes (page 489). I also love to pass a pestolike charmoula (page 131) at the table.

SERVES 6 TO 8

METHOD: Combination high and low heat

ROASTING TIME: About 1 1/4 hours

PLAN AHEAD: For best flavor and texture, season the meat 1 to 2 days before roasting.

WINE: Rich Cabernet or Cabernet-blend from California, Australia, or Chile, especially one with a few years of age.

One 2 ½- to 3-pound beef strip loin (also called top loin) or boneless rib roast, fat trimmed to about ¼ inch, tied at 1½-inch intervals

Kosher salt and freshly ground black pepper

1 tablespoon unsalted butter, at room temperature

1   **SEASON THE BEEF.** Sprinkle the meat generously all over with 1 ½ teaspoons salt and 1 teaspoon pepper (use slightly less if seasoning just before roasting). Refrigerate, uncovered or loosely covered, for 1 to 2 days. Let the roast sit at room temperature for 1 hour before roasting.

2   **HEAT THE OVEN.** Position a rack in the lower third of the oven and heat to 450 degrees (425 degrees convection). Smear the butter on all sides of the roast and place the meat on a roasting rack in a roasting pan just large enough to accommodate it (11 by 13 inches works well).

3   **ROAST.** Slide the roast into the oven. After 20 minutes, pour ½ cup room-temperature water into the bottom of the pan and lower the oven temperature to 300 degrees (275 degrees convection). Continue to roast until an instant-read thermometer inserted into the center of the roast registers about 120 degrees for rare and 130 degrees for medium-rare, another 45 to 55 minutes.

4   **REST.** Transfer the roast to a carving board to rest for 20 to 30 minutes. Skim any excess fat from the pan drippings and keep warm to serve with the beef.

5   **CARVE AND SERVE.** Cut the roast across the grain into ¼- to ⅓-inch-thick slices, snipping the strings as you go, and drizzle the pan juices over the slices before serving.

Shopping for Strip Loin Roast

STRIP LOIN ROASTS COME FROM THE PART OF THE STEER REFERRED TO AS THE SHORT LOIN—THE AREA BELOW THE RIB AND ABOVE THE SIRLOIN. IT'S actually from the same muscle as a rib roast, but slightly leaner and generally less expensive. Left whole, the long, rectangular strip loin weighs close to 10 pounds, but it's almost always broken down into highly marketable strip steaks (also called New York strip). Even if you don't see strip loin roasts in the meat case, chances are the butcher will have them in back, waiting to be sliced up into steaks. Most times all you need to do is ask for a strip loin roast and wait a few minutes while the butcher cuts one for you, but it can't hurt to call ahead and order the exact size you want and have it waiting for you.

PEPPERED TRI-TIP ROAST WITH CHIMICHURRI (PAGE 66)

PEPPERED TRI-TIP ROAST

The tri-tip is one of those in-between cuts that deliver robust flavor yet are well-marbled enough to remain tender and juicy when roasted at high heat—as long as you don't take it past medium. (I prefer tri-tip served medium-rare, about 125 degrees.) The only trick is figuring out which way to carve a tri-tip so the slices come out tender, but I tell you how (see Carving a Tri-Tip Roast, page 65).

The black peppercorns here need to be cracked—not ground—to create the crust you are after. The easiest way to crack peppercorns is with a mortar and pestle. If you don't have one, put the peppercorns on a cutting board and use the base of a small heavy saucepan and your body weight to coarsely crack them. My favorite way to serve this roast is to slather slices with chimichurri, a pestolike sauce from Argentina. Tri-tip is also wonderful with Homemade Steak Sauce (page 107), Garlic-Chile Mayonnaise (page 503), or Horseradish Cream Sauce (page 69). Slices of leftover peppered tri-tip make excellent steak sandwiches, so don't hesitate to make this if you're only two or three at home.

SERVES 4 TO 6
METHOD: High heat
ROASTING TIME: 25 to 35 minutes
PLAN AHEAD: For the best flavor, season the roast at least 1 hour and up to 24 hours ahead of cooking it.
WINE/BEER: Concentrated, intensely fruity/spicy red, such as a Sonoma or Lodi Zinfandel or a Barossa Shiraz; or a rich, dark Belgian-style ale.

One 1½- to 2-pound tri-tip roast (see Shopping for Tri-Tip, page 66)
1½ teaspoons freshly cracked black pepper

¾ teaspoon kosher salt
Chimichurri (page 66, optional)

1 **TRIM AND SEASON THE BEEF.** If there's a layer of heavy connective tissue on the roast, trim it off with a sharp knife (many butchers will have already removed this). Avoid removing too much external fat, as a little fat will baste the meat as it roasts, keeping it flavorful and juicy. If the surface feels wet, pat it dry with paper towels. Season the meat all over with the pepper and salt, rubbing so that all the seasonings adhere. Let the meat sit, uncovered, at room temperature for 1 to 2 hours before roasting. If seasoning it further ahead than that, cover it loosely with plastic wrap and refrigerate for up to 24 hours.

CONTINUED ON NEXT PAGE

Step-by-Step: Seasoning Tri-Tip Roast

1 A tri-tip roast, sometimes labeled triangle roast. **2** Season the meat all over with cracked black pepper and salt. **3** Place the tri-tip, fat-side up, on a a rack on a rimmed baking sheet or low-sided roasting pan.

2 **HEAT THE OVEN.** Position a rack near the center of the oven and heat to 400 degrees (375 degrees convection).

3 **ROAST THE MEAT.** Fit a shallow roasting pan with a flat rack if you have one. (If you don't, use the makeshift aluminum foil rack described on page 46.) Place the tri-tip fat side up on the rack and roast until the internal temperature of the thickest part of the roast, measured with an instant-read thermometer, reaches 120 degrees for rare, 125 to 130 degrees for medium-rare, 135 degrees for medium. Start checking after about 25 minutes; medium-rare (my preference) will take 30 to 35 minutes.

4 **REST.** Transfer the roast to a carving board, preferably with a trough and let it rest for about 10 minutes. Expect the temperature to rise about 7 degrees as the meat rests.

5 **CARVE AND SERVE.** Carve across the grain into thin slices as described on page 65 and serve with chimichurri, if desired.

CONTINUED ON PAGE 66

Carving a Tri-Tip Roast

Because of its irregular shape, a tri-tip can be confusing to carve. The key is figuring out which way the grain of the meat runs and then carving across the grain. With the triangular-shaped tri-tip, however, identifying the grain is not so cut-and-dried (pun intended). To carve it correctly, begin by orienting the leading point of the triangle so it faces 3 o'clock on the cutting board, with the two tail points at 7 o'clock and 11 o'clock. The grain runs horizontally from the leading point (at 3 o'clock) toward the tail side of the roast. Start carving thin vertical slices at the leading point, working your way back as the roast gets wider. (If you're left-handed, simply reverse the clockface, so the leading point faces 9 o'clock with the tail points at 5 o'clock and 1 o'clock.)

1 Resting the roast. If you don't have a carving board with a trough, set a cutting board inside a rimmed baking sheet to catch any juices. **2** Orient the tri-tip so that the leading point faces toward 3 o'clock (from the carver's point of view). **3** The grain in a tri-tip runs horizontally from the narrow tip back toward the wider base; by starting at the tip and slicing vertical slices, you're sure to carve across the grain. **4** The peppered tri-tip after slicing.

Shopping for Tri-Tip

THE TRI-TIP TAKES ITS NAME FROM ITS SHAPE: A NEAT LITTLE TRIANGULAR-SHAPED ROAST WITH THREE DISTINCT TIPS THAT COMES FROM THE SIRLOIN section (technically from the lower end of the bottom sirloin, underneath the hipbone). Sometimes labeled triangle roast, a single tri-tip weighs somewhere in the 2-pound range, and there are only two tri-tips per steer. Until recently, tri-tip was primarily a West Coast cut rarely seen in markets or butcher shops east of the Rockies. Happily, I've noticed more East Coast markets starting to carry tri-tip, although many still slice the modest roasts to sell as tri-tip or triangle steak. If you don't see tri-tip in the meat case, it's worth inquiring. Trust me, you'll discover a new favorite roast.

OPTION: CHIMICHURRI

If you're unfamiliar with chimichurri, imagine a sauce made with olive oil and a variety of different herbs, like pesto. Now give the pesto a bright vinegary kick and a bite of chile heat. This vibrant concoction comes from Argentina, where it's spooned onto the famous grass-fed beef. The warmth of the roasted or grilled meat aromatizes the herbs and spices in the sauce, and the olive oil mingles happily with the beef juices.

If you compare any number of chimichurri recipes, you'll find plenty of variation with two constants: all contain fresh oregano and some type of chile pepper. A traditional chimichurri uses *aji molido*, a crushed dried red chile from Argentina. In its place, I combine jalapeño, crushed red pepper flakes, and a bit of pimentón (smoked Spanish paprika). You may very well become inspired to play around with the various elements according to your taste. For instance, I am happy with half a jalapeño (with seeds), but you may amp this up or tone it down, or substitute another chile altogether.

Aside from partnering well with beef, chimichurri is delicious drizzled on slices of roasted or grilled poultry and fish. It also makes an excellent marinade for meat and poultry. I use it as a sandwich spread, either directly on the bread or stirred into mayonnaise. And I know of one cook who likes to fry eggs in a spoonful of chimichurri, which sounds quite good to me.

MAKES ABOUT 1/2 CUP

PLAN AHEAD: The infused oil should sit for at least an hour to cool before you add the parsley.

3 tablespoons packed fresh oregano leaves

2 tablespoons loosely packed fresh thyme leaves

⅓ cup extra-virgin olive oil

2 garlic cloves, minced

½ jalapeño (cut lengthwise) with seeds, stemmed and minced

Pinch of crushed red pepper flakes

2 tablespoons sherry wine vinegar

1 teaspoon paprika, sweet or hot, preferably pimentón

¾ teaspoon kosher salt, plus more to taste

¼ teaspoon freshly ground black pepper

⅓ cup coarsely chopped fresh flat-leaf parsley

1 **BRUISE THE HERBS.** Combine the oregano and thyme in a mortar and pound gently to bruise the leaves; this releases their flavors more than chopping and gives the sauce a smoother texture. If you don't have a mortar and pestle, coarsely chop the herbs.

2 **INFUSE THE OIL.** Combine the oil, garlic, jalapeño, and red pepper flakes in a small saucepan. Heat over medium heat until the oil is just hot but not simmering, about 2 minutes. Remove from the heat and stir in the oregano, thyme, vinegar, paprika, salt, and pepper. Set aside to cool and infuse at room temperature for 1 to 3 hours.

3 **STIR IN THE PARSLEY** and taste for salt and pepper. *The sauce keeps for several weeks in the refrigerator.*

STRAIGHT-UP ROAST BEEF (SLOW-ROASTED TOP ROUND)

When I crave straight-up roast beef—you know, the kind that gets thinly sliced and piled high in a good deli sandwich—this is what I have in mind. This humble roast will never receive the accolades of more luxurious cuts, like prime rib and strip roast, but it won't break the bank and has an excellent beefy taste. I like to roast a top round for Sunday supper, knowing that the leftovers will make first-rate sandwiches for the coming week.

To produce a roast that is juicy and rosy almost all the way to the edges, I roast it in a low oven (250 degrees). At this slow pace, you get nothing more than a drop or two of drippings, which is a good thing—all that juice stays right in the meat. To keep it tender, slice it as thin as you can; when carved into thick slabs, no matter how perfectly cooked, top round can be tough. If you're looking for an excuse to pull out the electric carving knife, here it is, as the thinner you can slice the beef, the more tender it seems.

Horseradish Cream Sauce (page 69) makes a fine accompaniment to the roast when served hot and a good sandwich spread for cold roast beef, too.

SERVES 4 TO 6, MORE IF MAKING SANDWICHES

METHOD: Combination sear and low heat

ROASTING TIME: 1 1/2 to 2 hours (plus 8 to 12 minutes to sear)

PLAN AHEAD: For the best flavor, salt the meat a day or two ahead of roasting.

WINE: Reds with forward fruit and softer tannins, such as a young California Merlot or Argentine Malbec.

One 2½- to 3½-pound top round roast, tied at 1½ inch intervals	Kosher salt and freshly ground black pepper 1 tablespoon peanut oil or grapeseed oil

1 **SEASON THE BEEF.** If seasoning in advance, sprinkle 1½ teaspoons salt and ¾ teaspoon black pepper over the entire surface and refrigerate, uncovered or loosely covered, for 24 to 28 hours.

2 **HEAT THE OVEN.** Position a rack near the center of the oven and heat to 250 degrees (225 degrees convection). Fit a shallow roasting pan, baking dish, or heavy-

duty baking sheet with a flat roasting rack, if you have one. You can also roast the meat directly on the pan.

3 **BROWN THE MEAT.** Pat dry the entire surface of the meat. If you didn't season in advance, season it now all over with salt and pepper. Heat a large heavy skillet over medium-high heat (cast iron works nicely). When the skillet is hot, add the oil, let it heat for several seconds, and place the meat in the pan. (The meat should sizzle the instant it hits the pan. If it doesn't, the pan is not hot enough; remove the meat, wait a minute, and try again.) Brown the roast on all sides, turning with tongs as you go, until it is nicely browned with a few dark, crusty spots on the ends, 8 to 12 minutes total. Transfer the meat to the roasting pan, placing it fat side up. Season the top generously with black pepper.

4 **ROAST** until an instant-read thermometer inserted in the center of the roast reads 115 degrees for very rare, 120 degrees for rare, and 125 degrees for medium-rare, 1½ to 2 hours. *With top round, I don't recommend roasting beyond medium-rare.*

5 **REST.** Transfer the meat to a carving board, preferably one with a trough, and leave to rest for 15 to 20 minutes. If you are making this for sandwiches, let it cool at room temperature for 1 to 2 hours before covering and refrigerating.

6 **CARVE AND SERVE.** Slice very thin and serve.

OPTION 1: HORSERADISH CREAM SAUCE

There is no better accompaniment to good roast beef than horseradish, but rather than serving it straight from the jar, I like to make an elegant little sauce by combining it with lightly whipped heavy cream and crème fraîche. (You can substitute sour cream for the crème fraîche, but the sauce will be denser and less creamy.) This is as good served with hot roast beef at the dinner table as it is slathered on bread for first-class roast beef sandwiches. It's also delicious with beef tenderloin. The sauce keeps for several days in the refrigerator.

MAKES ABOUT 1 1/3 CUPS

CONTINUED ON NEXT PAGE

½ cup heavy cream

½ cup crème fraîche or sour cream

⅓ cup prepared horseradish, drained

½ teaspoon dry mustard

Squeeze of fresh lemon juice

Kosher salt and freshly ground white
  pepper

IN A MEDIUM BOWL, whisk the heavy cream until it begins to thicken and form very soft peaks. Add the crème fraîche and whisk until thick. Fold in the horseradish and mustard. Season with lemon juice, salt, and pepper. Serve immediately or cover and refrigerate. You may need to give the sauce a quick whisk before serving if it has been refrigerated.

OPTION 2: SLOW-ROASTED TOP ROUND WITH CARAWAY AND MUSTARD SEEDS

This recipe pays tribute to the roast beef sandwiches, known as beef on weck, from my hometown, Buffalo, New York. There's nothing really special about the beef in a Buffalo beef on weck—it's all about the roll: a crusty kaiser roll topped with lots of pretzel salt and whole caraway seeds, known as a kummelweck roll (thus the nickname weck). The legend of these sandwiches goes back to a German tavern owner who was looking to sell more beer to people on their way to the 1901 Pan American Exposition. Topping the sandwich rolls with extra salt made his patrons thirsty for more beer. The caraway was incidental, but that's the flavor pairing that endures. I've never been able to find good kummelweck rolls outside Buffalo, so I season the beef itself with caraway before roasting. The result is divine, either carved hot and served for dinner or sliced cold and piled on a crusty roll. Don't forget the horseradish—either the sauce on page 69 or, for a classic sandwich, reach for the jar.

SERVES 4 TO 6, MORE IF MAKING SANDWICHES

METHOD: Combination sear and low heat

ROASTING TIME: 1 1/2 to 2 hours (plus 8 to 12 minutes to sear)

PLAN AHEAD: For the best flavor, season the meat a day or two ahead of roasting.

WINE/BEER: Rhône-blend with ripe red fruits and herbal notes, such as Gigondas, Vacqueyras, or Australian Grenache; or malty brown ale from the U.S. or the U.K.

1 tablespoon caraway seeds

1 teaspoon mustard seeds, yellow or black

Kosher salt and freshly ground black
  pepper

One 2 ½- to 3 ½-pound top round roast,
  tied at 1 ½ inch intervals

1 tablespoon peanut oil or grapeseed oil

1 **SEASON THE BEEF.** Crush the caraway and mustard seeds in a mortar or spice grinder just enough to crack open the seeds but not so much to make a powder. (I deliberately don't toast the spices here, since they get plenty toasted later when you sear the beef.) Combine with 1½ teaspoons salt and ¾ teaspoon black pepper. Rub this all over the entire surface of the beef and refrigerate, uncovered or loosely covered, for 24 to 28 hours.

2 **SEAR AND ROAST** as directed for Straight-Up Roast Beef, page 68.

Shopping for Top Round

THE *ROUND* CORRESPONDS TO THE THIGH SECTION OF A STEER, BELOW THE HIP AND SIRLOIN AND ABOVE THE KNEE AND SHANK. EVERY ROUND (THERE are two, obviously, on each steer) can be broken down into three muscle groups: top round, bottom round, and eye of the round. The way I remember which is which is simple. When a carcass is split into two sides and the sides are laid down on the cutting table, the top round is the part of the leg that will be on top, and the bottom on the bottom. For roasting, I much prefer the top round (which is also called the inside round, as it sits on the inside of the leg), because it's a slightly less used, finer-grained muscle than the bottom round (also called, not surprisingly, the outside round).

A full top round can weigh close to 15 pounds, but most markets will sell the round broken down into chunky little 2½- to 3½-pound roasts. If not, just ask. A top round roast shouldn't be difficult to come by, but it will need to be tied to keep its shape. The bottom round is even larger; a full one can weigh as much as 20 pounds. The eye of the round, incidentally, intersects the two rounds, running lengthwise. If you decide to roast either a bottom or an eye round, the only way to go is very slow and low, and plan to slice it thin.

HIGH-HEAT-ROASTED WHOLE BEEF TENDERLOIN

I think of a beef tenderloin as the little black dress of any cook's repertoire. Sure, other cuts may be more in vogue and have everyone talking, but you can't go wrong when you serve tenderloin. Admittedly, tenderloin is not the fullest-flavored cut of beef, and its silky texture doesn't offer the robust satisfaction you get from a rib roast, but it's exactly this understated elegance that makes tenderloin such a perennial crowd-pleaser. It's a cinch to carve, polite to eat (no wrestling with rugged steak knives), and it pairs beautifully with a range of sauces, such as the shallot and port wine sauce that follows or any of the other sauces that go well with beef, including the horseradish sauce on page 69 or the chimichurri on page 66.

To make the most of this luxurious cut of meat, I season it a day or so ahead; this enhances the flavor and texture of the beef, and it dries the surface just enough to help it sear more readily during roasting. Then I roast at a relatively high temperature—high enough to get a good sear on the meat, but not so high as to leave me with a smoke-filled kitchen before my fancy dinner party. With high-heat roasting, each slice of beef will have a graduated doneness; the outside will be quite well done and the inside will get more rare toward the center, a nice mix for people who like both. The one caution is that if you are not diligent, it's easy to go from perfectly cooked to overdone, as the high heat of the oven makes that transition happen fast. If I feel as though I will be too distracted to pay attention during roasting, I often opt to roast the tenderloin ahead and serve it at room temperature. Unlike fattier beef roasts, tenderloin is an excellent choice for a room-temperature buffet.

SERVES 8 TO 10

METHOD: High heat

ROASTING TIME: 30 to 45 minutes

PLAN AHEAD: For best flavor and texture, salt the beef 24 to 36 hours ahead.

WINE: A recent vintage of Cabernet Sauvignon from Napa Valley, Washington State, or South Australia's Coonawarra region; or a classified-growth from one of Bordeaux's top left-bank communes, such as St.-Julien.

1 whole trimmed beef tenderloin, 4 to 5 pounds (see pages 78 and 79)

2 teaspoons kosher salt

2 tablespoons extra-virgin olive oil

2 tablespoons cracked black peppercorns

1   **SALT THE BEEF.** Sprinkle the entire surface of the beef with the salt. Place it on a wire rack on a rimmed baking sheet and refrigerate, uncovered or loosely covered, for 24 to 36 hours.

2   **TIE AND PEPPER THE ROAST.** About an hour before roasting, remove the roast from the refrigerator. Tuck the thinner tail-like tip under the roast so you have an almost even thickness along the whole roast and, using kitchen string, tie the length of the roast at 2-inch intervals. Rub the entire surface with oil and sprinkle with black pepper, rolling and pressing so the pepper adheres. Let sit at room temperature for an hour.

3   **HEAT THE OVEN.** Position a rack in the center of the oven and heat to 425 degrees (400 degrees convection).

4   **ROAST.** Place the roast on a flat roasting rack on a heavy-duty rimmed baking sheet (the sides of a standard roasting pan will shield the roast from the oven's heat). Roast until an instant-read thermometer inserted in the thickest part of the tenderloin reads about 120 degrees for rare or 125 degrees for medium-rare, 30 to 45 minutes. (I don't recommend letting this roast get past medium-rare, since the hot oven temperature will quickly push it past medium into well-done territory, which means dry and disappointing.)

5   **REST, CARVE, AND SERVE.** Transfer to a cutting board, preferably one with a trough, and let rest, uncovered, for 15 minutes. Remove the strings and carve crosswise into ½-inch-thick slices. (If serving at room temperature, carve just before serving.)

OPTION: SHALLOT AND PORT WINE SAUCE

The elegance of beef tenderloin deserves an equally refined and delicious sauce. There's no flour (or other starch) thickener here, so this turns out thinner than some gravies, but the flavor remains bright and complex. What's great about this sauce is that you can make it

CONTINUED ON NEXT PAGE

ahead, independent of the meat. But please add any juices from the cooked tenderloin: they will make the sauce taste even better.

You will need either homemade beef stock or reconstituted demi-glace to make this sauce. Canned beef broth just won't cut it. If neither is in reach, consider one of the other sauce options, such as Horseradish Cream Sauce (page 69) or Creamy Mustard Sauce (page 77).

MAKES ABOUT 1 1/2 CUPS, ENOUGH FOR 8 TO 10 SERVINGS

4 tablespoons (½ stick) unsalted butter

¼ cup finely chopped shallots

1 teaspoon cracked black peppercorns

1 leafy sprig rosemary

3 tablespoons brandy, such as cognac

1 cup port wine, ruby or tawny

3 cups homemade beef stock or 1 ½ cups reconstituted demi-glace (see Shopping for Demi-Glace, page 75)

Kosher salt and freshly ground black pepper

1 **COOK THE SHALLOTS.** In a medium saucepan, melt 2 tablespoons of the butter over medium-low heat. Add the shallots and sauté until soft and translucent, about 3 minutes. Add the peppercorns, rosemary, and brandy.

2 **ADD THE LIQUID, REDUCE, AND STRAIN.** Increase the heat to medium-high and boil until the brandy is almost gone, about 1 minute. Add the port and bring to a simmer. Add the beef stock or demi-glace and continue to simmer over medium heat, whisking frequently, until reduced by about half if using beef stock, about 25 minutes, or simmer for 5 minutes if using demi-glace. Strain the sauce through a fine-mesh sieve into a clean saucepan, pressing to extract as much liquid as possible. Discard the solids. *The sauce may be made ahead up until this point and refrigerated for up to 2 days.*

3 **WHISK IN THE REMAINING BUTTER.** Set the sauce over low heat and bring to just below a simmer. Cut the remaining butter into ½-inch pats and, one by one, whisk them in. Taste for salt and pepper. Add any carving juices. Keep warm but do not let boil.

Shopping for Demi-Glace

DEMI-GLACE, AS YOU MAY IMAGINE FROM THE SPELLING, COMES FROM THE CLASSIC FRENCH COOKING REPERTOIRE, AND REFERS TO A VEAL STOCK THAT has been reduced significantly until it is halfway (*demi*) to a glaze (*glace*). The production of real demi-glace requires several days and a prodigious amount of beef and veal bones, along with aromatic vegetables, tomatoes, and seasonings. The resulting liquid is neither a stock nor a sauce but something in between, and is used as a base for a range of savory sauces. A well-made demi-glace (or "demi," as savvy cooks refer to it) will be smooth, meaty, and lightly syrupy without being cloying, and delivers a flavor that lasts on your palate like a sip of fine wine.

Today, few home cooks I know ever even consider making demi-glace, and only the finest restaurants continue the practice. Thankfully, there are a couple of commercial brands that work quite well and are increasingly available in gourmet markets and upscale grocery stores. Most often I rely on the More Than Gourmet brand, sold in 1.5-ounce, puck-shaped containers of veal and/or beef demi-glace (both are excellent). When shopping for other brands, look for an ingredient list that does not list salt or chicken fat as the primary ingredient and that contains a minimum of unrecognizable ingredients.

RECONSTITUTING STORE-BOUGHT DEMI-GLACE

Most brands of store-bought demi-glace have been reduced down further than the syrupy consistency of a true demi-glace as described above. Instead, they are apt to be as thick as tar and often need to be reconstituted before being added to a recipe. For instance, if you want to use store-bought demi-glace as a base for a sauce (as in the Shallot and Port Wine Sauce on page 73), place the entire 1.5-ounce container in a heatproof vessel and add 1 cup of hot water to dissolve. To use store-bought demi-glace as a stock base (for soups and braising liquid), add about 1½ cups of water for every 1.5-ounce package. In every case, consult the package directions and use your kitchen sense.

Besides reconstituting store-bought demi-glace to replace beef stock, using it straight from the package is a wonderful way to enrich any number of savory pan sauces. Simply whisk a little dollop of the thick concentrate into a sauce while simmering.

MODERATE-HEAT-ROASTED WHOLE BEEF TENDERLOIN WITH ROSEMARY AND FENNEL

Because the beef gets coated with a rub made with fresh rosemary and ground fennel, I roast it in a moderate oven to keep the seasoning from burning. Plus, the moderate heat ensures an even rosiness all the way through and widens the window of doneness, making it less likely that you will overcook the beef. Delicious on its own, the tenderloin is even better when paired with the quick-to-make mustard sauce that follows. Both the beef and the mustard sauce are also excellent at room temperature, making this a superb candidate for a make-ahead buffet.

SERVES 8 TO 10

METHOD: Moderate heat

ROASTING TIME: 40 to 50 minutes

PLAN AHEAD: For best flavor and texture, salt the beef 24 to 36 hours ahead.

WINE: Deeply flavored red with pronounced herbal notes such as Chateauneuf-du-Pape from France's Southern Rhône; or a dry red based on the Touriga Nacional grape from Portugal's Douro Valley.

1 tablespoon extra-virgin olive oil

1 tablespoon finely chopped fresh rosemary

1½ teaspoons fennel seed, ground to a coarse powder

2 teaspoons kosher salt

½ teaspoon freshly cracked black pepper

1 whole trimmed beef tenderloin, 4 to 5 pounds (see pages 78 and 79)

Creamy Mustard Sauce (page 77; optional)

1 **SEASON THE BEEF.** In a small bowl, combine the olive oil, rosemary, fennel, salt, and pepper. Stir to make a paste. Pat the beef dry with paper towels and rub the seasonings all over the surface of the meat. Place it on a rimmed baking sheet or large platter and refrigerate, uncovered or loosely covered, for 24 to 36 hours.

2 **TIE THE ROAST.** Remove the roast from the refrigerator. Tuck the thinner tail-like tip under the roast so you have an almost even thickness along the whole roast and, using kitchen string, tie the length of the roast at 2-inch intervals. Let it sit at room temperature for about an hour.

3 **HEAT THE OVEN.** Position a rack in the center of the oven and heat to 375 degrees (350 degrees convection).

4 **ROAST.** Put the roast on a flat rack, if you have one, on a rimmed baking sheet. Roast until an instant-read thermometer inserted in the center reads 120 degrees for rare, 125 degrees to 130 degrees for medium-rare, or 135 degrees for medium, 40 to 50 minutes.

5 **REST, CARVE, AND SERVE.** Transfer to a cutting board, preferably one with a trough, and let rest for 15 minutes. Remove the string and carve crosswise into ⅓- to ½-inch-thick slices. Pass the mustard sauce at the table, if using.

OPTION: CREAMY MUSTARD SAUCE

Delicious with hot beef tenderloin, this sauce is also good as a condiment for room-temperature beef and adds zing to roast beef sandwiches. Covered and refrigerated, it will keep for a few days.

MAKES ABOUT 2/3 CUP, ENOUGH FOR 8 TO 10 SERVINGS

½ cup crème fraîche

2 tablespoons Dijon mustard

2 teaspoons fresh lemon juice

Kosher salt to taste

IN A SMALL BOWL, whisk together the crème fraîche, mustard, and lemon juice. Season to taste with salt.

Shopping for Beef Tenderloin

NO MATTER WHERE YOU SHOP, THE PRICE OF BEEF TENDERLOIN ALWAYS ELICITS A SHOCK, AND FOR GOOD REASON. FOR EVERY 600-POUND (GIVE or take a couple hundred) steer, there are only two 4- to 5-pound trimmed tenderloins. True, there are only two flank steaks, tri-tips, and a few other specialty cuts, but none hold the same cachet (nor bear the price) of the tenderloin, for one simple reason: the tenderloin is, hands-down, the most tender, finely textured cut of beef ever. And while I understand that tenderness is not the be-all and end-all when it comes to judging quality, the appeal of the cut-it-with-a-butter-knife texture and mild taste persists.

A whole tenderloin is a single intact muscle, and as such, there's nothing at all complicated about ordering or purchasing one. The only decision is whether you want to have the butcher trim it for you or trim it yourself. If you shop at a market that sells large hunks of meat in Cryovac, then it's likely you'll be taking home an untrimmed tenderloin. If you're shopping at a full-service market, you will have a choice. It all depends on how much work you want to do at home and whether you want to try to save a few dollars. An untrimmed tenderloin will weigh close to 2 pounds more than a fully trimmed one, but the price per pound will be considerably less. In the end, the decision rests on how much time you want to invest, how skilled you are with your knife, and whether you want to deal with the trim (on the plus side, you'll end up with some first-rate scraps for a quick stir-fry or stroganoff).

If you let the butcher do the work for you, you will want to ask for a trimmed beef tenderloin with the chain (or side muscle) and silverskin removed. When you get it home, inspect it to be sure there is no silverskin left; there shouldn't be. If there are a few patches of fat on the roast, leave these, as they will help baste the roast as it cooks. If you do notice silverskin, remove it by sliding a sharp, thin-bladed knife under the bands of skin and stripping them off, doing your best not to remove much meat.

SUBSTITUTING A SMALLER TENDERLOIN ROAST

You don't need to wait until a dinner party of 8 to serve tenderloin. For a smaller group, look for what's known as a butt tenderloin, a partial tenderloin from the thicker, hip portion of the tenderloin. These weigh between 2 and 3 pounds and make a perfect little roast for 4 to 6 people. Because of the elongated shape of the tenderloin, these shorter roasts take about the same time to roast, so follow either recipe for the whole tenderloin, cutting the seasonings in half. You can also use a smaller tenderloin to make the Sear-Roasted Chateaubriand on page 80.

Trimming Whole Beef Tenderloin

THE FIRST STEP IN PREPARING AN UNTRIMMED TENDERLOIN IS TO USE YOUR HANDS TO PULL AWAY ANY THICK LAYER OF FAT COVERING THE MEAT. THEN locate what's known as the chain (or side muscle), a ragged strip of muscle that runs the length of the tenderloin and is readily apparent by its loose, coarse texture (distinctly different from the smooth, close-grained texture of the actual tenderloin). Starting at the narrow end of the tenderloin, pull the chain with your hands, tugging gently so it separates from the tenderloin proper; a clear, weblike membrane will be holding the two together. The lower part of the chain may pull free entirely by hand, but as you get toward the fatter end (this is the butt end, where the tenderloin was hooked around the pelvic bone), you will need a sharp, thin-bladed knife (a boning knife works best) to separate the chain from the tenderloin. Don't worry if bits of the chain muscle stay behind; you're better off leaving some chain muscle on the tenderloin than removing any precious bits of tenderloin with the chain.

Once the chain is removed, trim it and cut it into smaller pieces and save (or freeze) it for a stir-fry or a quick sauté. Finally, trim away any large hunks of fat from the tenderloin, but don't remove every speck. Then remove any bands of silverskin covering the meat by sliding a sharp, thin-bladed knife under them and stripping them off, angling the knife upward so you scrape silverskin without digging into the beef.

SEAR-ROASTED CHATEAUBRIAND

As much as I love to innovate and explore new flavors, there are times when I crave something classic, and Chateaubriand, especially when paired with béarnaise sauce, more than satisfies that craving. Chateaubriand has come to refer to the center, most indulgent portion of the beef tenderloin. Though you will often see it on restaurant menus (especially around Valentine's Day), as just big enough to serve two, a larger portion makes an exquisite offering for a small dinner party. While you can prepare and serve this cut as you would any cut of beef tenderloin, there is something deeply satisfying about the combination of the tender, almost silky meat and the rich, tarragon-infused butter sauce. One bite and you instantly recognize why this combination has stood the test of time. Because it is smaller than a whole tenderloin, the Chateaubriand is manageable enough to sear in a skillet before gently roasting, which results in a gorgeously browned exterior and an interior that's rosy and juicy.

SERVES 4 TO 6

METHOD: Combination sear and moderate heat

ROASTING TIME: 25 to 35 minutes (plus 8 minutes to sear)

PLAN AHEAD: For best flavor and texture, salt the beef 12 to 24 hours ahead.

WINE: Look for an aged classified growth Bordeaux (Pauillac or St.-Julien), or Napa Valley Cabernet Sauvignon.

One 2- to 2 ½-pound center-cut piece of beef tenderloin, trimmed of silverskin and any excess fat (see Shopping for Chateaubriand, page 81)

Kosher salt and freshly ground black pepper
1 tablespoon peanut oil or grapeseed oil
Béarnaise Sauce (page 82; optional)

1 **SEASON THE BEEF.** Sprinkle the entire surface of the beef with the salt and pepper (I use about 1 teaspoon salt and ½ teaspoon black pepper). Place it on a rimmed baking sheet on a wire rack and refrigerate, uncovered or loosely covered, for 12 to 24 hours.

2 **HEAT THE OVEN.** Position a rack in the center of the oven and heat to 375 degrees (350 degrees convection). Let the beef sit at room temperature for about 30 minutes as the oven heats.

3 **SEAR THE MEAT.** Heat a low-sided, 10-inch ovenproof skillet over medium-high heat until quite hot. Add the oil, and heat until shimmering, about 30 seconds. If the surface of the meat is not very dry, pat it dry with a paper towel. Lower the meat into the skillet and brown one side well. Turn with tongs to brown all sides, about 8 minutes total.

4 **ROAST.** Slide the skillet into the oven, and roast until an instant-read thermometer inserted in the center reads 120 degrees for rare, 125 to 130 degrees for medium-rare, or 135 degrees for medium, 25 to 35 minutes.

5 **REST, CARVE, AND SERVE.** Transfer beef to a carving board, preferably one with a trough, and let rest for 10 to 15 minutes before carving crosswise into ⅓- to ½-inch-thick slices. If serving with the béarnaise, spoon some sauce over each serving or transfer the sauce to a warmed sauceboat and pass it at the table.

CONTINUED ON NEXT PAGE

Shopping for Chateaubriand

DEPENDING ON WHERE YOU SHOP, YOU MAY FIND TWO DEFINITIONS FOR CHATEAUBRIAND. MOST AMERICAN COOKBOOKS (AND THE NATIONAL Livestock Board) describe Chateaubriand as a roast cut from the center portion of the beef tenderloin. Some chefs (notably French ones) and some butchers also use the term to denote a single tenderloin steak (about 1¼-inches thick). Since these smaller steaks are best suited to grilling and sautéing, when I talk about Chateaubriand in this book, I am referring to the larger cut. Some markets use the term filet mignon roast to avoid confusion. Whatever the name, shop for a chunk of tenderloin in the 2- to 2½-pound range. Most often Chateaubriand comes from the evenly shaped center section of the tenderloin, but many markets also take it from the thicker butt portion. Both are good choices.

OPTION: BÉARNAISE SAUCE

Béarnaise is a luxuriantly thick, rich sauce in the same family as hollandaise. Both rely on egg yolks, lots of butter, gentle cooking, and a good deal of whisking to make a thick yet light sauce. What sets béarnaise apart is the addition of a tangy reduction of shallots, tarragon, vinegar, and white wine that provides the perfect counterbalance to the buttery sauce. Making a good béarnaise is all about controlling the heat so that the yolks thicken but don't scramble. Because I work on a gas stove, which responds quickly to adjustments in the level of heat, I cook my sauce directly on the stovetop in my favorite Windsor pan (see What Is a Windsor Pan?, page 84). Some cooks find using a double boiler is a safer bet. If you go that route, you will have more room to whisk if you skip the conventional double boiler and instead set a medium-size metal bowl over a saucepan filled partway with water, being sure the bottom of the bowl sits *above* the surface of the water and not in it. Béarnaise also makes fish, eggs, and vegetables—I love it with asparagus—mighty tasty indeed.

MAKES ABOUT 1 CUP, ENOUGH FOR 4 TO 6 SERVINGS

¼ cup minced shallots (about 1 medium)

¼ cup dry white wine

¼ cup champagne or white wine vinegar

6 whole black peppercorns

Two 3- to 4-inch leafy sprigs tarragon, plus
   2 teaspoons finely chopped fresh tarragon

12 tablespoons (1½ sticks) unsalted butter

2 large egg yolks

Kosher salt and freshly ground black
   pepper

1 **MAKE THE SHALLOT-VINEGAR REDUCTION.** Combine the shallots, white wine, vinegar, peppercorns, and tarragon sprigs in a small saucepan. Bring to a simmer over medium-high heat and cook until you have only 2 tablespoons of liquid left and the shallots begin to look dry, about 5 minutes. Strain through a small fine-mesh strainer (I often use a tea strainer), pressing firmly on the solids, into a bowl or liquid measure. Discard the solids and let the liquid cool to room temperature.

2 **CLARIFY THE BUTTER.** Melt the butter in a small heavy-based saucepan over medium-low heat. Once the butter is melted, adjust the heat so it simmers gently (it will splatter some, but the idea is to control the heat so it doesn't pop and splatter wildly). Simmer until there appears to be no more foam rising to the surface, about 3 minutes. The butter will have separated into three parts: solids floating on top, a clear golden liquid, and more solids resting on the bottom of the pan. Remove from

the heat and spoon off just the thick foam from the surface, doing your best not to spoon away the clear liquid butter; don't worry about removing every last bit of foam. Set the butter aside in a warm spot; when you make the sauce, you need the butter to be warm enough that it doesn't solidify, but not so hot that it breaks the emulsion.

3   **MAKE THE EMULSION.** Combine the egg yolks with 1 tablespoon of the shallot-vinegar reduction and 1 tablespoon water in a heavy-based saucepan (a 1½- to 2-quart pan, preferably a Windsor pan, works well) or in a medium metal mixing bowl. Whisk the yolks vigorously, off the heat, until they are lighter in color and have gained a little volume, about 30 seconds.

    Set the saucepan over low to medium-low heat (if using the bowl for a double boiler, set the bowl over a pan of barely simmering water, making sure the bottom of the bowl does not touch the surface of the water). Heat the yolks, whisking constantly and vigorously, until the yolks lighten in color and thicken just enough so the whisk leaves tracks on the bottom of the pan (or bowl) as you drag it across, 2 to 3 minutes. (Do not try to rush this process; if the heat is too high, you risk scrambling the yolks and ruining the sauce.) Once the yolks are thickened, immediately remove the pan (or bowl) from the heat and whisk for another 30 seconds to slow the cooking.

4   **ADD THE BUTTER.** Begin whisking in the clarified butter, a tablespoon or so at a time, until the sauce is thick and voluminous. (If at any time the butter doesn't appear to incorporate into the sauce—in other words, if the sauce threatens to break—stop adding butter and whisk the sauce steadily until it comes back together.) Continue adding all of the clarified butter, pouring carefully so you don't add the milky solids that have sunk to the bottom.

5   **FINISH THE SAUCE.** Whisk in 1 teaspoon of the remaining shallot-vinegar reduction, ½ teaspoon salt, and the finely chopped tarragon. Season to taste with the remaining reduction, more salt, and pepper. Keep in a warm, but not hot, place until ready to serve. (I generally keep it near the back of the stove.)

What Is a Windsor Pan?

IF YOU MAKE A LOT OF SAUCES, I STRONGLY ENCOURAGE USING (AND buying if need be) a Windsor pan. The shape of a Windsor pan—a narrow base and flared sides—offers many advantages. A smaller base means less contact with the burner, making the pan less prone to accidental overheating; it cools more quickly when you remove it from the burner, which allows for more control. The wider top of the pan helps in both reduction sauces and emulsified sauces. For reduction sauces, the flared sides provide a lot of surface area for maximum evaporation. As the volume reduces, the surface area shrinks (as the sauce reduces down toward the narrower part of the pan), so you are less apt to scorch or over-reduce a sauce. When making emulsified sauces that require whisking, the wider top gives you more room to work, allowing you to incorporate a maximum amount of air, thus creating lighter, fluffier, more stable sauces. The best Windsor pans are heavy-based (for even heat) and include some type of highly conductive metal (such as copper or aluminum), making them quick to heat and easy to cool. The classic Windsor pan has a copper exterior with a nonreactive liner, but more common today is stainless steel construction with a layer of copper (or aluminum) sandwiched inside. For most of my sauce making, I use a 1½-quart Windsor pan. Well-equipped kitchens often include a larger Windsor pan, close to 4 quarts, that looks more like a deep sauté pan with splayed sides. These are good for making large quantities of sauce and for skillet roasting.

STANDING RIB ROAST (PRIME RIB)

My family celebrates Christmas around the table—or I should say tables. You see, when we all come together, we number close to 40 people. To feed this horde, we organize an elaborate sort of potluck. Various relations pitch in by bringing casseroles and salads as well as the requisite holiday ham and turkey, but for as long as anyone can remember, the centerpiece of the meal has been my father's glorious standing rib roast. Although he handed over the carving responsibilities in his later years, he insisted on making his roast beef well into his eighties. My father recently passed away, but we keep up the family tradition. Every time I make this standing rib roast recipe, I think of him and fondly remember his patriarchal generosity.

My father's approach to seasonings was minimalist: salt, pepper, dry mustard, and rosemary. I can just hear him remarking that if you buy a good piece of beef (which he always did), why would you muck it up with a bunch of other ingredients? I agree. Probably the biggest difference between my father's approach and mine is that he would roast the beef until, as he would say, "It looked pretty good." I am too anxious a cook for such a cavalier attitude, and I use a meat thermometer. Both our methods had the same goal: a roast that is bloody near the bone, rosy and juicy throughout, with some well-done pieces on the outside for those few who prefer it that way.

If you are serving more than sixteen people (and aren't supplementing with a ham and a turkey, as we do!), shop for a larger roast (see Shopping for Standing Rib Roast, or Prime Rib, page 87). A larger roast will be longer, not thicker, so it will roast in about the same time. In my house, it's unacceptable to serve prime rib without Yorkshire pudding, so I have included a recipe (page 88). You could also use the drippings to make British Roast Potatoes (page 499).

SERVES 12 TO 16

METHOD: Combination high and moderate heat

ROASTING TIME: 2 1/4 to 2 3/4 hours

PLAN AHEAD: For the best flavor, season the roast at least 1 day and up to 3 days before roasting it. The roast should sit at room temperature for 3 hours before roasting for most even cooking.

WINE: For such a special occasion, reach deep into the cellar for a "best bottle" of aged Cabernet from California, Washington, or Australia, or a fine classified Bordeaux from Pauillac or St.-Julien.

CONTINUED ON NEXT PAGE

One 5-rib standing rib roast (10 to 12 pounds), tied at intervals between the rib bones

Scant 2 tablespoons kosher salt

1½ tablespoons dry mustard

1½ tablespoons chopped fresh rosemary, or 2 teaspoons dried rosemary

Coarsely ground black pepper

1 **SEASON THE ROAST.** Sprinkle the roast all over, including the bones, with the salt. Rub the mustard over all the meat and then sprinkle rosemary and black pepper over the top. Set the roast rib side down on a baking sheet. Refrigerate, uncovered or loosely covered, for 1 to 3 days. Remove the roast from the refrigerator about 3 hours before you plan to roast it.

2 **HEAT THE OVEN.** Position a rack in the bottom third of the oven. (You will need room above to accommodate the large roast.) Heat the oven to 450 degrees (425 degrees convection).

3 **ROAST.** Place the roast rib side down in a heavy roasting pan not much larger than the meat (12 by 14 inches works nicely). Slide the roast into the oven with the bone ends facing the oven door. Roast until the outside begins to brown and sizzle, about 20 minutes. Without opening the oven, lower the temperature to 325 degrees (300 degrees convection). Continue roasting for another 1½ hours before beginning to check for doneness with an instant-read thermometer. Because this cut of meat is so large, there will be more carryover cooking than with smaller roasts (the internal temperature will rise as much as 10 to 15 degrees while the meat rests), which means you need to remove the meat at a lower temperature than for smaller roasts. For rare meat, take the roast out when it reaches 110 to 115 degrees; for medium-rare, 120 degrees, and for medium, 125 degrees. If the meat hasn't reached the desired doneness, wait another 10 to 15 minutes before checking again. Once the internal temperature reaches about 95 degrees, expect it to rise 8 to 10 degrees for every 10 minutes more in the oven.

4 **REST, CARVE, AND SERVE.** Transfer the roast to a carving board, ideally one with a large trough, and let it rest for 25 to 40 minutes. If the kitchen is cool or drafty, cover the roast loosely with foil. If you are making Yorkshire pudding to go with the roast, pour the beef drippings into a glass measuring cup and reserve, and set the hot roasting pan aside. Carve the meat as directed on page 90 and serve, spooning any carving juices over the meat.

CONTINUED ON PAGE 88

Shopping for Standing Rib Roast, or Prime Rib

MANY PEOPLE REFER TO A STANDING RIB ROAST AS PRIME RIB, AND DEPENDING ON THE SIZE OF THE ROAST, THIS MAY OR MAY NOT BE ACCURATE. The term *prime rib* derives from the first step in butchering, whereby a steer is divided into 8 large cuts, known as "primal cuts," one of which is the rib, or "primal rib." Prime rib is merely the more familiar, more appetizing name for the entire rib section, consisting of 7 rib bones and weighing upward of 20 pounds. You'll most likely find these gargantuan roasts at restaurants that specialize in prime rib, or, if your family is as large as mine, at big holiday gatherings. (The other niggling confusion regarding prime rib is that the term *prime* has nothing to do with the grade of the beef; for more on this, see Buying Good-Quality Beef, page 56).

Most of the time when you're shopping for a partial rib roast, you'll be looking for what is more correctly known as a rib roast or standing rib roast—a name meant to convey the regal way the roast stands tall on its rack of bones. Most butchers label these roasts according to the number of rib bones to indicate the size of the roast. Depending on the rest of the menu and who will be at the table, you can figure 1 rib for every 2 to 3 people. For instance, the 5-rib roast I call for on page 86 will serve 12 to 16 people. (Anything smaller than a 3-rib roast is no longer considered a standing rib roast; it becomes simply a rib roast, as on page 93.) Keep in mind, you're not serving the roast sliced into single "chops" the way you would pork or lamb (these are beef ribs we're talking about, and each one offers a hefty portion of meat). You can also shop by weight, figuring about 12 ounces per person. Some older cookbooks recommend 1 pound per person, but I can't imagine any group except for a crew of lumberjacks eating this much.

When buying a partial rib roast, you also can select between a leaner, more tender roast or fattier, more robust roast by simply specifying which end of the prime rib you want. Let me explain. A steer has 13 ribs, but the first 5 ribs are part of the shoulder section (or chuck) and, as such, are too tough and chewy for roasting. The prime rib starts with rib number 6 (the first rib below the shoulder) and runs through to include rib number 12, just above the saddle. (Number 13 goes with the midsection, or loin). Even though the same muscle runs the length of the prime rib, it varies from fattier and more robust near the shoulder to leaner and more tender as it gets closer to the saddle section. In other words, the lower number ribs (6 though 9) are richer and beefier, while the higher numbers (10 through 12) are leaner. The diameter of the roast also tapers in size, resulting in butchers referring to

CONTINUED ON NEXT PAGE

the shoulder end as the "large end" and the saddle end as the "small end." Other labels used to distinguish the ends are the "chuck end" or "blade end" for the larger, fattier, beefier end, while the leaner, more tender end goes by "loin end" and sometimes "first cut." Though the large-end roasts may have a more meaty flavor, I prefer the leaner roasts from the small end because they don't have unruly shoulder muscles that remain in the ribs from the large end.

Whatever rib roast you buy, you want a neat roast that includes only the rib-eye attached to an arching rack of rib bones. Nowadays, most meat markets sell rib roasts with the backbone (chine bone and featherbone assembly) already removed, but it's always good to check. Some markets will slice the meat off the bones and then tie it back on, which certainly makes carving easier. Either way, be sure the roast is tied at intervals between each rib bone. If not, you will want to do this at home with kitchen string. Otherwise the crispy top layer may peel away from the meat during roasting.

OPTION: YORKSHIRE PUDDING

As the name implies, this dish originated in Yorkshire, England. However, it's not a pudding at all. More like a wonderfully rich popover, it's a batter of eggs and milk enriched by beef drippings, baked until light and puffy. As the story goes, Yorkshire housewives always served the pudding as a separate course before the roast so their families would eat less of the more costly meat entrée. Nowadays it's served in small pieces alongside the meat as a delectable accompaniment. Though you can buy pans to make individual Yorkshire puddings, I prefer to bake it directly in the roasting pan so the batter can soak up all the savor of the beef drippings. Served this way, the pudding may not look as pretty, but its beef-suffused flavor more than makes up for any deficit in appearance.

Making the batter a few hours in advance will result in a lighter pudding. The pudding bakes for about 30 minutes—giving the roast time to rest and you time to organize the rest of the meal. These quantities work for a 12-by-14-inch roasting pan. If you're using a larger pan (such as 17-by-13-inch), use 4 eggs, ½ teaspoon salt, 2 cups milk, 1 ¾ cups flour, and the same amount of beef drippings and follow the recipe.

SERVES 12 TO 16
PLAN AHEAD: For best results, the batter should rest for 2 to 5 hours.

3 large eggs

½ teaspoon kosher salt

1½ cups whole milk

1⅓ cups all-purpose flour, sifted

¼ cup beef drippings

1 **MAKE THE BATTER.** In a medium mixing bowl, whisk together the eggs and salt until frothy. Whisk in the milk, followed by the flour, until well blended. Cover and refrigerate for 2 to 5 hours.

2 **HEAT THE OVEN.** Place a rack in the center of the oven and heat the oven to 450 degrees (425 degrees convection).

3 **HEAT THE DRIPPINGS.** Add the beef drippings to the roasting pan and heat in the oven until hot and sizzling, 4 to 6 minutes.

4 **BAKE.** Stir the batter. Slide out the oven rack holding the roasting pan just enough so you can pour the batter into the pan all at once. Don't worry about tilting the pan to spread it evenly; the batter is so liquid that it will spread on its own. Bake for 12 minutes. Lower the oven temperature to 350 degrees (325 degrees convection), rotate the pan front to back, and continue baking until the pudding is puffy and nicely browned, about 15 more minutes.

5 **SERVE.** Cut into small squares and serve immediately.

Carving Standing Rib Roast

HOW YOU APPROACH CARVING PRIME RIB DEPENDS ENTIRELY ON HOW YOU BOUGHT IT. IF THE MEAT WAS SLICED OFF THE BONE AND THEN TIED BACK on by the butcher (as is often the case), then it's merely a matter of snipping the strings, lifting the meat off the bones, and slicing the loaf-shaped roast across the grain into thick or thin slices as you like; I find that ¼- to ½-inch-thick slices please just about everyone.

If, however, the bones are still attached, you have two options. The first is the easier, but less showy. Start by standing the roast on its side, lengthwise, so the rib ends point toward the ceiling. Then, with a large carving knife, slice the meat away from the bones, doing your best to scrape the bones and leave as little meat on them as possible, and remove the meat in one large piece. Set the bones aside and slice the meat across the grain.

The other method for carving prime rib harkens back to the era when a waiter in a fancy restaurant might stand at a carving station ceremoniously serving up the prime rib; it is also sometimes referred to as the English method, evoking a sense of Old World decorum. Start by determining which end of the roast is larger, and then stand the roast up on one end with the larger end down. If the roast is at all wobbly, return it to its original position and cut a thin slice from the larger end to form an even base. Now, with the ribs toward the left (if you are right-handed), steady the roast by holding a carving fork firmly against the bones. With a carving knife, slice the meat from the outside horizontally in toward the bone, making even strokes and cutting ½- to ¾-inch-thick slices. When you reach the bone, continue holding the bones with the fork and slice down along them to free the slice. Use the fork and knife in combination to pick up the slice and transfer it to a platter or individual plate. Continue slicing horizontal slices until you've worked your way to the bottom.

Whichever way you carve, serve the beef on a warm platter (or individual plates) and spoon any carving juices over the meat before serving. If you'd like to offer the meaty bones, slice into individual bones and pile on a separate platter (or save them for Quick Deviled Rib Bones, page 91).

Quick Deviled Rib Bones

WINE: Young Zinfandel or Shiraz.

After serving prime rib, you'll be left with the meaty rib bones (that is, if your guests don't nab them to nibble on). Before you even think about giving them to the dog or, worse, throwing them out, try this quick yet irresistible recipe. Even if you don't think of yourself as the bone-gnawing type, I think you'll find these sizzling, crispy ribs irresistible. I like to enjoy one (or two) rib bones as an indulgent afternoon snack, or turn them into lunch by adding a tossed salad and some good bread.

Here's how to do it: Using a large chef's knife, carve down between the bones, separating the rack into individual ribs. Paint each with a thin coat of Dijon mustard (1 generous teaspoon per rib) and season with a pinch of salt and plenty of black pepper (the mustard and pepper "devil" the bones with their heat). Arrange the bones meat side up, without touching, on a baking sheet and bake at 450 degrees (425 degrees convection), flipping them once about halfway through, until sizzling and crispy on all sides, about 15 minutes. Serve hot with plenty of napkins, as deviled bones are best enjoyed eaten by hand.

ONE-HOUR ROSEMARY RIB ROAST

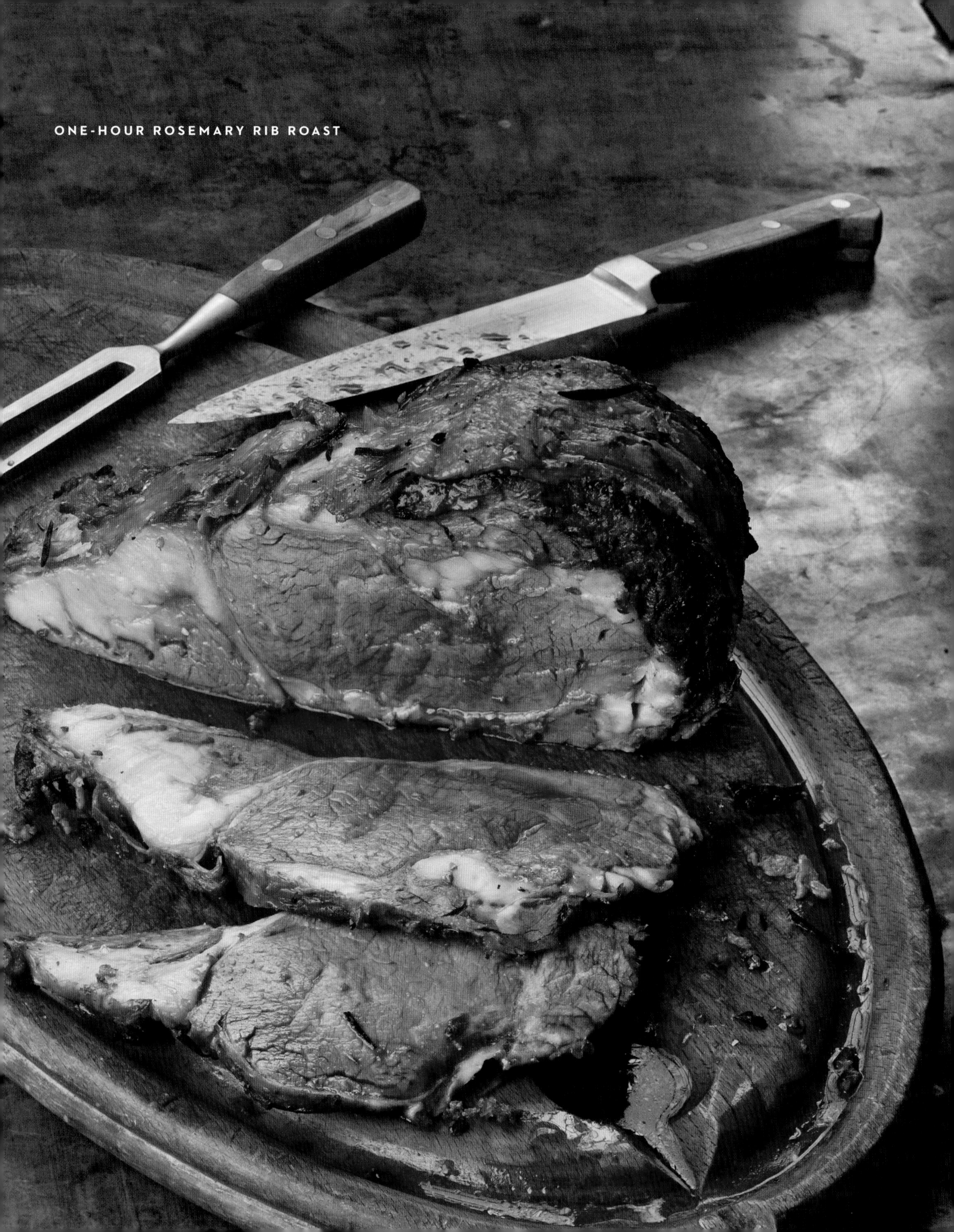

ONE-HOUR ROSEMARY RIB ROAST

If you think of beef rib roast as strictly holiday fare, something spectacular for a once-a-year gathering of a sizable crowd, you'll be pleased to discover this smaller but equally elegant version. This high-heat method works perfectly for a small rib roast. The very center slices are fiercely rare, and the outer slices come out medium-rare to medium.

To make serving easier, the beef gets carved off the bone and then tied back onto the bone before roasting. This provides the opportunity to slide rosemary sprigs between the bottom of the roast and the bones, which gives the roast a dramatic spiked appearance and adds a depth of flavor to the meat. I like to season the roast and wrap it in rosemary a day or two in advance, but 4 to 6 hours will do. The further ahead you season, the better the rosemary permeates the meat.

SERVES 6

METHOD: High heat

ROASTING TIME: 1 to 1 1/3 hours

PLAN AHEAD: Season the roast at least 4 hours and up to 2 days ahead. The meat should sit for at least 2 hours at room temperature before roasting.

WINE: Deeply flavored California or Washington State Merlot or Merlot blend.

One 2-rib beef rib roast (about 4 ½ pounds)

1 tablespoon kosher salt

1 garlic clove, crushed to a paste

Coarsely ground black pepper

12 to 14 fresh rosemary sprigs (3 to 4 inches each)

Horseradish Cream Sauce (page 69; optional)

---

1   **PREPARE AND SEASON THE ROAST** (as shown on page 95). If the butcher hasn't already carved the meat off the bone, do so as follows: Hold the roast with your nondominant hand so the rib ends point toward the ceiling. Now, resting your knife flat against the curved rack of rib bones, make several smooth incisions to cut the meat away from the bones, leaving a minimal amount of meat on the bones and without cutting into the meat. When you finish, you should have a neat rib-eye roast and a curved rack of rib bones. Season the meat all over with salt and black pepper, and rub with the garlic paste.

CONTINUED ON NEXT PAGE

Next wrap the roast in rosemary sprigs, a maneuver that may require a second pair of hands the first time you try it. Begin by laying out 3 lengths of kitchen string long enough to wrap generously around the roast. Set the rack of bones on the string, so one piece of string sits between the two bones and the other strings are on either side (everything doesn't need to be perfectly situated at this point). Now arrange 4 rosemary sprigs on the rack of ribs, so the sprigs run perpendicular to the direction of the ribs. With both hands, lift the rib roast and place it on the ribs (on top of the rosemary), putting the meat back where it was before the bones got carved off. Now the idea is to attach the remaining rosemary sprigs around the circumference of the roast, running in the same direction as the sprigs already lined up underneath. It can be tricky to hold the rosemary in place and tie the string, so if someone else is around, enlist help at least to secure the middle string. Once the rosemary is secured, set the roast on a tray or in a shallow baking dish and refrigerate, uncovered or loosely covered, for 4 hours or, preferably, 1 to 2 days. Let it sit at room temperature for 2 hours before roasting.

2 **HEAT THE OVEN.** Position a rack near the center of the oven and heat to 450 degrees (425 degrees convection).

3 **ROAST.** Place the roast on a heavy-duty rimmed baking sheet or in a shallow roasting pan not much bigger than the roast itself. (Since the rack of bones keeps the meat off the bottom of the pan, it doesn't need a roasting rack.) Roast, and don't be alarmed if the rosemary begins to smoke partway through. The meat will be fine. After 1 hour, check the progress by inserting an instant-read thermometer in the center. You are looking for an internal temperature of about 115 degrees for rare or 120 to 125 degrees for medium-rare. As you check for doneness, keep in mind that the high oven heat will cause the temperature to rise rapidly. Once the roast gets above 100 degrees, check every 5 minutes or so.

4 **REST, CARVE, AND SERVE.** Transfer the roast to a carving board, preferably one with a trough to catch any drippings, and rest for 20 to 30 minutes. Snip the strings, discard the charred rosemary, lift the meat off the bones, and slice into ¼- to ½-inch-thick slices. Spoon any juices over the meat as you serve it, and pass the horseradish cream sauce if you like. Offer the bones to whoever relishes gnawing on meaty bones—a very tasty part of the roast—or save them for Quick Deviled Rib Bones (page 91) for lunch or a snack the next day.

Step-by-Step: Seasoning Rosemary Rib Roast

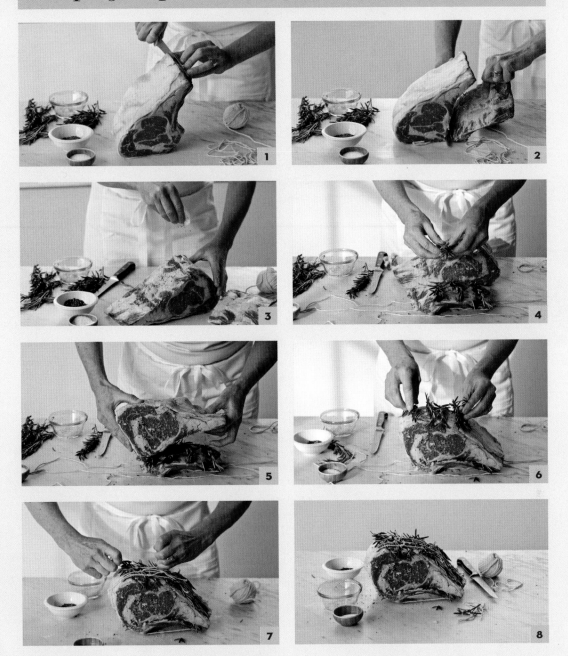

1 If the butcher hasn't already carved the meat off the bone, hold the top of the rib bones with your non-dominant hand and, with the blade of your knife, locate the inside surface of the rib bones. **2** Make several smooth incisions to cut the meat away from the bones, leaving a minimum amount of meat on the bones and without cutting into the meat. Finish by cutting the roast completely away from the curved rack of rib bones. **3** Season the meat all over with salt and pepper and rub with garlic paste. **4** Lay out 3 lengths of kitchen string long enough to generously wrap around the roast, and set the rack of bones on the string. Arrange four rosemary sprigs on the rack of ribs, so the sprigs run perpendicular to the direction of the ribs. Everything doesn't need to be perfectly situated at this point. **5** Lift the rib roast and place it back on the ribs (on top of the rosemary). **6** Arrange the remaining rosemary sprigs on top of the roast. **7** One by one, snug the strings and tie them so they hold the rosemary and bones in place. **8** One-Hour Rosemary Rib Roast, ready for roasting.

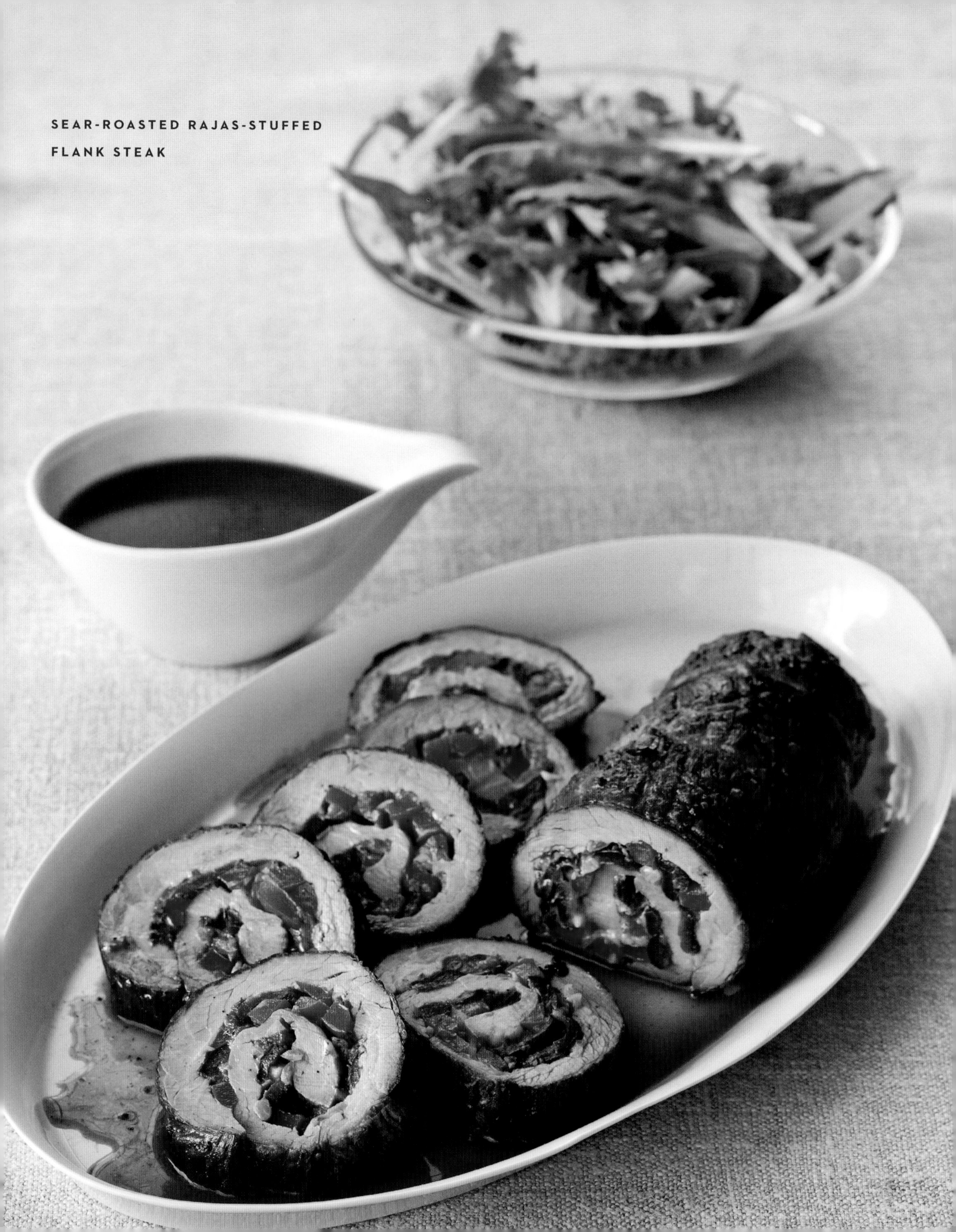

SEAR-ROASTED RAJAS-STUFFED FLANK STEAK

SEAR-ROASTED RAJAS-STUFFED FLANK STEAK

Flank steak, with its flat, rectangular shape, usually ends up on the grill or under the broiler, but by butterflying it and rolling it around a savory filling, you can transform this beefy cut into a wonderful roast. Once stuffed, the roast is seared in a hot skillet and then gently roasted in a low oven. It comes out rosy and tender in the center, with a swirl of filling and a handsome browned exterior. The flavorful pan drippings provide the basis for a quick pan sauce that comes together as the meat rests.

In this recipe, I stuff the beef with one of my favorite things in the world: rajas, a mix of roasted peppers, onion, and cheese. I also make this with a savory stuffing of sautéed mushrooms, shallots, and thyme (see the option on page 100). Once you get the hang of the method, feel free to experiment by coming up with your own variations. This recipe includes quite a few steps, including making the filling, but you can stuff the flank steak a day in advance to get ahead. In fact, the flavor will be even richer that way. Just be sure to cool the stuffing completely before assembling the roast.

SERVES 4 TO 6

METHOD: Combination sear and low heat

ROASTING TIME: 40 to 50 minutes (plus about 8 minutes to sear)

PLAN AHEAD: The filling must be cooked and cooled before you stuff the flank steak.

WINE/BEER: Medium-bodied red with youthful fruit and spice elements, like a Chilean Carménère or an Australian Grenache-Shiraz blend; or lighter Belgian ale.

One 1½- to 2-pound flank steak, preferably over ½-inch thick

Kosher salt and freshly ground black pepper

Rajas Filling (page 99)

2 tablespoons extra-virgin olive oil

¾ cup dry white wine or dry white vermouth, plus more as needed

½ cup homemade or store-bought low-sodium beef or chicken broth

¼ cup crème fraîche or heavy cream

CONTINUED ON NEXT PAGE

1 **HEAT THE OVEN.** Position a rack in the center of the oven and heat to 275 degrees (250 degrees convection). If working ahead, wait to heat the oven.

2 **BUTTERFLY THE FLANK STEAK** (as shown on page 103). Lay the flank steak on a cutting board with one of the shorter sides facing you. The grain of the meat should run vertically. Trim off any large bits of fat, but don't remove all of it. Holding a long sharp thin knife (I use a boning knife) parallel to the cutting board, begin slicing into one of the long sides of the steak so that you are cutting horizontally so you can open the steak like a book. It's a good idea to take your time, making careful knife strokes to avoid cutting through the steak. If you do happen to cut a hole in the meat, simply stop, realign your knife, and continue. As you slice, it can be helpful to place your noncutting hand on top of the steak to steady it. As best you can, move the knife in long sweeping motions and avoid sawing away. Stop slicing when you get within ½ inch of the other long side. Open the steak like a book. Lay a piece of plastic wrap over the butterflied steak, and with a meat pounder or rolling pin, pound the meat to create an even thickness, paying special attention to the center ridge where you opened the steak. You are not trying to make the steak significantly thinner, just to even it out.

3 **FILL AND ROLL THE STEAK** (as shown on page 103). Turn the butterflied steak so the center seam runs parallel to the counter edge; this means the grain of the meat will be running parallel to the counter edge as well. Season the cut side of the steak lightly with salt and pepper. Spread the cooled filling evenly over the steak, leaving about an inch clear along the edge farthest from you and along the two edges that run perpendicular to the counter edge (so the filling won't squeeze out when you roll up the steak).

   Starting at the edge closest to you, roll the steak jelly-roll style to enclose the filling, but not so tightly that you squeeze out any filling. Arrange the roll seam side down and secure it with kitchen string tied at 1¼-inch intervals. Season the outside with salt and pepper. *You can stuff the steak and keep it refrigerated overnight. Just let it sit at room temperature for 30 to 45 minutes while you wait for the oven to heat before roasting.*

4 **SEAR AND ROAST.** Heat the oil over medium-high heat in a large ovenproof skillet (I use a 12-inch heavy round skillet; an oval skillet will work as well). Pat the roast

dry. Lower the flank steak into the skillet and brown on all sides, turning with tongs, about 8 minutes total. Slide the skillet into the oven and, before closing the oven door, add ½ cup wine to the skillet. Roast the meat until an instant-read thermometer inserted in the center reads about 145 degrees, 40 to 50 minutes. If at any time during roasting the bottom of the skillet appears to be getting too brown, add another ¼ to ½ cup wine or water. Transfer the roast to a cutting board, preferably one with a trough, and let rest about 10 minutes.

5 **MAKE THE SAUCE.** Pour any excess fat from the roasting skillet, but don't pour away any of the good drippings. (Be careful not to grab the handle with a bare hand; I find it helps to drape a kitchen towel or pot holder over the handle as a reminder.) Set the skillet over medium-high heat. Add the remaining ¼ cup wine or vermouth to the pan and bring to a boil, scraping up the browned bits on the bottom of the pan with a wooden spoon. Immediately pour the liquid into a small saucepan and return to a boil. Add the broth and simmer briskly over medium heat until reduced by half, about 6 minutes. Add the crème fraîche or cream to the sauce and simmer until slightly reduced, 2 to 3 more minutes. Lower the heat to a gentle simmer and taste for salt and pepper. Keep the sauce warm until ready to serve.

6 **CARVE AND SERVE.** Add any juices accumulated on the cutting board to the sauce. Slice the steak into ½-inch-thick slices, snipping the strings as you go. Transfer the slices to individual plates or a serving platter, handling them gently so they don't unroll. If some of the stuffing falls out, simply serve it on top. Serve the meat with a little sauce poured over the top. Pass any extra sauce at the table.

RAJAS FILLING

The word *rajas* means "strips" in Spanish, and in the kitchen it refers to strips of roasted chile peppers or, in this case, strips of poblano and red bell peppers. Rajas relies primarily on poblano peppers, which have a complex, almost grassy flavor, but I include a small red bell pepper for sweetness and color. Delicious as a stuffing for flank steak, rajas also make a fantastic taco filling and may be served as a side dish, too.

MAKES ABOUT 1 GENEROUS CUP, ENOUGH TO STUFF ONE FLANK STEAK

CONTINUED ON NEXT PAGE

2 poblano peppers (see page 102)

1 small red bell pepper

2 tablespoons extra-virgin olive oil, plus
  more for rubbing

½ cup finely chopped white onions

Kosher salt and freshly ground black
  pepper

2 to 3 garlic cloves, minced

1 teaspoon dried oregano

½ teaspoon cumin seed, ground

½ teaspoon paprika, sweet or hot

½ cup shredded Monterey jack cheese
  (about 2 ounces)

2 tablespoons chopped fresh cilantro leaves
  and tender stems

1 **HEAT THE OVEN.** Position a rack near the center of the oven and heat to 375 degrees (350 degrees convection).

2 **ROAST THE PEPPERS.** Rub the peppers with a thin film of olive oil and arrange them on a baking sheet. Roast, turning with tongs after 20 minutes, until blistered all over and ready to collapse, 40 to 45 minutes. Transfer to a bowl, cover with plastic wrap, and set aside until cool enough to handle.

3 **PEEL AND SLICE THE PEPPERS.** When the peppers are cool, slip off their skins with your fingers. Rinsing the peppers washes away much of their flavor, so peel them without water. It's fine to leave a few bits of char. Once the peppers are peeled, slice them open, cut away the stems, and remove the clusters of seeds attached to the stems. Cut all the peppers into ¼-inch strips.

4 **MAKE THE FILLING.** Heat the 2 tablespoons of olive oil in a medium skillet (10 inches works well) over medium heat. Add the onions, season with salt and pepper, and sauté until tender but not brown, about 5 minutes. Add the garlic, oregano, cumin, and paprika. Continue to sauté until fragrant, another 2 minutes. Add the poblano and red pepper strips, stir, and sauté for 1 minute to combine the flavors. Transfer to a bowl and set aside to cool. Stir in the cheese and cilantro and taste for salt and pepper. *The filling may be made up to a day ahead and kept refrigerated.*

OPTION: MUSHROOM FILLING FOR SEAR-ROASTED FLANK STEAK

The pairing of beef and mushrooms always delivers great flavor and pleases most everyone. I like to use a combination of shiitake, cremini, and oyster mushrooms, but you can use whatever you like or looks good in the market. Once the mushrooms are sautéed, let them cool, and then use them in place of the rajas filling in the recipe for sear-roasted flank steak on page 97.

on page 97.

MAKES 1 SCANT CUP, ENOUGH TO STUFF 1 FLANK STEAK

WINE: Rich, earthy Grenache blend from France's Southern Rhône Valley, such as Chateauneuf-du-Pape or Gigondas.

1 pound mixed fresh mushrooms, such as shiitake, cremini, and oyster, cleaned and stem ends trimmed (see Cleaning Mushrooms, page 459)

1 tablespoon extra-virgin olive oil

1 tablespoon unsalted butter

Kosher salt and freshly ground black pepper

1 medium shallot, minced (about 3 tablespoons)

2 garlic cloves, minced

1 teaspoon fresh thyme leaves, roughly chopped

¼ cup homemade or low-salt chicken broth

¼ cup freshly grated Parmigiano-Reggiano cheese

2 tablespoons chopped flat-leaf parsley

1 **SLICE THE MUSHROOMS.** If you are using shiitakes, tear off and discard the stems (they are too fibrous to include). Slice the mushrooms very thin.

2 **SAUTÉ THE MUSHROOMS.** Heat the oil and butter in a large skillet (I like a 12-inch one) over medium heat. When the butter begins to foam, add the mushrooms and season with salt and pepper. Sauté, stirring frequently, until the mushrooms begin to wilt, about 3 minutes. Add the shallot, garlic, and thyme, and continue to sauté, stirring occasionally but not constantly, until the mushrooms start to brown, another 4 to 6 minutes. If the mushrooms release a lot of liquid, increase the heat slightly to evaporate most of the liquid so that the mushrooms will brown. Add the chicken broth, stir to deglaze the bottom of the pan, and simmer until the broth is mostly absorbed, about 1 minute. Remove from the heat and transfer to a bowl to cool.

3 **FINISH THE FILLING.** Stir the cheese and parsley into the mushrooms. Taste for salt and pepper. Set aside to cool. *The filling may be made up to a day ahead and kept refrigerated.*

Shopping for and Handling Poblano Chile Peppers

ONCE AVAILABLE ONLY IN LATINO MARKETS AND SOUTH OF THE BORDER, POBLANOS HAVE BECOME INCREASINGLY AVAILABLE IN SUPERMARKETS everywhere. Best recognized by shape and color, a fresh poblano is slightly smaller than a standard bell pepper, has a wavy triangular silhouette with broad shoulders and sides that often indent toward a pointy, upturned tip, and has shiny dark green skin. When buying poblanos, look for ones with a tight, almost polished appearance, without cuts or soft spots. They should feel heavy for their size, as the longer they sit in storage, the lighter they get.

The one tricky aspect of cooking with poblano chiles is that their heat level can vary from mild to jalapeño-hot, and there's really no way to tell until you taste the individual peppers. If you appreciate spicy food, as I do, you will probably enjoy the variance. Although I have certainly encountered a few extra-*picante* poblanos, I've never been unhappy eating them. Rather, I've always enjoyed their rich, complex flavor, no matter the burn. If you possess a more delicate palate, you may want to proceed with caution and sample the chile before adding it to any recipe. The best way to taste a chile you're not sure of is just to touch a piece to the tip of your tongue and wait a second. If there's no immediate burn, go ahead and take a small taste.

When you come across a poblano that's too high on the heat scale, there are a few ways to tame the fire. First, be sure to remove all the seeds and every bit of the veins (also called ribs, these are the source of the heat in a chile). If the pepper is still too hot for your taste, rinse it under cold water after roasting, or, for raw poblanos, soak for 10 to 20 minutes in lightly salted water and rinse. I advise these last steps only as a last resort, since they take away much of the chile's flavor.

Step-by-Step:
Butterflying and
Stuffing
Flank Steak

1 Begin slicing along one of the long sides of the steak so that you are cutting the steak horizontally in half. Press lightly with your non-cutting hand to firm the steak and make it easier to slice. **2** Continue slicing the steak in half, making careful, sweeping knife strokes, and begin to open up the steak like a book. Stop slicing when you get within 1/2-inch of the other long side. **3** Lay a piece of plastic wrap over the butterflied steak, and with a meat pounder or straight rolling pin (pictured here), pound the meat to create an even thickness, paying special attention to the center ridge. **4** Season the steak with salt and pepper, and spread the cooled filling evenly, leaving about an inch clear along the edge farthest from you, and along the two edges that run perpendicular to the counter edge. **5** Starting at the edge closest to you, roll the steak, jelly-roll style, around the filling. **6** Continue rolling to enclose the filling, but not so tightly that you squeeze out any filling. **7** Arrange the roll seam-side down and secure it with kitchen string tied at 1 1/4-inch intervals.

STEAKHOUSE-STYLE SEAR-ROASTED STRIP STEAK

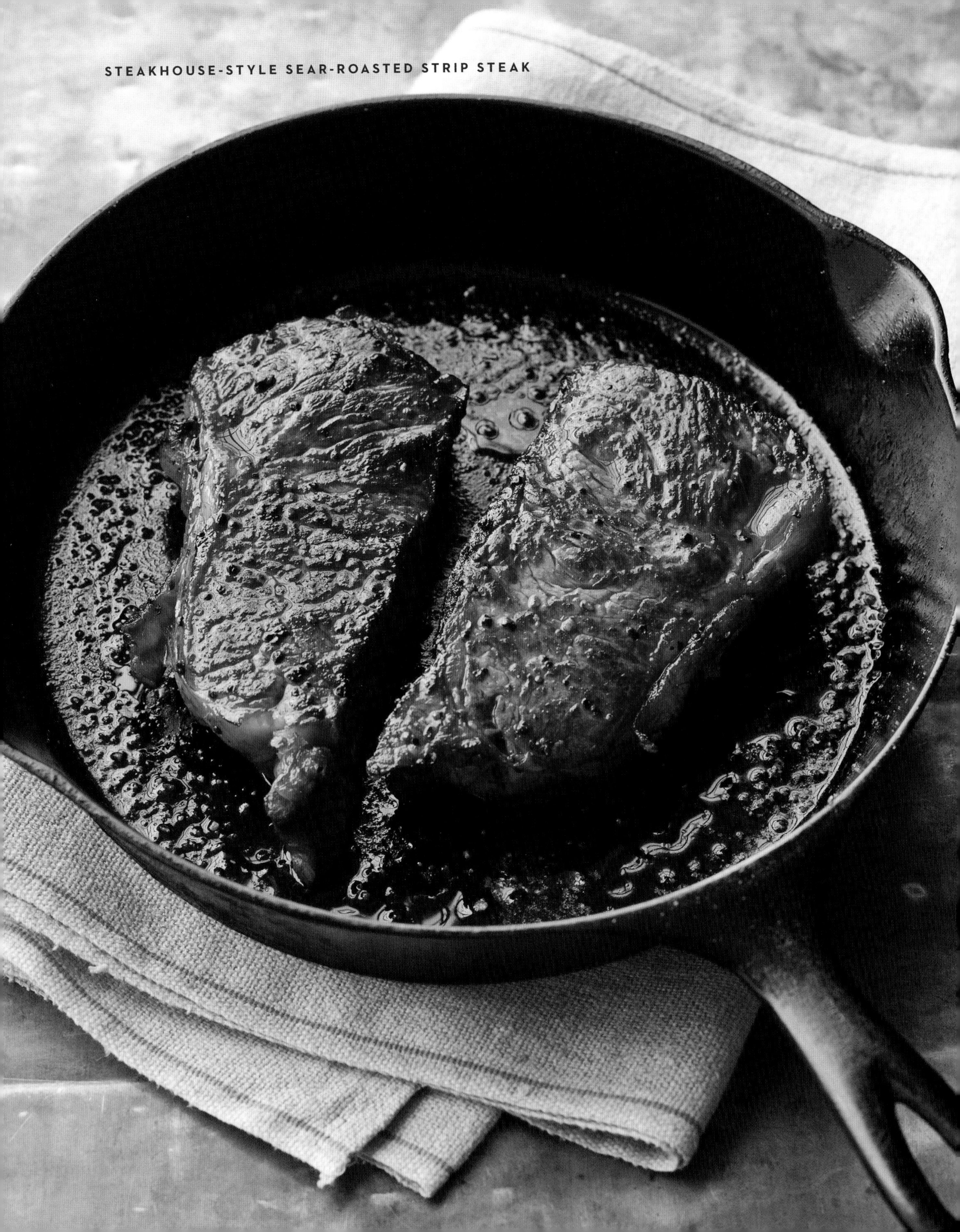

STEAKHOUSE-STYLE SEAR-ROASTED STRIP STEAK

There's something almost mythological about the experience of a good steakhouse steak, and I like to think it's more than just nostalgia. To me, a real steakhouse steak is thick, handsomely caramelized on the outside, with a meaty pink interior. You can replicate that steakhouse goodness at home by following a few tips and using one "secret" ingredient. To start, you need to season the steak very generously with salt and pepper. (And if you have ignored my calls for kosher salt so far, stop now; this is no place for table salt. Same goes for pepper; it must be freshly ground.) The seasonings go on right before sear-roasting, not sooner, because you want that contrast of the well-seasoned exterior and the pure beefy interior. The cooking method is a combination of a high-heat sear on the stove and then a finish in the oven for even cooking throughout. And that secret ingredient? Butter. A good smear of it just before the steak goes in the oven. The butter bastes the meat and mingles deliciously with the steak juices. Use anywhere from ½ to 1 tablespoon butter per steak, adding more if you're feeling luxurious, less if more restrained, but please don't skip it.

The best cut for sear-roasting is a boneless strip steak (also called New York strip or top loin) because of its elongated and compact shape. Plus it delivers the perfect combination of tender and meaty, and superb flavor. This might be a good time to splurge on a really good steak, maybe even one that's dry-aged or graded prime or both.

To serve steak in true over-the-top steakhouse fashion, plate one steak per person and be sure to have sharp steak knives on the table. For a more modest meal, divide the steaks in two. If you're up for it, make homemade steak sauce (see page 107), but be careful—it's addictive. Or smear each steak with a little blue cheese and chive butter (see page 111). Serve the steak with some creamed spinach and smashed potatoes, and the only thing missing will be the red leather banquettes and dim lighting.

SERVES 2 TO 4

METHOD: Combination sear and moderate heat

ROASTING TIME: 6 to 10 minutes (plus 2 minutes to sear)

WINE: Strip steak and Cabernet Sauvignon is a classic combination. Look for good bottlings from California's Napa and Alexander Valleys or Washington State.

CONTINUED ON NEXT PAGE

Two 12- to 14-ounce New York strip steaks,
  1 to 1½ inches thick
Kosher salt and freshly ground black
  pepper

2 tablespoons peanut oil, grapeseed oil, or
  other neutral-flavored vegetable oil
1 to 2 tablespoons unsalted butter, softened

1 **HEAT THE OVEN.** Position a rack near the center of the oven and heat to 375 degrees (350 degrees convection). Let the steaks sit at room temperature while the oven heats.

2 **HEAT THE SKILLET.** Place a large cast-iron or black metal skillet (a 12-inch skillet will hold two steaks nicely) over medium heat and heat the skillet while you season the steaks.

3 **SEASON THE STEAKS.** Sprinkle each steak aggressively all over with salt and pepper, turning the steak and pressing all sides down onto the seasonings that fall onto the work surface. You want the entire surface to be seasoned. If you prefer to measure, use ½ to ¾ teaspoon salt and ¾ to 1 teaspoon pepper per steak.

4 **SEAR THE STEAKS.** Once the pan is hot, increase the heat to high and add the oil to the pan, tilting to coat. When the oil begins to shimmer, after about 30 seconds, place the steaks side by side in the skillet. Let them sear without disturbing; nudging the steaks will interfere with the browning. After 2 minutes, lift the edge of one of the steaks to check whether it's well seared. If so, immediately flip both steaks and smear the tops with butter, dividing it equally. (If the steak isn't browned yet, continue to sear for another 45 seconds and check again.)

5 **ROAST.** Immediately transfer the skillet to the oven. After 6 minutes, start checking for doneness either by touching the meat (the steak firms up as it cooks) or by taking the internal temperature with an instant-read thermometer. Baste the steaks with pan juices each time you open the oven, and check again every 2 minutes until the steaks are done to your liking. Depending on what degree of doneness you're after and how often you open the oven to check on them, expect them to roast for 6 to 10 minutes, or until they reach 115 to 120 degrees internal temperature for rare, 120 to 125 degrees for medium-rare, and 125 to 130 degrees for medium.

6 **REST AND SERVE.** Immediately transfer the steaks to a cutting board—preferably one with a trough—to rest for 5 to 10 minutes. Serve on individual plates if serving 1 per person, or cut in half to share. Pour the pan drippings and any juices from the cutting board over the top of the steaks and serve.

OPTION 1: HOMEMADE STEAK SAUCE

I am the first to admit that I can be a bit of a snob when it comes to what I eat, and until recently I considered bottled steak sauce a desecration of a perfectly good piece of meat. I just couldn't get past the list of ingredients (especially ones like caramel color and xanthan gum). Trouble is, many of my best friends (including my husband) adore a dark, syrupy, sweet-tart sauce alongside a juicy steak. For me, the only reasonable solution was to develop a homemade version, and this one has a brightness and zing that I think surpasses the bottled ones. Now that I have such a delicious steak sauce, I've become a convert and love the way the tingly, complex flavors of the sauce taste on a beefy forkful of steak.

The sauce is best made ahead and left to cool before serving. It keeps, covered and refrigerated, for several weeks.

MAKES ABOUT 2/3 CUP

PLAN AHEAD: The raisins and zest need to soak for at least 4 hours.

2 strips orange zest, removed with a vegetable peeler (about 2 inches by ½ inch each)

1 strip grapefruit zest, removed with a vegetable peeler (about 3 inches by ½ inch)

¼ cup raisins

2 tablespoons gin or room-temperature water

⅛ teaspoon crushed red pepper flakes

One walnut-sized ball of tamarind pulp (see page 109), or 1 tablespoon tamarind or tart cherry juice concentrate

1 tablespoon extra-virgin olive oil or vegetable oil

¼ cup finely chopped onions

Kosher salt

1 garlic clove minced

¼ teaspoon ground cloves

⅛ teaspoon ground allspice

⅛ teaspoon ground cinnamon

2 tablespoons tomato paste

1 tablespoon sugar

½ cup fresh grapefruit juice (from 1 small grapefruit), preferably pink

⅓ cup fresh orange juice (from 1 small orange)

¼ cup red wine vinegar

CONTINUED ON NEXT PAGE

1 **SOAK THE CITRUS ZEST AND RAISINS.** Tear the orange and grapefruit zests into a few pieces each. Combine the zest, raisins, gin or water, and red pepper flakes in a small bowl. Cover tightly and let sit for 4 to 6 hours.

2 **SOAK THE TAMARIND PULP,** if using. Put the tamarind ball in a small bowl, add ¼ cup warm water, and use your fingers to help dissolve some of it. Set aside to soften for 5 minutes. Work the tamarind with your fingers to dissolve more of the pulp. Let sit for another 5 minutes, then work again with your fingers to dissolve more pulp. Strain through a fine sieve into a small bowl, pressing on the solids. Set the tamarind juice aside and discard the solids.

3 **SAUTÉ THE AROMATICS.** Heat the oil in a small saucepan over medium heat. Add the onions, season with a pinch of salt, and sauté until translucent, about 5 minutes. Increase the heat to medium-high, add the garlic, cloves, allspice, and cinnamon, and sauté until fragrant, another minute or so. Stir in the tomato paste and sugar and cook, stirring frequently, until the bottom of the pan begins to darken, about 1 minute. Add the soaked raisins and zest, stir, and simmer briefly until almost evaporated, about 15 seconds.

4 **ADD THE LIQUID AND SIMMER.** Add the grapefruit juice, orange juice, vinegar, and reserved tamarind juice (or tamarind or tart cherry juice concentrate, if using). Stir to combine, and adjust the heat so the sauce simmers steadily but doesn't boil violently. Continue simmering until the sauce is shiny and reduced by about one third, 15 to 20 minutes.

5 **STRAIN AND COOL.** Pour the sauce through a fine-mesh strainer, pushing firmly on the solids to extract as much liquid as you can. Cool to room temperature and taste for salt. Transfer to a clean jar, cover, and refrigerate for up to 3 weeks.

CONTINUED ON PAGE 111

Tamarind

IN THE WESTERN KITCHEN, WE RELY ON VINEGAR AND LEMON (OR LIME) JUICE AS OUR PRIMARY SOUR FLAVORINGS, BUT COOKS FROM INDIA TO IRAN AND Southeast Asia to Latin America rely instead on the somewhat more exotic fruit from the tamarind tree. The tree bears 3- to 4-inch, chalky brown, curved pods that contain a dark, sticky, tarlike edible pulp. To the uninitiated, the sweet-tart taste of tamarind can be shocking, even exhilarating. In some parts of West Africa and Southeast Asia, tamarind is eaten straight up as a fruit, but more often it is processed into a pulp and used to flavor everything from thirst-quenching cold drinks to soups, stews, and sauces with its uniquely concentrated sweet sourness.

Three forms of tamarind are available: whole pods, tamarind pulp, and tamarind concentrate. The best of these for cooking is the pulp (the pods require too much work, are hard to find, and are often too sweet, and the concentrate lacks the brightness of flavor of the pulp). Look for pulp in 8-ounce plastic-wrapped blocks at Asian markets or well-stocked supermarkets. Well wrapped, a block will keep in the refrigerator for about a year. To use, you need to reconstitute the pulp and extract all the juice. First tear off a small hunk and soak it in just enough warm water to cover, working it with your fingertips every 5 minutes or so until well softened and dissolved. Then strain it, pushing on the solids to extract all the juice.

If you can't find tamarind pulp, you may substitute 1 tablespoon of tamarind concentrate for a 1-inch ball of pulp. Alternatively, you can substitute tart cherry juice concentrate (available at health food stores), again using 1 tablespoon per 1-inch chunk of pulp.

STEAKHOUSE-STYLE SEAR-ROASTED STRIP STEAK (PAGE 105)
WITH BLUE CHEESE AND CHIVE BUTTER (PAGE 111) AND
MUSTARD-CRUSTED ROAST POTATOES (PAGE 493)

OPTION 2: BLUE CHEESE AND CHIVE BUTTER

A match made in heaven—blue cheese and steak. As the tangy butter melts on the hot steak, it mingles with the steak's juices to create an instant savory sauce. At home I make this with Jasper Hill Bayley Hazen blue cheese from Vermont, but you can use any high-quality blue. I like to store and serve the butter in a ramekin or small dish, but you may shape it into a roll using wax paper for a more formal presentation. This makes more than you'll need for 2 steaks, but it keeps for 10 days, tightly covered, in the refrigerator or for a month in the freezer. You might also try it on roast chicken or simply spread on a crusty baguette.

MAKES ABOUT 3/4 CUP

2 ounces creamy blue cheese, such as
   Roquefort, bleu d'Auvergne, or a favorite
   local cheese

8 tablespoons (1 stick) unsalted butter, at
   room temperature

1 tablespoon thinly sliced chives

1 scant teaspoon freshly ground black
   pepper

Kosher salt

1 **SEASON THE BUTTER.** Crumble the blue cheese into a small bowl and mash it with a fork until smooth. Add the butter and work to combine the two evenly. Add the chives and pepper and stir with a wooden spoon or rubber spatula until smooth. Taste for salt; the amount needed will vary depending on the saltiness of the cheese.

   Transfer to a small bowl or ramekin, wrap tightly, and refrigerate. Let the butter sit at room temperature for about 30 minutes before using.

2 **SERVE.** Scoop a generous tablespoon of butter onto the hot steak as it rests. The idea is that the heat of the steak will melt just enough of the butter to lightly sauce the steak and leave a small amount unmelted so it's still visible when it comes to the table.

ROASTED HAMBURGERS

Roasted hamburgers do, I admit, sound funny. But roasting has its advantages when it comes to burgers. With roasting, you can enjoy perfect burgers when the grill is buried in snow or a thunderous summer rainstorm keeps you inside. There's also no flipping, no flare-ups, and no stovetop splattering to contend with. But most important, roasting means the burgers cook more evenly and shrink less and therefore come out amazingly plump and juicy. (They don't develop the same crust that you get on a grill or in a skillet, but I think it's a fair tradeoff, as I sometimes find the crust on a burger too dry.)

The one trick to roasting burgers is to cook them on a flat wire rack set over a baking sheet. This allows the hot oven air to circulate and prevents the burgers from frying in their own grease. I will warn that burgers are best roasted in a clean oven. Because ground beef is fattier than most roasts, the burgers can (and will) spatter a fair amount. You'll have less smoke if you start with a clean oven. A thin layer of salt on the baking sheet also reduces smoking as the salt absorbs any spatters.

This recipe is written for 2 pounds of ground beef but is easily adaptable for more or less. Simply figure about 5 ounces of beef and ¼ teaspoon salt per burger. This gives you burgers that are not too paltry but not so large that you have to unhinge your jaw to eat them.

Finish the burgers with whatever condiments and toppings you like, or look to one of the options starting on page 114. If you want to toast buns for burgers, simply put the buns right on the oven rack for about 3 minutes.

SERVES 6

METHOD: High heat

ROASTING TIME: 10 to 16 minutes

WINE: Red zinfandel and hamburgers make one of the all-time best comfort food pairings. Look for recent vintages of old-vine Zinfandels from Sonoma's Dry Creek Valley or San Luis Obispo.

1 ½ teaspoons kosher salt, plus more for lining the pan

2 pounds ground beef, preferably chuck

1 tablespoon Worcestershire sauce

½ teaspoon freshly ground black pepper, or more to taste

6 toasted hamburger buns, English muffins, split focaccia, or slices of other favorite bread

Optional toppings: sliced Swiss or cheddar cheese, sliced tomato, lettuce, rings of sweet onion, and condiments (pickles, ketchup, and mustard)

1 **HEAT THE OVEN.** Position a rack in the center of the oven and heat to 475 degrees (450 degrees convection). Line a heavy-duty rimmed baking sheet with aluminum foil, and spread a thin layer of salt over the surface of the foil to absorb any drippings and prevent the oven from smoking. Arrange a wire rack so that it sits at least ¾ inch above the surface of the pan.

2 **SEASON THE BEEF.** Break the beef into 1- to 2-inch lumps with your hands and drop into a mixing bowl. Season with salt, Worcestershire, and a generous amount of black pepper. Mix gently, using your fingertips to break up the meat and incorporate the seasonings. Overhandling the beef will make for tough, dry burgers.

3 **SHAPE THE BURGERS.** Divide the meat into 6 portions. I like to eyeball even portions and arrange them, before shaping, on a large plate. This way I can add a little here and remove a little there until I have 6 equal-size lumps to start with. If you have a kitchen scale and are of an exacting nature, you can also weigh out 5.3 ounces of meat per burger before shaping. Lightly shape the beef into disks about 3¼ inches across and about 1 inch thick. Set the burgers at least 1 inch apart on the wire rack.

4 **ROAST THE BURGERS.** Roast the burgers for 10 to 16 minutes, checking on them either with an instant-read thermometer (the quickest way) or by cutting into one to peek. For medium-rare, look for 130 to 135 degrees; for medium, 140 degrees. (I don't recommend burgers cooked past medium but if you do, expect them to roast for about 20 minutes, or 160 degrees for medium-well.) If adding cheese, top the burgers with cheese when they are about 2 degrees away from being done to your liking and return them to the oven for 1 minute to melt the cheese.

5 **SERVE.** Transfer the burgers to buns, English muffins, split focaccia, or favorite bread and garnish as you like.

CONTINUED ON NEXT PAGE

OPTION 1: ROASTED MUSHROOM- AND CHEDDAR-STUFFED BURGERS

This recipe takes the basic roasted burger and adds a ton of flavor by stuffing each patty with sautéed mushrooms and grated cheddar. I call them my inside-out burgers.

SERVES 6

WINE: Young hearty Australian Shiraz or Shiraz-Cabernet blend.

2 tablespoons unsalted butter

8 ounces button mushrooms, finely chopped

Kosher salt and freshly ground black pepper

1 garlic clove, minced

¼ cup chopped fresh flat-leaf parsley

¼ cup grated cheddar cheese (about 1¼ ounces)

Roasted Hamburgers (page 112), prepared through step 2

1 **MAKE THE FILLING.** Melt the butter in a 12-inch skillet over medium heat. Add the mushrooms, season well with salt and pepper, and increase the heat to medium-high. Sauté, stirring frequently, until the mushrooms have released most of their liquid and started to brown, about 4 minutes. Stir in the garlic and the parsley. Remove from the heat and let cool. When cooled, stir in the cheese.

2 **SHAPE AND STUFF THE BURGERS.** Divide the seasoned hamburger meat into 12 even portions. Shape each portion into a thin 4-inch patty. Divide the filling evenly among 6 of the flat patties, centering the filling so it doesn't spill to the edges. Top each patty with another flat patty and pinch the edges and round the burger to make 6 evenly shaped burgers.

3 **ROAST.** Continue with the Roasted Hamburgers recipe at step 4.

OPTION 2: ROASTED PIMENTO CHEESE-STUFFED BURGERS

If you're from the South, you don't need me to convince you of the glories of pimento cheese (more affectionately known as PC), but if you're a born northerner like me, let me explain. Pimento cheese is a blend of grated cheese (usually Cheddar), chopped pimiento peppers, a bit of mayonnaise (though many swear by Miracle Whip) to bind, and some seasonings. For people who love it—the legions are many, and I count myself among them—pimento cheese goes into sandwiches, onto crackers, and, best of all, onto hamburgers. But here, instead of piling the PC on top of the burgers, I tuck a little into each one before roasting. As the burgers roast, the cheese melts, becoming irresistibly gooey and delicious.

As with all things, the quality of your pimento cheese depends entirely on the ingredients you use. For mine, I use a two-year old Vermont cheddar, and for the pimiento I reach for a jar of my favorite fire-roasted red peppers from Spain, known as piquillo peppers. You can use any roasted or pickled red pepper, sweet or hot to your taste.

SERVES 6

WINE/BEER: Rich spicy reds, such as Zinfandel or Shiraz blends; or a full-bodied brown ale.

⅓ cup grated sharp cheddar cheese (about 1⅔ ounces)

1½ tablespoons minced pimientos (or roasted red peppers)

1 tablespoon minced scallions

1½ teaspoons mayonnaise

A few dashes of hot sauce, such as Tabasco

Roasted Hamburgers (page 112), prepared through step 2

1 **MAKE THE PIMENTO CHEESE.** In a small bowl, stir together the cheddar, pimientos, scallions, mayonnaise, and hot sauce.

2 **SHAPE AND STUFF THE BURGERS.** Divide the seasoned hamburger meat into 12 even portions. Shape each portion into a thin 4-inch patty. Divide the pimento cheese evenly among 6 of the flat patties, centering the filling so it doesn't spill to the edges. Top each patty with another flat patty and pinch the edges and round the burger to make 6 evenly shaped burgers.

3 **ROAST.** Continue with the Roasted Hamburgers recipe at step 4.

BASIC ROASTED RACK OF LAMB

When I'm looking to make a special-occasion dinner but don't have a lot of time to fuss, rack of lamb is one of the first dishes I consider. The delicate arch of slender rib bones and the tender, distinctive meat bring a certain luxury to even the humblest table. Roasting and carving is an entirely straightforward affair—as long as you have a reliable meat thermometer in the house. My roasting method involves a quick sear on top of the stove followed by 20 to 30 minutes in a moderate oven. If you're entertaining, you can sear the lamb well before your guests arrive, which gives you a chance to wipe up any splatters and vent any smoke, and then quietly roast the racks during cocktails.

Depending on the setting, rack of lamb pairs with a range of side dishes, from simple to fancy, from roasted potatoes (page 488) and green beans to gratin dauphinoise and porcini risotto. Traditionalists may like mint jelly on the side, but I prefer a more exciting condiment, like my Fig, Mint, and Pine Nut Relish (page 118).

SERVES 4 TO 6

METHOD: Combination sear and moderate heat

ROASTING TIME: 20 to 30 minutes (plus 4 to 6 minutes to sear)

WINE: Classic rack of lamb does exceptionally well with a youthful Pinot Noir from the Russian River Valley or Carneros in California or Oregon's Willamette Valley.

2 racks of lamb (1 ¼ to 1 ½ pounds and 7 to 8 ribs each), trimmed (see Trimming and Frenching Rack of Lamb, page 125)

Kosher salt and freshly ground black pepper

1   **HEAT THE OVEN.** Position a rack near the center of the oven and heat to 350 degrees (325 degrees convection).

2   **TRIM THE LAMB.** If there is more than a thin layer of fat left on the racks, trim them so that only a thin layer remains. Do not attempt to remove all the fat, and be careful not to cut away any of the precious meat.

3   **SEAR THE RACKS.** Pat the lamb dry and season the meat all over with salt and pepper. Heat a heavy skillet (12-inch cast iron works well) over high heat. Lower one rack, meat side down, into the hot skillet. If there's room without crowding, sear

Carve into single chops by slicing between the rib bones (to carve into double chops, slice between every other rib bone). After resting, the bone ends should be cool enough that you can steady the rack with your fingertips; if they still feel hot, use a clean dishtowel to protect your fingers.

the other rack at the same time. It's okay if the bone ends extend over the side of the skillet (your objective here is to get a good sear on the meat; the bones don't need to brown). When the top is nicely browned, 2 to 3 minutes, turn with tongs and brown the bottom for 2 to 3 minutes. Remove and repeat with the second rack, if necessary. *This can be done up to 2 hours ahead. Leave the meat at room temperature.* (If you wish to protect the tips of the rib bones from possibly charring, cover them with a thin strip of aluminum foil. I don't bother as it doesn't affect the flavor, and I like the appearance of a little char.)

4 **ROAST.** Transfer the racks, bone side down, to a heavy-duty rimmed baking sheet or shallow roasting pan. You may need to interlock the bone ends to make the racks fit. If possible, arrange the racks so the meaty part faces the outside of the pan; this will help them to cook more evenly. Roast until an instant-read thermometer inserted in the center of the meat reads 125 to 130 degrees for rare to medium-rare, 20 to 25 minutes, or 135 to 140 degrees for medium-rare to medium, 25 to 30 minutes.

5 **REST, CARVE, AND SERVE.** Transfer the lamb to a carving board, preferably one with a trough, to rest for 5 to 10 minutes. Carve by slicing down between the rib bones, cutting into single rib chops (1 bone each, as shown above) or double rib chops (2 bones each) as desired. Serve, spooning any carving juices over the top.

CONTINUED ON NEXT PAGE

OPTION: FIG, MINT, AND PINE NUT RELISH

In place of traditional mint jelly, serve this bright tasting relish alongside roasted lamb (it's good with pork and chicken, too). If you're skilled at multitasking in the kitchen, make the relish as the lamb roasts. If there's already a lot going on, make it ahead of time. The relish can sit for several hours before serving, but the lamb is best served right away.

MAKES ABOUT 3/4 CUP, ENOUGH FOR 4 TO 6 SERVINGS

½ cup finely chopped dried figs, black mission, Turkish, or Calimyrna (about 3 ounces)

¼ cup coarsely chopped fresh mint

¼ cup pine nuts, lightly toasted and coarsely chopped

1 scant teaspoon minced garlic

1 teaspoon finely grated lemon zest

3 tablespoons extra-virgin olive oil

1 tablespoon fresh lemon juice

Kosher salt and freshly ground black pepper

IN A SMALL BOWL, combine the figs, mint, pine nuts, garlic, and lemon zest. Stir to combine. Drizzle in the oil and lemon juice. Season with salt and pepper to taste.

American Lamb vs. Imported Lamb

WHEN SHOPPING FOR LAMB, YOU MAY NOTICE A LOT OF lamb from New Zealand and Australia in American supermarkets. Even though these imports often cost less, I tend to prefer American, and not only because I generally champion the "eat local" mentality. (Cases have been made that lamb raised on grass elsewhere and flown here can actually have a smaller carbon footprint than lamb raised by our domestic suppliers.) More important is that I prefer the flavor and texture of American lamb. Most commercial American lamb comes from the West (primarily Colorado and California) and is fed a mix of grass and grain, which translates into rich, well-marbled meat with mild taste and tender texture. The breeds raised on American sheep farms tend to be larger than those raised elsewhere and offer a higher meat to bone ratio; you'll get more tender rib meat in relation to rack on the average rack of lamb, for example). There are also a growing number of small farms (in regions like the northeast and my home state of Vermont) raising heritage breeds, such as the Navajo-Churro, that thrive on pasture and forage-based feed systems. Expect these to have a slightly richer, wonderfully delicious lamb flavor.

If all you can find is lamb from down under (as is the case in many chain markets) or if the cheaper price of imported lamb tempts you, expect the lamb to be leaner and smaller than lamb bred here. Much of the New Zealand lamb is entirely grassfed and apt to have a stronger, more gamey flavor. Australian lamb tends to be somewhere between American and New Zealand in size and taste. Most imported lamb comes already broken down into retail cuts and vacuum sealed in plastic, meaning less variety of cuts in the meat case.

Icelandic lamb is relatively new to the American market and mostly found in high-end restaurants and specialty shops. The lambs are the smallest of all, with a very delicate flavor and tender, almost soft, texture.

CONTINUED ON NEXT PAGE

Finding the lamb you like best may take a bit of experimentation. There are many factors, including provenance, that affect flavor. For instance, feed, breed, and age all play a role in a complicated equation. (Though lamb sold in American markets must come from animals that are 4 to 12 months old, thus ensuring tender and mild meat; anything older would need to be labeled *yearling* or *mutton* and has a limited specialized audience.) My recommendation is to try several brands, including any locally raised if you're fortunate enough to frequent a market that carries it, and decide for yourself which you prefer.

Although lamb has springtime associations, good lamb is available year round at well-stocked supermarkets and smaller, specialty meat markets. The selection of cuts may vary according to where you shop, but I encourage you to ask if you don't see what you want. Most good markets will be happy to bring in what you are looking for as long as you are willing to wait a few days.

ROASTED RACK OF LAMB WITH CRUNCHY MUSTARD-HERB CRUST

I must confess to a certain sentimental attachment to this recipe: this is the first dish I ever cooked for my in-laws. At the time, they were merely my boyfriend's parents, but I knew I wanted to impress. Plus I'd already heard about my father-in-law's legendary wine cellar, and I was hoping to inspire him to reach for something special, and indeed he did. Sadly, I don't remember the exact wine or vintage, but dinner must have been a success, because the boyfriend became the husband, and his parents still fondly remember my rack of lamb.

Searing the lamb before painting the meat with seasoned mustard deepens the flavor and ensures that you won't have any flabby bits of fat under the crunchy coating. The quantities here make enough for 2 to 3 chops per person. If you're serving big eaters, add a third rack and increase all the other ingredients by one half.

SERVES 4 TO 6
METHOD: Combination sear and moderate heat
ROASTING TIME: 20 to 30 minutes (plus 4 to 6 minutes to sear)
WINE: Deeply flavored Rioja Reserva or Gran Reserva.

2 racks of lamb (1 to 1½ pounds and 8 ribs each), trimmed (see Trimming and Frenching Rack of Lamb, page 125)

2 tablespoons Dijon mustard

2 tablespoons extra-virgin olive oil

2 teaspoons fresh lemon juice

2 teaspoons finely chopped fresh rosemary or thyme

2 garlic cloves, minced

Kosher salt and freshly ground black pepper

¾ cup fresh bread crumbs (see Making Fresh Bread Crumbs, page 210)

1 **HEAT THE OVEN.** Position a rack near the center of the oven and heat to 350 degrees (325 degrees convection).

2 **TRIM THE LAMB.** If there is more than a thin layer of fat left on the racks, trim them so that only a thin layer remains. Keep in mind when trimming that the coating will adhere to any fat left on the rack, so leave on only as much as you (and your guests) are happy eating. Be careful not to cut away any of the precious meat.

CONTINUED ON NEXT PAGE

3 **SEAR THE RACK.** Pat the lamb dry and lightly season the meat all over with salt and pepper. Heat a heavy skillet (12-inch cast iron works well) over high heat. Lower one rack, meat side down, into the hot skillet. If there's room without crowding, sear the other rack at the same time. It's okay if the bone ends extend over the side of the skillet. When the top is handsomely browned, 2 to 3 minutes, turn with tongs and brown the bottom for another 2 to 3 minutes. Remove and repeat with the second rack, if necessary. *This can be done up to 2 hours ahead: leave the lamb at room temperature.*

4 **MAKE THE BREAD-CRUMB CRUST.** In a small bowl, whisk together the mustard, olive oil, lemon juice, rosemary or thyme, and garlic. Season lightly with salt and pepper. Spread the bread crumbs on a pie plate. Paint the seared lamb all over (the meat, not the bones) with the mustard mixture and roll the meaty side and meaty ends in the bread crumbs, pressing the crumbs so they adhere. Don't bother breading the back (bone) side. (You can cover the rib ends with a strip of aluminum foil to protect them from charring if you like; I rarely do.)

5 **ROAST.** Transfer the racks, breading side up (bone side down), to a heavy-duty rimmed baking sheet or shallow roasting pan. You may need to interlock the bone ends to make the racks fit. Arrange the racks so the meaty part faces the outside of the pan; this will help them to cook more evenly. Roast until an instant-read thermometer inserted in the center of the meat reads 125 to 130 degrees for rare to medium-rare, 20 to 25 minutes, or 135 to 140 degrees for medium-rare to medium, 25 to 30 minutes.

6 **REST, CARVE, AND SERVE.** Transfer the lamb to a carving board, preferably one with a trough, and let rest for 5 to 10 minutes. Carve by slicing down between the rib bones, cutting into single rib chops (1 bone each) or double rib chops (2 bones each), as desired. Serve.

OPTION: ROASTED RACK OF LAMB WITH OLIVE AND PARSLEY CRUST

This boldly flavored crust gives the lamb a decidedly Mediterranean flavor. Select whatever olive varieties you favor, or use a mix. Black olives (such as kalamata, nyçoise, or nyons) provide a deeper flavor, while green olives (such as lucques or picholine) tend to have a brighter, more vegetal character.

MAKES ENOUGH FOR 2 RACKS

WINE: Robust Provençal red, such as Bandol Rouge.

½ cup chopped black or green olives, or a
    mix (see above)

⅓ cup chopped fresh flat-leaf parsley

1 tablespoon fresh thyme leaves

2 garlic cloves, minced

1 anchovy fillet, rinsed, patted dry, and very
    finely chopped

1 teaspoon finely grated lemon zest

½ teaspoon Aleppo or Marash pepper
    flakes (see page 317)

1 tablespoon extra-virgin olive oil

2 racks of lamb (1 to 1½ pounds and 8
    ribs each), trimmed (see Trimming and
    Frenching Rack of Lamb, page 125)

Kosher salt and freshly ground black
    pepper

1   **MAKE THE OLIVE AND PARSLEY CRUST.** In a mortar or small bowl, combine the olives, parsley, thyme leaves, garlic, anchovy, lemon zest, and pepper flakes. Pound the mixture with a pestle, or mash it against the side of the bowl with a wooden spoon, to form a coarse paste. Stir in the olive oil.

2   **SEAR, COAT, AND ROAST THE LAMB.** Proceed with the recipe for Roasted Rack of Lamb with Crunchy Mustard-Herb Crust, omitting the mustard and bread crumbs and coating the racks with the olive paste after searing (step 4).

Shopping for Rack of Lamb

A RACK OF LAMB IS A SERIES OF LAMB RIB CHOPS LEFT AS ONE ROAST. A FULL RACK OF LAMB HAS 8 RIB BONES, STARTING FROM JUST BEHIND THE shoulder section and moving back toward the loin section. (You may also encounter 7- or 9-rib racks, the ribs dropped or added coming from the shoulder end.) Each rib consists of a nugget (also called the eye) of meat and the arcing rib bone. If you're cooking for 1 or 2, you can order a partial rack of 4 or 5 ribs. Specify that you want the rack cut from the loin end, where the eye of meat is the largest. Depending on the appetites around your table and the rest of the menu, figure 2 to 3 chops per person. Expect a single rack, depending on the type of lamb and how it's trimmed, to weigh between 1½ and 2 pounds. (For more on types of lamb see page 119.) A frenched rack will weigh between 1 and 1½ pounds. Each chop will offer about 2 ounces of meat.

When selecting a rack of lamb, check that the meat is deep red in color, with a firm, fine-grained texture. The layer of fat should be pearly white. Next check to see that the backbone (or chine bone) has been removed. Follow the underside of the arc of rib bones to the meaty bottom of the rack. If you find a hefty square-shaped set of vertebrae running the length of the rack, connecting the rib bones, then you'll want to ask for some assistance from behind the meat counter. Although the backbone helps the rack to stand upright, it is all but impossible to get through the backbone with an ordinary carving knife. Some butchers will leave the backbone in place but score it between the ribs with a saw in order to make carving easier. Theoretically, your carving knife will just glide between the ribs, finding the spot where the impenetrable backbone has been scored. In reality, it can be difficult, and frustrating, to find the exact spot. The best approach is to ask the butcher or whoever is manning the counter at the meat department to remove the backbone.

BUYING VACUUM-PACKED RACK OF LAMB

Many markets sell individually vacuum-sealed racks from New Zealand and Australia. These sealed racks typically have a muslin sheet covering the meat, which makes it a little trickier to assess its freshness. The best you can do is feel that the meat is firm and trust the market. When you cut open the plastic in your kitchen, give the meat a moment, since all vacuum-sealed meat releases an unpleasant (vaguely putrid) odor when first exposed to oxygen. Once the lamb has had a chance to breathe, check that it smells like fresh meat—somewhat sweet, heady but not spoiled.

Trimming and Frenching Rack of Lamb

ONCE YOU'RE CERTAIN THAT THE BACKBONE HAS BEEN REMOVED, THERE ARE TWO BASIC STAGES TO TRIMMING A RACK OF LAMB, ONE ESSENTIAL AND one optional. The first step involves removing most of the thick layer of fat that protects the meaty side of the rack. Depending on where you shop, this may already be done for you. It's easy enough to tell when you unwrap the lamb. If there is a solid, thick layer of fat covering the rack, then get out a sharp, thin-bladed knife and trim it away with careful, sweeping strokes; it should come away easily. Don't overtrim, and don't cut into the eye meat. Ideally, for roasting you want to leave a thin layer of fat (just under ¼-inch thick) to baste the meat. As you trim, focus on the fat covering the nugget of eye meat (in other words, the lamb chop), and do not fuss with the deposits of fat that sit above the eye meat. I've seen plenty of chefs and fancy butchers who like to trim lamb racks so that all that remains is the perfect nugget of eye meat—the chops look something like meat lollipops— but I don't agree. There are really two muscles that run the length of the rack, and I prefer to leave both intact. The primary, and most obvious, is the evident rib-eye muscle, or what we recognize as the chop. The smaller section of meat that runs along the top of the rib-eye (but separated from it by a band of fat) is known as the rib cap (sometimes called the deckle). If you aggressively attempt to remove all the fat from a rack of lamb, you will end up separating these two muscles and the rib cap will come away from the rack. Losing the rib cap is a waste of a tasty morsel of meat, and that little bit of cap fat that connects it to the bone adds succulence to the roast.

As you are deciding on how much fat to leave on the meat, think about how you are going to prepare the rack. For instance, if you are preparing Basic Roasted Rack of Lamb (page 116), there's no real harm in leaving a little extra. (Some of my friends relish the juicy deposits of fat on a lamb chop, while others want nothing to do with them.) If you are adding a crust to the rack, however, such as the olive and parsley one (page 123) or the mustard-rosemary one (page 121), you'll want to remove most, but not all, of the fat, because whatever fat you leave on gets covered with the coating and it's messy (and impolite) to carve it away at the table.

The second stage of trimming a rack of lamb involves trimming the tips of the rib bones to give the rack a decorative appearance. This technique is known as "frenching" the rack, and I leave it up to you whether or not you want to bother. The benefits of frenching the rack are mostly aesthetic: the long, delicate bones arcing upward make an elegant presentation. Frenching also makes it less messy to hold the rack while carving or to pick up a chop to nibble the last bits of meat from the bone. Having learned to cook in France, where you learned

CONTINUED ON NEXT PAGE

the proper way to do things and that's how you did them, I still take a certain satisfaction in spending the time to carefully strip every last bit of meat and sinew from the rib ends, but I confess, sometimes when I'm in a hurry or when my knives are dull, I don't bother.

If you do decide to dress up the rack by frenching it, you'll need a sharp knife (preferably a thin-bladed boning knife) and a stable cutting board. Start by laying the rack bone side down, so the meaty side faces you and the bones arc away. Now, using the tip of the knife, score a line perpendicular to the rib bones about 2 to 2½ inches from the ends of the rib bones. The ribs should be long enough for you to cut well above the meaty part of the rack with no risk of cutting into the eye meat. If you're not sure, make the cut closer to the rib ends. The idea is just to create a row of cleaned rib tips (they always remind me of a picket fence). Following your score line, cut through the fat and down to the bone. You can now easily remove most of the fat covering the bones by turning the knife away from you and, starting at the cut you've just made, sliding the blade along the flat side of the ribs away from the base of the rack until you reach the rib ends. Lift off the slab of fat and discard. Next use the tip of your knife to cut around each rib bone and remove the meat and fat between the bones. The ribs should now be nearly clean, but for the most professional appearance, scrape the ribs clean with a knife. Alternatively, use a dish towel to tear off any bits of meat or sinew.

Before roasting a frenched rack of lamb, many cooks like to protect the rib ends by covering them with a thin strip of foil. I usually don't bother as it doesn't affect the flavor and I rather like the primal appeal of slightly charred bone tips.

ROASTED RACK OF LAMB WITH SPICED HONEY GLAZE

This recipe takes a cue from the Moroccan kitchen and combines honey with a mix of warming spices balanced with fresh mint and a jolt of lemon juice. The resulting glaze provides a beguiling, mildly sweet, somewhat floral background for the rich meat. Also, the glaze caramelizes quickly in the hot oven, creating a beautiful brick-red finish.

This glaze works best with a mild floral honey, such as orange blossom, acacia, or fireweed. I like to serve the lamb with herb-flecked couscous (mint and parsley are especially good) or rice pilaf.

SERVES 4 TO 6
METHOD: High heat
ROASTING TIME: 25 to 30 minutes
WINE: Concentrated red with dried fruit character, such as an Amarone.

2 racks of lamb (1 to 1½ pounds and 8 ribs each), trimmed (see Trimming and Frenching Rack of Lamb, page 125)

¼ cup honey, preferably a mild-tasting variety such as orange blossom, acacia, or fireweed

2 tablespoons unsalted butter, melted

1 teaspoon paprika, preferably sweet

1 teaspoon cumin seed, toasted in a dry skillet and finely ground

¼ teaspoon ground ginger

Pinch of cayenne

Kosher salt and freshly ground black pepper

3 tablespoons fresh lemon juice

2 garlic cloves, minced

2 tablespoons chopped fresh mint

1 **HEAT THE OVEN.** Position a rack in the center of the oven and heat to 425 degrees (400 degrees convection). Line a small, low-sided roasting pan or heavy-duty rimmed baking sheet with heavy-duty foil (this makes it easier to clean the glaze from the pan).

2 **TRIM THE LAMB.** If necessary, trim the lamb so that only a thin layer of fat remains. Arrange the racks meat side up on the foil-lined pan. (You can cover the rib ends with a strip of aluminum foil to protect them from charring if you like; I rarely bother.)

CONTINUED ON PAGE 129

ROASTED RACK OF LAMB WITH SPICED HONEY GLAZE (PAGE 127);
QUICK-ROASTED SUGAR SNAP PEAS
WITH TOASTED SESAME SALT (PAGE 451)

3 **MAKE THE GLAZE.** In a small bowl, thoroughly combine the honey, butter, paprika, cumin, ginger, and cayenne. Generously season the rack all over with salt and pepper. Brush the surface with about half the glaze. (A heatproof silicone pastry brush works best here, but any pastry brush will do.) Transfer the remaining glaze to a very small saucepan and set aside.

4 **ROAST AND BASTE.** Roast, brushing the lamb after 10 minutes and then again every 5 minutes with the glaze that has dripped onto the roasting pan, until an instant-read thermometer inserted close to but not touching the bone reads 125 to 130 degrees for rare to medium-rare or 135 to 140 degrees for medium-rare to medium, 25 to 30 minutes.

5 **SIMMER THE GLAZE.** Meanwhile, add the lemon juice and garlic to the reserved glaze in the small saucepan. Bring to a simmer over medium-high heat and simmer gently until fragrant and slightly syrupy, 2 to 4 minutes. Keep a close eye on the glaze, as it can thicken and scorch very quickly; if it becomes gummy, add a teaspoon of water. Season with salt and pepper. Keep warm over very low heat.

6 **REST, CARVE, AND SERVE.** Let the lamb rest for 5 to 10 minutes on a cutting board (preferably with a trough). Carve the rack into single or double chops, cutting down between the bones. Add any juices from the carving board to the glaze, along with the fresh mint. Serve the chops with a little glaze drizzled over them.

BASIC ROASTED THICK-CUT LAMB LOIN CHOPS

Thick-cut lamb loin chops roasted in a super-hot oven make a quick and sumptuous supper. To avoid the smoke and mess that can sometimes come with high-heat roasting, I line the roasting pan with a layer of salt; this catches the drips and prevents them from smoking. If you have time to plan ahead, you can boost the flavor with a charmoula marinade (see option). Figure on 1 to 2 chops per person.

SERVES 4 TO 6
METHOD: High heat
ROASTING TIME: About 11 minutes
WINE: Medium-bodied red with supple fruit and soft tannins, such as a Chilean Cabernet or young Argentine Malbec.

Eight 1- to 1¼-inch-thick lamb loin chops (about 2 pounds)

Kosher salt and freshly ground black pepper

1   **HEAT THE OVEN.** Position a rack near the center of the oven and heat to 500 degrees (475 degrees convection). Let the chops sit at room temperature until the oven is well heated, at least 40 minutes.

2   **ROAST THE LAMB.** Cover a 10-by-6-inch area of a heavy-duty rimmed baking sheet with about a ¼-inch layer of salt. Set a rack over the baking sheet and arrange the chops on the rack. If necessary, adjust the chops or the salt so the meat sits above the salt; the salt doesn't have to cover the entire sheet, and the lamb should not be touching the salt. Roast until a thermometer inserted in the center of a chop registers about 135 degrees for medium-rare, about 11 minutes.

3   **REST AND SERVE.** Remove the chops to a serving platter to rest for 5 minutes before serving.

OPTION: ROASTED THICK-CUT LAMB LOIN CHOPS WITH CHARMOULA

Charmoula may best be described as a Middle Eastern pesto. My version is packed with fresh herbs like parsley, mint, and cilantro and enhanced with smoky paprika, toasted cumin, and plenty of garlic. I use some to marinate the lamb chops and serve the rest at the table as a finishing sauce. It's also good as a condiment for roast leg of lamb (page 142), roast strip loin (page 60), and roasted tri-tip (page 63).

SERVES 4 TO 6
METHOD: High heat
ROASTING TIME: About 11 minutes
PLAN AHEAD: The chops should marinate for at least 4 hours for best flavor and should sit at room temperature for an hour before roasting.
WINE: Medium-bodied, fruity Rhône-style blend based on Grenache, such as Côte du Rhône Villages or a young Australian Grenache blend.

2 large garlic cloves

1 ½ cups lightly packed fresh flat-leaf parsley leaves

½ cup lightly packed fresh mint leaves

¼ cup lightly packed fresh cilantro leaves and tender stems

1 tablespoon cumin seeds, toasted in a dry skillet and finely ground

1 tablespoon smoked sweet paprika (pimentón is good here)

1 teaspoon kosher salt

¼ teaspoon cayenne

6 tablespoons extra-virgin olive oil

1 tablespoon fresh lemon juice

Eight 1- to 1 ¼-inch-thick lamb loin chops (about 2 pounds)

1   **MAKE THE CHARMOULA.** With the food processor running, drop the garlic cloves into the feed tube and process until finely minced (this minces garlic more effectively than adding it before the machine is on). Scrape down the sides and add the parsley, mint, cilantro, cumin, paprika, salt, and cayenne. Pulse on and off to create a rough paste. With the machine running, slowly add 4 tablespoons of the olive oil.

Transfer 2 tablespoons of the charmoula to a small bowl. To the charmoula in the small bowl, add the remaining 2 tablespoons of olive oil and the lemon juice and whisk to combine. Cover and set aside for serving.

CONTINUED ON NEXT PAGE

2 **MARINATE THE LAMB.** Place the lamb chops in a large zip-top bag, pour the charmoula from the food processor into the bag, and rub the paste evenly over the chops. Seal and place the bag in a bowl or pie plate in case of leaks. Refrigerate at least 4 hours and up to 24 hours. Cover and refrigerate the reserved charmoula as well.

3 **ROAST THE LAMB.** Let the chops and the small bowl of charmoula sit at room temperature for 1 hour before roasting, and roast as directed in the recipe on page 130. Serve with the reserved charmoula on the side.

Shopping for Lamb Loin Chops

MY FAVORITE LAMB CHOPS FOR ROASTING ARE THICK LOIN LAMB CHOPS. CUT FROM THE SADDLE SECTION OF THE LAMB, LOIN CHOPS LOOK LIKE miniature porterhouse or T-bone steaks, with the recognizable T-shaped bone separating two fine-grained nuggets of meat. The smaller of the nuggets is the tenderloin, and the larger the loin. Loin chops are leaner than rib chops, but I find them every bit as tender and delicious. Plus, because loin chops have meat on both sides of the T-bone, they are heftier than rib chops, and 2 chops per person make a very generous serving. (Depending on what else is on the menu, modest appetites may be satisfied with only 1 chop.) For best results, choose chops that are at least 1 inch thick (preferably closer to 1¼ inches).

ROASTED BONELESS DOUBLE LAMB LOIN

Here's the crème de la crème of lamb roasts. This chic little roast somewhat resembles a beef tenderloin in shape and size, but it boasts a protective layer of fat that conceals the secret of its goodness: The roast actually consists of two lamb loins as well as two lamb *tender*loins all rolled together and tied into one neat cylindrical shape for a roast that delivers a maximum of flavor and tenderness.

To get a handsome brown exterior while keeping the inside rosy pink, I first sear the lamb in a skillet and then roast it in a moderate oven. The ranges for cooking times in the recipe account for the fact that lamb loins can range in size. Your best bet is to monitor the temperature with a good thermometer.

For a really special occasion, make the Lamb Demi-Glace (page 135) ahead of time and mix this deeply concentrated sauce with the pan drippings to create a "wow" kind of sauce to spoon over each serving of lamb. This satiny, meaty sauce means starting a day ahead, but since the lamb tastes best when seasoned in advance, the timing works out well. You can also skip the demi-glace, make a simple pan sauce, and still have an exceptional meal, but for a real uptown treat, it's worth the effort. Either way, serve this with roasted potatoes (page 488) and a heap of steamed asparagus or green beans.

SERVES 4 TO 6

METHOD: Combination sear and moderate heat

ROASTING TIME: 25 to 45 minutes (plus 8 minutes to sear)

PLAN AHEAD: For best flavor and texture, season the lamb 12 to 24 hours ahead.

WINE: Merlot-based blend from Pomerol or St.-Emilion in Bordeaux; or a Merlot from California or Washington State.

1 boneless, 2½- to 3-pound, double lamb loin roast (see Shopping for Boneless Double Lamb Loin Roast, page 137)

Kosher salt and freshly ground black pepper

1 tablespoon extra-virgin olive or grapeseed oil

3 tablespoons dry white vermouth, dry white wine, or water

Lamb Demi-Glace (page 135; optional)

1 to 2 tablespoons unsalted butter (optional)

CONTINUED ON NEXT PAGE

1   **TRIMMING AND SEASONING THE ROAST.** Evaluate the roast. It should have about ¼-inch thick fat cap covering the top side. If the fat seems excessively thick or if any patches are leathery or dried out, remove the strings and pare these away. Season the roast generously all over with salt and pepper (I use about 1½ teaspoons salt and ¾ teaspoon pepper). If necessary, re-tie the roast, securing a loop of butcher twine every 1 to 2 inches. If seasoning ahead, refrigerate, uncovered or loosely covered, for 12 to 24 hours.

2   **HEAT THE OVEN.** Position a rack near the center of the oven and heat to 350 degrees (325 degrees convection). Let the lamb sit at room temperature for at least 30 minutes as the oven heats.

3   **SEAR THE LAMB.** Heat a low-sided skillet (11- to 12-inch works well) over medium-high heat until quite hot. Add the oil, and heat until the oil shimmers, about 30 seconds. Sear the lamb, placing the fat side down first and turning with tongs, until well browned on all sides, about 8 minutes total. You may need to hold the roast in place with the tips of your tongs in order to evenly brown the rounded fat-side (its wont is to roll to one side or the other). Once nicely browned, set the roast fat-side up, and transfer the skillet to the oven.

4   **ROAST.** Roast until an instant-read thermometer inserted in the thickest part of the roast registers 120 to 130 degrees for rare to medium-rare, 25 to 35 minutes; or 130 to 135 degrees for medium, 35 to 45 minutes. Transfer the roast to a carving board, preferably one with a trough, and let rest for 10 to 15 minutes.

5   **MAKE A SAUCE.** Holding the skillet handle with a potholder or dishtowel (so as not to burn yourself), pour off any fat from the skillet, leaving the meat juices in the pan. Add the vermouth (or wine or water) and heat over medium, stirring with a wooden spoon to dissolve any drippings. Continue cooking until the liquid is reduced to about 2 tablespoons, about 2 minutes. If not using the Lamb Demi-Glace, keep this simple pan sauce warm to spoon over the carved roast.

If using the Lamb Demi-Glace, heat it gently to a simmer. Add the simple pan sauce to the demi-glace. Season to taste with salt and pepper. If the sauce tastes at all sharp or cloying (this can happen to reduction sauces), adjust the heat so the sauce is just below a simmer, and whisk in 1 to 2 tablespoons of the butter. (I often don't add the butter.)

6 **SERVE.** Carve the lamb into generous ½-inch thick slices, removing the strings as you go. Add any accumulated juices to the sauce and spoon a little over each serving. Pass any remaining sauce at the table.

OPTION: LAMB DEMI-GLACE

A demi-glace is a meat stock that has been simmered until it turns glossy and syrupy and the flavor becomes wonderfully concentrated. To make a lamb demi-glace, you'll need the bones that the butcher removed from the loin, which most butchers are happy enough to hand over. If those are not available, shop for a pound of lamb neck bones. Either way, ask the butcher to cut the bones into 1- to 2-inch pieces. Make the stock a day or two before you plan to roast the lamb—this gives it a chance to cool, allowing the fat to rise to the surface and be easily removed. If you plan to make the demi-glace while roasting the lamb, start at least 30 minutes before you roast the lamb, so the sauce and the meat will be ready at about the same time.

MAKES ABOUT 1/2 CUP, ENOUGH FOR 4 TO 6 SERVINGS

PLAN AHEAD: Make the stock a day ahead, so you can chill it and remove the fat before reducing it for the sauce.

1 pound lamb bones (the bones removed from the loin or neck bones), cut into 1- to 2-inch pieces

1 tablespoon tomato paste

1 carrot, cut into 2-inch chunks

1 medium onion, peeled and cut into quarters

1 celery stalk, preferably with leaves, cut into 2-inch chunks

2 garlic cloves, smashed and peeled

1 bay leaf

4 whole black peppercorns

Kosher salt

1 **BROWN THE BONES.** Heat the oven to 425 degrees (400 degrees convection). Smear the bones with the tomato paste (I find this is easiest to do with my fingers), doing your best to evenly coat the bones. Arrange the bones in a low-sided skillet or heavy roasting pan (8- to 9-inch works) and roast, turning once about halfway, until the bones are browned, about 25 minutes. Do not let the bones scorch or blacken; it's better to leave them a little underdone than burnt, as any scorch will taint the finished sauce.

CONTINUED ON NEXT PAGE

2 **MAKE THE STOCK.** With tongs, transfer the bones to a medium saucepan (3- to 4-quart, about 8 inches wide), leaving the drippings behind. Protecting your hand with a potholder or dishtowel, pour off and discard any fat from the skillet or roasting pan. Set the pan over low heat, add about ½ cup water, and bring to a simmer, scraping the bottom of the pan to dissolve any cooked on bits. Pour this over the bones in the saucepan. Add enough cold water to cover the bones by about 1 inch. Bring the water to a quiet simmer, skim off any foam that rises, and then add the carrot, onion, celery, garlic, bay leaf, peppercorns, and a small pinch of salt. Adjust the heat so the stock bubbles softly and steadily, and continue to gently simmer, skimming occasionally, until the stock is flavorful, 2 ½ to 3 hours. (Boiling or simmering too aggressively will cloud the stock and make it greasy tasting.) If at any time the level of liquid drops below the bones, add a bit more cold water. Be conservative when adding water as you don't want to overdilute the stock.

3 **STRAIN AND COOL.** Strain the stock though a fine-mesh sieve, discarding the solids. (If you don't have a fine-mesh sieve, line your strainer with a double layer of cheesecloth.) You should have 3 to 4 cups. Let cool to room temperature and then refrigerate until well chilled, several hours and preferably overnight to allow any fat to solidify on the surface.

4 **REDUCE THE STOCK TO MAKE THE DEMI-GLACE.** Scrape any hardened layer of fat from the lamb stock and discard. Transfer the stock to a small saucepan, and bring to a boil over medium heat. Adjust the heat so the stock simmers steadily, but not so much that it splatters and splashes. You want it to reduce in volume to about ½ cup of slightly thickened and satiny sauce. Expect it to take about 45 minutes. As the sauce reduces, proceed with searing and roasting the lamb (steps 3 and 4 on page 134). If the sauce is ready before the lamb, set it aside in a warm place without letting it further reduce. *The demi-glace can be made a day or two ahead and heated before serving.*

Shopping for Boneless Double Lamb Loin Roast

THE LOIN REFERS TO THE SADDLE PORTION OF LAMB. IT BEGINS JUST BELOW THE RIB SECTION (WHERE RACK OF LAMB AND RIB CHOPS COME FROM) AND runs down to just above the hip, or rump, section. The full lamb loin consists of two elongated loin muscles (comparable to beef NY strip loin) running down each side of the backbone, and two smaller tenderloins, each running along the inside of the backbone. To visualize how these two sets of muscles relate, imagine a lamb loin chop (it resembles a miniature T-bone steak). A lamb loin chop comes from splitting the full loin (or saddle) in half down the backbone and then sawing the halves crosswise into individual chops. When you look at a lamb loin chop, the larger eye of meat is the loin muscle, the smaller nugget comes from the tenderloin. A boneless double loin includes all the muscles from this cut—both loins and both tenderloins—but none of the bones, all neatly rolled up and tied into a handsome cylindrical roast.

In my experience, few markets display these roasts in their meat case, but if there are lamb loin chops on offer *and* if there's someone behind the meat counter with decent butchering skills, then it's merely a matter of asking. Explain that you want a boneless double lamb loin roast, sometimes called a rolled double loin roast. Confirm that the roast includes the two loins as well as both tenderloins—these should be tucked inside the rolled roast. If you are having trouble explaining yourself, you may try using the Uniform Retail Meat Identity Standards number: it's NAMP 232B. (This refers to an industry guidebook that strives to standardize retail meat cuts.) The advantage of having the roast cut and trimmed to order is that you can ask for all the corresponding bones. Ask that the bones are cut into 1- to 2-inch pieces, since they are better for making stock when cut up and it's a difficult task to do at home.

The size of your roast will depend on the provenance of the lamb. Expect a boneless lamb loin roast from American lamb to weigh 3 to 4 pounds, while one from New Zealand or Australian lamb will be closer to 2 pounds. The range in roasting times in the recipe reflects these size variances. As for which is better, it's a matter of personal preference; for more information, turn to American Lamb vs. Imported Lamb (page 119).

BASIC ROAST BONE-IN LEG OF LAMB

When I first thought about writing a book on roasting, this was the exact recipe I had in mind—a big bone-in leg of lamb, glistening and browned on the outside but revealing a rosy pink inside when sliced. When it comes to how well (or how rare) to cook the lamb, I like to remember what Richard Olney wrote in *Simple French Food*; "Preferences in degrees of doneness may legitimately vary from rare to pink (which means well done in France), but those who are nervous if flesh is not cooked until gray will never understand what a glorious thing roast lamb can be." Keeping this in mind, I've learned that most of my American friends (and family) prefer their lamb rosy but not blood red. I've given instructions for both below. Keep in mind when deciding the degree of doneness that a whole leg of lamb will provide you a range from more well done near the narrower shank to pinker toward the thick center. In my experience, there's always something to please everyone.

Lamb goes with many sides, but I like to offer something starchy (such as a potato gratin or a dish of white beans) and something green (perhaps minted peas or sautéed spinach).

SERVES 8 TO 10

METHOD: Combination high and moderate heat

ROASTING TIME: 1 1/2 to 1 3/4 hours

PLAN AHEAD: For the best flavor and texture, season the meat 1 to 2 days before roasting.

WINE: Côte de Beaune red Burgundy with age, such as a Pommard Premier Cru.

1 whole bone-in leg of lamb, 7 to 8 pounds, preferably with hip bone removed (see Shopping for Bone-In Leg of Lamb, page 141)

Kosher salt and freshly ground black pepper
1 tablespoon extra-virgin olive oil
¾ cup dry white wine or dry white vermouth

1   **TRIM THE LAMB.** Examine the leg of lamb to determine what kind of trimming and perhaps tying you need to do before seasoning. If the pelvic bones have been removed, you may find a loose flap of meat at the wide end of the roast. If so, secure this with skewers or sew it shut with a trussing needle and kitchen string. Using a thin-bladed sharp knife, trim any leathery membrane or excess fat from the exterior

of the lamb. You want to leave a thin (⅛-inch-thick) layer of fat to protect the meat from drying.

2 **SEASON THE LAMB.** Sprinkle the meat all over with salt and pepper (I use a heaping tablespoon of salt and about 1½ teaspoons of pepper). Set in a large baking dish and refrigerate, uncovered or loosely covered, for 1 to 2 days. Let the lamb sit at room temperature for about 2 hours before roasting.

3 **HEAT THE OVEN.** Arrange a rack in the lower third of the oven and heat to 450 degrees (425 degrees convection).

4 **ROAST THE LAMB.** Rub the surface of the meat with the olive oil. Place the lamb with the rounder, meatier side up in a roasting pan just large enough to accommodate it (it's fine if the tip of the shank rests on the edge of the roasting pan). Roast for 25 minutes and then pour the wine or vermouth over the lamb. Immediately lower the oven temperature to 325 degrees (300 degrees convection), and continue roasting until a meat thermometer inserted in the widest part of the leg (careful not to touch the bone) reaches 120 to 125 degrees for rare, about 1 hour from the time you lowered the oven heat; or 130 to 135 degrees for medium-rare, about 1¼ hours.

5 **REST.** Remove the lamb to a carving board (preferably one with a trough) to rest for 20 to 35 minutes. Tilt the roasting pan and spoon off as much of the clear fat as you can. Using a wooden spoon, scrape up the pan drippings (if they are too stuck to the pan to scrape up, add ¼ cup water to dissolve them). Set aside the pan drippings to drizzle over the carved lamb.

6 **CARVE AND SERVE.** Carve the leg of lamb (see Carving Bone-In Leg of Lamb, page 140), adding any juices from the carving board to the pan drippings. Serve drizzled with the pan drippings, or layer the slices in the roasting pan so they soak up the pan juices and serve family-style, from the roasting pan.

Carving Bone-In Leg of Lamb

THERE ARE TWO APPROACHES TO CARVING A WHOLE LEG OF LAMB. THE FIRST, AND PERHAPS MOST OBVIOUS, METHOD IS TO CARVE THE MEAT INTO LONG thin slices parallel to the bone, and the second, slightly more complicated method is to carve the meat across the grain. Both methods are sound and have their advantages, and I encourage you to use whichever seems best to you. For the first, arrange the lamb on a cutting board with the meatier side up (one side is always meatier than the other) and the shank end facing you. Steady the shank end either by holding it with a clean dish towel or by holding a carving fork against it. In your other hand, hold a long carving knife parallel to the bone and begin slicing thin slices (¼ inch or so) of lamb from the roast. Continue until you reach the leg bone. Flip the leg over and continue making lengthwise slices until you've left little meat on the bone. You'll be rewarded with a platter of handsome long thin slices of roast lamb. The downside of this approach, however, is that you carve the meat with the grain, so it's not as tender or juicy as it might be.

If you prefer carving across the grain, start the same way, by arranging the lamb on a cutting board with the meatier side up and the shank end facing you. Raise the shank end, holding it with a clean dish towel or cloth napkin, and carve off as large a piece of meat as you can by running your knife along the length of the leg bone. When you reach the wider hip portion, maneuver the knife to free the chunk of meat. Rotate the leg and repeat the process of carving the meat off the bone in two to three more large chunks. Once the leg bone is mostly clean (you can further trim it for leftovers later on), carve each chunk crosswise into ½-inch thick slices. (This technique is very similar to the one shown for slow-roasted goat leg on page 155.) In the end, you'll have a platter of smaller, less regular slices, but they will be slightly more tender and juicier.

Shopping for Bone-In Leg of Lamb

A WHOLE LEG OF LAMB ENCOMPASSES EVERYTHING FROM THE REAR SHANK UP TO THE SIRLOIN OR HIP REGION. THIS MEANS THAT IT CAN CONTAIN A number of bones, starting with the shank, then the leg bone, and finally a complicated pelvic configuration including a piece of the hip bone and tailbone. The difficulty for the home cook is that these pelvic bones are convoluted and pose a problem when it comes to carving. One solution is to purchase a half leg, meaning that the butcher has simply removed the entire sirloin (hip) and thus left you with a shorter roast containing two simple straight bones (leg and shank). The drawback is that the sirloin includes some of the meatiest and tastiest meat on the leg, plus the roast will be smaller, serving only 5 to 6 people. The better alternative is to ask the butcher to remove the hip bone (also called the aitch bone or pelvic bone). Removing the hip bone will leave loose flaps of meat at the wider end, but the butcher, or you, can neatly skewer these to secure them. You may also come across something called a semiboneless leg, also called an *American-style lamb leg*, which refers to a partially bone-in leg where the shank bone has been removed. Expect these to weigh a bit less (closer to 6 pounds), but they make a fine roast, although I miss the majesty of the shank bone. Some upscale markets will french the shank bone on a whole bone-in leg by cutting the tendons and exposing the end of the bone. This makes for a more dramatic presentation but doesn't affect the roasting. And finally, some butchers crack the shank bone—a practice I've never understood because it seems only to make the leg difficult to handle.

If you do bring home either a half leg or an American-style leg, follow the roasting technique given in the recipes but know that the roasting times may be less, so start checking for doneness after 45 minutes.

ROAST LEG OF LAMB WITH ANCHOVY, ROSEMARY, GARLIC, AND PIMENT D'ESPELETTE

For this recipe, I boost lamb's sweet flavor by studding the meat with a combination of fresh rosemary, garlic, and anchovies. Yes, anchovies. But don't be afraid—tucked into the meat, the anchovies dissolve during roasting, enriching the lamb with a delicious though elusive flavor that's far less assertive than you might think. In place of black pepper, I season the roast with *piment d'Espelette*; I love the way its light heat complements the lamb, but you can use hot paprika in its place. If you keep lard (or good bacon drippings), rub a little over the meat before roasting. It adds a wonderful richness to the drippings and helps deepen the caramelization of the surface. It's a trick I learned from an old Spanish cookbook.

SERVES 8 TO 10

METHOD: Combination high and moderate heat

ROASTING TIME: 1 1/2 to 1 3/4 hours

PLAN AHEAD: For the best flavor and texture, season the meat 1 to 2 days before roasting.

WINE: Deeply fruity red with herbal and spice notes and a touch of earthiness, like Garnacha-based reds from Navarra or Monastrell from Jumilla.

1 whole bone-in leg of lamb, 7 to 8 pounds, preferably with hip bone removed (see Shopping for Bone-In Leg of Lamb, page 141)

5 garlic cloves, cut into 20 thin slivers

4 anchovy fillets, rinsed, patted dry, and cut into 20 little pieces

4 leafy sprigs rosemary, cut into twenty 1-inch pieces

2 teaspoons kosher salt

2 teaspoons *piment d'Espelette* (see page 145)

1 to 2 tablespoons lard or extra-virgin olive oil

¾ cup dry white wine or dry white vermouth

1   **TRIM THE LAMB.** Examine the leg of lamb to determine what kind of trimming and perhaps tying you need to do before seasoning. If the pelvic bones have been removed,

you may find a loose flap of meat at the wide end of the roast. If so, secure this with skewers or sew it shut with a trussing needle and kitchen string. Using a thin-bladed sharp knife, trim any leathery membrane or excess fat from the exterior of the lamb. You want to leave a thin layer (⅛ inch) of fat to protect the meat from drying.

2   **SEASON THE LAMB.** Using the tip of a paring knife, make 20 small holes on all sides of the lamb. Stuff each hole with a sliver of garlic, a bit of anchovy, and a sprig of rosemary, leaving the tips of the rosemary sticking out. (It may help to gather the seasonings into a little "bouquet" and use the point of the knife to tuck a "bouquet" into each hole.) After you've studded the entire roast, season the surface with the salt and the *piment d'Espelette* (you use slightly less salt here than in the basic recipe because of the saltiness of the anchovies). Set in a large baking dish and refrigerate, uncovered or loosely covered, for 1 to 2 days. Let the lamb sit at room temperature for about 2 hours before roasting.

3   **HEAT THE OVEN.** Arrange a rack in the lower third of the oven and heat to 450 degrees (425 degrees convection).

4   **ROAST THE LAMB.** Rub the surface of the meat with the lard or olive oil. Place the lamb with the rounder, meatier side up in a roasting pan just large enough to accommodate it (it's fine if the tip of the shank rests on the edge of the roasting pan). Roast for 25 minutes and then pour the wine or vermouth over the lamb. Immediately lower the oven temperature to 325 degrees (300 degrees convection), and continue roasting until a meat thermometer inserted in the meatiest part of the leg reaches 120 to 125 degrees for rare, about 1 hour from the time you lowered the oven heat; or 130 to 135 degrees for medium-rare, about 1¼ hours.

5   **REST.** Remove the lamb to a carving board, preferably one with a trough, to rest for 20 to 35 minutes. Tilt the roasting pan and spoon off as much of the clear fat as you can. Using a wooden spoon, scrape up the pan drippings (if they are too stuck to the pan to scrape up, add ¼ cup water to dissolve them). Set aside the pan drippings to drizzle over the carved lamb.

6   **CARVE AND SERVE.** Carve the leg of lamb (see Carving Bone-In Leg of Lamb, page 140) and serve drizzled with the pan drippings, or layer the slices in the roasting pan so they soak up the pan juices and serve family-style, from the roasting pan.

CONTINUED ON NEXT PAGE

OPTION: TOMATO-FENNEL VINAIGRETTE FOR ROAST LEG OF LAMB

A surprising and delicious way to brighten up roast lamb, this vinaigrette is equally good with basic roast leg of lamb and with lamb that gets seasoned with anchovy, rosemary, garlic, and *piment d'Espelette*. Make the vinaigrette while the lamb roasts, then pour it into the roasting pan as the meat rests. The vinaigrette warms slightly and mingles with the savory pan drippings. If you're not a fan of fennel or are looking for an alternative, substitute whole cumin seeds and use fresh mint in place of the basil.

SERVES 8 TO 10; MAKES ABOUT 2 CUPS VINAIGRETTE; ENOUGH FOR 1 ROAST LEG OF LAMB

WINE: Full-bodied Sangiovese-based red from Tuscany, such as a Vino Nobile di Montepulciano or a Brunello di Montalcino.

1 pound ripe tomatoes, seeded and finely chopped (about 2 cups)

½ cup black olives, such as Kalamata or Niçoise, pitted and finely chopped

3 tablespoons red wine vinegar

1½ teaspoons fennel seeds, lightly toasted in a dry skillet and coarsely ground

Freshly ground black pepper

⅓ cup extra-virgin olive oil

1 Basic Roast Bone-In Leg of Lamb (page 138) or Roast Leg of Lamb with Anchovy, Rosemary, Garlic, and *Piment d'Espelette* (page 142)

⅓ cup thinly sliced, lightly packed fresh basil leaves

Kosher salt

1   **MAKE THE VINAIGRETTE.** In a medium bowl, combine the tomatoes, olives, vinegar, and fennel seeds. Season with pepper (I wait to add salt until the vinaigrette combines with the drippings, otherwise it may become too salty). Whisk in the olive oil and set aside.

2   **ROAST THE LAMB AS DIRECTED.** After transferring the lamb to the carving board in step 5, spoon and pour off as much of the excess fat from the roasting pan as you can. Using a wooden spoon, scrape up the pan drippings (if they are too stuck to the pan to scrape up, add 2 to 3 tablespoons water to dissolve them). Add the vinaigrette to the pan, stirring to combine with the drippings. Stir in the basil. Taste for salt and pepper. The vinaigrette should be warm but not hot.

3   **CARVE AND SERVE.** Carve the leg of lamb (see Carving Bone-In Leg of Lamb, page 140). Add any juices from the carving board to the vinaigrette. Spoon the warm vinaigrette over the slices and serve.

Piment d'Espelette

PIMENT D'ESPELETTE IS THE NAME OF A MILDLY HOT SEASONING FROM THE TOWN OF ESPELETTE IN THE BASQUE REGION OF FRANCE. THE NATIVE chile peppers are strung together after harvest and hung on buildings and barns to dry in the sun, then ground into a brick-red powder. Milder than cayenne, *piment d'Espelette* has a light heat and a unique, nuanced fruity sweetness. The smallish, bright red peppers are so treasured and unique to the surrounding region that they bear the same certification of origin (A.O.C., or *appellation d'origine controllé*) that designates many of the best wines of France. The most celebrated use for *piment d'Espelette*, perhaps, is to season the famous Bayonne hams before curing. In the kitchen, I like to use it to season eggs (scrambled or deviled), pasta, chicken, and meat—especially roast lamb. Shop for *piment d'Espelette* (sometimes labeled "ground espelette pepper") at specialty markets or on-line. You can also substitute hot (not smoked) paprika.

MECHOUI-STYLE ROAST LAMB

*M*echoui (pronounced mesh-*wee*) is a North African dish of heavily spiced whole lamb spit-roasted over an open fire until the meat can be easily torn away from the bones. Indeed, the traditional way to serve mechoui is directly from the fire, inviting guests to pull off bite-size pieces with their fingers and dip them into bowls of cumin-salt, a perfect accompaniment for the tender, juicy meat. At home, I mimic this festival dish by roasting a whole bone-in leg or shoulder of lamb in the oven until meltingly tender. To get those great spicy flavors as well as the succulence, I massage the meat with butter and spices. The spices ensure the meat has the perfume of North Africa while the butter keeps the roast moist and helps to develop a glistening crust.

I make *mechoui* more often with leg than shoulder because leg is easy to find and I love the results. A bone-in lamb shoulder, if you can find one, is also a great choice and turns out a bit closer to the real deal as shoulder meat has a more robust flavor, and the complicated bone structure means that picking the meat off by hand is really the only way to serve it. The cumin salt is optional, but it adds wonderful counterpoint to the tender, rich meat. Couscous and a carrot salad would make fine side dishes.

SERVES 8 TO 10 IF USING LEG; 6 TO 8 IF USING SHOULDER

METHOD: Combination high and moderate heat

ROASTING TIME: 3 1/2 to 4 1/2 hours

PLAN AHEAD: For best flavor and texture, season the meat 1 to 2 days before roasting.

WINE: Robustly flavored Spanish red, such as Monastrell from Jumilla or Garnacha (Grenache) from Priorat.

One whole bone-in leg of lamb, about 7 to 8 pounds, with hip bone removed (see Shopping for Bone-In Leg of Lamb, page 141), or one whole bone-in lamb shoulder, about 5 to 6 pounds

1½ tablespoons whole coriander seeds

1 tablespoon whole cumin seeds

2 teaspoons sweet paprika

½ teaspoon sugar

6 cloves garlic, smashed and peeled

Kosher salt

8 tablespoons (1 stick) unsalted butter, softened

For serving (optional): 2 tablespoons whole cumin seeds and 4 tablespoons fleur de sel

1 **TRIM THE LAMB.** Examine the leg of lamb to determine what kind of trimming and perhaps tying you need to do before seasoning. If the hip bone has been removed, you may find a loose flap of meat at the wide end of the roast. If so, secure this with skewers or sew it shut with a trussing needle and kitchen string. Now, using a thin-bladed sharp knife, trim any leathery membrane or excess fat from the exterior of the lamb. You want to leave a thin (⅛-inch) layer of fat to protect the meat from drying. (If using a lamb shoulder, don't trim aggressively at all; much of the pleasure of eating roast shoulder is the contrast between the crisp skin and the tender meat inside.)

2 **MAKE THE SPICE RUB.** Combine the coriander and 1 tablespoon cumin in a small, dry skillet and toast, shaking the pan a few times, over medium-low heat until fragrant and beginning to darken, 2 to 3 minutes. Let cool slightly and then grind to a coarse powder in a mortar or spice grinder. Transfer to a small bowl, and stir in the paprika and sugar. Combine the garlic and 2 teaspoons of salt in the mortar and pound to a paste (alternatively you can make the garlic paste with a chef's knife according to the directions on page 230). Add the garlic paste to the spices. Using a wooden spoon, work in the butter until evenly mixed.

3 **SEASON THE LAMB.** Using the tip of a paring knife, make a dozen or more 1-inch deep incisions in the meatiest part of the lamb. Rub the lamb all over with the seasoned butter, doing your best to smear some into the incisions. Set in a large baking dish and refrigerate, uncovered or loosely covered, for 1 to 2 days. Let the lamb sit at room temperature for 1 to 2 hours before roasting.

4 **HEAT THE OVEN.** Position a rack in the lower third of the oven and heat to 450 degrees (425 degrees convection).

5 **ROAST THE LAMB.** Place the lamb in a roasting pan (9 by 13 inches works well) just large enough to accommodate it (if roasting a leg, place the rounder, meatier side up; for a shoulder, place the skin side up). Roast for 25 minutes, and then lower the oven temperature to 325 degrees (300 degrees convection) and continue roasting, basting occasionally with any pan drippings, until the meat is meltingly tender and beginning to pull away from the bone, another 2½ to 3½ hours. I generally check for doneness by feel—it's done when the meat easily pulls away from the bone—but if you

CONTINUED ON NEXT PAGE

do use an instant-read thermometer, it should register 170 to 180 degrees. (Because of its smaller size, expect a shoulder to roast more quickly than a leg. Also, the complicated bone structure of a shoulder—ribs, blade bone, and arm—make it tricky to find a spot to check the internal temperature. The thickest, fleshiest spot tends to be near the arm bone.)

6 **MEANWHILE, MAKE THE CUMIN SALT, IF USING.** Lightly toast the 2 tablespoons cumin in a small, dry skillet over medium-low heat until just fragrant but not darkened, about 1 minute. Let cool slightly and transfer to a mortar (or spice grinder) and crush only to lightly crack the seeds. Combine with the fleur de sel and set aside.

7 **REST.** Remove the lamb to a carving board, preferably one with a trough, to rest for 20 to 35 minutes. Pour off any excess fat and deglaze the pan drippings with about ¼ cup of water, scraping and stirring to dissolve any cooked-on bits. Using a meat fork and tongs, pull the lamb apart into serving pieces. Drizzle over the pan drippings, and serve with either individual bowls of cumin salt for dipping or one larger one to pass at the table.

BASIC ROLLED BONELESS LEG OF LAMB ROAST

If you're looking for the quintessential roast lamb for a sit-down dinner party or a Sunday night family supper, here it is. This compact bundle of tender, flavorful meat serves 6 people easily without breaking the bank. The only hard part is deciding whether you want to take the purist route, seasoning with only salt and pepper and letting the sweet, musky flavor of the lamb stand on its own, or bump up the flavor by smearing the meat with an herb paste or surrounding the meat with vegetables in the roasting pan and turning it into a one-pot meal (see options that follow). Either way, you can't go wrong.

SERVES 6 TO 7

METHOD: Moderate heat

ROASTING TIME: 55 minutes to 1 1/2 hours

WINE: Herbal red with a touch of earthiness, such as Nero d'Avola from Sicily or a youthful Barbera from Piedmont.

One 2 ½- to 3-pound butterflied leg of lamb (see Shopping for a Butterflied Leg of Lamb, page 153)

Kosher salt and freshly ground black pepper

½ cup homemade or store-bought low-sodium chicken broth, beef broth, or water (optional)

¼ cup dry white wine or dry white vermouth (optional)

1 **TRIM THE LAMB.** Lay the lamb out flat on a cutting board. (If you weren't able to find a butterflied leg of lamb, refer to Butterflying a Boneless Leg of Lamb, page 153). Arrange it so the cut side is down and the outside faces up; you can identify the outside by the layer of subcutaneous fat. If there is more than a scant ⅛-inch layer of fat, pare it down with a sharp, thin-bladed knife (a boning knife works best) till it just barely covers the meat. Flip the meat and trim away any large clumps of fat from the cut side. Don't attempt to remove all the fat, and do your best not to cut any large holes in the meat or detach the membrane that holds the various muscle groups together.

CONTINUED ON NEXT PAGE

2 **SEASON THE LAMB.** *If you're using one of the flavored options below, skip this step; go to the flavor option recipe, follow the directions there, and then proceed with step 3.* If not using a flavor option, season the lamb liberally with salt and pepper on both sides. Use 1½ to 2 teaspoons salt if seasoning 6 hours or more in advance (seasoning in advance will make the lamb more flavorful), slightly less if seasoning right before roasting; use pepper to taste.

3 **ROLL AND TIE THE ROAST.** Roll the lamb up into a cylinder so the grain of the meat runs the length of the roast. Using kitchen string, secure the roll by tying loops of string at 1½-inch intervals along its length. Tie the loops securely but not so tightly as to tear into the meat. If the ends of the roll flap open, finish by weaving a long loop of twine lengthwise through the loops. *The lamb can be seasoned and tied up to 2 days ahead. Refrigerate the lamb, uncovered or loosely covered, if you plan to wait more than 2 hours before roasting.* Allow the lamb to sit at room temperature for 1 to 2 hours before roasting.

4 **HEAT THE OVEN.** Position a rack in the lower third of the oven and heat to 350 degrees (325 degrees convection).

5 **ROAST.** Place the lamb on a shallow roasting pan or heavy-duty rimmed baking sheet just a bit larger than the roast (8 by 12 inches or slightly smaller). Roast until an instant-read thermometer inserted into the meat reaches 120 to 125 degrees for rare, about 55 minutes; or 130 degrees for medium, 1¼ to 1½ hours. Transfer the lamb to a cutting board, preferably one with a trough, and let the meat rest for 20 to 30 minutes.

6 **MAKE A QUICK SAUCE (OPTIONAL).** If the pan drippings look appealing and you want a bit of pan sauce, start by tilting the roasting pan and pouring or spooning off the clear fat; stop before you discard any of the drippings, even if this means leaving some fat. Add the broth or water and the white wine or vermouth. Heat over medium heat, scraping up the drippings with a wooden spoon. Transfer the sauce to a small saucepan and simmer over medium-high heat until slightly reduced, about 4 minutes. Taste. If the liquid tastes watery, simmer a bit longer.

7 **CARVE AND SERVE.** Carve the meat into thick or thin slices as you like (I prefer them ½-inch thick), removing the kitchen string as you go. Add any carving juices to the pan sauce, if using. Serve.

OPTION 1: GREEN HERB STUFFING FOR ROLLED LEG OF LAMB

This piquant, verdant stuffing enhances the rich flavor of the lamb and provides a visual contrast to the rosy meat. Follow the recipe for Basic Rolled Boneless Leg of Lamb Roast (page 149), using the herb paste and these directions in place of step 2. For other flavoring options, use the olive and parsley crust from page 123 or the herbed spinach stuffing used in the pork tenderloin roulade on page 180.

MAKES ABOUT 1/2 CUP HERB PASTE

2 to 3 garlic cloves

1 cup loosely packed fresh flat-leaf parsley leaves

¼ cup loosely packed fresh mint leaves

1 tablespoon fresh oregano or marjoram leaves

2 anchovy fillets, coarsely chopped

1 teaspoon cracked black pepper

Kosher salt and freshly ground black pepper

½ teaspoon grains of paradise, crushed to a powder (see page 154; optional)

⅛ to ¼ teaspoon crushed red pepper flakes

2 tablespoons extra-virgin olive oil

One 2 ½- to 3-pound butterflied leg of lamb (see Shopping for a Butterflied Leg of Lamb, page 153)

1 **MAKE THE HERB PASTE.** Start the food processor, and with the motor running, drop in the garlic cloves. When finely minced, stop the motor, remove the top, scrape down the sides of the bowl, and add the parsley, mint, oregano, anchovies, cracked black pepper, ¾ teaspoon salt, the grains of paradise (if using), and the red pepper flakes. Replace the top and pulse on and off until the ingredients are evenly chopped. Pour in the olive oil and pulse briefly to create a rough paste.

2 **TRIM THE LAMB** as directed in step 1 of the Basic Rolled Boneless Leg of Lamb Roast on page 149.

3 **SEASON.** *Lightly* season both sides of the meat with salt and pepper, then arrange the lamb skin side down and spread the herb paste all the way to the edges, rubbing it in with your hands to get it into any crevices or gaps.

4 **ROLL, TIE, AND ROAST.** Proceed with step 3 of the rolled leg of lamb recipe. Gather any herb paste that falls out during rolling and tying and rub it over the surface of the lamb. If you stuff and tie the lamb in advance, you will find some liquid from the herb paste seeps from the meat as it sits. Pour this over the lamb just before roasting.

CONTINUED ON NEXT PAGE

OPTION 2: ROLLED LEG OF LAMB ROASTED ON A BED OF POTATOES AND CARROTS

Here's a way to get your meat and potatoes—and carrots—all in one dish. The vegetables soak up the delicious lamb juices and play up the natural sweetness of the meat.

SERVES 6 TO 8

METHOD: Moderate heat

ROASTING TIME: 55 minutes to 1 1/2 hours

WINE: Youthful, deeply fruity Pinot Noir from Oregon or New Zealand.

1 pound small red or white potatoes, cut in half if larger than a walnut

1 pound carrots, peeled and cut into 2-inch chunks

1 tablespoon extra-virgin olive oil, plus more for the pan

1 tablespoon fresh rosemary leaves, coarsely chopped

Kosher salt and freshly ground black pepper

One 2 ½- to 3-pound butterflied leg of lamb (see Shopping for a Butterflied Leg of Lamb, page 153)

1 TRIM, SEASON, AND TIE THE LAMB. Follow steps 1 through 4 of the recipe for Basic Rolled Boneless Leg of Lamb Roast (page 149).

2 ROAST THE LAMB AND THE VEGETABLES. Lightly oil a medium-sized roasting pan (14 by 12 inches works well). Combine the potatoes and carrots in the pan, drizzle with the olive oil, and season with rosemary, salt, and pepper. Toss to coat and arrange the vegetables around the perimeter of the pan to make way for the lamb. Place the lamb in the center and roast until an instant-read thermometer inserted in the meat reaches 120 to 125 degrees for rare, about 55 minutes; or 130 degrees for medium, 1¼ to 1½ hours. Stir the vegetables once or twice during roasting. Transfer the lamb to a cutting board, preferably one with a trough, and let the meat rest for 20 to 30 minutes.

Check that the potatoes and carrots are tender and nicely browned in spots. If not, return them to the oven to continue to roast as the meat rests. If they are ready, set them aside in a warm spot while the meat rests.

3 CARVE AND SERVE. Stir the vegetables so they are coated with pan drippings and serve alongside the sliced lamb. Carve the meat into ½-inch thick slices, removing the kitchen string as you go. Pour any carving juices over the meat as you serve.

Shopping for a Butterflied Leg of Lamb

ALTHOUGH MANY MARKETS SELL BONELESS LEG OF LAMB ALREADY ROLLED AND TIED INTO A NEAT BUNDLE, I FIND YOU GET A TASTIER AND LESS FATTY roast by purchasing a butterflied leg of lamb and rolling and tying it yourself. A butterflied leg of lamb will be a thick steaklike cut (anywhere from 1 to 2 inches thick) that rolls neatly into a cylindrical roast. Plus a butterflied leg allows more surface area if you're planning to season or smear.

A full boneless leg of lamb weighs close to 6 pounds, but I prefer to shop for a smaller, shorter roast, somewhere between 2½ and 3 pounds. These smaller cuts have the sinewy shank end removed, leaving you only the meatiest, most tender parts of the leg. If you can only find boneless lamb legs (and not butterflied), look for a leg with the shank end removed (sometimes labeled "short leg" or "half leg"), and butterfly as directed below.

BUTTERFLYING A BONELESS LEG OF LAMB

If the roast is tied or wrapped in any sort of net, remove the string or netting. Trim away any excess fat from the skin side. Ideally, there should be a scant ⅛ inch layer of clean white fat covering the roast. Sometimes there is a tough papery layer on top of the fat; this must be trimmed away before you get to the fat. Once you've trimmed the outside, turn the meat skin side down and open it up as best you can on the cutting board.

Start by removing any significant clumps of fat, taking care not to cut any large holes in the meat. Next, use a little judgment in deciding how much you need to butcher the meat. Depending on how the bones were removed, the meat may unroll much like a butterflied leg (thus your work is pretty much done), or it may hold together, leaving very little opportunity for stuffing. The goal here is to open up the roast some so that you have more surface area to season, but you don't want to cut too deeply into the meat. Using a sharp knife, make a few lengthwise incisions into the thicker sections of the roast and fold these open to flatten the roast.

Grains of Paradise

GRAINS OF PARADISE IS THE RATHER POETIC NAME OF A CARDAMOM-LIKE SPICE THAT WAS ENORMOUSLY POPULAR IN EUROPE FOR HUNDREDS OF years (starting around the time of Queen Elizabeth I) but that fell out of favor by the early nineteenth century. Happily, this pungent little seed seems to be making a comeback. In fact, last I checked, it had its own Twitter account (I am not kidding). The small reddish brown seeds are typically crushed before you use them (this is easily done in a mortar or a spice grinder) to release their peppery bite with hints of cardamom and ginger. Shop for grains of paradise, also known as Melegueta (or Malagueta) pepper, at specialty stores or on-line spice suppliers. You won't need much—a little goes a long way. You can substitute cardamom mixed in equal parts with black pepper plus a tiny pinch of dried ginger.

SLOW-ROASTED GOAT LEG WITH HARISSA, TOMATOES, AND ONIONS

Goat, popular just about everywhere in the world, seems to be finally catching on with American cooks. Though authentic Indian, Mexican, and Greek restaurants have long had goat on their menus, I've been excited to see it appear at increasingly more restaurants, and not just those that classify as ethnic eateries. And all I can say is, "it's about time," as there is much to love about this delectable meat. For one thing, the dark meat has a wonderful flavor best described as that of dry-aged beef with a hint of lamb. It's not gamey, but slightly musky, mildly sweet and earthy. When roasted, goat delivers a richness that belies the fact that the meat is remarkably lean—leaner than chicken or beef and higher in protein than both. This leanness does, however, mean taking care not to dry the meat out when roasting. I solve this by first rubbing the meat with harissa (a North African olive-oil and chile puree), which flavors and lubricates the meat. Then, after an initial blast of high heat, the goat roasts slowly, surrounded by wine-moistened tomatoes and onions that make a delicious side dish right in the roasting pan.

The best harissa to use here is Tunisian-style, which has a more complex flavor and a thicker texture than Moroccan-style (the type often sold in tubes). I like to make my own Tunisian-style puree, but you can also purchase it in jars and tins from specialty markets and on line. The best store-bought brand I've ever tasted comes from Les Moulins Mahjoub (see Sources & Resources, page 539).

SERVES 4 TO 6
METHOD: Combination high and low heat
ROASTING TIME: About 2 1/4 hours
PLAN AHEAD: For best flavor, season the goat 6 to 24 hours before roasting.
WINE: Young fruity Monastrell from Spain's Jumilla region.

CONTINUED ON PAGE 157

SLOW-ROASTED GOAT LEG WITH HARISSA, TOMATOES, AND ONIONS (PAGE 155)

One bone-in goat leg (about 4 pounds; see
 page 160)

1½ tablespoons jarred or homemade
 Tunisian-Style Harissa (page 158)

1½ pounds small ripe tomatoes (such as
 Roma), cored and cut into quarters

3 small onions (about 12 ounces), peeled
 and cut into ½-inch wedges

6 garlic cloves, peeled

2 tablespoons extra-virgin olive oil

Kosher salt and freshly ground black
 pepper

¾ cup dry white vermouth, dry white wine,
 or water

1   **TRIM AND SEASON THE GOAT.** Using a sharp, narrow knife (a boning knife
or paring knife) and your hands, peel and trim away the leathery membrane, known
as caul, and any thick patches of fat. Don't worry about trimming off every last bit
of fat (goat is quite lean and will benefit from a little fat), but you do want to remove
any tough caul membrane that pulls away in sheets to expose the meat below. Smear
the harissa over the entire surface of the meat. If seasoning ahead, cover loosely with
plastic wrap and refrigerate for 6 to 24 hours. Let sit at room temperature for about
an hour before roasting.

2   **HEAT THE OVEN.** Position a rack in the lower third of the oven and heat to 425
degrees (400 degrees convection).

3   **SEASON THE VEGETABLES.** Combine the tomatoes, onions, and garlic in a
bowl. Add the olive oil, season with salt and pepper, and toss to coat. Set aside.

4   **ROAST.** Place the goat in a roasting pan just large enough to hold it, and slide it
into the oven. After 15 minutes, slide the oven rack holding the roasting pan out
and tip the vegetables into the roasting pan, scattering them around the meat. Pour
the vermouth (or wine or water) over the meat, and slide the rack back in. Close the
oven, and reduce the temperature to 275 degrees (250 degrees convection). After 30
minutes at the lower temperature, baste the meat with the pan juices and stir the
vegetables; do this again every 20 minutes or so, flipping the leg over after about 1
hour at the lower temperature. Continue roasting, basting, and stirring, until an
instant-read thermometer inserted into the thickest part of the leg registers about
150 degrees, about 1 hour more.

CONTINUED ON NEXT PAGE

5 **REST.** Transfer the meat to a cutting board, preferably one with a trough, and let it rest for 20 to 30 minutes. Stir the vegetables, scraping the roasting pan to capture any roasted-on bits. Taste the vegetables for salt and pepper, and keep warm until serving.

6 **CARVE.** If you've ever carved a bone-in leg of lamb, you are on familiar ground here. Start by grabbing hold of the shank end (the narrow end) of the leg with your hand or a clean dish towel. Now, either carve thin lengthwise slices of meat from the roast, or, my preferred method (as shown on page 161), carve off large chunks of meat by sliding the knife as close to the bone as possible and then slice those chunks crosswise into thin slices. This method may look less dramatic and give you smaller slices, but it ensures that you carve the meat across the grain (which means more tender bites) and gives a better mix of doneness, as each slice contains some of the outside and inside of the roast.

In most cases, whole goat legs have the pelvic bone intact (this is the convoluted bone that runs laterally at the wide end of the leg; you can see it in photo 6 on page 161). Even the most expert carvers have trouble getting around this bone, so simply do the best you can.

7 **SERVE.** Transfer the sliced goat to a carving platter or individual plates. Surround with the tomatoes and onions and spoon any carving juices over the top.

TUNISIAN-STYLE HARISSA

Before I was lucky enough to visit Tunisia, the only harissa I knew was the Morrocan version, a thin paste made from dried chiles, tomato paste, and salt, and while I relied on it to spice my tagines and couscous, it wasn't something I couldn't live without. In Tunisia, however, I fell head over heels for their version, a puree of sun-dried local chiles, freshly ground spices, garlic, and fruity olive oil that offers an amazing depth of flavors as well as a nice bit of heat. Though I packed a few jars in my suitcase to take home with me, it eventually ran out, leaving me to experiment with making my own. The flavor—and heat index—will vary according to the chiles you use. I like a combination of guajillo chiles and New Mexico or pasillas for a harissa with some heat, but not too much. The final flavor will depend a great deal on the quality of olive oil, so use the best you can. In addition to using the paste as a marinade for meat, try adding a spoonful to sautéed onions when making soups and stews, or whisk a bit into eggs before scrambling them. Sometimes I just smear a bit onto a crust of bread for a snack. If you're like me, you'll want to double the recipe to make sure you don't run out. In fact, I am so addicted to the stuff that I usually stock my refrigerator with both my homemade harissa *and* jars of my favorite brand from Les Moulins Mahjoub (see Sources & Resources, page 539).

MAKES ABOUT 3/4 CUP

2 ounces of dried chiles, preferably a mix of
   guajillo and New Mexico or pasillas

1 teaspoon coriander seeds

½ teaspoon cumin seeds

¼ teaspoon caraway seeds

2 garlic cloves, coarsely chopped

¾ teaspoon kosher salt

3 tablespoon extra-virgin olive oil, plus
   more as needed

1   **SOAK THE CHILES.** Put the chiles in a medium bowl and cover with boiling water. If the chiles float, weight them down with a small plate. Let them sit until softened, about 25 minutes.

2   **TOAST THE SPICES.** Combine the coriander, cumin, and caraway in a small, dry skillet and heat over medium, shaking the pan to prevent burning, until fragrant and beginning to color, about 2 minutes. Transfer to a mortar or spice grinder, let cool, and grind to a fine powder.

3   **MAKE THE PASTE.** Outfit a food processor with a chopping blade, and, with the motor running, drop the garlic cloves into the feed tube. Process until finely minced. Drain the chiles, and tear them into medium-small pieces, removing and discarding the seeds and stems. Add the chiles to the food processor along with the ground spices and the salt. Process, stopping to scrape down the sides, to make a course puree. Add the olive oil, and process briefly to incorporate (avoid overworking the olive oil, as that can turn it bitter).

4   **PACK IN A JAR.** Transfer the paste to a clean glass jar—the paste may discolor plastic containers—packing it down with a small rubber spatula. Pour a thin layer of olive oil over the surface (this preserves the flavor and color). Put a lid on the jar, and refrigerate for up to 3 weeks. Top off with olive oil after each use.

Shopping for Goat

MOST GOAT MEAT SHOULD TECHNICALLY BE CALLED "KID" (OR BABY GOAT) MEAT, SINCE IT COMES FROM ANIMALS NO MORE THAN 2 TO 3 MONTHS OLD. (Meat from older animals would be too tough and lean for roasting.) Spanish markets use the term *cabrito* to designate young, milk-fed kid, while in Northern Europe, *chevron* is the term for young goat. Regardless of the name, you can tell that you're getting a young animal if the leg weighs in at less than 5 pounds. Look for goat at the farmers' market, ethnic meat markets (especially Middle Eastern stores), and specialty butchers. It's also available from several on-line suppliers (see Sources & Resources, page 539). You may find goat meat that is sold frozen, which I've never had any complaint with. Just be sure to allow 2 to 3 days for the leg to defrost, in its original wrapping, in your refrigerator.

If you do buy a fresh leg of goat from a full-service butcher, ask them to remove the pelvic bone. This complicated piece of the hip bone sits at the wide end of the leg and interferes with carving. Getting it out of the way before roasting is by no means essential, but it does make your life easier. If you do manage to get a leg without the pelvic bone, there will be a loose flap of meat where the bone once was. Secure this with kitchen string tied lengthwise, and then in several smaller loops around the wide end of the leg.

BONE-IN GOAT LEG BRUSHED WITH HARISSA BEFORE ROASTING

Step-by-Step: Carving Slow-Roasted Goat Leg

1 Grab hold of the shank end and carve off large chunks of meat by sliding the knife as close to the bone as possible. **2** Make a lateral slice into the meaty portion of the leg cutting down to the leg bone to free the chunk you sliced off. **3** Rotate the leg and slice down along the bone to remove another meaty section. **4** Continue rotating the leg and slicing along the bone until you have carved off as much meat as you can. **5** Slice the chunks of meat crosswise into serving portions. **6** Most goat legs have the pelvic bone intact (the curve-shaped bone above the knife blade). Maneuver the knife as best you can to carve around this bone.

CLASSIC PORK RIB ROAST
(RACK OF PORK) (PAGE
191) GARNISHED WITH
WATERCRESS

3

PORK

OVEN-ROASTED PORCHETTA
(PAGE 213)

PORK
RECITES

ANYONE WHO PAYS THE SLIGHTEST ATTENTION TO FOOD TRENDS KNOWS THAT THE PASSION FOR PORK HAS BEEN RUNNING HIGH. A RECENT *NEW York Times* headline on the subject read "Pig Is Big," and the past few years have seen a slew of books (recipe-based and otherwise) on the topic. Restaurant menus across the country proffer more pork than ever, everything from porchetta to double-cut heritage-breed pork chops. As more and more chefs, diners, and home cooks embrace pork for its deliciousness and versatility, perhaps we can finally put an end to that "other white meat" nonsense. For one thing, a good piece of pork is not white; it can be anything from pink to rosy to almost beefy-looking, depending on the cut, the provenance, and how it's been cooked. Also, "white meat" suggests a nondescript flavor, and this couldn't be further from the truth. Pork has a distinctive, slightly sweet taste, and there is no better, more direct way to appreciate its goodness than to roast it to perfect doneness.

The cuts of pork best suited to roasting can be divided into two categories: those from the top part of the animal (including tenderloin, rib roasts, boneless loin roasts, and even double-cut pork chops) and those from the shoulder and leg. The former includes the naturally tender, relatively lean roasts that are best cooked to medium and not beyond, while the shoulder and leg offer roasts that are more robust and most delicious when cooked until well done.

Let's start with the first category. The expression "living high off the hog" comes from the fact that the leanest and most expensive pork cuts—the tenderloin, rib roast, and boneless pork loin—come from the muscles that run along the top of a pig. These naturally tender, relatively lean cuts roast beautifully, but they do require care so they don't dry out in the oven. In the recipes that follow, you will find a number of tricks for keeping these cuts juicy—brining, wrapping in prosciutto, smearing with butter—but the real key to a delicious piece of roasted pork is to set the oven at a low to moderate temperature. High heat seems to abuse pork more than it does any other meat, causing it to shrink up and dry out. Also, a very hot oven makes it more likely that you'll sail right past the ideal doneness, thus ruining the roast. As for "ideal doneness," most people, myself included, prefer pork cooked to somewhere between 140 and 145 degrees, which will give you super-moist meat with a trace of pink. (Happily, the USDA has finally lowered the recommended "safe" doneness temperature for pork to 145 from 160 degrees—a temperature at which tender cuts of pork will be dry and definitely lack flavor.) There is also a growing appreciation among some chefs and serious eaters for medium-rare pork. If this is to your taste, you're looking for temperatures around 130 degrees; the meat will have a deep pink, slightly wet-looking center.

Pork shoulder and leg, in contrast, contain a good bit of connective tissue that remains tough unless cooked until well done and falling-off-the-bone tender. These bigger, fattier cuts also contain plenty of intramuscular fat, which bastes the meat as it cooks, so that even at the well-done stage of 180 degrees, the meat is tender and succulent. Roast these cuts low and slow and there is little to no worry of overcooking. In fact, the best doneness test for these is to prod the roast with a meat fork to see that the meat gives way.

Regardless of which type of pork roast you choose, much of what makes pork so popular is its versatility. I get a singular satisfaction from a simple pork roast seasoned only with salt and pepper, like the Classic Pork Rib Roast on page 191, but pork seems to absorb seasonings more readily than any other meat. Indeed, pork seems to possess a chameleon-like ability to take on the flavor of the rest of the ingredients in the dish, and it goes well with all kinds of flavors—everything from Mediterranean seasonings, to pungent soy-based Asian seasonings, to vibrant Caribbean seasonings, to the classic combination of pork with fruit. The recipes in this chapter range from straightforward sear-roasted pork tenderloin for a quick weeknight supper (page 169) to a spectacular Oven-Roasted Porchetta (page 213).

For the best results with these recipes, buy the best pork you can afford. Fortunately, as the pig's culinary fame has been rising, so has the availability of delicious, well-raised pork. I am especially partial to heritage pork. As opposed to factory-farmed pigs, which have been bred over the years to be very lean and as a result can have dry and bland meat, heritage breeds (such as Berkshire, Duroc, and Tamworth) generally have more fat, making the meat richer, moister, and more flavorful. These breeds also don't take well to industrialized farming, which means they are usually raised on smaller farms where they are not subject to confinement—a situation that is bad for both the pig and the environment. However, none of this is a guarantee based on the label "heritage." For that reason, the best practice is to ask around, find a market that carries meats produced on a small scale, or, if you live near a farmers' market, try some of the locally raised pork. To find sources for heritage pork in your area, visit the website for LocalHarvest (turn to Sources & Resources on page 539 for more information).

BASIC SEAR-ROASTED PORK TENDERLOIN WITH QUICK VERMOUTH PAN SAUCE; ORANGE-ROASTED CARROTS WITH GREMOLATA (PAGE 510)

BASIC SEAR-ROASTED PORK TENDERLOIN

This simple pork tenderloin is one of my go-to recipes for weeknight dinners when I want something quick and good. If I remember to season the pork ahead, the flavor is even better, but it's also excellent when seasoned at the very last minute. Most nights I'm happy with just salt and pepper, especially when I have a good piece of pork, but you can certainly up the ante with one of the options I suggest or improvise with your own seasonings. You can apply herb and spice rubs before searing, but anything at all wet or sticky (like miso-sesame paste or mustard-herb coating) should be added after searing and before roasting.

You'll notice that I sear the pork in a skillet and then transfer it to a small baking sheet to roast. This enables the narrow little tenderloin to roast evenly; if you leave it in the hot skillet, it cooks too quickly, especially the bottom. One tasty way to help justify the two-pan method is to turn the drippings left in the skillet into a little pan sauce as the pork roasts.

If you are 2 for supper, as we so often are at my house, a single tenderloin provides enough for dinner and a tasty sandwich or two the following day. Of course, if you've got more people to feed, simply double, or even triple, the recipe. One word of caution when multiplying the recipe: Be sure not to crowd the tenderloins when searing. Either use a skillet that is large enough to sear them side by side or sear them one at a time.

SERVES 2 TO 3

METHOD: Combination sear and moderate heat

ROASTING TIME: 13 to 18 minutes (plus 6 to 8 minutes to sear)

PLAN AHEAD: For the best flavor, season the pork 4 to 24 hours ahead.

WINE: Deeply flavored Zinfandel with spice and pepper notes from Sonoma or San Luis Obispo.

1 pork tenderloin (1 to 1¼ pounds), trimmed (see Trimming Pork Tenderloin, page 179)

½ to ¾ teaspoon kosher salt

Freshly ground black pepper

1 tablespoon grapeseed oil or other neutral-tasting oil

1 **SEASON THE PORK.** Pat the pork dry and season the entire surface with salt and pepper. *If seasoning ahead, set on a plate and refrigerate, uncovered or loosely covered, for 4 to 24 hours.*

CONTINUED ON NEXT PAGE

2   **HEAT THE OVEN.** Position a rack in the center of the oven and heat to 350 degrees (325 degrees convection). Let the pork sit at room temperature as the oven heats, 25 to 30 minutes. Pat the surface dry. Tuck the last 3 inches or so of the "tail" or narrow end of the tenderloin under the rest (this will help prevent it from overcooking) and tie it in place with a loop of kitchen string, as shown below. *(Some markets trim off this narrow tail, in which case you won't need to tuck and tie it.)*

3   **SEAR THE PORK.** Heat an ovenproof skillet (10 to 11 inches works well) over medium-high heat. When the skillet is quite hot, add the oil, swirling the pan to coat. Add the pork; if the tenderloin is a bit longer than the diameter of the pan, simply arrange the meat in a curve so it fits without forcing, as it will shrink some as it cooks. Sear, undisturbed, until brown on one side, about 2 minutes. Turn the tenderloin with tongs to brown all four sides, for a total of 6 to 8 minutes. Transfer the pork to a small rimmed baking sheet.

4   **ROAST THE PORK.** Roast until the internal temperature at the thickest point, measured with an instant-read thermometer, reaches 140 to 145 degrees, 13 to 18 minutes.

5   **REST, SLICE, AND SERVE.** Transfer the pork to a carving board, preferably one with a trough, to rest for 5 to 8 minutes. Remove the string if tied, carve the pork into ½- to 1-inch-thick slices, and serve.

Step-by-Step: Tucking and Tying Pork Tenderloin

1 Tuck the last 3 inches or so of the "tail" or narrow end of the tenderloin under the rest to help keep it from overcooking.   **2** Tie the "tail" in place with a loop of kitchen string.

OPTION 1: QUICK VERMOUTH PAN SAUCE

This classic technique for making a last-minute pan sauce offers plenty of room for improvisation. For instance, no vermouth? Substitute dry white wine. No wine? Try apple cider or orange juice. Or, for something a little headier, try Madeira, Marsala, or sherry. I call for fresh parsley, but most any fresh herb (or combination) will do, such as chives, thyme, basil, and/or summer savory. The bit of butter (or cream or crème fraîche) whisked in at the end adds a lovely richness and balance to the sauce. The more you add, obviously, the richer the sauce will be. I leave that up to you to decide. The sauce makes enough to serve 4 to 6 people, so if you sear-roast 2 tenderloins, you'll have a terrific entrée for a little dinner party.

MAKES ABOUT 2/3 CUP, ENOUGH FOR 4 TO 6 SERVINGS

WINE: Deeply fruity Monastrell with herb and spice notes from Spain's Jumilla region.

¼ cup finely minced shallots, scallions, leeks (white part only), or onions

¼ cup dry white vermouth

1 cup homemade or store-bought low-sodium chicken broth

1 to 2 tablespoons chopped fresh flat-leaf parsley (or other fresh herb)

2 to 4 tablespoons unsalted butter, heavy cream, or crème fraîche

AFTER TRANSFERRING the tenderloin to the baking sheet and into the oven (step 4), let the skillet cool slightly off the heat, 1 to 2 minutes (this prevents scorching the shallots when you add them to the pan). Add the shallots (or scallions, leeks, or onions) to the pan, return the pan to medium heat, and sauté, stirring frequently, until they are slightly softened, about 2 minutes. Add the vermouth, increase the heat to medium-high, and bring to a simmer. Scrape the bottom of the skillet with a wooden spoon to dissolve any drippings. Continue to simmer until the vermouth just barely covers the bottom of the skillet, another 2 to 3 minutes. Add the broth and simmer until reduced by about half, about 5 minutes. Stir in the parsley. Taste for salt and pepper. Set aside in a warm place until the pork is ready.

Just before serving, heat the sauce over medium heat to just below a simmer. Add any drippings from the roasting pan to the sauce. If using butter, cut it into ½-tablespoon-sized pats and whisk them in 2 at a time. Don't let the sauce boil, or the sauce may separate. The more butter you add, the thicker (and richer) the sauce will be. If using heavy cream or crème fraîche, add it all at once, increase the heat to medium-high, and allow the sauce to simmer until slightly thickened, 2 to 3 minutes.

After carving the pork, pour any meat juices into the sauce. Spoon some sauce onto each serving.

CONTINUED ON NEXT PAGE

OPTION 2: ORANGE- AND THYME-RUBBED SEAR-ROASTED PORK TENDERLOIN

This quick-to-make rub is a good riff on basic pork tenderloin. Vary the amount of orange to suit your palate. In other words, if you love the floral perfume of orange, use the full ½ teaspoon; if you prefer a subtler approach, use only ¼ teaspoon.

SERVES 2 TO 3

METHOD: Combination sear and moderate heat

ROASTING TIME: 13 to 18 minutes (plus 6 to 8 minutes to sear)

PLAN AHEAD: For the best flavor, season the pork 4 to 24 hours ahead.

WINE: Ripe jammy Grenache or Grenache blend from Australia.

2 teaspoons fresh thyme leaves, roughly chopped

¼ to ½ teaspoon finely grated orange zest

¼ teaspoon cumin seed, toasted in a dry skillet and ground

¼ teaspoon Marash or Aleppo pepper flakes (see page 318)

Kosher salt and freshly ground black pepper

1 pork tenderloin (1 to 1¼ pounds), trimmed (see Trimming Pork Tenderloin, page 179)

IN A SMALL BOWL, combine the thyme, orange zest, cumin, pepper flakes, ½ to ¾ teaspoon kosher salt, and several grindings of black pepper (I use about ¼ teaspoon). Follow the directions for Basic Sear-Roasted Pork Tenderloin, using this rub in place of the salt and pepper in step 1.

OPTION 3: SEAR-ROASTED PORK TENDERLOIN WITH ROSEMARY, CORIANDER, AND MUSTARD

This mustard-based paste turns a simple pork tenderloin into something fragrant and a little special without much effort.

SERVES 2 TO 3

METHOD: Combination sear and moderate heat

ROASTING TIME: 13 to 18 minutes (plus 6 to 8 minutes to sear)

PLAN AHEAD: For the best flavor, season the pork 4 to 24 hours ahead.

WINE: Earthy Grenache blend from France's Southern Rhône Valley, such as Gigondas or Vacqueyras.

1 ½ tablespoons Dijon mustard

1 ½ teaspoons finely chopped fresh
   rosemary

1 teaspoon extra-virgin olive oil or melted
   unsalted butter

1 garlic clove, minced

½ teaspoon coriander seeds, toasted in a
   dry skillet and lightly crushed

¼ teaspoon cracked black pepper

Kosher salt

1 pork tenderloin (1 to 1 ¼ pounds),
   trimmed (see Trimming Pork Tenderloin,
   page 179)

IN A SMALL BOWL, mash together the mustard, rosemary, oil or butter, garlic, coriander, black pepper, and a pinch of salt. Follow the directions for Basic Sear-Roasted Tenderloin through step 3, seasoning with salt and pepper ahead of time or before searing. After searing and before roasting, smear the mustard paste all over the pork. Finish roasting as the recipe directs.

OPTION 4: MISO-SESAME SEAR-ROASTED PORK TENDERLOIN

This Asian-inspired spice paste forms an alluringly spicy-sweet crust on the pork as it roasts. It's a good idea to line the baking sheet with foil, because some of the paste slides off the pork as it cooks.

SERVES 2 TO 3

METHOD: Combination sear and moderate heat

ROASTING TIME: 13 to 18 minutes (plus 6 to 8 minutes to sear)

PLAN AHEAD: For the best flavor, season the pork 4 to 24 hours ahead.

WINE: Full-bodied fruity white with a touch of sweetness, such as Alsace Riesling or Pinot Gris.

1 tablespoon dark or red miso (see page
   174)

1 tablespoon rice wine vinegar

2 teaspoons freshly grated ginger

1 teaspoon toasted sesame oil

1 teaspoon honey

1 pork tenderloin (1 to 1 ¼ pounds),
   trimmed (see Trimming Pork Tenderloin,
   page 179)

1 tablespoon sesame seeds, white or black

1 tablespoon chopped fresh cilantro

CONTINUED ON NEXT PAGE

IN A SMALL BOWL, stir together the miso, vinegar, ginger, sesame oil, and honey. Follow the directions for Basic Sear-Roasted Tenderloin through step 3, but go lightly on the salt (using no more than ½ teaspoon, as the miso adds a fair bit of salt). After searing and before roasting, smear the miso paste all over the pork. Finish roasting as the recipe directs. Sprinkle the sesame seeds and cilantro onto the pork as soon as it comes out of the oven.

Miso

AN ESSENTIAL ELEMENT OF THE TRADITIONAL JAPANESE PANTRY, MISO IS A FERMENTED SOYBEAN PASTE CALLED FOR IN A RANGE OF RECIPES INCLUDing pickles, dressings, marinades, and, most notably, the restorative miso soup that appears before almost every meal in Japanese restaurants. Depending on how the miso was made—in addition to soybeans, it may contain barley, rice, or other grains—the protein-rich paste ranges in color from mahogany to pale yellow and in texture from chunky and coarse to smooth. Miso classification is not standardized, so many cooks simply refer to the varieties as light or dark, with tastes described as anything from winy and sweet to bitter and faintly chocolatey. A cook well versed in Japanese cooking may stock several favorite types of miso for various uses, but I find that a single tub of red (or dark) miso is plenty for my kitchen. I love the pungent, vaguely sweet, earthy saltiness in dressings, marinades, and spice pastes.

Shop for miso in the refrigerated section of a health-food store or Asian market. It comes packaged in tubs and bags. Once opened, a tub will last 2 to 3 months in your refrigerator. (Tubs and jars store better than bags, so transfer bagged miso to a small plastic tub or jar after opening.) Keep it tightly sealed, and use a clean spoon or utensil each time you scoop into it.

SEAR-ROASTED PORK TENDERLOIN WITH FENNEL TWO WAYS

Anytime I see fennel and pork paired up, I'm hooked. There's just something about the way the mildly sweet, anise-scented vegetable plays against the similarly sweet taste of pork that I find impossible to resist. So when I spied this particular pairing while flipping though an old copy of *Gourmet* magazine, I knew I'd be trying it. Though I have since tweaked that recipe, I owe a nod to Ian Knauer, the magazine's food editor at the time, for setting me on the path to what has become a favorite way to prepare pork tenderloin. There is a double dose of fennel in this recipe; the tenderloin gets seasoned with fennel seeds (and fresh thyme) before it is gently roasted on a bed of buttery, wine-simmered fennel slices. (Make it a triple dose by garnishing the roast with additional fennel fronds, if you like.) To round out the meal, serve with rice or, even better, creamy polenta.

SERVES 5 TO 6
METHOD: Combination sear and moderate heat
ROASTING TIME: About 18 minutes (plus 6 to 8 minutes to sear)
PLAN AHEAD: For the best flavor, season the pork 4 to 24 hours ahead.
WINE: Deeply flavored Sangiovese-based red from Tuscany, like a Chianti Riserva or Brunello di Montalcino.

1 tablespoon fresh thyme leaves, roughly chopped

2 teaspoons fennel seeds, lightly toasted in a dry skillet and coarsely crushed

Kosher salt and freshly ground black pepper

2 pork tenderloins (1 to 1¼ pounds each), trimmed (see **Trimming Pork Tenderloin, page 179**)

2 medium fennel bulbs, trimmed (see page 480)

2 tablespoons extra-virgin olive oil

3 garlic cloves, minced

½ cup dry white wine or dry white vermouth

1 to 2 tablespoons chopped fennel fronds for garnish (optional)

1½ tablespoons unsalted butter, at room temperature

1 **SEASON THE PORK.** In a small bowl, combine the thyme, fennel seeds, 1 teaspoon salt, and a few grindings of black pepper. Pat the pork dry and rub this mixture

CONTINUED ON NEXT PAGE

over the entire surface. *If seasoning ahead, set on a plate and refrigerate, uncovered or loosely covered, for 4 to 24 hours.*

2 **HEAT THE OVEN.** Position a rack in the center of the oven and heat to 350 degrees (325 degrees convection). Let the pork sit at room temperature as the oven heats, about 25 to 30 minutes. Pat it dry if any moisture remains on the surface. Tuck and tie the tail end of the tenderloin, if needed, as shown on page 170.

3 **SLICE THE FENNEL.** Cut the fennel bulbs in half lengthwise through the core. Lay each half cut side down on a cutting board and slice lengthwise into ¼- to ⅓-inch-thick slices.

4 **SEAR THE PORK.** Heat a large ovenproof skillet (a 12-inch pan works well) over medium-high heat. When the skillet is very hot, add the oil, swirling the pan to coat. Add the pork tenderloins, arranging them so they don't overlap (if the pan is crowded, sear them one at a time). Sear, undisturbed, until brown on one side, about 2 minutes. Turn the tenderloins with tongs to brown all four sides, for a total of 6 to 8 minutes. Transfer to a plate.

5 **SAUTÉ THE FENNEL.** Return the skillet to medium heat. Add the fennel, season with salt and pepper, and sauté, stirring frequently, until browned in spots, about 5 minutes. Add the garlic and sauté it briefly. The fennel and garlic will seem somewhat dry, but that's fine for now. Pour in the wine or vermouth, cover, and lower the heat to medium-low. Simmer the fennel until crisp-tender, about 12 minutes.

6 **ROAST.** Remove the fennel from the heat. Arrange the pork on the fennel so the tenderloins do not touch. Smear the butter over the pork and transfer the skillet to the oven. Roast until the internal temperature at the thickest point, measured with an instant-read thermometer, reaches 140 to 145 degrees, about 18 minutes.

7 **REST, SLICE, AND SERVE.** Transfer the pork to a carving board, preferably one with a trough, to rest for 5 to 8 minutes. Taste the fennel and season to taste with salt and pepper. Keep in a warm spot. Carve the pork into ½- to 1-inch-thick slices, removing the string if tied. Spread the fennel out onto a serving platter, arrange the pork on top, and drizzle the juices over it, or, for individual plates, spoon some fennel onto each plate, prop a few slices of pork alongside, and drizzle any juices on top. Garnish with fennel fronds, if you like, and serve immediately.

SPICE-CRUSTED ROAST PORK TENDERLOIN

Rolling pork tenderloin in a flavorful bread-crumb coating before roasting gives it an enormous boost in flavor and appearance. I include a little melted butter in the breading to help it brown up and turn crunchy in the oven. I like the combination of coriander seeds, mustard seeds, and fennel seeds, but feel free to play around with your own favorite spice mixtures. As always, you will get the most flavor if you toast and grind your own spices. Here I leave the seeds a little coarse, so they add some texture as well as flavor.

SERVES 5 TO 6

METHOD: Combination high and moderate heat

ROASTING TIME: 22 to 27 minutes

WINE: Young concentrated Australian Shiraz or Shiraz blend with jammy fruit and pepper-spice notes.

1½ teaspoons mustard seeds, yellow or brown

1½ teaspoons coriander seeds

1 teaspoon fennel seeds

¼ cup plain yogurt, preferably whole milk or low-fat

2 garlic cloves, minced

1 teaspoon Dijon mustard

Kosher salt and coarsely ground black pepper

2 pork tenderloins, 1 to 1¼ pounds each, trimmed (see Trimming Pork Tenderloin, page 179)

¾ cup panko or fresh bread crumbs (see Making Fresh Bread Crumbs, page 210)

2 tablespoons unsalted butter, melted, plus more as needed for the baking sheet

2 tablespoons chopped fresh flat-leaf parsley

1 **TOAST THE SPICES.** Combine the mustard, coriander, and fennel seeds in a small skillet over medium heat. Toast, shaking the skillet occasionally, until fragrant and the mustard seeds just begin to pop, 1 to 2 minutes. Let cool slightly. Grind very coarsely in a mortar or spice grinder. Do not grind to a powder; you want the spices to have some texture.

CONTINUED ON NEXT PAGE

2 **MAKE THE MUSTARD COATING.** In a small bowl, combine the yogurt, garlic, mustard, ¾ teaspoon salt, and several grindings of pepper (I use ¼ to ½ teaspoon). Stir until well mixed. Using your hands or a rubber spatula, spread this mixture all over the two tenderloins. *The pork can be slathered with the yogurt mixture and refrigerated for up to 4 hours before roasting.*

3 **HEAT THE OVEN.** Position a rack in the center of the oven and heat to 450 degrees (425 degrees convection). Lightly butter a heavy-duty rimmed baking sheet. Let the pork stand at room temperature as the oven heats, 25 to 30 minutes.

4 **COAT THE PORK.** In a shallow baking dish, combine the panko or bread crumbs, butter, parsley, and toasted spices. If the tenderloins have very thin tails, tuck these under (making a blunt end and giving the tenderloins a more even thickness) and tie with kitchen string as shown on page 170. Roll the tenderloins in the bread-crumb mixture, pressing down so the crumbs and spices adhere to the meat. Put the tenderloins on the baking sheet, gather up any remaining crumbs and spices, and pat them on top of the pork.

5 **ROAST, REST, AND CARVE.** Roast the tenderloins for 10 minutes and then lower the oven temperature to 325 degrees. Continue roasting until an instant-read thermometer inserted in the center of each tenderloin reads 140 to 145 degrees, 12 to 17 minutes longer. Transfer the pork to a carving board and let it rest for 5 to 8 minutes. If you tied the tail ends, snip and remove the string; some of the breading will fall off. Carve the tenderloins into ½-inch-thick slices. When serving, include any crumb coating that might have fallen off during carving.

Trimming Pork Tenderloin

PORK TENDERLOIN COMES PRETTY MUCH READY TO ROAST, WITH ONE SMALL EXCEPTION: A STRIP OF CONNECTIVE TISSUE, KNOWN AS SILVERSKIN, THAT NEEDS TO BE removed. Silverskin is made up of an aptly named protein, elastin, that remains elastic and chewy unless cooked very slowly over a long period of time, as in braising. When we're roasting, the silverskin doesn't have a chance to dissolve, so it's better to remove it. Here's how.

Choose the sharpest, thinnest blade you have (I like to use a boning knife). Start at the fatter end of the tenderloin, where the silverskin is most prominent. Slide the tip of the knife just under a strip of silverskin about ¾-inch wide, holding the blade parallel with the surface of the meat, and then tilt the blade so it scrapes along the silverskin. With your other hand, take hold of the freed end of the silverskin and keep a light tension on it as you slide the knife in the other direction. The goal is to remove the silverskin without cutting into the meat. You will not get the full width of the silverskin in one swipe; instead, remove it in two or three narrow bands. It's fine to leave a few specks of silverskin in place.

If a few larger bits of fat are present, you can tear them away with your hands. Do not, however, trim every little speck of fat from the tenderloin. The meat itself is so lean that a little external fat will help baste it during roasting.

1 Slide the blade of a knife just under a strip of silverskin about 3/4-inch wide, holding the blade parallel with the surface of the meat, then tilt the blade so it scrapes along the silverskin. **2** With your non-cutting hand, keep light tension on the silverskin. The goal is to remove only the silverskin without cutting into the actual meat. **3** You will not get the full width of the silverskin in one swipe; instead, remove it in two or three narrow bands. It's fine to leave a few specks of silverskin in place.

PORK TENDERLOIN ROULADE STUFFED WITH HERBED SPINACH WITH A QUICK PAN SAUCE

*R*oulade comes from the French word *rouler*, meaning "to roll," and refers to the method of rolling a thin piece of meat around a small amount of flavorful stuffing. After roasting, each slice of this roulade presents a handsome—and appetizing—pinwheel design of tender pork swirled around herbed spinach. In order to make the tenderloin thin enough to roll, you need to butterfly and flatten it. Fortunately, this requires nothing more than a sharp knife and something solid to pound with (a meat pounder is ideal, but a rolling pin or a small, sturdy skillet will also do). If you've never done this, no worries—I give full instructions in the recipe and provide photographs on page 187.

I use spinach seasoned with herbs and a bit of cheese as my basic stuffing, but once you get the technique down, there's no limit to stuffing options. I've included one of my favorites—featuring port-soaked dried fruit—but feel free to create your own. You will need anywhere from ⅓ to 1 cup of stuffing (the more assertive the flavor, the less you need). Take care that the filling isn't too wet—it should be spreadable, not spoonable—and don't include any uncooked meats.

SERVES 3 TO 4

METHOD: Combination sear and moderate heat

ROASTING TIME: 18 to 24 minutes (plus 8 minutes to sear)

PLAN AHEAD: You can stuff and roll the pork 8 to 24 hours ahead, but the dish is also good when rolled right before roasting.

WINE: Young vintage of a Côte de Beaune red Burgundy, such as Volnay or Pommard.

FOR THE PORK AND THE STUFFING

1 ½ tablespoons unsalted butter

¼ cup finely chopped shallots

2 teaspoons fresh thyme leaves, roughly chopped

¼ teaspoon crushed red pepper flakes

Kosher salt and freshly ground black pepper

5 ounces baby spinach, or 5 ounces frozen leaf spinach, thawed and squeezed dry (about ½ cup)

1 tablespoon finely chopped fresh flat-leaf parsley, dill, basil, or a mix

2 tablespoons freshly grated Parmigiano-Reggiano cheese

2 tablespoons pine nuts, lightly toasted in a dry skillet and coarsely chopped

Pinch of freshly ground nutmeg

1 pork tenderloin (1 to 1 ¼ pounds), trimmed (see Trimming Pork Tenderloin, page 179)

1 tablespoon extra-virgin olive oil or grapeseed oil

FOR THE SAUCE

1 tablespoon unsalted butter

1 tablespoon finely chopped shallots

2 tablespoons brandy (such as cognac) or dry sherry

¾ cup homemade or store-bought low-sodium chicken broth

2 tablespoons crème fraîche or heavy cream

1 **HEAT THE OVEN.** Position a rack in the center of the oven and heat to 325 degrees (300 degrees convection). *If you are stuffing and rolling the tenderloin in advance, wait to heat the oven until 30 minutes before roasting.*

2 **MAKE THE STUFFING.** Heat the butter in a medium skillet (9 to 10 inches) over medium heat. Add the shallots, thyme, and red pepper flakes. Season with salt and pepper. Cook, stirring, until just tender, about 3 minutes. If using fresh spinach, increase the heat to medium-high, add the spinach and another pinch of salt, and cook, tossing frequently with tongs, until well wilted, about 2 minutes. If using frozen spinach, stir in the spinach and season lightly with salt. Remove from the heat and set aside to cool to room temperature.

Just before spreading the stuffing, squeeze any excess liquid from the spinach mixture, then stir in the herb(s), Parmigiano, pine nuts, and nutmeg. Taste the filling for salt and pepper.

CONTINUED ON NEXT PAGE

3   **BUTTERFLY THE TENDERLOIN** (as shown on page 187). Arrange the trimmed tenderloin on a stable cutting board. Using a sharp boning knife or chef's knife, start at one end of the tenderloin (either end is fine) and make a horizontal incision along its entire length. Do your best to make the incision at the center of the tenderloin's thickness. Continue slicing through the tenderloin, peeling back the top half as you go and being very careful to stop about ½ inch before you actually cut the tenderloin in two. You want the two halves to be as close to even as possible, but don't worry if they are slightly uneven. Fold back the top half and open the tenderloin like a book. Lay a piece of plastic wrap over the cut surface and, using a meat pounder, a rolling pin, or a small heavy pan, begin pounding the pork with solid but not heavy blows. The idea is to flatten and expand the meat without crushing it or making any holes. Glancing blows (in other words, striking the meat at a slight angle rather than dead on) work best. Continue pounding until the meat is an even thickness of ¼ to ⅓ inch.

4   **STUFF AND ROLL THE PORK.** Examine the butterflied pork so you can identify the direction of the grain of the meat (it helps to remember that the grain runs the length of the tenderloin). When you stuff and roll the pork, you want to keep this grain running lengthwise, so that you will cut *across* the grain when you slice the roast into little pinwheel slices. Arrange the tenderloin with the longer side toward the front of the cutting board and the grain running parallel to the counter edge. Season the surface sparsely with salt and pepper.

Use your hands or a rubber spatula to spread the stuffing evenly over the pork, leaving a 1½- to 2-inch border along the far edge of the meat. Starting at the edge closest to you (the one that has the filling right up to the edge), roll the tenderloin into a snug tube shape. Place it seam side down on the cutting board and tuck under the narrow tail at one end of the roll so that you have a more or less even thickness. Secure the roll by tying loops of kitchen string at 2- to 3-inch intervals along its length (you will have 5 to 6 ties). *You can refrigerate the roulade, uncovered or loosely covered, for 8 to 24 hours at this point. Let it sit at room temperature as you heat the oven.*

5   **SEAR THE PORK.** Heat a large skillet (12 inches) over medium-high heat. Add the oil, tilting the pan to cover the surface. Add the pork, seam side up or to one side (sometimes the first side sticks to the pan, and this could cause the filling to come out if the seam side was down). Sear the pork, turning with tongs to brown all but one

side, for a total of about 8 minutes. When you turn the pork to brown the final side, transfer the skillet immediately to the oven (the bottom side will brown in the oven).

6 **ROAST THE PORK.** Roast, turning the pork once after 10 minutes so the bottom doesn't overcook, until an instant-read thermometer inserted at the thickest point reaches 140 to 145 degrees, 18 to 24 minutes.

7 **REST.** Transfer the pork, seam side down, to a carving board, preferably one with a trough, to rest while you make the pan sauce.

8 **MAKE THE SAUCE.** Off the heat, add the butter to the skillet. Holding the skillet handle with a pot holder or dish towel, tilt the pan to distribute the butter and prevent it from burning. Return the skillet to medium heat (be sure not to grab the skillet handle bare-handed, as it is still hot). Add the shallots and sauté, stirring a few times, until softened, about 2 minutes. Add the brandy or sherry, scraping the bottom of the skillet with the spoon to dissolve any drippings (including any bits of stuffing that may have escaped from the roast) and cook until evaporated, about 1 minute. Add the chicken broth and any juices on the cutting board, and simmer vigorously until reduced by a little more than half, about 4 minutes. Add the crème fraîche or cream and simmer another minute or two. Taste and season with additional salt and pepper if needed.

9 **CARVE AND SERVE.** Slice into ½-inch-thick slices (if the blade seems to tear the meat, try a serrated edge), snipping the strings as you go. Stir any juices that are released into the sauce. Arrange 2 to 4 slices on each plate and spoon some sauce over each serving. Pass any remaining sauce at the table.

CONTINUED ON PAGE 185

PORK TENDERLOIN ROULADE WITH FIG-CHERRY STUFFING AND
PORT WINE SAUCE; GOOSE-FAT-ROASTED POTATOES (PAGE 497)

OPTION: PORK TENDERLOIN ROULADE WITH FIG-CHERRY STUFFING AND PORT WINE SAUCE

This elegant little roast makes the most of the match-made-in-heaven combination of pork and fruit. The dried figs and cherries get macerated in a little port wine to soften the texture and deepen their flavor. A little bit of minced prosciutto adds just the right savory note.

SERVES 3 TO 4

METHOD: Combination sear and moderate heat

ROASTING TIME: 18 to 24 minutes (plus 8 minutes to sear)

WINE: Ripe, jammy old-vine Zinfandel from Sonoma's Dry Creek Valley or Alexander Valley.

FOR THE PORK AND THE STUFFING

1 tablespoon unsalted butter

¼ cup finely chopped onions or shallots

Kosher salt

¼ cup coarsely chopped (about ½ inch) dried figs, Turkish, black mission, or Calimyrna

2 tablespoons finely chopped dried tart cherries

¼ cup ruby port

1 teaspoon fresh rosemary, minced

1 bay leaf, preferably fresh

½ teaspoon finely grated orange zest

Freshly ground black pepper

1 ounce prosciutto or other thin-sliced country ham, minced (about ¼ cup)

1 pork tenderloin (1 to 1¼ pounds), trimmed (see Trimming Pork Tenderloin, page 179)

1 tablespoon extra-virgin olive oil or grapeseed oil

FOR THE SAUCE

1 tablespoon unsalted butter

¼ cup finely chopped shallots

2 tablespoons ruby port

¾ cup homemade or store-bought low-sodium chicken broth

1 to 2 tablespoons crème fraîche or heavy cream

1   **HEAT THE OVEN.** Position a rack in the center of the oven and heat to 325 degrees (300 degrees convection). *If you are stuffing and rolling the tenderloin in advance, wait to heat the oven until 30 minutes before roasting.*

CONTINUED ON NEXT PAGE

2 **MAKE THE STUFFING.** Heat the butter in a small skillet (8 inches) over medium heat. Add the onions or shallots and a pinch of salt and sauté, stirring frequently with a wooden spoon, until the onions soften, about 6 minutes. Add the figs, cherries, port, rosemary, and bay leaf. Lower the heat to a gentle simmer and simmer until the fruit is very soft, about 5 minutes. Increase the heat to a vigorous simmer and simmer until most of the liquid has evaporated, another 3 minutes. Add the orange zest and several grinds of black pepper. Remove from the heat and set aside to cool. Once cool, remove the bay leaf and stir in the prosciutto. Taste and season with additional salt and pepper if needed.

3 **BUTTERFLY, STUFF, AND ROAST THE PORK.** *Follow steps 3 through 7 for Pork Tenderloin Roulade Stuffed with Herbed Spinach (on pages 180–83) using the fig-cherry stuffing in place of the spinach.*

4 **MAKE THE SAUCE.** After transferring the pork to a cutting board (ideally one with a trough) to rest, add the butter to the skillet used to roast the pork. Holding the skillet handle with a pot holder or dish towel, tilt the pan to distribute the butter. Return the skillet to medium heat (be sure not to grab the skillet handle bare-handed, as it's still very hot). Add the shallots and sauté, stirring a few times with a wooden spoon, until softened, about 2 minutes. Add the port, scraping the bottom of the skillet with the spoon to dissolve any drippings (including any bits of stuffing that may have escaped from the roast), and cook until almost evaporated, about 1 minute. Pour in the chicken broth and any juices on the cutting board and simmer vigorously until reduced by a little more than half, about 4 minutes. Add the crème fraîche or cream and simmer again for a minute or so. Taste and season with additional salt and pepper if needed.

5 **CARVE AND SERVE.** Slice into ½-inch-thick slices (if the blade seems to tear the meat, try a serrated edge), snipping the strings as you go. Stir any juices that are released into the sauce. Arrange 2 to 4 slices on each plate and spoon some sauce over each serving. Pass any remaining sauce at the table.

Step by Step: Butterflying and Stuffing Pork Tenderloin Roulade

1 Make a horizontal incision along the entire length of the tenderloin. Try to cut at the center of the tenderloin's thickness so the two halves are even. **2** Continue slicing through the tenderloin, peeling back the top half as you go, and stopping about 1/2-inch before you cut the tenderloin in two. Fold back the top half and open the tenderloin up like a book. **3** Lay a piece of plastic wrap over the cut surface and pound with a meat pounder (or rolling pin or heavy pan) until the meat is an even thickness of 1/4 to 1/3 inch. **4** Season the surface sparsely with salt and pepper. **5** Spread the stuffing evenly over the pork, leaving a 1 1/2- to 2-inch border along the far edge. Starting at the edge closest to you (the one that has the filling right up to the edge), roll the tenderloin into a snug tube shape. **6** Secure the roll by tying a loop of kitchen twine at 2- to 3-inch intervals the length of it.

SEAR-ROASTED DOUBLE-CUT PORK CHOP FOR TWO

A double-cut pork chop provides the perfect solution when you're cooking for 2 and want the satisfaction of a big pork roast without being overwhelmed by leftovers. Start by brining a single chop with juniper, allspice, and peppercorns to amp up the flavor and the texture. Then treat the chop as a mini-roast, searing it first and roasting it in a moderate oven until just done. The result: 2 servings of juicy, flavorful roasted pork. Round out the meal with roasted carrots (page 510) and wild rice. If you really want to put on the ritz, serve the pork with a generous spoonful of Fig, Mint, and Pine Nut Relish (page 118). Don't forget the candles.

I know some restaurants serve one double-cut pork chop per person, but even taking the weight of the bone into account, 20 to 24 ounces of meat is too much for me, even for the most indulgent occasion. Of course, if you're up for it, simply double the recipe. For a weeknight dinner, brine the chops just before you go to bed the night before, drain them in the morning, wrap them in plastic wrap, and then roast them after work.

SERVES 2
METHOD: Combination sear and moderate heat
ROASTING TIME: 25 to 35 minutes (plus 9 minutes to sear)
PLAN AHEAD: The pork needs to brine for 6 to 8 hours. If you need to make it further ahead, remove the pork from the brine after that time, cover, and refrigerate for up to 2 days before roasting.
WINE: Spicy Cabernet-Shiraz Blend from Australia's Barossa Valley.

5 cups cool water (about 50 degrees)

⅓ cup kosher salt

3 tablespoons brown sugar, dark or light

1 tablespoon molasses

6 juniper berries, lightly crushed

1 teaspoon whole black peppercorns, cracked

¼ teaspoon whole allspice berries, cracked

1 double-cut center-cut pork loin chop (1⅛ to 1½ pounds; see Shopping for a Double-Cut Pork Chop, page 190)

1 tablespoon grapeseed oil or other neutral-flavored oil

½ cup dry white vermouth or dry white wine, plus more as needed

1 tablespoon unsalted butter, softened

1 **BRINE THE PORK.** In a deep bowl, combine the water, salt, brown sugar, molasses, juniper berries, peppercorns, and allspice berries. Stir until the salt and sugar dissolve. Add the pork chop and weight it with a plate to keep it submerged. Refrigerate the pork in the brine for 6 to 8 hours. *If you are not ready to roast the chops after 6 to 8 hours, remove them from the brine, pat them dry, wrap in plastic wrap, and refrigerate. Discard the brine.*

2 **HEAT THE OVEN.** Position a rack in the center of the oven and heat the oven to 350 degrees (325 degrees convection). Remove the pork from the brine, pick off any spices, and dry thoroughly. Discard the brine.

3 **SEAR THE PORK.** Heat a small ovenproof skillet (8 inches works well) over medium-high heat until hot. Add the oil, give the pan a swirl to coat with the oil, and sear the pork chop, starting with the cut faces, about 3 minutes per side. Then sear the fatty top side, another 3 minutes.

4 **ROAST THE CHOP.** When all three sides are nicely browned, stand the chop upright (bone side down) and smear the butter all over the top of the chop. Being careful to avoid splatters, pour the vermouth or wine over the pork. Transfer the skillet to the oven and roast, basting every 10 to 15 minutes by spooning the pan juices over the meat. If at any time the skillet appears to be drying out, add another ¼ cup of vermouth or wine. Continue to roast until an instant-read thermometer inserted in the thickest part registers 140 to 145 degrees, 25 to 35 minutes.

5 **REST AND CARVE.** Transfer the pork chop to a cutting board to rest for 8 to 10 minutes. Taste the pan drippings for salt and pepper (I don't bother skimming the fat as this adds richness) and set aside in a warm place. If the chine bone was removed, cut down between the rib bones to separate the "roast" into 2 pork chops and serve. If the chine bone has not been removed, you'll need to carve the meat away from the bone as follows: using a thin-bladed carving knife and holding it so it runs perpendicular to the bone ends, start at the top of the ribs, on the meat side, and cut the meat away from the bones, following the contour of the ribs as you go. When you reach the juncture where the ribs meet the backbone, angle the knife sideways and free the pork from the bone. Slice the meat crosswise into thick or thin slices, according to your taste (I find ½-inch-thick slices are meaty without being too thick). If you and

CONTINUED ON NEXT PAGE

your dinner partner enjoy meaty bones, place the bone assembly on a separate plate to serve as a shared lagniappe, or little bonus. If it's a more formal occasion, save the meaty bones to snack on later. Drizzle any pan drippings and/or carving juices over the meat and serve immediately.

Shopping for a Double-Cut Pork Chop

RECENTLY THE *NEW YORK TIMES* PRONOUNCED THE DOUBLE-CUT PORK CHOP "THE BAR STEAK OF THIS GENERATION," AND IF THIS IS TRUE, THESE CHOPS MAY soon appear in every meat case. In the meantime, it may help to know more about what you're after in order to purchase one. There's really nothing at all exotic about a double-cut pork chop; it's just 2 center-cut rib chops left together. If your market sells bone-in center-cut pork rib roasts and there's someone who knows how to operate the meat saw behind the counter, it's a simple matter of asking that person to cut off 2 ribs in one piece. You do want to make sure the ribs come from the center cut, not the shoulder or the sirloin.

Some butchers trim away much of the surface fat and scrape the rib bones clean, in much the way they french lamb chops and racks. If given the choice, I prefer to leave the chops untrimmed. Any extra fat will baste the meat as it cooks, and scraping the bones seems a waste of good loin meat to me. Depending on how the chop has been trimmed, a double-cut chop will weigh between 1⅛ and 1½ pounds.

Double-cut chops come with or without the chine bone—the rigid, squared-off portion of the backbone that attached to the ribs—and both styles are suitable for roasting. Without the chine bone, a double chop will weigh less and therefore roast more quickly—closer to 25 than 35 minutes. The other difference is how you deal with the bones after roasting. The thing about the chine bone is this: The hefty bone is nearly impossible to cut through at home. If, like me, you are the kind of cook (and eater) who cherishes the meaty bones from a roast almost as much as the meat itself, then having the chine bone removed before roasting will make it a cinch to divide the roast into two bone-in pork chops for serving. When I get a double chop with the chine bone intact, I opt to serve the meat without the bones on the side. It's not quite as satisfying, but it's probably more genteel than serving one big chunk of bone for 2 people to share. If you've not discovered the pleasures of nibbling on bones once the roast meat is gone, I urge you to dig in. You may be surprised by the amount of flavor and satisfaction found in the meat closest to the bone.

CLASSIC PORK RIB ROAST (RACK OF PORK)

A center-cut pork rib roast, still on the bone, may well be the quintessential pork roast. These handsome roasts stand majestically on their arcing rib bones and are easily carved into juicy pork chops for serving. Indeed, this is the kind of roast you want to present at the table and serve family-style, having the diners pass their plates as you carve. The only challenge is that the lean meat of the center loin can dry out, even when roasted at low heat. To insure against this, I let it sit for a day in a flavorful brine seasoned with garlic, rosemary, honey, and red pepper flakes. This step adds time to the preparation, but it also adds plenty of juiciness and flavor.

To make this the centerpiece of a dinner party, make Apricot and Pistachio Dressing (page 193) to go alongside.

SERVES 6

METHOD: Combination sear and moderate heat

ROASTING TIME: About 1 1/2 hours (plus 5 to 8 minutes to sear)

PLAN AHEAD: For the best flavor and texture, brine the pork for at least 18 hours and up to 24 hours.

WINE: Deeply flavored Grenache-Shiraz blend from Australia or California Merlot-blend.

5 cups cool water (about 50 degrees)

⅓ cup kosher salt

2 tablespoons brown sugar, light or dark

¼ cup honey

3 sprigs fresh rosemary (4 to 5 inches each)

2 garlic cloves, smashed and peeled

¼ teaspoon crushed red pepper flakes

One 4- to 5-pound center-cut bone-in pork rib roast (6 to 8 ribs), with the chine bone removed or cracked (see Shopping for Pork Rib Roasts, page 196)

1 **BRINE THE PORK.** In a large bowl or a 2-quart measuring cup, stir together the water, salt, brown sugar, and honey and stir until the salt and sugar have dissolved. Stir in the rosemary, garlic, and red pepper flakes.

Place the rib roast in a large zip-top plastic bag. (If you don't have a large enough bag, place the pork in a deep bowl.) Add the brine. If using the bag, press out any

CONTINUED ON PAGE 193

CLASSIC PORK RIB ROAST (RACK OF PORK) (PAGE 191), GARNISHED WITH WATERCRESS

extra air, seal, and set in a deep baking dish to catch any leaks that may occur. If using a bowl, add more water if needed to cover the pork and cover with plastic wrap. Chill for 18 to 24 hours. About an hour before roasting, remove the pork from the brine. Let drain and then pat dry with paper towels. Let stand at room temperature 1 hour.

2   **HEAT THE OVEN.** Position a rack in the center of the oven and heat to 325 degrees (300 degrees convection). If you have not already done so, remove the pork from the brine and let sit at room temperature while the oven heats.

3   **SEAR THE PORK.** Heat a large heavy ovenproof skillet (10 to 12 inches) over medium-high heat. Place the pork roast fat side down in the skillet and cook until the fat is browned, 5 to 8 minutes. Turn the pork roast (tongs and a meat fork are handy tools here) so it sits fat side up.

4   **ROAST AND REST.** Transfer the skillet to the oven and roast until an instant-read thermometer inserted into the center of the pork registers 140 degrees, about 1½ hours. Transfer the pork to a carving board, preferably one with a trough, to rest for 15 minutes.

5   **SLICE AND SERVE.** Carve by slicing down between the rib bones to divide the roast into chops. Drizzle any carving juices over the chops and serve immediately.

OPTION: APRICOT AND PISTACHIO DRESSING

I believe that much of the reason some cooks cling to the notion of a crown roast is so they can have stuffing. To squelch that argument, I make a fragrant bread dressing that bakes separately while the pork roasts. (I differentiate stuffing from dressing, as the former goes inside the roast while the latter cooks alongside.) The flavors go especially well with mild-flavored pork roast, adding excitement and texture to the plate. Dried figs can easily take the place of the apricots for a slightly different (deeper and sweeter) flavor.

SERVES 12 TO 14
PLAN AHEAD: The apricots need to soak for 4 to 8 hours.
WINE/BEER: Fruity young Zinfandel; or traditional English Old Ale with a combination of fruity, earthy, and malty flavors.

CONTINUED ON NEXT PAGE

8 ounces dried apricots, quartered (about 1½ cups)

¾ cup sweet white wine, such as Muscat or Essencia

14 cups 1-inch cubes country-style white bread (about 1¼ pounds)

8 tablespoons (1 stick) unsalted butter, plus more for the dish

2 yellow onions, chopped (about 3 cups)

4 celery stalks, chopped

3 garlic cloves, minced

1 tablespoon chopped fresh rosemary

Kosher salt and freshly ground black pepper

1 cup unsalted pistachios, lightly toasted in a dry skillet and coarsely chopped

1 to 1½ cups homemade or store-bought low-sodium pork or chicken broth

1 **SOAK THE APRICOTS.** Place the apricots and wine in a small bowl. Cover and let soak for 4 to 8 hours.

2 **TOAST THE BREAD.** Position a rack in the center of the oven and heat to 350 degrees (325 degrees convection). Arrange the bread cubes in a single layer on a rimmed baking sheet and bake until dry, about 15 minutes. Cool. If you plan to bake the dressing right away, lower the oven temperature to 325 degrees (300 degrees convection).

3 **COOK THE AROMATICS.** Melt the butter in heavy large skillet (11 to 12 inches) over medium heat. Add the onions, celery, garlic, and rosemary. Sprinkle with salt and pepper. Cover the skillet and cook until the vegetables are soft, stirring occasionally, about 15 minutes. Transfer the vegetables to a large bowl.

4 **ASSEMBLE THE DRESSING.** Butter a large baking dish (ideally 10 by 14 inches). Add the apricots with their soaking liquid, the bread cubes, and the pistachios to the cooked vegetables and toss well to combine. Add enough broth to moisten the dressing but not make the bread soggy; you should be able to mound it on a large spoon. Taste for salt and pepper. Transfer the dressing to the baking dish. *The dressing can be assembled up to 2 hours ahead and kept at room temperature, covered with foil.*

5 **BAKE THE DRESSING.** If necessary, heat the oven to 325 degrees (300 degrees convection). Cover the baking dish tightly with foil (buttering the underside of the foil prevents it from sticking) and bake the dressing for 45 minutes. Uncover and bake

until it begins to brown, about another 20 minutes. Serve hot. The dressing is best served soon after baking. If you need to keep it warm, cover with foil and set in a low oven (250 degrees) for up to 40 minutes.

HONOR GUARD ROAST OF PORK AFTER
SEARING AND BEFORE ROASTING
(PAGE 197)

Shopping for Pork Rib Roasts

FOR FLAVOR AND PRESENTATION, NOTHING RIVALS A RACK OF PORK. THE ARCHED ROW OF CONNECTED RIB BONES PROVIDES A NATURAL ROASTING rack. The top side of the meat is protected by a generous cap of fat—thicker than anywhere else on the loin—that naturally bastes the meat as it roasts.

When ordering a bone-in rib roast, you may find it easiest to specify how many ribs you want, keeping in mind that each rib represents 1 pork-chop-sized serving. Although there are up to 11 ribs in the loin, the first 3 ribs are involved in the shoulder blade assembly, which is difficult to carve and less majestic than a true rack of pork. For this reason, it's best to ask for a *center rib roast* (meaning no blade section and no sirloin), or specify that you want the roast to come from what's called the "small end" in butcher's parlance (this is the end closest to the sirloin, or hip, and while the overall dimensions are smaller, it actually has the largest eye, or lean chop meat). Also, it's wise to limit the roast size to 8 ribs (thus 8 chops) maximum. If you're feeding more people, consider roasting two racks (see Honor Guard Roast of Pork, page 197). It's easiest to figure 1 rib (1 chop) per person (plus one or two extra for good measure). I've seen recipes that suggest 2 ribs/chops per person, but aside from the occasional teenage nephew or ravenous guest at my table, I find most people are satisfied with a single chop, especially when there are a few side dishes (including the dressing on page 193) and maybe a salad. If you're unsure, err on the side of a few extra ribs, as it's hard to complain about having cold roast pork for sandwiches the next couple of days.

When you're at the market, be sure to check that the butcher has removed the chine bone (backbone) before you take the roast home. It's a simple procedure and takes only a moment, but it does require a bandsaw. The chine bone is easily recognizable as the hefty, squared-off strip of bone that runs along the base of the ribs. If the chine bone is left in place, the roast will be impossible to carve well. Many butchers and markets leave the chine bone in place but saw through it between the chops, supposedly to facilitate carving. In my experience, the cuts are never in the right place, the rack is unwieldy to carve, and the whole thing is a mess. Instead, politely request that the butcher fully remove the chine for you. The rib bones will stay in place and serve to hold the rack together. I also recommend that you (or the butcher) tie the rack between every other (or every) rib with kitchen string; this will promote the most even cooking and reward you with neat, compact slices.

Honor Guard Roast of Pork

AN HONOR GUARD ROAST IS MY ANSWER TO A CROWN ROAST. OVER THE YEARS, WHEN LOOKING FOR A SHOWSTOPPING MENU CENTERPIECE FOR A large dinner party, I've sometimes attempted a crown roast of pork—the name given to 2 rib roasts (or racks) curved and tied together to form a crown shape. While the roast was always impressive to look at, I found that the eating never held up to the spectacle. Not only did the crown shape make the roast too large for even my roomiest roasting pan, it also made it difficult to roast the pork properly—the meat on the inside of the crown is sheltered from the oven heat and thus cooks more slowly than that on the outside. To make matters worse, many cookbooks (particularly older ones) instruct you to fill the center of the crown with some type of stuffing (usually bread- or rice-based) which only makes the meat roast more unevenly. The much smarter—and, in fact, easier—way to make a memorable pork roast is to create an honor guard. The name (also "guards of honor") refers to the image of two rows of ceremonial guards standing facing each other with weapons (swords or firearms) lifted and crossed to form a covered pathway. To make an honor guard roast, arrange 2 evenly sized rib roasts with their bone sides facing each other and interlace the rib bone ends (you'll want to have the butcher clean, or French, the rib bones). There's none of the intricate trussing required with a crown roast, and best of all an honor guard is as easy to roast as a straight-up pork rib roast. If you are afraid you'll miss the stuffing, make it separately and serve it alongside the pork.

Here's how to make an honor guard roast to serve 12 to 14 people: Double the recipe for Classic Pork Rib Roast (page 191), shopping for two 4- to 5-pound center-cut bone-in pork rib roasts (with the chine bone removed or cracked). You want a total of 14 to 16 rib bones. Ask the butcher to french the rib bones—in other words, to strip the meat away from the ends so the bone ends are exposed, thus making it possible to interlace them. The results will be most dramatic if you find 2 evenly shaped roasts, but this is not a deal-breaker.

Follow the instructions for brining the roasts (step 1), doubling the brine amounts. After brining, sear the roasts one at a time as directed in step 3. Now comes the exciting part. After searing, let the roasts cool slightly so you can handle them. Arrange them with the fat side out, facing each other, and maneuver them so the bones interlace (as shown on page 195). Loop kitchen string around the roasts in several spots and tie it so the roasts are secure but not squeezed. Stand the roasts in a roasting pan large enough to hold them without leaving too much extra space, and roast as directed. Expect the honor guard roast to take 10 to 20 minutes longer than a single roast.

CONTINUED ON NEXT PAGE

To serve, transfer the pork to a large carving board, preferably one with a trough. After about 15 minutes of rest, set the roast at the head of the table and carve by cutting down between the chops, alternating sides and removing the strings as you go. If you've made Apricot and Pistachio Dressing (page 193), scoop some onto each plate and prop the pork chop on top.

British Pork Roast

IF YOU'VE EVER BEEN LUCKY ENOUGH TO DINE ON OR SHOP FOR ROAST PORK LOIN IN ENGLAND, YOU MAY HAVE BEEN SURPRISED TO FIND THAT THE ROAST comes with skin intact, roasted up to deliver plenty of crispy, browned, irresistible cracklings. Long ago, our pork loins were sold the same way, but the practice is no longer common. If you do buy your pork directly from a farm (or, as I often do, from a market that buys directly from small farms), it's worth inquiring about getting a rack with the skin in place. It's a little extra work, but you'll be rewarded with a spectacular roast and plenty of delicious pork cracklings. The trick is to score the rind at ½-inch intervals, using a very sharp sturdy knife (a box cutter works well, too). The Brits go for horizontal scoring, running in the same direction as the bones, and I find this easier and more fetching than a cross-hatched pattern, but either will do. (For more, see A Note on Pig Skin, or Rind, page 235.) Once scored, brine the roast as described in step 1 of the Classic Pork Rib Roast recipe (page 191). Then, after draining and discarding the brine, set the pork skin side up on a tray or in a baking dish and refrigerate it, uncovered, for 1 to 2 days. This drying period is essential to getting the crispiest, cracklingest skin you can. To roast, heat the oven to 450 degrees (425 degrees convection) and roast for 20 minutes. Then reduce the oven heat to 350 degrees (325 degrees convection) and roast as directed in step 4 of the recipe on page 191.

PROSCIUTTO-WRAPPED BONELESS PORK LOIN WITH RHUBARB AND SAGE

As much as I love the way moderate-heat roasting preserves the delicate texture of pork loin, it comes at the expense of a handsomely browned exterior. To solve this, here I rub the roast with sage and orange zest and then drape it with a few thin slices of prosciutto before it goes into the oven. Even at low heat, the prosciutto will brown and crisp slightly, giving the pork a lovely look while adding a salty edge. Don't trim any fat from the prosciutto, as the fat helps baste the meat as it roasts.

The rhubarb roasts right alongside the meat, transforming into a sweet-tart condiment. Pink peppercorns impart a seductively spicy floral nuance to the rhubarb (although you can leave them out if you like). Rhubarb season is in the early spring, with a second, smaller season in the fall; when it's not in season, substitute plums or apples.

SERVES 4 TO 5

METHOD: Moderate heat

ROASTING TIME: 1 hour and 10 to 15 minutes

PLAN AHEAD: If you have time, season the pork up to a day ahead and refrigerate it, covered with plastic wrap. Its flavor will be better, although it will be quite good when roasted right away.

WINE: Young Amarone, a concentrated red from Italy's Veneto region.

2 to 3 garlic cloves

1 tablespoon chopped fresh sage plus 1 teaspoon minced sage

½ teaspoon finely grated orange zest

Kosher salt

½ teaspoon whole black peppercorns

3 tablespoons extra-virgin olive oil, plus more for drizzling

One 2 ½ pound boneless pork loin (see Shopping for Boneless Pork Loin Roasts, page 201)

4 thin slices prosciutto (about 2 ounces)

1 ½ pounds rhubarb, trimmed, peeled if necessary, and cut into ½-inch pieces

3 tablespoons brown sugar, light or dark

1 ½ teaspoons pink peppercorns, finely ground (optional)

CONTINUED ON NEXT PAGE

1   **HEAT THE OVEN.** Position a rack in the center of the oven and heat to 325 degrees (300 degrees convection).

2   **MAKE THE RUB.** Smash the garlic a few times in a mortar. Add the chopped sage, orange zest, ¾ teaspoon salt, and the peppercorns and mash together to create a smooth paste. (If you don't have a mortar and pestle, use a chef's knife as directed on page 230 to make the paste.) Stir in 2 tablespoons of the olive oil and rub the garlic mixture over the entire surface of the pork. *You can rub the pork with the paste up to a day ahead and refrigerate it, uncovered or loosely covered.*

3   **DRAPE THE PORK WITH PROSCIUTTO.** Arrange the pork in a medium-sized roasting pan or baking dish (there should be plenty of extra room to hold the rhubarb; I use an 11-by-13-inch pan). Leaving just the very ends of the roast exposed, drape slices of prosciutto crosswise over the pork loin, starting at one end, overlapping slices to cover the entire surface, and tucking any excess prosciutto under the roast. Drizzle the top of the roast lightly with olive oil.

4   **ROAST THE PORK AND PREPARE THE RHUBARB.** Roast the pork for 45 minutes. Meanwhile, toss the rhubarb with the brown sugar, pink peppercorns, if using, and minced sage, and season with a pinch of salt. Toss and set aside. After the pork has roasted for 45 minutes, remove it from the oven. Add the remaining tablespoon of olive oil to the rhubarb, toss to coat, and spread the rhubarb around the pork in the roasting pan. Return the pan to the oven and continue roasting until an instant-read thermometer inserted into the roast reads about 140 to 145 degrees, another 25 to 30 minutes.

5   **REST, SLICE, AND SERVE.** Transfer the pork to a carving board (ideally one with a trough) to rest for 10 to 15 minutes. Stir the rhubarb so it combines with any pan drippings; it will be soft and resemble a compote. Taste and season with additional salt, if needed, and keep it warm until serving. Carve the pork into ¼- to ½-inch-thick slices. Stir any juices from the cutting board into the rhubarb. Place a few slices of pork on each serving plate and serve with a generous spoonful of rhubarb alongside.

Shopping for Boneless Pork Loin Roasts

WITHOUT THE PRESENCE OF THE RIB, BLADE, OR HIP BONES TO HELP YOU UNDERSTAND WHERE BONELESS PORK LOIN ROASTS COME FROM, YOU must rely mostly on labels. Fortunately, your choices are relatively few: blade-end, sirloin, center-cut, and last, but certainly not least, tenderloin.

Blade-end roast is my favorite boneless pork loin roast, because it's a little fattier and therefore juicier than cuts from the center of the loin. A blade-end roast isn't as picture-perfect as the center cut, because it has two muscles (part of the rib-eye and part of the shoulder) rather than the one rib-eye muscle of the center cut, but any shortfall in appearance is made up for in flavor. Another advantage of the blade-end roast is that it tends to be shorter and stouter than a center roast, so it cooks more evenly and is less apt to dry out. Blade-end roasts run anywhere from 2 ½ to 4 pounds.

A *sirloin roast* is another good choice for a boneless pork roast. A little smaller than a blade-end roast (only about 2 ½ to 3 pounds), the sirloin is a bit leaner than the blade end, so extra care must be taken to retain moisture (brining and slow cooking are two good solutions).

Center-cut pork loin is often my first choice for bone-in pork roasts, because these are easiest to carve, but when it comes to boneless, I prefer the slightly fattier, meatier roasts listed above, because the long narrow shape of the center cut makes it prone to drying out. Center-cut roasts are popular, however, and easy to find. Brining is always good insurance to keep a center cut juicy and flavorful (see Maple-Brined Boneless Pork Loin Roast, page 207). In the end, as long as you're careful not to overcook the roast, you'll be rewarded with a handsome, easy-to-carve, delicious meal.

One thing to be aware of when buying center-cut pork loin roasts is that many markets tie 2 boneless roasts together, one on top of the other, to form a thicker roast. Sometimes the 2 loins are tied so tightly that you need to look twice to see that there are 2 pieces. Personally, I don't have much use for these double roasts. I find they have all the downsides of center-cut roasts (a tendency to dry out and taste bland) and yet they take longer to cook.

Pork tenderloin is the smallest and most unique roast from the loin. If you imagine the full loin running all the way from the hog's shoulder to just above the rump, then the pork tenderloins (there are two on each hog) run along either side of the backbone, tucked well underneath the area just below the ribs. It's the fact that the tenderloins are so well protected

CONTINUED ON NEXT PAGE

and therefore little used that makes the meat so fine-textured and delicate. "Tenderloin" is an apt name for these narrow little roasts, as there is no more tender cut.

A single pork tenderloin can run anywhere from 8 ounces to close to 1½ pounds, depending on its provenance and how it is trimmed. Lately I've seen markets selling trimmed-down tenderloins that barely tip the half-pound mark. I find these cook too quickly and are at risk of drying out when roasted; they are best grilled or cut into medallions and sautéed. For roasting, you will do better to find ones in the 1- to 1¼-pound range. If you end up with something larger, simply add a few minutes to the roasting time.

SAUSAGE- AND PRUNE-STUFFED ROAST PORK LOIN WITH BRANDY CREAM SAUCE

As much as I love roast pork loin for its fine texture and mild flavor, I sometimes want a roast with a bigger wow factor—the kind of dish that your family or friends will remember long after the plates are cleared. That's when I turn to this: a boneless pork loin stuffed with a lavish mixture of sausage, brandy-soaked prunes, and herb-flecked sautéed onions and served with a brandy-spiked cream sauce. *This* is special-occasion cooking. Wow with a capital W.

The method I use for stuffing the roast is not the fanciest way to do it—some recipes have you tunnel a hole through the center of the meat; others involve an intricate butchering procedure that leaves you with a spiral-stuffed roast—but what I like about this simple butterflying technique is that it gives you a thick layer of stuffing running through the center of the roast, which helps guarantee moist and perfectly cooked results. You can also stuff the pork a day ahead, another reason this is a great recipe for entertaining.

SERVES 6 TO 8

METHOD: Combination high and moderate heat

ROASTING TIME: 1 1/4 hours

PLAN AHEAD: You can stuff the roast up to 24 hours ahead.

WINE/BEER: Old-vine Zinfandel from California; or aged Belgian Saison.

CONTINUED ON NEXT PAGE

Scant ½ cup pitted prunes, chopped into ½-inch pieces (about 3 ounces)

¼ cup brandy, such as cognac

1 tablespoon and 2 teaspoons extra-virgin olive oil

1 tablespoon unsalted butter

1 yellow onion, finely chopped (about 1 cup)

1 garlic clove, minced

2 teaspoons finely chopped fresh sage or rosemary

Kosher salt and freshly ground black pepper

4 ounces pork sausage meat (I prefer sweet Italian), casings removed if necessary

¼ cup fresh bread crumbs (see Making Fresh Bread Crumbs, page 210)

1 teaspoon finely grated lemon zest

One 3-pound boneless pork loin (see Shopping for Boneless Pork Loin Roasts, page 201)

⅔ cup dry white wine or dry white vermouth

3 to 4 tablespoons crème fraîche or heavy cream

1 teaspoon plum or currant jelly

Fresh lemon juice, as needed

1 **SOAK THE PRUNES.** Put the prunes in a small bowl and pour the brandy over them. Set aside to soak for 20 to 40 minutes.

2 **MAKE THE STUFFING.** Heat the 1 tablespoon of oil and the butter in a medium skillet (8 to 10 inches) over medium heat. Add the onion, garlic, and 1 teaspoon sage or rosemary. Season with salt and pepper and cook, stirring occasionally, until the onion is just tender, about 5 minutes. Add the sausage and cook, flipping and breaking up any large chunks with a wooden spoon, until browned in spots and cooked through, about 6 minutes. Depending on the kind of sausage you use, you may or may not have an excess of fat in the pan. In most cases I like the added richness of the fat, so I include it all in the stuffing but if the sausage seems to be swimming in fat, you may want to drain some off. Transfer the sausage and onion to a bowl.

Set a small sieve over a small bowl or glass measure and strain the brandy from the prunes. Press on the prunes lightly to extract as much brandy as you can. Add the prunes to the stuffing mixture and reserve the brandy to use later (after roasting) for sauce-making. Stir the bread crumbs and lemon zest into the stuffing mixture. Season to taste with salt and pepper. Chill the stuffing in the refrigerator for 10 to 20 minutes to make it easier to handle. *If you're stuffing the pork ahead, chill the stuffing completely (at least 30 minutes) before stuffing the roast.*

3 **BUTTERFLY THE PORK.** Start by arranging the pork loin fat side up on the cutting board. Place your noncutting hand on top of the pork and, with a sharp knife (I like a boning knife), make a lengthwise slit down one long side of the loin, aiming to make the top and bottom an even thickness. Keep cutting, using a sweeping motion and peeling back the top as you go until you've almost cut the roast in half. Stop cutting when you're about 1 inch from the edge, and fold back the top half to open the meat flat like a book. Now, with the point of the knife, make a lengthwise slit down the center of each half, about ¼-inch deep and running parallel to the "spine" of the butterflied roast; these slits will give the stuffing a little more room to expand. With the palm of your hand, or using a meat pounder with a very light touch, press the meat to flatten it slightly.

4 **STUFF AND TIE THE ROAST.** Season the cut surfaces of the roast with salt and pepper. Mound the stuffing onto the bottom side of the butterflied loin (the top side is the side with the layer of fat on the outside), leaving about a ½-inch border at the edge. Fold the top half over and use your hands to snug the roast into shape. Using kitchen string, tie the roast at 1- to 1½-inch intervals, securely but not so tightly as to squeeze out the stuffing. Season the outside all over with salt and pepper and the remaining teaspoon of sage or rosemary. *The pork may be made ahead up to this point and refrigerated, uncovered or loosely covered, overnight. Be sure to cover the prune-soaking brandy with plastic wrap; otherwise it may evaporate. When ready to roast, remove the pork from the refrigerator and let stand at room temperature while the oven heats.*

5 **HEAT THE OVEN.** Position a rack in the center of the oven and heat to 450 degrees (425 degrees convection).

6 **ROAST THE PORK.** Set the pork fat side up in a small roasting pan or flameproof dish that holds it without too much extra space (about 9 by 13 inches works well). Rub the surface with the remaining 2 teaspoons olive oil. Roast for 15 minutes. Lower the oven temperature to 325 degrees (300 degrees convection) and continue roasting until an instant-read thermometer inserted into the meat (check the stuffing, too) registers 145 to 150 degrees, about another hour.

CONTINUED ON NEXT PAGE

7 **REST THE PORK AND MAKE THE SAUCE.** Transfer the pork to a carving board, preferably one with a trough, and let it rest in a warm spot for at least 10 minutes while you make the sauce. Pour off and discard any excess fat from the roasting pan. Set the pan over high heat, add the reserved brandy from soaking the prunes, and bring to a boil. Quickly add the wine or vermouth so as not to scorch the pan and evaporate all the brandy, and scrape the bottom with a wooden spoon to dislodge any browned bits. If any bits of stuffing have fallen out, capture these, too (if you can resist stealing them as a cook's treat). Transfer the liquid to a small saucepan and boil until reduced by half, about 5 minutes. Add the crème fraîche or cream and boil until slightly thickened, another 3 minutes. Lower the heat, whisk in the jelly, and taste. Season to taste with salt and pepper. If the sauce tastes flat, add a few drops of lemon juice.

8 **SLICE AND SERVE.** Carve the roast into ½-inch slices, removing the strings as you go. If the slices don't hold together completely, simply place them back together as you arrange them on individual plates or a platter. Spoon a little sauce over the meat and serve.

MAPLE-BRINED BONELESS PORK LOIN ROAST WITH APPLES, ONIONS, AND MUSTARD BREAD CRUMBS

When I was kid, pork for dinner always meant there would be apples somewhere on the plate, even if just a spoonful of applesauce. In coming up with my own version of pork with apples, I wanted to honor this classic combination by making the apples more prominent and more appealing. So I nestle the pork on a bed of apples and onions, and during roasting in a moderate oven, the fruit and vegetables soak up the juices from the pork and caramelize into a seductively delicious savory compote.

You'll see as you read through this recipe that there are a few steps. In addition to making a brine—a mix of maple syrup, garlic, and rosemary—I glaze the roast with maple syrup and apple cider for a beautiful exterior, and I finish the dish with some crunchy mustard bread crumbs. While all of this takes more time and effort than opening a jar of applesauce, I guarantee that the result, an intriguing combination of homey and sophisticated, makes it all worthwhile.

SERVES 4 TO 5

METHOD: Moderate heat

ROASTING TIME: 1 to 1 1/4 hours (plus 10 minutes to sear)

PLAN AHEAD: For the best flavor and texture, brine the pork for at least 18 hours and up to 24 hours.

WINE/BEER: A rich, spicy Australian GSM (Grenache-Shiraz-Mourvèdre); or deeply flavored Export Stout ale.

CONTINUED ON NEXT PAGE

FOR THE BRINE

5 cups cool water (about 50 degrees)

⅓ cup kosher salt

¼ cup pure maple syrup, preferably Grade B

3 sprigs fresh rosemary (3 to 4 inches each)

1 teaspoon whole black peppercorns

4 garlic cloves, smashed (you can leave the skin on)

2 bay leaves, preferably fresh

One 2- to 2 ½-pound boneless pork loin, preferably a blade-end roast (see Shopping for Boneless Pork Loin Roasts, page 201), tied at 2-inch intervals along its length

FOR ROASTING THE PORK

1 pound tart, crisp apples (3 to 4 apples), such as Granny Smith, Jonagold, or Winesap, peeled, cored, and cut into 1-inch chunks (about 3 cups)

1 large yellow onion, thinly sliced (about 2 cups)

1 teaspoon finely chopped fresh rosemary

2 tablespoons extra-virgin olive oil

1 tablespoon unsalted butter, melted

Kosher salt and freshly ground black pepper

2 cups fresh apple cider

1 tablespoon pure maple syrup, preferably Grade B

1 tablespoon Dijon mustard

FOR THE BREAD CRUMBS

¾ cup fresh bread crumbs (see page 210)

2 tablespoons unsalted butter, melted

2 teaspoons Dijon mustard

½ teaspoon finely chopped fresh rosemary

1 **MAKE THE BRINE.** At least 18 hours before roasting, combine the water with the salt and syrup and stir to dissolve the salt. Add the rosemary, peppercorns, garlic, and bay leaves.

2 **BRINE THE PORK.** If you have a sturdy gallon-size bag (zip-top freezer bags are best), this is the neatest route. Place the roast in the bag, pour in the brine, and seal. If the brine doesn't completely surround the pork, either squeeze out some of the air, or, if needed, add a little cold water. Set the bag in a bowl or dish to guard against leaks and refrigerate. Otherwise, place the roast in a large bowl (deeper rather than wider works best) and pour the brine over it. If necessary, add just enough extra cold water to cover the roast completely. Cover with plastic wrap and refrigerate for at least 18 hours and up to 24 hours. About 1 hour before roasting, remove the pork from the brine (discard the brine) and let sit at room temperature.

3 HEAT THE OVEN AND PREPARE THE APPLES AND VEGETABLES. Position a rack in the center of the oven and heat to 325 degrees (300 degrees convection). If you have not done so already, remove the pork from the brine and let sit at room temperature.

Put the apples, onion, and rosemary in a bowl, drizzle with 1 tablespoon of the olive oil and the melted butter, and season with salt and pepper. Toss to coat. Spread the apple-onion mixture in the bottom of a shallow-sided roasting pan that will hold the pork roast with only 2 to 3 inches around the sides to spare (I use an 11-by-13-inch pan). Set aside.

4 MAKE THE GLAZE. Heat 1 cup of the cider in a small saucepan over medium-high heat. Bring to a boil and continue to boil until reduced to about ⅓ cup of syrupy glaze, about 12 minutes. Remove from the heat and whisk in the maple syrup and mustard. Set aside.

5 BROWN THE PORK. Heat a large skillet (10 inches will do) over medium-high heat. Add the remaining 1 tablespoon of oil to the skillet and pat the pork dry. As soon as the oil is hot, brown the pork, turning with tongs, until browned on all sides, about 10 minutes total. Using tongs, set the pork fat side up on the apples and onions.

6 DEGLAZE THE PAN. Return the skillet to high heat. Add the remaining 1 cup cider and bring to a boil, scraping the bottom of the pan with a wooden spoon to bring up the tasty browned bits. Continue to boil until reduced by half, about 8 minutes. Pour the reduced cider over the apples and onions in the roasting pan, being careful not to pour the liquid over the pork.

7 GLAZE THE PORK. Brush about half the reserved glaze over the top side of the pork.

8 ROAST THE PORK. Roast, brushing after 45 minutes with the remaining glaze, until an instant-read thermometer inserted in the center registers 140 to 145 degrees, about 1 to 1¼ hours.

9 PREPARE THE BREAD CRUMBS. In a medium bowl, stir together the bread crumbs, melted butter, mustard, and rosemary. Season to taste with salt and pepper.

CONTINUED ON NEXT PAGE

10 **REST THE ROAST** and toast the bread crumbs. Transfer the pork to a carving board, preferably with a trough, to rest for 10 to 15 minutes. Stir the apple-onion mixture (it will be very soft and like a compote) and taste for salt and pepper. Set in a warm place. Meanwhile, increase the oven temperature to 375 degrees (350 degrees convection). Spread the bread crumbs on a small baking sheet and toast in the oven, stirring often, until golden brown and crispy, 10 to 12 minutes.

11 **CARVE AND SERVE.** Remove the strings, and carve the roast into slices (I like ¼-inch-thick slices, but thicker is fine), pouring any carving juices into the apple-onion compote. For family-style service, scrape the compote onto a serving platter and top with pork slices. For individual plates, spoon some of the apple-onion mixture onto each plate and serve the pork alongside. Sprinkle the bread crumbs over the top and serve immediately.

Making Fresh Bread Crumbs

WHEN A RECIPE CALLS FOR FRESH BREAD CRUMBS, IT CAN BE TEMPTING TO REACH INSTEAD FOR THE CANISTER OF DRIED BREAD CRUMBS TUCKED IN the back of the cupboard from the last time you made crabcakes, but I urge you to reconsider. Fresh bread crumbs are about as different from their dried counterpart as fresh pasta is from dried. And like pasta, both have their place. I use dried bread crumbs (especially panko, the Japanese-style bread crumbs described on page 408) to coat foods for frying, for example. But fresh bread crumbs give you a whole new level of texture and taste experience. They add loft and tenderness to otherwise dense mixtures such as the filling in Sausage- and Prune-Stuffed Roast Pork Loin (page 203). Homemade fresh bread crumbs can also be flavored and toasted; in the Maple-Brined Boneless Pork Loin Roast (page 207), for example, buttery, toasted bread crumbs add a crunchy counterpoint to the meaty pork and soft apple-onion compote. In both these applications, packaged dried crumbs would taste gritty in their place.

Making your own bread crumbs requires little more than giving a few pieces of bread a spin in the food processor. That said, there are some things to consider. Bread crumbs are best made from bread that is a little dry—in other words, day-old bread or a type of white bread, such as a ciabatta, Italian bread, or even English muffins, that starts off on the drier side. (If the bread is too moist, the crumbs will be gummy and clump up in the food processor.) Every loaf of bread is different, so it may take some experimenting to find out which breads make good crumbs. I have tried countless times to dry out fresh bread by toasting it before grinding it into crumbs, but the resulting crumbs are never as good as crumbs made from day-old bread. Consider making bread crumbs anytime you find yourself with a surplus of bread that's beginning to get stale. Frozen airtight, the crumbs will keep for a few weeks. They lose some of their fluffiness in the freezer, but they are still better, in most cases, than packaged dried crumbs.

To make fresh bread crumbs: Cut away any thick or excessively dark crust; this is especially important for hearth breads, where the crust can become tooth-breakingly hard when the bread dries out. Tear or cut the bread into 1-inch pieces and drop these into a food processor fitted with the chopping blade. Don't fill the processor much more than one-third full. Run the machine, pulsing off to check the progress, until you have a mix of small and tiny pieces—everything from a pea size to the size of coarse sand. You are not trying to get the crumbs all the same size—their irregular shapes are much of the textural appeal of fresh bread crumbs. If you don't have a food processor (or don't want to haul it out for a small job), either grate the bread on the largest holes of a box grater or simply tear the bread into the tiniest pieces possible and then chop them with a large chef's knife. (This final method is tedious, no doubt, but if you've got a good kitchen conversation going or something worthwhile on the radio, it can be a relaxing task.) Expect an ounce of stale bread to give you about ½ cup of fresh bread crumbs.

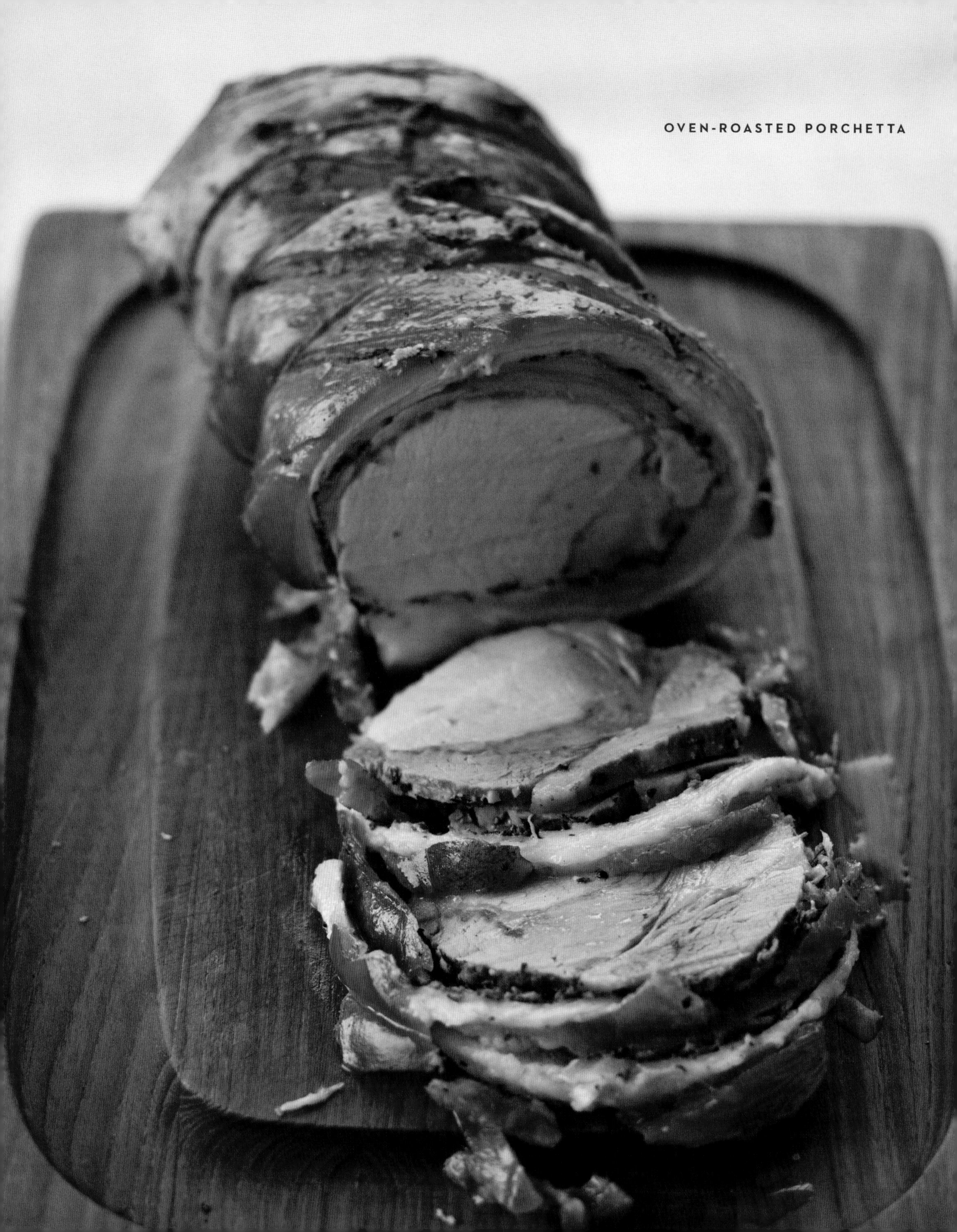

OVEN-ROASTED PORCHETTA

OVEN-ROASTED PORCHETTA

For years I've fantasized about making porchetta—herb- and garlic-infused pork roasted over an open fire until meltingly tender, with skin that's crisp and crackly. In Italy, where the dish hails from, porchetta almost always begins with a whole pig, which gets gutted, boned, seasoned, tied, and spit-roasted to perfection. While I can be an ambitious cook, the prospect of wrangling a whole pig over an open fire in my small (and very wooded) yard always overwhelmed me. Then came an *ah-ha!* moment during a trip to New York City, specifically during a visit to a popular storefront eatery aptly named Porchetta. Waiting in line for my porchetta sandwich, I watched as the cook behind the counter sliced the meat, not from a whole pig, as I had always imagined, but from a single roast, albeit one unlike any I had ever seen. There was a large eye of juicy meat in the center, surrounded by an unctuous layer of dripping fat, all encased in crackling skin. Back home, I did some research and learned that Sara Jenkins, the talented chef-owner of Porchetta, creates her version by wrapping skin-on pork belly (the part of the pig from which we get bacon) around a pork loin. Brilliant!

This version remains a fairly bold undertaking for most home cooks, mainly owing to the fact that pork belly, though super-popular with chefs, is not (yet!) a common supermarket cut. (For more on that, see Shopping for a Porchetta Roast, page 217.) Once you have the right cut, however, the only hard part is picking which of your friends and family deserve to come join you for such a delicious meal. (Do leave any fat-phobic folks off the guest list, as porchetta is hearty fare.) Serve the pork with sautéed greens (think spinach or Swiss chard) and something soft and comforting, like polenta, mashed potatoes, or white beans. Any leftover meat will make amazing sandwiches, especially when stacked on good crusty bread with braised broccoli rabe and sweet red pepper spread as shown on page 218.

SERVES 10 TO 12 WITH LEFTOVERS

METHOD: Combination high and moderate heat

ROASTING TIME: 2 1/2 to 3 1/2 hours

PLAN AHEAD: For the best flavor, season the pork at least 24 hours ahead of roasting.

WINE: A Nebbiolo-based red, like that bottle of Barolo or Barbaresco you've been saving for a special occasion.

CONTINUED ON NEXT PAGE

1 center-cut pork loin with the belly flap
    attached, preferably with skin on (8 to 9
    pounds), or 1 boneless center-cut pork
    loin (about 5 pounds) plus 1 pork belly
    (4 to 5 pounds)
4 to 6 garlic cloves, minced
Kosher salt
Coarsely ground black pepper

1½ tablespoons chopped fresh rosemary
1 tablespoon chopped fresh sage
1 tablespoon chopped fresh thyme
1 tablespoon fennel seeds, toasted and
    ground to a coarse powder
1 tablespoon finely grated lemon zest
½ teaspoon crushed red pepper flakes

1   **TRIM THE PORK AND SCORE THE RIND.** If you purchased a pork loin with the belly attached, unroll the roast so the skin side is down. Examine the belly portion and determine whether you need to trim away any of the top layer of fat. If the roast came without skin, turn it over and also trim away some of the fat from the top side if need be. All pork bellies have prodigious amounts of fat; how much you leave in place is a matter of personal preference. Ideally you want a layer just under ½-inch thick, so if the butcher has left more than this, use a large chef's knife to pare it down. (The fat can be saved for rendering or other use.)

Now arrange the belly, whether separate or attached to the loin, so it is skin side up on a stable surface and, using a box cutter, utility knife, or other razor-sharp knife, carefully (but firmly) score the rind in parallel lines about ½-inch apart, cutting through the rind and just into the fat (about ¼-inch deep) without cutting through to the meat. The lines can go in any direction that appeals to you.

If you've got a separate pork loin and pork belly, check that the outermost fat layer of the pork belly is less than ½-inch thick. If needed, trim it down. Next, drape the belly (skin side up) around the pork loin (without tying it), just to get a sense of how it will fit. It doesn't have to be perfect, but if it extends more than 1 inch over the ends of the loin, trim it down and save the trimmings for another use. If there's a gap on the underside because the belly doesn't reach all the way around, that's fine. Also, if you've got a separate piece of pork skin, drape this over the roast and trim it to fit (poultry shears or utility scissors are useful here).

Now arrange the belly, whether separate or attached to the loin, so it is skin side up on a stable surface and, using a box cutter, utility knife, or other razor-sharp knife, carefully (but firmly) score the rind in parallel lines about ½-inch apart, cutting through the rind and just into the fat (about ¼-inch deep) without cutting through to the meat. The lines can go in any direction that appeals to you.

2   **SEASON AND TIE THE ROAST** (as shown on page 216). In a small bowl, combine the garlic, 1½ tablespoons salt, 2 teaspoons black pepper, the rosemary, sage, thyme, fennel, zest, and red pepper flakes. For the single-piece roast, unroll the belly flap and sprinkle the seasonings evenly over the belly and the roast, rubbing lightly so the seasonings adhere. Roll the flap around the loin; if the skin is a separate piece, drape it over, and secure the whole porchetta at 1- to 2-inch intervals with kitchen string. For the 2- or 3-piece roast, sprinkle half the seasonings all over the loin and the other half on the meat side of the belly, rubbing lightly so they stick, and then wrap the belly (skin side out) over the loin, so the belly covers the top side (fat side) of the roast thoroughly and any gap is on the bottom (or rib side). If the skin is a separate piece, drape it over the top. Secure the entire ensemble with kitchen string, tying loops at 1- to 2-inch intervals.

Season the surface of the roast lightly but evenly with salt and pepper (about ¾ teaspoon each), getting some into the score marks as well. Set the roast on a tray or in a baking dish and refrigerate, uncovered or loosely covered, for 24 to 48 hours. Let the pork sit at room temperature for 1 to 2 hours before roasting.

3 **HEAT THE OVEN.** Position a rack in the lower third of the oven and heat to 500 degrees (475 degrees convection).

4 **ROAST.** Place the pork seam side down on a roasting rack in a sturdy roasting pan just large enough to accommodate it. Roast for 25 minutes and then reduce the oven temperature to 325 degrees (300 degrees convection). Continue to roast until an instant-read thermometer inserted into the center of the roast registers 140 to 145 degrees, another 3 hours or so—but it's a good idea to start checking the temperature after another 2 hours.

5 **REST AND CARVE.** Transfer the roast to a carving board, preferably one with a trough. Let rest for at least 25 minutes (the roast can easily sit at room temperature for an hour and not suffer). Carve into ¼- to ½-inch-thick slices, removing the strings as you go and doing your best to give each serving a bit of the crackling rind. If the rind is too tough to slice through easily (or if it was a separate piece to begin with), remove it in larger chunks and transfer it to a second cutting board, where you can chop it into pieces to serve alongside the sliced roast.

Step-by-Step: Seasoning and Tying Porchetta

1 The makings for porchetta: boneless pork loin, pork belly, and herb rub. **2** Sprinkle half the seasonings all over the loin. **3** Sprinkle the rest of the seasonings on the meat side of the belly, rubbing lightly so they stick. **4** Wrap the belly around the loin, so that the belly covers the top side (fat side) of the roast. **5** If there is a gap in the belly, make sure it goes on the bottom of the roast. **6** Secure the entire ensemble with kitchen string, tying loops at 1- to 2-inch intervals. The belly may extend over the loin (as above), or it may not. Both ways are fine.

Shopping for Porchetta Roast

To MAKE THIS PORCHETTA, YOU WILL HAVE TO SHOP AT A SPECIALTY MEAT MARKET, ONE THAT GOES BEYOND THE STANDARD SUPERMARKET fare. (Plus, the best porchetta is made from well-marbled, flavorful heritage breeds of pigs not found at most supermarkets.) Basically, there are three parts to a porchetta roast: the boneless loin roast, the belly, and the skin. Ideally the butcher will be able to give you all three in one piece: the pork loin and belly with the skin still on the belly. If not, you can buy a loin and a belly (with or without the skin) separately. Constructing the roast is not difficult as long as you have some kitchen string and a little understanding of how it goes together.

The loin is the thick, straplike muscle that runs along either side of the spine (parallel to the backbone); since we're dealing with only one loin, imagine just one of those long back muscles. To grasp how the belly relates to the loin (and if it's not too macabre for you to compare your own anatomy to that of a pig), place one hand on your own back muscle right near the bottom of your ribs (that's the loin) and then slide your hand to the front of your body. Voilà—there you are, the belly. So if the butcher bones out the loin without separating the belly flap from the back, you'll have a pork loin with a long flap of streaky belly (fresh bacon) that you can wrap around the loin. (The British refer to this cut as a "long middle," which makes sense, as it comes from the middle of the pig and, well, it's long.)

I prefer the loin with the belly attached because it makes a neat porchetta. When you order the pork loin with the belly attached, ask the butcher to trim the belly fat down to just under a ½-inch-thick layer on the inside. Trimming the belly this way gives you the ideal balance of fat and lean. Also request a roast with the rind, or skin, attached. If the rind has already been removed, request a piece of pork rind large enough to wrap around the roast. (If the butcher shop has access to pork loin with the belly still attached, it should be able to get you a sheet of fresh pork rind as well.) Simply wrap this around the roast before you tie it in step 2 of the recipe.

Many meat markets, however, will not be able to provide you with a single pork loin–belly flap combo. In this case you'll need to buy a separate boneless loin (preferably center-cut) and a slab of fresh pork belly that closely corresponds in length so it will wrap neatly around the loin. It's impossible to give exact dimensions since every roast differs, but again, if you explain to the butcher what you're after, he or she should be able to help. The belly should be long enough to cover the loin from end to end, but it doesn't have to reach all the way around the circumference. For directions on wrapping the belly around the loin, go to step 1 in the recipe.

The makings for first-rate porchetta sandwiches include braised broccoli rabe, roasted red pepper spread, and crusty bread (or rolls). Slather the pepper spread on the bread, pile on thinly sliced porchetta, top with greens (both the pork and greens are best warm or at room temperature), and drizzle over any pan drippings. Make your own pepper spread (using both sweet and hot peppers) or use one of the many premade pepper relishes available, ranging from sweet to spicy. For a traditional South Philly–style roast pork sandwich, forgo the pepper spread and top the braised greens and pork with sliced sharp provolone.

BONELESS PORK BLADE ROAST (BOSTON BUTT)

Plump and glistening, a boneless pork blade roast, also known as Boston butt, is an ideal dish to serve to your best company but affordable enough for a family supper. Unlike the leaner pork loin and tenderloin, cuts from the shoulder are best roasted until well done, but thanks to a generous amount of interlacing fat, the meat self-bastes, leaving you with incomparably juicy results. Each time I carve a blade roast—a task as simple as slicing a loaf of bread—I nab a taste and nearly go weak in the knees. It's that good. Most often I season the roast with nothing more than salt and pepper, but it's also delicious rubbed with flavorings, such as the one on page 222.

This recipe calls for a partial pork blade roast—only about 3 pounds—which is perfect for a small dinner party. For a larger gathering, purchase a whole boneless blade roast (or Boston butt) and cook it according to the directions on page 222.

SERVES 4 TO 6

METHOD: Moderate heat

ROASTING TIME: 2 1/2 to 3 hours

PLAN AHEAD: The pork tastes best if seasoned 18 to 48 hours ahead.

WINE: Rich, fruity Grenache blends with pepper-spice notes from either the Rhône Valley or Southern Spain.

One 2½- to 3¼-pound boneless pork blade roast (Boston butt), without skin (see Shopping for Pork Shoulder Roasts, page 223)

Kosher salt and freshly ground black pepper
⅓ cup dry white wine or dry white vermouth

1 **SEASON THE ROAST.** If the roast is tied, cut the strings. Depending on how the shoulder was boned, the roast may or may not unroll, but your objective is to do your best to season the inside as well as the outside of the hunk of meat. Start by placing the roast fat side down on a cutting board and pulling it apart a little to expose more of the interior. I sometimes make a few vertical cuts into the thicker parts of the meat, which enables me to open it up further and season it from the inside out. Don't go overboard slicing into the meat, but if you can manage to open it out some (a sort of butterfly

CONTINUED ON NEXT PAGE

technique), you will season the meat better. Sprinkle salt and pepper generously all over the meat, turning it to season the fat side as well (I use 1 to 1¼ teaspoons salt and ¾ teaspoon pepper). After seasoning, gather the roast back together, using both hands to shape it into a neat, compact shape (I find a thick, plump shape turns out a juicier roast than a long, narrow one.) Tie the roast at 1½-inch intervals with kitchen string. If there are loose flaps at either end, tie a loop around the circumference to hold these in as well. For the best flavor, refrigerate the pork, uncovered or loosely covered, for 18 to 48 hours. (You can roast the pork immediately, and it will still be quite good.) Let the pork sit at room temperature for 1 to 2 hours before roasting.

2 **HEAT THE OVEN.** Position a rack in the lower third of the oven and heat to 350 degrees (325 degrees convection). Set the roast fat side up in a low-sided roasting dish just large enough to hold it (an 11-inch skillet or oval gratin dish works well).

3 **ROAST.** Turn the roast after 1 hour and pour the wine or vermouth over the top. Continue roasting, turning again after another hour, until the roast is nicely browned and an instant-read thermometer inserted in the center registers 175 to 180 degrees, a total of 2½ to 3 hours.

4 **REST.** Transfer the roast to a carving board, preferably one with a trough, and let rest for 20 to 25 minutes. Tilt the roasting pan and spoon off the clear fat. Pour about ¼ cup water into the pan and stir with a wooden spoon to dissolve the cooked-on drippings. Keep the drippings in a warm spot to drizzle over the roast pork.

5 **CARVE AND SERVE.** Carve the pork into ¼-inch slices, removing the strings as you go. Add any juices from carving to the pan drippings and drizzle a little of the drippings over the sliced meat.

OPTION 1: BONELESS PORK BLADE ROAST WITH FINGERLING POTATOES, CARROTS, AND SHALLOTS

Roast hefty chunks of vegetables alongside the pork to create a comforting one-pot meal. I call for fingerling potatoes, carrots and shallots, but you can swap out the potatoes for turnips, the carrots for parsnips, and the shallots for onions. You get the idea. For even more flavor, rub the pork with the *arista* rub on page 222 before roasting.

SERVES 4 TO 6

METHOD: Moderate heat

ROASTING TIME: 2 1/4 to 2 1/2 hours

WINE: An aged bottle of a California Meritage blend of Cabernet and Merlot.

One 2 ½- to 3 ¼-pound boneless pork blade roast (Boston butt), without skin (see Shopping for Pork Shoulder Roasts, page 223)

1 pound fingerling potatoes, left whole if smaller than 1 inch in diameter, or cut into 1 ½-inch pieces

1 pound carrots, peeled, halved lengthwise (or quartered if large), and cut into 2-inch pieces

1 pound shallots, peeled and, if large, cut in half from stem to root end

1 tablespoon extra-virgin olive oil

2 teaspoons fresh thyme leaves, roughly chopped

Kosher salt and freshly ground black pepper

FOLLOW THE RECIPE for Boneless Pork Blade Roast, using a larger roasting pan (12 by 15 inches will work). Combine the potatoes, carrots, and shallots in the roasting pan *before* placing the pork in it (step 3). Add the olive oil and season with thyme, salt, and pepper. Toss to coat evenly, and arrange the vegetables around the perimeter of the pan to make room for the pork. Set the pork in the center. Don't worry if a few pieces of vegetables are under the pork; much of the appeal of this dish is how some of the vegetables turn out crispy and brown and others remain soft and soaked in roasting juices.

Roast as directed, giving the vegetables a stir when you turn the roast. In step 5, while the pork is resting, use a slotted spoon to scoop the vegetables onto a serving tray and keep them warm. Evaluate the pan drippings. The vegetables may have absorbed all the drippings, but if you do find plenty of drippings, spoon off any clear surface fat, add ¼ cup water, and stir to dissolve any caramelized bits. Add any carving juices to the drippings and drizzle them over the sliced pork.

CONTINUED ON NEXT PAGE

OPTION 2: ROASTED WHOLE BOSTON BUTT

Perfect for a casual dinner party, an open-house, or a houseful of weekend guests.

SERVES 10 TO 12

PURCHASE A WHOLE BONELESS pork blade roast (Boston butt) weighing about 6 pounds (without skin). Prepare it as directed for Boneless Pork Blade Roast, seasoning with 1 tablespoon kosher salt and 1¼ teaspoons freshly ground black pepper. (This also works very nicely with *Arista* Rub for Boneless Pork Blade Roast). Roast as directed, adding about 1 hour to the roasting time, so the roast will take a total of 3¼ to 3½ hours.

OPTION 3: *ARISTA* RUB FOR BONELESS PORK BLADE ROAST

Arista appears on many Italian menus. It refers to roast pork seasoned with an alluring blend of Mediterranean seasonings, namely herbs and garlic. While many recipes use pork loin, I find pork shoulder absorbs the seasonings better than the leaner loin. According to culinary lore, the name *arista* originated at a fifteenth-century dinner served in Florence to Greek bishops who were there for an ecumenical summit. The bishops were so pleased with their meal of succulent seasoned pork that they exclaimed "Aristos!" which means "excellent" in Greek. I don't know about the veracity of this tale, but I appreciate the urge to shout with pleasure when served a plate of well-seasoned, juicy pork shoulder. For the most delicious results, season the pork at least 24 hours before roasting. This makes enough for one 2½- to 3¼-pound boneless pork blade roast. For a whole boneless pork butt, increase the salt to 1 tablespoon and double the other seasonings.

WINE: Nero d'Avola-based red from Sicily, such as Cerasuolo di Vittoria.

4 cloves garlic, smashed

1 to 1¼ teaspoons kosher salt

2 teaspoons finely chopped fresh rosemary

2 teaspoons finely chopped fresh sage

1 teaspoon freshly ground black pepper

1 teaspoon finely grated lemon zest

COMBINE THE GARLIC and salt in a mortar and pound until you have a smooth paste. (If you don't have a mortar and pestle, you can make the paste using a chef's knife; see Making Garlic Paste Without a Mortar and Pestle, page 230). Stir in the rosemary, sage, pepper, and zest. Rub this mixture over the pork in place of salt and pepper.

Shopping for Pork Shoulder Roasts

THE BEST WAY TO MAKE SENSE OF PORK SHOULDER ROASTS IS TO UNDERSTAND A LITTLE OF HOW A BUTCHER BREAKS DOWN A PIG. FOR STARTERS, A WHOLE pork shoulder is a formidable chunk of meat, weighing in at around 15 pounds, and unless you buy directly from a small, independent producer or meat packer, you aren't likely to find a whole pork shoulder roast. Instead, almost every pork shoulder is divided into two similar but distinct roasts. The top half of the shoulder, including the blade bone, is widely known as *Boston butt* or *blade roast*. The bottom half, including a portion of the arm and shank bone, is called *picnic shoulder*. Both parts of the shoulder roast wonderfully, but I approach them a little differently.

BLADE ROAST/BOSTON BUTT

The Boston butt is the more popular, smaller, and more expensive of the two shoulder roasts. This square-cut hunk of meat offers plenty of rich-tasting lean meat laced with fat and connective tissue that melts to succulence when roasted at a moderate temperature. Many chefs praise the Boston butt for having the perfect fat-to-muscle ratio for slow-cooked barbecue, and I agree, but I also find that it makes a wonderful sliced roast when roasted in a moderate oven for about 2 ½ hours.

Bone-in versions of Boston butt contain a portion of the shoulder blade and the upper arm, which makes them difficult to carve. For this reason, I prefer the boneless version. Just be sure the roast is well tied, so all the various muscles that make up this part of the shoulder stay intact.

Over the years I've heard a number of far-fetched stories as to how this cut got its odd name, but the explanation that seems the most reasonable comes from the National Pork Board. The story relates to the casks or barrels, referred to as butts, that were used centuries ago to store and ship everything from hog parts to beer. The particular way the shoulder was butchered in New England (the source for pork in the years before the Midwest became the nation's pork supplier) became known as "Boston butt." Other names include "Boston-style butt," "Boston shoulder," "pork butt," and "shoulder blade Boston-style." Also, just to add to the confusion, when a recipe calls for "pork shoulder" but indicates something under 12 pounds, you are safe to assume that it refers to Boston butt. Expect a Boston butt to weigh 6 to 9 pounds if it contains the bone and 4 to 6 pounds when boneless. Once the bone has been removed, Boston butt is quite often broken down into several smaller roasts. I recommend picking up a 2 ½- to 3-pound roast the next time you're thinking of serving pork to 4 to 6 lucky people around the table. A whole butt will serve 10 to 12.

CONTINUED ON NEXT PAGE

PICNIC SHOULDER

Before I started working on this book, I'll admit, I didn't have much use for the picnic shoulder. When braising and stewing, I found that this lower part of the whole shoulder was too fatty, leaving a thick layer of grease to skim off the resulting braise or stew. When it comes to roasting, however, I love the way this generous layer of subcutaneous fat bastes the meat as it roasts, so in the end, much of the fat sits in the bottom of the roasting pan and you are left with a succulent, juicy, fall-apart-tender pork roast. In addition, a bone-in picnic shoulder contains the easy-to-navigate round bones of the upper and lower arm, making it rather easy to work around when it comes to carving. And finally, picnic shoulders often come with the skin, or rind, intact, which translates into plenty of crispy cracklings and an impressively handsome roast. (For more on pork rind, see page 235.)

Picnic shoulders run slightly larger than Boston butts, weighing in at 8 to 10 pounds bone-in and 6 to 8 pounds when boneless, but they actually yield less meat than the Boston butt (because there's a bigger bone). The picnic shoulder does, however, give you the most amount of delectable skin for cracklings. Some cooks like to remove the skin and roast it separately to ensure consistent cracklings, but I like the way you get some crunchy hard bits and some rich, gooey bits when you roast it with the skin on.

FAUX PORK BARBECUE (BASIC SLOW-ROASTED PICNIC SHOULDER)

This is one of those "fix it and forget it" roasts that can serve a crowd and that invites people to casually dig in. The roast takes 8 to 9 hours, but there's no real work on your part other than to score the skin, an essential step that allows the seasonings to penetrate the meat and, most importantly, enables a good portion of the fat beneath the skin to render and turn the skin crisp and crackly. After the long, slow roast, the pork will emerge nicely browned, with a mix of crispy skin and skin that is soft and unctuous. I love both. If you crave a maximum of extra-crispy skin, you can brown the roast at the very end. It means using another pan, but if you're a crackling fiend, it is worth it. Usually I wait and see how crispy the skin turns out before I decide. Every shoulder seems to turn out just a little differently.

My favorite way to serve this roast is to let it rest for a generous hour after roasting and then shred the meat to resemble southern-style pulled pork. If you want to go whole hog (pun intended), douse the meat with a zesty barbecue-style sauce. I've included a recipe for my favorite vinegar-based sauce, but you can use any sauce you like—be it homemade or from a jar. For sandwiches, pile the meat into soft rolls, drizzle a little extra sauce on top, layer on a spoonful of coleslaw, and dig in.

If you can't find a picnic shoulder or prefer the meatier Boston butt, this recipe works equally well for both cuts.

SERVES 8 TO 10 (OR MORE, DEPENDING ON HOW YOU SERVE IT; SEE NOTE ON PAGE 230)

METHOD: Combination high and low heat

ROASTING TIME: 8 to 9 hours

PLAN AHEAD: The roast cooks for at least 8 hours. It also tastes best if seasoned a day or two ahead of roasting.

WINE: California old-vine Zinfandel or Shiraz from South Australia's Barossa Valley.

1 bone-in, skin-on pork picnic shoulder (about 7 pounds; see Shopping for Pork Shoulder Roasts, page 223)

4 teaspoons kosher salt

Freshly ground black pepper

1½ to 2 cups barbecue sauce (optional), Bubba's Vinegar-Based Barbecue Sauce (page 228), or use your own favorite

CONTINUED ON NEXT PAGE

1 **SCORE THE RIND.** Using a box cutter, utility knife, or other razor-sharp knife, firmly (but carefully) score the rind in parallel lines ⅓- to ½-inch apart. Score deep into the fat (about ½-inch deep), but avoid cutting into the meat. Turn the roast and score the rind on the bottom and sides as well. It's impossible to keep the same parallel pattern on the bottom and sides, but do your best to score as much of the rind as you can without getting reckless. This task requires a bit of force and can be dangerous. (Photos 1 and 2 on page 237 show scoring the rind.)

2 **SEASON THE ROAST.** Sprinkle the meat all over with salt and pepper. Set it on a baking sheet or other tray and refrigerate, uncovered or loosely covered, for 18 to 48 hours. Let the pork sit at room temperature for 1 to 2 hours before roasting.

3 **HEAT THE OVEN.** Position a rack in the lower third of the oven and heat to 450 degrees (425 degrees convection). Set the pork roast skin side up on a rack set in a sturdy roasting pan (14 by 12 inches). Slide the roast into the oven and roast for 30 minutes.

4 **REDUCE THE OVEN TEMPERATURE.** Reduce the oven temperature to 250 degrees (225 degrees convection) and continue roasting until the meat is fork-tender and pulling away from the shank bone, 8 to 9 hours. Begin checking the roast after 3 hours to see that it is browning evenly; if not, rotate the pan on the oven rack. Check again every 2 hours. In most cases, there's no need to flip the roast, but if after 5 hours you notice that the underside is not browning, flip the meat and let it roast skin side down for a few hours. It should finish roasting right side up.

5 **TEST FOR DONENESS.** The most reliable doneness test is to insert a meat fork into the wide end of the roast and gently pull. If a chunk of meat pulls away easily, the roast is done. Be careful not to tear the meat from the roast; just tug it to get a feel. Also, check to see that the meat at the shank end of the roast has contracted, leaving the bone exposed some. If you're unsure, check the internal temperature with an instant-read thermometer; you're looking for something in the 175- to 185-degree range. Remove the roast from the oven.

6 **OPTIONAL: BROWN THE ROAST.** If you want lots of extra-crispy skin, increase the oven heat to 450 degrees (425 degrees convection). Using a meat fork and another sturdy implement (I find a big wooden spoon works), maneuver the roast onto a heavy-duty rimmed baking sheet (this prevents the pan drippings from catching fire

or scorching in the super-hot oven). Return the roast to the oven and roast just until the skin appears deeply browned, just shy of scorching, about 10 minutes.

7 **REST AND CARVE (OR SHRED).** Transfer the roast to a carving board, preferably one with a trough. Let the roast rest for 30 minutes or up to 2 hours. You can cover it loosely with foil, but you will lose some of the crispness of the skin. I tend to leave it uncovered, as it will stay plenty warm enough unless the kitchen is terribly cold. Whether you're slicing or shredding, begin by cutting away the rind with a large knife. It will lift off in a few sections. Set aside for now (although I can never resist tearing off a few bits to nibble on while I carve the meat).

There are two ways to carve: chop or shred. Chopping tends to be more efficient, but you get a more authentic pulled-pork texture if you shred. Either way, start by pulling the meat apart into large sections. It will separate naturally at the fatty seams. Transfer a section at a time to a second cutting board. To shred, you'll need two table forks. With one fork in each hand, start pulling the meat apart; it will naturally tear into fibers along the grain. Keep going until you have small bite-sized pieces. If the meat won't shred easily, don't agonize. Chopped pork is just as delicious and tender. To chop, cut a section across the grain into ½-inch slices, then chop again into bite-sized pieces. Pile the pieces onto a shallow serving dish.

As you shred or chop a picnic shoulder, you will encounter ample amounts of unctuous fatty bits. How you handle these is a matter of personal taste, and perhaps consideration of the sensibilities of your guests. For instance, if I'm serving a crowd of enthusiastic nose-to-tail pork-eaters who relish every part of the pig, I leave on all the fat. If I'm serving the roast to folks I know won't appreciate such a super-rich meal, I trim off some of the fat.

Once the meat is broken down, move the skin to the cutting board and, using a cleaver or large chef's knife, chop it into bite-sized pieces. If you come across some pieces that seem tooth-breakingly hard, discard them. Expect to find a mix of crackly-crispy bits and some softer, gummier pieces. I like both, but if you prefer crispy to chewy—or if the skin is just too gummy—heat the oven to 450 degrees (425 degrees convection), spread any soft-chewy bits of skin in a skillet or on a baking sheet, and roast them until crisp, 5 to 10 minutes.

As with the fatty bits and how you determine your own fat-to-lean ratio in the final mix, you can either mix the skin right in with the rest of the meat (you get more textural contrast this way or serve it in a separate dish.

CONTINUED ON NEXT PAGE

8 **ADD SAUCE, IF USING, AND SERVE.** Drizzle any juices from the carving board onto the meat. Pour about ¾ cup barbecue sauce, if using, over the meat to moisten. Add more as needed. Mix and taste for seasoning. If you've kept the skin separate, don't moisten it with sauce. Simply scatter a few bits over each serving or pass them separately. Pass extra sauce at the table.

OPTION 1: BUBBA'S VINEGAR-BASED BARBECUE SAUCE

My first taste of real barbeque came on a vacation in the Outer Banks of North Carolina. Early in the trip, hungry after a day on the water, we stopped at Bubba's Bar-B-Que roadside restaurant, excited by the thick smoke billowing out of the back of the building and the alluring smell of barbecued pork. The sauce at Bubba's falls firmly into the non-tomato-based, thin, vinegary category of eastern North Carolina–style barbecue, and my first taste of chopped slow-cooked pork shoulder liberally doused with the sharp, slightly sweet, mildly spicy sauce was a revelation. We ate at Bubba's several times that week and even bought a bottle of the sauce to bring home. Of course, the exact formula for the sauce is a well-guarded family secret, but I'm very happy with my version. It adds just the right amount of acidity, sweetness, and zing to balance the richness of slow-roasted pork.

MAKES ABOUT 1 1/2 CUPS

¾ cup cider vinegar

¾ cup white wine or champagne vinegar

¼ cup brown sugar, light or dark

2 tablespoons ketchup

1 tablespoon dried mustard

1 tablespoon soy sauce

1 tablespoon peanut oil or vegetable oil

1 teaspoon sweet paprika

1 teaspoon crushed red pepper flakes

COMBINE ALL the ingredients in a small saucepan. Heat over medium heat, whisking, until the sugar is dissolved and everything is well combined. Simmer for 2 minutes. Set aside to cool. Serve at room temperature. *The sauce keeps for several weeks, covered, in the refrigerator.*

OPTION 2: SPICE-RUBBED SLOW-ROASTED PORK PICNIC SHOULDER

I often season a picnic shoulder with no more than salt and pepper and let the deliciousness of the pork itself prevail, but then there are those times when I'm after something a little more complex and bold. For these occasions, I mix together a selection of compatible spices and rub the mixture onto the pork a day or two before roasting. My favorite mixtures tend to combine a few warming spices (like ginger and Chinese five-spice) with something hot (think garlic and chiles), but I encourage you to invent your own combinations. Simply keep the amount of salt constant.

SERVES 8 TO 10 (OR MORE, DEPENDING ON HOW YOU SERVE IT)

METHOD: Combination high and low heat

ROASTING TIME: 8 to 9 hours

PLAN AHEAD: The roast cooks for at least 8 hours. It also tastes best if seasoned a day or two ahead of roasting.

WINE: Young Malbec from the Mendoza region of Argentina.

4 garlic cloves, crushed

1 teaspoon freshly grated ginger

4 teaspoons kosher salt

2 tablespoons brown sugar, light or dark

1 tablespoon dried mustard

1 teaspoon freshly ground black pepper

¾ teaspoon Chinese five-spice powder

¾ teaspoon crushed red pepper flakes

1 bone-in, skin-on pork picnic shoulder (about 7 pounds; see Shopping for Pork Shoulder Roasts, page 223)

1   **MAKE THE SPICE PASTE.** Combine the garlic and ginger in a mortar. Add a teaspoon of salt and work the garlic and ginger into a paste using the pestle. If you don't have a mortar and pestle, use a chef's knife on a cutting board (see page 230). If using a mortar, add the remaining 3 teaspoons salt, brown sugar, dried mustard, black pepper, five-spice powder, and red pepper flakes. (If you've made the paste on a cutting board, transfer to a small bowl and stir in the remaining ingredients.)

2   **SEASON THE PORK.** Score the rind as directed in step 1 of the Faux Pork Barbecue recipe. In step 2, season the roast with the spice paste in place of salt and pepper, rubbing the paste over the entire surface of the roast and into the incisions in the skin. Do your best to distribute it evenly, but don't obsess. The seasonings will permeate the entire roast as it sits. Set it on a baking sheet or other tray and refrigerate, uncovered or loosely covered, for 18 to 48 hours. Let the pork sit at room temperature for 1 to 2 hours before roasting.

3   **ROAST, REST, AND CARVE (OR SHRED)** as directed. Serve with or without the optional barbecue sauce.

A Note on How Many People a Pork Shoulder Serves

I'VE SEEN A SLOW-ROASTED PICNIC SHOULDER SERVE AS MANY AS 20 PEOPLE AND AS FEW AS 8. IT ALL DEPENDS ON HOW YOU SLICE (OR SHRED) IT AND how you serve it. If you are carving the roast and serving slices, it won't go as far as if you shred it; you can expect a sliced picnic shoulder to serve 8 to 10. If you shred the meat, you'll end up with about 10 to 12 cups of chopped meat, enough for 16 to 24 sandwiches, depending on the size of the rolls and the appetites. And finally, there is the whole Jack Sprat equation to consider. Some people prefer leaner meat and others relish the fatty bits. When you're carving a slow-roasted picnic shoulder, you'll find plenty of both—as well as all the deliciously rich skin.

Making Garlic Paste Without a Mortar and Pestle

A MORTAR AND PESTLE SITS PRETTY HIGH ON MY LIST OF ESSENTIAL KITCHEN TOOLS, AND I FREQUENTLY USE IT TO QUICKLY TURN OUT A SMOOTH GARLIC puree. There are times, however, when I'm traveling and in someone else's kitchen, that I have to do without. Happily, a decent chef's knife does a fine job of making a quick garlic paste, although it does take just a bit longer than using a mortar. Start by chopping the garlic on a sturdy cutting board. Sprinkle a measure of salt over the chopped garlic (the salt will act as an abrasive and help break down the garlic). Now drag the flat side of your knife back and forth across the chopped garlic, pressing down on the top of the blade to crush the garlic. As you work, you will spread the garlic into a thin paste. As the smear of garlic gets too thin, gather it back up with the knife and continue. After a minute or two of this smearing and gathering, the garlic will turn into a creamy paste. Transfer to a small bowl and continue with the recipe.

PERNIL AL HORNO (CUBAN-STYLE MARINATED SLOW-ROASTED PORK PICNIC SHOULDER)

This is my version of the classic Latin American dish of slow-roasted pork shoulder seasoned with a heady mixture of garlic, oregano, and citrus (I use a combination of limes and oranges to approximate the sour oranges of the Caribbean). It makes a festive party centerpiece, especially because it's simple to carve—it mostly falls off the bone—and people can fight over the cracklings, or *cuentos*, as they are called in Cuba. For the complete experience, serve this with a dish of black beans and rice and tostones and/or sweet plantains on the side.

Be sure to season the pork in advance so the citrus and seasonings have a chance to work their way through the entire roast.

SERVES 8 TO 10

METHOD: Combination high and low heat

ROASTING TIME: 8 to 9 hours

PLAN AHEAD: The roast tastes best if marinated for at least 24 hours.

WINE/BEER: Fruity off-dry rosé; or India Pale Ale.

1 tablespoon cumin seeds

1 tablespoon whole black peppercorns

6 garlic cloves, smashed

1 tablespoon dried oregano

1 tablespoon kosher salt

⅛ teaspoon cayenne

⅔ cup fresh orange juice

⅓ cup fresh lime juice

2 tablespoons extra-virgin olive oil

1 bone-in, skin-on pork picnic shoulder
  (about 7 pounds; see Shopping for Pork
  Shoulder Roasts, page 223)

CONTINUED ON PAGE 233

PERNIL AL HORNO (PAGE 231)

1 **MAKE THE SPICE RUB AND MARINADE.** Place the cumin seeds in a small skillet and heat over medium-low heat until lightly toasted about 2 minutes. Let cool. Combine the cumin and peppercorns in a spice grinder or a mortar and grind coarsely. Add the garlic, oregano, salt, and cayenne. Grind again to form a rough paste. Set aside. In a small bowl, combine the orange juice, lime juice, and oil. Set this aside as well.

2 **SCORE THE RIND AND MARINATE THE PORK** (as shown on page 237). Using a box cutter, utility knife, or other razor-sharp knife, firmly (but carefully) score the rind in parallel lines ⅓- to ½-inch apart. Score deep into the fat (about ½-inch deep), but avoid cutting into the meat. Turn the roast and score the rind on the bottom and sides as well. Using a sharp paring knife, poke several holes in the cut side of the pork (the side with no skin). Rub the entire surface of the roast with the spice paste, doing your best to get some of the paste into the incisions in the skin. If you have a plastic bag large enough to hold the pork, place it in one (Reynolds large oven bags work well). Otherwise, place the pork in a deep bowl just large enough to hold it. Pour the marinade over the roast and massage it to coat it evenly. Place the bag in a baking dish or large bowl in case it leaks, and refrigerate for 24 to 48 hours, turning occasionally to redistribute the marinade. Remove the pork from the marinade (reserve the marinade) and let it sit at room temperature, uncovered, for 1 to 2 hours before roasting; this dries the skin to help it crisp in the oven.

3 **HEAT THE OVEN.** Set a rack in the lower third of the oven and heat to 450 degrees (425 degrees convection).

4 **ROAST THE PORK.** Set the roast skin side up on a rack set in a sturdy roasting pan (14 by 12 inches works well). Roast for 30 minutes, then reduce the oven temperature to 250 degrees (225 degrees convection). Combine the reserved marinade with ½ cup cool water and pour this over the meat. Continue roasting, basting every 2 to 2 ½ hours with the drippings until the meat is fork-tender and pulling away from the shank bone, 8 to 9 hours. If at any time the liquid evaporates, add about ½ cup of water to the pan. If after 5 hours you notice that the underside is not browning, flip the meat and let it roast skin side down for a few hours before righting it. It should finish roasting right side up.

CONTINUED ON PAGE 235

PERNIL AL HORNO (PAGE 231) SERVED WITH RICE AND BEANS

5 **TEST FOR DONENESS.** The best doneness test is to insert a meat fork into the wide end of the roast and gently pull. If a chunk of meat pulls away easily, the roast is done. Be careful not to tear the meat from the roast; just tug it to get a feel. Also, check to see that the meat at the shank end of the roast has contracted, leaving the bone exposed some. If you're unsure, check the internal temperature with an instant-read thermometer; you're looking for something in the 175- to 185-degree range.

6 **REST AND CARVE.** Let the pork rest, uncovered unless the kitchen is very cold, for about 30 minutes. Unless you have a very sharp knife, it's easiest to begin by carving off the rind. If you notice parts of the rind that are soft and chewy, not crisp, cut them into smaller pieces and place them in a skillet or on a rimmed baking sheet. Place the skin in a 450-degree (425-degree convection) oven until crisp, 5 to 10 minutes. Thinly slice the pork and chop the rind into crackling bits to put on each plate. Spoon any juices that run from the meat over it as you carve.

A Note on Pig Skin, or Rind

WHETHER YOU REFER TO IT AS SKIN OR RIND (AND I USE BOTH THROUGHOUT THIS CHAPTER), GETTING A PORK ROAST WITH THE SKIN INTACT IS A REAL bonus for pork lovers. The skin protects the meat as it roasts, basting it with the underlayer of fat, and best of all, it offers some of the most satisfying eating on the whole pig. But getting pork rind just right can be tricky. The goal is wonderfully crisp, almost crinkled or puffed skin that's easy to chop into bite-sized tidbits that crunch noisily between your teeth and release just the right amount of tasty pork fat. But the rind can also turn out gummy and soft and, while tasty, difficult to enjoy, as it sticks to your teeth and pretty well locks your jaws together. And then there's what I've heard Chinese chefs refer to as "scorpion skin," when the skin forms an impenetrable sheath, too tough to chop, much less to chew.

Pork skin is basically an amalgam of protein, fat, and water, and your job as a cook is to enable the moisture and fat to release as the protein sets into a crispy, crunchy shell. If the moisture remains trapped, the skin will turn out gummy and leathery. And if the fat doesn't release, the skin will be greasy. The technique I use to get the best cracklings is twofold. First I score the rind, cutting down through the tough skin and into the fat layer below but not cutting into the meat. This allows the fat to render during roasting and helps to crisp the rind. You can score as the British do, in horizontal stripes ¼- to ½-inch apart, or in the

CONTINUED ON NEXT PAGE

more American fashion of a diamond cross-hatch pattern. Both are effective, but I find the horizontal pattern slightly easier to master. Second, I presalt the entire surface of the roast—the rind and the score marks—and let it sit, uncovered, in a refrigerator for at least a day before roasting. This draws moisture from the rind, making it dry and more likely to turn crisp when heated. Rubbing a little oil on the rind can also encourage crisping. Acid and alcohol help break down the rind, too, and are used in many marinades.

Even using these techniques, I often find parts of the rind, especially any nooks or creases on irregularly shaped pork legs and shoulders, that won't crisp no matter how well I score or salt. In these instances, I lift these off after roasting and return them to a hot oven (450 degrees or 425 degrees convection) for about 10 minutes to crisp up.

Finally, if you're an absolute fanatic for crispy cracklings, you may want to try a technique from food writer Christopher Tan. Chinese chefs have often brushed pork skin with an alkali solution (such as baking soda dissolved in water), but I have never liked the unpleasantly soapy, chemical taste. Neither did Tan, so he devised an ingenious solution: he first scalds the pork skin with a solution of boiling water and baking soda (using 1 ½ tablespoons for 5 cups of water), then proceeds to score and season the pork. The baking soda and boiling water denature the skin enough so that it will break down during roasting, but the highly diluted solution doesn't leave any unpleasant flavor residue. In the recipes in this chapter, I don't employ Tan's solution, as I am happy enough with my simpler scoring and salting technique, but if you're the kind of cook who enjoys extra steps, by all means give it a try.

Step-by-Step: Scoring and Seasoning Pork Picnic Shoulder

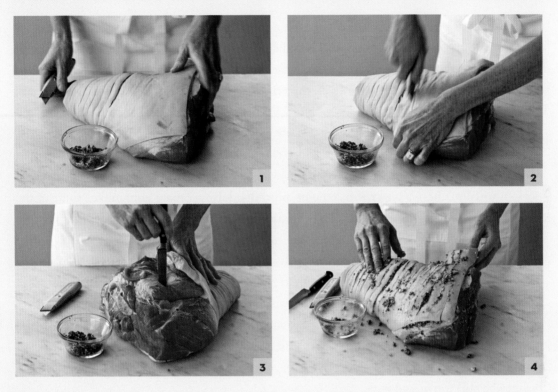

1 Using a box cutter (or utility knife or other razor-sharp blade), score the rind in parallel lines 1/3- to 1/2-inch apart. **2** Apply a bit of force, but work carefully so as not to cut into the meat—and keep your other hand out of the way of the blade. **3** Use a sharp paring knife to poke several holes in the skinless side of the pork. **4** Rub the entire surface with the spice paste.

ROASTED WHOLE FRESH HAM (PORK LEG ROAST)

A whole fresh ham is about as impressive a roast as you can find, feeding upwards of 20 people at a relatively low price. The substantial roast is meatier than a pork loin, but it's not as rugged as a pork shoulder. But before I get too carried away extolling the virtues of fresh ham, I want to be sure we're all on the same page about exactly what it is. A fresh ham is an uncooked and uncured hind leg of pork. What it is *not* is salted or smoked or treated in any way, which, to be honest, is what most of us imagine when we hear the word *ham*. A whole bone-in fresh ham, which includes the plump rump portion down to the shank, can weigh between 17 and 22 pounds and provides an abundance of robust and juicy roast pork. If you don't have a big crowd, keep in mind that leftover roast ham makes some of the best pork sandwiches in the world. You can also buy smaller roasts from the hind leg (see Shopping for and Carving Fresh Ham, page 241).

When roasting a fresh ham—no matter its size—I like to blast it in a hot oven at first to brown the outside. Then I let it finish slowly at a more moderate oven temperature so it stays moist and tender. To keep the drippings from scorching, I pour some beer into the bottom of the roasting pan. A fresh ham tastes best when cooked until the juices run clear and the meat around the bone is cooked through, and as with any large roast, it's imperative to let the meat rest for a good long while before serving; I've waited up to 2 hours and found the meat to be still warm and moist.

SERVES 20 TO 24

METHOD: Combination high and moderate heat

ROASTING TIME: About 5 hours

PLAN AHEAD: For the best flavor, season the pork 2 to 3 days ahead.

WINE/BEER: Luscious, full-bodied Alsace Pinot Gris; or refreshing pale ale.

1 whole fresh ham, 18 to 20 pounds, preferably bone-in or partially boned (see Shopping for and Carving Fresh Ham, page 241)

Kosher salt and freshly ground black pepper

24 ounces pale lager-style beer (such as Labatt, Miller, or Pilsner Urquell), or as needed

1 **SCORE AND SEASON THE PORK.** If the pork has its rind, use a box cutter, utility knife, or other razor-sharp knife to firmly (and carefully) score the rind so the lines are ¾- to 1-inch apart. Score deep into the fat (about ½-inch deep), but avoid cutting into the meat. Turn the roast and score the rind on all sides. If the rind has been removed, simply score the fat, again being careful not to cut into the meat. Combine 3 tablespoons of salt and about 1½ teaspoons of black pepper. (If your ham is larger than 18 pounds, add another ½ teaspoon salt per extra pound; if smaller, take away a pinch. The pepper can remain constant.) Sprinkle and rub the mixture all over the pork, being sure to season inside the score marks. If the pork has been boned, get the seasoning into any loose flaps of meat. If the large end has been tied where the hipbone has been removed, it's a good idea to remove the strings to get the seasoning into the flaps and then retie. Arrange the roast on a wire rack set above a tray to catch any drips and refrigerate, preferably uncovered, for 2 to 3 days.

2 **HEAT THE OVEN.** Set the roast skin side up on a rack set in a large sturdy roasting pan (16 by 13 inches works well). Let it sit at room temperature for 1 to 2 hours before you plan to roast. Position a rack on the lowest or second lowest setting in the oven and heat to 475 degrees (450 degrees convection).

3 **ROAST THE HAM.** Roast for 25 minutes, then reduce the oven temperature to 325 degrees (300 degrees convection). Pour enough beer into the roasting pan (not over the pork) to cover the bottom by ¼ to ½ inch. Continue to roast, rotating the pan if one side seems to brown more quickly than the other, and adding more beer if the pan threatens to dry up, until the juices run clear when you pierce the meat and an instant-read thermometer inserted into the thickest part registers about 145 degrees, another 4 to 4½ hours. (The temperature will continue to rise about 10 degrees as the meat rests.)

4 **REST THE ROAST AND DEGREASE THE DRIPPINGS.** Transfer the roast to a large cutting board (ideally one with a trough) or rimmed baking sheet to rest for at least 45 minutes. (I've let it rest for more than 2 hours with no sacrifice in quality.) Scrape the drippings from the pan into a liquid measuring cup or a gravy separator and spoon or pour off most of the fat. Taste the drippings; if they are too salty, add a little water to them. Set the drippings aside and warm before serving.

CONTINUED ON NEXT PAGE

5 **CARVE AND SERVE.** Remove the crispy skin (if your ham had skin to start) and chop it into bite-sized pieces. If the skin isn't crisp in parts, spread out any soft or gummy pieces on a baking sheet or in a skillet and place in a 450-degree (425-degree convection) oven until crisp, 5 to 10 minutes.

If the roast is partially boned, carve it into thin slices (about ¼ inch) and serve.

If the bones are intact, use a sturdy small knife and your hands (or a meat fork) to free chunks of meat from the roast (you are basically trying to identify muscle groups and cut and/or pull these away from the bone). Once you've removed a good-sized chunk, identify the grain (the way the muscle fibers run) and slice across the grain into slices ¼- to ½-inch thick. Continue removing chunks of pork and slicing until you have enough to serve your guests. (Any leftovers will stay more moist if left unsliced.)

Drizzle pan juices over each serving (or pass the pan juices at the table) and garnish each serving with bits of cracklings if you have them.

OPTION: SPICE RUB FOR FRESH HAM

Fresh ham, like all pork, takes well to a variety of seasonings. Use any of your favorite spice rubs, or try this smoky-sweet version.

MAKES ENOUGH FOR 1 WHOLE (18- TO 20-POUND) FRESH HAM

1 tablespoon cumin seeds	1 teaspoon paprika, preferably sweet
2 teaspoons coriander seeds	1 teaspoon chili powder
½ teaspoon allspice berries	¼ teaspoon ground cloves
2 bay leaves	¼ teaspoon cayenne

COMBINE THE CUMIN, coriander, and allspice in a small dry skillet over medium-low heat and toast, shaking frequently, until fragrant, about 2 minutes. Transfer to a mortar or spice grinder and let cool. Tear the bay leaves into small pieces and add them to the toasted spices. Grind to a coarse powder. Mix in the remaining spices. Add the spice mix to the salt and pepper in the Roasted Whole Fresh Ham recipe on page 238 and season and roast as directed in the recipe.

Shopping for and Carving Fresh Ham

THE AVAILABILITY OF FRESH HAM VARIES FROM REGION TO REGION, BUT ANY MARKET THAT CARRIES A GOOD VARIETY OF FRESH PORK SHOULD BE ABLE TO get you one with a few days' notice. When you talk to the person in the meat department, stress that you want a *fresh* ham; it may help to underscore your request by saying, "You know, a pork leg for roasting." Once you are sure that your butcher knows you're looking for raw, uncured pork, you may want to inquire about getting it partially boned. While I enjoy the primal appearance of the fully bone-in leg, it's not the neatest roast to carve. In fact, it's almost a stretch to call it *carving*, as it's more a matter of separating large hunks at a time and slicing them up as you go. If you want a tidier approach, ask your butcher to remove the hipbone (also called the aitch bone) and possibly the leg bone. A fully boneless ham will be easiest of all to carve, but it lacks a certain majesty. At least with the semi-boneless leg, the shank bone remains and sticks out from one end, giving the roast shape and heft.

For a smaller crowd, consider a partial fresh ham. Ask for either the rump (or sirloin) or the shank portion. The shank half is neater and looks more like the iconic ham we all recognize. Plus a bone-in shank-end ham is easier to carve than a bone-in rump-end ham. But the rump end is a bit meatier and contains the most tender of the leg muscles, the top round. Both weigh 8 to 10 pounds and will serve 10 to 12 people.

To roast a smaller ham: Season the ham, using about ½ teaspoon of salt per pound, slightly less for a boneless roast. Season and roast according to the directions in the recipe, but expect a half ham to be cooked through in 2 to 3 hours.

To carve a bone-in shank-end ham, start at the large end and slice down until you hit the bone. Continue making a few more ¼- to ½-inch-thick slices (they will remain attached to the bone) and then turn your knife parallel to the bone and cut toward the center of the roast to free the slices. Continue, making a few more slices at a time and then running your knife along the bone to free them. Once you're near the narrow end of the roast, turn the roast and repeat on another side. Continue carving until you've carved enough to serve everyone at the table. (Leftovers keep best when uncarved.)

To carve a boneless rump-end ham, remove the strings and slice into ¼- to ½-inch slices. *To carve a bone-in rump-end ham,* use a sturdy small knife and your hands (or a meat fork) to free chunks of meat from the roast (you are basically trying to identify muscle groups and cut and/or pull these away from the bone). Once you've removed a good-sized chunk, identify the grain (the way the muscle fibers run) and slice the chunk into thin slices across the grain. Continue until you have enough sliced pork to serve your guests.

ORANGE- AND PINEAPPLE-GLAZED HAM WITH CHIPOTLE

This is the archetypal holiday ham. You start with a fully cured, fully cooked ham and roast it in a moderate oven until heated through. Even though the ham doesn't technically *need* to be cooked, gentle roasting does wonders to improve the taste and texture. To give the ham its classic burnished appearance, the top gets painted with an orange-pineapple-chipotle glaze toward the end of roasting, and the ham is finished in a hot oven. Not only does the glaze make the ham look picture-perfect, but it adds just the right sweet-tart-spicy element to the meat. I like to add a splash of tequila to my glaze, but you can forgo this if there's none in the house or if it's not your style.

This recipe is for a half ham, enough to serve 10 to 12 as a main course, more on a buffet. For a bigger group or an open house, buy a whole ham (12 to 16 pounds), double the glaze, and expect the ham to take 1 to 2 hours longer to cook.

SERVES 10 TO 12
METHOD: Combination moderate and high heat
ROASTING TIME: 2 3/4 to 3 1/2 hours
WINE/BEER: Medium-sweet Auslese Riesling from the Rheingau or Rheinhessen; or traditional English nut-brown ale.

1 fully cooked bone-in ham, 6 to 8 pounds (see Shopping for a Ham, page 244)

½ cup canned pineapple chunks in heavy syrup

½ cup orange marmalade

¼ cup brown sugar, light or dark

2 tablespoons Dijon mustard

2 tablespoons silver or gold tequila (optional)

1 to 2 teaspoons finely chopped chipotle peppers (from can of chipotle peppers in adobo sauce)

1 **HEAT THE OVEN.** Position a rack in the lower third of the oven and heat to 325 degrees (300 degrees convection). Let the ham sit at room temperature as the oven heats, about 30 minutes. If you like, line a shallow roasting pan just large enough to accommodate the ham (I use a 9- by 13-inch one) with heavy-duty aluminum foil (this makes it easier to clean).

2 **TRIM AND SCORE THE HAM.** Examine the ham; if the skin is intact, peel it away. Some hams only have pieces of tough rind; trim these away. If the fat is thicker than ¼ inch, use a sharp knife to trim it down to about ¼ inch—enough to baste the meat as it cooks. Score the fat in a diamond pattern, being careful not to cut down into the meat and making the score lines about 1 inch apart. Place the ham fat side up in the roasting pan.

3 **ROAST.** Slide the ham into the oven and roast, rotating the pan if it appears to be browning on one side more than the other, until an instant-read thermometer inserted into the thickest part registers about 125 degrees, 2½ to 3 hours.

4 **MEANWHILE, MAKE THE GLAZE.** As the ham roasts, drain the pineapple, reserving the juice, and chop coarsely. In a saucepan, combine the pineapple chunks and juice with the marmalade, brown sugar, mustard, tequila, if using, and chipotle. Bring to a simmer over medium heat and stir to combine. Remove from the heat and set aside.

5 **GLAZE THE HAM.** When the ham has reached 125 degrees remove it from the oven and increase the oven temperature to 400 degrees (375 degrees convection). Paint or smear the top of the ham with three-quarters of the glaze and return it to the oven. Roast, spooning the remaining glaze over the ham after 10 minutes, and continue to roast until the surface is nicely caramelized and sizzling, 20 to 30 minutes.

6 **REST.** Transfer the ham to a large carving board and let it rest for about 25 minutes (longer is fine, too).

7 **CARVE AND SERVE.** Carve, starting at the large end and slicing down until you hit the bone. Continue making a few more thin slices (they will remain attached to the bone) and then turn your knife parallel to the bone and cut toward the center of the roast to free the slices. Continue, making a few more slices at a time and then running your knife along the bone to free them. Once you're near the narrow end of the roast, turn the roast and repeat on another side. Serve hot or warm.

Shopping for a Ham

THE HAM YOU WANT FOR ROASTING IS SOMETIMES REFERRED TO AS A *CITY HAM* TO DISTINGUISH IT FROM A *COUNTRY HAM*. I'VE ALSO HEARD PEOPLE USE the term *supermarket ham*, but this doesn't always apply, as there many great mail-order sources for city hams (see Sources & Resources, page 539). Bottom line, you want a fully cured, brined, smoked, and cooked ham. A true country ham, in contrast, has been salted and cured but not smoked or cooked. (These include the famous American southern hams like Smithfield and the European hams, such as prosciutto, Iberico, and Serrano, which are not at all suited to roasting and glazing.) The best city hams are 100 percent pure ham, with no water or "natural juices" added. They can be quite expensive, but their exquisite taste and lean texture make them worth the cost. If you're looking for a good ham but don't want quite such a splurge, look for a fully cooked ham that contains no more than 10 percent added water or "natural juices." Lesser-quality hams contain anywhere from 15 to 50 percent added water and other juices, and the flavor and texture suffer accordingly. Whatever you do, avoid pressed or canned hams, which contain, in addition to large amounts of water and sodium, gelatin and often other additives. For the best texture, buy bone-in or semiboneless (sometimes labeled shankless) ham. When the ham producer removes all the bones, it reshapes the meat into a neat ham shape, a process that can toughen the meat. For roasting, I don't recommend spiral ham. While these nifty hams may be convenient to carve, they are best eaten cold, as heating tends to dry them out. Hams are also sold with or without skin. If you're planning to glaze the ham as I do (page 242), buying a skinless ham will save you the step of removing the skin, but it's an easy enough process, so either will do.

Finally, some producers also offer *partially cooked hams*. These are less common but can also be quite good. Use the same criteria as when evaluating a fully cooked ham (that is, the best will have a minimum of added water and will include the bone). If you do buy a partially cooked ham, you'll need to roast it longer, until the internal temperature reaches 160 to 165 degrees (this means adding about 5 minutes per pound cooking time to the recipe on page 242).

CHAR SIU (CHINESE ROAST PORK)

C *har siu* is the kind of dish that induces cravings, and when I get a hankering, nothing else will do. Tender pork, with just enough fat on it to make things interesting, gets slathered with a classic Chinese marinade (think soy sauce, hoisin, ginger, and scallion) and gently roasted to keep the interior supple while the outside becomes lacquered and sizzling. The Chinese accomplish this by suspending boneless strips of meat on forks or special hooks to roast. (The phrase *char siu* translates as "fork-roasted" and refers to this particular Cantonese method.) But with my method—arranging marinated pieces of pork on a rack and turning them often as they roast—you can easily duplicate this luxurious dish at home.

If you've seen and eaten *char siu* in a Chinese restaurant, you've probably noticed the lustrous red sheen, which these days comes from food coloring. I leave the food coloring out; the results may not be as eye-catching, but the flavor is just as good (and maybe better).

Traditional *char siu* is made from boneless strips of pork shoulder, and you could certainly buy a whole shoulder and cut it into strips yourself. However, boneless country-style ribs, which most supermarkets carry, make an excellent and more convenient substitution. Serve the pork with some fragrant white rice, Asian noodles, or sandwiched in a soft bun for *cha siu baau*. A crunchy fresh cucumber salad is a fitting accompaniment.

SERVES 4

METHOD: Combination moderate heat and broiling

ROASTING TIME: About 1 1/4 hours (plus 6 minutes to broil)

PLAN AHEAD: The pork needs to marinate for 8 to 12 hours.

WINE/BEER: Fruity medium-sweet white such as German Auslese Riesling; or light-bodied lager with spice notes.

CONTINUED ON NEXT PAGE

¼ cup plus 2 tablespoons hoisin sauce (see page 247)

3 tablespoons soy sauce

3 tablespoons brown sugar, light or dark

3 tablespoons sherry, preferably dry, or bourbon

1½ tablespoons finely chopped fresh ginger

1 teaspoon rice wine vinegar

¾ teaspoon Chinese five-spice powder

¼ teaspoon freshly ground white pepper

1½ pounds boneless country-style pork ribs

1 **MAKE THE MARINADE.** In a small bowl, combine the hoisin, soy, brown sugar, sherry or whiskey, ginger, vinegar, five-spice powder, and pepper.

2 **TRIM THE RIBS.** Boneless country-style pork ribs are generally sold in strips that are 3 to 4 inches long and of varying widths. For this recipe, you want them to be 1 to 1½ inches wide, and in many cases this means cutting them in half lengthwise. You don't need to get out your ruler; just approximate and cut them into strips as evenly as you can without wasting any. Don't trim away much of the fat, as it serves to baste the meat as it roasts.

3 **MARINATE THE RIBS.** Set aside ⅓ cup of the marinade to use as a glaze, cover, and refrigerate. Place the ribs in a large zip-top plastic bag and pour the remaining marinade over them. Massage the bag to coat the meat evenly and refrigerate for 8 to 12 hours.

4 **HEAT THE OVEN.** Position an oven rack about 8 inches from the broiler element. Heat the oven to 325 degrees (300 degrees convection). Let the pork sit at room temperature as the oven heats, about 25 to 30 minutes. Line a rimmed baking sheet with heavy-duty aluminum foil and place a wire rack, preferably one ¾- to 1-inch high, on it.

5 **ROAST.** Remove the ribs from the marinade, reserving the excess marinade, and arrange them evenly spaced on the rack. Roast, turning every 20 minutes and brushing with the reserved marinade, until they are completely fork-tender and almost falling apart, about 1¼ hours. Stop brushing with the marinade about 10 minutes before they are done, and discard any remaining marinade. (Because the marinade was in contact with the raw pork, you don't want to use it without fully cooking.)

6 **GLAZE.** Remove the ribs from the oven and set the broiler to high. Brush the ribs on one side with the reserved glaze and broil them until sizzling and dark in spots on the glazed side, about 3 minutes. Flip, paint with the remaining glaze, and broil until the second side is dark and sizzling, another 2 to 3 minutes. Serve hot.

Hoisin Sauce

IF YOU'VE EVER HAD PEKING DUCK OR *MU SHU*, YOU WILL RECOGNIZE HOISIN AS THE BASE FOR THE DARK, GLOSSY SAUCE THAT GOES ON THE CREPES OR BUNS before you fill them with meat. Hoisin belongs to the vast soy-based family of Chinese sauces, and the traditional recipe contains sugar, garlic, chiles, and spices in addition to fermented soybeans. Hoisin sauces can be thick and jammy or thinner and pourable, and the color ranges from reddish brown to inky. The best have a provocative sweet-smoky character with a good hit of spiciness from the chiles and garlic. Lesser brands can be cloying and blunt. Look for jars or cans of hoisin sauce in the international section of a well-stocked supermarket or in Asian markets. I prefer Koon Chun brand. Once opened, hoisin sauce should be stored in the refrigerator, where it will keep for months. Use it as a base for marinades for meat, such as *Char Siu* (page 245). I also like to smear it on meats and poultry just before roasting or grilling for a last-minute flavor boost.

BASIC ROASTED SAUSAGES

This is more of a technique than a recipe, but I include it here because I think it's something every busy cook needs to know. For the longest time, I thought the only way to cook good sausages was to grill them, or, in a pinch, sauté them. That all changed when I got a copy of the book *Charcuterie*, by Michael Rhulman and Brian Polcyn, and I stumbled across this line: "Roasting is the easiest way to cook sausages." I practically slapped my forehead. Of *course* it is! Roasting sausages require much less tending—a single flip halfway through cooking—and there is no splatter to deal with. When I roast sausages, I use a very hot oven and preheat the skillet to give the sausages a little extra sear. I also like to include a little sliced onion in the pan, because it cooks in the same time as the sausages and soaks up some of the wonderful flavor. You can easily add sliced bell peppers, or eliminate the vegetables altogether.

I typically roast a combination of sweet and hot Italian sausages, but whatever you choose, know that the quality of the dish rests almost entirely on the quality of the sausages. Buy the best you can find. The timing here is for sausages that are about 1 inch in diameter. For smaller sausages, such as merguez, check them sooner, and slice the onion even more thinly. To serve, cut the sausages in half on a sharp angle; this makes it easy for people to take varying amounts and choose which sausages they like if you're serving more than one kind. Serve the sausages with some sautéed or braised greens (I especially like kale) as a main dish or slice them into smaller pieces for an appetizer.

SERVES 3 TO 4 AS A MAIN COURSE, 6 AS AN APPETIZER

METHOD: High heat

ROASTING TIME: 20 to 35 minutes

WINE: Lighter fruity Pinot Noir from California or Cru Beaujolais, such as Brouilly or St. Amour.

1 tablespoon peanut oil or grapeseed oil

1 medium yellow onion (about 6 ounces), sliced about ⅓-inch thick (optional)

Kosher or coarse sea salt and freshly ground black pepper

1 pound Italian sausage links, preferably a mix of sweet and hot

1 **HEAT THE OVEN.** Position a rack in the center of the oven and heat to 400 degrees (375 degrees convection).

2 **PREHEAT THE SKILLET.** Slide a 12-inch ovenproof skillet into the oven to heat for 5 minutes. Add the oil, tilt the pan to coat, and return to the oven for another 2 minutes. (The hot pan helps the sausages brown nicely.)

3 **ROAST.** Scatter the onion slices, if using, in the skillet, and season with a pinch of salt and pepper. Place the sausages on top. Roast, flipping the sausages and giving the onions a little stir after 10 minutes, until the sausages are cooked through and juices run clear when pierced with a knife, 20 to 25 minutes total. To check for doneness, insert an instant-read thermometer into the thickest part of a sausage; it should read 150 to 160 degrees.

4 **SERVE.** If cutting the sausages in half, let them rest for a few minutes before doing so. Transfer the sausages and onions to a warmed serving platter or individual plates and serve hot.

TANDOORI-STYLE ROASTED
CHICKEN LEGS (PAGE 319)

CHAPTER

4

CHICKEN & POULTRY

CHICKEN & POULTRY

RECIPES

BASIC ROAST CHICKEN (PAGE 263)

A ROAST CHICKEN MAY WELL BE THE ULTIMATE EXPRESSION OF ROASTING. YOU START WITH A GOOD BIRD (MORE ON THAT LATER), SEASON IT, SLIDE it into a heated oven, and an hour or so later you have a delicious dinner, impressive enough for company and easy enough for a weeknight supper. And yet for all its simplicity, roasting a chicken can intimidate and even baffle the most accomplished cooks.

When I set out to write this book, I decided I needed to understand how such a simple dish could cause so much kitchen anxiety, and this meant getting to the bottom of all the varying methodology. Over the course of several months, I embarked on a quest, testing every chicken-roasting technique I'd ever thought of or heard about. I presalted and I brined; I stuffed seasonings under the skin and filled cavities with lemons and herbs; I propped birds up on all kinds of roasting racks; I trussed them and I rubbed them with butter. I blasted chickens at super-high heat and I roasted them gently at moderate heat. I used convection and nonconvection ovens. I started them breast side down and turned them from side to side as they roasted. I basted and I glazed. In the end, I can now honestly say that with few exceptions, every method turned out a tasty roast chicken. What I discovered ultimately is that there is no single "best" way to roast a chicken. Instead, there are *different* ways, each with its own benefits. The one constant I found, in all of my testing, however, is the huge benefit of presalting chicken a day ahead of roasting. I can't stress enough how much this simple step improves the flavor and texture of the bird. (For more on presalting, see page 257.)

In this chapter you will find a few different approaches to roast chicken that take into account a number of variables, including who is coming to dinner, how much time you have, how much effort you want to exert, and what flavors and texture you're after. The chapter opens with my Basic Roast Chicken (page 263), a beautifully straightforward way to turn out a great roast chicken with little fuss. But I also offer an option that produces a lovely little pan sauce, or *jus* (page 268), or, if you want to make an even more involved sauce, try Roasted Chicken with Lemony Garlic-Parsley Pan Sauce (page 280). If you're looking to bump up the flavor, you might choose to smear herb butter under the skin (page 269) or add a spice rub (page 269) that leaves the chicken fragrant and infused with warm spice flavor. If you want maximum crispy skin and don't mind doing some quick butchery, try Crispy Butterflied Roast Chicken (page 287). For a one-pot Sunday supper, buy a bigger bird and roast it along with some hearty root vegetables, as directed on page 271. And for times when you want to roast chicken pieces and not a whole bird, you'll find recipes for everything from thighs and legs to breasts and even wings, and along with each, I provide instructions for getting moist meat and crispy skin—the ultimate goal of roast chicken.

While chicken takes up much of this chapter, I also show you how to roast a number of other birds, such as turkey, quail, Cornish game hen, duck, and goose. In each section you'll find basic recipes outlining the roasting method that best matches the qualities of the type of poultry. Goose, for example, benefits from being steamed, simmered, or even poached before roasting to melt away a considerable portion of its fat (see the recipe on page 365, which calls for steaming the goose before roasting, a proposition that's easier than it sounds). A whole duck benefits greatly from slow roasting (see page 355); the relatively low heat renders fat and cooks the tougher leg meat to tender, braiselike perfection.

No matter which kind of bird you are roasting, in part or in whole, there are a few poultry-specific roasting principles to keep in mind.

Buy a good chicken (or other bird)

I cannot emphasize enough that your roast poultry can only be as good as the bird itself. In all my chicken-roasting trials, the best-tasting chickens were always the ones from the producers who raise their flocks with an eye toward flavor and quality. In other words, the better the farmer, the better the chicken. I go out of my way (and I urge you to do the same) to eschew chicken from the big brand-name commodity producers, whose intentions are to raise poultry as quickly as possible at the least expense. Without going into the gruesome details of what goes on at large-scale factory farming operations, I can say that the bottom line is, you really can taste the difference. The meat from a well-raised chicken will be flavorful, delicate, and a little sweet, with a pleasantly meaty texture, tender but not flaccid. The factory-farmed birds, in contrast, will be bland at best, with a dry, somewhat chalky texture at worst.

The one detail worth mentioning about industrially raised poultry is that the chickens are typically water-chilled after processing (quick chilling is essential to food safety), whereas small producers and specialty butchers (such as kosher or halal) are more apt to air-chill their poultry. Wet chilling produces inferior-tasting chickens, because the birds actually absorb a percentage of the water they are soaked in, making them plumper but blander. This added water can also affect cooking times, causing the chickens to cook faster because the water conducts heat so readily, but the water also runs out during cooking, so the results are drier. Air chilling maintains more of the integrity of flavor and texture of the natural chicken, and perhaps best of all, the skin of an air-chilled chicken will brown up much more readily (and will be crisper) when roasted.

That said, as much as I am an advocate for buying naturally raised meats and poultry, I know that it's not always possible for everyone to eat that way all the time, whether because of financial reasons, time constraints, or market access. My answer is to eat fewer chickens but buy the better (and inherently more expensive) ones when I do.

Presalt poultry

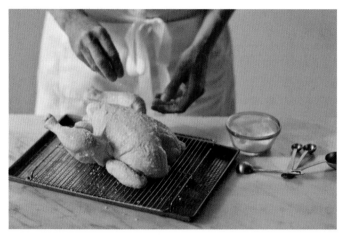

Presalt chicken 8 to 48 hours before roasting. Set it on a wire rack before refrigerating for best results.

I am always amazed at how dramatically something as simple as salting ahead of time improves the flavor and texture of roasts. I've given a full explanation of the science behind salting on page 26, but nowhere are the effects more apparent than on a simple roast chicken; the salt not only adds flavor but also works to make the chicken more tender. Then there's the skin. The combination of the salt and a period to air-dry in the refrigerator definitely promotes a crispier skin. I can tell you how delicious it turns out, but you really have to try it for yourself to see.

Salting itself takes only a few minutes, but you do need to plan ahead, as the chicken needs to be salted a day or so before you roast it for the magic to happen. Because I think this step improves a roast chicken so much, I've gotten into the habit of salting the bird soon after I get it home from the grocery store, so that it's ready to roast the next day or the day after that.

Here's how do it: Unwrap the chicken over the sink and drain it if necessary. Remove the giblets if there are any, saving them if you like (see page 348 for more about giblets). Pat the chicken dry inside and out with paper towels. Then measure out ½ to a scant ¾ teaspoon of kosher salt per pound of chicken. Why the range? It depends in part on your taste for salt; I go for the full amount, but some people may prefer less. You should also use the smaller amount if you're salting for less than the minimum amount of time. If you use the larger amount for a shorter time, the surface of the chicken will taste too salty because the salt hasn't had time to penetrate and disperse evenly. (Even if you are on a low-sodium diet and use only a fraction of the recommended amount of salt, letting the chicken air dry for a day or two will result in crisper skin.)

Once you have measured the correct amount of salt, sprinkle it all over the surface of the chicken, including the back, thighs, and drumsticks, and put a little into the cavity as well.

Now is the time to add other seasonings—black pepper, if you like, as well as any other spices or herbs you're using. The reason is twofold. As the salt makes its way through the chicken, it will take in the other flavors as well. Also, as the salted chicken sits in the refrigerator, its skin dries out and becomes taut; spices sprinkled on just before roasting don't adhere as well unless you add some sort of lubricant, such as butter or olive oil.

Arrange the salted chicken on a wire rack (a cake cooling rack or roasting rack works well) set in a baking dish or on some kind of tray to catch any drips. (The rack allows the air to circulate and promotes crisper skin all over, but it's not absolutely necessary. If space is tight or you don't have a rack that fits, just set the chicken in a dish.) Refrigerate—ideally uncovered, but a loose covering of plastic wrap is fine—for at least 8 hours and up to 48 hours. (The optimum time is in 24 to 36 hours, but a little less or more won't hurt.) When you remove the chicken from the refrigerator, the surface will be dry with no trace of salt. All the salt will have been absorbed into the meat, leaving none to brush or rinse away. Let the chicken sit at room temperature for an hour before roasting.

Recommended Salt Amounts for Presalting Chicken

3-pound chicken
　　whole: 1 ½ to 2 teaspoons
　　butterflied: 1 ¼ to 1 ¾ teaspoons

3 ½-pound chicken
　　whole: 2 to 2 ½ teaspoons
　　butterflied: 1 ½ to 2 teaspoons

4-pound chicken
　　whole: 2 teaspoons to 1 tablespoon
　　butterflied: 1 ¾ to 2 ½ teaspoons

4 ½-pound chicken
　　whole: 2 ¼ to 3 ½ teaspoons
　　butterflied: 2 to 2 ¾ teaspoons

The amount of salt you choose depends on your taste, how long ahead you plan to salt, and the size of your bird.

These amounts are based on using Diamond Crystal kosher salt. Other kinds of salt may require adjustments (see page 29).

Why I don't rinse poultry

Anyone who has followed a poultry recipe from my earlier book, *All About Braising*, may be surprised by the title of this section. Yes, it's true: Throughout the braising book, I begin every poultry recipe by telling you to rinse the bird and then pat it dry, and for years I mindlessly rinsed poultry (especially chicken) as soon as I took it out of its packaging. Then, as I began developing recipes for this book, I was standing in my kitchen about to hold a perfectly wholesome chicken under my kitchen faucet and I had one of those rare moments of revelation. I realized that rinsing was not only unnecessary, it was a bad habit. For starters, many of us rinse poultry because we think it's more sanitary; in other words, we are somehow washing off any potential pathogens. The problem here is that by rinsing, you are actually spreading any harmful bacteria all over your kitchen sink, so unless you scrub your entire sink (and any counter surfaces that may have been splashed) with some sort of cleaning agent afterward, you are doing more harm than good. Also, unless you severely undercook your poultry (see page 260), any bad microbes will be killed during cooking.

Beyond the food safety question, rinsing poultry can have a negative effect on the appearance and taste of your recipes, especially when roasting. One of the primary goals of roasting is to develop a handsome brown crust, and this requires having a dry surface—the less moisture it has, the better the surface will crisp and brown. Wet poultry skin also has the unfortunate tendency to stick to the pan or roasting rack, so that it tears when you try to remove it. From a flavor standpoint, when we rinse, we are essentially washing away flavor, and worse, we water down the chicken's natural flavor. More so than red meat and pork, chicken (and other poultry) has a natural ability to absorb a good deal of water. When you're brining, this is a good thing, because the chicken will soak up the flavors and salt in the brine, which will enhance its flavor. Plain tap water, however, does nothing but dilute the natural juices and leave the chicken waterlogged and bland. Plus unsalted water added to poultry during rinsing merely leaks out during cooking, leaving the meat drier than it would be otherwise. Now the only time you'll find me rinsing poultry is if I've accidentally dropped it on the kitchen floor, in which case the quicker, the better.

To truss or not to truss?

Proper trussing refers to tying poultry into a snug bundle so the legs are tucked neatly and tightly alongside the breast and the wings are secured—again, tightly—behind the neck. The practice goes back to the days of spit-roasting, when an improperly trussed fowl would roast unevenly or, worse, flop off the spit and into the fire. Given the two reasons still cited by modern cooks for trussing—the chicken cooks more evenly and it looks prettier—I disagree with the former but can't argue with the latter. Since roasting relies on hot oven air circulating around the food, trussing actually interferes, by securing the legs close to the chicken body and protecting them (especially the joints) from the oven heat. As a result, the thigh joints of a trussed bird can take a very long time to roast, unless you are conscientious about turning so the chicken roasts back side up for a period. As for producing a more handsome bird, yes, a trussed bird will have a somewhat more polite, less splayed stance than an untrussed one, but unless you're snapping photos before you carve, I'm guessing no one will complain. If you like the notion of trussing, I suggest a compromise: Ignore any complicated cat's-cradle-style trussing instructions and simply tie the two drumsticks together with kitchen string. This approach gives you a prettier bird that roasts as evenly as an untrussed one.

What about basting?

I've written extensively on basting in the Principles of Roasting (page 23), but it's important to add one note about basting chicken. Since the basting liquid is somewhat cooler than the oven air (the liquid can't be hotter than 212 degrees without evaporating), it actually cools the breast and thereby slows the cooking, especially during the last half of the roasting time. Opening the oven door to baste also slows the cooking of the entire bird. However, most chickens don't release enough liquid on their own to make basting worthwhile, and since the whole notion of a simple roast chicken should be just that—simple—I don't usually bother to baste, unless I'm roasting a very big bird or I'm looking to enrich the pan drippings. If you'd like to go the extra step, consider adding some wine, broth, water, or other liquid to the pan at the beginning of roasting (or partway through if you want to give the drippings a chance to caramelize on the bottom of the dry pan). This added liquid then becomes your basting liquid.

Is it done yet?

Regardless of what roasting technique you use, the best chicken is one that's cooked to doneness and not too far beyond. An overcooked chicken loses much of its flavor and juiciness, while an undercooked bird is unappealingly pink and rubbery and possibly even unsafe. As with all roasts, a recipe can provide estimated cooking times, but the actual cooking time varies from oven to oven—and from chicken to chicken. There's also an element of personal taste, so it's up to the cook to determine exactly when to pull the chicken from the oven. With practice, you will be able to judge doneness easily by using your senses, but until you trust these, you may want to confirm by checking the internal temperature.

LOOK FOR VISUAL CLUES FOR DONENESS. When you can smell the aroma of roast chicken in the kitchen, it's time to open the oven and check it out. First, pierce the underside of a thigh with a skewer or the tine of a meat fork to see if the juices are pale. They don't need to be absolutely clear, but they should be mostly clear with only a faint trace of pink; if they are dramatically streaked with red, keep roasting. You can also test by inserting a meat fork, wooden spoon, or sturdy tongs into the cavity and tilting the chicken forward so the juices run into the roasting pan. As the chicken cooks, the juices in the cavity first become murky and pinkish gray (an indication that the chicken is not done). When the chicken is ready, the juices in the cavity will be mostly clear with some darker red streaks. You don't need to wait for the juices to be completely clear; this is a sign that the chicken is overdone. Also look at the drumsticks: The skin will begin to shrink back around the knobby ends as the chicken reaches doneness. You can try wiggling a drumstick in its socket; if the chicken is cooked through, it will feel somewhat loose.

USE A THERMOMETER TO DOUBLE-CHECK. To be on the safe side, it's a good practice to insert an instant-read thermometer into the thigh of a whole bird to check for doneness (see How to Take a Chicken's Temperature, page 262). In the recipes in this book, I generally recommend that the thighs register 170 degrees. But at the risk of sounding unhelpful, I encourage you to decide for yourself what temperature best suits your taste. If you prefer chicken firmer, aim high (say, 175 degrees). If you value juiciness above all, stay on the low end of the scale (165 degrees). Many chefs, particularly French or French-trained ones, pull the chicken out of the oven at 160 degrees. At this temperature, the chicken is safe to eat (salmonella cannot survive temperatures above 160 degrees), but it may still seem underdone for some tastes. So what's a cook to do? I would suggest that there is some flexibility in deciding when the chicken is done and that there is no single magic temperature at which chicken goes from underdone to overdone. The correct doneness temperature depends on several factors: whether it's white meat or dark meat, whether the bird has been salted or brined, what kind of chicken it is, and, perhaps most important, what your preference is. Here are a few things that will help you determine your preferred doneness:

• Dark meat tolerates higher temperatures than white meat does. In fact, dark meat begins to turn tender and succulent at temperatures above 165 degrees. I've enjoyed it cooked as high as 185, even 190, with no trace of drying out. That said, even the most thoroughly cooked chicken may have tinges of red around the thigh joint. Don't be alarmed; as long as the thigh and leg meat registers above 160 degrees, the chicken is safe to eat. When I am roasting only dark meat (as in Basic Roast Chicken Thighs, page 311), I prefer the legs well done (180 to 190 degrees), so that they nearly fall off the bone and are satisfyingly tender. When roasting a whole chicken, however, I reach a compromise, leaving the dark meat at 170 degrees so the breast won't overcook.

• Presalting (or brining) does wonders for keeping chicken moist even as the temperature climbs. For instance, a chicken breast that has not been presalted will have already lost much of its moisture (and flavor) as the temperature reaches 165, whereas a presalted one can be cooked upwards of 175 degrees and still be tender and moist.

How to Take a Chicken's Temperature

Start with the chicken cavity facing you and insert the probe of an instant-read thermometer into the inside of the thigh, between the thigh and the breast. Maneuver the probe so you pierce the meatiest part of the thigh without hitting the leg socket. It's best to take two or three readings, noting the lowest temperature, just to be sure you're not hitting a bone or fat deposit that could throw off the reading. Also take care not to push the thermometer so far that it comes out the other side, where you'll be reading the air temperature (trust me, I've done this often). You can double-check the thicker end of the breast, up near the neck opening, which should be in the 170-degree range, but I rarely do, as I've never known the breast to be underdone if the thighs are cooked through.

BASIC ROAST CHICKEN

This is what I make when I want a straight-up, no-fuss, delicious roast chicken. The keys here are buying a good chicken *and* buying the right size chicken (4 pounds or less) so that you can roast it quickly in a hot oven to crisp the skin. (A bigger chicken requires moderate heat to cook evenly, so if that's what you bring home from the market, turn to Sunday Supper Roast Chicken, on page 271). Another secret to a superb roast chicken is seasoning the bird ahead of time (anywhere from 8 to 48 hours). To my mind, one of the greatest of kitchen miracles is the way a couple teaspoons of salt improve the taste and texture of a chicken when applied ahead of time.

Once you've bought a good chicken and seasoned it ahead if you've had time, then it's merely a matter of setting it on a few thick slices of onion or lemon (my choice is usually based on what I have on hand) in a gratin dish or large skillet, popping it into a hot oven, and waiting for it to be done. A shallow-sided pan like a skillet or flameproof gratin dish, is essential to prevent a pale underside. The onion and/or lemon slices eliminate the need for a roasting rack while keeping the skin from sticking to the bottom of the pan. They also add a bit of good flavor to the drippings, the lemon some piquancy and the onion an earthy sweetness. (You can even use both together, though you'll have half a lemon and half an onion left over.)

I love this recipe as much for its simplicity as for its reliability. It's just plain good. Most times I serve it unadorned, doing nothing more with the pan drippings than drizzling them directly over the carved chicken—or just sopping them up with a crust of bread to snack on when on one's looking. Other times, especially if company's coming, I turn the pan drippings into a quick *jus* to drizzle on after carving (see page 268). You can also jazz up the chicken by giving it a spice rub, like the one on page 269, or by smearing a flavored butter (page 269) under the skin. I sometimes pass a stand-alone sauce such as Romesco (page 291) or a chutney to spoon onto the plate.

SERVES 3 TO 4

METHOD: High heat

ROASTING TIME: 1 to 1 1/4 hours

PLAN AHEAD: For the best-tasting, juiciest chicken possible, presalt the chicken at least 8 hours and up to 48 hours before roasting.

WINE: Richer whites, like a well-oaked Chardonnay, pair beautifully with basic roast chicken, as well as with the simple *jus* and herb-butter options.

One 3½- to 4-pound chicken

Kosher salt and freshly ground black
  pepper

1 lemon or 1 medium onion, ends cut off,
  cut into ½-inch-thick rounds

2 teaspoons extra-virgin olive oil or
  unsalted butter, softened

1 **TRIM AND SEASON THE CHICKEN.** Over the sink, remove the giblets (they should be tucked into the cavity) and discard or reserve for another use. Hold the chicken over the drain and let any juices run out. Pat it dry inside and out with paper towels. With your fingers, pull away and discard any large deposits of fat from the neck or body cavity opening. If you are presalting the chicken, refer to the directions and salt amounts on pages 257–58. If not presalting, season the chicken generously all over with salt and pepper, including the cavity. Let the chicken stand at room temperature for about 1 hour before roasting.

2 **HEAT THE OVEN.** Position a rack in the center of the oven and heat to 400 degrees (375 degrees convection).

3 **ROAST THE CHICKEN.** Arrange the lemon or onion slices in a single layer in the center of a large ovenproof skillet (11 to 12 inches) or a flameproof gratin dish (8 by 11 inches); you can also use a small, low-sided roasting pan. Place the chicken on top of the lemon or onion slices and tuck the wing tips back so they are secure under the neck bone. Rub the olive oil or butter evenly over the breast and legs and roast, with the legs facing the rear of the oven (the back of the oven is usually hotter, so this helps the legs cook more quickly than the breast). Continue roasting until the juices run clear with only a trace of pink when you prick the thigh and an instant-read thermometer inserted in the thickest part of the thigh (without touching bone) registers 170 degrees, 1 to 1¼ hours. Lift the chicken with a meat fork or sturdy tongs inserted in the cavity and carefully tilt to pour the juices from the cavity into the roasting pan.

4 **REST AND CARVE.** Transfer the chicken to a carving board (preferably one with a trough) and let it rest for 10 to 20 minutes before carving and serving.

5 **PREPARE THE DRIPPINGS AND SERVE.** Examine the drippings in the pan and decide whether you'd like to use them or simply ignore them (both are fine approaches). To use the drippings, remove the onion and/or lemon, scraping off any juices adhering to the slices before discarding (resist the impulse to squeeze the lemon, as it can add too much bitterness). Tilt the pan to evaluate the drippings. If a lot of clear fat is floating on the surface, spoon it off (you can save it to make a vinaigrette, as directed on p. 268, or discard). If there's only a thin layer of fat, I leave it, as I like the richness it adds. Use a wooden spoon to scrape up any caramelized bits. Now you can use the roasting pan as a serving dish and return the carved pieces to the pan, turning them so they get coated with the drippings. Alternatively, scrape the drippings onto the carved chicken; you won't have enough to sauce the chicken, you're merely getting every last drop of flavor. Finally, if the drippings are cooked onto the roasting pan, warm the pan over medium heat and add a few tablespoons of water (or chicken broth or dry white wine if you have it handy) to dissolve them, and drizzle them over the carved chicken.

CONTINUED ON PAGE 268

Carving a Chicken

THE GOAL IS TO CARVE THE CHICKEN INTO 2 DRUMSTICKS, 2 BONE-IN THIGHS, 2 WINGS, AND CHUNKS OF BONELESS BREAST MEAT. I FIND THIS METHOD GIVES just the right assortment of light and dark meat so that everyone at the table gets something they like. Before you begin, have a serving platter or the roasting pan nearby to arrange the pieces as you carve; even a large cutting board becomes crowded once you start breaking down the bird. Choose a comfortable, sharp knife (I prefer an 8-inch blade), and I find a meat fork or a pair of locking tongs indispensable for holding the hot bird while I carve.

Begin with the legs facing you, and slit the loose skin between the leg and the breast. Using the fork (or tongs), bend the leg away from the breast, pushing it toward the cutting board to expose the ball-and–socket joint where the thigh-bone connects to the back. Now maneuver the tip of the knife into the leg joint and slice though the cartilage (you should not have to cut through bone, but you may need to wiggle your knife to find the right spot). Remove the leg, doing your best to get as much of the meat that tucks around underneath the chicken as you can. Set the leg skin side down on the cutting board, and separate it into a thigh and drumstick by slicing neatly through the knee joint (again, you're cutting easily through cartilage, if you encounter bone, reposition your knife). Next, remove the wing assembly by slicing into the very top of the breast and cut through the shoulder joint where the wing meets the breast. Removing the wing this way turns it into a tasty portion offering a juicy nugget of breast meat along with crispy skin and dark wing meat. Finally, carve the breast meat off the carcass by slicing lengthwise flush with the breastbone, doing your best to remove all the breast meat and leaving the breastbone as clean as possible.You can leave the breast whole, or, if you want to serve a mix of white and dark meat, place the breast skin side up on the cutting board and slice it crosswise into ¾- to 1-inch-thick pieces, being mindful of keeping the crisp skin attached to each piece. Repeat on the second side of the chicken. After carving, check the carcass to see if you've left any large pieces of meat. If so, carve them off and tuck them onto the platter. Pour any juices that have accumulated on the cutting board over the chicken or into the pan drippings or any pan sauce you may be making, and serve immediately.

Step by Step: Carving a Chicken

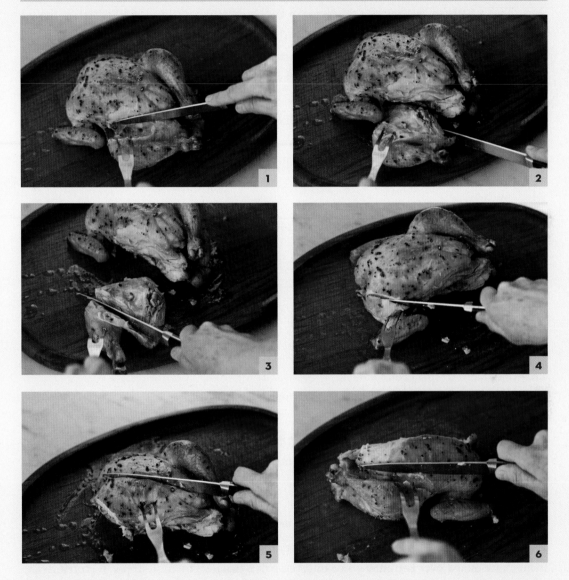

1 Slit the loose skin between the leg and the breast, and bend the leg away from the breast, pushing it toward the cutting board. **2** Once you expose the ball-and-socket joint, slice though the cartilage and remove the leg, doing your best to get as much of the meat that tucks around underneath the chicken as you can. **3** Set the leg skin side down on the cutting board, and separate it into a thigh and drumstick by slicing neatly though the knee joint. **4** Remove the wing by slicing into the very top of the breast and cutting through the shoulder joint where the wing meets the breast. **5** Remove the breast meat by slicing lengthwise flush with the breastbone, doing your best to remove all the breast meat and leaving the breastbone as clean as possible. Leave the breast whole, or slice crosswise. **6** Turn the chicken and repeat on the second side.

OPTION 1: GREEN SALAD WITH A VINAIGRETTE MADE FROM PAN DRIPPINGS

A simple lettuce salad makes a fine accompaniment to roast chicken, and one way to give that salad a little more flavor—and to make the most of what's on hand—is to use the fat skimmed off the pan drippings in place of most of the olive oil for the dressing. I generally get about 2 tablespoons fat from a basic roast chicken, to which I add 1 tablespoon extra-virgin olive oil. You can play around with this ratio according to how much fat your chicken renders and your own taste.

This is not like a hot-bacon vinaigrette where the dressing wilts the greens. The chicken fat will be warm to start, but by the time you skim it and whisk it in, it will have cooled to room temperature. Try this with tender Boston lettuce or something sharper, such as arugula or frisée, or a combination.

MAKES ABOUT 1/4 CUP, ENOUGH TO DRESS A LETTUCE SALAD FOR 3 TO 4

1 tablespoon minced shallots

1 tablespoon wine vinegar, preferably red or sherry

¼ teaspoon Dijon mustard

Kosher salt and freshly ground black pepper

2 tablespoons fat skimmed from the roasting pan (substitute some olive oil if there is not enough fat from the chicken)

1 tablespoon extra-virgin olive oil

AS THE CHICKEN RESTS, whisk together the shallots, vinegar, and mustard. Season lightly with salt and pepper. Whisk in the fat and the olive oil. Drizzle over the greens, toss, and serve.

OPTION 2: BASIC ROAST CHICKEN WITH A SIMPLE *JUS*

With a modicum of effort and one or two more ingredients, you can turn the pan drippings from Basic Roast Chicken into a savory *jus*, or pan sauce. The first step is to retrieve the giblets before roasting (with the exception of the liver, which should be saved for another use or discarded; for more on giblets, see page 348). Arrange them in the skillet or roasting pan alongside the lemon or onion slices in step 3 before placing the chicken on top. The giblets roast alongside the chicken and enhance the flavor of the pan drippings—it's as if you're making a little roasted chicken broth. Then, after the chicken has roasted for 25 minutes, pour ¼ to ½ cup of dry white wine, dry vermouth, chicken broth, or water over the breast. (Use the larger amount if the pan is very dry.) Continue to roast as directed.

After transferring the chicken to a carving board to rest in step 4, set the skillet or roasting pan over a burner set to medium heat and evaluate the drippings. If there is less than ½ cup of liquid, or if there are a lot of caramelized and cooked-on drippings on the bottom of the pan, add ¼ to ½ cup more dry white wine, vermouth, chicken broth, or water to the pan and scrape to deglaze. If there is plenty of liquid in the pan, skip the deglazing step. Remove the giblets and the lemon or onion slices and discard. (Scrape any drippings from the lemon or onion, but don't squeeze the lemon as its juices can be bitter.) Transfer the *jus* to a small saucepan or heatproof measuring cup and skim off any visible surface fat. Taste, and add a few drops of fresh lemon juice and season with salt and pepper as needed. Keep warm while carving, and add any chicken juices from carving to the *jus*. You should have about ½ to ⅔ cup of *jus*—plenty to serve 3 to 4 people. Moisten each serving with a little *jus* and pass any extra at the table.

OPTION 3: BASIC ROAST CHICKEN WITH HERB BUTTER

Rubbing a little bit of flavored butter (also called compound butter) under the chicken skin adds good flavor and richness to any roast chicken. It also helps to crisp up the skin. You can use your own favorite flavored butter or a purchased butter such as truffle butter, or you can make a basic herb butter simply by mixing together 2 tablespoons of softened unsalted butter and 2 heaping teaspoons of chopped fresh herbs of your choice. I'm particularly fond of sage and rosemary with chicken, but thyme and parsley are also delicious, and a mix of several herbs is good too. Use your fingertips to gently loosen the skin over the breast and thighs of the chicken, starting at the cavity opening, and work most of the butter under the skin, smearing it over the breast and thighs. (If you're presalting the chicken, you can rub the butter under the skin before or after you salt.) Rub a small amount of butter (the little bit left on your hands will do) over the surface of the chicken, mostly on the breast but some on the thighs and legs. Roast as directed in the Basic Roast Chicken recipe. You can use this same method with your favorite pesto; use about ⅓ cup and slather it under the skin in the same way.

OPTION 4: SPICE-RUBBED BASIC ROAST CHICKEN

A homemade spice rub adds a fragrant and somewhat exotic note to Basic Roast Chicken. The only downside of this recipe is that the crispy spiced skin is so good that the cook may have to restrain herself or himself from tearing bits off to snack on as the chicken rests.

CONTINUED ON NEXT PAGE

You can improvise with any favorite spice combinations, but I turn to this one often. The cinnamon is subtle, adding just a little intrigue without overpowering.

MAKES ENOUGH SPICE RUB FOR ONE WHOLE 3 1/2- TO 4-POUND CHICKEN

PLAN AHEAD: For the best flavor, season the chicken 24 to 48 hours ahead.

WINE: Youthful, fruity Pinot Noir from California's Carneros or Russian River Valley.

1 teaspoon whole coriander seeds	½ teaspoon ground cinnamon
1 teaspoon whole cumin seeds	Pinch of cayenne
1 teaspoon paprika, sweet or hot	Kosher salt
½ teaspoon freshly ground black pepper	One 3 ½- to 4-pound chicken

IN A DRY SKILLET over medium heat, toast the coriander and cumin seeds, shaking frequently, until fragrant and slightly darkened, 1 to 2 minutes. Let cool and then grind to a powder in a mortar or spice grinder. Transfer to a small bowl and combine with the paprika, black pepper, cinnamon, and cayenne. Add salt (if presalting, use the amount of salt called for in the chart on page 258; otherwise, just add salt to taste). Rub the spice rub all over the outside of the chicken and rub a little inside the cavity. Proceed as directed in the Basic Roast Chicken recipe.

SUNDAY SUPPER ROAST CHICKEN WITH BACON AND ROOT VEGETABLES

This one-dish meal deserves to be the centerpiece of a cozy family supper or a casual gathering of friends. It's not meant to be fancy or elegant; it's just very tasty and satisfying. For the full effect, you'll need a relatively big chicken, one that's 5 to 5½ pounds—sometimes labeled as oven-roasters. (If you can only find smaller chickens, see the option that follows.) To prevent the breast from drying out I use a moderate oven, and I sneak some diced bacon under the skin before roasting. As the bacon slowly renders its fat, it moistens the breast while imparting some smoky goodness. For even more flavor, I brush the bird with melted butter mixed with balsamic vinegar and honey. This tangy-sweet glaze turns the breast gorgeously brown and more than makes up for any loss of browning you get from roasting in a moderate oven. The root vegetables—think carrots, parsnips, turnips, and beets (the choice is yours, as long as they're hardy)—share the roasting pan with the chicken. Not only does this allow the vegetables to soak up plenty of savory juices as they roast, but there's also one less pan to clean.

SERVES 4 TO 6

METHOD: Moderate heat

ROASTING TIME: About 1 1/2 hours

PLAN AHEAD: For the best-tasting, juiciest chicken, presalt the chicken at least 8 hours and up to 48 hours before roasting.

WINE/BEER: Fruity young Garnacha blend from Navarra Spain or Côte du Rhône Villages; or a rich export-style Stout.

CONTINUED ON PAGE 273

SUNDAY SUPPER ROAST CHICKEN WITH BACON AND
ROOT VEGETABLES (PAGE 271)

One 5- to 6-pound chicken

1 medium-thick slice of bacon (about 1 ounce), diced

Kosher salt and freshly ground black pepper

2½ to 3 pounds mixed root vegetables, such as carrots, potatoes, parsnips, beets, turnips, celery root, and/or rutabaga, trimmed, peeled or scrubbed if left unpeeled, and cut into 1½- to 2-inch pieces (about 5 cups)

2 tablespoons extra-virgin olive oil, plus more as needed

1 tablespoon dried herbes de Provence (see page 275), plus more as needed

1½ tablespoons unsalted butter

1½ teaspoons balsamic vinegar

1 teaspoon honey

1 medium onion, ends cut off, cut into ½-inch-thick rounds

1 **TRIM AND SEASON THE CHICKEN.** Over the sink, remove the giblets and discard or reserve for another use. Drain off any liquid and dry the chicken inside and out with paper towels. Pull off and discard any large deposits of fat from the neck or body cavity opening. Use your fingertips to gently loosen the skin over the breast of the chicken, starting at the cavity opening, and push the diced bacon under the skin, doing your best to spread it evenly over the breast. If you are presalting the chicken, refer to the directions and salt amounts on pages 257–58, but use the amount suggested for a 4-pound chicken because of the extra salt in the bacon. If not presalting, season the chicken generously all over with salt and pepper. Let the chicken stand at room temperature for about 1 hour.

2 **HEAT THE OVEN.** Position a rack in the center of the oven and heat to 375 degrees (350 degrees convection).

3 **SEASON THE VEGETABLES.** Place all of the vegetables except the red beets, if using, in a large mixing bowl; if you're using red beets, place them in a separate bowl so they don't stain the other vegetables. Drizzle with the 2 tablespoons oil and season with the 1 tablespoon herbes de Provence, salt, and pepper, tossing to coat. (For beets, add just enough oil to coat very lightly and a pinch of the herbes, salt, and pepper.)

4 **MAKE THE GLAZE.** Melt the butter in a small saucepan. Whisk in the vinegar and honey and set aside in a warm place.

CONTINUED ON NEXT PAGE

5 ROAST THE CHICKEN AND VEGETABLES. Arrange the onion slices in a single layer in the center of a low-sided roasting pan (I use a 14-by-12-inch pan). Set the chicken breast side up on the onion slices and tie the legs together using kitchen string, if you want the bird to look spiffy when it comes out of the oven (see page 259 for more on trussing).

Arrange the vegetables all around. They should be in a dense single layer, but don't worry if they are a little crowded; they will shrink as they roast. Slide the chicken into the oven, preferably with the legs facing away from the door. After 25 minutes, brush the breast and drumsticks with some of the glaze and nudge the vegetables around with a metal spatula to promote even cooking (don't worry if you can't stir them thoroughly; it's nice to have some more browned than others). Continue roasting, brushing on additional glaze and stirring the vegetables at 20-minute intervals, until the chicken juices run clear with only a trace of pink when you prick the thigh and an instant-read thermometer inserted in the thickest part of the thigh (without touching bone) registers 170 degrees, a total of 1⅓ to 1⅔ hours. If at any point the chicken seems to be getting darker on one side than the other, rotate the pan in the oven.

6 REST, CARVE, AND SERVE. Transfer the chicken to a carving board (preferably one with a trough to catch the juices) and let it rest for about 20 minutes. Leave the sliced onions in the pan with the other vegetables, and give all the vegetables a good stir with a metal spatula, scraping up any browned bits and coating them with pan juices. Poke a few different vegetables with the tip of a knife to be sure they are nice and tender; if not, return the pan to the oven for 10 minutes or so to finish roasting the vegetables as the chicken rests. If the vegetables are done, set them aside in a warm spot as the chicken rests. Carve the chicken (see page 266) and serve it with the vegetables, stirring the vegetables before serving so they are coated with pan drippings.

OPTION: SUNDAY SUPPER LITTLE ROAST CHICKENS AND ROOT VEGETABLES

If you can't find a large roasting chicken or you simply prefer smaller birds (or because, like me, you sometimes want more wings and legs to go around), substitute two 3- to 3¼-pound chickens in the recipe above. Cut the vegetables into 1-inch pieces (as opposed to 1½- to 2-inch chunks) to accommodate a shorter roasting time. You'll also need a larger roasting pan (13 by 16 inches works) or a heavy-duty rimmed baking sheet. Expect the chickens to be done in 1 hour to 1 hour and 10 minutes.

Herbes de Provence

HERBES DE PROVENCE IS A BLEND OF DRIED HERBS THAT CAPTURES THE ESSENCE OF THE SUN-SOAKED MEDITERRANEAN CUISINE OF THE REGION OF Provence in southeastern France. At its origin, the term referred to homemade blends local cooks concocted from the wild herbs growing in the arid inland area known as haute Provence. Today jars and tins of herbes de Provence are sold in the spice section of most well-stocked supermarkets and specialty food shops. (The most recognizable brand comes in a small clay crock under the label Aux Anysetiers du Roy.) Whatever the brand, the blend commonly includes thyme, summer savory, marjoram, rosemary, basil, bay leaf, fennel seed, and lavender flowers.

SKILLET-ROASTED CHICKEN

This is the roast chicken recipe for cooks—and eaters—who are finicky about getting the back of a chicken as browned as the breast. The key is to preheat a large, heavy skillet—ideally a 12-inch cast-iron one—in a very hot oven until the skillet is ripping hot. Then you place the whole chicken directly on the hot surface to give the meaty thighs a head start and insure that the back gets as brown as the top. Following the initial blast of heat, lower the oven temperature to enable the chicken to cook through without drying out. Adding ¼ cup of dry vermouth or white wine or water about halfway through roasting achieves two purposes: It helps prevent the chicken from sticking to the skillet and it forms the base for a flavorful little pan sauce.

As with most of my chicken recipes, I suggest presalting for the best flavor (see page 257). Another flavor boost: smearing a bit of soft butter under the skin, which bastes the chicken and helps the exterior to brown and crisp. To really make the most of this step, use a good, high-butterfat butter, such as Vermont Butter & Cheese Creamery or Kerrygold.

SERVES 3 TO 4
METHOD: Combination high heat and moderate heat
ROASTING TIME: About 55 minutes
PLAN AHEAD: For the best-tasting, juiciest chicken possible, presalt the chicken at least 8 hours and up to 48 hours before roasting.
WINE: Rich, fuller whites, such as well-oaked Chardonnay.

One 3½- to 4-pound chicken
Kosher salt and freshly ground black
  pepper
1½ tablespoons unsalted butter, softened

¼ cup dry vermouth, dry white wine,
  or water
½ lemon (if making the sauce)

1 **TRIM AND SEASON THE CHICKEN.** Over the sink, remove the giblets (they are usually tucked into the cavity). Reserve them for another use or discard. Hold the chicken over the drain and let any juice run out. Pat the chicken dry with paper towels inside and out. With your fingers, pull away and discard any large deposits of fat from the neck or body cavity opening. If you are presalting the chicken, refer to the directions and salt amounts on pages 257–58. If not presalting, season the chicken all over with salt. Let the chicken stand at room temperature for about 1 hour.

2 HEAT THE OVEN AND A SKILLET. Position a rack in the center of the oven and heat to 450 degrees (425 degrees convection). After the oven has heated for 30 minutes, slide a large heavy-duty skillet (I prefer a 12-inch cast-iron one) into the oven and heat the skillet for 20 minutes.

3 BUTTER THE CHICKEN. While the skillet heats, gently loosen the skin over the breast and thighs of the chicken, starting at the body cavity opening. With your fingers, work most of the butter under the skin. Spread it over the breast and thighs, being careful not to tear the skin. Rub the remaining butter over the surface of the chicken, concentrating on the breast but smearing a thin film on the back and legs as well. Grind some pepper over the breast and legs; it will adhere to the butter rubbed on the skin. Tuck the wing tips back so they are secure behind the neck opening.

4 ROAST AND REST THE CHICKEN. Put the chicken in the skillet breast side up and roast for 10 minutes. Without opening the oven, lower the temperature to 350 degrees (325 degrees convection) and continue roasting. After another 15 minutes, pour the vermouth, wine, or water over the chicken. Be careful when you open the oven, as the initial blast of high heat may have created some smoke; this will calm down as the oven temperature moderates. Continue roasting until the juices run clear with only a trace of pink and an instant-read thermometer inserted into the thickest part of the thigh (without touching bone) registers 170 degrees, another 30 minutes (for a total cooking time of about 55 minutes).

Lift the chicken by grasping the cavity with tongs or a meat fork and carefully tilt it to pour the juices into the roasting pan. Transfer the chicken to a carving board (preferably one with a trough) to rest for 10 to 20 minutes.

5 MAKE A QUICK PAN SAUCE, IF YOU LIKE. Using a pot holder, return the skillet with the pan juices to a burner set over medium heat. If there appears to be more than 2 or 3 tablespoons of fat, skim and spoon some off, but don't remove all the fat, as it gives richness to the sauce. Add a squeeze of lemon juice and bring to a simmer, stirring with a wooden spoon to dissolve any cooked-on drippings. Season with salt and pepper, if needed, and keep the sauce warm.

6 CARVE AND SERVE. Carve the chicken (see page 266). Add any juices released during carving to the sauce, if using, and serve the chicken with the sauce spooned over it.

CONTINUED ON NEXT PAGE

OPTION: **SKILLET-ROASTED CHICKEN WITH SHREDDED CABBAGE SLAW**

This wonderful way of serving roast chicken comes from my friend Maura O'Sullivan, a very talented (and generous) chef in Burlington, Vermont. The idea is simple, but it's genius. All you do is shred up some cabbage while the chicken roasts. Pile the cabbage on a serving platter and drizzle the warm savory juices from the roasting pan right over it. Then you carve the chicken into pieces and arrange them on the cabbage to serve; the hot chicken pieces wilt the cabbage slightly yet leave it crunchy enough to be refreshing. While you could serve just about any roast chicken this way, I prefer Skillet-Roasted Chicken because of the generous amount of buttery drippings it creates—enough to "dress" the slaw amply.

I make this dish in late summer, when the first heads of crunchy green cabbage appear at the farmers' market, but you can make it anytime and use any cabbage you like, including red and Savoy. Unless you find a very small head (as you may at the farmers' market), you will need to halve or even quarter the cabbage to get the amount you need (about 8 cups shredded). No matter what cabbage you use, the key is to slice it thinly. If you own a mandoline, this would be a good time to use it.

SERVES 3 TO 4

PLAN AHEAD: The slaw is quick to make, but the cabbage will have a nice crisp texture if you salt it 1 to 2 hours before serving, so begin this step before you heat the oven for the chicken.

WINE: Rich, deeply fruity Pinot Gris from Alsace or Oregon.

One 1- to 1¼-pound cabbage, green, Savoy, or red

Kosher salt

Juice from ½ lemon

Freshly ground black pepper

Skillet-Roasted Chicken, made through step 5, pan juices reserved in the skillet

Olive oil, if needed

1 **SLICE AND SALT THE CABBAGE.** Cut the cabbage into wedges and cut away the core. Shred the cabbage quarters by thinly slicing crosswise. Ideally, the shreds should be no more than ⅛-inch thick, and you should have about 8 cups. Put the cabbage in a colander and set the colander over a larger bowl. Sprinkle with 1 tablespoon salt, toss to coat, and set aside at room temperature for 1 to 2 hours, tossing to redistribute the salt every 30 minutes or so. The salt will draw some moisture out of the cabbage, which is why the colander is in the bowl. Just before serving, taste a shred of cabbage for salt. Sometimes the released moisture rinses away most of the salt; other

times the cabbage tastes too salty. If that is the case, rinse the cabbage quickly under cold water and squeeze it dry. If the cabbage tastes just right, simply give it a good shake to eliminate excess moisture.

2 **SEASON AND DRESS THE CABBAGE.** While the chicken rests, pile the shredded cabbage onto a large serving platter. (I use a 15-by-12-inch oval platter.) Squeeze the juice from the ½ lemon over the cabbage and season it generously with black pepper.

Reheat the pan juices from the chicken, if necessary, scraping the skillet to capture any cooked-on drippings. You want about 2 tablespoons fat as well as the juices in the pan. If there looks to be too much fat, spoon some off. If, however, there is very little fat in the pan, add a tablespoon of olive oil (think of this as a salad dressing). Drizzle the juices over the cabbage and toss lightly with tongs to distribute. Taste for seasoning.

3 **CARVE AND SERVE.** Carve the chicken (see page 266) and arrange the pieces on top of the cabbage, covering as much of the slaw as you can. Pour any juices that have accumulated on the cutting board over them and serve immediately, being sure to provide a large serving spoon to scoop up the slaw and juices.

ROASTED CHICKEN WITH LEMONY GARLIC-PARSLEY PAN SAUCE

This roast chicken is a little dressy, thanks to a flavorful pan sauce based on ordinary ingredients you are likely to have on hand: lemon, parsley, white wine, and garlic. Best of all, the sauce gains a depth of flavor thanks to two classic roasting techniques: using a roasting rack and basting. The rack lifts the chicken off the bottom of the pan and allows the drippings to caramelize as they fall and hit the hot pan. The result is darker, more savory drippings, but you do have to take care not to let the drippings get too dark—toasty brown drippings we want, scorched we don't. To avoid burned bits, I add a measure of chicken broth partway through roasting. I also toss the giblets (if they came tucked into the chicken) into the roasting pan so that they roast alongside the chicken and further enrich the drippings. The giblets get discarded before serving, but they leave behind tremendous flavor—it's like making roasted chicken broth right in the pan. Basting also deepens the flavor of the liquid; each time I spoon the drippings over the chicken, they become richer-tasting. The final secret to this sauce is the garlic, which roasts right along with the chicken to become sweet and tender. To finish, push the softened garlic cloves through a sieve to make a puree that adds body and sweetness to the sauce.

SERVES 4

METHOD: High heat

ROASTING TIME: 1 to 1 1/3 hours

PLAN AHEAD: For the best-tasting, juiciest chicken, presalt the chicken at least 8 hours and up to 48 hours before roasting.

WINE: Intensely fruity and herbal Sauvignon Blanc from New Zealand's Marlborough region or South Africa.

One 3½ to 4-pound chicken, preferably
   including giblets
1 lemon, cut in half
Kosher salt and freshly ground black
   pepper
8 garlic cloves, peeled
1 teaspoon extra-virgin olive oil

4 to 5 sprigs fresh flat-leaf parsley plus ½
   cup chopped parsley
1¼ cups homemade or store-bought low-
   sodium chicken broth, or as needed
½ cup dry white wine or dry vermouth plus
   more as needed

1   **TRIM AND SEASON THE CHICKEN.** Over the sink, remove the giblets (they should be tucked into the cavity). Reserve the heart, neck, and gizzard. (Discard the liver or save it for another use.) Hold the chicken over the drain and let any juice run out. Pat the chicken dry inside and out with paper towels. With your fingers, pull away and discard any large deposits of fat from the neck or body cavity opening. If you are presalting the chicken, refer to the directions and salt amounts on pages 257–58. If not presalting, rub the chicken all over with one lemon half, squeezing the lemon as you go to release the juice (save the spent lemon half), and season the chicken generously all over with salt and pepper. Let the chicken stand at room temperature for about 1 hour.

2   **HEAT THE OVEN.** Position a rack in the center of the oven and heat to 400 degrees (375 degrees convection).

3   **ROAST THE CHICKEN.** In a medium, low-sided roasting pan or flameproof gratin dish (about 8 by 11 inches), toss the garlic and reserved giblets (neck, heart, and gizzard) with the olive oil. Set a roasting rack over the garlic and giblets. If you presalted, now rub the chicken all over with one lemon half, squeezing the lemon as you go to release the juice. Put the squeezed lemon half in the chicken's cavity along with the parsley sprigs and reserve the remaining lemon half for the sauce. If desired, use kitchen string to tie the legs together (this gives the roasted chicken a more presentable appearance). Fold the wing tips back so they stay tucked behind the neck bone. Put the chicken breast side up on the roasting rack.

    Roast the chicken, with the legs facing the rear wall of the oven, for 25 minutes. After 25 minutes, open the oven door and pour ¾ cup of broth over the breast of the chicken; the broth will baste the breast and drain into the roasting pan. Continue roasting, basting the chicken once or twice as it roasts by spooning the pan drippings

CONTINUED ON NEXT PAGE

over the top and adding more broth to the pan by ¼ cupfuls if the pan appears to be drying out, until the juices run clear with only a trace of pink when you prick a thigh and an instant-read thermometer inserted in the thickest part of the thigh (without touching bone) registers 170 degrees, another 35 to 55 minutes (the time will depend somewhat on how many times you open the oven door to add broth).

4 **MAKE THE SAUCE.** Lift the chicken with tongs or a meat fork and carefully tilt it to pour the juices from the cavity into the roasting pan. Transfer the chicken to a carving board (preferably one with a trough to catch any juices) and let it rest for 10 to 20 minutes.

Strain the pan juices through a sturdy fine-mesh strainer set over a heatproof measuring cup, pressing on the solids to force the garlic pulp through. Spoon the visible fat from the surface with a small spoon. You should have at least ½ cup of liquid; if you have less, add enough broth to compensate.

On top of the stove, set the roasting pan over medium heat. Add the wine or vermouth to the pan and scrape the bottom of the pan with a wooden spoon to dislodge any browned bits. As soon as the wine begins to simmer, add the strained pan juices. Continue to stir until heated through, about 1 minute. Add a generous squeeze of juice from the reserved lemon half (about 2 teaspoons) and the chopped parsley and stir. Season to taste with salt and pepper, and keep the sauce warm.

5 **CARVE AND SERVE.** Carve the chicken (see page 266), adding any juices from the cutting board to the sauce. Drizzle each serving with a little sauce and serve.

GINGER ROAST CHICKEN AND ELBOW MACARONI WITH TOMATOES AND PAN SAUCE

This is what I call a sleeper recipe. At first glance it doesn't look like much—a whole chicken rubbed with a little fresh ginger, roasted, and served alongside elbow macaroni tossed with diced tomatoes and the roasting juices. Exactly what makes this dish so remarkable is hard to pinpoint, but there's a wonderful alchemy that occurs when the chicken, ginger, and tomato all come together. It's comforting, a little exotic, and truly delicious. To create a maximum of pan juices—since these become the sauce for the noodles—I add the giblets to the roasting pan and pour a bit of white wine over the chicken partway through roasting. During roasting, the drippings, the wine, and the roasted giblets cook together, creating a savory *jus*. The chicken also roasts on a rack to encourage the drippings to caramelize a bit as they hit the hot pan, developing even more flavor. I make this year-round using canned tomatoes, but if you make it in the summer, by all means use fresh ripe tomatoes.

The inspiration for this dish come from *Lulu's Provençal Table*, by Richard Olney, one of my favorite cookbooks of all time. When I first read the recipe, I was immediately taken with the idea of tossing roasting juices onto hot pasta. In this version, I've tweaked the flavors and method some, but the concept of combining tomatoes, ginger, and pan drippings remains true to the original. I confess that I did experiment with other shapes of pasta, thinking that a different shape might make the dish more sophisticated, but I returned to the simplicity and familiarity of elbow macaroni. If you decide to branch out, choose a short shape with enough squiggle, such as cavatappi, to hold the sauce.

SERVES 3 TO 4

METHOD: High heat

ROASTING TIME: 1 to 1 1/3 hours

PLAN AHEAD: For the best flavor, season the chicken 8 to 24 hours ahead of roasting.

WINE: Youthful fruity Provence rosé or Grenache-based rosé from Navarra Spain.

CONTINUED ON PAGE 285

GINGER ROAST CHICKEN AND MACARONI WITH TOMATOES AND PAN SAUCE (PAGE 283)

1 tablespoon plus 2 teaspoons peeled and grated fresh ginger, divided

2 tablespoons extra-virgin olive oil

Kosher salt and freshly ground black pepper

One 3½- to 4-pound chicken, preferably with giblets

Juice of 1 lemon

¾ cup dry vermouth or dry white wine

12 ounces dried elbow macaroni

2 to 3 garlic cloves, chopped

One 14½-ounce can diced tomatoes, with juices, or 1 scant pound fresh tomatoes, peeled, seeded, and chopped (see Peeling and Seeding Tomatoes, page 435)

¼ cup chopped fresh basil or flat-leaf parsley, plus sprigs for garnish, if desired

1 **SEASON THE CHICKEN.** In a small bowl, combine 1 tablespoon of the ginger, 2 teaspoons of the olive oil, 1 teaspoon salt, and ¾ teaspoon pepper.

Over the sink, remove the giblets from the chicken, if there are any (they are usually tucked into the cavity). Reserve all but the liver. (Discard the liver or save it for another use.) Hold the chicken over the drain and let any juice run out. Pat the chicken dry inside and out with paper towels. With your fingers, pull away and discard any large deposits of fat from the neck or body cavity opening. Then, using your fingertips and starting at the cavity opening, gently loosen the skin over the breast and thighs of the chicken. Once the skin is loose, rub about three quarters of the ginger mixture under the skin, over the breast and thighs. Rub the rest inside the cavity. Smear the surface all over with about 1 teaspoon olive oil. Season the breast liberally with more salt and pepper. Tuck the wing tips back so they are secure under the neck bone. If you are seasoning the bird ahead of time, refrigerate it for at least 8 hours and up to 48 hours, uncovered or lightly covered with plastic wrap. Refrigerate the giblets too, if using. If you are not seasoning that far in advance, let the bird stand at room temperature to allow some of the rub's flavoring to penetrate; it can safely stay at room temperature for up to 2 hours.

2 **HEAT THE OVEN.** Position a rack in the center of the oven and heat to 400 degrees (375 degrees convection).

3 **ROAST THE CHICKEN.** If you have giblets, put them in a medium, low-sided roasting pan or gratin or baking dish (about 8 by 12 inches). Set a roasting rack over the giblets and put the chicken breast side up on the rack. Squeeze the lemon juice over the chicken and put it in the oven, with the legs facing the rear wall. After 25 minutes, open the oven door and pour the vermouth or wine over the chicken. If at any

CONTINUED ON NEXT PAGE

time the liquid in the pan appears to dry up, add ¼ cup water to the pan. Continue roasting, basting the chicken once or twice by spooning the pan drippings over the breast, until the juices run clear with only a trace of pink when you prick the thigh and an instant-read thermometer inserted in the thickest part of the thigh (without touching bone) registers 170 degrees, another 35 to 55 minutes.

Lift the chicken out of the pan, using a fork or tongs to steady it, and carefully tilt it to pour the juices from the cavity into the roasting pan. Transfer the chicken to a carving board (preferably one with a trough). Discard the giblets, but reserve all the juices in the pan.

4 **COOK THE MACARONI.** About 10 minutes before the chicken is done, bring a large pot of well-salted water to a boil. While the chicken rests, warm a wide, shallow serving dish or bowl big enough for the cooked macaroni; I like to use a 2- to 3-quart gratin or baking dish. A pasta bowl works as well. Cook the macaroni until tender but not mushy, about 7 minutes or according to the package instructions.

5 **MEANWHILE, MAKE THE SAUCE.** In a medium skillet (10 inches), heat the remaining 1 tablespoon olive oil over medium heat. Add the garlic, the remaining 2 teaspoons ginger, and a pinch of salt. Cook, stirring, until fragrant and just golden, about 1 minute (lower the heat if the garlic threatens to scorch). Add the tomatoes and their juices and increase the heat to high. Cook, stirring often, evaporating some of the juice, until the tomatoes begin to brown in spots, about 8 minutes. (They won't get very brown because of the liquid, but you want to see a few caramelized bits.) Taste for salt and pepper. Remove from the heat and immediately stir in the basil or parsley.

6 **SAUCE THE MACARONI, CARVE THE CHICKEN, AND SERVE.** Drain the macaroni and transfer it to the warmed serving dish. Add the sauce along with all the juices from the roasting pan (don't skim the fat from the roasting pan juices; you want it to enrich the pasta). Toss well, taste, and season as needed with salt and pepper. Carve the chicken (see page 266), add any carving juices to the macaroni, and serve the chicken alongside the macaroni. Garnish with herb sprigs, if desired.

CRISPY BUTTERFLIED ROAST CHICKEN

If I had to pick one way to roast a chicken for the rest of my life, this might well be it. Butterflying the bird and flattening it before it goes in the pan may add an additional step, but the payoff is enormous. Not only does the chicken cook more evenly—and more quickly—but all of the skin, even the skin on the tops of the thighs, becomes gorgeously crispy. To get the most benefit from the technique, use a heavy-duty rimmed baking sheet or a low-sided roasting pan. A deep pan will shield the chicken from the hot oven heat and prevent the skin from browning evenly. As for a roasting rack, you have a choice. A flat rack does promote crisp skin all the way to the very edges of the chicken, but in my experience, the difference between using a rack and not using one is incremental. Both methods give you a handsomely browned chicken with plenty of crisp skin to go around.

Removing the backbone leaves you with the basis for a good pan sauce, as you can roast the backbone (and any giblets that came with the bird) alongside the chicken. The meaty bits caramelize during roasting and enrich the pan drippings, and then it's simply a matter of adding a little dry white wine or vermouth to the pan while the chicken rests. Keep in mind that this isn't a fancy or developed sauce, merely a little savory goodness to drizzle over each serving. And it certainly doesn't preclude the addition of a more substantial sauce or condiment, such as the full-flavored Romesco Sauce that follows. When it comes to serving, you will discover another reason to love butterflied roast chicken: Carving is a breeze.

SERVES 3 TO 4

METHOD: High heat

ROASTING TIME: About 50 minutes

PLAN AHEAD: For the best-tasting, juiciest chicken, presalt the bird (after butterflying it) at least 4 hours and up to 24 hours ahead.

WINE: For white, go with a well-oaked Chardonnay; for red, choose a fruity young California or Oregon Pinot Noir or Beaujolais Villages.

One 3½- to 4-pound chicken

Kosher salt and freshly ground black
  pepper

About ¼ cup dry white wine or dry
  vermouth, if needed (if making pan sauce)

½ lemon, if needed (if making pan sauce)

CONTINUED ON PAGE 289

CRISPY BUTTERFLIED ROAST CHICKEN (PAGE 287)
WITH OPTIONAL ROMESCO SAUCE (PAGE 291)

1 **BUTTERFLY THE CHICKEN.** Over the sink, remove the giblets from the chicken, if there are any (they are usually tucked into the cavity). Reserve all but the liver. (Discard the liver or reserve it for another use.) Hold the chicken over the drain and let any juices run out.

Set the chicken breast side down on a cutting board, as shown on page 290. Using poultry shears, kitchen scissors, or a sturdy knife, cut down along one side of the backbone, starting at the neck and cutting through the ribs on each side. You may need to apply a little extra muscle where the thigh joint meets the backbone. If you wiggle the shears around, you can sometimes find the cartilage that holds the joint in place and snip right through it. If not, just keep at it until you chop clear through the bone. Repeat along the other side of the backbone, so the backbone comes away in a narrow strip. Cut the backbone into 2-inch pieces and reserve it along with the giblets if you have them. Pull off and discard any large lumps of fat attached to the underside of the chicken. Cut away any excess of loose skin near the neck.

Flip the chicken over so it's breast side up. With the heels of your hands, press heavily on the breastbone to crack it slightly; you may need to lean your full body weight into it. Once cracked, the chicken should lie relatively flat and its legs should be situated so the "knees"—the joints between the thighs and the drumsticks—are facing inward, giving the chicken a knock-kneed appearance. If they have flopped outward, reorient them. Push each wing tip up over the top of the breast, folding and tucking the wing behind the "shoulder." Pat the chicken dry all over with paper towels.

2 **SEASON THE CHICKEN.** Presalt the chicken, if you like, according to the directions and amounts on pages 257–58, and season with black pepper. If not presalting, season the chicken generously all over with salt and black pepper just before roasting.

3 **HEAT THE OVEN.** Position a rack in the center of the oven and heat to 450 degrees (425 degrees convection). Let the chicken sit at room temperature for about 40 minutes while the oven heats. (This is less time than for a whole chicken because the butterflied bird warms up faster.)

4 **ROAST THE CHICKEN.** Put the backbone and the reserved giblets on a heavy-duty rimmed baking sheet or in a shallow roasting pan large enough to hold the bird without crowding or leaving too much space around it (about 10 by 15 inches). Set a flat roasting rack over them and lay the chicken on the rack, breast side up. (If you

CONTINUED ON PAGE 291

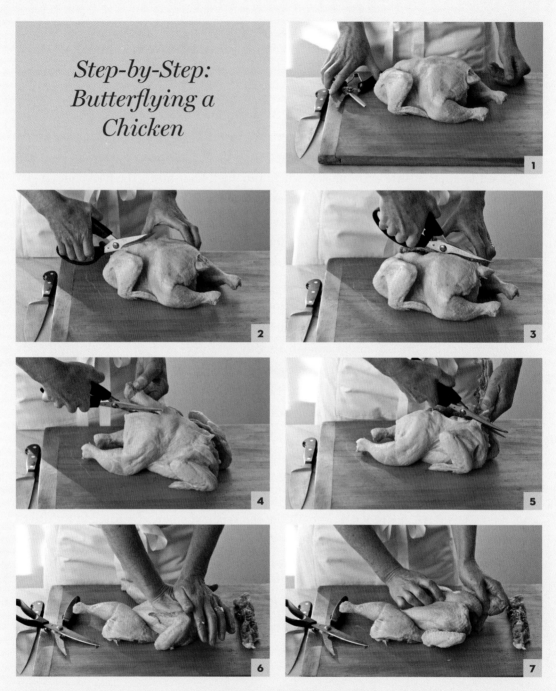

Step-by-Step:
Butterflying a
Chicken

1 Set the chicken breast side down on a cutting board. **2** Using poultry shears (or kitchen scissors), cut down along one side of the backbone starting at the neck and cutting through the ribs on each side. **3** You may need to apply a little extra muscle where the thigh joint meets the backbone. **4** Turn the chicken so the legs are facing you, and repeat along the other side of the backbone. **5** Remove the entire backbone. **6** Flip the chicken over so it's breast side up, and press heavily on the breastbone to slightly crack it; you may need to lean your full body weight into it. **7** Push each wing tip up over the top of the breast, folding and tucking the wing behind the respective "shoulder." Make sure the "knees" are facing inward, and not flopped out.

don't have a flat roasting rack, place the chicken directly on the baking sheet with the backbone and giblets around the edges.) Roast. If the drippings seem to be getting too dark or start to scorch during roasting, pour about ½ cup of water into the pan. Continue roasting until the skin is crisp and well browned in spots, the juices run almost clear when you prick the breast, and an instant-read thermometer inserted in the thigh (without touching bone) registers 170 degrees, about 50 minutes. Transfer the chicken to a cutting board (preferably one with a trough to collect juices) to rest for 10 to 20 minutes.

5 **MAKE A QUICK PAN SAUCE, IF YOU LIKE.** Pour any juices from the pan into a small saucepan, discarding the backbone and giblets. (If a lot of browned bits are stuck to the roasting pan, add the wine or vermouth to the pan and scrape with a wooden spoon to dislodge. If they still won't come up, heat the roasting pan over medium heat to dissolve the drippings.) Bring the juices in the saucepan to a boil, whisking. Taste the sauce; if it tastes a little flat, add a few drops of lemon juice and season to taste with salt and pepper.

6 **CARVE AND SERVE.** Halve the chicken by cutting straight down the center of the breastbone. Next cut each whole leg (thigh and drumstick) away from each breast half and cut the legs into thighs and drumsticks. Cut each breast half crosswise in half, leaving the wing assembly attached to the upper portion. When finished, you will have 8 pieces (as shown on page 288). Pour any juices from the cutting board into the pan sauce, if making. Drizzle a few teaspoons of sauce—you won't have much, just enough to anoint the meat—over the chicken and serve.

OPTION: ROMESCO SAUCE

Romesco sauce, a thick, smoky, brick-red puree featuring roasted red peppers, is one of my favorite accompaniments to roast chicken. Closer to a pesto than a long-simmered sauce, it originated in Spain, in the region of Catalonia. For my version, I roast red bell peppers along with a couple of ripe tomatoes and a few garlic cloves. These are then pureed with toasted slices of crusty bread and almonds, which impart the characteristic coarse, nutty texture. Serve the sauce warm or at room temperature, spooned onto plates alongside carved chicken, or pass a bowl of it at the table. It's also good with roasted vegetables, pork, and fish, tossed with pasta, and as a sandwich spread.

MAKES ABOUT 2 CUPS

CONTINUED ON NEXT PAGE

METHOD: Moderate heat

ROASTING TIME: 40 to 45 minutes

WINE: Crianza Rioja from Spain or young Italian Barbera with tart acidity.

4 garlic cloves, unpeeled

2 large or 3 small red bell peppers (1 pound total)

2 medium tomatoes (8 ounces total)

¼ cup plus 1 tablespoon extra-virgin olive oil

Kosher salt

2 thin slices rustic bread (each about ¼-inch thick and 5 inches across; about 1 ½ ounces)

¼ cup slivered almonds

2 tablespoons sherry vinegar

¼ teaspoon piménton (smoked Spanish paprika)

¼ teaspoon crushed red pepper flakes

1 **HEAT THE OVEN.** Position racks in the lower and upper thirds of the oven and heat to 375 degrees (350 degrees convection).

2 **ROAST THE VEGETABLES.** Line a rimmed baking sheet with parchment paper. Put the garlic, peppers, and tomatoes on the baking sheet and drizzle with 1 ½ teaspoons olive oil. Season lightly with salt and toss to coat. Slide the vegetables onto the top rack and roast, turning them with tongs once or twice during roasting, until the vegetables have dark spots on them, the tomatoes have split, and the peppers have begun to collapse, 40 to 45 minutes. Transfer the peppers to a bowl and cover tightly with plastic wrap to steam until cool enough to handle, about 30 minutes. Let the garlic and tomatoes cool on the baking sheet.

3 **MEANWHILE, TOAST THE BREAD AND ALMONDS.** Drizzle the bread slices on all sides with about 1 ½ teaspoons olive oil and place directly on the top oven rack to toast until golden and crisp, about 10 minutes. Spread the almonds on a small rimmed baking sheet and place on the lower rack to toast until lightly browned and fragrant, about 10 minutes. Let the bread and nuts cool.

4 **PEEL AND SEED THE PEPPERS.** Working over a bowl to catch any juices, peel the skin from the peppers. (Resist rinsing them, as that will wash away some flavor.) Once peeled, gently tear the stem and core away from the flesh of each pepper and discard the stem and seeds. (Don't obsess over removing every last seed and/or charred bit.) Drop the peppers into the bowl of a food processor. Add any collected juices, straining the juices if necessary to remove seeds or skin.

5 **PUREE THE SAUCE.** Break the toasted bread into bite-sized pieces and add it to the food processor. Slide the garlic cloves out of their skins and add them. Pinch off the tomato skins and add the tomatoes to the food processor too. Add the almonds, vinegar, piménton, red pepper flakes, and ¾ teaspoon salt. Pulse to a coarse puree. With the machine running, add the remaining ¼ cup olive oil; process just long enough to incorporate the oil, as overprocessing can turn the sauce bitter. Season to taste with salt. Don't be shy with the salt—this sauce should be bold.

6 **SERVE OR STORE.** Serve warm or at room temperature. The sauce will keep, covered tightly in the refrigerator, for at least a week. Reheat it gently in a saucepan or let come to room temperature before serving. Taste before serving, as refrigeration can mute the flavors. If it tastes at all bland, add a splash of sherry vinegar and a pinch of salt.

CRISPY BUTTERFLIED CHICKEN (PAGE 287) ROASTED ON A RACK ABOVE THE GIBLETS AND BACKBONE

BASIC ROASTED CHICKEN PIECES

This recipe gives a good mix of light and dark meat without calling for any last-minute carving. It's an ideal casual family supper. The challenge is to roast both breast and leg pieces to doneness at about the same rate. I achieve this by lowering the oven to a moderate temperature, and as I check for doneness, if some pieces are ready before the others, I nab them with a pair of tongs and keep them in a warm spot for 5 minutes or so while the other pieces finish cooking. Coating the chicken pieces with a little oil or melted butter before roasting helps them to brown up nicely. When all the pieces are done, you're left with a slick of tasty drippings in the roasting pan. You can certainly ignore them—perfectly understandable for a weeknight supper—or you can drizzle them as is over the chicken or add a splash of wine and/or broth to make a quick, flavorful sauce.

You can use whatever chicken parts you like here (a mix of light and dark or all of one or the other) as long as they are bone-in and skin-on. The basic recipe calls for nothing beyond salt and pepper, but if you want something a little more exciting, try Thai-Style Roast Chicken Pieces with Lemongrass, Red Peppers, and Shiitakes (page 298), Roast Chicken Pieces Dijonnaise (page 302), or Roasted Chicken Pieces with Apricots, Olives, and Oranges (page 304).

SERVES 4
METHOD: Moderate heat
ROASTING TIME: 40 to 45 minutes
PLAN AHEAD: For best flavor and texture, season the chicken 4 to 24 hours in advance.

One 3½- to 4-pound chicken, cut into 8 to 10 pieces (see How to Cut Up a Raw Chicken, page 296), or 2¾ pounds of skin-on, bone-in chicken pieces
Kosher salt and freshly ground black pepper

1 tablespoon extra-virgin olive oil or melted unsalted butter
½ cup dry vermouth or dry white wine and/or store-bought low-sodium chicken broth (optional)

1 **TRIM AND SEASON THE CHICKEN.** Trim away any loose skin flaps or fatty deposits. Season the chicken generously all over with salt and pepper (I use 1 to 1½ teaspoons salt and a few good grindings of pepper). Refrigerate, preferably uncovered, for at least 4 hours and up to 24 hours.

2   **HEAT THE OVEN.** Position a rack in the center of the oven and heat to 375 degrees (350 degrees convection). Let the chicken sit at room temperature as the oven heats.

3   **ROAST AND REST THE CHICKEN.** Arrange the chicken skin side up in a shallow roasting pan or on a heavy-duty rimmed baking sheet (about 9 by 13 inches). Drizzle the tops with the oil or butter. Roast until the chicken is brown, a paring knife slides easily into a thigh or drumstick, and the juices from a breast piece run mostly clear with only a trace of pink (an instant-read thermometer inserted in the thickest part of any breast pieces should register about 170 degrees, and about 180 degrees for leg pieces), 40 to 45 minutes. If some of the chicken pieces are dramatically thicker or fatter than others, they may take longer. Remove any smaller pieces as they are done and set them aside in a warm place while the others finish cooking. Let the chicken rest on a serving platter or cutting board (preferably with a trough) for about 5 minutes.

4   **MAKE A QUICK PAN SAUCE, IF YOU LIKE, AND SERVE.** As the chicken rests, scrape any pan drippings into a small saucepan. If they are stuck to the pan, add ¼ cup water, set it over medium heat, and scrape to dissolve any cooked-on bits. Let the drippings settle and skim off any excess fat (don't worry about leaving some fat; it will enrich the sauce). Add the vermouth, wine, and/or broth, bring to a simmer over medium-high heat, and simmer to reduce by about one third. Season to taste with salt and pepper. Add any juices that have accumulated under the chicken as it rested and spoon over the chicken to serve. If you are not making pan sauce, serve the chicken with any pan drippings drizzled over the top, if desired.

How to Cut Up a Raw Chicken

WHENEVER A RECIPE CALLS FOR CHICKEN PARTS, I ENCOURAGE YOU TO BUY A WHOLE CHICKEN AND CUT IT UP YOURSELF, FOR SEVERAL REASONS. FOR one thing, a whole chicken is generally less expensive than parts. Plus packaged chicken parts tend to vary in size, which can make them difficult to roast evenly. As a bonus, cutting up your own chicken rewards you with those tasty, sauce-building pieces (namely the wing tips, the back, the neck, and the giblets) that are missing from packaged parts. The directions for cutting up a chicken that follow are detailed, but if you follow them once or twice straight through, you should get the hang of it and soon be able to do it without instruction.

To start, you'll need a sharp, sturdy chef's knife, a large cutting board, and it's helpful to have a good pair of poultry shears (or a solid pair of kitchen scissors) on hand. (Raw chicken is something you need to isolate and to be able to thoroughly clean up after—knives, hands, surfaces, and all.) Over the sink, remove the giblets (they are usually tucked into the cavity) and reserve or discard them. Hold the chicken over the drain and let any juice run out. Pat dry inside and out with paper towels. With your fingers, pull away and discard any large deposits of fat from the neck or body cavity opening.

Set the chicken on its back on the cutting board so the wings face you. Pull on the wing tips to unfold the joints and cut off the outermost segment of each wing (set it aside with the giblets). Turn the bird so the legs are near you. Tug at one drumstick to pull the leg away from the body, and with the tip of the knife, cut through the skin that bridges the body to the leg. Cutting the skin closer to the leg will leave the breast skin most intact. Once you've cut through the skin, you will see the spot where the thigh bone connects to the backbone. To judge where to separate the leg from the body, put down the knife and bend the leg back and away from the body, popping this leg joint. This will expose the ball-and-socket joint so you can see right where to cut. Pick up the knife and separate the leg from the body, using the tip of the knife to cut right through the cartilage that holds this joint together cutting as close to the backbone as possible. This is an easy cut and should not require any real force on your part. If you find yourself wrestling with bone, reposition the knife and try again. The idea is to separate the joint by cutting around the bones, not through them. Repeat with the second leg.

Set one leg skin side down on the cutting board. Locate the strip of white to yellow fat that runs crosswise, separating the drumstick from the thigh. With the knife, cut along this line and down through the joint. Again, you should not have to cut through any bone, just the cartilage that secures the joint. Repeat with the second leg.

The next step requires your most aggressive cutting, as you separate the backbone from the breast. If you have poultry shears, they work well here. If not, the chef's knife will do the job. If using shears, turn the chicken over so you are looking at the back. Starting from the leg end, cut up one side of the back and continue cutting up through the rib bones until you reach the neck. You are aiming to isolate the bony back portion and leave the rest intact. Repeat on the other side of the backbone, so that you're removing a 1- to 1½-inch-wide strip. If you are using a chef's knife, stand the carcass up so that the leg end is facing up. With the knife, whack though the ribs on both sides of the backbone to separate it. When you get to the neck, you'll have to cut away on either side to free the entire backbone. Set the backbone aside with the wing tips and giblets.

Lay the breast skin side up on the cutting board and straighten the skin over the breast so it's not pulled to one side or stretched. Using your sturdy knife and steady pressure, cut down through the center of the breast, separating it into two halves, each with a wing bone attached.

Grab one wing with your noncutting hand and wiggle it against the breast so that you can feel where the shoulder joint is. Holding the knife in your other hand and pressing the wing against the breast, cut at an angle to separate the wing from the breast by slicing through the joint and slicing a ½- to 1-inch piece of breast away with it. Tug on the wing to open the joint as you slice through the cartilage; the wing with the small piece of breast meat should release. If you strike solid bone, reposition the knife and try again for the socket. Repeat with the other breast half.

You will now have 8 pieces of chicken: 2 thighs, 2 drumsticks, 2 breasts, and 2 wings— enough to serve 4 to 6 people, depending on the size of the bird. The breast halves may be significantly larger than the other pieces. If you'd like more evenly sized pieces, go ahead and cut each breast in half crosswise, which leaves you with 10 pieces: 2 thighs, 2 drumsticks, 4 breast pieces, and 2 wings. The backbone, wing tips, and giblets can be used for stock right away or frozen for future use.

THAI-STYLE ROAST CHICKEN PIECES WITH LEMONGRASS, RED PEPPERS, AND SHIITAKES

What I love about this recipe is the combination of the familiar—chicken pieces—and the exotic, in this case the enticing sweet/salty/sour/hot flavors of Southeast Asia. A quickly made spice paste featuring fresh ginger, cilantro, garlic, chiles, and fish sauce gets rubbed all over the cut-up chicken before the pieces roast on a bed of bell peppers and shiitake mushrooms. In the not-too-hot oven, the flavors mingle and fill the kitchen with the most wonderful aroma. On the plate, the finished dish is as visually appealing as it is delicious. All you need is some jasmine or basmati rice or your favorite Asian noodles to round out the meal.

You can buy a small chicken to cut up into individual pieces, but you can also use already cut-up pieces, light and dark or all of one or the other, depending on your preference.

SERVES 4

METHOD: Moderate heat

ROASTING TIME: 40 to 45 minutes

PLAN AHEAD: Rub the chicken with the spice paste at least 4 hours and up to 24 hours before roasting.

WINE/BEER: Fruity off-dry Riesling or Chenin Blanc; or a classic pilsner.

FOR THE SPICE PASTE

½ cup loosely packed fresh cilantro leaves and stems

2 tablespoons coarsely chopped fresh ginger (from a 1- to 1 ½-inch piece ginger)

2 tablespoons thinly sliced lemongrass (see page 300)

2 garlic cloves, chopped

1 small shallot, chopped (about 2 tablespoons)

1 jalapeño or serrano, stemmed and coarsely chopped, seeded or not according to taste

2 tablespoons Asian fish sauce (see page 301)

1 tablespoon brown sugar, light or dark

Kosher salt

2 tablespoons peanut oil or other neutral-tasting oil

FOR THE CHICKEN

One 3½- to 4-pound chicken, cut into 8 to 10 pieces (see How to Cut Up a Raw Chicken, page 296), or 2¾ pounds of skin-on, bone-in chicken pieces

10 ounces shiitake mushrooms, cleaned, stems removed (see Cleaning Mushrooms, page 459), and caps halved or quartered

1 large red bell pepper, stemmed, ribs removed, and cut into ¼-inch strips

1 tablespoon peanut oil or other neutral-tasting oil

1 **MAKE THE SPICE PASTE.** Combine the cilantro, ginger, lemongrass, garlic, shallot, jalapeño or serrano, fish sauce, brown sugar, ¼ teaspoon salt, and oil in a blender or small food processor. Puree to a coarse paste. *(The spice paste will keep for days covered tightly in the refrigerator.)*

2 **TRIM AND SEASON THE CHICKEN.** Trim away any loose skin flaps or fatty deposits. Rub the chicken pieces all over with half of the spice paste. Use your hands to coat all of the pieces evenly, and work some of the spice paste under the chicken skin. Cover with plastic wrap and marinate in the refrigerator for at least 4 hours and up to 24 hours.

3 **HEAT THE OVEN.** Position a rack in the center of the oven and heat to 375 degrees (350 degrees convection). Let the chicken sit at room temperature as the oven heats.

4 **SEASON THE VEGETABLES.** Combine the mushrooms and red pepper in a shallow roasting pan or baking dish (9 by 13 inches works well). Toss the vegetables with the remaining spice paste and the 1 tablespoon oil. Nestle the chicken pieces skin side up in the pan on top of the vegetables.

5 **ROAST.** Slide the chicken and vegetables into the oven, and roast, stirring the vegetables after about 20 minutes to help them to cook evenly. (Don't worry if the pan is too crowded to stir the vegetables thoroughly; you will simply end up with some bits browner than others.) If there are drumsticks, turn these partway through roasting so the skin on both sides will crisp (thigh and breast pieces don't need to be turned, since there is skin on only one side). Continue roasting until the chicken is brown, a paring knife slides easily into a thigh or drumstick, and the juices from a breast run mostly clear with only a trace of pink (an instant-read thermometer inserted in the thickest

CONTINUED ON NEXT PAGE

part of any breast pieces should register about 170 degrees, and about 180 degrees for leg pieces), a total of 40 to 45 minutes. If some of the chicken pieces are dramatically thicker or fatter than others, they may take longer. Remove any smaller pieces as they are done and set them aside in a warm place while the others finish cooking.

6 **REST AND SERVE.** Let the chicken rest for about 5 minutes. Stir the mushroom and pepper strips with a wooden spoon or metal spatula so they are coated with any pan drippings and serve them alongside the chicken. Drizzle on any juices that accumulated as the chicken rested.

Lemongrass

LEMONGRASS IS A PERENNIAL TROPICAL GRASS USED TO ADD A DISTINCTIVE LEMONY, FLORAL PERFUME TO MANY DISHES THROUGHOUT SOUTHEAST ASIA. A single lemongrass stalk has a bladelike shape and looks something like a large, woody, grayish green scallion. Once difficult to find outside of Asian grocery stores, lemongrass now turns up in most well-stocked produce sections, often near the fresh ginger and tropical fruits. Expect the stalks to be anywhere from 12 to 18 inches long, but the actual length matters little, since it's only the bottom, more bulbous 4 to 6 inches of the stalk that get used. Choose stalks with bulbs that feel dense and firm when you squeeze. Avoid those that feel excessively light, hollowed out, or brittle—an indication that they've dried out.

To use lemongrass, first slice off any dried root end (usually about ¼ inch at the base of the stalk). Then discard the outer, more fibrous sheaths to reveal the paler, more tender heart (it will still be fibrous but is not as woody as the outer layers). Once you've exposed the heart, use a knife to cut off the top 6 to 10 inches of the stalk and discard. Now you can slice, mince, or smash the bulb as directed. Keep in mind that even after you've removed the toughest parts of the plant (the root end, the outer layers, and the top), the bulb is still fibrous and must be pulverized (as in the spice paste on page 298), chopped very finely (a very sharp knife helps here), or left in large pieces and removed from a soup or stew before serving (just as you would remove a bay leaf). Wrap any unused lemongrass in plastic and keep in the refrigerator for several weeks or the freezer for a few months.

Fish Sauce

THOUGH FISH SAUCE (*NUOC NAM* IN VIETNAMESE AND *NAM PLA* IN THAI) IS INDEED MADE FROM FERMENTED FISH, IT DOES NOT NECESSARILY IMPART A fishy flavor to dishes (despite what it smells like straight from the bottle). Instead, its savory, salty notes, usually tempered in recipes by assertive flavors like ginger, lime, and chiles, add a unique depth of flavor that helps characterize Southeast Asian cooking. You can usually find fish sauce in the supermarket with other Asian ingredients. As with most traditional ingredients, there are grades and various styles of fish sauce, but unless you immerse yourself in Vietnamese, Thai, and Filipino cuisines (which use fish sauce the most), the distinctions won't much matter. Some of the soundest advice I've ever heard comes from the Vietnamese cooking authority (and blogger) Andrea Nguyen. Andrea recommends buying a premium brand—it's an instance where you really do get what you pay for. She also prefers the thinner, amber-red sauces over dark, coffee-colored or thicker sauces, explaining that the lighter-style sauces have a more refined, more balanced taste. A glass bottle will also give you a cleaner, purer flavor and will hold up better than plastic. A brand that meets all these criteria is a Vietnamese sauce called Three Crabs (recognizable by the illustration of three crabs on the label). Andrea also wisely reminds us to make sure the bottle is standing upright in the shopping bag, as the bottles are often poorly sealed and a little leakage will make the inside of your car (or your reusable shopping bag) smell like rotten fish for a long time to come. Much like soy sauce, fish sauce has an indefinite shelf life. Store it in a dark cupboard if you use it often, or in the refrigerator if you only use it occasionally.

ROAST CHICKEN PIECES DIJONNAISE

The magic of this recipe is its simplicity, and this technique for roasting a cut-up chicken has long been a favorite of French housewives. A coating of mustard marinates the chicken pieces, adding flavor and tenderizing ever so slightly. Just before the chicken goes into a moderate oven, each piece gets a generous dollop of crème fraîche, and then a little vermouth or dry white wine goes into the pan. As the chicken roasts, the cream thickens and absorbs the drippings to create a rich, winy sauce that needs only a few minutes of simmering to finish. Serve steamed rice (white or brown, depending on your predilection) or buttered noodles on the side to absorb the sauce. Or, for a comforting homey supper, arrange the chicken on slices of buttered toast and spoon plenty of sauce over the top.

SERVES 4

METHOD: Moderate heat

ROASTING TIME: 40 to 45 minutes

PLAN AHEAD: The chicken needs to marinate in the mustard for at least 1 1/2 hours before roasting.

WINE: Crisp, herbal Sauvignon Blanc from France's Loire Valley, such as Sancerre, Pouilly Fumé, or Quincy.

One 3½- to 4-pound chicken, cut into 8 to 10 pieces (see How to Cut Up a Raw Chicken, page 296), or 2 ¾ pounds of skin-on, bone-in chicken pieces

⅓ cup Dijon mustard

Kosher salt and freshly ground black pepper

¼ cup dry vermouth or dry white wine, plus more as needed

½ cup crème fraîche

Juice from ½ lemon

2 teaspoons chopped fresh tarragon, chervil, or flat-leaf parsley

1 **MARINATE THE CHICKEN.** Combine the chicken and mustard in a large stainless steel or glass bowl. Season lightly all over with salt (keep in mind that the mustard contains salt) and pepper. Toss (your hands work best here) to coat all sides of the pieces evenly, massaging some of the mustard under the chicken skin as well. Cover the bowl with plastic wrap and marinate at room temperature for 1 ½ hours or in the refrigerator for 4 hours.

2 **HEAT THE OVEN.** Position a rack in the center of the oven and heat to 375 degrees (350 degrees convection).

3 **ROAST THE CHICKEN.** Transfer the chicken, skin side up, to a shallow roasting pan or baking dish large enough to hold all the pieces without overlapping or crowding (about 9 by 13 inches). Pour ¼ cup of vermouth or wine around the chicken (not over it, or you'll wash off the mustard) and dollop the crème fraîche onto the chicken pieces; don't worry about distributing it evenly, as it will melt off the chicken as soon as it meets the heat of the oven. Once or twice during roasting, spoon the drippings over the chicken. If the pan drippings appear to be drying out, add another ¼ cup vermouth or wine. If there are leg pieces, turn these partway through roasting so the skin on both sides will brown (thigh and breast pieces don't need to be turned, since there is skin on only one side). Continue roasting until a paring knife slides easily into a thigh or drumstick, the juices from the breast run mostly clear with only a trace of pink, and an instant-read thermometer inserted in a thick piece of chicken (without touching bone) registers about 170 degrees for any breast pieces and about 180 degrees for leg pieces, about 45 minutes. If some of the chicken pieces are dramatically thicker or fatter than others, they may take longer. Remove any smaller pieces as they are done and set them aside in a warm place while the others finish cooking. When all the pieces are done, if they appear pale and not at all golden (this may happen, depending on your oven), turn the broiler to high, set the chicken about 6 inches from the broiler, and brown for 3 to 4 minutes.

4 **SIMMER THE SAUCE AND SERVE.** Transfer the chicken pieces to a serving platter and cover lightly with foil. Using a heatproof rubber spatula, scrape the pan juices into a small saucepan. If the juices are too thick to collect, loosen them by adding a few tablespoons of vermouth or wine. Bring to a boil over medium-high heat and simmer until reduced by about half, 4 to 8 minutes. I don't bother skimming the fat from the sauce because I like the way it emulsifies into the crème fraîche to add richness and flavor. However, you can skim any surface fat before the sauce boils, if you like.

Add 1 to 2 tablespoons lemon juice (to taste) and the herbs to the sauce. Taste for salt and pepper. If the sauce tastes flat, add a little more lemon juice. Serve the chicken with the sauce spooned over the top.

ROASTED CHICKEN PIECES WITH APRICOTS, OLIVES, AND ORANGES

Roasted apricots, olives, and oranges may be novel to some guests—and cooks—but I get raves every time I serve this. The combination pays tribute to the Spanish kitchen and gives a finger-licking sweet-savory gloss to cut-up chicken pieces. To truly marry the flavors of the chicken and the fruit, marinate them together overnight, along with a few other Spanish-inspired ingredients: vinegar, olive oil, honey, and pimentón. During roasting, the marinade cooks down to a glaze, and the chicken turns out temptingly tender and moist and infused with a spicy sweetness. For the olives, I like a mix of meaty green and black ones, such as Picholine and Lucques for green and Kalamata for black, preferably pitted just before adding to the marinade for easier eating. Serve rice or couscous on the side or some good crusty bread to mop up some of the delicious juices.

SERVES 4
METHOD: Moderate heat
ROASTING TIME: 40 to 45 minutes
PLAN AHEAD: The chicken needs to marinate for 6 to 24 hours.
WINE: Young Chenin Blanc with ripe fruit and herbaceous notes.

¼ cup red wine vinegar

2 tablespoons extra-virgin olive oil

2 tablespoons honey

1½ teaspoons dried oregano

1 teaspoon pimentón or paprika, sweet or hot

1 teaspoon kosher salt

Freshly ground black pepper

1 small navel orange

½ cup olives, preferably a mix of green and black

One 3½- to 4-pound chicken, cut into 8 to 10 pieces (see How to Cut Up a Raw Chicken, page 296), or 2 ¾ pounds of skin-on, bone-in chicken thighs and drumsticks

½ cup dried apricots (about 12)

1   **MARINATE THE CHICKEN:** In a small bowl, whisk together the vinegar, oil, honey, oregano, pimentón or paprika, salt, and a few grindings of pepper. Grate enough zest of the orange to add 1 teaspoon of zest to the marinade (a microplane

rasp-style grater works best). Then trim the stem and blossom ends from the orange, and cut it in half lengthwise. Cut each half horizontally into ⅓-inch-thick half-moons. Pit the olives, if desired (it makes the dish easier to eat).

Combine the chicken, orange slices, olives, and apricots in a large stainless steel or glass bowl. Pour the marinade over them and toss to coat all pieces. Cover the bowl with plastic wrap and refrigerate for at least 6 hours and up to 24 hours, turning the chicken pieces once or twice during this time to help insure that they marinate evenly.

2 **HEAT THE OVEN.** Position a rack in the center and heat the oven to 375 degrees (350 degrees convection). Line a 17-by-14-inch rimmed baking sheet with heavy-duty foil; the honey-based marinade can scorch around the edges of the pan and make a mean mess. Transfer the chicken, skin side up, along with the marinade, oranges, apricots, and olives, to the baking sheet and let sit at room temperature while the oven heats. Do your best to tuck the pieces of fruit and olives under the chicken to protect them from the heat of the oven, but don't obsess over this at all, as some will inevitably brown more than others, and this only adds to the appeal of the dish.

3 **ROAST THE CHICKEN.** Roast, turning the chicken pieces over after about 20 minutes (tuck any pieces of fruit back under the chicken when you turn it, as they may char if left on top of the chicken pieces), until the chicken is nicely browned, a paring knife slides easily into the thighs and drumsticks, and the juices run mostly clear from any breast pieces when pierced with the tip of a knife, 40 to 45 minutes. (An instant-read thermometer inserted in a thick piece of chicken, without touching bone, should register about 170 degrees for any breast pieces and about 180 degrees for legs.) If some of the chicken pieces are much bigger than others, they may take longer. Remove any smaller pieces as they are done and set them aside in a warm place while the others finish cooking.

4 **SERVE.** Transfer the chicken pieces to a serving platter and scatter with the olives, apricots, and oranges. Evaluate the pan juices. If there is a lot of surface fat, tilt the pan to pour this off. Use a wooden spoon or heatproof rubber spatula to stir the pan juices and scrape up any cooked-on drippings; avoid any drippings near the edge of the pan that have become too dark and charred during roasting. Drizzle the pan drippings over the chicken and serve.

BASIC SEAR-ROASTED CHICKEN BREASTS

The traits that make chicken breast so undeniably popular—its leanness and delicate flavor—also make it challenging to roast well. Trouble is, when roasted at a high temperature, the tender, all-white meat of a chicken breast dries out, but when roasted at a low temperature, the skin doesn't brown well. My solution is twofold. First I enhance the juiciness quotient of the chicken by salting it ahead or giving it a quick brine (the former requires starting a day ahead, but the latter can be done in the afternoon before dinner). Then, before roasting, I sear the chicken in a skillet over high heat to give it a handsome and flavorful exterior. It then gets finished in a moderate oven, where it can gently roast to doneness without drying out. Choose bone-in, skin-on chicken breasts here. The bone and skin protect the meat some, also preventing it from drying out. Do your best to find breasts in the 8- to 10-ounce range. Bigger ones can be difficult to cook through and awkward to serve—one is too large for a single portion and too small to share. Some bone-in breasts need a little trimming to make them more manageable (and prettier on the plate); you'll find instructions for doing so in step 1 of the recipe.

A properly roasted chicken breast tastes superb on its own, but if you want to dress it up, try one of the creamy sauces that follow, starting on page 308, or garnish with your favorite chutney or salsa.

SERVES 4

METHOD: Combination sear and moderate heat

ROASTING TIME: 25 to 35 minutes (plus about 5 minutes to sear)

PLAN AHEAD: For the best-tasting, juiciest chicken, presalt the chicken at least 8 hours and up to 24 hours before roasting. If you don't have that much time, brine the breasts for 2 to 4 hours before roasting (see option 1 on page 308).

WINE: Lighter-bodied Chardonnay with a touch of oak, or a light, fruity Pinot Noir.

4 bone-in, skin-on chicken breasts (8 to 10 ounces each)

Kosher salt

1 tablespoon peanut oil, other neutral-tasting oil, or extra-virgin olive oil

1 tablespoon unsalted butter

Freshly ground black pepper

1 **TRIM THE CHICKEN BREASTS.** Bone-in chicken breasts often include a bony rib section that offers little meat and makes the breast appear gargantuan on the plate. To determine whether the bones need trimming, examine the breasts: If you find a strip of thin rib bones extending along the length of the tapered edge of the meaty breast, remove this portion (ribs and skin) with a pair of poultry shears (or heavy-duty kitchen scissors). It's okay to leave some of the rib bones attached where they are tucked up under the actual breast meat. The idea is to neaten the edge, but do *not* cut into the thick part of the breast meat. Save the ribs if you are making a pan sauce, or freeze for stock-making at a later date. Smooth the skin over the breast meat (sometimes it gets pushed to one side when packaged) and trim any excessively long or loose flaps. Ideally the skin should neatly cover the breast meat.

2 **PRESALT OR BRINE THE CHICKEN BREAST.** Sprinkle a generous ¼ teaspoon salt on both sides of each breast (for a total of 1 heaping teaspoon for all 4 breasts). Arrange them skin side up on a tray or shallow baking dish and refrigerate, uncovered or loosely covered with plastic wrap, for 8 to 24 hours. (For more on presalting, see page 257.) If you don't have time to presalt, brine the breasts as directed on page 308.

3 **HEAT THE OVEN.** Position a rack in the center of the oven and heat to 325 degrees (300 degrees convection). Let the chicken sit at room temperature while the oven heats.

4 **SEAR THE CHICKEN.** Heat a large (preferably 12-inch) ovenproof skillet over medium-high heat for about a minute. (If the chicken was quick-brined, pat it dry; presalting leaves the surface quite dry, so you rarely need to dry it before cooking). Add the oil and butter and heat until the butter is beginning to brown but not smoking. Sear the breasts, skin side down, until nicely browned, about 5 minutes. If you trimmed the rib pieces from the breasts, toss them into the pan while the chicken is browning and give them one flip with tongs; they will enhance the pan drippings.

5 **ROAST THE CHICKEN.** Once the chicken is nicely browned, turn the pieces skin side up. Season the top with black pepper to taste. Transfer the skillet to the oven and cook until the juices run mostly clear with only a trace of pink when you pierce the breast with a skewer or tip of a paring knife and an instant-read thermometer inserted in a thick piece of chicken (not touching bone) registers 165 degrees, 25 to 35 minutes, depending on the size of the chicken pieces.

CONTINUED ON NEXT PAGE

6 **REST AND SERVE.** Transfer the chicken to a serving platter or warm dinner plates and set in a warm spot to rest for 5 to 10 minutes. Discard the rib pieces, if using. Drizzle any drippings from the skillet over the chicken before serving, if desired, or use them to make one of the optional pan sauces (below and on page 309).

OPTION 1: QUICK BRINE FOR SEAR-ROASTED CHICKEN BREASTS

For times when it's impractical to salt the chicken breasts a day in advance, a quick brine serves well. Makes enough brine for 4 bone-in, skin-on chicken breasts.

⅓ cup kosher salt

3 tablespoons granulated sugar or brown sugar

IN A MEDIUM MIXING BOWL, combine the salt and sugar with 5 cups of cool water (about 50 degrees), stirring until the sugar and salt dissolve. Submerge the trimmed chicken breasts in the brine; if they bob above the surface, rest a plate on top of them to keep them submerged. The chicken can soak at room temperature for up to 2 hours; for longer than that, refrigerate the chicken. Because this is a fairly strong brine, don't let the chicken stay in it for longer than 4 hours.

OPTION 2: SEAR-ROASTED CHICKEN BREASTS WITH CREAMY SHERRY-TARRAGON SAUCE

If you prep and measure the ingredients while the chicken roasts, this luxurious little sauce is easy to pull together as the chicken rests after roasting.

MAKES ABOUT 2/3 CUP, ENOUGH FOR 4 SKIN-ON, BONE-IN CHICKEN BREASTS

WINE: California Sauvignon Blanc-Semillon blend with a hint of oak.

Basic Sear-Roasted Chicken Breasts, cooked through step 5

1 medium shallot, minced (about 3 tablespoons)

¼ cup dry sherry, such as fino

¾ cup homemade or store-bought low-sodium chicken broth

¼ cup heavy cream or crème fraîche

2 teaspoons chopped fresh tarragon

Kosher salt and freshly ground pepper

1 **SAUTÉ THE SHALLOT.** Transfer the roasted chicken to plates or a platter to rest; remove the rib bones from the pan if you included them. While the chicken rests, use a pot holder or kitchen towel to grasp the skillet handle and carefully pour off all but a thin film of fat. Be careful not to pour off any of the tasty brown drippings or chicken juices. (If the chicken was especially lean, there may be very little fat to pour off.) Heat the skillet over medium heat, add the shallot, and sauté just until fragrant, about 1 minute.

2 **DEGLAZE.** Pour in the sherry, scraping to dissolve the browned bits stuck to the bottom of the pan and simmer for about 1 minute. (Keep in mind that the skillet handle may still be hot.) Add the broth and bring to a simmer. Adjust the heat so the sauce simmers steadily but does not boil aggressively, and continue to simmer until it has reduced by about one third, 5 minutes or so.

3 **FINISH THE SAUCE AND SERVE.** Add the cream or crème fraîche and simmer until lightly thickened, about 2 more minutes. Just before serving, add the tarragon and any juices that accumulated while the chicken rested. Season to taste with salt and pepper. Spoon the sauce over the chicken breasts and serve immediately.

OPTION 3: SEAR-ROASTED CHICKEN BREASTS WITH CREAMY GINGER-LIME SAUCE

This fragrant sauce really brightens up chicken. Serve some jasmine rice on the side to soak up any extra.

MAKES ABOUT 2/3 CUP, ENOUGH FOR 4 SKIN-ON, BONE-IN CHICKEN BREASTS

WINE: Fruity but dry Muscat or Gewürztraminer from Alsace.

Basic Sear-Roasted Chicken Breasts, cooked through step 5

1 tablespoon grated fresh ginger

1 garlic clove, minced

¼ cup sake or dry vermouth

¾ cup homemade or store-bought low-sodium chicken broth

¼ cup heavy cream or crème fraîche

½ lime

Kosher salt and freshly ground black pepper

1 to 2 tablespoons chopped fresh cilantro, flat-leaf parsley, or basil (Thai basil is especially nice), or a mix

CONTINUED ON NEXT PAGE

1 **SAUTÉ THE AROMATICS.** Transfer the roasted chicken to plates or a platter to rest; remove the rib bones from the pan, if using. While the chicken rests, use a pot holder or kitchen towel to grasp the skillet handle and carefully pour off all but a thin film of fat. Be careful not to pour off any of the tasty brown drippings or chicken juices. (If the chicken was especially lean, there may be very little fat to pour off.) Heat the skillet over medium heat, add the ginger and garlic, and sauté just until fragrant, about 1 minute.

2 **DEGLAZE.** Pour in the sake or vermouth, scraping to dissolve the browned bits stuck to the bottom of the pan and simmer for about 1 minute. (Take care and remember that the skillet handle may still be hot.) Add the broth and bring to a simmer. Adjust the heat so the sauce simmers steadily but does not boil aggressively, and continue to simmer until it has reduced by about one third, 5 minutes or so.

3 **FINISH THE SAUCE AND SERVE.** Add the cream or crème fraîche and simmer until lightly thickened, about 2 more minutes. Add a squeeze of lime juice and salt and pepper to taste. Just before serving, add the chopped herbs and any juices that accumulated as the chicken rested. Spoon the sauce over the chicken breasts and serve immediately.

BASIC ROAST CHICKEN THIGHS

When I'm shopping for a simple and satisfying weeknight dinner, I often reach for a package of chicken thighs. Not only do chicken thighs offer robust flavor, they're also easy on the cook. Their dark meat fares well when roasted at high temperatures, which means they cook quickly. And because chicken thighs taste best when well done, and because the succulent meat doesn't dry out even when a little overcooked, roasting them is virtually worry-free. You don't even need a thermometer to test for doneness. You can easily tell when thighs are done by look and feel; the skin has crisped and become a beautiful golden brown, the meat is tender enough to pull away with a fork, and the juices run clear. This same technique works just as well for chicken drumsticks, so if you're a devotee of drumsticks, by all means go that route. You can also buy whole chicken legs (thighs and drumsticks intact), so you have a little of both.

The basic recipe requires nothing more than salt and pepper. But if you are in the mood for a little more flavor, rub the thighs with spices, marinate them, or finish them with a bright-flavored vinaigrette just before serving. You can try one of my recipe options starting on page 313 or use your own favorite dressing or marinade. If you make your own vinaigrette, make it a little sharper than you would for a green salad by adding more vinegar or lemon juice to balance the richness of the chicken meat.

SERVES 4

METHOD: High heat

ROASTING TIME: 30 to 40 minutes

PLAN AHEAD: Though not as critical as with a whole roast chicken, presalting the chicken 4 to 24 hours in advance will deepen the flavor and make the skin even crispier.

WINE: Fruity young red, such as a California or Oregon Pinot Noir or Beaujolais Villages.

8 bone-in, skin-on chicken thighs or drumsticks (2 ½ to 3 pounds), or 4 whole chicken legs (see page 313)

Kosher salt and freshly ground black pepper

1 tablespoon extra-virgin olive oil

CONTINUED ON NEXT PAGE

1   **TRIM AND SEASON THE CHICKEN.** Trim away any large deposits of fat or extra flaps of skin from the chicken. (You want the skin to cover the flesh neatly as best it can, but you can do away with any excess.) Season the chicken generously all over with salt and pepper (I use a total of about 1¼ to 1½ teaspoons salt and several generous grindings of black pepper). *You can do this 4 to 24 hours in advance and refrigerate the chicken, preferably uncovered, until 30 to 40 minutes before roasting.*

2   **HEAT THE OVEN.** Position a rack in the center of the oven and heat to 450 degrees (425 degrees convection). Let the chicken sit at room temperature while the oven heats.

3   **ROAST THE CHICKEN.** Arrange the chicken pieces skin side up on a large rimmed baking sheet with room between them. Drizzle with the olive oil, rubbing to coat all surfaces of the thighs or drumsticks. Roast, turning the drumsticks once halfway through cooking (thigh pieces don't need to be turned, since there's only one skin side), until the juices run clear when you pierce the chicken with a knife and the meat begins to pull away from the bone, 30 to 40 minutes. (I prefer the visual and tactile doneness tests here, but you can check the internal temperature with an instant-read thermometer; it should be 180 to 190 degrees.) The degree of doneness depends on personal preference; if you like your chicken fall-off-the-bone tender, roast to the higher temperature.

4   **SERVE.** Let the chicken rest on the roasting pan or on a serving platter for about 5 minutes before serving. If desired, drizzle the pan drippings over, or if the drippings appear especially greasy, pour off the excess fat and then scrape them over the chicken. Serve 2 thighs per person.

A Note on Chicken Legs

THE TERM *CHICKEN LEG* CAN BE SOMEWHAT CONFUSING, BECAUSE THERE ARE TWO PARTS TO A CHICKEN LEG—DRUMSTICK AND THIGH—YET *LEG* CAN also refer only to the drumstick. (I use leg to refer to the whole assembly.) At the market you may find a selection of bone-in thighs, drumsticks, and whole legs, or you may find only whole legs, which are sometimes labeled *chicken quarters* or *chicken leg quarters*.

If you do purchase whole legs, you may need to do a quick bit of butchery, as some whole legs come with a portion of the backbone still attached, which should be remove before roasting to make eating more pleasant. The backbone is easy enough to spot. Simply turn the leg skin side down; if the thigh piece has a rigid, complicated bony part running along the outside edge, that is the backbone. Remove it with a pair of strong kitchen scissors or poultry shears. Backbones aren't much good for dinner, but they add a great depth of flavor to chicken stock, so set it aside or freeze it for later use.

For roasting, I prefer to separate the legs into thighs and drumsticks, because they cook more evenly, with a maximum of crispy skin and no worry that the meat around the joint is undercooked. To separate a leg into 2 pieces, set it skin side down on a cutting board and locate the line of yellow or white fat that runs crosswise at the point where the thigh meets the drumstick. Slice down along this line to separate the leg into 2 pieces. If you prefer to roast whole legs intact, simply add about 5 minutes to the cooking time.

OPTION 1: SPICE-RUBBED ROAST CHICKEN THIGHS WITH CILANTRO-LIME VINAIGRETTE

A quickly made spice rub and a tangy vinaigrette brighten the flavor of roast chicken legs.

SERVES 4

METHOD: High heat

ROASTING TIME: 35 to 40 minutes

WINE/BEER: Fruity, un-oaked Chardonnay from Australia or New Zealand; or a classic pilsner.

CONTINUED ON NEXT PAGE

1 ½ teaspoons cumin seeds

1 teaspoon coriander seeds

8 bone-in, skin-on chicken thighs or
   drumsticks (2 ½ to 3 pounds), or 4 whole
   chicken legs (see page 313)

Kosher salt and freshly ground black
   pepper

1 lime

1 garlic clove, very finely chopped

3 tablespoons extra-virgin olive oil

2 tablespoons coarsely chopped fresh
   cilantro

1 **TRIM AND SEASON THE CHICKEN.** Put the cumin and coriander seeds in a small skillet over medium heat and toast, shaking once or twice, until fragrant, about 3 minutes. Cool and grind the spices in a mortar or spice grinder. Trim the chicken legs as directed in step 1 of the Basic Roast Chicken Thighs recipe. Sprinkle the cumin and coriander over the legs and season generously with salt and pepper. (I use 1 ¼ to 1 ½ teaspoons of salt and several generous grinds of black pepper.) *This may be done 4 to 24 hours in advance and refrigerated, preferably uncovered, until 30 to 40 minutes before roasting.*

2 **HEAT THE OVEN** and roast the chicken as directed in steps 2 and 3.

3 **MAKE THE VINAIGRETTE.** Zest enough lime to get ½ teaspoon of finely grated zest (a rasp-style microplane grater works best). In a small bowl, whisk together the zest, 2 tablespoons fresh lime juice, and the garlic. Whisk in the olive oil and cilantro. Season to taste with salt and pepper.

4 **SERVE.** Spoon or pour off the excess fat from the roasting pan, and scrape the drippings into the vinaigrette. Whisk to combine. Just before serving, drizzle the vinaigrette over the chicken legs.

OPTION 2: GARLICKY ROAST CHICKEN THIGHS WITH LEMON AND HERBS

The inspiration for this version of roast chicken thighs comes from a recipe contributed by Bill Devin, an exporter of Spanish foods, to *Fine Cooking* magazine many years ago. It's such a good recipe that I find myself making it all the time, tweaking the flavors by adding a good dose of Marash or Aleppo pepper, a type of crushed red pepper that adds a sweet, earthy depth to the dish. The method stays more or less true to Devin's original by marinating chicken thighs overnight in a garlic–olive oil paste and then roasting them on a throne of lemon and a little heap of herbs. Everything mingles together in the oven, giving you citrusy, garlicky, spicy, and herb-infused pieces of roast chicken. For a real Spanish feast, serve these with a spoonful of Romesco Sauce (page 291) on the side. Sautéed spinach and grilled bread make quick and delicious sides.

SERVES 4

METHOD: High heat

ROASTING TIME: 35 to 40 minutes

PLAN AHEAD: For a depth of garlic flavor, rub the chicken with the garlic at least 4 hours and up to 24 hours before roasting.

WINE: Citrusy Sauvignon Blanc from New Zealand or California with pronounced herbal notes.

1 large or 2 small garlic cloves

Kosher salt

½ teaspoon Marash or Aleppo pepper (see page 317)

2 tablespoons extra-virgin olive oil

8 bone-in, skin-on chicken thighs, or drumsticks or a mix (2 ½ to 3 pounds; see A Note on Chicken Legs, page 313)

1 to 2 lemons

8 small sprigs rosemary or 8 small sprigs thyme or a combination

1   **MAKE A GARLIC PASTE.** With a mortar and pestle, smash the garlic cloves, a heaping teaspoon of salt, and the Marash or Aleppo pepper to a paste. (Alternatively, use a chef's knife to finely mince the garlic with the salt and pepper; for detailed instructions, see Making Garlic Paste Without a Mortar and Pestle," page 230.) Mix the paste with the olive oil until emulsified.

CONTINUED ON NEXT PAGE

2 **TRIM AND SEASON THE CHICKEN.** Trim the chicken thighs (and/or drumsticks) as directed in step 1 of the Basic Roast Chicken Thighs recipe. Using your fingers, rub the garlic paste over all the chicken, carefully lifting the skin from the meat in order to rub the paste under the skin but without fully detaching the skin. Transfer the chicken to a zip-top bag or baking dish to marinate. Cover lightly with plastic wrap and refrigerate for 4 to 24 hours.

3 **HEAT THE OVEN** as directed in step 2. Let the chicken sit at room temperature before roasting.

4 **ROAST THE CHICKEN.** Slice the lemon or lemons to get 8 slices (discarding the end pieces that are mostly pith and skin with no flesh), each about ¼-inch thick. Arrange the lemon slices about 1½ to 2 inches apart on a heavy-duty rimmed baking sheet. Top each slice with one or two herb sprigs and then set a piece of chicken on top of each. Roast as directed in step 3.

5 **SERVE.** Serve the chicken by sliding a metal spatula under each piece to scoop up the lemon, herbs, and chicken and transferring them to individual plates or a serving platter. There may be plenty of lemony pan juices. Tilt the pan to determine whether you want to skim off the layer of surface fat (your decision will depend on how much there is and your appetite). Once you've skimmed as much fat as you care to, taste the pan juices for salt and pepper. They should taste tart, with a pleasantly bitter edge from the lemon slices. Drizzle them over the chicken and serve.

OPTION 3: BLACK OLIVE, ORANGE, AND MINT VINAIGRETTE

This is one of my go-to vinaigrettes when I want a quick sauce for roasted poultry or meat. Delicious drizzled over Basic Roast Chicken Thighs, it's also superb with roast Cornish game hens (see recipe page 330) as well as with lamb and full-flavored fish such as salmon.

MAKES 3/4 CUP

WINE: Youthful, dry rosé from Southern France, such as Tavel.

1 large orange

3 small sprigs fresh mint plus 1 tablespoon chopped mint

1 small shallot, minced

1½ teaspoons Dijon mustard

1 tablespoon white wine vinegar

Freshly ground black pepper

⅓ cup extra-virgin olive oil

12 Kalamata olives, pitted and coarsely chopped

Kosher salt, if needed

WITH A VEGETABLE PEELER, peel the zest from the orange in strips, being careful to avoid the white pith underneath. Squeeze the juice from the orange into a small saucepan; it's okay if some pips fall in, as the juice will be strained later. Add the strips of zest and the sprigs of mint. Heat the pan over medium heat and cook at a gentle boil until reduced to about 2 tablespoons, about 6 minutes. Pour the liquid through a fine strainer into a small bowl, pushing down on the solids to extract all the juice. Let cool briefly and then add the shallot, mustard, vinegar, and black pepper to taste; whisk until smooth. Gradually whisk in the olive oil; the sauce should thicken and emulsify slightly as you go. Stir in the olives and chopped mint. Taste for pepper and salt—I usually add a pinch of salt and a few grinds of pepper, but the vinaigrette may be salty enough because of the olives. It will keep, covered and refrigerated, for a couple of days.

Aleppo and Marash Pepper

I DON'T REMEMBER WHO FIRST TURNED ME ON TO THESE TWO REMARKABLE DRIED RED PEPPERS, BUT I WISH I DID, SO I COULD THANK THEM FOR INTRODUC-ing me to two of the world's greatest spices. While slightly different in taste (and I like to keep both in the pantry, using them interchangeably), Aleppo and Marash are related vari-eties of chile peppers named after the places where they are traditionally grown: Aleppo from the eponymous city in northern Syria, and Marash from the former name of the city of Kahramanmaras in southeastern Turkey. But it's not just the peppers themselves that are special, it's the way they are processed. In both cases, the chile peppers are harvested when they are fully red and ripe, then split open, cored, seeded, and left to dry in the sun until leathery but not brittle, and then coarsely ground. The resulting spices are dark red and slightly moist, much softer than the typical shardlike crushed red pepper flakes that most of us are used to. If you look closely at ordinary crushed red pepper flakes, you notice both seeds and flakes of the dried pepper. Aleppo and Marash peppers are both seeded before being ground, which results in a more delicate texture and milder heat. The softer texture makes these spices ideal for blending with a little olive oil, vinegar, or lemon juice to create a simple paste for rubbing on poultry and meats before roasting (I also love this paste as a spread for grilled cheese and roast turkey sandwiches).

From a flavor standpoint, Aleppo and Marash can best be described as sweet with a distinct yet mild heat similar to that of a ripe red New Mexico chile, and with an earthy, rich, full flavor. I've heard them described as something like a medium-hot chili powder (the blended kind) with a hint of smoky chipotle. For me, there really is no substitute. Aleppo and Marash pepper both perform as a sort of secret ingredient in my kitchen, and I add them to everything from scrambled eggs to pasta sauce. Indeed, I often reach for one or the other when a dish needs just a little something to boost its flavor. However you use these remark-able spices, keep in mind that they will dry out and fade in your spice cabinet. They are best used within a few months of purchase, while the texture is still soft and the flavor rich. According to Paula Wolfert, a leading authority on Eastern Mediterranean cuisine, the best of these peppers available domestically is the Marash pepper sold by Zingerman's. I also buy Aleppo from Penzeys (see Sources & Resources, page 539) or other quality spice merchants.

TANDOORI-STYLE ROASTED CHICKEN LEGS

Authentic tandoori chicken takes its name from a *tandoor*, an enormous cylindrical clay pot used in Indian cooking. The "oven" is heated by a layer of hot coals on the bottom of the pot, and skewers of poultry (or meat) are then suspended above the coals to roast. The combination of the very hot dry air and the heated clay gives foods cooked in a *tandoor* a distinctive earthy character. Even without a *tandoor* at home, you can come deliciously close to the real thing by starting with a traditional yogurt-based tandoori marinade, roasting at a very high temperature, and serving the chicken on a bed of charred onions with fresh cilantro and lime.

If you've eaten tandoori chicken in an Indian restaurant (or in India), you may recall the vivid red-orange hue of the roasted meat. This comes from a natural dye added to the marinade for the sole purpose of appearance. If you want the authentic experience, purchase tandoori coloring at a specialty food store or by mail-order (see Sources & Resources, page 539) and add a few drops to the marinade. I find that the golden pieces of chicken flecked with crisp bits of cooked-on marinade are gorgeous enough without the added coloring. One word of caution when using a yogurt-based marinade: The natural enzymes in yogurt are such effective meat tenderizers that the chicken can become mushy if left in the marinade for more than 6 hours. Serve the chicken with fragrant basmati rice.

SERVES 4 TO 6

METHOD: High heat

ROASTING TIME: 20 to 25 minutes

PLAN AHEAD: The chicken legs need to marinate for at least 4 hours and no more than 6.

WINE: Off-dry blush wine such as White Zinfandel, or slightly sweet Chenin Blanc or Riesling.

CONTINUED ON PAGE 321

TANDOORI-STYLE ROASTED CHICKEN LEGS (PAGE 319)

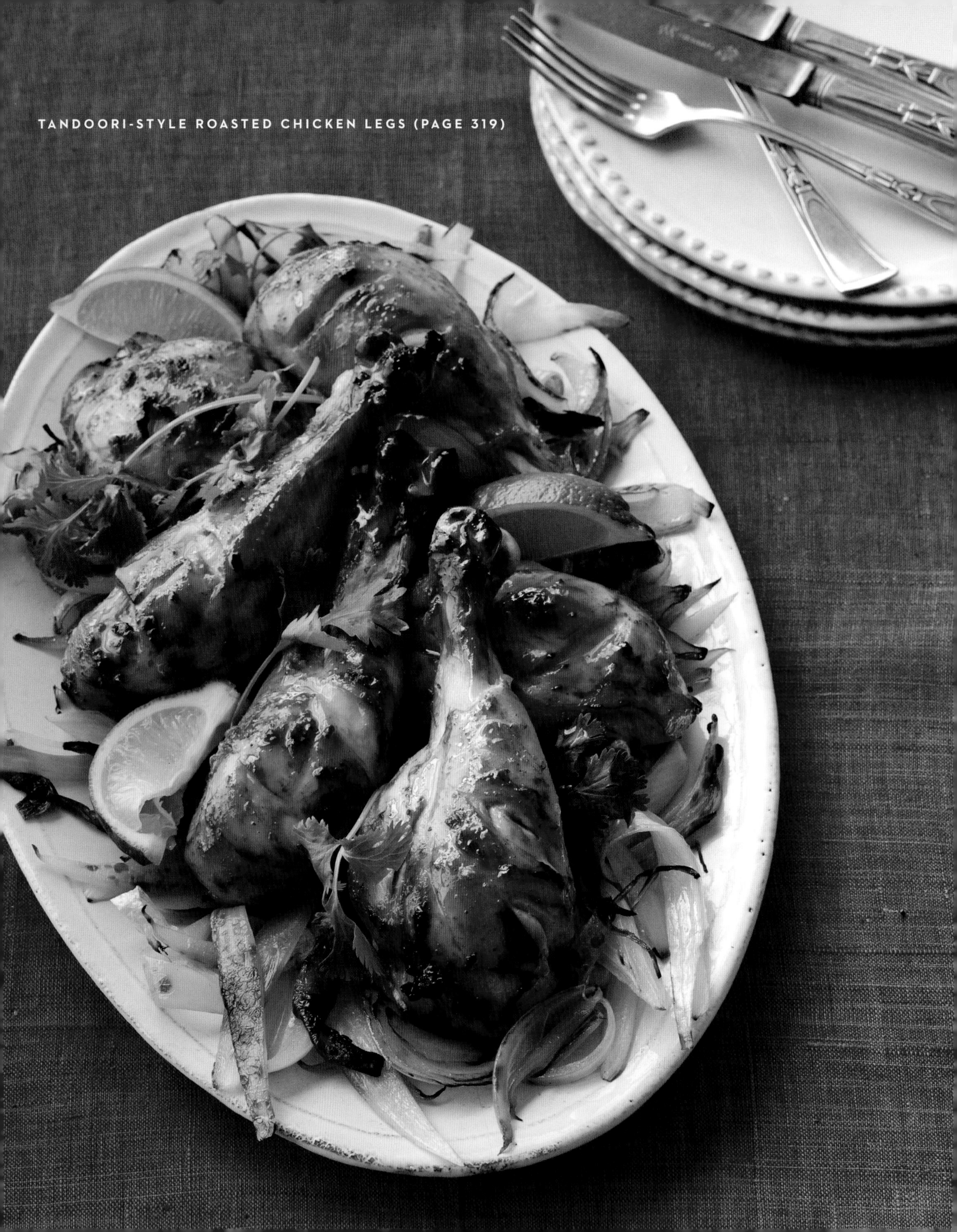

2 ½ pounds bone-in, preferably skinless,
   chicken drumsticks, thighs, or a
   combination

FOR THE MARINADE

½ cup plain yogurt, whole-milk or low-fat

3 garlic cloves, minced

2 tablespoons finely grated fresh ginger
   (from a 1- to 1 ½–inch piece)

2 teaspoons fresh lime juice

1 ½ teaspoons cumin seeds, toasted and
   ground

1 teaspoon garam masala (see page 323)

1 teaspoon kosher salt

½ teaspoon paprika, sweet or hot

¼ teaspoon cayenne

FOR ROASTING AND SERVING

3 tablespoons unsalted butter, melted

1 large white onion (about 12 ounces)

1 tablespoon peanut oil or other
   neutral-tasting oil

Kosher salt

¼ cup lightly packed fresh cilantro leaves
   and tender stems, coarsely chopped

1 lime, cut into wedges

1   **MARINATE THE CHICKEN.** If necessary remove the skin from the chicken pieces. With a paring knife or boning knife, cut diagonal slashes about ½-inch deep into the fleshy parts of the chicken pieces. Make 3 to 4 slashes in each piece, about 1 inch part. Transfer the chicken to a zip-top bag or baking dish.

In a small bowl, combine the yogurt, garlic, ginger, lime juice, cumin, garam masala, salt, paprika, and cayenne. Toss the chicken with the marinade, massaging the pieces so the marinade gets into the slits and evenly covers all surfaces. Seal the bag or cover the dish with plastic wrap and refrigerate for 4 to 6 hours.

2   **HEAT THE OVEN.** Position a rack in the center of the oven and heat to 500 degrees (475 degrees convection). Let the chicken sit at room temperature as the oven heats, at least 30 minutes.

3   **ROAST THE CHICKEN.** Arrange the chicken pieces skin side up about 2 inches apart on a broiler pan or on a wire rack set above a heavy-duty rimmed baking sheet, leaving on as much of the marinade as possible. You can scrape any extra marinade

CONTINUED ON NEXT PAGE

onto the chicken, as long as it doesn't puddle up on the pan; it will cook down and make a sort of crust on the chicken as it roasts. Drizzle the top of the chicken pieces with 1 tablespoon of the melted butter. Roast, flipping the chicken after about 10 minutes and drizzling with another tablespoon of butter. (Start the onions at this point; see step 4.) Continue roasting until tender and cooked through, 20 to 25 minutes total. The best doneness test is to cut into a piece with a paring knife to see that it's cooked throughout and the meat pulls away from the bone easily. If you use an instant-read thermometer inserted into a thick piece of chicken (not touching bone), it should register 180 to 190 degrees.

4 **MEANWHILE, CHAR THE ONION.** Cut the onion in half lengthwise (through the root end) and trim the ends, cutting the base at an angle to remove the root end. Slice each half crosswise into ¼-inch half-moons. With your fingers, separate the half-moons into shreds.

Heat a heavy 8- or 9-inch skillet (cast iron is best) over high heat until very hot, about 2 minutes. Add the oil, immediately swirl the pan to distribute the oil, and add the onions. Do not stir until the onions begin to color, then add a pinch of salt and sauté, stirring occasionally, until charred in spots and slightly softened, about 8 minutes. Transfer the onions to a warm serving platter and cover with foil.

5 **SERVE.** Transfer the chicken to the serving platter, nestling the pieces among the onions. Drizzle the remaining tablespoon of butter on top, sprinkle with cilantro, and arrange the lime wedges around the edges. Cover with foil and let sit for 5 to 10 minutes to allow the chicken to rest and the flavors to meld. Serve the chicken accompanied by the charred onion and lime wedges.

Garam Masala

GARAM MASALA IS A HIGHLY AROMATIC SPICE MIX OFTEN USED IN INDIAN COOKING. THE SPICES, WHICH ARE TOASTED AND GROUND, CAN INCLUDE cumin, coriander, cardamom, cinnamon, black pepper, cloves, and others. You can find garam masala at markets that specialize in spices and, obviously, in Indian markets. I avoid generic supermarket blends of preground spices like garam masala, because most will have lost much of their flavor and vibrancy. If you don't have access to good (and fresh) spice blends, you'd do well to make your own garam masala.

Here's how: Break open 3 or 4 green cardamom pods, discard the pods, and put the seeds in a small skillet. Smash a small cinnamon stick (about 2 inches) with a rolling pin to break it into small pieces and add these to the skillet. Add 2 tablespoons cumin seeds, 2 tablespoons coriander seeds, 2 teaspoons whole black peppercorns, ½ teaspoon whole cloves, and 1 dried bay leaf. Heat the spices over medium heat, shaking or stirring often, until fragrant, darker in color, and just showing the first signs of smoking, about 2 minutes. Immediately transfer them to a bowl or plate to cool. When cool, grind to a fine powder in a mortar or spice grinder. This makes about ⅓ cup. Store in an airtight container for a month or so.

TOASTED SPICES POUNDED IN A MORTAR AND PESTLE

ROASTED BUFFALO WINGS

Maybe it's because I grew up in Buffalo, New York, but I just love good chicken wings. And by *good* I mean wings that are crispy on the outside, not greasy or dense with a heavy breading. The insides need to be tender, and your lips should burn just slightly from their spicy, buttery sauce.

Eating out, I've been served more mediocre wings than exceptional ones. So out of frustration, I set out to perfect chicken wings at home. The secret to most restaurant chicken wings is that they're deep-fried and then tossed in a copious amount of butter. Not having a deep fryer in my kitchen and hoping to get away with a little less butter, I landed on a great solution that turns out wings that are superior to most. The answer is high-heat roasting. To get that crispy exterior, I roast the wings on a wire rack so they sit above the roasting pan. This allows the oven heat to circulate around the wings, making them super-crispy. Then, as soon as the wings are done, I toss them with a good—but not ridiculous—amount of melted butter mixed with enough hot sauce to add a little kick but not enough to make your eyes water or your cheeks flush. If you want hotter, add more hot sauce. For suicidal, use one of those X-rated habenero-based hot sauces (but you're on your own if you do).

For the complete Buffalo experience, serve the wings with blue cheese dip (homemade is best) and carrot and celery sticks. If you want your wings a little more chichi, brush them with a balsamic-honey glaze (see option 2) and skip the blue cheese. Whichever way you serve them, keep in mind something that every bartender in Buffalo knows: Good wings make you thirsty for frosty-cold beer. Make sure you have plenty on hand.

SERVES 3 TO 6

METHOD: High heat

ROASTING TIME: About 50 minutes

WINE/BEER: Recent vintage of Zinfandel with spice notes; or a zesty lager.

3 pounds whole chicken wings or 2 ½ pounds trimmed chicken wings (about 12 whole wings or 24 chicken wing pieces; see Shopping for Chicken Wings, page 327)

1 tablespoon extra-virgin olive oil

Kosher salt and freshly ground black pepper

2 tablespoons unsalted butter, melted

2 tablespoons hot sauce, such as Tabasco, or to taste

Blue Cheese Dip (page 326; optional)

Raw carrot and celery sticks (optional)

1   **HEAT THE OVEN.** Position a rack in the center of the oven and heat to 400 degrees (375 degrees convection). Line a heavy-duty rimmed baking sheet with heavy-duty aluminum foil and outfit it with a wire rack that sits at least ¾ inch above the surface (if the rack is larger than the baking sheet, you can set it on the rim of the baking sheet, which will hold it the right distance from the surface). The rack needs to be large enough to hold all the wings without crowding; use 2 pans and racks if necessary.

2   **TRIM AND SEASON THE WINGS.** Whether you bought whole wings (that is, 3 sections still attached at the joints) or trimmed wings (whole wings with the wing tip removed), cut them into serving pieces: the flat middle segment and the meaty drumette (so named because it resembles a miniature drumstick). Using the tip of a sharp knife, locate the spot at each joint where you can easily divide the wings into pieces by cutting through cartilage and not bone. If there are wing tips, set them aside (or freeze them) for making stock at another time. (Although you can roast the wing tips, there's virtually no meat to speak of, and they are better saved for the stockpot.) Put the drumettes and middle sections in a large bowl and toss with the oil, 1 teaspoon salt, and a few grindings of black pepper to coat.

3   **ROAST THE WINGS.** Arrange the wings on the wire rack, making sure there is some space around each wing. (If they're too crowded, they won't get crisp.) Roast, turning the wings over after 20 minutes. When turning the wings, I find it's easiest to take the pan out of the oven, close the oven door (to retain the heat), and turn each wing over with tongs. Continue to roast for another 20 minutes and flip again. Before returning the wings to the oven after the second flip, increase the heat to 450 degrees (425 degrees convection). Continue roasting until the wings are nicely browned and crisp and a paring knife slides easily into the meaty part, another 7 to 10 minutes. If in that time the wings don't get brown and crisp but are cooked through, remove them from the oven and set the broiler to high. Position the wings 5 to 6 inches from the broiler and broil, keeping a close eye on them, until crisp, about 2 minutes. Turn and broil the second side, another minute.

4   **MAKE THE SAUCE.** As the wings are roasting, combine the melted butter and hot sauce and keep warm. (I start with 2 tablespoons hot sauce, but if you like more, or if the bottle you have isn't particularly hot, add more.)

CONTINUED ON NEXT PAGE

5 **SAUCE AND SERVE.** Transfer the wings to a large bowl and toss well (using tongs or a large rubber spatula) with the butter sauce until thoroughly coated. Let the wings sit for a few minutes to absorb the flavor of the sauce before serving. Taste for salt and heat, and sprinkle with salt and splash with a little more hot sauce if needed. Toss again. Serve with the dip and carrot and celery sticks, if desired, and plenty of napkins.

OPTION 1: BLUE CHEESE DIP

This recipe makes enough for one batch of wings and then some, depending on how many carrot and celery sticks you put out and how deeply people dip. You can also serve it as a chip dip, a baked potato topping, or a dressing for crisp lettuces. The dip is only as good as the blue cheese you use. Choose one that's somewhat creamy and not terribly sharp, such as Maytag blue or bleu d'Auvergne. At home in Vermont, I make this with one of the locally made blue cheeses, such as Boucher Blue.

MAKES ABOUT 3/4 CUP

¼ cup mayonnaise

¼ cup sour cream

½ cup crumbled blue cheese (about 2 ounces), at room temperature

½ teaspoon cider vinegar

Kosher salt and freshly ground black pepper

2 tablespoons milk, if needed (preferably whole or 2 percent)

STIR TOGETHER the mayonnaise and sour cream in a small bowl. Add the blue cheese and vinegar, and season with a pinch of salt and a good dose of black pepper. Stir with a wooden spoon or rubber spatula, mashing the blue cheese to incorporate it until the dip is creamy and only small bits of cheese are visible. Don't overwork the dip, or it may turn an unpleasant grayish green. If the dip seems too thick, stir in a few drops of milk. This dip will keep, covered, for several days in the refrigerator, but for best flavor let it sit at room temperature for about 20 minutes before serving.

OPTION 2: BALSAMIC-HONEY-GLAZED WINGS

For something a little more uptown, make a sticky, salty-sweet glaze in place of the butter-and-hot-sauce mixture. To give the glaze a hint of heat, stir in a smidgen of hot chile paste such as *sambal oelek*, a chile-based condiment used in Southeast Asian cooking and sold in specialty and ethnic markets. You could also use a splash of any favorite hot sauce or paste, from Tabasco to Harissa (page 158). Delicious hot, these wings are equally good served at room temperature, making them great for a buffet or a picnic.

SERVES 3 TO 6
BEER: Pale ale or India pale ale with a balance of malty sweetness and hoppy bitterness.

3 pounds whole chicken wings or 2 ½ pounds trimmed chicken wings (about 12 whole wings or 24 chicken wing pieces; see Shopping for Chicken Wings, below)

⅓ cup balsamic vinegar

2 tablespoons soy sauce

1 tablespoon honey

¼ teaspoon hot chile paste (such as *sambal oelek*)

1 tablespoon unsalted butter

1 tablespoon finely chopped chives or scallions

FOLLOW THE RECIPE for Roasted Buffalo Wings, reducing the salt to ¼ teaspoon in step 2. As the wings roast (step 4), combine the balsamic vinegar, soy sauce, honey, and chile paste in a small saucepan. Bring to a boil, reduce the heat, and simmer until syrupy and reduced by half, about 10 minutes. Add the butter and set aside in a warm spot until the wings are done. In step 5, toss the wings with the balsamic-honey glazed. Sprinkle with the chives or scallions just before serving.

Shopping for Chicken Wings

CHICKEN WINGS ARE GENERALLY SOLD IN THREE DIFFERENT WAYS: WHOLE, WHOLE BUT TRIMMED (MEANING THE WING TIPS HAVE BEEN REMOVED AND discarded), or cut up and packaged as drumettes and middle segments. Unfortunately, it's rare to find a market that sells just drumettes, which is too bad, as most people prefer them for their higher meat-to-bone ratio.

If buying whole wings, you can expect to lose 2 to 3 ounces per pound when you trim away the wing tips, which is why I call for 3 pounds of whole wings and 2 ½ pounds trimmed wings. Trimmed wings require just one cut through the joint to separate the wing into its two serving pieces. Cut-up wings are ready to roast, no knife work required.

ROAST QUAIL WITH SHALLOTS

Roast quail merits a special occasion and an appreciative guest list. Each diminutive bird offers a few perfect bites of lean meat with a rich but decidedly ungamey flavor, making 1 an ideal first course and 2 a satisfying entree. Quickly seared on top of the stove and then roasted in a hot oven, the dark meat retains just a faint trace of rosiness, leaving it tender and tasty. If time allows, preseason the quail with salt, pepper, and fresh thyme to greatly improve the flavor and succulence. I also brush them with a mixture of sherry vinegar and honey and roast them on a bed of wine-simmered shallots to create a savory compotelike accompaniment. Provide steak knives so your guests can carve the breast meat off, but please lead by example and pick up the legs and thighs to nibble the meat off the bone. It's the most satisfying way to savor these wonderful birds.

SERVES 4 AS A MAIN COURSE, 8 AS A FIRST COURSE

METHOD: High heat
ROASTING TIME: 20 to 25 minutes (plus 8 to 10 minutes to sear)
PLAN AHEAD: For the best flavor and texture, season the quail 4 to 24 hours ahead.
WINE: Vibrant Tempranillo red, such as a young Crianza.

Kosher salt and freshly ground black pepper

8 quail (about 5 ounces each)

2 teaspoons chopped fresh thyme

3 tablespoons mild-tasting honey, such as acacia or orange blossom

3 tablespoons sherry vinegar

2 tablespoons extra-virgin olive oil

2 tablespoons unsalted butter

6 medium shallots (about 8 ounces), thinly sliced

¾ cup herbal, dry white wine, such as Albariño or Verdejo

1 **SEASON THE QUAIL.** Pat dry the quail and sprinkle all over with salt and pepper (I use about 1 teaspoon salt and several grindings of pepper). Sprinkle a teaspoon of thyme over the birds as well. Set on a tray or in a baking dish and refrigerate, uncovered or loosely covered, for 4 to 24 hours.

2 **HEAT THE OVEN AND TRUSS THE QUAIL.** Position a rack in the center of the oven and heat to 400 degrees (375 degrees convection). Let the quail sit at room temperature as the oven heats. Tie the legs of each quail together using a loop of kitchen

string. Fold the wing tips back and tuck them behind the neck bone. In a small bowl, whisk together the honey and vinegar, and set it aside for basting.

3 **SEAR THE QUAIL.** Heat a large (12 inch works well) ovenproof skillet over medium-high heat for about 1 minute. Add the oil and 1 tablespoon of butter and heat until the butter stops foaming, less than 1 minute. Arrange 4 quail breast side down in the skillet, and brown them on all sides—3 to 4 minutes on each breast and about 2 minutes on each back—turning with tongs. Transfer to a plate or platter and repeat with the remaining quail.

4 **SAUTÉ THE SHALLOTS.** Return the skillet to medium heat, add the remaining tablespoon butter and then the shallots. Season with salt, pepper, and the remaining teaspoon of thyme and sauté, stirring frequently, until softened, about 6 minutes. Add ½ cup wine and bring to a simmer. Remove from the heat and arrange the quail, breast side up, on the shallots. Brush the birds generously with the honey-vinegar mixture.

5 **ROAST.** Transfer the quail to the oven. After about 10 minutes, brush the breasts and legs with the remaining honey mixture and continue to roast until the juices run clear when the thigh is pricked with a meat fork and the breast meat feels firm with only a slight give, 20 to 25 minutes. (Because of their small size, I have had little success checking the internal temperature with an instant-read thermometer, but if you want to try, you are looking for something in the range of 145 to 155 degrees.)

6 **REST THE QUAIL, FINISH THE SHALLOTS, AND SERVE.** Transfer the quail to a platter or cutting board (preferably one with a trough) to rest. Set the skillet with the shallots over medium-high heat and add the remaining wine. Bring to a simmer, scraping with a wooden spoon to loosen any browned bits. Simmer until the liquid almost evaporates, about 4 minutes. Taste for salt and pepper. Serve the quail on top of the shallots, pouring any juices that accumulated during resting over them.

BASIC ROASTED CORNISH GAME HENS

I'm always a little surprised that people don't roast Cornish game hens more often. These compact birds offer the perfect balance of being a little out of the ordinary without being too exotic for timid palates. Contrary to the name, there is nothing remotely gamey about Cornish hens. In taste and texture they resemble a very tender, delicate chicken—and an all-white-meat chicken at that.

One whole Cornish game hen serves 2 people generously, and I like to split the hens before roasting for two reasons. A split hen is more elegant, and there's no last-minute carving. Also, the split hens roast quickly and evenly in a hot oven, giving you the ideal combination of crisp skin and juicy meat. The recipe serves 4, but it can easily be scaled down for an intimate dinner for 2 or scaled up for a dinner party. Cornish game hens need no sauce, but you can dress them up with a fancy cherry–port wine sauce (page 335) or by making a stuffing to go under the skin (page 333).

SERVES 4
METHOD: High heat
ROASTING TIME: 20 to 25 minutes
PLAN AHEAD: For the best-tasting, juiciest hens, presalt the birds (after splitting them) for at least 8 hours and up to 48 hours.
WINE: Mature bottle of Côte de Beaune red Burgundy, such as Pommard or Volnay.

2 Cornish game hens (1 ½ to 2 pounds each)	1 tablespoon unsalted butter, melted
Kosher salt and freshly ground black pepper	

1   **SPLIT THE HENS.** Place a hen breast side down on a cutting board. Using poultry shears or kitchen scissors, remove the backbone by cutting up along one side, then cutting down along the other side. Flip the hen over and flatten it by pressing down on the breastbone with your palms. With a sturdy chef's knife, split the hen in two along the breastbone. Extend the wings on each side and chop off the last two joints. (All these trimmings—the backbones and the wing tips—are great for making stock,

so reserve or freeze them for future use.) Remove and discard any large deposits of fat. Repeat with the remaining hen. Presalt the hen by sprinkling a generous ½ teaspoon of salt and a pinch of black pepper all over each half. Refrigerate, uncovered, for 8 to 48 hours.

2 **HEAT THE OVEN AND SEASON THE HENS.** Position a rack in the center of the oven and heat to 450 degrees (425 degrees convection). Let the hens sit at room temperature while the oven heats.

3 **ROAST.** Arrange the hens skin side up on a heavy-duty rimmed baking sheet with an inch or two between them, and brush the tops with the melted butter. Roast, rotating the pan after 10 or 12 minutes, until they are nicely browned, the juices run clear when you prick the thigh, and an instant-read thermometer inserted in the thickest part of the thigh registers 170 to 175 degrees, 20 to 25 minutes.

4 **REST AND SERVE.** Let the hens rest at least 5 minutes before serving. If desired, drizzle the drippings from the pan over the hens before serving. If the drippings appear especially greasy, pour off the excess fat and then scrape the drippings over the hens.

Some Colorful Cornish Game Hen History (and a Shopping Note)

I NEVER GAVE MUCH THOUGHT TO THE ORIGINS OF THESE DIMINUTIVE BIRDS UNTIL A 2005 ARTICLE IN THE *SAN FRANCISCO CHRONICLE* CAPTURED MY interest. According to the article, the Cornish game hen is a hybrid developed by a Frenchwoman, Alphonsine "Te" Makowsky, who retired with her husband to Connecticut from Manhattan in 1946. Once in the countryside, Mrs. Makowsky, who had grown up on a farm in France, returned to her agrarian roots and began raising and selling guinea hens—a popular breed at the time. After a fire destroyed the flock in 1949, she promised her customers more hens. But without any guinea hens to restart her brood, she had to improvise. As the story goes, she set out to cross-breed other varieties to create a plump-breasted, short-legged little bird. Crossing various chickens and game birds, including Cornish game cocks, a White Plymouth Rock hen, and a Malayan fighting cock, Makowsky developed the breed we now know as the Cornish game hen. Her new variety was so popular that she never returned to raising guinea hens. The Makowskys sold their farm and moved to Florida in 1967. Mrs. Makowsky died in 2005, at age ninety-two.

Today Cornish game hens can be found year-round in most supermarkets, fresh or frozen, depending on their popularity in the region. The official name is Rock Cornish game hen, but you often see them sold as Cornish hens or simply game hens. The petite size and remarkable tenderness result from the fact that they come to the market in as little as 4 to 6 weeks, weighing anywhere from 1 to 2 pounds. For splitting and roasting, select a hen on the upper end of this range. The 1-pound birds are a little meager for 2 full servings. As with chicken, most supermarket brands of Cornish game hens are factory-raised birds (often with familiar brand names like Tyson). However, more small poultry farms are diversifying their offerings to include breeds like Cornish hens. From the ones I've been lucky enough to taste, this is very good news indeed.

ROASTED CORNISH GAME HENS WITH PROVENÇAL STUFFING

This inspiration for a briny, bold-tasting stuffing that goes under the hens' skin comes from Provence, where anchovies, garlic, capers, and parsley are a classic combination. Don't be afraid of that anchovy; it does not make the bird taste fishy. Instead it imparts a robust flavor that rounds out the garlic and capers. The hens here roast at a slightly lower temperature than Basic Roasted Cornish Game Hens (page 330), because the cheese in the stuffing could get too dark at the higher temperature. A little wine added to the pan before roasting makes the basis for a pan sauce that captures all the elements of the dish. Serve with Blasted Broccoli (page 461) and fresh egg pasta tossed with olive oil and butter.

SERVES 4
METHOD: High heat
ROASTING TIME: 20 to 25 minutes
PLAN AHEAD: The hens may be stuffed and seasoned 3 to 4 hours ahead.
WINE: Deeply flavored Grenache-based red from Southern France, such as Chateauneuf-du-Pape or Gigondas.

1 garlic clove, coarsely chopped

1 anchovy fillet, rinsed and patted dry

1 tablespoon capers, drained and rinsed

1 teaspoon whole fennel seeds, lightly toasted and coarsely ground

3 tablespoons chopped fresh flat-leaf parsley

2 tablespoons fresh goat cheese

1 tablespoon extra-virgin olive oil, plus more for brushing

2 Cornish game hens (1½ to 2 pounds each)

Kosher salt and freshly ground black pepper

¼ cup dry white wine or dry vermouth

1   **MAKE THE STUFFING.** Using a mortar and pestle or the flat side of a chef's knife (see Making Garlic Paste Without a Mortar and Pestle, page 230), mash the garlic and anchovy to a paste. Add the capers and fennel and continue to pound until roughly combined. Transfer to a small bowl. Add the parsley, goat cheese, and olive oil and stir to combine.

CONTINUED ON NEXT PAGE

2 **SPLIT THE HENS.** Place a hen breast side down on a cutting board. Using poultry shears or kitchen scissors, remove the backbone by cutting up along one side and down along the other side. Flip the hen and flatten it by pressing down on the breastbone with your palms. With a sturdy chef's knife, split the hen in two along the breastbone. Extend the wings on each side and chop off the last two joints. (Save the trimmings for making stock or discard.) Remove and discard any large deposits of fat. Repeat with the remaining hen.

3 **SEASON THE HENS.** Gently loosen the skin over the breast and thigh by running your index finger under the skin to separate it from the meat, being careful not to tear the skin. Insert one quarter of the stuffing under the skin of a hen half and work it so it evenly covers the breast and thigh meat. Smooth the skin back to its original position and repeat with the remaining hen halves. Season the hens lightly all over with salt and pepper. *The hens may be prepared up to this point and refrigerated, loosely covered, for several hours (the stuffing may dry out if left completely uncovered, but covering the birds tightly can prevent the skin from crisping in the oven).*

4 **HEAT THE OVEN.** Position a rack in the center of the oven and heat to 425 degrees (400 degrees convection). Let the hens sit at room temperature while the oven heats.

5 **ROAST.** Arrange the hens skin side up on a heavy-duty rimmed baking sheet with room around them and brush the tops with olive oil. Pour the wine or vermouth onto the baking sheet. Roast, rotating the pan after 10 or 12 minutes, until the hens are nicely browned, the juices run clear when you prick the thigh, and an instant-read thermometer inserted in the thickest part of the thigh registers 170 to 175 degrees, 20 to 25 minutes. Transfer the hens to a serving platter to rest.

6 **MAKE A QUICK PAN SAUCE AND SERVE.** Carefully scrape the pan drippings into a small saucepan. Spoon off any surface fat and set over medium heat. Bring to a simmer and taste for salt and pepper; the drippings will probably be quite salty because of the stuffing. Add any accumulated juices from the hens, drizzle a little sauce over each hen, and serve.

ROASTED CORNISH GAME HENS WITH CHERRY-PORT WINE SAUCE

Cornish game hens make an excellent focal point for a dinner party menu. A bronzed split bird looks elegant and a little unexpected on the plate, but it also has a flavor that's sure to please everyone. The cherry–port wine sauce for this recipe makes the entrée glamorous enough for your best china, yet most of the work, from prepping the chicken to starting the sauce, can be done well ahead, preferably the day before. The deep flavor of the sauce depends on a Cornish game hen broth made by simmering the backbones and wing tips in chicken broth (kitchen pros refer to this as a "double stock," and it's often a secret weapon in restaurant sauce-making). Making the broth ahead also means you can preseason the hens, a step that greatly improves their flavor and texture. While it takes a little planning to work this way, it does leave you free on the afternoon of your dinner party to polish the silver and prepare the rest of the menu. Mustard-Crusted Roast Potatoes (page 493) and steamed green beans would be lovely alongside.

You can use either unsweetened or sweetened dried cherries for the sauce. I like the purity of unsweetened cherries, but they can be hard to find. Fortunately, the sauce tastes equally wonderful with the more common sweetened ones. If the finished sauce tastes a tinge too sweet for you, add a few drops of red wine vinegar to balance the flavor.

SERVES 8

METHOD: High heat

ROASTING TIME: 20 to 25 minutes

PLAN AHEAD: The hens need to be split and seasoned 8 to 24 hours ahead of roasting; for less work on the day you are serving, make the broth ahead too.

WINE: Dry red from the Douro Valley of Portugal based on the Touriga Nacional grape.

CONTINUED ON NEXT PAGE

1 tablespoon finely chopped fresh thyme plus 2 small sprigs thyme

1 tablespoon finely chopped fresh sage plus 2 small sprigs sage

Kosher salt and freshly ground black pepper

4 Cornish game hens (1½ to 2 pounds each)

2 teaspoons extra-virgin olive oil

½ cup coarsely chopped shallots plus 1 tablespoon minced shallots

2 cups homemade or store-bought low-sodium chicken broth

⅓ cup ruby port

⅓ cup dried cherries, sweetened or unsweetened

2 tablespoons unsalted butter, melted

1 tablespoon all-purpose flour

1 **MAKE THE HERB RUB.** In a small bowl, combine the chopped thyme and sage with 1 tablespoon kosher salt and several good grindings of black pepper.

2 **SPLIT AND SEASON THE HENS.** Place a hen breast side down on a cutting board. Using poultry shears or kitchen scissors, remove the backbone by cutting up along one side and down along the other side. Chop or break the backbone into two pieces and set it aside. Flip the hen and flatten it by pressing down on the breastbone with your palms. With a sturdy chef's knife, split the hen in two along the breastbone. Extend the wings on each side and chop off the last two joints, reserving the wing tips with the backbone. Remove and discard any large deposits of fat. Repeat with the remaining hens.

Season the split hens all over with the herb rub, rubbing gently so the herbs adhere. Arrange the hens skin side up on a heavy-duty rimmed baking sheet and refrigerate, preferably uncovered, overnight or up to 24 hours.

3 **MAKE THE BROTH.** Pat the reserved bones dry. Heat the oil over medium-high heat in a medium saucepan. Add the bones and sauté, stirring a few times, until browned on all sides, about 8 minutes. Add the chopped shallots and sauté until just beginning to soften, about 4 minutes. Add the chicken broth and herb sprigs. Adjust the heat to a gentle simmer and simmer the broth until it has a sweet, chickeny flavor, 30 to 40 minutes. Strain, pressing gently on the solids, and discard the solids. You should have about 1 cup of broth, depending the dimensions of the saucepan and how gently the broth simmered. Don't worry if you have slightly more or less; you'll be able to adjust when you make the sauce. Cool the broth to room temperature. Cover and refrigerate, preferably overnight.

4 **HEAT THE OVEN.** Position a rack in the center of the oven and heat to 450 degrees (425 degrees convection). Let the hens sit at room temperature while the oven heats.

5 **SOAK THE CHERRIES.** While the oven heats, combine the port and the cherries in a small saucepan and bring to a simmer. Remove from the heat and let sit at room temperature to soak.

6 **ROAST THE HENS.** Brush the tops of the hens with the butter. Roast, rotating the pan after 10 or 12 minutes, until the hens are nicely browned, their juices run clear when you prick the thigh, and an instant-read thermometer inserted in the thickest part of the thigh registers 170 to 175 degrees, 20 to 25 minutes. Transfer the hens to a serving platter and let rest at least 5 minutes.

7 **MAKE THE SAUCE WHILE THE HENS ROAST.** Skim the fat from the surface of the chilled broth and reserve 1 tablespoon of it (if the broth did not chill overnight, do your best to skim the liquid fat from the surface with a wide spoon). Heat the broth to just warm in a saucepan (or in a microwave oven). Heat the 1 tablespoon reserved fat (you can substitute butter, if you like) in a small saucepan over medium heat. Add the 1 tablespoon minced shallots and sauté, stirring occasionally, until the shallots are tender, about 1 minute. Stir in the flour and cook, whisking gently, for about 30 seconds. Strain the port through a fine sieve into the saucepan, reserving the cherries (don't press down on the cherries; you want to leave them plump with juice). Whisk for another 30 seconds. Slowly whisk in the warmed broth, adjusting the heat to maintain a steady simmer. Simmer, whisking occasionally, until the sauce is the texture of a medium gravy and reduced to about ½ cup, anywhere from 1 to 5 minutes. The more broth you start with, the longer it will take to reduce it. Stir in the reserved cherries and any remaining soaking liquid. Season to taste with salt and pepper. Keep the sauce warm as the hens finish roasting.

8 **SERVE.** Just before serving, pour any accumulated pan drippings from the hens into the sauce. Serve each hen half with a little sauce spooned over the top. Pass any remaining sauce at the table.

BASIC ROAST TURKEY
WITH GRAVY

Every fall, food magazines put a roast turkey on the cover with some newfangled version of the classic holiday bird. Call me old-fashioned, but I don't see any reason to smoke, barbecue, or deep-fry a turkey when it takes so beautifully to roasting—the easiest method of all. A few years back, brining—soaking a whole turkey in a salt-and-sugar bath before roasting—was all the rage. While that method yields tender and juicy results, it's a big hassle. Think about it: You need to find a container that will hold both the bird and a lot of water, and you have to keep it all cold. What I recommend instead is a dry brine. Like a wet brine, a dry brine tenderizes and intensifies flavor, but all you need to do is rub the bird with some salt (and other seasonings, such as the pimentón in option 2 on page 344) and clear out enough space in the fridge to accommodate it. No coolers, garbage bags, or lobster pots required.

When it comes time to roast, you'll want a strong roasting pan with a sturdy roasting rack (I find a U-shaped one works best to cradle the turkey). To help brown the skin, the turkey goes into a very hot oven, but to promote even cooking of this relatively large roast, I immediately lower the temperature to a moderate 350 degrees (325 degrees if you are using a convection oven). If you have the time and inclination to baste the breast, by all means do. Basting will help prevent the skin from getting too dark and enrich the drippings, but an unbasted bird is equally delicious. I find that my decision to baste or not depends largely on where the conversation is more lively, the kitchen or the living room.

This recipe calls for making a rich roasted turkey broth as a base for the gravy; don't skip this step if you want outstanding gravy. I advise making the broth a day or two ahead of time, usually at the same time you season the turkey. (If you're super-organized, you can even make the broth a month ahead and freeze it. If you travel by car for the holiday, the frozen-solid tubs of turkey broth double as ice packs for your cooler.) When it comes time to roast the turkey, some of the broth goes into the roasting pan to enhance the drippings, another flavor boost for the gravy. I even use the fat skimmed off the pan drippings to make the roux that thickens the gravy. In the end, you will have a few cups of leftover broth, which you can use to moisten the dressing or save it for turkey soup. You will need to purchase turkey parts to make a proper broth. If these are absolutely unavailable, substitute chicken parts; the gravy won't have quite as deep a turkey flavor, but it will still be head and shoulders above a water-based gravy.

SERVES 10 TO 12

METHOD: Combination high heat and moderate heat

ROASTING TIME: 2 1/2 to 3 hours

PLAN AHEAD: The turkey needs to be seasoned 24 to 48 hours in advance; it's best to make the broth in advance too.

FOR THE TURKEY BROTH

5 to 6 pounds turkey parts (neck, wings, legs), plus the giblets

1 large carrot, chopped into 2-inch pieces

1 large onion, chopped into 2-inch pieces

1 celery stalk, chopped into 2-inch pieces

1 bay leaf

½ teaspoon kosher salt

½ teaspoon whole black peppercorns

FOR THE TURKEY AND GRAVY

Kosher salt and freshly ground pepper

One 13- to 14-pound turkey, preferably fresh (see Choosing a Turkey, page 345), with the wishbone removed (see Removing the Wishbone, page 349)

2 tablespoons unsalted butter, if needed

2 tablespoons brandy

¾ cup dry white wine or dry vermouth

⅓ cup all-purpose flour

1 **MAKE THE TURKEY BROTH 1 TO 2 DAYS AHEAD.** Position a rack in the center of the oven and heat to 450 degrees (425 degrees convection). If you have a cleaver or a seriously large kitchen knife, hack any larger turkey parts into 3- to 4-inch pieces. Otherwise, leave them as is. (Chopping extracts slightly more flavor from the bones than leaving them whole, but if you don't happen to have a cleaver, it's not worth damaging your knives—or, worse, yourself!) Arrange the turkey pieces in a roasting pan large enough to accommodate them in a single layer (12 by 14 inches works well). Roast for 30 minutes. Using tongs, turn the pieces over. Don't worry if they stick to the pan; any caramelized bits will only add flavor to the broth. Continue roasting until the turkey pieces are browned on the other side, another 25 to 30 minutes.

If you are planning to season the turkey at this time, unwrap it now and retrieve the giblets from the cavity. Save the liver for another use (or discard it) and set the remaining giblets (neck, heart, and gizzard) aside. If you are making the broth in advance and have not yet purchased the turkey, you do not need the giblets. The broth will still be excellent.

Using tongs, transfer the roasted turkey pieces to a large soup pot or stockpot

CONTINUED ON NEXT PAGE

(4- to 5-quart size). Add the reserved giblets, if you have them. Place the roasting pan over 1 or 2 burners, depending on its size, and heat over high heat. Add 2 cups of water to the pan, scraping with a wooden spoon to loosen any cooked-on drippings. Pour this into the stockpot. Add enough cold water to the stockpot to just cover the turkey pieces (I start with 7 to 8 cups) and place it over medium-high heat. Push down on the pieces with a wooden spoon as you add the water to be sure they are not floating, which would cause you to add too much more water. Bring to a boil, reduce the heat to medium-low, and skim off any foam or murky particles that rise to the top. Add the carrot, onion, celery, bay leaf, salt, and peppercorns and return to a simmer. Simmer gently, uncovered, for 2½ to 3 hours (if the turkey pieces were not chopped up, simmer for a little longer, 3½ to 4 hours), checking occasionally to be sure the liquid covers the solids at all times. It's okay if a wing tip or another piece sticks above the surface, but the bones should remain fairly well covered.

Strain the broth through a fine-mesh sieve into a large bowl, pressing gently on the solids with a wooden spoon. Discard the solids, let the broth cool to room temperature, and then cover and refrigerate it overnight or up to 2 days (for longer storage, freeze the broth). You should have about 2 quarts. Once the broth has chilled thoroughly, remove the layer of surface fat. If you glean flavorful fats for cooking, save this. Otherwise, discard it.

2   **SEASON THE TURKEY.** Combine 2 tablespoons salt and 1 teaspoon pepper. Sprinkle the mix liberally all over the turkey, starting on the back, then sprinkling a little into the cavity, and finally turning the turkey breast side up and seasoning the breast and legs. Place the turkey on a wire rack set over a rimmed baking sheet or large platter and refrigerate, preferably uncovered (but loosely covered is fine), for 1 to 2 days.

3   **HEAT THE OVEN.** Remove the turkey from the refrigerator and let stand at room temperature for 2 hours before roasting (this will help it roast more evenly). There is no need to rinse or wipe the seasonings off the turkey. The skin will be dry and taut. Discard any liquid that has pooled beneath the turkey. Position a rack in the lowest part of the oven and heat to 450 degrees (425 degrees convection).

4   **ROAST THE TURKEY.** Tuck the wings behind the neck bone and tie the legs together with kitchen string, if you like; this step is not necessary, but the turkey will look nicer coming out of the oven. Transfer the turkey to a roasting pan fitted with a

large roasting rack. Pour 1½ cups of the turkey broth into the bottom of the roasting pan. Slide the turkey into the oven and immediately lower the heat to 350 degrees (325 degrees convection). Roast, rotating the pan after about 1¼ hours and covering the breast with foil during the last 45 minutes if it seems to be getting too dark, for 2½ to 3 hours. If desired, baste by spooning the pan drippings over the breast every 45 minutes or so. (If after about 2 hours the thighs and legs don't appear to be browning, see page 342.)

The turkey is done when the juices from the thigh run mostly clear with only a trace of pink and an instant-read thermometer inserted into the meaty part of the thigh registers about 170 degrees. Make sure the thermometer doesn't hit bone and that the probe doesn't go all the way through so that it's reading the temperature of the oven air. It's a good idea to take the temperature in a few spots to get an accurate reading.

5 **HEAT THE BROTH WHILE THE TURKEY ROASTS.** When the turkey is close to done, pour about 4 cups of broth into a saucepan and heat to just below a simmer (you can heat the broth in a microwave oven if stove space is limited). Keep warm. (You will have about 2½ cups of broth leftover to use for stuffing or to save for soup.)

6 **REST THE TURKEY.** When the turkey is done, grab both sides of the roasting rack with oven mitts and, being careful so the turkey doesn't slip, tilt the turkey so the juices pour from the cavity into the roasting pan. Now transfer the bird to a large carving board by lifting it off the rack with oven mitts or a double thickness of kitchen towels and moving it to the carving board (it's a good idea to enlist help here, asking someone to hold the roasting rack for you and having someone else bring the carving board close). Set the turkey in a warm spot to rest for at least 30 minutes. (If it's drafty, loosely tent foil over the top.)

7 **DEGREASE THE PAN DRIPPINGS AND DEGLAZE THE ROASTING PAN.** Lift the roasting pan with sturdy oven mitts and pour the liquid from the pan into a large glass measuring cup (4-cup size) or a heatproof bowl. Don't bother to scrape the pan at this point. Let the drippings settle so the fat rises to the top. Spoon about 4 tablespoons fat off the top and into a medium saucepan (if there are not 4 tablespoons of fat, add enough butter to make up the difference), and set aside (to make the roux). Spoon off and discard any additional fat from the drippings and set the drippings aside for a minute.

Set the roasting pan over two burners over medium-high heat and pour in the

CONTINUED ON NEXT PAGE

brandy and wine or vermouth. Bring to a boil, scraping with a wooden spoon to loosen the browned bits on the bottom. Pour the measuring cup (or bowl) of degreased drippings into the roasting pan along with 1 cup of the heated broth. Boil, stirring once or twice, until reduced by about half, about 10 minutes. Set aside.

8 **MAKE A ROUX.** Heat the reserved fat in the medium saucepan over medium-low heat. Whisk in the flour until smooth and cook for 2 to 3 minutes. Gradually whisk in the roasting-pan drippings. Still whisking, add the remaining 3 cups of heated broth. Simmer, whisking occasionally, for about 10 minutes. Season to taste with salt and pepper.

9 **SERVE.** Carve the turkey (see How to Carve a Turkey, page 347). Arrange the carved turkey on a platter and serve with the gravy in a gravy boat alongside.

What to Do If the Turkey Legs and Thighs Aren't Browning

AS LONG AS YOUR ROASTING RACK HOLDS THE TURKEY UP HIGH ENOUGH IN THE ROASTING PAN, THE THIGHS AND LEGS WILL USUALLY BROWN ENOUGH without any fuss. But if the thighs and legs don't appear to be browning enough, you can give the turkey a flip toward the end of roasting to brown the backside. I generally like to avoid turning a turkey midway through roasting, because it's messy and a little tricky, but it certainly can be done, as long as you don't mind manhandling a hot, slippery, 14-pound beast. *Here's how:* Select a sturdy pair of oven mitts or two double thicknesses of kitchen towels to protect your hands (you will want to send these right to the laundry basket afterward). Take the roasting pan from the oven and set it on a heatproof surface on the counter. Grab hold of the turkey (using the mitts or towels), putting one hand on either side, right around the thigh, and lift, being careful not to tilt the turkey and douse yourself with hot juices. It does help to have someone stand by if the rack threatens to stick a bit. Turn the turkey so it is breast side down and return it to the oven. Roast until the back is golden, about 35 minutes, and then repeat the flip so the turkey finishes roasting breast side up. Expect the turkey to take about 20 minutes longer to roast to compensate for the time out of the oven.

OPTION 1: CLASSIC HERBED BREAD DRESSING

You will notice that my basic turkey recipe does *not* call for stuffing. The primary reason is that as much as I appreciate the flavor of stuffing cooked inside a turkey, the stuffing actually compromises the quality of the finished roast. By packing the cavity with a dense bread stuffing, you prevent the oven heat from circulating inside the bird and slow down the cooking, so the exterior ends up cooking more rapidly than the center leaving you with dried-out breast meat and undercooked dark meat. As much as traditionalists don't want to hear it, an unstuffed turkey roasts more quickly and evenly. Also, there's the food safety dilemma: Stuffing packed into the bird will not cook through to a safe temperature until the rest of the turkey is overdone. My solution is to bake the stuffing separately in a baking dish, which makes it technically a dressing.

Here's my favorite bread dressing—nothing fancy, just lots of herbs, celery, onions, and, yes, butter. If you've made roast turkey broth, you'll have enough leftover broth to moisten the dressing, a neat trick to make it taste as though it baked right inside the bird. The amount of liquid you add will depend on the bread. You can dry bread cubes by spreading them out on a baking sheet and leaving them out uncovered overnight or by heating them in a low (275-degree) oven until they feel dry, about 15 minutes. If the bread isn't dried, it will become soggy, making the dressing mushy.

SERVES 10 TO 12

12 tablespoons (1½ sticks) unsalted butter, plus more for the dish

3 cups chopped onions

2½ cups chopped celery, including leaves

1 garlic clove, finely chopped

1½ tablespoons chopped fresh or 1½ teaspoons dried sage

1½ tablespoons chopped fresh or 1½ teaspoons dried thyme

2 teaspoons celery seeds

Pinch of grated nutmeg

Pinch of ground cloves

Kosher salt and freshly ground black pepper

¼ cup chopped fresh flat-leaf parsley

One 12- to 16-ounce loaf of good white bread, cut into ½-inch cubes (about 10 cups), stale or lightly toasted (see headnote)

1½ to 2 cups turkey broth or homemade or store-bought low-sodium chicken broth, as needed

CONTINUED ON NEXT PAGE

1 **COOK THE VEGETABLES.** In a large skillet (11 to 12 inches) over medium heat, melt 4 tablespoons of the butter. Add the onions, celery, garlic, sage, thyme, celery seeds, nutmeg, and cloves. Season with a good pinch of salt and several grindings of black pepper. Cook, covered, until the onions are very soft, 10 to 14 minutes. Remove from the heat and stir in the parsley. *This may be done several hours ahead; keep at room temperature.*

2 **COMBINE THE VEGETABLES AND THE BREAD.** In a large bowl, toss the sautéed vegetables with the bread cubes. Melt 4 tablespoons of butter and pour it over the dressing along with ½ cup broth. Toss to coat. Continue to add broth until you have a dressing that is moist enough to mound on a spoon but not soggy (usually 1 to 1½ cups). Taste and adjust for salt and pepper.

3 **HEAT THE OVEN.** Butter a large baking dish (ideally 10 by 14 inches, but 9 by 13 inches will do) and heat the oven to 350 degrees (325 degrees convection), unless you have room alongside the turkey, in which case the oven will already be heated. Spoon the dressing into the baking dish. Dot the top with the remaining 4 tablespoons butter. Cover the dish with foil (buttering the underside of the foil helps prevent sticking) and bake until heated through, 45 to 50 minutes. Uncover and continue to bake until the top is crunchy, another 15 to 20 minutes.

4 **SERVE.** Serve hot or warm directly from the baking dish. Stuffing may be kept warm, covered with foil, in a low oven (250 degrees) for up to 40 minutes.

OPTION 2: PIMENTÓN-RUBBED ROAST TURKEY

For a simple but remarkable twist on basic roast turkey, add a bit of pimentón—Spanish smoked paprika—to the salt and pepper. Pimentón pairs beautifully with turkey and adds just enough heat and smoke to make the flavor more intriguing, but not enough to put off traditionalists. Plus it gives the turkey a gorgeous burnished appearance. Follow the recipe for Basic Roast Turkey, adding 1 tablespoon pimentón to the salt and pepper when seasoning the turkey (step 2).

WINE: Supple red with spicy red fruits, such as Pinot Noir from California's Carneros or Russian River Valley regions or the Willamette Valley in Oregon.

If You Stuff the Turkey After All

AS MUCH AS I URGE ANYONE WHO WILL LISTEN TO FORGO STUFFING THE TURKEY AND INSTEAD COOK THE STUFFING IN A CASSEROLE DISH, I RESPECT the adherence to tradition that prevents cooks from being swayed. If you simply can't face the prospect of a turkey without stuffing, or if you have a family who will revolt if you even suggest roasting an unstuffed bird, then please keep in mind a few things: Only put warm stuffing in a raw turkey if the oven is preheated and the turkey is going directly in to start roasting. If you're stuffing the turkey ahead, make sure the stuffing is well cooled. Stuff the turkey lightly; the less densely you pack the stuffing, the better chance there is that the oven heat will penetrate, and bread stuffing expands as it cooks and absorbs turkey juices. Finally, be sure to check the internal temperature of the stuffing as well as of the turkey. The stuffing has absorbed all the turkey juices during roasting (that's exactly why people like it so much), so it needs to reach at least 165 degrees to be safe to eat.

Choosing a Turkey

FOR MOST PEOPLE, CHOOSING A TURKEY IS A ONCE-A-YEAR (THANKSGIVING) OR TWICE-A-YEAR (THANKSGIVING AND CHRISTMAS) PROPOSITION. AS A FAN of turkey, I think this is too bad. I'm all in favor of roasting a big turkey to kick off a week-end with a house full of guests or to celebrate a big birthday. No matter when you do decide to roast a whole turkey, chances are it will be for a special occasion, so choosing the most delicious bird can take on an added importance.

If you shop at supermarkets, you cannot help but notice the mass-market turkeys that start crowding the coolers and freezers around the fall holidays. Even though these birds are affordable, I find them to be quite tasteless, with an unpleasant, almost soft texture. I know that in recent years some of the self-basting commercial birds have gotten positive reviews in blind taste tests, but I have never been impressed. If you want to experience the real flavor of turkey, I encourage you to choose a fresh, old-fashioned breed (also called a heritage turkey). Will it cost more? Yes. But the difference in price is worth it for a special occasion.

Prized for their rich flavor and beautiful plumage, heritage turkeys, which include breeds like American Bronze, Bourbon Red, Jersey Buff, Narragansett, and White Holland, are the ancestors of the common Broad-Breasted turkey, which makes up almost all of the supermarket turkeys sold today. The main thing that sets these old-fashioned breeds apart is that the birds are more mature than the commercial breeds when brought to market;

CONTINUED ON NEXT PAGE

commercial turkeys can reach market weight in as little as 18 weeks, while heritage breeds take anywhere from 24 to 30 weeks. This added time makes a big difference in flavor; an older turkey simply has more flavor, yet it is not so old that its meat is tough. On the contrary, a heritage turkey has a better meaty texture—not the soft, almost mealy texture of a turkey that has grown too big too fast. Sometimes heritage birds are described as being a bit gamey, but I disagree, I think they just taste more like turkey.

Another great advantage of heritage breeds is that they don't grow to the gargantuan size of commercial breeds, and that is a good thing. The average turkey sold today (at Thanksgiving) is close to 28 pounds, and while such a bird will feed an army, it is nearly impossible to cook evenly. The bigger the turkey, the longer it takes to cook and the more likely it is to dry out. You will get much better results roasting a moderate-sized turkey, something in the 12- to 15-pound range. If you have a very large gathering, simply roast two smaller birds. I know this may sound radical, but it makes a huge difference in time, texture, and flavor, and you get the bonus of more legs and wings and crispy skin to go around (and two carcasses for even better day-after turkey soup). Trust me. It took me a few years to convince my own family of the merits of the smaller turkey, but now every Thanksgiving we roast two turkeys (you do need two ovens), and the meat turns out perfect and everyone is happy.

You can find heritage turkeys at some specialty food markets, but you may also want to find a local farm raising birds for the holidays (check out Local Harvest's website for help). Mail-order is another option (see Sources & Resources, page 539), though shipping can be pricey. Also, because there are not as many of these rarer breeds available, you would do well to order yours well ahead of the holiday.

If a heritage turkey is not a possibility, the best choice when shopping for a supermarket turkey is a kosher one. Because kosher turkeys are treated with salt during processing, they offer a full flavor and a juicy texture. (If you do buy a kosher turkey, skip presalting; just rub the outside with any spices you want to use an hour before cooking and roast as directed.)

And finally, a word on fresh versus frozen turkey. Over the years I've tasted excellent roast turkey from both fresh and frozen birds; I've also tasted disappointing examples of both types. As much as "fresh" always sounds more appealing, what really matters is the turkey itself. If a producer starts with a top-quality turkey (for instance, a heritage bird raised on a humanely-run farm) and properly freezes it using a high-tech commercial-grade freezer, and then you properly defrost it at home (in the refrigerator in its original packaging, over a period of several days), you will indeed enjoy a superb frozen turkey. If, however, you buy a top-quality turkey that was frozen in the freezer compartment of someone's refrigerator (where meat freezes very slowly and thus suffers textural damage) and then thaw and roast that bird . . . well, the results will be greatly inferior. In the debate between fresh and frozen, what really matters is the quality of the meat or poultry to begin with *and* the freezing process itself. However, a fresh turkey is much more convenient than a frozen one, as there's no worry about making sure it's properly defrosted—a task that always seems to take longer than anticipated.

How to Carve a Turkey

THE MOST CHALLENGING PART TO CARVING A ROAST TURKEY—AT LEAST AT OUR FAMILY THANKSGIVING—IS FINDING THE SPACE TO DO SO. WITH SO MUCH else going on in the kitchen, from side dishes to biscuits and pies, it can be difficult to find the space you need to carve a turkey properly, but your life will be much easier if you do. Here's what you need: the turkey, set on a large carving board, preferably one with a trough; a second large cutting board alongside; and a platter on which to pile the meat as you go. Obviously, you'll also need a sharp knife (preferably at least 8 inches long) and a sturdy meat fork. Once the turkey has rested a good 30 minutes, you should be able to grab hold of a drumstick with your hand, but it's also a good idea to outfit yourself with a clean dish towel for any moments when you want to grab the still-hot turkey.

First, orient the turkey so the drumsticks are facing you, and with either your meat fork or your noncarving hand, push one leg away from the body until the leg folds back and you expose the ball joint where the thigh meets the back. Using the tip of the knife, cut away the thigh so the entire leg comes free from the carcass. Do your best to cut as far down on the thigh as you can, reaching down under the back to keep as much meat attached to the thigh as possible. Transfer the leg to the cutting board, skin side down. Cut the leg into two pieces—thigh and drumstick—by cutting through the "knee" joint, maneuvering the knife until you find the joint. To get plenty of sliced dark meat, carve the meat off the thigh by slicing along the length of the bone, turning the thigh as you go to get all the meat. Transfer the thigh meat to the serving platter. You can do the same with the drumstick (slice the meat off parallel to the bone), or you can place the whole drumstick on the serving platter, if you know there's someone at your table who appreciates drumsticks. Repeat the process with the second leg.

Once both legs are off and sliced, turn your attention to the breast. The best way to carve the breast for efficiency and quality is not the classic way of making long thin slices following the contour of the breastbone. While this approach has a certain Norman Rockwell charm, you end up slicing the white meat *with* the grain, which makes it taste drier than it needs to. Instead, the objective is to remove the entire breast and then slice it crosswise. Begin by steadying the turkey with the fork and making a long vertical slice all the way along one side of the breastbone. Continue cutting down and angling out as you glide the knife along the breastbone and ribcage to remove the entire breast in a single piece. This will be easier

CONTINUED ON NEXT PAGE

if you've removed the wishbone in advance (see page 349), but either way, it can get a little tricky as you near the wing joint. Simply do your best to maneuver the knife tip to leave a minimum of white meat behind on the carcass. Transfer the breast to the cutting board and now cut it crosswise into ¼- to ½-inch-thick slices being careful to slice through the skin so every slice gets a bit of skin. Transfer these slices to the serving platter. Repeat with the second side of the breast.

Return to the carcass and remove the wings, folding them back and cutting between the joints. Add these to the serving platter if you have the kind of eaters who like the crisp skin. There's not enough meat on most wings to bother trying to carve it off. Finally, look over the carcass for large pieces of meat you may have left behind. Turn the turkey over and see if you've left behind the "oysters," two poker-chip-sized nuggets of succulent dark meat that sit right above the leg joint and are almost always left behind by all but the most experienced carvers. In my family, I leave these behind on purpose, so when everyone descends on the platter of carved meat in the dining room, my brother-in-law (with whom I sometimes share carving duties) and I hang back in the kitchen to enjoy our prize. In fact, I think the team approach to carving a turkey, especially at the holidays, is the way to go. Have one person breaking down the bird—carving off the legs and breast—and then have the second person carve these into individual slices. It's faster and more in keeping with the communal spirit of the occasion.

Giblets

WHEN YOU PURCHASE WHOLE POULTRY (ESPECIALLY TURKEYS AND CHICKENS), GIBLETS ARE PART OF THE DEAL, AND IN THE SPIRIT OF WASTE NOT, want not, it's worthwhile to know a little more about what they are and how to use them. *Giblet* (pronounced with a soft *j* sound) is the general term given to the handful of edible organs, typically the heart, liver, and gizzard, sold with poultry. The neck is often included in the mix, and so I include it in a general discussion on what to do with giblets. Turkey giblets will also sometimes include the tail, a bulbous fatty piece that can be used like the rest. Most poultry producers gather the giblets (after processing) and place them in a small bag, which they tuck into the body cavity. When roasting a whole bird, be sure you check both cavities for such a bag before you start.

The most obvious use for giblets (with the exception of the liver) is to add them to your next batch of broth (they keep in the freezer for several months). The liver should not be used for broth, as it will turn the liquid bitter and cloudy. My favorite use for poultry liver is to sauté it in butter, season it aggressively with salt and pepper, deglaze with a little brandy, and chop it up to smear on toast for a snack. Alternatively, you can save up the livers (in the freezer) until you have enough to make a batch of pâté.

Another way to use giblets is to toss them (again, no liver) into the roasting pan (I suggest this in a few recipes, such as Basic Roast Chicken with a Simple *Jus*, page 268) to enrich the drippings. After roasting, discard them (or chop the meat and feed it to the dog). You can also make a simple giblet broth by simmering the neck, heart, and gizzard with aromatics (such as celery, onion, carrot, and bay leaf) and enough cold water to cover by about an inch. For chicken, simmer about 25 minutes; for turkey, 50 minutes. Once simmered, strain and use the broth for sauce-making or another recipe calling for broth. The strained-out giblets can then be chopped into fine dice and added to gravy, stuffing, or even salads. When chopping the gizzard, first trim away and discard the tough membrane. The heart may be chopped as is. For the neck, remove any skin, pull the meat away from the bone, and tear it into shreds.

Removing the Wishbone

WE ALL KNOW WHAT A WISHBONE LOOKS LIKE, BUT NOT EVERYONE KNOWS THAT REMOVING THE WISHBONE *BEFORE* ROASTING MAKES CARVING ANY poultry, especially the larger birds, like turkey and goose, much easier. The wishbone sits as a sort of collarbone atop the breast, its apex a piece of cartilage at the tip of the breast-bone and the two "arms" reaching to shoulder joints at their end points. The trouble is that the tip portion of the breast meat on each side runs up under the span of the wishbone. As a result, leaving the wishbone intact makes it difficult to carve the breast from the carcass neatly. Thankfully, the bone structure on every bird (from Cornish hen to turkey) is pretty much the same, so once you learn how to remove one wishbone, you basically know how to remove them all.

To remove the wishbone, arrange the bird breast side up on a cutting board with the neck facing you. Pull back the skin flap to reveal the meat around the neck opening. If you've never done this operation before, you may not immediately recognize the wishbone, as it's covered with a thin layer of meat. Just feel around with your fingers until you locate the familiar thin, inverted-V-shaped bone. Using the tip of a sharp, rigid knife (I recommend a boning knife or sturdy paring knife), scrape along the inside of the "arms" of the wishbone, freeing it, and then slide the knife under to release the underside. Scrape free as much as you can. The easiest approach is to slip a finger under one side at a time and yank to remove it—one arm at a time. If you're hoping to retrieve the wishbone intact, you'll need to free up the cartilaginous tip with the knife before lifting. Then you can scrub it clean and let it sit on a windowsill until dry enough to use to make a wish.

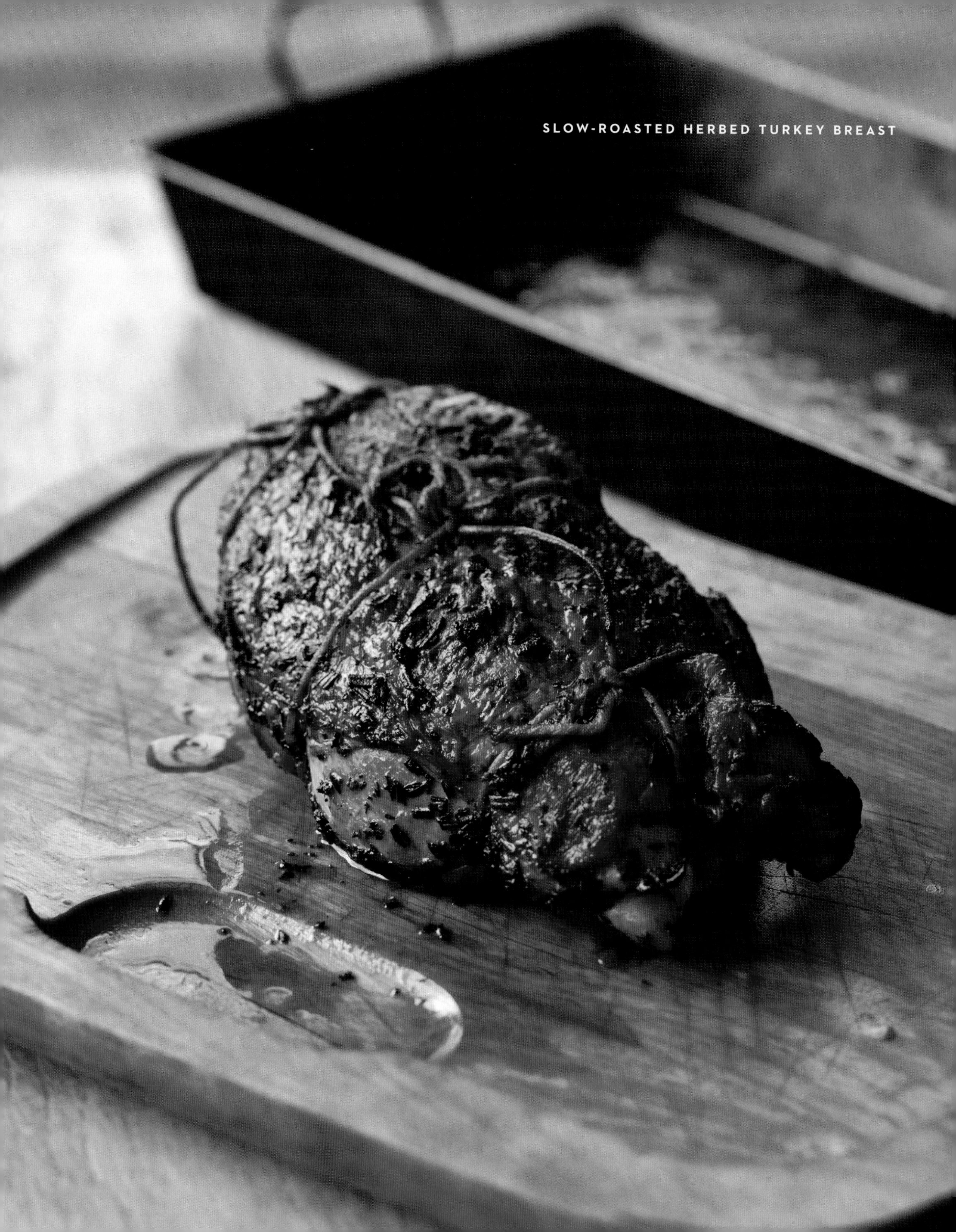

SLOW-ROASTED HERBED TURKEY BREAST

SLOW-ROASTED HERBED TURKEY BREAST

As much as I enjoy roasting a whole turkey, there are occasions when I crave the taste of roast turkey but don't want to bother with the whole bird. Fortunately, a single boneless turkey breast becomes a wonderful little roast, ideal for a small dinner party or a relaxed family supper. I will sometimes make this when there are only 2 or 3 of us at the table, knowing that I can look forward to superb turkey sandwiches later in the week. A single breast weighs between 2 and 3 pounds. For this recipe, you want one with the skin on, but no bones. This gives you a compact roast that will have a handsome, browned exterior and be a cinch to carve.

There are two keys to keeping the turkey breast moist and flavorful. First, the turkey gets rubbed with an herb paste ahead of time, so the salt and seasonings can work into the meat. I use a full complement of herbs—sage, rosemary, and thyme—but you could certainly create your own combinations based on what's growing on the windowsill or sitting in your refrigerator. Then you want to sear the breast in a skillet before roasting it in a low oven, where it can cook through without drying out. I like to serve this with roasted potatoes and something green, like string beans or a salad. The meat is so moist that it doesn't need gravy. Trust me.

SERVES 4 TO 6

METHOD: Combination sear and low heat

ROASTING TIME: 1 1/2 to 1 3/4 hours (plus 12 minutes to sear)

PLAN AHEAD: The turkey needs to be rubbed with an herb paste 6 to 24 hours before roasting.

WINE: One of the most versatile of all wine pairings—anything from fruity dry and off-dry whites, such as Riesling, Chenin Blanc, and Pinot Gris, to lighter reds, such as a young vintage of Pinot Noir or Beaujolais.

2 garlic cloves

1¼ teaspoons kosher salt

3 tablespoons extra-virgin olive oil

2 teaspoons finely chopped fresh sage

2 teaspoons finely chopped fresh thyme

2 teaspoons finely chopped fresh rosemary

½ teaspoon freshly ground black pepper

¼ teaspoon celery seeds

1 boneless turkey breast half (about 2 ½ pounds), with skin

CONTINUED ON NEXT PAGE

1 **MAKE THE HERB PASTE.** Combine the garlic and salt in a mortar and pound until you have a smooth paste. (If you don't have a mortar, make the paste using a chef's knife; see Making Garlic Paste Without a Mortar and Pestle, page 230.) Transfer to a small bowl and stir in 2 tablespoons olive oil, herbs, pepper, and celery seeds.

2 **SEASON AND TIE THE TURKEY BREAST.** Smear the turkey breast all over with the herb paste, using your fingers to slide some of the paste under the skin, being careful not to loosen the skin completely. Using your hands, arrange the turkey breast in a neat shape, tucking the edges under so the breast sits plumply on the cutting board. Now tie the breast, using 2 to 3 loops of kitchen string to secure it in a cylindrical shape and looping a longer string from end to end to keep the roast compact. Place the roast on a wire rack on a baking sheet or tray and refrigerate, preferably uncovered, for 6 to 24 hours. Let the roast sit at room temperature for about an hour before roasting.

3 **HEAT THE OVEN.** Position a rack near the center of the oven and heat to 300 degrees (275 degrees convection).

4 **SEAR THE TURKEY.** Heat a large skillet (11 to 12 inches) over medium-high heat. Add the remaining tablespoon oil and heat until the oil shimmers. Sear the turkey skin side down, maneuvering it and turning it from side to side with tongs so the skin side sears evenly, about 6 minutes. Turn the turkey skin side up and brown lightly on the bottom, another 2 to 3 minutes. Transfer the turkey, skin side up, to a shallow roasting pan or baking dish not much larger than it is (about 8 by 12 inches).

5 **ROAST.** Slide the turkey into the oven and roast until the juices run mostly clear with a trace of pink and an instant-read thermometer inserted in the thickest part registers about 165 degrees, 1½ to 1¾ hours. Let the turkey rest for 20 minutes.

6 **CARVE AND SERVE.** Remove the strings and carve the turkey across the grain into ¼- to ½-inch-thick slices. There will be few, if any, pan drippings (because of the preseasoning and slow cooking), but if there are a few, drizzle these over the meat.

SLOW-ROASTED HERBED TURKEY BREAST (PAGE 351); AT RIGHT SERVED
WITH MAPLE-ROASTED BUTTERNUT SQUASH AND APPLES (PAGE 518)

WHOLE ROAST DUCK WITH HOISIN SAUCE (AKA LAZY PERSON'S PEKING DUCK)

WHOLE ROAST DUCK WITH HOISIN SAUCE (AKA LAZY PERSON'S PEKING DUCK)

I love Peking duck, the kind you get at Chinese restaurants with its super-crispy skin and the accompanying paper-thin pancakes and hoisin sauce for wrapping it in. I love it so much that I thought I would recreate the dish at home for this book. I knew that authentic Peking duck requires a lengthy preparation process, including a step that involves stringing the duck up in front of a fan for a period of time, but I was gung-ho. At least at first. I went through the rigmarole of blanching a whole duck several times, then hanging it on my screen porch for hours to dry, and finally glazing it multiple times before roasting. In the end I was exhausted, and the results weren't measurably better than what I can get from my favorite Chinese restaurant. I decided to rethink what I was really after, which is this: incredibly crackly, crisp skin and the sweet Asian accent of the hoisin sauce. Taking a cue from my roast chicken recipes, I decided to try presalting the duck to get that crisp skin. Though this takes some planning ahead—the seasoned duck needs at least 24 hours in the refrigerator—it's much easier, and less unsightly, than hanging a duck from the rafters.

The duck then slow-roasts in order to render its fat and cook the tougher leg meat to tender, braiselike perfection. I start with the duck breast side down, as this helps render some of the thick layer of fat under the skin. Prodigious pricking of the skin with a sharp knife also helps release this fat as it melts. As with Peking duck, the meat will almost be falling off the bone, and it will be moist and tender thanks to the natural basting from the bird's own fat. After carving, I like to serve each person a bit of breast meat and dark meat, rounding out the meal with steamed rice and crisp-tender stir-fried bok choy. For a full-on Peking duck experience, chop or shred the roasted duck into bite-size pieces, making one platter of tender meat and another of crispy skin. Serve with warm Chinese pancakes (also called Mandarin pancakes and available in Chinese markets), chopped scallions, sliced cucumbers, and more hoisin. You can also take the minimalist route and enjoy the simple goodness of plain slow-roasted duck by following the directions on page 357.

CONTINUED ON NEXT PAGE

SERVES 4

METHOD: Combination moderate heat and high heat

ROASTING TIME: 2 1/4 to 2 1/2 hours (plus 10 minutes to glaze)

PLAN AHEAD: The duck needs to be seasoned at least 24 and up to 48 hours ahead of roasting.

WINE: Medium-sweet Riesling with tart acidity, such as Auslese Rieslings from the Rheingau, Rheinhessen, or Pfalz regions of Germany.

FOR THE SPICE RUB AND THE DUCK

1 tablespoon kosher salt

2 garlic cloves, minced

2 teaspoons finely grated orange zest

1¼ teaspoons coriander seeds, lightly toasted

1¼ teaspoons Chinese five-spice powder

½ teaspoon freshly ground white pepper

1 Pekin (Long Island) duck (5 to 6 pounds), giblets removed (see Shopping for Duck, page 360)

FOR THE GLAZE

3 tablespoons hoisin sauce

2 tablespoons orange liqueur, such as Grand Marnier or Triple Sec (or you can substitute orange juice)

1 tablespoon honey

1 teaspoon toasted sesame oil

1 **TRIM AND SEASON THE DUCK.** In a mortar or spice grinder, grind the salt, garlic, zest, coriander seeds, five-spice powder, and pepper into a coarse paste.

Make 20 to 30 small slits in the duck skin, using a sharp paring knife held parallel to the surface so that you pierce the skin and fat without cutting into the meat. Be sure to make slits on the back and thighs as well as the breast. Rub about two thirds of the spice mixture into the duck cavity and then rub what remains all over the skin. Set the duck on a rack set over a baking sheet and allow to air-dry in the refrigerator for at least 24 hours and up to 48 hours.

2 **HEAT THE OVEN.** Position a rack in the center of the oven and heat to 325 degrees (300 degrees convection). Let the duck sit at room temperature as the oven heats.

3 **ROAST THE DUCK.** Arrange the duck breast down on a roasting rack in a roasting pan (about 12 by 14 inches) and roast for 1¼ hours. Remove the pan from the oven and spoon or pour off most of the fat. (A turkey baster can make this job easier.) Using sturdy tongs inserted in the duck's cavity, flip the duck over. Pierce the skin again all over the breast and legs with a knife. Return the duck to the oven to continue roasting until the meat around the thighs feels tender when prodded (a skewer should penetrate the thigh with no resistance), the legs feel loose in their joints, and an instant-read thermometer inserted into the thickest part of the thigh (without touching bone) registers 175 degrees, another 1 to 1¼ hours. *(You can roast the duck a day ahead to this point; see page 359.)*

4 **GLAZE AND BLAST THE DUCK.** Remove the duck from the oven and increase the oven temperature, preferably to 500 degrees convection, if you have it, or to 525 degrees standard. In a small bowl, whisk together the hoisin sauce, orange liqueur, honey, and sesame oil. Carefully transfer the duck (on the roasting rack) to a rimmed baking sheet. Paint the breast and legs with about half the glaze and return the duck to the hot oven. Paint again after 5 minutes, and continue roasting until crispy and mahogany-colored, about 3 minutes in a convection oven, 5 minutes in a standard oven.

5 **LET REST AND CARVE.** Transfer the duck to a carving board, ideally one with a trough, and let it rest for 5 to 10 minutes before carving. Carving a duck is much like carving a small version of a goose, so you can refer to the directions on pages 372 and 373. Be sure each person gets both breast meat and a thigh or leg.

OPTION: PLAIN SLOW-ROASTED DUCK

You can use the preseasoning and slow roasting method from the Whole Roast Duck with Hoisin Sauce recipe with just about any flavors you like, including just simple salt and pepper. Just be sure to use at least 1 tablespoon of salt per bird in the presalting step. Follow the trimming and roasting instructions (steps 1–3). Omit the glaze, but do give the duck that final blast of heat to brown it beautifully.

WINE: New World Pinot Noir from Russian River Valley or Oregon's Willamette Valley.

WHOLE ROAST DUCK WITH HOISIN SAUCE
SERVED PEKING-STYLE

A Restaurant Make-Ahead Trick for Whole Roast Duck

I LEARNED A GREAT MAKE-AHEAD TRICK FOR ROAST DUCK—REALLY FOR ANY ROAST BIRD—FROM BOSTON CHEF JODY ADAMS. THINGS MOVE QUICKLY IN A busy restaurant kitchen, and as Jody says, "It's hell to break down a whole duck when it's hot for service." So Jody and her cooks roast the ducks a day in advance. Then, before the customers arrive, they can calmly carve the ducks while cool (both the ducks and the cooks who are just starting dinner service). The ducks get portioned, and then when an order comes in, the portions are blasted in the hot oven to heat and crisp them up. This is a great technique for the home cook to keep in mind, especially for stress-free entertaining.

Brushing Slow-Roasted Duck Breast (page 362) with hoisin glaze

In the case of Whole Roast Duck with Hoisin Sauce, follow the recipe through step 3. After roasting, let the duck cool at room temperature (without glazing). Cover and refrigerate for up to 24 hours. To serve, carve the duck into pieces and put them skin side up on a heavy-duty rimmed baking sheet. Heat the oven to 500 degrees convection (525 degrees standard if you don't have convection). Let the duck sit at room temperature as the oven heats. Slide the duck into the oven and heat for 5 minutes, then brush with about half the glaze. Continue heating, brushing again with glaze after another 5 minutes. Expect carved pieces of cold duck to take 10 to 15 minutes to heat through and get crisp.

LEFT: For the full Peking duck experience, serve sliced or shredded roasted duck with warm Chinese pancakes (also called Mandarin pancakes and available in Chinese markets), sliced scallions and/or cucumbers, and hoisin or plum sauce. To eat, spread a bit of hoisin (or plum) sauce on a pancake, top with duck, scatter on scallions (and/or cucumbers), roll it up, and eat with your fingers. Make sure everyone gets a bit of crispy skin in each pancake.

Shopping for Duck

WHOLE DUCK

Long Island duck, sometimes called Pekin, is the most widely available duck variety and can be found in most well-stocked markets. Fortunately, this popular breed makes fine eating, and its generous size (5 to 6 pounds) provides enough rich, dark meat to serve 4 people. Some producers apply the term *duckling* to their birds, but this is merely a marketing ploy meant to underscore their tenderness. Long Island ducks are a fast-growing breed that come to market at a young age, not more than 8 weeks, so whether the duck is labeled *duck* or *duckling*, you can expect the same tender, fatty bird. In most markets, look for whole ducks in the freezer section; when handled properly, freezing does nothing to diminish the quality of the meat. To defrost, leave the duck in its original wrapping, place it on a baking dish to catch any drips, and allow 2 full days in the refrigerator to defrost.

Some specialty markets and mail-order sources carry other breeds, such as the Muscovy, a smaller, leaner duck. I prefer the larger Long Island ducks, because when I roast a duck, I want enough meat to serve a small dinner party—which to me means at least 4 people. If you're the sort of cook who roasts a whole duck for 2 people, by all means seek out one of these smaller birds.

DUCK BREAST

Duck breasts, often labeled by their French name, *magrets,* can be found fresh or frozen in specialty markets and many upscale supermarkets and through mail-order sources (see Sources & Resources, page 539). They are typically sold in vacuum packages of one or two to the pack. Unlike chicken, with which we face the choice among bone-in, boneless, skin-on, and skinless, duck breasts are always sold boneless and skin-on. The most commonly available come from Moulard (or Mullard) ducks, the larger of the two species commercially available. (Long Island, or Pekin, is the second type, and is more often sold whole; see Whole Duck, above.) Moulard has a more robust, beefier flavor than Long Island, and I find its heftier size works perfectly for the sear-roasting technique in my recipe. On occasion I have seen a third variety of duck breast, those from Muscovy ducks, a smaller, South American breed (sometimes called Barbarie). Muscovy ducks share characteristics of the Moulard and Long Island in that they are robust and beefy like the former but smaller like the latter. Not all markets, however, specify species. The best way to tell is by size: If the breast is in the 12- to 14-ounce range, it's Moulard. If by chance you come across a smaller breast (around 8 ounces), it's Long Island.

A NOTE ON WILD DUCK

If you are a hunter, or friendly with any duck hunters, you know that wild ducks differ dramatically from their plump, fatty, domesticated counterparts. The few times I've been the benefactor of a hunter's bounty, I've received dressed ducks weighing as little as 8 ounces and none more than 2 pounds. The best way to roast these lean, bony birds is to brush them with some kind of fat (butter or oil) or wrap them in bacon and roast at relatively high heat (450 degrees) until the breast meat is rosy pink, about 30 minutes. (The slow-roast method I advocate for farm-raised ducks would leave wild duck dried out.) Let the ducks rest for 10 minutes or so, then carve off the breast and serve. The thighs are too tough and stringy to eat as is, so transfer them to a small covered pot with a little bit of broth and braise them in a 300-degree oven until they are tender, another hour or so. They make a fine lunch the next day, or the basis for pasta sauce.

SLOW-ROASTED DUCK BREAST

I think of duck breast as the rib-eye steak of the poultry world. The rich, rosy red meat of a perfectly cooked duck breast delivers the same sort of primal satisfaction that you get from a good thick steak. The key phrase in that sentence is "rosy red." Overcook duck breast and you'll miss much of what makes it so wonderful. Despite its thick layer of fat, the actual meat is quite lean (leaner, in fact, than either chicken or turkey). As a result, you need to take a little care when cooking duck breast in order to get it just right. Fortunately, sear-roasting—browning and crisping the duck on the stove before transferring it to a very low oven to gently finish cooking—is nearly foolproof for turning out perfectly cooked duck breast. Not only is this method much less nerve-racking than the high-heat, fast-paced stovetop method often used for duck breast, but the hands-off finish also gives you time to prepare the rest of the meal.

Another benefit of searing the breast before roasting is that you wind up with a few tablespoons of marvelous rendered duck fat. Reserve it right in the skillet and use it to sauté greens—spinach and watercress are my favorites—to serve alongside the duck. (Or reserve the fat to use later; just don't throw it away.) Along with the greens, I like to serve creamy polenta topped with roasted cherries (page 534). The contrast of colors and flavors is truly exceptional.

SERVES 4 TO 6
METHOD: Combination sear and low heat
ROASTING TIME: About 50 minutes (plus 6 minutes to sear)
WINE: Older vintage of red Burgundy from the Côte de Nuits, such as Gevrey-Chambertin or Morey-St.-Denis.

2 Moulard duck breasts (*magrets*), about 12 ounces each (see page 360)

Kosher salt and freshly ground black pepper

1 **SCORE THE DUCK SKIN AND FAT.** Pat the duck breasts dry with paper towels. Using a sharp paring knife or boning knife, score the skin and fat in a cross-hatch pattern, making the cuts about ½-inch apart. The key here is to cut down through the fat without exposing the meat. Go slowly at first, until you get a sense of how deeply you can cut while leaving a thin layer of the fat (about ⅛-inch) uncut. Season the breasts well all over with salt and pepper. Leave the seasoned duck at room temperature while the oven heats.

2　**HEAT THE OVEN.** Position a rack in the center and heat the oven to 200 degrees (175 degrees convection).

3　**SEAR THE DUCK.** Have ready a small roasting pan or small heavy-duty rimmed baking sheet outfitted with a flat roasting rack.

Heat a large, heavy skillet (10 to 12 inches, and I prefer cast iron) over medium-high heat until hot. Add the duck breasts skin side down and cook, without moving them, until the skin is deeply browned, about 6 minutes. The duck should sizzle, but it shouldn't splatter wildly or smoke. If the skin appears to be browning too fast and there is a risk of burning, lower the heat slightly.

Transfer the duck, skin side up, to the rack on the roasting pan or baking sheet. A good amount of duck fat will be left behind in the skillet. Reserve the fat in the pan to sauté greens to go along with the duck, as described above, or pour it into a heatproof container (leave any solids behind in the pan) to save for another time.

4　**ROAST THE DUCK.** Slide the duck into the oven and roast until medium-rare (an instant-read thermometer inserted in the thickest part registers 145 to 150 degrees), about 50 minutes. (If you like your duck seriously rare—I don't—you can take it out when it reaches 135 degrees; begin checking after 25 minutes.)

5　**REST, SLICE, AND SERVE.** Transfer to a cutting board and let the duck rest for about 5 minutes before carving. Slice each breast crosswise into ¼- to ⅓-inch thick slices and serve.

CHRISTMAS ROAST GOOSE
WITH GRAVY AND OPTIONAL
POTATO-SAGE STUFFING; SLOW-
ROASTED GRAPES (PAGE 527)

CHRISTMAS ROAST GOOSE WITH GRAVY

Roast goose ranks as one of the most magnificent and festive dishes of all time. It conjures up images of historic yuletide feasts, and it remains the iconic Christmas dinner in England. I also like to treat friends to a roast goose on New Year's Eve—one big luxurious meal before all those pesky resolutions kick in. Indeed, a plump, glistening, crisp-skinned goose transforms any winter dinner party into something festive and memorable. Goose is definitely made for that season. To fully appreciate the rich, all-dark, almost beefy meat, you'll want the kind of hearty appetite that only cold weather can bring.

My basic recipe includes a luxuriously thick gravy. Because goose tastes best when roasted until well done, it is also delicious filled with a savory stuffing, such as the potato-sage one on page 369. You can also use any favorite bread stuffing (figure 5 to 6 cups well-seasoned stuffing). If you happen to possess a covered oval roaster this is an ideal time to use it, as the goose gets steamed before roasting, a step that helps to render its abundant fat, and therefore needs to be covered (for more on steam roasting, see page 371). If your roaster doesn't have a cover, use heavy-duty aluminum foil.

SERVES 6 TO 8

METHOD: Combination steam and moderate heat

ROASTING TIME: 2 to 2 1/2 hours (plus 40 minutes to steam)

PLAN AHEAD: Season the goose and make the broth for the gravy a day or two before roasting.

WINE: A fine aged Rioja Gran Reserva from Spain or Barbaresco from Italy.

One 9- to 12-pound goose, with giblets (see
  Shopping for Goose, page 374)

Kosher salt and freshly ground black
  pepper

1 tablespoon peanut oil or other
  neutral-tasting oil

1 medium onion, coarsely chopped

1 carrot, chopped into 1-inch pieces

1 celery stalk, chopped into 1-inch pieces

2 to 3 sprigs fresh thyme

1 bay leaf

¼ teaspoon whole black peppercorns

¾ cup dry red wine, Madeira, tawny port,
  or dry sherry

2 tablespoons reserved goose fat or
  unsalted butter

3 tablespoons all-purpose flour

2 tablespoons currant or plum jelly

CONTINUED ON NEXT PAGE

1   **TRIM AND SEASON THE GOOSE.** Look over the goose carefully to determine whether any pinfeathers or quills (the small feather tips) are present; they're most often found around the legs. Remove any you find with strong tweezers or pliers. Pull the giblets out of the cavity and set aside, reserving the liver for a stuffing, if desired (see Giblets, page 348). Tear off any loose deposits of fat inside the two cavity openings, neck and tail. To make for easier carving later on, you may want to remove the wishbone (see Removing the Wishbone, page 349.) Next, cut off and reserve the outermost joints of each wing, leaving only the section nearest the breast still attached. (Some geese come with the wing tips already removed, so you may not need to do this.) Set the wing tips (if present) aside with the giblets. Using a sharp skewer or a thin paring knife, prick holes in the skin around the lower breast and thighs. Try to poke through the skin without cutting into the meat beneath. (The holes will allow fat to release from under the skin during cooking.) Finally, season the goose generously inside and out with salt and pepper. Set the goose on a rack over a rimmed baking sheet and refrigerate, uncovered, for 1 to 2 days.

1 Pull the giblets out of the cavity (they are often found in a small bag) and set aside. **2** Tear off the loose deposits of fat from inside the two cavity openings, neck and tail. **3** Prick holes in the skin around the lower breast and thigh with the tip of a sharp knife or skewer, without cutting into the meat beneath.

2   **MAKE THE BROTH.** Assemble the reserved giblets and trimmings; they should include the neck, a heart, a gizzard, the wishbone, if you removed it, and 2 wings, if not removed before you bought the goose (but no liver—it's bad for broth making). With a cleaver or heavy knife, hack the neck and wings (if present) into 3- to 4-inch pieces. Pat dry with a paper towel, and dry the giblets as well.

Heat the oil in a 5-quart stock pot over medium heat. Add the bones and giblets.

Sauté, turning occasionally, until browned on all sides, about 10 minutes. Add the onion, carrot, celery, thyme, and bay leaf and stir. Add 4 cups of water (or enough to just cover the bones), the peppercorns, and a small pinch of salt and bring to a gentle boil. Immediately reduce the heat and simmer gently, uncovered, for 2 hours. The bones should remain just barely covered by liquid; if the broth boils too hard, you may need to add more water just to barely cover the solids. Strain into a large bowl through a fine-mesh sieve, pressing gently on the solids with a wooden spoon. Discard the solids and cool the broth to room temperature before refrigerating. You should have 1¾ to 2 cups broth. *The broth will keep for 4 days in the refrigerator, 6 months in the freezer.*

3 **STEAM THE GOOSE.** Put the goose breast side up on a rack set in a large, sturdy roasting pan with sides at least 3 inches high. (If you have a covered roasting pan, this is a great time to use it.) Set the pan on the top of the stove over your largest burner and add 1 to 2 inches of water. Cover the roasting pan tightly with its lid or heavy-duty foil. Bring to a boil and lower the heat so the water gently simmers. Steam the goose for 40 minutes, checking the liquid occasionally to make sure it's simmering. Turn off the heat, carefully uncover (so as not to burn yourself with the steam), and let the goose sit until cool enough to handle, about 30 minutes.

4 **HEAT THE OVEN.** Position a rack in the lower third of the oven and heat to 325 degrees (300 degrees convection).

5 **GATHER THE GOOSE FAT.** Using sturdy pot holders or a double thickness of dish towels, lift the roasting rack and goose out of the roasting pan and set aside on a tray or cutting board to catch any drips. Pour the steaming liquid from the roasting pan into a clean vessel and leave at room temperature until cool. When the liquid and fat are cool enough to handle, separate them, using a gravy separator or pouring off as much fat as you can. Save the fat but discard the liquid. Set aside 2 tablespoons of the fat for the gravy and reserve the rest for future cooking. (When you get to the point where it's difficult to pour off fat cleanly, pour the liquid into a glass vessel and refrigerate until the fat solidifies. Then simply spoon off the white fat and discard the water.) *If stuffing the goose, do so now.*

6 **ROAST THE GOOSE.** Return the roasting rack and goose to the roasting pan. Transfer to the oven and roast until the meat on the drumsticks feels soft when

CONTINUED ON NEXT PAGE

pressed (your finger should leave a slight impression where you press) and the skin is beginning to pull away from the drumstick end, about 2 hours if unstuffed and 2½ hours if stuffed. If unsure, prick the thigh with a sharp knife, being sure to cut all the way through to the meat. If the juices run pink, roast for another 20 minutes or so. If the juices are clear or if very few juices run, the goose is done. The internal temperature of the thigh meat should be about 180 degrees, as measured with an instant-read thermometer inserted in the thickest part of the thigh (without touching bone). If the bird is stuffed, check that the stuffing reaches 170 degrees. Remove the goose from the oven. If the skin is not deeply browned and crisp, increase the oven heat to 425 degrees (400 degrees convection). Transfer the roasting rack with the goose on it to a heavy-duty rimmed baking sheet (this way you can brown the goose without burning the pan drippings) and roast for an additional 15 minutes to brown the skin.

Set the goose in a draft-free spot to rest for 20 to 45 minutes. If the kitchen is cool, tent foil loosely over it.

7 **MAKE THE GRAVY.** Pour off any excess grease from the roasting pan, being careful to leave behind all the tasty drippings. Place the roasting pan over medium heat on the largest burner and add the wine, Madeira, port, or sherry, stirring and scraping with a wooden spoon to loosen all the browned bits stuck to the pan. Bring to a boil and reduce by about half, stirring often, about 3 minutes. Scrape the contents of the roasting pan into a fine-mesh strainer set over a 1-quart glass measuring cup or bowl. Let the liquid settle before skimming off any surface fat.

In a medium saucepan over medium-low heat, heat the reserved 2 tablespoons of goose fat or butter. Whisk in the flour, reduce the heat to low, and continue cooking, whisking regularly, until smooth, about 3 minutes. Slowly whisk in the strained liquid from the roasting pan. Bring to a simmer and cook over low heat, whisking regularly, until thickened, about 3 minutes. Add about half of the reserved broth and bring to a simmer, whisking. Once the sauce begins to thicken, continue adding broth until the gravy is a consistency you like. Continue simmering, whisking occasionally, until any floury taste disappears, about 8 minutes. Whisk in the jelly until melted. Season to taste with salt and pepper and set aside in a warm place while you carve the goose.

8 **CARVE AND SERVE.** Carve and serve the goose with the gravy on the side. (For help, see Carving a Roast Goose, page 372.)

OPTION: POTATO-SAGE STUFFING

The idea of mashed potato stuffing comes from Pennsylvania Dutch country, and it's my favorite way to stuff a goose. There's a certain flavor magic that happens when the rich juices from the goose baste the dense potato filling. I add a little apple and celery to the stuffing as well, for a hint of sweetness and a bit of crunch. It's also a nice way to use up the reserved goose liver, if you like.

MAKES ABOUT 5 1/2 CUPS OF STUFFING, ENOUGH FOR ONE 9- TO 12-POUND GOOSE

PLAN AHEAD: Make the stuffing while the goose steams and cools.

2 ½ pounds russet potatoes, peeled and cut into golf-ball-size chunks

Kosher salt

2 tablespoons unsalted butter or rendered goose fat or bacon fat

1 large onion, finely chopped

Freshly ground black pepper

1 small garlic clove, minced

1 goose liver (optional), chopped into ½-inch pieces

2 celery stalks, with leaves, coarsely chopped

1 large tart apple, such as Granny Smith, cored and chopped into ½-inch pieces (about 1 ½ cups)

2 tablespoons chopped fresh sage

1 teaspoon finely grated lemon zest

Christmas Roast Goose with Gravy (page 365), prepared through step 5

1 **BOIL AND MASH THE POTATOES.** Place the potatoes in a large pot and cover with cold water. Salt the water generously and bring to a boil over medium-high heat. When the water boils, reduce to a strong simmer—the potatoes shouldn't bash around in the pot—and simmer until the potatoes are tender enough to pierce easily with a metal skewer or fork, about 20 minutes. Drain well. Return the drained potatoes to the pot, place over low heat, and shake and stir for 1 to 2 minutes to remove excess moisture. You should see a starchy film form on the bottom of the pot. Mash the potatoes, using a hand masher or a ricer. I find the stuffing is best with lump-free potatoes, so do the best you can to smooth them out.

2 **SAUTÉ THE AROMATICS.** Heat the butter or rendered fat in a large skillet (10- to 11-inches) over medium heat. Add the onion, season lightly with salt and pepper, and sauté, stirring frequently until soft and lightly browned, about 6 minutes. Add the

CONTINUED ON NEXT PAGE

garlic and chopped liver, if using, and cook, shaking the pan, until the liver changes color, about 4 minutes. (If not using the liver, sauté until the garlic is fragrant, only about 2 minutes.) Add the celery, apple, sage, and zest. Season with salt and pepper and cook another 3 minutes to meld the flavors. Fold this mixture into the mashed potatoes. Season to taste with salt and pepper.

3 **STUFF AND ROAST THE GOOSE.** Using a large spoon, loosely fill both cavities of the steamed and cooled goose with the stuffing. Roast as directed, starting with step 6 on page 367.

Steam Roasting

THE CHALLENGE TO ROASTING GOOSE IS DEALING WITH THE GENEROUSLY THICK LAYER OF SUBCUTANEOUS FAT THAT COVERS THE BREAST AND THIGHS. Geese, like ducks, are genetically designed to collect this protective, calorie-rich layer of fat under their skin in order to sustain them during their long migrations. Even when these fowl are farm-raised (as all commercially available geese are), they still boast an abundance of soft white fat. When properly roasted, the fat melts away, leaving just enough to nicely lubricate the meat and render the skin marvelously crisp and delicious. As a bonus, the cook is left with a generous amount of glorious goose fat, one of the most delicious cooking fats known to man.

The best way to roast a goose involves an initial moist-heat phase. Before roasting, the bird is steamed, simmered, or even poached to melt away a considerable portion of the fat. In addition, a goose needs to roast slowly in order to melt even more fat away from the meat as it cooks. In the end, goose is best roasted until well done. Unlike other poultry, which turns dry and tough as it overcooks, goose actually turns tender and succulent when cooked to an internal temperature of 180 degrees.

For the steaming technique, I took a cue from Julia Child in *The Way to Cook* and steam the goose in a covered roasting pan directly on top of the stove instead of in the oven, as many recipes direct. The reason? If you steam a goose in the oven, you have to haul the hot, heavy roasting pan containing a 10-pound goose plus a good amount of simmering water and liquid fat onto the countertop without sloshing and spilling. When you steam on the stove, you only have to lift out the roasting rack holding the goose and then pour off the steaming liquid and fat.

Carving a Roast Goose

IF YOU'VE EVER CARVED A LARGE CHICKEN OR A TURKEY, YOU'RE ON FAMILIAR GROUND WHEN CARVING A GOOSE. START BY ARRANGING THE GOOSE ON A large and stable cutting board (as shown on page 373) and grabbing a thin-bladed carving knife. If you've stuffed the goose, use a large spoon to transfer the stuffing to a serving platter (remember both cavities). Pull one wing away and tilt the carcass slightly so you can get the knife into the joint where the wing attaches to the breast. Remove one wing at a time. Now use a kitchen towel to grab hold of one leg and cut through the skin where the leg and breast meet. Once the skin is cut, pry the leg away from the body—it may feel somewhat stiff, but with a slight force you should be able to push it away from the body. Still holding the leg, tilt the carcass to expose the ball-and-socket joint where the thigh meets the backbone and cut through the joint to remove the leg section. (It helps to know that the thigh joint on a goose is a little lower than on a turkey, so you may need to wiggle a little to locate it.) The objective is to get the fat little nugget of meat (referred to as the "oyster") that sits right up against either side of the backbone while cutting easily through the joint. Repeat with the other leg.

Now turn your attention to the breast. Using the tip of your knife, make a long incision along the length of one side of the breastbone. The breastbone on a goose is high and wide, so you may have to do a little exploratory cutting to find the place where the breastbone ends and the meat begins. Once you find the place to start, continue carving in long, sweeping strokes to remove one entire side of the breast in one single piece. As you carve, try to feel the blade gliding along the bone, leaving as little meat behind on the carcass as possible. When you get down toward the end of the breast, free the entire breast half and place it on the carving board. Repeat with the second breast half. Once you have removed both halves, carve them crosswise (across the grain) into ¼- to ½-inch thick slices.

Transfer the carved breast meat to a platter and return your attention to the legs. One at a time, set them skin side down and separate each into a thigh and a drumstick by slicing through the knee joint. Then slice the meat from the thigh, carving parallel to the bone. You can also carve the meat off the drumstick (although there is very little) or offer the drumsticks to anyone who likes to gnaw meat off a bone.

Pour any juices from carving into the gravy, if you are making gravy. Serve each person some breast and leg meat.

Step by Step: Carving a Goose

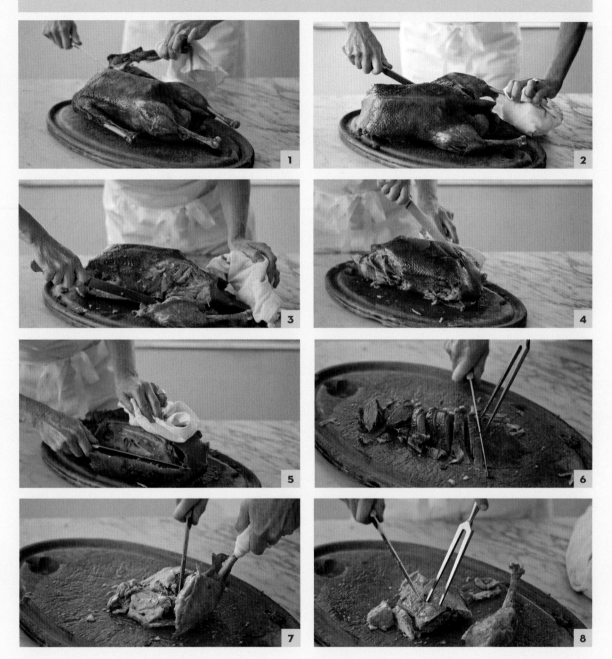

1 Pull one wing away, and tilt the carcass slightly so you can get the knife into the joint where the wing attaches to the breast. Repeat with the second wing. **2** Grab hold of one leg (protecting your hands with a towel) and cut through the skin where the leg and breast meet. Pry the leg away from the body with a slight force until you are able to push it away from the body. Cut through the joint to separate the leg from the body. **3** Repeat with the second leg. **4** Make a long incision along the length of one side of the breastbone. Continue carving in long, sweeping strokes, trying to feel the blade gliding along the breastbone. **5** Remove one entire side of the breast in one single piece. Repeat with the second breast half. **6** Carve each breast crosswise (across the grain) into slices. **7** One by one, turn the legs skin side down and separate each into a thigh and a drumstick. **8** Slice the meat from the thigh, carving parallel to the bone.

Shopping for Goose

ABOUT THE ONLY TIME YOU'LL FIND FRESH GOOSE IS AROUND CHRISTMAS, AND USUALLY ONLY IN BIG CITIES AND IN UPSCALE FOOD MARKETS. (YOU CAN also mail-order them from certain purveyors; see Sources & Resources, page 539.) In many markets, no matter the time of year, frozen is the only option (look for goose in the freezer case alongside the turkeys, ducks, and Cornish hens). The good news is that when properly thawed, there's no significant difference between the fresh and the frozen. If you do buy a frozen goose, allow several days for it to thaw in your refrigerator before cooking.

Fresh or frozen, all geese sold in commercial markets are young, domesticated birds. Farm-raised geese grow fast; in as little as 16 weeks, they can reach anywhere from 8 to 16 pounds. I recommend roasting a modest-sized goose, about 9 to 12 pounds. As geese grow larger, they get bonier but not much meatier. In fact, I once roasted and carved a 12-pounder and a 16-pounder side by side and was stunned to see that the 16-pound goose yielded only about 6 ounces more meat. Smaller birds are also easier to handle and more reliably tasty and tender.

Geese, like ducks, have a somewhat elongated, torpedo-shaped carcass, with wider and deeper cavities than chickens and turkeys. As a result, they always seem to look as though they'll serve more people than they actually will. A 9- to 12-pound goose generously serves 6 to 8 people. To serve 10 people, stuff the goose, add a few extra side dishes, and make a little extra gravy. For more guests, you'll want a second goose.

As with all meats and poultry, the more you know about the source, the better likelihood you will have of buying a first-rate product. If you're willing to do a little homework and spend a little more money, you can find some excellent free-range, humanely raised geese from the Amish and Mennonite farms in Pennsylvania Dutch country. Regardless of where you buy your goose, brace yourself: A whole goose can run anywhere from $50 to $150, depending on its size and provenance.

Leftover Roast Goose

IF YOU'RE CONSIDERING ROASTING A GOOSE BUT DON'T HAVE 6 TO 8 PEOPLE TO INVITE TO DINNER, DON'T LET THAT STOP YOU. LEFTOVER ROAST GOOSE IS AKIN to leftover roast beef. It's delicious thinly sliced or shredded and served cold or at room temperature. Treat it like a first-rate cold cut—on a sandwich or salad or as the centerpiece of plowman's lunch, with a little sweet chutney or spicy mustard and some pickled vegetables alongside. In fact, the esteemed English food writer Elizabeth David suggests in *Elizabeth David's Christmas* (published posthumously in 2008) that despite all the fuss over the traditional Christmas goose, roast goose is best served cold. I don't know that I'd go that far, but I agree that it's a rare treat and greatly appreciated by anyone lucky enough to get a taste.

WHOLE ROASTED RAINBOW
TROUT (PAGE 433)

FISH & SHELLFISH

HERB-ROASTED SHRIMP WITH
PANCETTA (PAGE 387)

FISH & SHELLFISH

RECIPES

EAFOOD MAY NOT BE AT THE TOP OF YOUR MIND WHEN YOU THINK OF ROASTING, BUT I'M GUESSING THAT IF MORE PEOPLE KNEW HOW TO ROAST fish (and shellfish) at home, they would do so more often. For one thing, it's easy; with roasting, there's no worry about having the delicate flesh stick to the pan or grill. Plus seafood roasts evenly in the oven, leaving your hands free to finish the rest of the meal. But best of all are the lightly golden crust and the moist, just-cooked center that come as a result of roasting fish. Unlike the case with hefty cuts of meat and large birds, the time fish spends in the oven is measured not in hours but in minutes, often 20 or less, which makes it a perfect weeknight choice.

By nature, fish and shellfish are more delicate than any of the land animals that we eat. This delicacy means we don't have to worry about tenderizing any tough connective tissue during cooking, but it also means that we want to preserve this quality so the fish we serve is succulent and tasty. The best method I've found to do this is high-heat roasting (with one exception—see Slow-Roasted Wild Salmon Fillets, page 418). In some cases I first sear the fillets in a skillet on the stove to brown the surface, and in all cases the fish roasts at a temperature upwards of 400 degrees.

In most of my fish recipes I offer two doneness tests. The primary (and most helpful) test is to peek inside, by nicking the fish with the tip of a sharp knife, to see that the center looks done. The second is to check the internal temperature: Most fish and shellfish are best between 130 and 140 degrees, when they will be firm but still moist. (Some seafood enthusiasts prefer certain fish, especially salmon, cooked to only 120 degrees, as I've indicated in the recipes.) The only problem with the temperature method is that many pieces of seafood are too thin to monitor effectively with any but the most sophisticated thermometer. Also, because the texture is so delicate, excessive prodding with a probe can deteriorate the finished dish. As you cook your way through this chapter, I encourage you to use both your sense of touch and your sight to judge doneness, and of course if you are ever unsure, use the thermometer for a second opinion.

You may notice that I have more recipes for salmon than any other kind of seafood. This is deliberate. For one thing, I know from my teaching that people cook more salmon than any other kind of fish. Even people who say they don't particularly care for seafood often like salmon. Salmon's popularity means that it's easy to find in most markets. But the real reason

I include so many salmon recipes is that its high fat content (all those good-for-you fish oils that we keep reading about) makes it hard to overcook. The extra richness helps keep the fish moist and succulent even if you do manage to overcook it a little. In other words, when it comes to roasting, there is not a lot of fretting with this fish. Salmon's richness keeps its texture supple at many levels of doneness, from rare to well-done. I also like the fact that I can pick up a couple of fillets for a simple dinner or buy a whole side of salmon for a spectacular dinner-party entrée.

Beyond salmon, there are many other great seafood choices for roasting. Halibut, haddock, swordfish, cod, and sablefish all benefit from a super-hot oven, which browns the outside of the fish nicely while leaving the inside tender and moist. I also love to roast a whole fish (page 427); the skin, bones, and head help keep the meat moist during roasting, and the presentation is always dramatic. Shellfish can also be roasted, and you'll find recipes here for shrimp, scallops, and, perhaps more surprisingly, clams and oysters.

Many of the recipes in this chapter have the benefit of being straightforward to prepare yet special enough for company. About the only tricky part about roasting seafood is making sure you start with the best product possible. Because fish has a short shelf life, this can be a challenge, but not an insurmountable one. My best advice is to find a market you like (and trust), where you feel comfortable asking questions, and ask for a sniff of whatever you're considering buying. While it may feel awkward to lean over the counter nose first, one quick whiff is all it takes to know whether the fish will be sweet and delicious or pungent and unpleasant. Fresh fish will also be bright and moist, not dull and tacky. If the skin is in place, it should be shiny. Fillets should glisten and look firm. If the flesh gaps or looks at all dried out, move on. It also helps to be flexible when you're at the fish counter. For example, some of the recipes here will work with different fish; make the choice between, say, tuna and salmon when you get to the market and see (and smell) which is best that day.

Fish choices that go beyond freshness

When I first learned to cook, choosing a piece of fish at the market came down to deciding what looked (and smelled) the freshest. I learned to examine the eyes (they should be bright) and the flesh (it should be shiny, not matte) and to sniff (it should smell like a fresh sea breeze, not a foul one). I knew nothing about asking where the fish came from or how it was caught. Much has changed in the thirty-some years since. While freshness remains paramount in selecting seafood, a conscientious shopper now must think beyond what might taste good for dinner and consider the status of our oceans, lakes, and streams. If you pay even the slightest attention to current environmental news, you know that many of our favorite fishes are in serious danger of being overfished while others are being domesticated (farmed) with mixed success. Fish remains the last wild food available on the open market, and we have a long way to go in terms of learning how to manage and sustain our supplies. Stories about the decline of tuna and certain species of wild salmon or articles on some of the problematic issues associated with farming fish don't just make the scientific journal covers; they are the subject of features in the *New York Times* and *Time*. And I admit that I sometimes feel overwhelmed by the complexities of our seafood supply, and my worries over the fate of the world's fisheries can quell my appetite for fish. But then I will have a delicious dinner at a restaurant dedicated to sourcing only sustainable seafood, or I will read about a pioneer in environmentally sound fish farming or learn of the revival of a once endangered fishery, and I will feel optimistic that fish can remain a healthy part of our diet—as long as we pay close attention to the choices we make. In the end, the next few decades are apt to bring many changes in our relationship with the sea and the food it generates. For now, I think of fish as a special treat on the dinner table, and I am willing to pay accordingly.

In creating recipes for this chapter, I have done my best to highlight fish that are considered sustainable species, but the situation is in a state of constant flux. I urge you to consult programs like Seafood Watch (a program from the Monterey Bay Aquarium), which puts out and updates a sustainable seafood guide, listing "Best Choices" and "Good Alternatives" as well as suggestions about which fish to avoid (see Sources & Resources, page 539). In the meantime, here are some considerations for the fish I use in this chapter.

COD. For centuries the seemingly limitless stores of cod made it one of the most important market fish in the world. Twentieth-century overfishing, however, changed all that. As of this writing, supplies of Atlantic cod (especially those from Canadian waters) have dwindled dramatically, to the point that the fish is becoming endangered. Today the only healthy Atlantic cod fisheries are those in Iceland and the northeast Arctic, where the fishing is primarily done with hook and line and bottom longline so as not to damage the sea floor and deplete the remaining stocks. Conscientious consumers avoid buying Atlantic cod, with the exception of Icelandic and northeast Arctic. Alternatively, longline-caught Pacific cod (also known as true cod, Alaska cod, and gray cod) makes a good (and environmentally friendly) choice for now. Harvested from the waters off Oregon to the Bering Sea, Pacific cod has the same lean, sweet flavor as Atlantic cod.

HADDOCK. A member of the cod family (which also includes pollock and whiting), haddock is sometimes labeled *scrod* (another name for baby cod). All haddock comes from the Atlantic Ocean, and for years this delicately flavored, firm-fleshed fish represented a huge part of the eastern seafood industry. By 1995 strict regulations were implemented to end overfishing. Today the numbers of haddock are rebounding, and there is a growing market for haddock caught with hook and line, a fishing technique that avoids unintended (and wasteful) by-catch and reduces the environmental damage of the more traditional trawl-caught haddock. Hook-and-line-caught haddock will cost more than trawl-caught, but it's the better choice for the overall health of the ocean.

HALIBUT. There are two species of halibut, Atlantic and Pacific, but the Atlantic populations have been largely depleted by overfishing, so it is rare to see Atlantic halibut in the market anymore. (And a conscientious shopper does best to avoid it.) Look instead for Pacific, in particular Alaskan, halibut. The Northwest harvest is limited by strict fishing regulations, and the season generally runs from April through December.

RAINBOW TROUT. For those cooks interested in provenance, most rainbow trout in the country come from fish farms in Idaho. As of this writing, rainbow trout is considered a "best choice" type of seafood in terms of environmental and biological concerns. All rainbow trout sold in the United States is farm-raised, and trout are especially efficient at converting feed into protein, which means they produce less waste—and therefore fewer pollutants—than other farm-raised species.

SALMON. I much prefer the cleaner taste and firmer texture of wild salmon to that of most farm-raised salmon, but I would be foolish—and selfish—to think that I could eat as much wild salmon as I like. As Paul Greenberg points out in his important book *Four Fish: The Future of the Last Wild Food,* our appetite for salmon long ago outstripped the natural supply, especially as we've diminished many of the great salmon breeding grounds over the course of the past two centuries. In fact, there are no remaining commercial supplies of wild Atlantic salmon. In order to meet the demand, farm-raised Atlantic salmon has become big business, and you only need to glance at most supermarket fish counters to see that farm-raised salmon dominates.

Much has been written in recent years about the environmental impact and health concerns related to farm-raised salmon, but fortunately pioneers in marine biology are working to find better, safer, and healthier ways to raise salmon. When shopping for farm-raised salmon, look for fish raised in "closed," "contained," or "tank" systems and avoid those raised in open net pens. This may take some research and inquiries on your part, but the more consumers ask these questions, the quicker suppliers will respond.

As for wild salmon, I think of it as a special treat to be enjoyed and appreciated but never taken for granted. Also, keep in mind that some of the remaining wild salmon fisheries are in better shape than others. Alaskan wild salmon and wild-caught salmon from Washington are both "ocean-friendly choices," as Seafood Watch puts it. But wild-caught salmon from California and Oregon should be avoided. (For more on shopping for wild salmon, see page 420.)

SCALLOPS. Most sea scallops sold in the United States are wild-caught in the northeastern waters of the Atlantic, from Canada to New Jersey. From an environmental perspective, the fisheries to the north are in better shape than more southerly ones, so your best choice for scallops is those that come from the Northeast and Canada.

SHRIMP. In order to satisfy our national appetite, more than 85 percent of all the shrimp we eat is imported from giant shrimp farms located primarily in Asia and Central America. Not only has this driven down the price of domestic shrimp, but these industrial aquacultural enterprises wreak far-reaching environmental, economic, and social damage. The Worldwatch Institute, a global environmental organization, refers to the waters in which farm-raised shrimp grow as a "chemical cocktail," and researchers warn about the health risks of eating imported shrimp. I find the notion of industrial shrimp farms unappetizing, and my experience as a cook has taught me that wild-caught shrimp simply taste better. More and more markets now list the origin on the signs in the case, but if not, the person behind the counter should be able to tell you, since it will have been marked on the bag or box.

STRIPED BASS. Anyone who has been paying attention to the state of our oceans may remember that the wild striped-bass fishery along the Atlantic coast of the United States and Canada nearly collapsed in the 1980s, but thanks to careful management, the stocks have recovered, and we can now happily (and in good conscience) eat wild striped bass. At the same time, striped-bass fish farms are reported to have a relatively low impact on the surrounding environment or other aquatic species. Farm-raised striped bass are actually a hybrid of wild and white bass.

SWORDFISH. If you were paying attention to the state of our oceans in the late 1990s, you may remember the "Give Swordfish a Break" campaign, which resulted in prominent chefs across the country removing the popular fish from their menus. Fortunately, fishery management has allowed the swordfish stocks to rebuild, and today we can responsibly enjoy swordfish in moderation. Swordfish migrate great distances and can be found in oceans all over the world, but keep in mind that some regions are better managed than others. When shopping for swordfish, look for harpoon- or hook-and-line-caught fish. Avoid imported swordfish caught using longlines—the most common and efficient method for catching swordfish, which also captures large numbers of endangered sea turtles, sharks, and seabirds.

TUNA. Much has been said and written about the overfishing of tuna around the globe, but fortunately for those of us who appreciate its meaty taste and steaklike texture, it is still possible to find good tuna. Even though both yellowfin and albacore populations are in pretty good shape as of this writing, I encourage you to be sure to buy only troll- or pole-caught tuna; with these fishing methods, there is no by-catch, so they pose less risk to other sea life, including several endangered species.

HERB ROASTED SHRIMP WITH PANCETTA

HERB-ROASTED SHRIMP WITH PANCETTA

The idea to roast pancetta-wrapped shrimp on a bed of hardy herbs came to me at the end of a beach vacation one summer. It was our last dinner, and I had a surplus of fresh herbs plus a chunk of pancetta on hand. I made a quick trip to the seafood market for fresh shrimp, and I had the makings of a meal special enough to celebrate the end of a great week but simple enough to leave time for one last walk on the beach before dinner.

First I spread the herb sprigs out on the bottom of a gratin dish; then I wrapped the shrimp in pancetta and arranged them on top of the herbs. During roasting, the herbs act as a sort of rack, keeping the shrimp up off the bottom of the pan and infusing them (and the entire house) with their marvelous aromas. I also poured a little white wine into the pan before roasting to absorb the herb flavors. The strained wine gets poured over the shrimp just before serving, anointing them with the essence of herb flavor. The results were so delicious that I found myself making this over and over again at home.

For herbs, use any of the hardier Mediterranean varieties—think rosemary, thyme, oregano, marjoram, and fresh bay leaves. I prefer a combination of two or more, but in the spirit of the dish, use what you have on hand. I love serving the pancetta-wrapped shrimp on a mound of rice or, if I'm feeling up for it, a heap of creamy risotto, but you may prefer them all by themselves. A fresh salad of cucumbers and tomatoes would be a refreshing side dish. The shrimp can be wrapped in pancetta and arranged on the bed of herbs up to 6 hours before roasting—which leaves plenty of time for that beach walk.

SERVES 4

METHOD: High heat

ROASTING TIME: About 14 minutes

WINE: Dry Tempranillo-based rosé from the Navarra or Rioja regions of Spain.

CONTINUED ON NEXT PAGE

1 ¼ to 1 ½ pounds large or jumbo (16/20 or bigger) shrimp (see Shopping for and Preparing Shrimp, page 391), peeled and deveined

2 teaspoons extra-virgin olive oil

2 garlic cloves, minced

Kosher salt and freshly ground black pepper

Handful of fresh herbs (¾ to 1 ounce), such as rosemary, thyme, oregano, and/or bay leaves

¼ pound thinly sliced pancetta

¼ cup dry white wine or dry vermouth

1 **HEAT THE OVEN.** Position a rack in the center of the oven and heat to 425 degrees (400 degrees convection).

2 **SEASON THE SHRIMP.** In a large bowl, toss the shrimp with the olive oil, garlic, a nice pinch of salt, and plenty of black pepper. Toss to coat.

3 **MAKE A BED OF HERBS AND WRAP THE SHRIMP.** Arrange the herb sprigs (and bay leaves, if using) on the bottom of a low-sided baking dish or gratin pan (the dish needs to be large enough to hold the shrimp in a single layer; I use a 10-by-14-inch gratin dish). Unroll the pancetta (this may mean peeling off the outer casing) so that each slice resembles a crooked slice of bacon. Count the slices of pancetta and the shrimp and cut the pancetta into enough pieces so you have one per shrimp. Wrap each shrimp with a piece of pancetta and place the shrimp on the herbs, leaving a little space between them. *The shrimp may be prepared up to this point up to 6 hours ahead and kept refrigerated. Let sit at room temperature for 20 minutes before roasting.*

4 **ROAST THE SHRIMP.** Pour the wine or vermouth into the dish. Roast until the pancetta is crisp and the shrimp are sizzling and cooked through, flipping the shrimp halfway through, 12 to 18 minutes. (The larger the shrimp, the longer they take.)

5 **STRAIN THE PAN JUICES AND SERVE.** Using tongs, transfer the shrimp to a serving platter or individual plates. (If you are serving the shrimp with rice, set the shrimp directly on top.) Set a fine-mesh sieve over a bowl and dump the herbs and cooking liquid into the sieve. Save a few sprigs of herbs for garnish, if you like (or discard), and drizzle the liquid over the shrimp; there will be only a tablespoon or two, but it will be intensely flavored. Serve immediately.

GARLIC-ROASTED SHRIMP WITH TOMATOES, CAPERS, AND FETA

This dish is based on a recipe that dates back to when Craig Claiborne and Pierre Franey were collaborating and writing for the *New York Times*. The original involves making a tomato sauce and cooking the shrimp in two separate skillets on the stove before combining everything (in a third pan!), topping it with feta, and finishing it in the oven. I loved the combination of the spicy tomato sauce, sweet shrimp, and creamy feta, but it always bugged me that the recipe dirtied so many dishes. So I decided to streamline the process, roasting the shrimp right along with the tomatoes and capers. Then, once the shrimp are sizzling, I top them with crumbled feta and roast just long enough for the cheese to soften and the shrimp to cook through. I find it every bit as delicious as the original, especially with a bit of ouzo or vodka added to the marinade. And it's oh, so much easier.

The finished dish deserves to be served family-style, right from the gratin dish—it's that pretty. Accompany it with a pot of rice or olive-oil-drenched orzo, and put a basket of good crusty bread on the table.

SERVES 4

METHOD: High heat

ROASTING TIME: About 14 minutes

WINE: Crisp rosé with a touch of herbs and earth from Southern France, such as Bandol or Tavel.

1½ pounds large (16/20) shrimp (see Shopping for and Preparing Shrimp, page 391), peeled and deveined

3 tablespoons extra-virgin olive oil

2 garlic cloves, minced

1 teaspoon dried oregano, preferably Greek

¼ to ½ teaspoon crushed red pepper flakes

1 tablespoon ouzo or vodka (optional)

Kosher salt

One 14.5-ounce can diced tomatoes, drained, or 1¾ cups peeled, seeded, and chopped tomatoes (from about 1 pound ripe plum tomatoes; see page 435)

2 tablespoons capers, drained

2 ounces feta cheese, crumbled (about ½ cup)

3 tablespoons shredded fresh basil (optional)

CONTINUED ON NEXT PAGE

1 **HEAT THE OVEN.** Position a rack in the center of the oven and heat to 425 degrees (400 degrees convection).

2 **MARINATE THE SHRIMP.** In a large bowl, toss the shrimp with 2 tablespoons olive oil, the garlic, oregano, pepper flakes (if you like spice, use the larger amount), ouzo or vodka, if using, and a good pinch of salt. Toss to coat and set aside at room temperature for 30 minutes while the oven heats.

3 **ROAST THE SHRIMP AND TOMATOES.** Spread the tomatoes in a single loose layer in the bottom of a small shallow roasting pan or large gratin dish (I use an oval one that's 10 by 14 inches). Drizzle the remaining tablespoon of olive oil over the tomatoes and scatter the capers in the dish. Arrange the shrimp on top in a single layer and use a rubber spatula to scrape any marinade remaining in the bowl over the shrimp. Roast until the shrimp are sizzling and beginning to turn pink, about 8 minutes.

4 **ADD THE FETA.** Remove the dish from the oven and, using tongs, flip the shrimp over. Scatter the feta over the top and return to the oven until the shrimp are just cooked through and the feta has softened, another 6 minutes. (Cooked feta holds its shape, so don't wait for it to melt.)

5 **SERVE.** Top the shrimp with basil, if using, and serve immediately, using a large serving spoon to transfer the shrimp and tomatoes to plates.

Shopping for and Preparing Shrimp

SHOPPING FOR SHRIMP

Unless you live in the Gulf states or southern Atlantic coastal regions, where shrimp are caught locally, most of what is sold has been previously frozen. Fortunately, shrimp freeze well, and when properly thawed are of the same high quality as freshly caught shrimp. In fact the best strategy if truly fresh shrimp are unavailable is to buy frozen shrimp and allow time to thaw them at home. The reason is that once thawed, the shrimp deteriorate quickly, even in the seafood case at the market.

I much prefer wild-caught shrimp, which deliver a sweet, fresh taste without the overly rubbery texture and bland character of their imported counterparts. Wild caught shrimp are becoming a little easier to find thanks to a burgeoning Wild American Shrimp Certification Program (if your market doesn't stock these shrimp, ask). If no wild-caught shrimp are available, domestic farm-raised shrimp are at least subject to FDA approval, so while they may never match the quality of wild shrimp, you can take comfort in knowing that the farmers aren't relying on banned chemicals, as overseas producers sometime do. A final thought: Be on the lookout for additives, primarily sodium bisulfite and sodium tripolysulphate. Dipping shrimp in solutions containing these salts lengthens shelf life and prevents moisture loss. Unfortunately, this practice has a negative impact on flavor and texture. All additives must be listed on the box or bag, so you can always ask before you buy.

Whatever shrimp you buy, avoid any with a mushy or broken appearance or with yellowish, dry patches or little black spots on the shell. (Some varieties of shrimp have dark stripey markings on the shell; these are fine. The black spots you need to avoid are small dots indicating decay.)

I prefer to buy shrimp with the shells on. For one thing, peeled shrimp cost more, since you pay for the peeling. Plus I find that the shells protect the integrity of the shrimp and preserve their moisture, so I like to leave them on as long as possible. But it does mean you'll have to peel them yourself.

A NOTE ON SHRIMP SIZES

We've all gotten a laugh at the oxymoronic moniker *jumbo shrimp*, but actually figuring out what constitutes small, large, and jumbo shrimp can be rather complicated. Unfortunately, the size categories of shrimp are not standardized, so what one market labels *jumbo* another may call *extra-large* or even plain old *large*. The least confusing approach is to look for the weight count—this tells you how many shrimp there are on average in each pound. For instance, 16/20 means there will be anywhere from 16 to 20 shrimp per pound. Other com-

CONTINUED ON NEXT PAGE

mon sizes are 21/25 and 26/30. As the numbers go up, the shrimp get smaller and the price goes down. When it comes to the really large shrimp (sometimes labeled *colossal* or *super colossal*), the size no longer includes a range, but specifies exactly the number of shrimp per pound. For instance, U-12 means 12 shrimp per pound, U-15 means 15 per pound, and so on. This size information should appear on the signage in the seafood case. If not, ask. For roasting, I prefer 16/20 count shrimp (I figure 5 to 6 per person) because they are large enough to hold up in a hot oven without overcooking but not so large as to break the bank. If you choose smaller or larger shrimp, keep in mind that the cooking time will vary accordingly.

THAWING FROZEN SHRIMP

The ideal way to defrost shrimp is in the refrigerator. Remove the shrimp from the bag and put them in a colander. Set the colander in a larger bowl and leave the shrimp on the bottom shelf of the refrigerator for 16 to 24 hours. I don't bother covering them, but if you prefer, you can cover loosely with plastic wrap.

If you don't have a day to spare, place the shrimp in a heavy-duty plastic bag and immerse the bag in cold (not warm) tap water. Change the water every 20 minutes so that it doesn't warm up to room temperature. You want the temperature as cool as possible; anything close to 40 degrees will thaw the shrimp. I've seen many cooks (and professional chefs) run cold water directly over the shrimp to speed the thawing process. While this does thaw the shrimp quickly, the running water leaches a good deal of moisture, and therefore flavor, from the shrimp.

PEELING AND DEVEINING SHRIMP

These days, shell-on shrimp often come with the shell already slit open along the back. You simply peel back the shell and pull it off in sections. If the shells are not already cut open, turn the shrimp so its underside faces up and, starting at the fat end, use your fingers to pull apart the first few sections of the shell. Once the upper half of the shell splits open, take hold of the peeled top part in one hand and the tail in the other and tug gently to separate the shell from the meat. Don't pull too hard, or you may tear the delicate shrimp in two. If the shell doesn't come away easily, split open a few more sections and try again. To remove the "vein" that runs along the shrimp's back (it's actually the digestive tract), use a sharp paring knife to make a shallow cut along the back—just deep enough to expose the vein—all the way down to the tail. Now slide the tip of the knife under the vein to loosen it and pull it out with your fingers. If the vein breaks, just continue until you've removed all of it. The vein is harmless but can feel gritty and unpleasant to eat. Many cooks leave the tail on for aesthetic reasons, others remove the tails along with the shell to make the shrimp easier to eat.

QUICK-ROASTED SCALLOPS WITH SRIRACHA AND LIME

I appreciate sea scallops for their sweet, clean taste and their meaty texture. I also love how incredibly easy they are to roast. To keep lean scallops juicy, I coat them before roasting in a mixture of Sriracha, mayonnaise, lime juice, and a pinch of sugar—an addictive combination of spicy heat, tanginess, and sweetness. To cook through without drying out, the scallops roast in a super-hot oven for a few minutes and then get glazed under the broiler just enough to tinge the surface brown.

Sriracha is a Thai-inspired hot chile sauce that has recently gained popularity in many American kitchens. It's becoming easy to find at the supermarket (look in the Asian or international aisle or near other kinds of hot sauce). But if you can't find it, substitute ½ teaspoon hot sauce, such as Tabasco.

If scallops aren't your thing (or if you're just in the mood for something else), the technique in this recipe works with shrimp and thick chunks of halibut or sablefish. I serve this as a main course accompanied by something green, like steamed asparagus spears or stir-fried bok choy.

SERVES 4

METHOD: Combination high heat and broil

ROASTING TIME: 7 to 8 minutes

WINE: Slightly sweet Riesling with vibrant acidity from Germany's Rheingau region or Mosel Valley.

Butter, for the pan

1 ½ pounds large dry scallops (see Shopping for Scallops, page 395)

¼ cup mayonnaise

1 teaspoon Sriracha (see page 396)

1 teaspoon fresh lime juice

¼ teaspoon sugar

1   **HEAT THE OVEN.** Position a rack about 6 inches away from the broiler element of the oven and heat to 500 degrees (475 degrees convection). Line a heavy-duty rimmed baking sheet with foil and lightly butter the foil (otherwise the sauce can make the scallops stick).

CONTINUED ON NEXT PAGE

2 **PREPARE THE SCALLOPS.** Most sea scallops have a small, opaque, tough muscle on one side that attaches the scallop to the shell, and while not inedible, it is rubbery and best peeled off and discarded. As you handle the scallops, check for sand. If they feel at all gritty, rinse them quickly under cold water and pat dry. Do not submerge the scallops, as they like to soak up water and consequently won't roast as well.

3 **MAKE THE COATING.** In a small bowl, stir together the mayonnaise, Sriracha, lime juice, and sugar. Put the scallops in a large bowl, add 1 tablespoon of the sauce, and toss gently with a rubber spatula to coat. Reserve the remaining sauce.

4 **ROAST THE SCALLOPS.** Arrange the scallops on the baking sheet with at least an inch between them. Roast for 5 minutes. Remove the pan from the oven and heat the broiler on high. Flip the scallops one by one (tongs work well for this) and dollop a small spoonful of the remaining sauce on each scallop. Return the scallops to the oven and broil until the tops are beginning to brown in spots and the scallops are just cooked through, another 2 to 3 minutes (the timing depends on their size). If you're uncertain about doneness, nick a scallop with a sharp knife and peek to see. It should be mostly opaque, with a trace of translucence at the center. Serve immediately.

Shopping for Scallops

FOR ROASTING, YOU WANT WHOLE, EVENLY SIZED SCALLOPS AND NOT A LOT OF LITTLE PIECES, WHICH MAY MEAN ASKING THE PERSON BEHIND THE COUNTER to pick out whole ones for you. Few markets offer a choice of scallop sizes (the way they do for shrimp); most scallops are somewhere between the diameter of a quarter and a half-dollar (or ¾ to 1¼ ounces each). The smaller, gumball-sized bay scallops aren't suitable for roasting.

Good scallops range in color from ivory to grayish pink to coral, and they feel somewhat sticky but never slimy. Always look for untreated or *dry scallops*, which means they have not been treated with a sodium solution as a preservative. Untreated scallops are more expensive, but their rich, sweet flavor and ability to brown beautifully are worth every extra penny. Markets are supposed to label scallops as *dry* or *wet* (sometimes referred to as *treated* or *water added*). If there's no label but the scallops are uniformly opaque, stark white, and sitting in a pool of milky liquid, there's a very good chance they've been treated, so ask. The seller is legally compelled to give you an honest answer.

Another classification that appears in high-end fish markets is *diver scallops*. Most commercial scallop operations harvest scallops by dragging a chain-mesh net along the bottom of the ocean. Diver scallops are those caught by hand—one at a time—by a scuba diver. They tend to be enormous (I've seen them with shells as large as dinner plates and meat as much as 3 inches across). In addition to their size, diver scallops are rarely gritty, since they don't get dragged along the sea floor. They are, however, always expensive. If you splurge on diver scallops, expect them to take a few more minutes to roast because of their size.

You may also come across scallops labeled *day boat*, which indicates that the fishermen went out for a single day and returned to market with fresh, unadulterated scallops. Be forewarned, however, that there are no official classifications for diver or day-boat scallops, and some unscrupulous fishmongers may attach the names to any large scallop just to increase the value. This is yet another reason to try to buy seafood from a reputable source.

Frozen scallops (or previously frozen, meaning thawed by the retailer) can be a good option, and they are certainly preferable to scallops that have been sitting too long in the fish case. (The label *FAS* means "frozen at sea.") Just be sure the scallops are whole and there are not too many ice crystals in the bag or on the scallops, which would indicate that they've been poorly stored. Thaw frozen scallops in their original packaging in a bowl (or other dish, to catch any drips) in the refrigerator for 16 to 24 hours.

Sriracha

FOR MOST AMERICANS, MYSELF INCLUDED, SRIRACHA HAS COME TO MEAN A PARTICULAR BRAND OF HOT SAUCE PRODUCED BY HUY FONG FOODS IN Rosemead, California. Packaged in an easily recognizable clear plastic squeeze bottle with a bright green top, a proud rooster logo, and white lettering spelling out *Sriracha Hot Chili Sauce*, this bright red sauce has gained a cultlike following of cooks who like a little spice in their food. (Many fans refer to it knowingly as "rooster sauce.") I, for one, am never without a bottle of Sriracha in the refrigerator, and I have friends who carry a bottle along on backpacking trips to add excitement to otherwise bland campfire meals.

Made from fresh red jalapeños, garlic powder, vinegar, sugar, and salt, and thicker than southern American hot sauces like Tabasco and Texas Pete's, the sauce provides a jolt of chile heat tempered by sweetness. I often reach for it in place of ketchup on a burger. I also use it to perk up eggs, dressings, marinades, and stews, and as you'll see from the quick-roasted scallops recipe on page 393, it does wonders for simple roast seafood.

Huy Fong Sriracha, however, is not an authentic Thai sauce. In Thailand, the word *sriracha* (also spelled *siracha*) refers generically to a seasoned puree of red chiles—often homemade—used as a condiment for grilled and deep-fried dishes. The sauce varies from spicy hot to mildly sweet, depending on the chiles and the cook. (The original name comes from a seaside village on the Gulf of Thailand, Sri Racha.) The Huy Fong version was created by David Tran, a Chinese man born in Vietnam who immigrated to the United States. With his Sriracha, Tran aspired to make a sauce that would appeal to a range of cultures, and indeed, the ingredients list on the bottle appears in five languages, including French and Spanish. Seeing that you can now buy Huy Fong Sriracha in every sort of Asian market as well as at suburban supermarkets and Wal-Mart, it would seem that Mr. Tran succeeded in producing a sauce with multicultural appeal. All I know for sure is that I love the stuff.

ROASTED OYSTERS OR CLAMS

Perhaps I shouldn't call this a recipe, but I can't resist including it, because it has changed my life—or at least changed the way I think about eating oysters and clams at home. Until I stumbled upon this easy method to roast bivalves, I confess that I rarely prepared them at home. I always managed to talk myself out of shucking them to serve on the half shell or add to stews and chowders—it just seemed like too much of a production. But learning how to roast them couldn't be simpler, and the oysters (or clams) basically shuck themselves. You will need a box (or bag) of rock salt, the kind you sprinkle on the ice in an old-fashioned hand-cranked ice cream maker. Then it's merely a matter of lining a rimmed baking sheet with the salt, heating it in a hot oven, and roasting the oysters or clams on top. The salt acts as a kind of heat sink, absorbing the oven's heat so the bivalves cook more readily. It also stabilizes them so they don't tip over on their round shells and spill out their precious juices. I often serve them with nothing more than melted butter with a squeeze of lemon and a dash of Tabasco, but a zingy salsa or the barbecue sauce option on page 399 is a fine way to go.

SERVES 4 TO 6 AS AN APPETIZER
METHOD: High heat
ROASTING TIME: 5 to 15 minutes
WINE/BEER: Tart, fruity rosé; or a classic pilsner, such as Pilsner Urquell.

Rock salt, to line the baking pan

12 tablespoons (1½ sticks) unsalted butter

1 to 1½ tablespoons fresh lemon juice (from ½ lemon)

Kosher salt

24 fresh oysters or clams, scrubbed

Tabasco sauce, for serving

1 **HEAT THE OVEN.** Position a rack in the center of the oven and heat to 475 degrees (450 degrees convection). Pour about ¼ inch of rock salt onto a heavy-duty rimmed baking sheet large enough to hold the oysters or clams in a single layer.

2 **MELT THE BUTTER.** Combine the butter and lemon juice in a small saucepan and melt over medium-low heat. Season with a pinch of salt. Keep warm over a low burner or in a warm spot.

CONTINUED ON PAGE 399

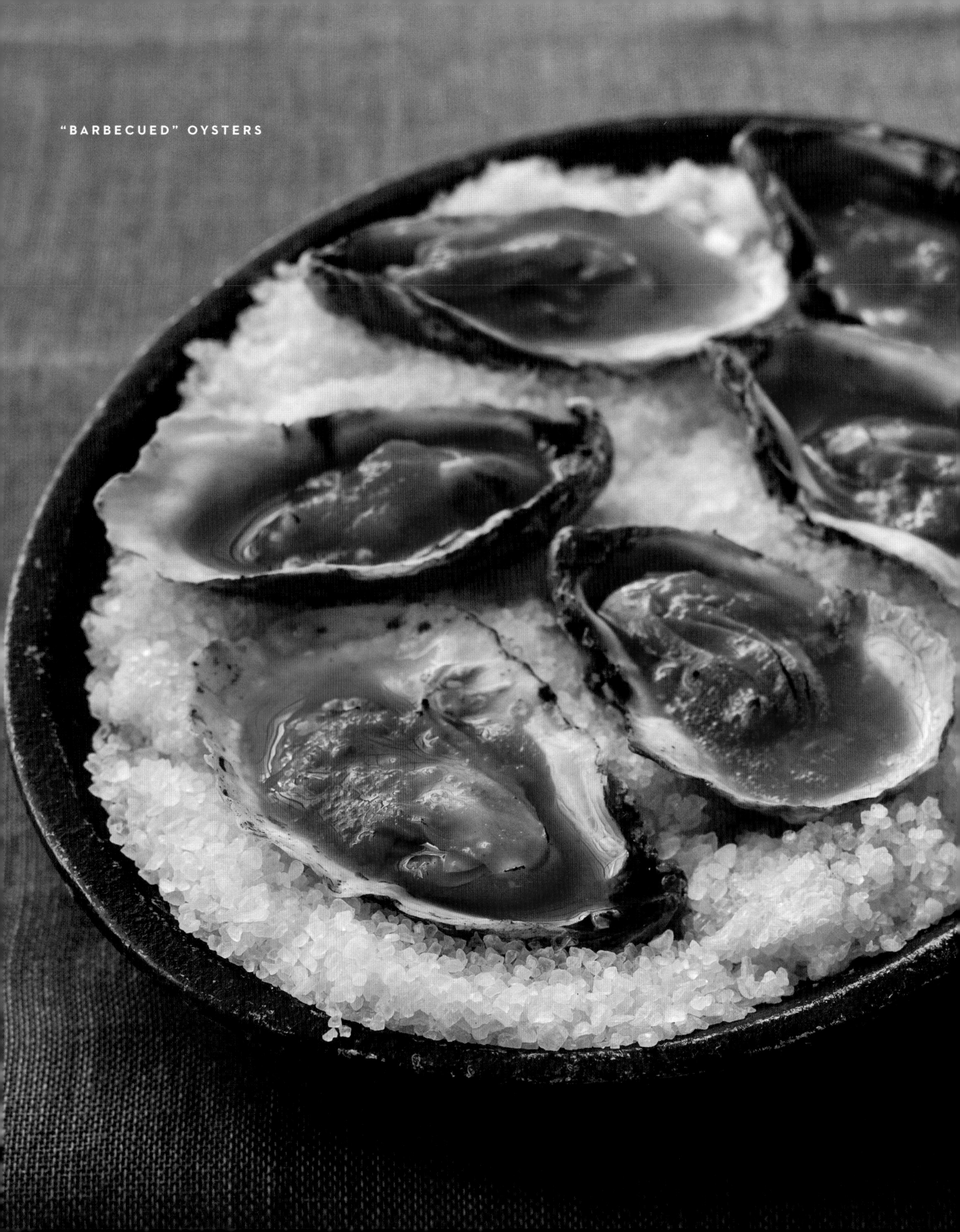

"BARBECUED" OYSTERS

3   **ROAST.** Once the oven is fully heated, arrange the oysters or clams on the rock salt; if the shells are deeper and more rounded on one side than on the other, be sure this side sits on the salt. Nestle the shells so they are stable. Slide the pan into the oven and roast until the shells pop open, 5 to 15 minutes depending on the size of the shells. You know that the shells have popped open when you can see a gap between the tops and bottoms. If any shells don't pop open, pry them open with a butter knife. If the meat inside appears dried and shriveled or has an off odor, discard. Otherwise, it's fine to eat.

4   **SERVE.** The top shells should lift right off, but you may need to slide a small knife (a table or butter knife usually works) along the top shell to release the meat. Either remove the shells in the kitchen and transfer the oysters or clams to a serving platter, doing your best not to tip the shells and lose the flavorful juices, or leave them on the salt for each person to open as they eat.

Set the melted butter and Tabasco alongside. (I often serve the butter in the saucepan, but you can transfer it to ramekins or individual dipping bowls.) Have on hand small forks to lift the oysters or clams and dip them in the butter.

OPTION: "BARBECUED" OYSTERS

One of the benefits of traveling with friends who love to eat as much as I do is that they are always willing to take a detour for something tasty. Such was the case several years ago when my friend Robin Schempp and I were headed from San Francisco to Napa Valley for a conference. Having time on our hands, Robin suggested a detour up the coast to Tomales Bay for barbecued oysters. A cold fog seemed to follow us the whole way, and I'll admit that the added hours in the car began to feel like a foolish idea—until we spotted Tony's Seafood Restaurant, with its packed parking lot and windows overlooking the very bay where the oysters are harvested. We grabbed a table, ordered a plate of barbecued oysters and a couple of Anchor Steams, and settled in. The oysters arrived on paper plates (doubled up to support the weight), each one sitting plumply atop a half shell, bubbling hot and swimming in a generous pool of reddish garlicky sauce. It took restraint to let them cool enough to eat, and then it took only one taste for me to know that these were definitely worth the detour. I don't remember how many plates of oysters we polished off that afternoon, but I do know that when we had finally had our fill, the fog had lifted and we took a long walk before climbing back in the car.

CONTINUED ON NEXT PAGE

Here's my version of the tangy, slightly sweet, garlic-laced sauce that pairs perfectly with briny oysters. Start by roasting the oysters according to the recipe above. Then, after popping off their shells, spoon a bit of the sauce onto each oyster and return them to the oven for a minute or two. Serve plenty of good bread for sopping up every last drop of sauce.

MAKES ABOUT 3/4 CUP SAUCE, ENOUGH FOR 24 OYSTERS

BEER: Pale ale with a balance of malty sweetness and bitter hops.

12 tablespoons (1½ sticks) unsalted butter

2 garlic cloves, minced

2 tablespoons Sriracha (see page 396), or 1 tablespoon ketchup and a splash of hot sauce, such as Tabasco

1 tablespoon ketchup

1 tablespoon fresh lemon juice

¾ teaspoon Worcestershire sauce

Pinch of cayenne

Kosher salt

MELT THE BUTTER in a small saucepan over medium-low heat. Whisk in the garlic, Sriracha, ketchup, lemon juice, Worcestershire sauce, cayenne, and salt to taste. After roasting in step 3 above, remove the oysters from the oven and leave the oven on. Using a kitchen towel or an oven mitt to protect your hand, carefully lift off and discard the top shell of an oyster. If the shell doesn't come away easily, slide a small knife along it to release the meat. This can be a tricky process, as the shell and the liquid are hot, but try your best not to topple the bottom shell and spill the juices. Repeat with the remaining oysters. Divide the sauce among them, spooning about 1½ teaspoons on each, and return them to the oven to heat for 2 minutes. Serve hot.

ONE-DISH ROASTED HADDOCK WITH LEMONY POTATOES

I have a fondness for one-pot meals. I just love the mingling of flavors that happens when different ingredients get tucked in together. That there is less cleanup is a benefit too. This one starts with thinly sliced potatoes and lemons layered together to make a potato-lemon gratin of sorts. The lemon, peel and all, contributes an appealing citrusy tang, with just the right touch of bitterness to play off the potatoes and the fish. In order to cook everything in one pan, the potatoes and lemons get roasted until almost done. Only then are they topped with the fish fillets, which get quickly roasted during the last 15 minutes. In the end, the fish comes out cooked just enough, while the potatoes and lemons are tender and flecked with tasty toasty browned bits.

Once you try this recipe, you'll see that it's highly adaptable. For instance, you can substitute other thick delicate fillets, such as cod, halibut, or snapper, for the haddock. And instead of thyme, try oregano or parsley or a combination of both. For a briny, salty note, add capers or chopped olives to the potatoes. You get the idea.

SERVES 4
METHOD: High heat
ROASTING TIME: About 1 hour
WINE: Youthful fruity Sauvignon Blanc from New Zealand or South Africa.

¼ cup extra-virgin olive oil, plus more for the pan

1½ pounds medium red or white potatoes, scrubbed

1½ small lemons, scrubbed

4 teaspoons chopped fresh thyme

2 to 3 garlic cloves, minced

¾ teaspoon Marash or Aleppo pepper (see page 318)

Kosher salt and freshly ground black pepper

4 haddock fillets (6 to 7 ounces each), about 1 inch thick

1 **HEAT THE OVEN.** Position a rack in the center of the oven and heat to 400 degrees (375 degrees convection). Lightly oil a gratin or baking dish large enough to hold the fish in a single layer with plenty of room around the edges (a 10-by-14-inch dish works well).

CONTINUED ON NEXT PAGE

2 **START ROASTING THE POTATOES AND LEMONS.** Slice the potatoes into ¼-inch rounds and toss them into a large bowl. Slice the whole lemon into ¹⁄₁₆- to ⅛-inch rounds, discarding the stem and blossom ends of the fruit, and using the tip of a paring knife, flick out the seeds from the rounds. Add the lemon rounds to the bowl with the potatoes. Drizzle 3 tablespoons of the olive oil over and toss to coat. Season with 3 teaspoons of the thyme, the garlic, ½ teaspoon of the Marash or Aleppo pepper, and salt and pepper to taste. Toss again to mix evenly. Tip the potato and lemon slices into the baking dish and spread them into a loosely even layer without compacting them. Roast, gently turning with a large spoon after about 20 minutes (try not to break too many potatoes, but don't worry if you do), until the potatoes are just tender and beginning to brown, 40 to 45 minutes.

3 **SEASON THE FISH.** Drizzle the remaining tablespoon of olive oil over the fish fillets and season on all sides with the remaining 1 teaspoon thyme, ¼ teaspoon Marash or Aleppo pepper, and salt and pepper to taste. Set aside or, if the kitchen is warm, refrigerate until the potatoes are almost tender.

4 **ROAST THE FISH.** Once the potatoes are just tender and beginning to brown, give them one more gentle stir and arrange the fish on top. Squeeze the juice from the remaining ½ lemon over the fish and roast until the fish is just cooked through, another 12 to 18 minutes, depending on the thickness of the fillets. (The easiest way to check for doneness is to poke a paring knife into the fillet and peek to see that the center is no longer translucent; waiting for it to flake means overcooking. If you test with an instant-read thermometer, look for it to register 130 to 140 degrees.)

5 **SERVE.** Serve immediately, scooping up some of the potatoes and lemon slices with each piece of fish.

QUICK-ROASTED HALIBUT STEAKS WITH BASIL-MINT BROWNED BUTTER AND ALMONDS

Halibut is an easy fish to love. The snowy white fish is mild enough to please timid eaters, while any true seafood enthusiast will appreciate its exquisite texture and sweet taste. The advantage to roasting halibut steaks, as opposed to fillets, is that there is less danger of overcooking, because the bone helps keep the fish moist even when roasted at high temperatures. To add some richness and flavor, I smear the steaks with butter before roasting and then make a quick brown butter sauce spiked with almonds (they toast right in the butter), orange zest, basil, and mint. The sauce comes together as the halibut roasts. You'll even have time to steam some green beans or dress a simple green salad to accompany the fish.

SERVES 4

METHOD: High heat

ROASTING TIME: 15 to 20 minutes

WINE: Medium-bodied white wine with crisp acidity and light herbal accents, such as Albariño from Spain or Orvieto from Italy.

6 tablespoons (¾ stick) unsalted butter, softened, plus more for the pan if using

4 halibut steaks (7 to 8 ounces each), preferably 1¼-inches thick (see Shopping for Halibut Steak, page 405)

Kosher salt and freshly ground black pepper

¼ cup coarsely chopped almonds, preferably from whole skin-on almonds

1 teaspoon finely grated orange zest

1 tablespoon chopped fresh mint

1 tablespoon chopped fresh basil

Fresh lemon juice, to taste

CONTINUED ON NEXT PAGE

1 **HEAT THE OVEN.** Position a rack in the center of the oven and heat to 450 degrees (425 degrees convection). Line a heavy-duty rimmed baking sheet with parchment paper or lightly butter the pan.

2 **SEASON AND ROAST THE FISH.** Divide 1 tablespoon of butter among the halibut steaks and spread it over the entire surface. Season the fish all over with salt and pepper. Arrange on the baking sheet at least 2 inches apart. Roast until opaque and almost cooked through, 15 to 20 minutes, depending on the thickness of the steaks. The easiest way to check the doneness is to nick the fish with the tip of a paring knife to peek inside; remove it from the oven when the flesh near the bone appears mostly opaque with a hint of translucence. You can also check for doneness with an instant-read thermometer; it should read between 130 and 140 degrees.

3 **MEANWHILE, MAKE THE SAUCE.** Heat the remaining 5 tablespoons of butter in a medium sauté pan over medium heat until it begins to foam, 3 to 4 minutes. Add the chopped almonds and cook until the almonds are toasty and the butter is nicely browned, another 3 to 4 minutes. Remove from the heat and set aside in a warm spot.

4 **FINISH THE SAUCE AND SERVE.** Once the fish is done, let it rest for a few minutes while you finish the sauce. Return the sauté pan to medium heat, stir in the orange zest, mint, and basil, and season with salt and pepper. Heat until fragrant, about 1 minute, and add a squeeze of lemon juice. Transfer the steaks to serving plates and spoon the browned butter and almonds over each. Serve immediately.

Shopping for Halibut Steak

Halibut belongs to the family of fish known as flatfish, along with sole, flounder, and turbot. Unlike round fish, such as salmon and trout, which have eyes on either side of their heads and swim upright, flatfish have both eyes on top of their heads and wide, flat bodies the color of sand, which enable them to lie flat on the sea floor and hide from predators. What this means for the cook is that round fish have 2 meaty fillets, often called sides, as in a side of salmon, and flatfish actually have 4 fillets, 2 from the top and 2 from the bottom. Halibut steaks are created when the fish is cross-cut and therefore has 4 sections of meat separated by a cross-shaped bone. At the fish counter, choose halibut that looks glossy and firm and smells sweet. You can also find previously frozen halibut year-round in many markets.

The recipe on page 403 calls for small halibut steaks in the 7- to 8-ounce range—perfect for single portions. Oftentimes these individual steaks will actually be a larger steak cut down the middle, leaving you with 2 sections of meat with only a portion of the cross-shaped bone. If all that's available is larger steaks, buy 2 steaks in the 12- to 14-ounce range and plan to divide them in half to serve. I prefer to do this after cooking, as leaving them intact while roasting will help keep them moist. To divide a large cooked halibut steak into portions, use a paring knife to cut through the skin and separate the individual portions. Then with the knife and a fork, gently pry the fillets away from the bone, trying your best to keep them intact.

PANKO-CRUSTED ROAST COD FILLETS WITH HORSERADISH AND DILL

In my recipe-testing notes for this dish, I used capital letters: "VERY simple, VERY tasty, and elegant." Translation: This is one of those ultra-useful recipes that's quick enough for a weeknight but impressive enough for company. Fresh cod fillets are coated in Japanese bread crumbs (panko) and then roasted in a hot oven to create a delectable contrast between the light, crunchy breading and the delicate flakes of cod. Hints of horseradish, dill, and lemon brighten the flavor.

At the fish counter, request fillets from the thick end (away from the tail). If you do end up with thinner tail pieces, tuck the thinnest part under to create a double thickness so they don't cook too quickly and dry out. If finding good cod proves a challenge (see page 382), striped bass and haddock are good alternatives. Sautéed spinach or another tender green makes a good side dish.

SERVES 4
METHOD: High heat
ROASTING TIME: 10 to 12 minutes
WINE: Youthful rosé sparkling wine from California, such as Schramsberg or Domaine Carneros.

4 tablespoons unsalted butter, melted, plus more for the pan, if using

¾ cup panko (see page 408)

2 tablespoons finely chopped fresh dill, plus sprigs for garnish (optional)

1 heaping tablespoon prepared horseradish, excess liquid gently squeezed or drained off

2 teaspoons finely grated lemon zest

1 teaspoon Dijon mustard

Kosher salt and freshly ground black pepper

Four 1- to 1¼-inch-thick cod fillets (about 6 ounces each), preferably Pacific cod

Lemon wedges, for serving (optional)

1   **HEAT THE OVEN.** Position a rack in the center of the oven and heat to 425 degrees (400 degrees convection). Line a heavy-duty rimmed baking sheet with parchment paper or lightly butter the pan.

CONTINUED ON NEXT PAGE

2 **MAKE THE BREADING.** In a medium bowl, combine the panko, 2 tablespoons of the melted butter, the dill, horseradish, lemon zest, and mustard. Season with a light pinch of salt and a little pepper and stir to combine.

3 **BREAD THE FILLETS.** Season the fillets on all sides with salt and pepper. Arrange them skin side down on the baking sheet, leaving plenty of room between them. Fold any thin tail ends under to make a thicker fillet; you want them all to be 1 to 1¼ inches thick. (If thinner, check for doneness sooner.) Top each fillet with some of the panko mixture, dividing it evenly among the fillets and pressing lightly so it adheres to the top of each fillet. Gather up any bits of breading that may fall off and pat them on as well. Drizzle the remaining 2 tablespoons of melted butter evenly over the topping.

4 **ROAST AND SERVE.** Roast until the panko is light brown and crunchy in spots and the fish is mostly opaque (just cooked through), with a trace of translucence in the center (you'll have to nick a piece to peek inside), 10 to 12 minutes, depending on the thickness of the fillets. If you're unsure about doneness or don't want to cut into a fillet, you can use an instant-read thermometer to check that it's between 130 and 140 degrees. Serve immediately, scooping up any breading that may fall onto the baking sheet. Garnish the plates with lemon wedges and fresh dill, if desired.

Panko

PANKO IS PACKAGED, JAPANESE-STYLE BREAD CRUMBS WITH A FLAT, ALMOST SHARDLIKE SHAPE. EXCEEDINGLY LIGHT, THEY CAN PRODUCE A CRUNCHY coating that stays crisp longer than most other bread crumbs. They also tend to absorb less oil, making them a superb choice for pan- and deep-frying, and they are delicious sprinkled on top of a casserole before baking. Panko is made from bread without crusts, which explains its white color. Once an uncommon sight except in Asian markets, you can find panko these days in any well-stocked supermarket. The brands with the lightest texture and best flavor come from Japan. Some markets sell both "fine" and "large" panko, indicating the size of the flakes. (I prefer the large, but either will do.) If you don't want to buy a whole box of panko, some fish counters will package up a small tub for you, since many markets now use it to bread their in-house recipes.

BASIC SEAR-ROASTED SALMON FILLETS

The practice of pan-searing fillets on a hot stove and finishing them in the oven comes from restaurant line cooks, who understand the value of high heat for developing deep flavor as well as a handsomely browned surface. These adrenaline-fueled professionals also know that having 5 to 7 minutes (the time the fillets are in the oven) "hands-free" allows them to whip up a finishing sauce or fulfill other orders. At home, I make sure I've got the rest of the meal ready before I start cooking the salmon—things move quickly once the pan gets hot. But I still value the few minutes the fish takes to roast in the oven; that's when I toss the salad and call everyone to the table.

For everyday meals, I season sear-roasted fillets with nothing more than salt and pepper and serve them unadorned, letting the rich taste of the fish stand on its own. For something a little fancier, I season the salmon with a simple spice rub before searing or drizzle it with a brightly flavored sauce, vinaigrette, or pesto afterward (recipes follow).

The recipe here is for 4 fillets, but you can easily apply this technique to fewer or more. For 2 fillets, use a 9-inch skillet (as in the photos on pages 410 and 411) and half the amount of oil for searing. For more than 4 fillets, use a larger skillet or work in batches and transfer the fillets to a heavy-duty rimmed baking sheet after searing to roast.

SERVES 4

METHOD: Combination sear and high heat

ROASTING TIME: 5 to 7 minutes (plus 1 to 2 minutes to sear)

WINE: Light-bodied, high-acid whites, such as Northern Italian Pinot Grigio, Albariño, or un-oaked Chardonnay from New Zealand.

4 center-cut salmon fillets (about 6 ounces each, preferably 1 inch thick), skin-on, pin bones removed (see page 417)

Kosher salt and freshly ground black pepper

2 tablespoons peanut oil, grapeseed oil, or other neutral tasting oil

1 **HEAT THE OVEN.** Position a rack near the center of the oven and heat to 425 degrees (400 degrees convection). Let the salmon sit at room temperature as the oven heats.

CONTINUED ON PAGE 411

SEAR-ROASTED SALMON FILLETS (PAGE 409)

2 **HEAT THE SKILLET AND SEASON THE FISH.** Set a 12-inch ovenproof skillet over medium-high heat and heat for 1 to 2 minutes. Meanwhile, pat the fish dry and season it liberally on all sides with salt and pepper. (Or season with a spice rub, such as the one that follows.)

3 **SEAR.** Add the oil to the skillet. When it begins to shimmer, lower in the fillets one by one, skin side up. Sear, without disturbing, until one side is nicely browned, lifting with a metal spatula (use a fish spatula if you have one) to check that it's well seared before committing to flipping, 1 to 2 minutes. Flip the fillets and immediately transfer the skillet to the oven.

Flipping the salmon after searing the non-skin side first; lifting the edge of a fillet with a metal spatula to check that it's well seared before committing to flipping.

4 **ROAST.** Roast until the thickest part of the fillets are just firm to the touch, 5 to 7 minutes. If unsure, poke the tip of a paring knife discreetly into a fillet and check to see if it's done to your liking (I prefer it medium-rare, which is slightly translucent in the center). You can also test with an instant-read thermometer; 120 to 125 degrees will give you rare, 130 to 135 degrees medium-rare, and 140 degrees medium.

5 **SERVE.** Remove the skillet from the oven, remembering to use a pot holder or kitchen towel to grab hold of the hot handle. Serve right away.

CONTINUED ON NEXT PAGE

OPTION 1: GARAM MASALA SPICE RUB

This aromatic spice rub works well on tuna as well as on salmon. Sprinkle it all over the fish in step 2, before cooking.

MAKES ABOUT 1 1/2 TABLESPOONS, ENOUGH FOR 4 FILLETS

WINE: Off-dry fruity Riesling or Chenin Blanc.

1 ½ teaspoons garam masala (see page 323)

1 teaspoon cumin seeds, toasted briefly in a dry skillet and ground

1 teaspoon coriander seeds, toasted briefly in a dry skillet and ground

¼ teaspoon dry mustard

¼ teaspoon cayenne

1 teaspoon kosher salt

COMBINE THE SPICES AND SALT in a small bowl. The spice rub will keep in a cool, dry place for 2 to 3 weeks, though its flavor will diminish over time.

OPTION 2: ARUGULA-PISTACHIO PESTO

I like to make this in the late spring, when wild salmon and tender arugula make their first appearance at the market. Pistachios underscore the spring-green color and taste. The brightly flavored pesto comes together in a flash, and a little dollop of it goes a long way in dressing up the salmon fillets. The sauce can be made several hours ahead and kept refrigerated.

MAKES ABOUT 2/3 CUPS, ENOUGH FOR 4 SERVINGS

WINE: Herbal crisp white, such as Sauvignon Blanc from California or New Zealand.

1 garlic clove, peeled

About 2 ½ cups lightly packed baby arugula leaves (about 2 ½ ounces)

About ¼ cup loosely packed chopped fresh chives, mint, or flat-leaf parsley, or a combination

¼ cup unsalted pistachios, lightly toasted

2 tablespoons freshly grated Parmigiano-Reggiano cheese

1 tablespoon fresh lemon juice, plus more to taste

3 to 4 tablespoons extra-virgin olive oil

Kosher salt and freshly ground black pepper

WITH THE FOOD PROCESSOR running, drop the garlic into the feed tube and process until finely minced (this minces garlic more effectively than adding it before the machine is on). Scrape down the sides and add the arugula, herbs, pistachios, and cheese. Pulse the machine several times until you have a coarse paste. Scrape down the sides. With the motor running, pour in the lemon juice and enough olive oil to make a smooth paste. Season to taste with salt, pepper, and additional lemon juice, if needed. Spoon onto sear-roasted salmon fillets just before serving.

OPTION 3: CHIVE-SHALLOT BUTTER

As much as I appreciate the luxurious richness of classic butter sauce on a perfectly cooked piece of fish, these delicate sauces are fussy to make and require a lot of last-minute whisking—and worrying. In their place, I like to create flavored butters, simply a matter of mashing softened butter with herbs and other seasonings. This one is enhanced with chives as well as shallots cooked in white wine, and is perfect with a sear-roasted salmon fillet. It's also good on sear-roasted tuna (page 421), whole roasted trout (page 433), and steak.

If you grow your own chives, pick a chive flower or two, pull the tiny pink-purple blossoms from it, and sprinkle those over the fish. They add flavor and color to the dish. The butter may be made well ahead and keeps for 10 days refrigerated. You may even consider doubling the recipe and freezing half (it will last at least a month if well wrapped) for future good eating.

MAKES ABOUT 1/4 CUP, ENOUGH FOR 4 SERVINGS

WINE: Medium-bodied white with little or no oak, such as Assyrtiko from Greece, Grillo from Sicily, or Pinot Blanc from Alsace.

¼ cup dry white wine or dry vermouth

1 tablespoon finely chopped shallots

⅓ cup coarsely chopped fresh chives

Kosher salt

4 tablespoons unsalted butter, at room
   temperature

½ teaspoon Dijon mustard

1 teaspoon fresh lemon juice

Freshly ground black pepper

1 COOK THE SHALLOTS. Combine the wine or vermouth and shallots in your smallest saucepan. Simmer over medium heat until the liquid is mostly evaporated, about 5 minutes; keep a close eye on it so the shallots don't scorch. Set aside to cool.

2 FLAVOR THE BUTTER. Pound the chives with ¼ teaspoon salt in a large mortar to make a coarse paste (or grind in a small food processor). Place the butter in a mix-

CONTINUED ON NEXT PAGE

ing bowl and, using a wooden spoon or paddle beater, beat until smooth. Scrape down the sides. Add the wine-shallot mixture, the pounded chives, and the mustard and lemon juice and stir until everything is evenly incorporated. Season with salt and pepper. If you plan to serve the butter within a few hours, scrape it into a small ramekin. Cover and refrigerate if working ahead, but let it sit at room temperature for about 15 minutes before serving. *If you are making the butter a day or more in advance (or if you've doubled the recipe), shape it into a log for easier storage and serving, as follows: Lay a sheet of wax paper or plastic wrap (about 12 by 14 inches) on the counter. Scrape the butter into a rectangular shape 2 to 3 inches long near one edge of the paper or plastic. Wrap the edge of the paper or plastic over the butter and shape it into a log. Continue rolling to tighten and shape the log. Twist the ends and refrigerate or freeze.*

3 **SERVE.** If the butter is in a ramekin, scoop about 1 tablespoon onto each fish fillet immediately after roasting. (For butter shaped in a log, slice a ¼- to ½-inch disk off and place on the fish). The idea is that the heat of the fish will melt just enough of the butter to sauce it lightly and leave a small amount unmelted so it's apparent when it comes to the table.

A Fish Spatula

IF YOU COOK FISH AT HOME ON A REGULAR BASIS, A FISH SPATULA BELONGS IN YOUR collection of hand tools. A classic fish spatula resembles an ordinary pancake turner, except that the metal head is elongated and flared so the business end is wider than the part where the turner meets the handle. The thin-gauge, flexible metal head is designed to flip and lift delicate fish fillets without tearing them (it also works well for eggs and fishcakes). This spatula is also characterized by long vertical slots designed to drain away oil (when frying) or liquid (when poaching).

ROAST SIDE OF SALMON WITH HERBED YOGURT SAUCE

This recipe comes by way of my sister-in-law, Carolyn. She loves to throw big dinner parties, and she has a knack for planning menus that not only are delicious but also enable her to do most of the work *before* her guests arrive so she can thereby enjoy the party as much as everyone else. Her roast salmon fits the bill perfectly: striking to look at, delicious, and easy on the host. Much of the work can be done ahead, and the rest is hands-off cooking. Most of the time, Carolyn forgoes carving and presents the whole handsomely glazed salmon on a platter, a move that provides the *ta-da* moment of the party. Guests then help themselves, buffet-style. The salmon is equally delicious served at room temperature alongside a salad of mixed greens—perfect for summer entertaining.

This recipe works best with farm-raised salmon, because its high fat content keeps it moist even though the high-heat roasting cooks the salmon well-done all the way through. The creamy marinade and sauce (flavored with dill, tarragon, or basil—the choice is yours) also help. For a very large group, this recipe is easily multiplied. Simply figure about 6 ounces of fish per person. Any leftovers make an exquisite addition to scrambled eggs the morning after.

The ultimate success—and reliability—of this recipe depends on getting a good thick salmon fillet. You want a single piece of fillet that is at least 1½ inches at the thickest part; anything smaller cooks too quickly. Depending on the variety of salmon (and thus the size of the fish), this may mean buying a whole side, a partial fillet, or even 2 center-cut fillets. Just keep in mind that anytime you need to request a partial side, ask for the thickest portion. It will hold up best to high-heat roasting.

SERVES 8
METHOD: High heat
ROASTING TIME: About 15 minutes
WINE: Medium-bodied white with herbal notes and citrusy acidity, such as Austrian Grüner Veltliner or New Zealand Sauvignon Blanc.

CONTINUED ON NEXT PAGE

⅓ cup plain yogurt, whole-milk or low-fat

⅓ cup mayonnaise

3 tablespoons honey mustard

⅓ cup chopped fresh chives

⅓ cup chopped fresh dill, tarragon, or basil

½ teaspoon dry mustard

Finely grated zest and fresh juice from 1 large lemon

Kosher salt and freshly ground black pepper

One thick 3-pound salmon fillet, skin-on, pin bones removed (see page 417)

1 **HEAT THE OVEN.** Position a rack in the center of the oven and heat to 450 degrees (425 degrees convection). Line a heavy-duty rimmed baking sheet with parchment paper. (The parchment will help greatly when it comes time to serve.)

2 **MAKE THE SAUCE.** In a small bowl, whisk together the yogurt, mayonnaise, and honey mustard. Stir in the herbs, dry mustard, lemon zest, and lemon juice and season with salt and pepper to taste. *The sauce may be made up to 1 day ahead, covered and refrigerated.*

3 **MARINATE THE FILLET.** Place the salmon skin side down on the baking sheet. Spoon about ⅓ cup of the sauce onto the fillet and, using a rubber spatula or the back of a spoon, spread it evenly to coat the entire surface. Do your best to keep the sauce on the fish. Spoon up any sauce that drips off and drizzle it on top. Transfer the remaining sauce to a serving dish with a gravy spoon or small ladle and set aside. *The salmon can stay in the marinade for up to 40 minutes at room temperature. Any longer than that can deteriorate the texture.*

4 **ROAST.** Roast the salmon, turning the baking sheet once halfway through, until the fish is opaque in the center, about 15 minutes (probe the thickest part of the fillet with a paring knife to check for doneness). If the surface is not at all browned but the interior is done, remove the salmon from the oven, turn the broiler to high, and position a rack about 6 inches below the heating element. Once the broiler has heated, set the salmon under it until just barely browned, less than 1 minute. Let the salmon rest for about 5 minutes; if you like to warm your serving platter, now is a good time. Simply slide it into the turned-off oven to warm slightly.

5 **SLICE, SAUCE, AND SERVE.** The easiest way to transfer the whole fillet to the serving platter is to hoist it by holding both sides of the parchment so the salmon hangs, as if in a sling, and lower it onto the platter. Then, with the tip of a small knife

or a pair of scissors, trim away the parchment around the fish so the only parchment that remains is directly under it. An alternate method requires a little more finesse but leaves you with a neater serving platter: Slide two thin metal spatulas under the salmon fillet, starting from either end and sliding toward the center (the longer the spatulas, the easier this is). When you feel you're supporting the bulk of the fillet, lift gently and quickly transfer to the platter; this may leave the skin behind on the parchment, but that is fine.

Using a large knife and a metal spatula (a pie server works nicely), cut the fillet crosswise into serving pieces. The fish won't carve neatly; it's more a matter of digging into it and scooping up a piece of the size you're after. If the skin is still intact, scrape the pieces off the skin, leaving it behind on the serving platter. Spoon some sauce generously over the top and pass any remaining sauce at the table.

Removing Pin Bones from Salmon Fillets

TO CHECK FOR PIN BONES, A SERIES OF FILAMENT-LIKE BONES THAT RUN DOWN THE THICK CENTER OF THE FILLET, DRAG A FINGER DOWN THE surface of the salmon. If you feel a row of small bumps—the ends of the pin bones—you'll need a pair of needle-nose pliers, sturdy tweezers, or a paring knife to remove them. (If you don't feel anything, the fishmonger has removed them already.) How to use pliers or tweezers is obvious; simply grab hold of the end of each and yank. With a paring knife, choke up on the knife with your thumb and forefinger; using the side of the blade, grab the bone between your thumb and the blade, and give a pull, trying not to dig into the flesh. If the pin bones are especially tenacious, take it as a good sign; the tougher they are to remove, the fresher the fillet is.

SLOW-ROASTED WILD SALMON FILLETS

Roasting salmon slowly with low heat leaves it incredibly moist, practically creamy and custardy inside. The method is especially well suited for wild salmon. In addition to creating the excellent texture, slow roasting accentuates the true flavor of wild salmon: sweet, rich, and buttery.

If I can find (and afford) wild king salmon (see Shopping for Wild Salmon, page 420), it's always my first choice for slow roasting. No other species gives you such luxuriously fat fillets. If you bring home a thinner fish, you'll want to roast it for less time. Whichever you choose, buy the thickest fillet you can, preferably from the head end of the fish. Both skinless and skin-on fillets work well in this recipe. For best results, leave the fillet in 1 or 2 pieces for roasting and divide it into portions at the table. If you want to add a sauce, try Arugula-Pistachio Pesto (page 412) or Tomato-Orange Relish (page 434). If you find fresh peas or asparagus at the market, either makes a fine side dish.

SERVES 4

METHOD: Low heat

ROASTING TIME: 25 to 40 minutes

WINE: A recent vintage of rosé Champagne or domestic rosé sparkling wine.

1½ pounds wild salmon fillet (page 420), preferably 1½ to 2 inches thick, left in 1 or 2 pieces, skin-on, pin bones removed (page 417)

2 teaspoons extra-virgin olive oil

2 tablespoons minced fresh chives

½ teaspoon finely grated lemon or orange zest

Kosher salt and freshly ground black pepper

1 **HEAT THE OVEN.** Position a rack in the center of the oven and heat to 250 degrees (225 degrees convection). Line a heavy-duty rimmed baking sheet with aluminum foil (this makes cleanup easier) and set a wire rack on top (a cake cooling rack works well.

2 **SEASON THE FISH.** Lightly oil both sides of the salmon and arrange it skin side down on the roasting rack. In a small bowl, combine the chives and the lemon or orange zest. Smear the chive mixture evenly over the top of the fillet and then season

generously with salt and pepper. Let the salmon sit at room temperature for a full 30 minutes. (Because the oven temperature is so low, the fish will cook more evenly if it doesn't start super-cold.)

3   **ROAST THE SALMON.** Roast until medium-rare or medium, 25 to 40 minutes, depending on the thickness of the fillet. The easiest way to test for doneness is to nick a thick portion of the fillet with the tip of a knife and peek inside to see if the center is done to your liking. For medium-rare (my preference for wild salmon), the center should be moist and deep red. Medium will be less red but still moist. (You can test with an instant-read thermometer; 120 to 125 degrees will give you rare, 130 to 135 degrees medium-rare, and 140 degrees medium.) If you're roasting sockeye salmon, keep in mind that it tends to dry out more quickly than other types of wild salmon, so take care not to overcook. Slow-roasting fish often draws out rather unsightly little globs of whitish albumin (the same protein found in egg whites). Usually the albumin falls through the roasting rack, but if there are any visible spots, simply wipe them away before serving.

4   **SERVE.** Using a large metal spatula, transfer the salmon to a cutting board, sliding the spatula between the skin and the fillet to remove the skin. Using the side of the spatula or fish server, divide the fish into portions and serve.

Shopping for Wild Salmon

FOR A SPECIAL TREAT, I PREFER WILD-CAUGHT PACIFIC SALMON TO THE UBIQUI-TOUS FARM-RAISED ATLANTIC SALMON FOR BOTH FLAVOR AND HEALTH REA-sons. Wild Pacific salmon are caught in the northern Pacific, mostly in Alaskan waters, as they migrate from late spring through autumn and sometimes even into early winter. The availability of the various Pacific species changes as the season progresses. For instance, the season kicks off in mid-May with Copper River king and sockeye, and then coho. Chums and pinks come last. There are definite flavor differences between the varieties, and I get most excited about king and sockeye for their richness and full flavor. King salmon, as its name suggests, is the largest of all, and bears the highest price tag to match. Prized for their high fat content and clean, sweet taste, king salmon fillets can range in color from deep red to pale—almost white. You may also find king salmon labeled Chinook (the native name) or named after the river in which it was caught, such as Copper River king, Yukon River king, and so on. Regardless of color, true king salmon is easy to spot by the thickness and size of the fillets (and the price). It's not at all unusual to find fillets up to 2 inches thick and 8 inches across—ideal for roasting, especially because the fat content helps keep the fish moist whether roasted at high or low temperature.

The less expensive sockeye and coho are also good choices. Both are smaller than king and have a firmer texture. Sockeye fillets are closest to king in their rich, fattier texture and are best recognized by an intensely deep red color. Coho (also called silver) is the leanest of the three choices, and while still delicious, it has the mildest flavor and flakiest texture.

BASIC SEAR-ROASTED TUNA STEAKS

Sear-roasting thick tuna steaks leaves them nicely browned on the outside and perfectly rosy and moist on the inside. The roasting time depends largely on the thickness of the steaks and, of course, your doneness preference. Expect a 1½-inch steak to take a full 6 minutes, while a 1-inch steak will be done in closer to 5 minutes. Personally, I think it's a crime to cook a gorgeous piece of tuna any more than medium-rare, so I keep a close eye on it, checking it often. A good piece of tuna needs nothing more than salt and pepper, but you might like to dress it up with Wasabi-Ginger Mayonnaise or Black Olive Vinaigrette (recipes follow).

SERVES 4

METHOD: Combination sear and high heat

ROASTING TIME: 5 to 7 minutes (plus about 3 minutes to sear)

WINE: Fruity young red wines without too much oak or tannin, such as Pinot Noir from Oregon's Willamette Valley or New Zealand's Central Otago region.

1 ¼ to 1 ½ pounds tuna steaks (1 to 1 ½ inches thick), preferably yellowfin or albacore (see Shopping for Tuna, page 423)

Kosher salt and freshly ground black pepper

2 tablespoons peanut oil, grapeseed oil, or other neutral-tasting oil

1 **HEAT THE OVEN.** Position a rack near the center of the oven and heat to 425 degrees (400 degrees convection). Let the tuna sit at room temperature as the oven heats.

2 **HEAT THE SKILLET AND SEASON THE FISH.** Set a 12-inch ovenproof skillet over medium-high heat and heat for 1 to 2 minutes. Meanwhile, pat the fish dry and season it liberally on all sides with salt and pepper.

3 **SEAR.** Add the oil to the skillet. When it begins to shimmer, lower in the steaks, one by one. Sear, without disturbing, until one side is nicely browned and doesn't stick

CONTINUED ON NEXT PAGE

to the pan when you lift it with a metal spatula (use a fish spatula if you have one) to check that it's well seared, about 3 minutes. Flip the steaks and immediately transfer the skillet to the oven.

4 **ROAST.** Roast until the thickest part of the steaks are just firm to the touch, 5 to 7 minutes. If unsure, poke the tip of a paring knife discreetly into a steak and check to see if it's done to your liking (I prefer it rare to medium-rare, which is still quite rosy in the center). You can also test with an instant-read thermometer; 120 to 125 degrees will give you rare, and 130 to 135 degrees medium-rare.

5 **SERVE.** Remove the skillet from the oven, remembering to wrap the handle in a pot holder or kitchen towel so you don't accidentally grab hold of it. With a large knife, cut the steaks into individual portions. Serve immediately.

OPTION 1: WASABI-GINGER MAYONNAISE

Creamy and sharp, a dollop of this on top of tuna or salmon makes a perfect accompaniment. And if you have any leftover tuna, this mayonnaise makes a killer tuna salad. I also love to use it as a dressing for coleslaw. Look for wasabi powder where you find other Asian ingredients in the supermarket; it's widely available.

MAKES A SCANT 1/2 CUP, ENOUGH FOR 4 SERVINGS

WINE: Young white wines with residual sweetness, lower alcohol, and high acid, such as Kabinett and Spätlese Rieslings from Germany or Rieslings from Washington State.

1 tablespoon wasabi powder	½ teaspoon soy sauce
1 lime	⅓ cup mayonnaise
1 ½ teaspoons finely grated fresh ginger	Kosher salt

IN A SMALL BOWL, moisten the wasabi powder with 2 teaspoons cool water. Stir to make a paste and let sit for about 10 minutes. Meanwhile, grate ½ teaspoon of zest from the lime (a rasp-style microplane grater works best) and squeeze 1 tablespoon of juice. Add the lime zest and juice to the wasabi along with the ginger and soy sauce. Add the mayonnaise, stir to combine, and season to taste with salt (about ¼ teaspoon usually suffices). May be made up 1 day in advance, covered, and refrigerated.

OPTION 2: GREEN OLIVE VINAIGRETTE

The meaty taste of tuna (or swordfish) stands up nicely to a drizzle of this vibrantly flavored vinaigrette. Serve green beans and potatoes with the tuna and you've got all the elements of a beautifully deconstructed salade Niçoise.

MAKES ABOUT 1/2 CUP, ENOUGH FOR 4 SERVINGS
WINE: Youthful, crisp Grenache-based rosé from Southern France.

⅓ cup coarsely chopped fresh flat-leaf parsley

¼ cup green olives, such as picholine or lucques, pitted

2 tablespoons capers, drained

1 garlic clove, chopped

2 teaspoons red wine vinegar

¼ cup extra-virgin olive oil

Kosher salt, if needed

COMBINE THE PARSLEY, olives, capers, garlic, and vinegar in a mini food processor and blend to a coarse puree. Add the olive oil and puree briefly, just until incorporated. If you don't have a mini food processor, chop all the ingredients (except the olive oil) as finely as you can. Transfer to a bowl and whisk in the oil. Taste for salt (it may not need any). The vinaigrette may be made several hours ahead and refrigerated, but do serve it at room temperature. Drizzle a little of the vinaigrette over each serving of sear-roasted tuna.

Shopping for Tuna

THE TWO KINDS OF TUNA THAT ARE AVAILABLE IN MOST MARKETS (AND FISHED FROM RELATIVELY HEALTHY OCEAN STOCKS) ARE YELLOWFIN AND ALBACORE. The larger yellowfin, usually the more expensive of the two, has deep pink to medium-red flesh and a rich flavor. Albacore, which tends to be less expensive, has a paler color, a softer texture, and a milder flavor. For roasting, shop for tuna steaks that are at least 1 inch thick; if you prefer tuna very pink in the center, go with even thicker, up to 1½ inches. Because individual tuna steaks are often too large for a single serving, you'll want to shop for total weight, not a certain number of steaks. At home, I like to leave the steaks whole and cut them into individual servings after roasting, not before. This helps prevent me from overcooking the pricey fish, as smaller steaks cook more quickly and are more likely to dry out in the hot oven.

SEAR-ROASTED SWORDFISH STEAKS

I used to steer away from swordfish at the market, because I couldn't seem to master cooking the thick, meaty steaks. My few attempts at broiling, grilling, and sautéing ended in either dried-out or undercooked steaks. Then I tried sear-roasting—starting the fish on top of the stove and finishing them in the oven—and *Eureka!* That was the secret I was after. The fish comes out cooked through but not dried, and every time I am impressed by how something so meaty-looking can be so delicate and sweet. I enhance the flavor of this rich fish by basting the steaks with a little butter as they cook and then drizzling it over the fish to serve. The flavor and texture of swordfish are best when it is cooked all the way through, but it will dry out if overcooked.

SERVES 4

METHOD: Combination sear and high heat

ROASTING TIME: 5 to 10 minutes (plus about 3 minutes to sear)

WINE: Un-oaked Chardonnay from Australia or New Zealand or Assyrtiko from Santorini.

1¼ to 1½ pounds swordfish steaks (1 to 1½ inches thick; see Shopping for Swordfish, page 426)

Kosher salt and freshly ground black pepper

2 tablespoons peanut oil, grapeseed oil, or other neutral-tasting oil

2 tablespoons unsalted butter, cut into chunks

1 **HEAT THE OVEN.** Position a rack near the center of the oven and heat to 400 degrees (375 degrees convection). Let the swordfish sit at room temperature as the oven heats.

2 **HEAT THE SKILLET AND SEASON THE FISH.** Set a 12-inch ovenproof skillet over medium-high heat and heat for 1 to 2 minutes. Meanwhile, pat the fish dry and season it liberally on all sides with salt and pepper.

3 **SEAR.** Add the oil to the skillet. When it begins to shimmer, lower in the steaks, one by one. Sear, without disturbing, until one side is nicely browned and doesn't stick to the pan when you lift it with a metal spatula (use a fish spatula if you have one) to check that it's well seared, about 3 minutes. Flip the steaks, dot the tops with the butter, and immediately transfer the skillet to the oven.

4 **ROAST.** Roast, basting the steaks with the butter once, until the fish feels firm to the touch, 5 to 10 minutes, depending on the size and thickness. If unsure, insert an instant-read thermometer into the center of one steak; it should read about 145 degrees. Swordfish should not be served rare.

5 **SERVE.** Remove the skillet from the oven, remembering to wrap the handle in a pot holder or kitchen towel so you don't accidentally grab hold of it. With a large knife, divide the steaks into individual portions as needed. Serve immediately, spooning some of the butter over each serving as desired.

OPTION: SWEET-AND-SOUR GOLDEN RAISIN RELISH

This relish is inspired by the classic Italian dish of swordfish with agrodolce sauce, a sweet-and-sour sauce often made with golden raisins. The tangy sauce pairs beautifully with the rich taste of swordfish, and it's also good on roast pork and chicken. A tablespoon of mint stirred in at the end adds a nice bright note, but if there's none growing on the windowsill or in the garden, the relish is delicous without.

MAKES ABOUT 3/4 CUP, ENOUGH FOR 4 SERVINGS

WINE: Fruity sparkling wine with crisp acidity, such as Prosecco or Cava.

1 tablespoon extra-virgin olive oil	½ cup golden raisins
1 small shallot, finely chopped	1 tablespoon sugar
1 anchovy fillet, finely chopped	2 teaspoons champagne vinegar
1 teaspoon chopped fresh thyme leaves	Kosher salt
1 teaspoon yellow mustard seeds	1 tablespoon chopped fresh mint (optional)

HEAT THE OIL in a small saucepan over medium-low heat. Add the shallot, anchovy, and thyme and cook, stirring frequently, until the shallot is tender, about 3 minutes. Add the mustard seeds and heat until the shallots brown lightly, about 2 minutes. Add the raisins,

CONTINUED ON NEXT PAGE

sugar, vinegar, a pinch of salt, and enough water to barely cover. Lower the heat and simmer until the raisins are plump and the liquid has become syrupy, about 15 minutes. Cool to room temperature before serving. Taste for salt, and stir in the mint, if using, just before serving. *The relish may be stored in the refrigerator for 2 weeks.*

Shopping for Swordfish

UNLESS WE SPEND TIME ON COMMERCIAL FISHING DOCKS, FEW OF US WILL EVER SEE A WHOLE SWORDFISH, BUT IT IS AN IMPRESSIVE FISH, WEIGHING anywhere from 50 to 1000 pounds, with its "sword" extending as much as 5 feet on the largest specimens. At the market you will see *wheels* or *logs*, round or half-moon-shaped sections of the fish. Swordfish varies in color from creamy white to pink, depending on its diet, but there seems to be no real corollary between color and taste. The fat content can also vary, but it's not always easy to tell by looking. Your best tactic when shopping for swordfish is to look for bright, shiny steaks. The more recently cut from the wheel, the better, and if the steaks in the case look dull or at all dried-out, I often ask the fishmonger to slice off a fresh one. Like tuna, swordfish steaks often have dark red areas, called bloodlines, and you should check that these are bright and not dark or brown. As with all fish, the smell should be mild. For roasting, you want steaks that are 1 to 1½ inch thick, which may mean buying 1 or 2 large steaks and then dividing them into individual portions after roasting.

BASIC WHOLE ROASTED STRIPED BASS

I love serving a whole roasted fish to friends. For one thing, it's not something people do often, so right off the bat you've made something special. Plus you get incredible flavor by roasting the fish right on the bone. And did I mention that it's easy? The recipe calls for a relatively large fish—about 7 pounds, which is about the biggest fish I can fit in my oven without breaking it down into fillets. For smaller fish, subtract about 3 to 5 minutes from the cooking time for every pound (see the option that follows for an example). For anything smaller than 2 pounds, follow the higher-heat roasting technique used in the recipe for Basic Whole Roasted Rainbow Trout (page 433). When you're figuring serving sizes, aim for 10 to 12 ounces per person to account for the weight of the bones and head.

If you want to add an herbal note to the fish, stuff the belly with a handful of herbs before roasting. It won't clobber you with bold flavor, but you'll get a lovely little nuance of, say, parsley, tarragon, or dill. To best appreciate the exquisite, mild flavor of striped bass, I often serve it with nothing more than a thin drizzle of my best olive oil, a squirt of lemon, and a pinch of fleur de sel. When I want a little more pizzazz, I skip the lemon and olive oil and serve it with a boldly flavored sauce, such as the Celery Leaf Salsa Verde or the Hot-and-Sweet Soy-Cilantro Sauce that follow. A classic hollandaise would also be lovely here.

SERVES 10

METHOD: High heat

ROASTING TIME: 40 to 55 minutes

WINE: Citrusy Sauvignon Blanc with bright herbal notes from France's Loire Valley, such as Sancerre or Quincy.

1 whole striped bass (6 to 7 pounds), scaled, cleaned, gutted, and gills removed

Kosher salt and freshly ground black pepper

Small bunch of fresh herbs, such as flat-leaf parsley, tarragon, or a mix (optional)

3 tablespoons extra-virgin olive oil, plus more for serving

Lemon wedges, for serving

Fleur de sel, for serving (optional)

CONTINUED ON NEXT PAGE

1 **HEAT THE OVEN.** Position a rack in the center of the oven and heat to 375 degrees (350 degrees convection). Line a large, heavy-duty rimmed baking sheet with parchment paper.

2 **PREPARE THE FISH.** Check the inside of the fish to make sure it's clean. If necessary, give the fish a quick rinse. Place it on a sturdy work surface, and with a sharp knife cut 3 to 4 angled slashes into the thickest part of the body, cutting about halfway to the bone and about 2 inches apart. Flip the fish and cut similar slashes on the other side. Use poultry or utility sheers to trim the tail flush with the body (this prevents the tail from burning and helps the fish fit in the oven). Season the cavity with salt and pepper. Place the herbs, if using, into the cavity, folding the stems as necessary so they fit. Rub the olive oil over the entire outside surface of the fish, even inside the slashes, and season all over with salt and pepper, again remembering to season the slashes. Arrange the fish on the baking sheet, placing it on a diagonal if necessary so it fits; don't worry if the head and tail extend somewhat over the sides of the pan.

3 **ROAST THE FISH.** Roast until opaque but still moist at the thickest part of the back (check by inserting a knife along the backbone of the fish, at the thickest part, and prying the top fillet away from the bone; it should come away easily but still be moist nearest the bone), 40 to 55 minutes, depending on the size and thickness of the fish. An instant-read thermometer inserted in the thickest part should read 130 to 140 degrees.

4 **CARVE AND SERVE.** If carving at the table, transfer the fish to a carving board, using the parchment paper to do so. Otherwise, carve directly on the roasting pan. (For carving directions, see Carving a Large Whole Fish, page 431.) Serve immediately, drizzling each portion with a thread of olive oil and passing the lemon wedges and fleur de sel, if using, at the table.

OPTION 1: ROASTED SMALLER WHOLE STRIPED BASS

For a 2½- to 3-pound striped bass, follow the recipe above, making only 2 angled slashes in each side and reducing the olive oil to 1½ tablespoons in step 2. Roast for 30 to 35 minutes, or until opaque but still moist at the thickest part of the back. An instant-read thermometer inserted in the thickest part of the fish should read 130 to 140 degrees. Expect a 2½- to 3-pound fish to feed 4 people.

OPTION 2: CELERY LEAF SALSA VERDE

I learned to turn celery leaves into a sprightly condiment from Judy Rodgers, the super-talented chef at Zuni Café in San Francisco. Like any resourceful chef, Judy deplores waste and so came up with a way to transform the often-discarded celery leaves into a bright and vibrant salsa. Judy makes hers quite peppery and serves it alongside grilled meats; I dialed back the heat for mine so as not to overwhelm the delicate fish. For best flavor and texture, use the innermost celery stalks, referred to as the heart. You will need 2 medium-size lemons to provide enough zest and juice, and remember it's best to grate the zest *before* you juice the fruit. The recipe is easily doubled if you're roasting a big fish.

MAKES ABOUT 1 CUP, ENOUGH FOR 4 TO 6 SERVINGS

PLAN AHEAD: For best flavor, make the salsa an hour or 2 ahead and leave it at room temperature. (Refrigerate the salsa if holding for longer than that, but let it come to room temperature to serve.)

WINE: Tart, medium-bodied white with youthful fruit, such as Mâcon from Burgundy.

6 scallions, white and pale green parts, minced

⅓ cup finely chopped celery heart, including the leaves

⅓ cup lightly packed chopped fresh flat-leaf parsley leaves

3 tablespoons capers, drained and chopped

2 tablespoons chopped tarragon leaves

1 tablespoon Dijon mustard

2 teaspoons finely grated lemon zest

2 tablespoons fresh lemon juice

Pinch of crushed red pepper flakes

½ cup extra-virgin olive oil

Kosher salt and freshly ground black pepper

IN A SMALL BOWL, combine the scallions, celery, parsley, capers, tarragon, mustard, lemon zest, lemon juice, and crushed red pepper flakes. Whisk in the olive oil. Season to taste with salt and pepper. Spoon the salsa over each serving of fish, and pass any extra at the table. Store any leftovers in the refrigerator and let come to room temperature before serving.

CONTINUED ON NEXT PAGE

OPTION 3: HOT-AND-SWEET SOY-CILANTRO SAUCE

Just a thin drizzle of this sweet/sour/salty sauce adds a distinct Asian flair to all kinds of fish, and I especially enjoy it with striped bass. Because it packs a punch, a little goes a long way. These days you can find both hoisin sauce and chile paste in the Asian section of most supermarkets; if not, you may need to visit an Asian market. Once you have the ingredients on hand, this takes just a minute to prepare. If you want to make it a few hours ahead, however, you can; just add the cilantro at the last minute to keep it pretty and green. Double the recipe if serving a crowd.

MAKES ABOUT 1/3 CUP, ENOUGH FOR 4 TO 5 SERVINGS

WINE/BEER: Medium-sweet Riesling, such as Auslese wines from the Mosel or Rheingau in Germany; or a light traditional lager with spice notes.

2 tablespoons soy sauce

2 tablespoons rice vinegar or champagne vinegar

2 teaspoons hoisin sauce (see page 247)

1 teaspoon honey

¼ teaspoon ground chile paste (such as *sambal oelek*)

2 tablespoons finely chopped fresh cilantro

COMBINE THE SOY sauce, vinegar, hoisin sauce, honey, and chile paste in a small bowl. Whisk to combine, making sure you haven't left a clump of honey. Stir in the cilantro right before serving. Pass the sauce at the table with a small spoon for drizzling over the fish.

Shopping for Striped Bass

STRIPED BASS ARE ALSO KNOWN AS *ROCKFISH*, AND FISHERMEN COMMONLY USE THE MORE COLLOQUIAL *STRIPERS*. BOTH WILD AND FARM-RAISED STRIPED bass are available in fish markets across the country. Which you have access to may depend on where you shop (or fish), but they are interchangeable in the kitchen. If you were to do a side-by-side comparison, you might notice that the taste of the wild-caught is slightly brighter and cleaner, but both offer delicate, white, delicious meat. All whole fish should have clear eyes, shiny, taut skin, and a faint, almost sweet (some say cucumber-like) aroma. If the smell is at all assertive, choose another fish.

Carving a Large Whole Fish

I F YOU'VE NEVER CARVED A BIG WHOLE FISH BEFORE, IT WILL HELP TO FIRST CON-
CEPTUALIZE THE GOAL: CREATING NEAT BONELESS PORTIONS AND REMOVING
the skeleton intact. The approach that I outline below serves both an aesthetic and a practical purpose: The portions have more eye appeal than a heap of shredded bits, and careful carving means you're much less likely to encounter bones when you sit down to eat.

Carving fish differs from carving meats, because roasted fish is tender enough to pull
away from the bone and divide into individual portions without a sharp knife. In fact,
attacking the fish too aggressively only serves to mash the thin, hairlike bones into the
flesh, making eating unpleasant. The classic tool for carving whole fish is a blunt-edged fish
serving knife. This specialized (and old-fashioned) implement looks like a cross between a
pie server and a wide-bladed table knife, but fortunately, since few of us have these in our
kitchen drawers, a large soup spoon, a small serving spoon, or even a small spatula will work
quite well. The trick is to hold the spoon with the bowl facing down (the opposite from how
you eat with it) and use the dull edge and rounded bowl to nudge the fillets away from the
bone. With a spatula, you use the backside to gently work the fillets from the bone. You can
use a table fork in your other hand, or your fingers.

To carve, it's helpful first to outline the fillets by cutting the skin with a paring knife,
since the skin is often tougher than the delicate flesh. Begin by cutting through the skin
all the way around the outside of the fish, making the cut on the inside of the fins so they
remain on the fish. Next run the tip of the knife down the center line, cutting the skin and
separating the top fillet into 2 long fillets. Now, using the edge of the spoon or the back of
the spatula, edge the top half of the fillet (the side that runs along the back of the fish) onto
a serving platter. With a large fish, don't expect to lift the fillet in one piece, and you may
need to cut the skin in order to separate it into 2 or 3 pieces. Next remove the belly side of
the fillet.

Now you've exposed the backbone. With your hands, grab the fish's tail and pull to lift
the bones off the bottom fillet, working slowly so as not to lift away any of the fillet below.
When you get to the head, use your spoon to detach any meat that wants to remain attached
to the bone. Discard the head and backbone. Check the bottom fillet and scrape away any
bones that remain. Divide the bottom fillet in half along the center line and divide into
serving pieces. Don't worry if the fillets don't remain entirely intact; the tender flesh flakes
apart easily.

BASIC WHOLE ROASTED RAINBOW TROUT

Even though I know that commercial rainbow trout comes from fish farms, the sight of the speckled, shiny fish with a pinkish line running from gill to tail (the bit of color that earns them their name) makes me wistful for camping trips and freshwater streams. Thankfully, I don't have to deal with the vagaries of trying to cook the fish over a campfire (not to mention the gutting and cleaning in the great outdoors) and instead can rely on a hot oven to roast them to perfection. Brushing the surface with a little melted butter before roasting helps the skin to crisp and brown up.

Rainbow trout fillets vary from ivory to pink, but the flavor is always mild and tasty. For a light meal, serve the fish as is. For something fancier, try the Tomato-Orange Relish recipe that follows. Good accompaniments for roasted trout are rice (pilaf is especially nice) and sautéed summer squash.

SERVES 2

METHOD: High heat

ROASTING TIME: 18 to 20 minutes

WINE: Light, citrusy whites, such as Pinot Grigio, Albariño, and Grüner Veltliner.

2 whole trout (about 12 ounces each; see page 437), cleaned, gutted, and preferably boneless

Kosher salt and freshly ground black pepper

4 to 6 thin lemon slices

4 sprigs fresh herbs, such as flat-leaf parsley, dill, thyme, or a combination

1½ tablespoons unsalted butter, melted

1   **HEAT THE OVEN.** Position a rack in the center of the oven and heat to 450 degrees (425 degrees convection). Line a heavy-duty rimmed baking sheet large enough to hold the fish with parchment paper.

2   **SEASON THE FISH.** Check the inside of the fish to make sure it's clean. If necessary, give the fish a quick rinse. Season the inside with salt and pepper. Layer the lemon slices inside and top with the herbs, folding the stems if necessary so they fit. Brush the butter over the entire outside surface of the fish and season all over with salt and pepper.

CONTINUED ON NEXT PAGE

3 **ROAST THE FISH.** Roast until the skin is crispy and browned and the flesh is opaque but still moist at the thickest part of the back (check by inserting a knife along the backbone of the fish, at the thickest part, and prying the top fillet away from the bone; it should come away easily but still be moist nearest the bone), 18 to 20 minutes, depending on the thickness of the fish. An instant-read thermometer inserted in the thickest part should read 130 to 140 degrees.

4 **SERVE.** Transfer the fish to serving plates and serve immediately.

OPTION: TOMATO-ORANGE RELISH

This recipe comes from my friend Roy Finamore, who coauthored a fish cookbook and knows a thing or two about what tastes good alongside fish. He made this to serve with my roasted whole trout, but it's also wonderful spooned on a sear-roasted salmon or tuna fillet. The relish is thick, almost like a jam, and its flavor is remarkably fresh, bright, citrusy, and sweet, especially when made with tomatoes picked at the height of the season. While the relish can be refrigerated overnight, it will lose some of its zing; for best flavor, let it come to room temperature before serving. The recipe can easily be doubled—just use a bigger skillet.

MAKES ABOUT 2/3 CUP, ENOUGH FOR 2 TO 4 SERVINGS

PLAN AHEAD: The relish tastes best at room temperature (not hot), so make this at least 30 minutes ahead of serving.

WINE: Young, fruity Pinot Gris from Alsace or Oregon's Willamette Valley.

1½ tablespoons extra-virgin olive oil	½ teaspoon chopped fresh thyme
¼ cup minced shallots	Kosher salt and freshly ground black pepper
½ pound ripe beefsteak tomatoes, peeled, seeded, and chopped (see page 435)	½ teaspoon finely grated orange zest
	2 tablespoons fresh orange juice
1 tablespoon vodka or grappa	1 teaspoon capers, drained

HEAT A SMALL SKILLET (6-inch works well) over medium-high heat. When the pan is hot, add the oil and shallots. Sauté, stirring often, until the shallots are translucent but not browned, about 1 minute. Add the tomatoes, vodka or grappa, thyme, a pinch of salt, and a grinding of pepper. Bring to a gentle boil, then lower the heat and simmer, stirring every once in a while, until the tomatoes have thickened and there is little to no liquid left in the pan, about 6 minutes.

Remove from the heat and stir in the orange zest, orange juice, and capers. Taste and season again with salt and pepper. Transfer the relish to a serving bowl and let cool to room temperature before serving.

Peeling and Seeding Tomatoes

I TRIED TO SHORTEN ROY'S ORIGINAL TOMATO RELISH RECIPE BY NOT BOTHER-ING TO PEEL AND SEED THE TOMATOES, BUT THE BITS OF SKIN ARE UNPLEASANT and the flavor isn't as refined (at least now you know this extra work is worth it and not some chef's affectation). In fact, many recipes featuring fresh tomatoes benefit from this step. Fortunately, there's a quick method for slipping off the skins without paring away any of the delicious flesh.

Bring a medium pot of water to a boil. Have ready a mixing bowl filled with ice water. Using a sharp knife, cut an *X* in the bottom (blossom end) of each tomato; you only really need to score the skin, so try not to cut too deeply. When the water boils, lower a few tomatoes in and keep them in the hot water for about 30 seconds. Remove with a slotted spoon and transfer immediately to the ice water to stop them from cooking. After about 30 seconds, remove from the water and, starting at the *X*, where the skin is loose, peel the skin off. If the skins don't slip off easily, return the tomatoes to the boiling water for another 15 seconds. The objective is to release the skin without cooking the tomato.

To seed the tomatoes, cut them crosswise across the equator—in other words, halfway between the stem end and the blossom end. Holding one half in your hand over a bowl, squeeze *very* gently, and with a fingertip of the other hand pry the seeds out of each segment. Next remove the core and chop the tomato as directed in your recipe.

WHOLE ROASTED RAINBOW TROUT WITH BACON AND BASIL

When I'm not roasting whole trout, I'm apt to pan-fry them in a skillet of bacon drippings. Here I use that same combination, but I arrange the strips of bacon on top of the trout before roasting. It's easier than pan-frying, and you get that same wonderful play of flavors between the sweet, almost fruity taste of trout and the salty, meaty taste of bacon. To bolster the flavor, I also stuff each trout with a handful of fresh basil and a couple of orange slices. Serve these on your biggest dinner plate, so you have room to set aside the basil and orange slices (as well as any bones) as you eat.

Be sure to use a top-quality bacon here (I like Nueske's Applewood Smoked). I find that thin- or medium-sliced bacon roasts best. Thick-sliced tends to overwhelm the fish. You could substitute pancetta for a less smoky taste. Be warned, however, that the bacon fat may smoke some as it roasts, especially if you haven't recently cleaned your oven.

SERVES 2
METHOD: High heat
ROASTING TIME: About 20 minutes
WINE: Slightly sweet Riesling from Germany or Chenin Blanc from Washington State.

2 whole trout (about 12 ounces each; see page 437), cleaned, gutted, and preferably boneless

4 thin orange slices

4 leafy sprigs fresh basil

Kosher salt and freshly ground black pepper

3 slices thin- or medium-cut bacon (about 1½ ounces)

¼ cup fresh orange juice

1 **HEAT THE OVEN.** Position a rack in the center of the oven and heat to 425 degrees (400 degrees convection).

2 **SEASON THE FISH.** Check the inside of the fish to make sure it's clean. If necessary, give the fish a quick rinse. Season the inside with salt and pepper. Layer the orange slices inside and top with the basil, folding the stems if necessary so they fit. Season the outside of the fish with salt and pepper. Cut the strips of bacon in half

crosswise so you have 6 shorter strips and arrange the strips, slightly overlapping and at an angle, so they cover the body of each fish. The tail and head will be exposed. Place the fish side by side on a heavy-duty rimmed baking sheet.

3 **ROAST THE FISH.** Roast until the bacon is crisp and the flesh of the fish is opaque but still moist at the thickest part of the back (check by inserting a knife along the backbone of the fish, at the thickest part, and prying the top fillet away from the bone; it should come away easily but still be moist nearest the bone), about 20 minutes, depending on the thickness of the fish. An instant-read thermometer inserted in the thickest part of the fish should read 130 to 140 degrees.

4 **SERVE.** Transfer the fish to plates. Pour off all but a few teaspoons of fat from the baking sheet, being careful not to pour off any drippings. (Different bacon releases varying amounts of fat, so you may have a lot or barely any.) Add the orange juice to the pan and scrape with a wooden spoon to combine the drippings and juice. Drizzle this over the fish and serve.

Shopping for Rainbow Trout

WHOLE RAINBOW TROUT ARE THE ONE WHOLE FISH I CAN PRETTY MUCH RELY ON FINDING AT EVERY SEAFOOD COUNTER, AND AS SUCH, THEY'VE become my standby for an easy fish dinner. Occasionally labeled *golden trout*, whole rainbow trout range from 12 to 16 ounces each, which, once you subtract the weight of the skeleton, translates to 6 to 8 ounces of roasted fillet—perfect for a generous single serving. Some markets sell the fish boneless (also referred to as butterflied), which means that they have removed the entire backbone while leaving the head and tail intact. Starting with a boneless trout makes your life easier when it comes time to serve—and eat.

ROASTED BRUSSELS SPROUTS WITH CAPERS AND LEMONY BROWNED BUTTER (PAGE 469)

VEGETABLES & FRUITS

RECIPES

ROASTING MAY BE THE SIMPLEST WAY TO PREPARE VEGETABLES. JUST CUT THEM UP, TOSS THEM WITH SOME FAT, SEASON THEM, AND SLIDE THEM into the oven. But the results are *so* good, and the technique offers limitless possibilities in terms of flavorings, finishing touches, and combinations of vegetables. In fact, the biggest challenge I had in putting together this chapter was restricting the number of recipes so that it didn't take over the whole book. In the pages that follow you will find plenty of recipes for the usual suspects—things like roasted potatoes and roasted root vegetables—but some of the tastiest roasted vegetables are the ones you least expect, such as broccoli (page 461), sugar snap peas (page 451), eggplant (page 476), and Brussels sprouts (page 469). Seriously: If you have never had roasted Brussels sprouts, prepare yourself—they are a revelation.

The marvel of roasting vegetables is how, more than any other cooking technique, roasting concentrates flavors, making the vegetables taste like better versions of themselves. The dry heat of the oven caramelizes the vegetables' natural sugars, giving them an irresistible sweetness and plenty of deliciously browned edges. This natural sweetness means that roasted vegetables welcome bold flavorings, like a zingy vinaigrette, a pungent pecorino, salty anchovies, and aromatic citrus. Because roasting makes most vegetables soft in the center, they also benefit from the addition of something crunchy, like toasted nuts and bread crumbs. In this chapter you will find all kinds of enhancements for plain roasted vegetables.

You will also find a handful of roasted fruit recipes. Roasting fruit follows the same principles as roasting vegetables, and because fruits have even more natural sugars than vegetables, they caramelize and become even sweeter in the oven. Roasted fruits make marvelous desserts, such as Maple-Roasted Apples with Candied Nuts (page 521) and Butter-Roasted Plums with Vanilla, Ginger, and Rum (page 531), but they also work on the savory side of things. For instance, serve Slow-Roasted Grapes (page 527) alongside roast pork, or try Roasted Cherries with Creamy Polenta (page 534) with roast duck.

As you cook your way through the recipes in this chapter, I encourage you to begin to create your own flavor variations. To help you on your way, here are a few guiding principles and tips.

CUT THE VEGETABLES OR FRUITS INTO EVEN-SIZED PIECES. Whether you're cutting Brussels sprouts into quarters or chunking a hefty butternut squash into cubes, make an effort to keep all the pieces the same size so they will cook at the same rate. If you're mixing vegetables (as in Herb-Roasted Roots, page 507), cut any denser, slower-cooking ones into smaller pieces and leave more tender, higher-moisture ones in larger pieces. In general, I aim for pieces between ¾ inch and 2 inches square. Anything smaller will cook too quickly and dry out, and anything over 2 inches doesn't leave enough cut surfaces to give you the desired ratio of crunchy crust to soft interior that so often defines roasting. If the vegetables are wet, or if you rinse them in water, dry them thoroughly before roasting for best results.

PICK A PAN AND LINE IT WITH PARCHMENT PAPER (OR NOT). My favorite pan for roasting vegetables is a heavy-duty rimmed baking sheet. The rim ensures the vegetables don't fall off when you stir them partway through roasting (a step that promotes even cooking). The low sides are also ideal for getting maximum moisture evaporation and subsequent browning. I am a big proponent of lining the pan with parchment paper before roasting vegetables, and here's why: First, the best part of many roasted vegetables is the delectable crunchy end bits, but these can easily get stuck to the pan, especially with tender vegetables like eggplant and endive. If you line the pan with parchment, these crunchy bits don't stick to the pan but stay part of the vegetable pieces. Second, parchment makes cleanup a breeze. One downside of lining the pan with parchment, however, is that it can be a little tricky to stir the vegetables during roasting without shifting the paper. The best technique is to hold the paper down with one oven-mitted hand and stir with the other. I also understand that not everyone stocks parchment in the kitchen and you may prefer to limit your use of disposable paper. Another solution is to line the pan with a reusable silicone mat (often called a *Silpat*) if you have one. These are especially useful when roasting fruits because their sugars tend to caramelize and stick to the pan. Thankfully, the recipes work just as well with or without a pan liner.

COAT THE VEGETABLES OR FRUITS WITH SOME FAT. Because vegetables and fruits contain virtually no fat, you need to coat them lightly with something that helps conduct the heat so they brown nicely and don't merely shrivel up in the hot oven. (The fat also helps seasonings stick.) Olive oil, butter, and goose or duck fat are all good choices. The vegetables should be lightly coated but not swimming in fat—you want them to roast, not fry. You can do this in a bowl and then transfer them to the roasting pan, or you can toss them right on the baking sheet. The advantage of the bowl is that it's more efficient and easier to get all the vegetable pieces evenly coated. The disadvantage is that you've dirtied another dish. Also, if you've lined the pan with parchment paper, tossing the vegetables directly on the sheet takes a little care so you don't ruffle up the parchment.

SEASON WELL. Use an ample amount of salt when seasoning vegetables; while you don't want them to taste too salty, you do want enough salt to bring out their flavor. The best way to know if your vegetables are properly seasoned before roasting is to take a nibble. Even if you are roasting something that you wouldn't normally eat raw, there's no better way to tell. If you toss the vegetables with your hands, as I most often do, you can simply lick a finger to get a sense of whether you've added enough salt, pepper, and whatever else you're using. (But do wash it if you plan to toss the vegetables again!)

SPREAD THE VEGETABLES OR FRUITS OUT IN A SINGLE LAYER. Piling up the vegetables or fruits will cause them to steam and not brown, so be sure they are in a single layer with some space in between. (The exception to this is leafy vegetables like cabbage, which will cook down quite a bit and can therefore afford to be piled up to start.)

ROAST WITH HIGH HEAT (BUT YOU CAN BE FLEXIBLE). Most of the recipes in this chapter call for a hot oven—above 400 degrees. This high temperature effectively drives the moisture from tender, fresh, high-moisture vegetables, leaving their flavors and sugars concentrated. Of course, roasted vegetables are often a side dish for roasted meat, poultry, or fish, and I am all for the efficiencies of sharing an oven. Since vegetables are less fussy than meat when it comes to temperature, I recommend that you adhere to whatever temperature the meat, poultry, or fish requires and adjust the vegetable cooking time accordingly. For instance, if a chicken roasts at 400 degrees and the recipe calls for roasting the vegetables at 450 degrees, simply use the lower temperature and expect the vegetables to take a little longer.

DRESS THEM UP OR SERVE THEM PLAIN. Beyond salt and pepper, roasted vegetables offer several opportunities to up the flavor ante before, during, and after roasting. For ideas, read through the recipes in this chapter to find instances where I add spice and herbs before roasting, or a glaze partway through, or a sprightly vinaigrette just before serving. Then go ahead and experiment with your own favorite flavors.

QUICK-ROASTED GREEN BEANS AND SHALLOTS WITH GARLIC AND GINGER JUICE

Here's a boldly flavored side dish that comes together quickly. Roast the green beans and shallots together, which takes 20 minutes or less, and then toss with finely chopped garlic and ginger juice. Though the juice seems to evaporate as soon as it hits the hot beans, it leaves behind its spicy bite and wonderful aroma. You can use either prepared ginger juice or, for the best flavor, make it yourself, starting with grated fresh ginger. If you do opt for the convenience of prepared ginger juice (available at specialty food markets—a good one is made by The Ginger People), use the leftover to enlighten salad dressings, marinades, and, perhaps my favorite, cocktails.

SERVES 4 TO 5
METHOD: High heat
ROASTING TIME: 15 to 20 minutes

One 1½-inch piece of fresh ginger, peeled (about 2 ounces), or 1 tablespoon bottled ginger juice

1 pound green beans, trimmed

2 to 3 shallots, sliced into rings about ¼-inch thick

2 tablespoons extra-virgin olive oil

Kosher salt and freshly ground black pepper

1 garlic clove, finely minced

2 tablespoons coarsely chopped fresh cilantro or mint, or a combination

1 **HEAT THE OVEN.** Position a rack near the center of the oven and heat to 450 degrees (425 degrees convection). If desired, line a heavy-duty rimmed baking sheet with parchment paper.

2 **MAKE THE GINGER JUICE, IF NECESSARY.** Grate the ginger finely, using a microplane or ceramic ginger grater. When you have grated about 2 tablespoons, squeeze the grated ginger over a small, sturdy fine-mesh sieve set over a bowl. Try to extract as much liquid as you can. (If you don't have a small sieve, either squeeze the

CONTINUED ON NEXT PAGE

grated ginger in a bit of cheesecloth or simply place it in the palm of one hand, squeeze your fist closed, and press the fingertips of your other hand against the place where the juice runs out to act as a sort of strainer.) Continue squeezing until you have 1 tablespoon fresh juice. Reserve the juice and discard the grated ginger.

3 **ROAST.** Combine the beans and shallots on the baking sheet, arranging them in a loose layer. Drizzle with the olive oil, season with salt and pepper, and toss gently to coat. Roast, tossing once or twice with tongs, until the beans are tender, browned in spots, and beginning to shrivel and the shallots are browned in spots, 15 to 20 minutes.

4 **SEASON AND SERVE.** Transfer to a bowl. Immediately add the garlic and ginger juice and toss to coat. Add the fresh herbs, toss, and season with additional salt if needed. Serve warm or at room temperature.

ROASTED ASPARAGUS BUNDLES WRAPPED IN BACON

The idea of wrapping bacon around a handful of asparagus and roasting the bundles at high heat is genius—and not mine. It comes by way of a dear friend whom I worked with in France years ago. Though American by birth, Randall Price has lived in France for as long as I've known him, and his cooking and his sensibilities are French through and through. That explains why Randall, like all good French cooks, takes care to peel the spears and then trim them to be all the same length. I agree that peeling is worthwhile, but I'm more apt to leave the ends uneven, since I hate to waste any edible part of my favorite spring vegetable. I find fat asparagus spears work best for this recipe, because you get a better ratio of tender centers and crispy bacon, but use whatever looks freshest.

The combination of salty, crisp bacon and tender, sweet asparagus makes this a sensational first course, either by itself or on top of lightly dressed baby greens. You can also serve it as a side dish with chicken, lamb, salmon, or tuna. Randall has been known to turn this into a fabulous brunch dish by topping the bundles with poached eggs and hollandaise sauce and serving them over toasted brioche. But don't forget, he thinks he's French; you and I can substitute English muffins for the brioche in this delicious take on eggs Benedict. If you're looking for a warm hors d'oeuvre, try the prosciutto option that follows. The individually wrapped spears are more finger-food-friendly.

SERVES 4
METHOD: High heat
ROASTING TIME: 24 to 30 minutes

1 pound asparagus, preferably thick and at least 8 inches long (see Shopping for Asparagus, page 449)

4 slices thin-cut bacon
Freshly ground black pepper

1   **HEAT THE OVEN.** Position a rack near the center of the oven and heat to 425 degrees (400 degrees convection). If desired, line a heavy-duty rimmed baking sheet with parchment paper.

CONTINUED ON NEXT PAGE

2 **TRIM AND WRAP THE ASPARAGUS.** Snap off the woody bases of the asparagus and peel as needed (see Trimming and Peeling Asparagus, page 450). Divide the asparagus into 4 bunches (the number of spears per bundle will depend on how thick or thin they are). If you like, trim the ends so the spears are all the same length. Bundle the asparagus by wrapping a strip of bacon around each bunch, winding the bacon like the stripe on a barbershop pole, so that just the tips and ends of the asparagus remain exposed. Do not stretch the bacon or wrap it too tightly; it will shrink as it cooks and tighten its hold. Evenly space the bundles on the baking sheet and season generously with pepper.

3 **ROAST.** Slide the pan into the oven. When the bacon on top begins to sizzle, usually after about 12 minutes, flip each bundle over with tongs. Continue roasting until the bacon is crisp and the asparagus tender, another 12 to 15 minutes. Transfer to a serving platter or dinner plates and serve hot.

OPTION: ROASTED PROSCIUTTO-WRAPPED ASPARAGUS SPEARS

Follow the recipe above, substituting 4 ounces of prosciutto for the bacon. Cut the prosciutto slices in half lengthwise (please don't cut away any of the fat) and wrap each strip around a single spear, spiraling it to leave only the tip and base exposed. Arrange on the baking sheet, spaced about 1 inch apart, season with pepper, and drizzle with a few teaspoons of olive oil (this makes up for the fact that prosciutto is leaner than bacon). Roast as directed, flipping with tongs once after about 8 minutes, until the prosciutto is crisp and the asparagus tender, another 12 minutes (for about 20 minutes total). Sprinkle a little grated Parmesan over the top, if you like, and serve warm or at room temperature.

Shopping for Asparagus

FEW THINGS SIGNIFY SPRING AS DEFINITIVELY AS THE APPEARANCE OF TALL, VERDUROUS STALKS OF ASPARAGUS AT THE FARMERS' MARKET. SURE, MOST grocery stores sell those neat rubber-banded bunches of pencil-thin spears from South and Central America year-round, but for us northerners, asparagus is the first substantial food crop to pop up each spring and is therefore great cause for celebration. The season for local asparagus lasts about a month, and I, for one, tend to go a little asparagus-mad, eating it as often as I can, trying to get my fill.

When shopping for asparagus, there are a few things to keep in mind. First off, there's the whole thick vs. thin debate. After years of hearing from experienced cooks and respected food authorities on why one surpasses the other, I've come to conclude that both thick and thin have their merits—and I'll take whichever appears fresher. Unlike many spring vegetables, such as carrots, for which the first baby bunches of spring are the slimmest and most tender, every asparagus plant (or crown, as the perennial root system is called) produces both pencil-thin and big fat spears during its productive life cycle of about fifteen years. While some varieties are bred to be generally thinner or taller, the thickest spears always come from healthy plants in their prime, yet those same vigorous plants also send up a few skinny stalks alongside the fat ones. When the plants are very young and just starting to produce and again as they advance in age, they produce a greater percentage of slender spears. In other words, thick or thin has no real bearing on quality. As to which are more tender, it's not a question of girth but of freshness. Pencil-thin spears can be tender enough to nibble raw, but if they sit too long in storage or on the supermarket shelf, they will dry out and toughen. Thicker spears possess a thicker, tougher outer skin (which I like to peel), but the insides are incredibly tender, and because they are so plump, there's more to them, so they're juicier and often more satisfying than the thin ones. As to which to buy when, you may decide on the basis of how you plan to serve the vegetable. For instance, when I am looking to serve asparagus unadorned as a simple side dish, I prefer the thick. When I am chopping it up to add to pasta or salad, the thinner spears work best. For roasting, I love them both.

Whether thick or thin, look at the tips to judge freshness. The tips should be tight, pointed, and dry. As asparagus matures, the individual spear tips open out or unfurl (*fern out* is the gardeners' term for what happens when the spears are left in the ground to go to seed). For the cook, this unfurling indicates that the spear will be tough and woody because of an increase in a fibrous compound known as lignin (also found in wood, hemp, and linen). In addition to being an indicator of age, the tips also tell of its freshness; the tip is the most delicate part of the spear, and therefore the first to deteriorate when stored too long or

CONTINUED ON NEXT PAGE

improperly. Make sure the tips aren't at all damp or mushy, a bad sign. This is especially problematic in those tightly bound bunches sold in supermarkets, which, although handy, spoil easily. Finally, the spears should be firm and smooth. Any shriveling or wrinkling means they're old and drying out.

STORING ASPARAGUS

If you've bought a bunch of asparagus that's tightly bound, first remove the rubber bands or wires that hold it. Store it loose in an open plastic bag in the produce drawer for several days. If you're lucky enough to get your hands on just-cut spears (either from the farmers' market or from someone's garden), treat them as you would fresh flowers: Trim about ½ inch from the bunch and stand the spears in a glass or jar of cold water; they will actually continue to grow for a day or two. Arrange a plastic bag loosely over the top to retain moisture. Refrigerate until ready to use, but no more than a couple of days.

Trimming and Peeling Asparagus

EVEN THE FRESHEST, MOST TENDER ASPARAGUS SPEAR WILL HAVE A WOODY BASE THAT REMAINS TOUGH AFTER COOKING AND THUS NEEDS TO BE removed. The trick is to remove only the fibrous base and not much more. The most common way to do so is to snap the woody ends off the raw spears one by one. Simply hold the base of a stalk in one hand, then place your other hand 2 to 3 inches up and gently bend the stalk until it snaps. If it doesn't yield and snap, move your second hand another inch up the stalk and try again. By starting close to the bottom of the spear and keeping your hands close together, you're sure to snap the spear at the lowest possible point. If you randomly bend the stalk, you're likely to toss away a good portion of the tender part.

Once the ends are snapped off, you need to decide whether or not to peel the asparagus. Pencil-thin spears generally don't need peeling. If in doubt, take a nibble. If the outside seems tough, remove it. When it comes to thicker spears, I always peel. While this may seem overly fussy, the experience of having to chew through a tough outer layer greatly diminishes the pleasure of eating the tender, juicy spears. It's an example of when a little extra prep work can turn an ordinary dish into an extraordinary one. It's easiest to peel asparagus when it's lying flat on a cutting board. Use a standard vegetable peeler and, starting an inch or two below the tip, use light pressure to strip off the thin outer layer. With very fat spears, apply more pressure as you reach the base, where the peel gets thicker. The appearance will tell you whether you've gone deep enough—the darker green of the fibrous outer layer is apparent to the eye.

QUICK-ROASTED SUGAR SNAP PEAS WITH TOASTED SESAME SALT

Fresh sugar snap peas are so sweet, tender, and crunchy that I can hardly resist munching them out of hand, but they are never more delectable than when quickly roasted in a hot oven. The pods stay crisp and their sugars intensify as they bronze up in the oven's heat. They make a delicious alternative to steamed peas alongside roast lamb or poultry. I also like to serve them at room temperature as a vegetable salad.

Toasted sesame salt (*gomasio*), a traditional Japanese condiment, is sold in little jars in Asian markets, but it's easy enough to make at home. Plus when you make it yourself, you can be sure the sesame seeds are fresh. I like to make a double or triple batch and use it to season everything from popcorn, to salads, to hardboiled eggs and seafood.

SERVES 4
METHOD: High heat
ROASTING TIME: About 12 minutes

1 pound sugar snap peas

2 tablespoons white or black sesame seeds, or a mix (preferably not hulled)

¼ teaspoon kosher salt

2 tablespoons extra-virgin olive oil

1 **HEAT THE OVEN.** Position a rack in the center of the oven and heat to 475 degrees (450 degrees convection). If desired, line a heavy-duty rimmed baking sheet with parchment paper.

2 **STRING THE PEAS.** Check to see if the peas have strings—a fibrous thread that runs from the stem end to the tail end of each peapod. Do so by snapping off the stem end with a paring knife or your thumbnail and pulling down toward the tail end. If you pull away a thread that runs down the seam of the pod like a zipper, then the peas need to be destrung. Check both the inside and the outside curve of the pod, starting at the tail end and pulling up as you check the second side, removing any strings as you go. If there are no strings (some snap pea varieties are stringless), simply trim off the stem ends.

CONTINUED ON PAGE 453

QUICK-ROASTED SUGAR SNAP PEAS WITH TOASTED SESAME SALT

(PAGE 451)

3 **MAKE THE SEASONED SALT.** Spread the sesame seeds out in a small dry skillet over medium-low heat and cook, stirring almost constantly, until fragrant and, if using white seeds, lightly golden, 2 to 3 minutes total. (If using hulled white seeds, expect them to toast in less than 1 minute.) Immediately pour the seeds onto a plate to cool. When cooled, combine them with the salt in a mortar or spice grinder. Grind together to form a coarse powder. It's okay to leave some sesame seeds whole for texture and appearance.

4 **ROAST.** Arrange the peas on the baking sheet in a single layer. Drizzle with the olive oil and toss to coat. Roast, turning once or twice with a spatula, until the pods are slightly bronzed in spots, beginning to shrivel, but still crisp, about 12 minutes.

5 **SEASON AND SERVE.** As soon as the peas are ready, transfer to a serving bowl and sprinkle with sesame salt. Serve hot, warm, or at room temperature.

CHILE-ROASTED "CANDY" CORN

I dubbed this "candy" corn the first time I made it, as a friend and I mindlessly polished off half a pan's worth of these addictive niblets of chewy sweetness while dreaming up ways to serve them. Because this dish is so intensely sweet, with just a touch of heat, it's best to think of it more as a relish or condiment than as a full-on side dish. Beyond eating this "candy" corn out of hand, try it alongside grilled steak or chicken. I also add it to all manner of salads and salsas (I've included one favorite on page 456). And it's great stirred into creamy guacamole.

Corn and chile make one of those perennially happy flavor combinations, like tomatoes and basil or apples and cinnamon. For the truest chile flavor, I use pure chile powder, such as ground ancho (my favorite) or ground chipotle, and not the spice blend referred to as chili powder (which is a mix of ground chiles and other seasonings). If you want to take your "candy" corn in another direction, feel free to use another spice; for instance, ground cumin is especially good. Another option is to toss the corn with bacon drippings in place of olive oil to give the whole dish a meaty, smoky edge—perfect for serving with pork chops. Or leave the spice out altogether to enjoy the pure, intense taste of roasted corn.

This is really best with fresh corn off the cob, but you can use frozen if you have a hankering for this out of season (see Using Frozen Corn, page 455).

MAKES ABOUT 2 CUPS, ENOUGH FOR 4 TO 6 SERVINGS
METHOD: High heat
ROASTING TIME: 10 to 15 minutes

2 to 2 ½ cups fresh corn off the cob (from 6 ears), or frozen corn kernels, defrosted and dried

1 tablespoon extra-virgin olive oil

Kosher salt and freshly ground black pepper

⅛ teaspoon ground chile powder (see headnote)

1 **HEAT THE OVEN.** Position a rack near the center of the oven and heat to 500 degrees (475 degrees convection). If desired, line a heavy-duty rimmed baking sheet with parchment paper.

2 **SEASON AND ROAST.** Spread the corn kernels on the baking sheet. Drizzle the olive oil over the corn and season with the salt, pepper, and chile powder. Toss to coat. Roast, stirring every 5 minutes so the kernels on the outside don't burn before the others are browned, until all the kernels are tinged with brown and slightly shriveled, 10 to 15 minutes. Serve warm or at room temperature.

CONTINUED ON NEXT PAGE

Getting Fresh Corn Off the Cob

HUSK THE CORN, REMOVING AS MUCH SILK AS YOU CAN BY RUBBING YOUR HAND ALONG THE EAR. IF YOU CAN'T GET ALL THE SILK, RUB THE EAR WITH A dry kitchen towel to remove any stubborn hairs. Cut off the stem end of each ear to give you a sturdy base on which to stand the ear. Hold the ear, tip end up, firmly on a cutting board (or inside a shallow bowl if you don't want to scatter kernels all over). Using a sharp knife and a sawing motion, slice the kernels from the ear, removing a few rows at a time. Go slowly at first, until you get a sense of how deeply to cut. You don't want to remove the fibrous base of the kernels, and you definitely don't want to cut into the woody core. After a few rows, you'll get a sense of how deeply to cut. (If you like, save the leftover, still-juicy cobs to make corn stock. You can also scrape the cobs clean with the back side of a knife, strain the scrapings through a fine-mesh sieve, and add the sweet, milky juices to salad dressing or soup.) Each ear will give you ⅓ to ½ cup of kernels.

Using Frozen Corn

SINCE THE SEASON FOR LOCAL CORN ON THE COB IS HEARTBREAKINGLY BRIEF IN MY PART OF THE COUNTRY, I SOMETIMES FIND MYSELF CRAVING CORN AT the wrong time of year. Fortunately, even if you are not the kind of person with the inclination (and space) to put up your own food, frozen corn is available in every supermarket. Look for bags or boxes labeled "shoepeg"; the kernels tend to be the most tender and least fibrous. Whatever you buy, make sure the ingredient list contains corn only. The easiest way to thaw frozen corn is overnight in the refrigerator. Avoid rinsing it in water to quick-defrost, since this makes it too wet to roast. However you defrost the corn, it's a good idea to spread it out on a clean dish towel to dry before roasting. If the corn is too wet, it will steam rather than roast.

OPTION: ROASTED CORN, TOMATO, AND BLACK BEAN SALAD/SALSA

Here's a great recipe that calls for roasted corn, from a sensational cook (and friend), Sarah Mitchell Duddy. Serve it as a side dish with hamburgers and call it salad or serve it as a dip for tortilla chips and call it salsa. It makes great picnic fare too, since it travels well and pairs beautifully with summertime foods. For best flavor, however, do not refrigerate it; the cold will mute its flavors and mar the texture of the tomatoes.

MAKES ABOUT 4 CUPS, ENOUGH FOR 6 TO 8 SERVINGS

Chile-Roasted "Candy" Corn, at room
  temperature

1 pint cherry tomatoes, quartered

1 cup cooked or canned black beans,
  drained and rinsed

¾ cup finely chopped red bell peppers

¼ cup finely chopped red onions

2 teaspoons minced jalapeño (from about
  ½ jalapeño, seeded or not, to your taste)

2 tablespoons fresh lime juice

1 tablespoon extra-virgin olive oil

½ teaspoon ground cumin, preferably
  freshly ground from toasted seeds

3 to 4 tablespoons chopped fresh cilantro

Kosher salt and freshly ground black
  pepper

TOSS THE ROASTED CORN with the tomatoes, beans, bell peppers, red onions, jalapeño, lime juice, olive oil, cumin, and cilantro. Season with salt and pepper to taste and serve.

QUICK-ROASTED MUSHROOMS WITH PINE NUTS AND PARMESAN

Roasting mushrooms at a high temperature leaves them browned on the outside but keeps them so juicy they burst with a sort of mushroom broth when you bite into one.

My favorite mushrooms to roast are small cremini. The caps are small enough to leave whole, and they have more flavor than plain white mushrooms. You can also make this with small portabellos, which are virtually the same as cremini but a little bigger. If you use large portabello caps, expect them to take about 10 minutes longer to roast. You can also play around with a mix. Just be sure the mushrooms are fresh and not at all shriveled or dried out.

Serve these mushrooms as a side dish with anything meaty, from a grilled steak to roast lamb. They're also substantial enough to serve as a first course, perhaps with a few slices of buttered toast for soaking up the rich juices (as shown on page 458). Sometimes I spear them with toothpicks and pass them as an hors d'oeuvre. As long as you chop the pine nuts finely, they shouldn't fall off.

SERVES 3 TO 4
METHOD: High heat
ROASTING TIME: 15 to 18 minutes

1 tablespoon pine nuts

1 pound small cremini, button, or portabello mushrooms, cleaned and stem ends trimmed (see page 459)

2 tablespoons unsalted butter, melted

1 tablespoon extra-virgin olive oil

1 tablespoon chopped fresh thyme

Kosher salt and freshly ground black pepper

Parmigiano-Reggiano cheese

1 **HEAT THE OVEN.** Position a rack in the upper third of the oven and heat to 425 degrees (400 degrees convection). If desired, line a heavy-duty rimmed baking sheet with parchment paper.

2 **TOAST THE PINE NUTS.** Spread the pine nuts on a small baking sheet or in a small ovenproof skillet and toast until lightly browned, 1 to 2 minutes. (Watch vigilantly; pine nuts have a high oil content and therefore brown up very quickly.) Dump

CONTINUED ON PAGE 459

CROSTINI WITH
QUICK-ROASTED
MUSHROOMS WITH
PINE NUTS AND
PARMESAN
(PAGE 457)

the toasted nuts onto a cutting board to stop cooking. Let cool slightly, then chop finely.

3 **ROAST.** Put the mushrooms in a large bowl. Drizzle with the butter and olive oil and sprinkle with the thyme. Season generously with salt and pepper. Toss to coat. Spread the mushrooms on the baking sheet in single layer so they are not piled up. Roast, turning once after about 10 minutes, until tender and browned, another 5 to 8 minutes.

4 **FINISH AND SERVE.** Transfer the mushrooms to a serving dish (you can also return them to the bowl you seasoned them in). Sprinkle the pine nuts over the mushrooms and grate cheese over them (start with a couple of tablespoons and add more to taste). Taste for salt and pepper and serve hot or warm.

Cleaning Mushrooms

THE MAXIM THAT MUSHROOMS ARE THIRSTY LITTLE SPONGES THAT BECOME WATERLOGGED IF THEY GET SO MUCH AS SPLASHED WITH WATER HAS BEEN etched into my kitchen consciousness. In recent years, however, several credible sources have debunked this myth by weighing mushrooms, dousing them with cold water, and then reweighing them. The result: The water-washed mushrooms don't weigh any more than they did dry, meaning that they aren't at all spongelike and don't soak up water. So if you like to wash all produce thoroughly, go ahead and wash the mushrooms—as long as you do it *immediately* before using them. Mushrooms will deteriorate very rapidly if left wet, so unless you're planning to add them directly to something liquid (soup, sauce, etc.), it's important to wipe them dry immediately after washing. The two most common methods for washing are to give them a quick rinse with a sprayer or to swish them around in a bowl of cold water. If you're roasting or sautéing, you have to be extra-sure to dry mushrooms thoroughly—damp ingredients don't brown up very well at all.

Now that I've said all this, if, like me, you've always cleaned mushrooms simply by wiping the surfaces with a paper towel, there's no reason to change your ways. For very dirty mushrooms (the "dirt" on cultivated mushrooms is actually a specific type of sterilized compost), I sometimes use a damp towel.

BLASTED BROCCOLI

BLASTED BROCCOLI

Roasting is not what usually comes to mind when preparing broccoli, but try it once and you'll be hooked. The hot air of the oven blasts the broccoli tips to turn them toasty brown and sweet while the stems cook crisp-tender. Delicious on its own, roasted broccoli is even better when drizzled with the Kalamata Vinaigrette that follows.

You can serve roasted broccoli hot from the oven or at room temperature (it will hold for hours undressed). If you plan to serve it with the vinaigrette, wait until just before serving to drizzle the dressing on.

SERVES 4
METHOD: High heat
ROASTING TIME: 15 to 20 minutes

1½ pounds broccoli	**Kosher salt and freshly ground black**
3 tablespoons extra-virgin olive oil	**pepper**

1 **HEAT THE OVEN.** Position a rack in the center of the oven and heat to 450 degrees (425 degrees convection). If desired, line a heavy-duty rimmed baking sheet with parchment paper.

2 **TRIM THE BROCCOLI.** If you bought broccoli by the head (as opposed to just crowns), cut the stalks away from the broccoli crowns, reserving both the crowns and the stalks. Tear off any leaves from the stems, trim the bottoms, and peel away the thick fibrous outer layer before slicing the stalks ½-inch thick. Cut the crowns into individual florets so the stem end is no more than ½-inch thick; avoid cutting through the buds as much as you can (it's impossible to avoid cutting through the buds entirely).

3 **ROAST.** Put the broccoli on the baking sheet, drizzle with the olive oil, season with salt and pepper, and toss to coat. Spread into an even layer and roast, stirring once about halfway through to insure even cooking, until the stems are just tender and the tops are nicely browned, 15 to 20 minutes.

4 **SERVE.** Transfer the roasted broccoli to a serving platter or bowl and serve warm or at room temperature.

CONTINUED ON NEXT PAGE

OPTION: KALAMATA VINAIGRETTE

Though the anchovy is listed as optional in this dressing, I highly recommend you use it. Its savory but not overtly fishy flavor goes really well with roasted broccoli.

MAKES ABOUT 1/3 CUP, ENOUGH FOR 4 SERVINGS

1 garlic clove, minced

1 anchovy fillet (optional), minced

2 tablespoons fresh lemon juice

¼ cup kalamata olives, pitted and finely chopped

2 tablespoons extra-virgin olive oil

Freshly ground black pepper

Kosher salt, if needed

1   **WHISK** together the garlic, anchovy, if using, and lemon juice in a small bowl. Let sit for 2 minutes to infuse the flavors. Add the olives, olive oil, and several grindings of black pepper and whisk well to combine. Taste for salt; the vinaigrette may not need any with the olives and anchovy.

2   **DRIZZLE** the vinaigrette over hot or room-temperature Blasted Broccoli and serve.

SLOW-ROASTED CAULIFLOWER WITH CORIANDER AND ONION

Slow-roasting cauliflower makes it seductively tender and brings out its inherent sweetness. While the florets don't get as crisply browned as they would if roasted at high heat, they transform into a sort of *über* cauliflower—a more intense version of themselves. The addition of coarsely ground coriander and mustard seeds adds bright hits of flavor, while the onion adds its own sweetness. Serve this alongside a simply prepared roast or steak and dinner is suddenly interesting. Or pile the florets onto a pretty plate and serve them as a snack with drinks (provide toothpicks for spearing them).

The inspiration for this recipe comes from Jody Adams, one of Boston's most renowned chefs. Adams combines broccoli and cauliflower, two cruciferous cousins, but over the years I've come to prefer the simplicity of all cauliflower. If you want to make a combination dish, cut 1 pound of broccoli into florets, combine the broccoli with the cauliflower, and increase the seasonings by rounding the teaspoons. Expect it to serve 6.

SERVES 3 TO 4
METHOD: Moderate heat
ROASTING TIME: 1 1/4 to 1 1/2 hours

1 medium head cauliflower (about 2 pounds)

1 large red or sweet onion, cut into 1/2-inch wedges

2 tablespoons extra-virgin olive oil

1 1/2 teaspoons coriander seeds, coarsely ground

1 1/2 teaspoons mustard seeds, brown or yellow, coarsely ground

1/4 teaspoon crushed red pepper flakes

Kosher salt and freshly ground black pepper

Juice from 1/2 lemon

Chopped fresh parsley (optional)

1 **HEAT THE OVEN.** Position a rack in the center of the oven and heat to 325 degrees (300 degrees convection). If desired, line a heavy-duty rimmed baking sheet with parchment paper.

CONTINUED ON NEXT PAGE

2 **SEPARATE THE CAULIFLOWER INTO FLORETS.** Trim away any green leaves from the cauliflower. Turn the cauliflower upside down and, using a small knife, cut around the thick core to remove it (I typically toss the fibrous core into the compost, but it can be saved and added to slow-cooked soups and stews or cooked with potatoes before mashing.) Separate the head into individual florets that are about 1½ inches wide across the top and just about as long.

3 **SEASON.** In a large mixing bowl, combine the cauliflower, onion, olive oil, coriander, mustard, red pepper flakes, and salt and pepper to taste. Toss to distribute the seasonings.

4 **ROAST AND SERVE.** Transfer the vegetables to the baking sheet, spreading them evenly. Roast, turning every 30 to 40 minutes, until tender and starting to brown in spots, 1¼ to 1½ hours. Squeeze a little lemon juice over the cauliflower and sprinkle with parsley, if you like. Serve hot or warm.

ROASTED CAULIFLOWER "STEAKS" WITH CRUNCHY PARSLEY-PINE NUT BREAD CRUMBS

The trick to this recipe is slicing the head of cauliflower, core and all, into thick slabs, or "steaks," as opposed to the usual florets. This creates a maximum surface area to caramelize and crisp up in the hot oven, providing a wonderful contrast with the melting, almost juicy texture of the inside. While the cauliflower "steaks" are superb on their own, I like to dress them up with a crunchy bread-crumb topping made with lemon zest, golden raisins, and plenty of fresh parsley.

When you slice a head of cauliflower this way, you'll get 2 or 3 intact center "steaks" that make a dramatic visual impact. The slices toward the outside won't be quite as stunning, but they will be equally delicious. Since I tend to take an egalitarian approach to serving, I usually cut each center slab in two and give everyone a little bit of both, the "steaks" and the more crumbled end pieces. In addition to making a great side for actual steaks, the slabs make a fine first course, served hot or at room temperature. If you do make this ahead, wait to add the bread-crumb topping until just before serving; it will maintain its crunch this way. You can also chop the cauliflower into bite-size bits and toss it, along with the bread-crumb mixture, into a bowl of hot pasta, adding a little of the pasta cooking water, to make an exceptional pasta dinner.

SERVES 4 TO 5

METHOD: High heat

ROASTING TIME: About 30 minutes

½ cup fresh bread crumbs (see Making Fresh Bread Crumbs, page 210)

¼ cup plus 1 tablespoon extra-virgin olive oil

3 tablespoons pine nuts

1 medium head cauliflower (about 2 pounds)

Kosher salt and freshly ground black pepper

¼ cup chopped fresh flat-leaf parsley

3 tablespoons golden raisins

1 teaspoon finely grated lemon zest

CONTINUED ON NEXT PAGE

1 **HEAT THE OVEN.** Position a rack in the center of the oven and heat to 375 degrees (350 degrees convection).

2 **TOAST THE BREAD CRUMBS AND NUTS.** Spread the bread crumbs on a small baking sheet, drizzle with 1 tablespoon olive oil, toss, and spread in an even layer. Bake the bread crumbs, stirring once or twice so they cook evenly, until golden brown and toasty, about 9 minutes. Meanwhile, spread the pine nuts on another small pan (a little skillet works) and toast alongside the bread crumbs until lightly toasted, about 8 minutes. Set both aside to cool.

3 **INCREASE THE OVEN TEMPERATURE** to 450 degrees (425 degrees convection). If desired, line a heavy-duty rimmed baking sheet with parchment paper.

4 **TRIM THE CAULIFLOWER.** Remove any leaves. Trim the base of the cauliflower core so that it is slightly recessed but do not remove it. Stand the cauliflower upright and, with a large chef's knife, cut it lengthwise into ½- to ¾-inch slices. Do your best to slice evenly. The center few slices will remain more or less intact, but the outer slices may crumble. Don't let this worry you; the idea is to create as many flat cut surfaces as you can without reducing the head to crumbs. Put the slices (and the crumbled or broken bits) on the baking sheet. Drizzle with the remaining ¼ cup olive oil. Season with salt and pepper and turn gently to coat, spreading the olive oil over the surfaces to insure that they are evenly coated.

5 **ROAST,** turning the pieces once or twice partway through so they cook evenly, until nicely browned and the tip of a paring knife easily penetrates the stems, about 30 minutes.

6 **MEANWHILE, MAKE THE BREAD-CRUMB TOPPING.** Place the toasted pine nuts, parsley, raisins, lemon zest, and a pinch of salt in a food processor and pulse several times until coarsely chopped. Transfer to a small bowl, add the toasted bread crumbs, and season to taste with salt and pepper.

7 **SERVE.** Transfer the cauliflower to a serving platter or individual plates. Just before serving, sprinkle with the bread-crumb mixture.

Romanesco Broccoli

ROMANESCO BROCCOLI MAY NOT BE AS READILY AVAILABLE AS ITS MORE PEDESTRIAN COUSINS, BROCCOLI AND CAULIFLOWER, BUT I SNAP IT UP whenever I find it. I love this exotic-looking vegetable, both for its Gaudiesque appearance and for its flavor. Especially when roasted, it seems to combine the almost nutty taste of cauliflower and the greener, grassy taste of broccoli. Plus, Romanesco's tight-head configuration makes it ideal for slicing in thick slabs and preparing according to the recipe for Roasted Cauliflower "Steaks" with Crunchy Parsley–Pine Nut Bread Crumbs. You can also roast it as you would conventional broccoli (see page 461).

ROASTED BRUSSELS SPROUTS WITH CAPERS AND LEMONY BROWNED BUTTER

I imagine Brussels sprouts were on the list of most hated vegetables for many of my generation growing up, but that's only because our mothers didn't know to splash the mini-cabbagey vegetables with olive oil and roast them in a hot oven until they were utterly tender and sweet. Gone are any traces of the slippery texture we associate with cabbage and, best of all, that strong sulfurous smell. In fact, these sprouts taste so good that you may have to restrain yourself from popping one after another into your mouth before they hit the table.

Roasted Brussels sprouts are wonderful on their own, and I often prepare them that way, but here's how I make them when I want a real show-stopper: As the sprouts roast, brown up a few tablespoons of butter in a skillet, add some capers and lemon, and toss this over the sprouts before serving. The contrast between the earthy vegetables and the sprightly lemon-caper dressing makes them irresistible.

Serve these alongside everything from roast beef to the Thanksgiving turkey. I've even been known to make supper out of a poached egg, a few slices of crisp bacon, and a generous serving of roasted sprouts. Thankfully, the recipe is easily doubled (or tripled), although if you roast more than 1½ pounds, you will have to use 2 baking sheets in order to give the sprouts plenty of room to brown up during roasting. If you make these ahead, keep them at room temperature and add the browned butter at the last minute.

SERVES 4
METHOD: High heat
ROASTING TIME: 20 to 25 minutes

1 pound Brussels sprouts, trimmed

2 tablespoons extra-virgin olive oil

Kosher salt and freshly ground black pepper

3 tablespoons unsalted butter

1 teaspoon mustard seeds, yellow or brown

2 tablespoons capers, drained

1 teaspoon fresh lemon juice, plus more if needed

CONTINUED ON NEXT PAGE

1 **HEAT THE OVEN.** Position a rack in the center of the oven and heat to 425 degrees (400 degrees convection). If desired, line a heavy-duty rimmed baking sheet with parchment paper.

2 **CUT AND SEASON THE BRUSSELS SPOUTS.** Depending on their size, cut the Brussels sprouts in halves or quarters; you want them to be small enough to be bite-sized. Place in a large bowl and toss with the olive oil and salt and pepper to taste. Arrange the sprouts in a single layer on the baking sheet. Don't worry if some of the leaves fall off. Include these when roasting; they will crisp up, adding a nice crunch to the dish.

3 **ROAST.** Slide the Brussels sprouts into the oven and roast, turning once or twice with a metal spatula to promote even cooking, until the sprouts are tender throughout and smaller bits or leaves that have fallen off are browned and crunchy, 20 to 25 minutes. Test for doneness by piercing a sprout with the tip of a paring knife, but to be sure, nab one off the baking sheet, let it cool slightly, and taste; it should be tender and sweet.

4 **MEANWHILE, MAKE THE BROWNED BUTTER.** As the sprouts roast, melt the butter in a small skillet or heavy saucepan (it should be no more than 6 inches across or the butter will burn). Cook over medium heat until the butter is melted. Add the mustard seeds, increase the heat to medium-high, and cook, watching the pan carefully and swirling frequently, until the butter begins to foam and turns golden brown, about 2 minutes. Add the capers and lemon juice—the butter will sizzle—and immediately remove from the heat. Season with salt and pepper to taste and keep warm until the Brussels sprouts are ready.

5 **SERVE.** Transfer the Brussels sprouts to a serving dish and add the browned butter. Toss to coat. Taste for salt, pepper, and lemon and serve immediately.

This recipe came to me when I was furtively eating all the crunchy bits of loose leaves that had fallen off a pan of roasted Brussels sprouts before serving the dish proper. They were as irresistible and addictive as good potato chips. Granted, people may look at you funny if you serve a platter of Brussels sprout chips, but I find they make a delightful—and delicious—garnish to everything from a simple fish fillet to a mound of mashed potatoes. Try sprinkling them on top of the bowl of mashed sweet potatoes at your next Thanksgiving. When shopping for Brussels sprouts to make chips, buy larger sprouts, which are easiest.

SERVES 4 TO 8 AS A GARNISH

METHOD: High heat

ROASTING TIME: About 15 minutes

½ pound Brussels sprouts

1 tablespoon extra-virgin olive oil

Kosher salt and freshly ground black pepper

1 **HEAT THE OVEN.** Position a rack in the center of the oven and heat to 450 degrees (425 degrees convection). If desired, line a heavy-duty rimmed baking sheet with parchment paper.

2 **SEPARATE THE BRUSSELS SPROUTS INTO LEAVES.** Using a paring knife, trim the base from the Brussels sprouts, cutting it flush with the base of the sprout. Using your fingers, start peeling the leaves from the outside of each spout; do your best to keep the leaves as whole as possible, but it's fine if some tear. As you get toward the center and the leaves become too tight to remove easily, pick up the paring knife and remove the core to free the innermost leaves. Finish separating the innermost leaves and pile all the leaves on the baking sheet. Drizzle the olive oil over them and sprinkle with salt and pepper. Toss to coat. Spread the leaves out in even layer.

3 **ROAST** until almost all leaves are brown in spots and crisp, tossing occasionally, about 15 minutes. Serve hot.

BUTTER-ROASTED CABBAGE STRIPS WITH CARAWAY AND MUSTARD SEEDS

One of the best things about roasting is the way it turns the ordinary into the extraordinary. Take, for instance, cabbage, a vegetable often synonymous with *dull*. But shred it, toss it with melted butter, caraway seeds, and mustard seeds, and roast till it's tender, sweet, and ever so slightly browned, and you've got a tasty and, dare I say, exciting side dish for any occasion. If you can find it, use Savoy cabbage, the one with the crinkly edges; the flavor will be sweeter still. For even more flavor, offer some grated aged Gouda cheese at the table and let folks sprinkle it over the cabbage. Choose a Gouda that's been aged for at least eighteen months—the older, the better. Its rich, buttery, somewhat nutty flavor makes a great accent to the sweetness of the cabbage.

SERVES 6
METHOD: Moderate heat
ROASTING TIME: About 30 minutes

4 tablespoons unsalted butter

1 teaspoon caraway seeds, coarsely ground in a mortar or spice grinder

1 teaspoon mustard seeds, brown or yellow

1 small head green cabbage (about 1½ pounds), preferably Savoy

Kosher salt and freshly ground black pepper

¼ cup grated aged Gouda cheese, for serving (optional)

1   **HEAT THE OVEN.** Position a rack in the center of the oven and heat to 350 degrees (325 degrees convection). If desired, line a heavy-duty rimmed baking sheet with parchment paper.

2   **MELT THE BUTTER** in a small saucepan. Add the caraway and mustard seeds and set aside in a warm place while you prepare the cabbage.

3   **SHRED THE CABBAGE.** Quarter the cabbage and remove the core. Slice each quarter crosswise into ⅓-inch-thick pieces. You should have about 12 cups. Pile the cabbage onto the baking sheet. Don't worry that the cabbage is piled high; it will shrink significantly in the hot oven. Pour the melted butter over the cabbage and season with salt and pepper. Toss to coat thoroughly and spread in an even layer.

4   **ROAST,** tossing and turning over with tongs every 10 minutes, until it is tender with crispy brown edges, about 30 minutes. Taste for salt and pepper.

5   **SERVE HOT OR WARM,** with some grated Gouda at the table, if you like.

ROASTED ENDIVE WITH SHERRY VINEGAR

Until recently, I was pretty stuck on braising as the best way to prepare endive. That all changed at a holiday party when the host served a platter of golden, tender roasted endive drizzled with sherry vinegar as a part of an appetizer buffet. The rather unassuming platter of endive was flanked by a number of sexier offerings—sizzling oysters Rockefeller, a heap of gougères (aka French cheese puffs), and a handsome potato–goat cheese galette—but in the end, the roasted endive was the taste everyone was talking about long after someone had snagged the last one.

The wonder of roasting endive is how it mellows the vegetable's natural bitterness, leaving a more nuanced balance of sweet backed by just a hint of bitter. The melting texture is downright seductive too. Beyond making a superb appetizer, either warm or at room temperature, roasted endive is excellent as a side dish with roast chicken or pork. I've also enjoyed it for lunch alongside a grilled cheese sandwich. If you're serving it as finger food, be warned that it can be a little messy to eat—the halved heads are hard to bite through, yet too big for a single bite. Putting a sharp paring knife on the platter is helpful, as is a stack of napkins.

SERVES 4 TO 6
METHOD: High heat
ROASTING TIME: 25 to 30 minutes

6 to 8 heads Belgian endive (about 1½ pounds)

1 tablespoon extra-virgin olive oil

½ teaspoon sugar

Kosher salt and freshly ground black pepper

2 to 3 teaspoons sherry vinegar

1 **HEAT THE OVEN.** Position a rack in the center of the oven and heat to 400 degrees (375 degrees convection). If desired, line a large heavy-duty rimmed baking sheet with parchment paper.

2 **TRIM.** Inspect the endive for any bruised or discolored spots. Remove any outer leaves that look less than pristine. Trim the thinnest sliver off the base of any that

appear browned or dried out. (Endive is grown in a controlled environment and not in dirt and therefore doesn't need careful washing. However, if the heads seem at all dirty, give them a quick rinse.) Cut each head in half lengthwise from core to tip.

3 **SEASON THE ENDIVE.** Place the endive in a large bowl. Drizzle on the olive oil and season with the sugar, salt, and pepper (I use about ½ teaspoon salt and several generous grindings of black pepper). Toss gently to coat and arrange the endive cut side up on the baking sheet. It's fine if the pieces are touching, but they should not be squeezed together. If any leaves have fallen off, tuck these under the heads.

4 **ROAST.** Transfer the baking sheet to the oven and roast, turning the heads with tongs after 15 minutes so they are cut side down. If the endive near the edges of the pan is browning more than the endive near the center, you may want to remove the pan from the oven and take a moment to rearrange the pieces. Continue roasting until tender and lightly caramelized, about 25 to 30 minutes total.

5 **SERVE.** Transfer the endive to a serving platter or individual plates, and immediately sprinkle with the sherry vinegar to taste. Roasted endive may be served hot from the oven or at room temperature.

ROASTED EGGPLANT WITH CUMIN AND PIMENTÓN

I have to pace myself whenever I make this, because I can quickly eat much more than my share—and sometimes even before dinner is served. There's just something irresistible about the combination of the browned exterior and tender, almost creamy insides of roasted eggplant. Cutting the eggplant into cubes maximizes the cut surfaces so you get even more deliciously browned edges. The cubes shrink considerably when roasted at high temperatures, so make more than you think you'll need. For best results, I encourage you to line the baking sheet with parchment before roasting. This will help prevent the tender eggplant from sticking to the baking sheet and collapsing as you attempt to stir the cubes during roasting.

The cumin and pimentón lend a certain Mediterranean flair, amplifying the eggplant flavor without dominating. The dish is best in the summer and early fall, when eggplants are at their peak. Serve this, warm or at room temperature, as a side dish alongside steak, grilled seafood, and roasted chicken. You can also turn it into a salad with the simple addition of balsamic vinegar and fresh basil (see the option that follows).

SERVES 4
METHOD: High heat
ROASTING TIME: 25 to 30 minutes

1 ½ pounds eggplant, preferably small Italian eggplants (see Selecting and Handling Eggplant, page 478)

¾ cup extra-virgin olive oil

1 ½ teaspoons cumin seeds, toasted and ground

½ teaspoon pimentón (smoked Spanish paprika)

Kosher salt and freshly ground black pepper

1 **HEAT THE OVEN.** Position a rack in the center of the oven and heat to 450 degrees (425 degrees convection). Line a large heavy-duty rimmed baking sheet with parchment paper.

2 **CUBE AND SEASON THE EGGPLANT.** Trim the stem end off the eggplants and cut each into ¾- to 1-inch cubes. (Leave the skin intact to add textural interest.) Put the eggplant in a large bowl. Drizzle the olive oil and sprinkle the cumin and

pimentón over it, season with a generous amount of salt and pepper, and toss well to coat. Don't worry if every cube doesn't look coated; eggplant soaks up such a prodigious amount of oil that you'd have to add too much to fully coat every bit. Spread the eggplant out on the baking sheet in an even layer. The pan will be crowded, but the eggplant will shrink as it roasts.

3 **ROAST,** turning the eggplant with a spatula after about 10 minutes and every 5 minutes after that, until shrunken in size, tender throughout, and browned on the outside, 25 to 30 minutes.

4 **SERVE.** Transfer to a serving bowl and serve hot, warm, or at room temperature.

OPTION: ROASTED EGGPLANT SALAD WITH FRESH BASIL

Serve this salad with anything from the grill. It's also fine picnic fare, as it's just as good at room temperature as it is warm. Roast the eggplant as directed above. After roasting (step 3), transfer the eggplant to a shallow serving bowl and sprinkle with ½ to 1 teaspoon balsamic vinegar. Slice ¼ cup fresh basil leaves into ¼-inch-thick ribbons (see below) and add to the bowl. Toss. Taste for salt and pepper and serve warm or at room temperature. If you're making this ahead, wait to add the basil until just before serving.

Slicing Fresh Basil

FRESH BASIL BRUISES EASILY, AND WHEN THIS HAPPENS, THE TENDER GREEN LEAVES WILT AND DISCOLOR. FORTUNATELY, WITH A LITTLE CARE YOU CAN slice basil without bruising so that it stays fresh and verdant. Start by removing the leaves from the stems by pinching them off at their base. Stack several leaves on the cutting board (4 or 5 leaves is a good number to start with; with practice, you can stack more). Now, with the center rib of the leaves running parallel with the edge of the counter, roll the stack of leaves up as if you were rolling a cigar. Roll snugly but without squeezing or crushing. Using a large knife with a sharp blade, slice the roll of basil leaves, cutting strips as thin or as thick as you like. After cutting, fluff the sliced basil; you'll see that you've made a neat little heap of ribbon shapes. The French refer to this cut as a *chiffonade*, from the word for shreds or rags. You can use the same technique for shredding any leafy green, particularly tender ones such as lettuce.

Selecting and Handling Eggplant

IN MY LAST BOOK, *ALL ABOUT BRAISING*, I WROTE A BRIEF PASSAGE ABOUT SHOPPING FOR EGGPLANT DESCRIBING THE TWO BASIC TYPES, GLOBE AND Asian varieties. Since then I've learned from my students that it would be helpful to provide a bit more in-depth information.

Technically a fruit, eggplant is a member of the same nightshade family as tomatoes, potatoes, and peppers. Countless varieties are cultivated all over the world (especially in climates with long, hot growing seasons), ranging from glossy deep purple to lavender, pink, striped, and ivory and with contours from bulbous and pear-shaped to slender and banana-shaped.

The biggest and most common (and typically least expensive) variety is referred to as American or standard globe eggplant. These teardrop-shaped fruits range in length from 6 to over 10 inches. Overall, American eggplants tend to be less flavorful than other types but are useful for their high flesh-to-skin ratio, which makes for quick chopping into large or medium chunks. Their wider diameter is also a plus when slicing into large rounds for frying. Next in popularity is Italian eggplant, similar in shape and color to American but smaller in size—only a few inches in diameter and 5 to 8 inches long. Italian eggplant is more delicate and sweeter in flavor than its larger cousin. Chinese eggplant, easily identified by its pale violet skin and cylindrical, slender shape, has the most delicate taste of all market varieties. Japanese eggplants are smaller than Chinese, with a narrow, pointy shape and the same dark purple skin as the American and Italian varieties. As more and more markets, especially farmers' markets, branch out into unique and heirloom varieties, I encourage you to experiment with new types to find ones you like best.

Regardless of the variety, the sweetest, best-tasting eggplants are those that are harvested just before peak maturity. Eggplants lose their glossy appearance if left too long on the plant. As this happens, their flesh turns spongy and bitter. When you cut into an eggplant at its peak, the seeds should be pale and tender; as the plant matures, the seeds darken, becoming unpleasantly large and hard. Avoid this by choosing eggplants with glossy, taut skin. The fruits should feel heavy for their size and not at all wrinkled, dull, or puffy. Avoid any with welts or pits (signs of decay). The stem (or calyx) should be a fresh green, with no signs of rot or mold. Eggplants do not store well. Temperatures of less than 45 degrees cause deterioration (indicated by dark, soft spots on the skin), but room temperature is too warm, so store them in the warmest part of your refrigerator for no more than a day or two.

CRISPY ROASTED FENNEL WEDGES WITH THYME

When I sent this recipe to one of my recipe testers to try, her testing notes came back saying "Sweet! Hot! Bold! Bursting with flavor!" Roasting concentrates the sweetness of the fennel and underplays its licorice flavor. In fact, I know non-fennel-lovers who happily gobble up these.

You can serve the crisp-tender fennel wedges hot from the oven or at room temperature. I like them as a side dish with chicken and pork. The little wedges are also easy to eat as finger food, making them an unexpected hors d'oeuvre in place of humdrum carrot and celery sticks. For a real treat, sprinkle the wedges with Coriander-Fennel Salt (page 503) or serve them with a dipping sauce, such as Garlic-Chile Mayonnaise (page 503).

SERVES 3 TO 4 AS A SIDE DISH, 6 AS AN HORS D'OEUVRE

METHOD: High heat

ROASTING TIME: 35 to 45 minutes

1 large or 2 small fennel bulbs (about 1½ pounds untrimmed)

2 tablespoons extra-virgin olive oil

3 to 4 leafy sprigs fresh thyme

Pinch of crushed red pepper flakes

Kosher salt and freshly ground black pepper

1 **HEAT THE OVEN.** Position a rack in the center of the oven and heat to 425 degrees (400 degrees convection). If desired, line a heavy-duty rimmed baking sheet with parchment paper.

2 **TRIM AND CUT THE FENNEL INTO WEDGES.** Trim the fennel as described on the next page. Once trimmed, stand each bulb of fennel upright on its base and cut it in half lengthwise, from stalk end through the base. Cut each half into ½-inch wedges. Each wedge should have a little bit of the core in order to keep it from falling apart.

CONTINUED ON NEXT PAGE

3 **SEASON AND ROAST.** Combine the fennel, olive oil, thyme, red pepper flakes, and salt and pepper to taste in a large bowl and toss to coat. Spread the fennel out cut side down on the baking sheet. Roast, using tongs to turn the wedges over every 12 to 15 minutes. Continue to roast until the fennel is tender when pierced with the tip of a paring knife and nicely browned, 35 to 45 minutes.

4 **SERVE.** Taste for salt and pepper and transfer the fennel to a serving bowl or platter. Discard the thyme sprigs (the leaves will have fallen off during roasting). Serve the fennel hot, warm, or at room temperature.

Trimming Fennel

THE FIRST STEP TO TRIMMING FENNEL IS TO REMOVE THE STALKS WHERE THEY MEET THE BULB, AND THE BEST APPROACH IS TO CUT EACH STALK individually at an angle, following the contours of the bulb. If you simply lop off the stalks in one fell swoop, you will either leave too much stalk on the sides of the bulb or cut away a chunk of good sweet fennel flesh at the top. I don't find much use for the stalks beyond the compost heap, but you can add a few to a vegetable, fish, or poultry broth to contribute a hint of anise. You may also save a tablespoon or so of the innermost fronds (these are the most tender) for garnish.

If the bulb has a few bruises, slashes, or brown spots, use a vegetable peeler to trim them from the base and any outer leaves. You can also use the vegetable peeler to shave off any dried or brown surface from the root end. (If it seems I'm being extreme by shaving only the thinnest bit from the fennel, it's because the bulbs can be expensive and I hate waste.) If, however, any outer parts are especially brown or sad-looking, peel these off. Once trimmed, proceed according to the recipe directions. For recipes in which the fennel gets cooked (as opposed to a salad of raw shaved fennel), I often leave the core intact. Its somewhat coarser texture adds interest to the dish.

ROASTED FENNEL, RED ONION, AND ORANGE SALAD

Chomping my way through a refreshing salad of shaved raw fennel, red onion, and fresh orange not too long ago, I got to thinking about the possibilities of roasting the trio to create a whole new taste. After a little experimentation, I came up with this visually stunning and sensationally good salad. As the individual flavors—the sweet licorice taste of the fennel, the soft pungency of the onion, and the floral ambrosia of the orange—mingle in the hot oven, they trade qualities until everything seems to taste bolder, sweeter, and better. If you're not used to eating citrus peel, you're in for a tasty surprise. The bits of orange rind become tender as they cook and provide just a trace of bitterness that offsets the sweetness of everything else.

If you stock your pantry with a range of extra-virgin olive oils, use your everyday oil for roasting and choose one of your fancier oils for drizzling over the salad just before serving. This salad is best appreciated slightly warm or at room temperature. It also travels well and can be made a day ahead, so it's ideal for a buffet or winter picnic. Because the flavors are so intense, make sure the portions are on the small side.

SERVES 4
METHOD: High heat
ROASTING TIME: 35 to 45 minutes

1 large or 2 small fennel bulbs (about 1
  pound untrimmed)
1 medium red onion
1 small navel orange, scrubbed

2 tablespoons extra-virgin olive oil, plus
  more for drizzling
Kosher salt and freshly ground black
  pepper

1 **HEAT THE OVEN.** Position a rack in the center of the oven and heat to 400 degrees (375 degrees convection). Line a heavy-duty rimmed baking sheet with parchment paper (this prevents the oranges from sticking to the pan).

CONTINUED ON NEXT PAGE

2 **PREPARE THE VEGETABLES AND ORANGE.** Trim the fronds from the fennel (see page 480). Stand a bulb on its base on the cutting board and cut it in half lengthwise, cutting from the core end to the stem end. (If the bulb is more oblong than round, as some are, you will create two halves that are thinner and flatter rather than thicker and bulbous.) Use a paring knife to remove most of the core from each half (no need to get it all out). Lay each half flat on the cutting surface and cut crosswise into ¼–inch-thick crescent-shaped slices. Toss onto the baking sheet and repeat with the second fennel bulb if you have two.

Cut the onion in half, cutting from root to stem end. Peel and remove the root end from both halves. Slice the onion halves crosswise into ¼–inch-thick half-moons and add to the fennel.

Next, slice about 1½ inches off each end of the orange and reserve (you'll use these later to squeeze over the salad). Stand the orange up on one cut end and cut it lengthwise in half, and then cut each half lengthwise in half again, leaving you with 4 pieces. Arrange each quarter with a cut side down and slice crosswise into ¼-inch-thick quarter-moon-shaped pieces. Add the orange to the fennel and onion. Drizzle the olive oil on top and season well with salt and plenty of pepper. Toss to coat and arrange as best you can in an even layer on the baking sheet.

3 **ROAST,** stirring with a spatula after 15 minutes to insure even cooking and again every 10 minutes or so. The vegetables close to the edge of the pan will brown more quickly than those in the center, so stirring and then shaking the pan to restore an even layer helps everything cook at the same rate. Continue roasting until the vegetables and orange are tender and the outer edges are beginning to caramelize, 35 to 45 minutes.

4 **FINISH AND SERVE.** Transfer to a serving dish (I like to use a wide, shallow bowl). Let cool for at least 15 minutes or to room temperature. Squeeze the juice from one of the reserved orange ends over the salad and taste. If it tastes a little flat, add a pinch of salt and squeeze the other orange piece over it. Drizzle with a little of your best olive oil and serve warm or at room temperature.

SLOW-ROASTED SWEET ONIONS WITH SHERRY VINAIGRETTE

To call this "slow-roasted" is no exaggeration. It takes close to 2 hours in a low oven to render thick slices of sweet onion tender yet still juicy enough to take center stage in this surprising salad.

Summer is the season for sweet onions, such as Vidalia, and this undemanding recipe makes a perfect accompaniment to steaks from the grill. If the weather is hot, make it in the morning before the house heats up and serve it at room temperature. The onions, with their sherry vinaigrette are also excellent with lamb, grilled or roasted. If you crave a little green in your salad, toss a few leaves of butter or Bibb lettuce with a tablespoon of the vinaigrette, arrange the leaves on a platter or plate, and then top with the dressed onions. A little feta crumbled on top would be welcome as well. If fresh thyme is unavailable for the vinaigrette by all means substitute fresh mint, marjoram, or dill.

SERVES 3 TO 4
METHOD: Low heat
ROASTING TIME: About 1 3/4 hours

2 sweet onions (about 1 ½ pounds), such as Vidalias, Texas Sweets, or Walla Wallas (see Selecting and Handling Sweet Onions, page 485)
6 tablespoons extra-virgin olive oil
Kosher salt and freshly ground black pepper

1 teaspoon minced shallots (about ½ small shallot)
2 teaspoons chopped fresh thyme
1 tablespoon sherry vinegar

1 **HEAT THE OVEN.** Position a rack in the center of the oven and heat to 275 degrees (250 degrees convection). If desired, line a heavy-duty rimmed baking sheet with parchment paper.

CONTINUED ON NEXT PAGE

2   **SLICE AND SEASON THE ONIONS.** Peel the onions and cut them crosswise into ½–inch-thick rounds, discarding the root and stem ends. Arrange the onions on the baking sheet, leaving the rounds whole, without separating them into rings. Drizzle about 3 tablespoons of olive oil over the onions and season with salt and pepper. Turn the onions over to coat all sides with oil and season with salt and pepper again.

3   **ROAST.** Slide the baking sheet into the oven and roast, flipping the onions once after 45 minutes so both sides roast evenly, until very tender, with only a few browned or crisp spots on the outsides of the rings, about 1¾ hours total. Let cool slightly.

4   **MAKE THE VINAIGRETTE.** In a small bowl, combine the shallots, thyme, and vinegar with a pinch of salt and a grinding or two of pepper. Let sit as the onions roast. When the onions are close to ready, gradually whisk in the remaining 3 tablespoons of olive oil. Season to taste with salt and pepper.

5   **DRESS AND SERVE.** With clean hands, separate the onions into rings and pull off and discard any brittle outer layers (or nibble on these as a crunchy kitchen snack). Arrange the onions in a loose pile on a serving platter and drizzle the vinaigrette over them. Toss gently to distribute the dressing. Serve warm or at room temperature. *The onions will keep overnight, covered and refrigerated. Let them come to room temperature before serving.*

Selecting and Handling Sweet Onions

SWEET ONIONS ARE A FAMILY OF HYBRID ONION VARIETIES PRIZED FOR THEIR SWEET, MILD FLAVOR AND JUICY TEXTURE. THEIR CHARACTERISTIC SWEETNESS results not only from a higher level of sugar but, more importantly, from very low levels of the sulfuric compounds that give regular onions their pungency and punch. Sweet onions have very specific soil and climate requirements, which explains why their production remains limited to certain regions. In fact, many of the best-known varieties take their names from the places where their seeds were first developed: Walla Walla, Washington; Maui, Hawaii; Texas; and Vidalia, Georgia. As sweet onions have become more popular, several of these original growing regions have expanded. For instance, today some twenty counties in Georgia are legally allowed to trademark their onions as Vidalia. Additionally, other trademarked varieties, such as SpringSweets and Texas 1015s, are popping up. In the Northeast, I've also seen New York sweet onions in markets.

Whatever the name, sweet onions are much more perishable than other onion varieties, and as such require a bit more vigilance when shopping. Choose firm onions that feel heavy for their size, indicating that they are juicy and fresh. Avoid onions with soft spots, discoloration, or gashes. A good onion will smell mild, not pungent. Any papery skin should be smooth and dry. Although high-tech storage facilities do enable some markets to sell sweet onions year-round, you'll always find the best (that is, the freshest) in the summer months, when sweet onions are at their peak. Vidalias and Texas Sweets run from late April through June. Walla Wallas are available from mid-June through September. Maui onion season runs longer than any other—February through November—but the shipping distance for most regions makes Maui onions scarce and rather pricey.

Because sweet onions spoil quickly, it's best to buy them not more than a week before you plan to use them. For short-term storage—a couple of days—keep them loose in a dry, well-ventilated, dark cupboard right alongside your regular onions. For longer storage, wrap each onion in a paper towel and store in the produce drawer in the refrigerator. The onions will keep longer if they don't touch each other. The Vidalia Onion Committee recommends hanging onions in the legs of clean sheer pantyhose with a knot tied between each one. Personally, I find it easier to just buy a few at a time while they are in season.

ROASTED BELL PEPPERS WITH TOMATO AND GARLIC

The inspiration for this recipe comes from Elizabeth David's revelatory 1950s book on Italian food. Tucked away in the hors d'oeuvres and salad chapter is an unassuming little paragraph on how to make *peperoni alla piemontese* (Piedmont-style bell peppers). David instructs us to split bell peppers in half, remove the seeds, and scatter the halves with garlic, anchovy, tomatoes, butter, and oil before roasting in a moderate oven until just tender. It's easy to be unimpressed by such a simple formula, but the combination of flavors turns out something utterly delicious, and quite pretty too. I've refined the recipe somewhat by making a flavored butter; I smash the garlic and anchovy into a paste and blend it into a knob of butter. As the butter melts, it bathes the peppers with garlicky, briny flavors. And you simply won't believe how good this smells until you make it yourself.

The peppers make splendid hors d'oeuvres eaten out of hand (with plenty of napkins) or set on top of a little crostini. A few on a plate make a nice sit-down first course, especially when paired with a soft cheese, such as chèvre, ricotta, or fresh pecorino, and they're great as part of a buffet. Serve them warm or at room temperature, which means you can make these ahead of serving.

SERVES 4 TO 6
METHOD: Moderate heat
ROASTING TIME: 30 to 40 minutes

2 small garlic cloves, peeled and smashed

2 anchovy fillets, chopped

Kosher salt

1 tablespoon unsalted butter, at room temperature

2 bell peppers (about 12 ounces total), red and/or yellow

1 medium-large tomato

Freshly ground black pepper

2 tablespoons extra-virgin olive oil

2 tablespoons chopped fresh flat-leaf parsley

1   **HEAT THE OVEN.** Position a rack in the center of the oven and heat to 350 degrees (325 degrees convection). Lightly oil a 13-by-9-inch gratin pan or similar-size baking dish.

2 **FLAVOR THE BUTTER.** Combine the garlic and anchovies in a small mortar, add a pinch of salt, and smash and grind to form a paste (if you don't have a mortar, follow the directions for Making Garlic Paste Without a Mortar and Pestle on page 230, adding the anchovies to the garlic). Add the butter and work together with a wooden spoon until well combined.

3 **PREPARE THE PEPPERS AND TOMATO.** Halve the peppers lengthwise and remove the core, seeds, and soft membrane-like ribs. Cut each half lengthwise into 1½-inch-wide strips. You should get 6 or 8 little boat-shaped strips from each pepper. Arrange the strips skin side down in the baking dish. Core the tomato and cut it into the same number of wedges as you have pepper strips. Using a sharp paring knife, carve the juicy seed pockets away from each tomato slice (and discard) so you are left with meaty strips of tomato (these seedless strips of tomato are sometimes called fillets). Season the tomato strips lightly with salt and pepper, turning to season all sides.

4 **ASSEMBLE AND ROAST.** Divide the seasoned butter among the pepper boats, spreading a small amount on each one. Top with a piece of tomato. Drizzle the olive oil over the top. Roast until the pepper and tomato pieces are tipped with brown and the pepper is just barely tender, 30 to 40 minutes. If any of the tomatoes have slipped off their perches, simply slide them back on.

5 **SERVE.** Sprinkle the peppers and tomatoes with parsley and serve warm or at room temperature, either directly from the baking dish or on plates with the juices poured over the top.

SIMPLE ROASTED POTATOES

Roasted potatoes are just as likely to find their way to the table on a busy weeknight as at a festive holiday meal. No matter how many other dishes there are on the menu—or how fussy my guests are—I can count on the fact that everyone loves potatoes, especially when they're roasted up to be creamy and tender inside and crisp and brown on the outside. This recipe can easily be scaled up or down according to how many mouths you're feeding (just be sure not to overcrowd the pan). Figure about ⅓ pound of potatoes per person (a little less if you have other side dishes and a little more if you expect big appetites). If you're planning this as a side dish for a roast and want to cook the potatoes in the same oven, you can lower the oven to 350 degrees or raise it to 425 degrees to suit your needs. The potatoes will take a little more or less time to cook accordingly. After roasting, potatoes can be held in a warm oven for up to an hour before serving—another reason they're so terrific for entertaining.

The classic recipe calls for small red potatoes, but you can also roast white potatoes, yellow potatoes, fingerlings, or any of the interesting heirloom varieties showing up in the markets lately. Since most lower-starch potatoes have thin skins, they don't need to be peeled before roasting. Just scrub them with a vegetable brush and dry them thoroughly (wet skins will interfere with browning). Round, bite-size creamer potatoes or the wobbly, oblong fingerlings can be roasted whole, while larger potatoes need to be cut up into chunks or wedges. For more on which varieties to use, see Choosing Potatoes for Roasting, page 495.

I like to sprinkle the potatoes with a little fresh thyme (and/or rosemary) before roasting, but it's merely an accent, and an optional one at that. If you want full-on Herb-Roasted Potatoes, see the option on page 489.

SERVES 4 TO 6
METHOD: Moderate heat
ROASTING TIME: 50 to 60 minutes

2 pounds waxy potatoes, left whole if very small, halved, or cut into 1-inch chunks

3 tablespoons extra-virgin olive oil or a blend of olive oil and melted butter

1 tablespoon chopped fresh thyme or rosemary, or a combination (optional)

Kosher salt and freshly ground black pepper

1 **HEAT THE OVEN.** Position a rack in the center of the oven and heat to 375 degrees (350 degrees convection). If desired, line a heavy-duty rimmed baking sheet with parchment paper.

2 **SEASON THE POTATOES.** Spread the potatoes in a single layer on the baking sheet. Drizzle with the oil, sprinkle with the herbs, if using, and season with salt (I use about 1 teaspoon) and plenty of pepper. Toss to coat well.

3 **ROAST.** Slide the potatoes into the oven. After about 20 minutes, give them a stir with a metal spatula to promote even browning. Continue roasting, tossing a few more times to prevent sticking, until the potatoes are very tender throughout (check by piercing a potato with a fork or a skewer; it should sink easily into the tender flesh) and the skins are somewhat shriveled and crisp, 50 to 60 minutes total. If in doubt, err on the side of cooking them a little longer—potatoes are better slightly overdone than underdone.

4 **SERVE HOT,** or cover loosely with foil and keep warm in a low oven (200 degrees) for up to 1 hour before serving.

OPTION: HERB-ROASTED POTATOES

These get a double dose of herbs—hardy herbs before roasting and tender herbs after—plus a splash of lemon to brighten the whole. They are especially good alongside fish, pork, and poultry.

FOLLOW THE recipe for Simple Roasted Potatoes but use only olive oil for the fat and toss the potatoes with 2 tablespoons of any combination of chopped fresh rosemary, thyme, savory, marjoram, and sage before roasting. As soon as the potatoes are done, toss with 3 tablespoons of any combination of chopped fresh flat-leaf parsley, chives, and chervil and the juice of 1 lemon.

A Note on Why Roasting Potatoes Sometimes Stick to the Pan

OVER THE YEARS I HAVE RECEIVED MORE THAN A FEW FRANTIC PHONE CALLS FROM FRIENDS AND RELATIVES IN THE MIDDLE OF DINNER PREPARATIONS WHO are perplexed by roasting potatoes that seem stuck to the pan and are starting to fall apart. The call usually goes something like this: "I went to stir the potatoes after they'd been in the oven for a while, and they're all stuck to the pan, and when I try to unstick them, they fall apart. What do I do?" If I wanted to be unhelpful, I could suggest lining the pan with parchment paper before roasting, but no one wants to hear this 20 minutes before dinner is meant to be on the table. My best advice? Leave the potatoes alone. Stop stirring and let them roast all the way through. When they are done, try again—to gently unstick them with a metal spatula and then let them roast another 5 to 10 minutes. Usually this does the trick. They may not be as evenly browned as you might like, but at least they will be more or less intact.

After the second or third time I heard about this dilemma, I started to wonder why this might occur. I came to several conclusions. The most obvious reasons are (1) the pan is too crowded, (2) it's the wrong kind of potato (see page 495 for information on the right kind of potato), or (3) the potatoes were wet (or even damp) before roasting. Happily, these are all mistakes we can correct through experience. The more troublesome reason for sticking potatoes is not a question of technique; it has to do with the seasonality of potatoes. The fresher the potatoes, the higher the moisture content and the more likely it is that they will stick to the pan and fall apart. Even though most commercial growers "cure" their potatoes by drying them in a controlled environment over a period of time, there are still seasonal variances in the amount of moisture in potatoes. I find that potatoes I buy in the late winter and early spring are most prone to this problem. In the end, the best solution is to line the roasting pan with parchment paper, make sure the potatoes are dry, don't crowd the pan, and relax. They'll still be tasty, even if they're not perfect.

ROASTED FINGERLING POTATOES WITH RED BELL PEPPERS, FENNEL, AND MARJORAM

This combination comes from a girls' getaway weekend on Martha's Vineyard at the tail end of summer. We had gone to the farmers' market in the morning without a plan for dinner and simply bought what looked good—fingerling potatoes, shiny red bell peppers, and fresh fennel. Back at the house, I realized we didn't have much in the way of pots or pans, nor did we want to get involved in a multicourse meal, so I cut up the vegetables—slicing the fennel relatively thinly to make it more of an accent than a central player—and piled everything onto a baking sheet. I seasoned the lot with fresh marjoram, tossed it with olive oil, and slid the pan into the oven. The dish was a triumph, and I have since made it countless times at home. I never tire of the lively play of flavors and the colorful appearance. It's ideal for those times when I am hungry for both a starch and a vegetable but only want to make a single side dish. On the Vineyard, we enjoyed it with grilled swordfish caught that day; it's also a great accompaniment to steaks and chops.

SERVES 4 TO 6
METHOD: Moderate heat
ROASTING TIME: 50 to 60 minutes

1 large or 2 small red bell peppers (about 10 ounces total), cored and seeded

1 small fennel bulb (about 12 ounces untrimmed), trimmed as described on page 480

1 ½ pounds fingerling potatoes, such as Russian bananas or French fingerlings, cut in half lengthwise and cut again into quarters if very large

3 tablespoons extra-virgin olive oil

1 tablespoon chopped fresh marjoram

Kosher salt and freshly ground black pepper

CONTINUED ON NEXT PAGE

1 **HEAT THE OVEN.** Position a rack in the center of the oven and heat to 375 degrees (350 degrees convection). If desired, line a heavy-duty rimmed baking sheet with parchment paper.

2 **CUT UP THE PEPPER AND FENNEL.** Cut the pepper or peppers into 1-inch chunks. Cut the fennel bulb in quarters lengthwise, and then cut each quarter cross-wise into ⅓-inch-thick slices.

3 **SEASON THE POTATOES.** Spread the potatoes in a single layer on the baking sheet. Add the peppers and fennel. Drizzle the oil and scatter the marjoram on top, season with salt and pepper, and toss to coat well.

4 **ROAST AND SERVE.** Slide the pan into the oven. After about 20 minutes, give the vegetables a stir with a metal spatula to promote even browning. Continue roasting, tossing a few more times to prevent sticking, until the potatoes are very tender throughout (check by piercing a potato with a fork or skewer; it should sink easily into the tender flesh) and the skins are somewhat shriveled and crisp, 50 to 60 minutes. The fennel will be browned in spots and the peppers will be tender. Serve hot.

MUSTARD-CRUSTED ROAST POTATOES

This is one of those recipes that may cause you to do a double-take. Yes, it really does call for coating the potatoes with ⅓ cup of mustard and a splash of lemon juice before roasting, but trust me, all that liquidy goo roasts up to a crusty coating. There's also a bit of garlic, rosemary, and crushed red pepper in the mix. The potatoes start out looking yellow and wet, but they finish with a golden brown crustiness and an intriguing depth of flavor. Perhaps most amazing of all is that they are not overly mustardy, simply tangy and delicious. One friend who made them reported that her five-year-old son ate them with gusto! At the same time, they are impressive and reliable enough to serve to your best company. Try these with roast chicken, pork, or beef.

SERVES 4 TO 6
METHOD: High heat
ROASTING TIME: 50 to 55 minutes

⅓ cup Dijon mustard

3 tablespoons extra-virgin olive oil

1 tablespoon fresh lemon juice

2 garlic cloves, minced

1 tablespoon chopped fresh rosemary

½ teaspoon Aleppo or Marash pepper (see page 318) or ¼ teaspoon crushed red pepper flakes

Kosher salt and freshly ground black pepper

2 pounds red potatoes, cut into ¾- to 1-inch cubes

1   **HEAT THE OVEN.** Position a rack in the center and heat the oven to 400 degrees (375 degrees convection). If desired, line a heavy-duty rimmed baking sheet with parchment paper.

2   **MAKE THE COATING.** In a large mixing bowl, whisk together the mustard, olive oil, lemon juice, garlic, rosemary, Aleppo or Marash pepper or crushed red pepper flakes, and salt and pepper to taste. Add the potatoes and toss to coat.

CONTINUED ON PAGE 495

MUSTARD-CRUSTED ROAST POTATOES (PAGE 493)

3   **ROAST AND SERVE.** Transfer the potatoes to the baking sheet and spread them in a single layer. Scrape the bowl with a rubber spatula and drizzle any leftover coating onto the potatoes. Roast, tossing with a spatula a few times and shaking to restore an even layer, until the potatoes are crusty on the outside and tender throughout, 50 to 55 minutes. Serve hot.

Choosing Potatoes for Roasting

YOU CAN ROAST PRETTY MUCH ANY POTATO, BUT I PREFER THE LOWER-STARCH VARIETIES, SUCH THE EASY-TO-FIND RED POTATOES OR THE MORE INTEREST-ing specialty potatoes such as fingerlings. Low-starch potatoes are also referred to as *waxy* or *creamer potatoes*, and these two terms aptly describe the dense, almost velvety texture of low-starch potatoes and why they are so good roasted. Lower starch also means higher sugars, thus giving them a better chance of browning up. To my mind, the ultimate roasted potato is one with a creamy, smooth, dense interior and a crispy brown exterior.

All potatoes can be classified by their starch content, and as the starch content goes up, the interior turns from dense and smooth to fluffy and dry. The highest-starch potato is the russet (and related varieties). I reserve these for times when I want this lighter, drier interior (as when making Oven Fries, page 501, or British Roast Potatoes, page 499, or plain old baked potatoes). Because they are drier and somewhat friable, high-starch potatoes need to be parboiled before roasting; otherwise they will crumble in the pan.

Of course, very few things in the kitchen (or in life, for that matter) are black and white, and a number of potato varieties fall into the medium-starch category, most notably Yukon Gold. These are a fine choice for roasting, and certainly if you have a bag in your kitchen and have a yen for roasted potatoes, there's no need for a special trip to the market. If you did a side-by-side tasting with low-starch potatoes, you might notice that medium-starch potatoes are somewhat less creamy inside, but they will still roast up beautifully. Other medium-starch varieties include all-purpose white potatoes and California whites (sometimes called long whites).

On a final note, be sure to look for more unconventional (and more flavorful) specialty potatoes, such as French fingerling, Carola, Russian banana, or other heirloom varieties with fanciful names. These are also excellent for roasting. If an unfamiliar variety catches your eye at a farmers' market, just ask the farmer if it's creamy or low-starch—or better yet, just ask which potatoes are best for roasting. The grower will know. Specialty potatoes are most widely available in the fall and early winter.

GOOSE-FAT-ROASTED POTATOES WITH ROSEMARY
(SHOWN WITH JAR OF RENDERED GOOSE FAT)

GOOSE-FAT-ROASTED POTATOES WITH ROSEMARY

T his is more of a technique than an actual recipe. Once you make these potatoes a few times, you'll learn that you don't really need to measure the ingredients, just as long as there's enough fat to coat the potatoes and the pan is big enough to hold the potatoes in a loose single layer. You can play around with different herbs (thyme and bay are both good) or toss in a few whole garlic cloves for good measure. The only key here is preheating the skillet and then preheating the fat. This ensures that the potatoes begin to sizzle the instant they hit the pan and thereby turn extra-crisp and don't absorb too much fat. The potatoes turn out remarkably creamy and sweet inside, with a delectably browned exterior. You can use any waxy or all-purpose potato variety (such as round reds or small Yukon Golds), but this recipe is the perfect place to showcase specialty potatoes. French fingerlings and Russian bananas are two of my favorites. If the potatoes are very small—say, the size of a walnut—leave them whole. For anything larger, cut them in half (or quarter them), since more cut sides mean more crispy edges. Fingerlings cook best when halved lengthwise.

I realize that not every cook stores a tub of goose fat in the refrigerator (or freezer), but these potatoes alone are worth tracking some down. Goose fat adds a savory richness to food unmatched by any other fat, with the exception of duck fat. The two are more or less interchangeable. If you roast your own goose or duck (see recipes on pages 365 and 355), you'll have plenty of fat left over for several batches of potatoes. Otherwise, it's available at specialty butchers and markets and on-line (see Sources & Resources, page 539).

SERVES 3 TO 4
METHOD: High heat
ROASTING TIME: About 40 minutes

1 pound small, waxy or all-purpose potatoes, such as fingerlings, creamers, or baby Yukon golds

2 to 3 tablespoons goose fat (duck fat may be substituted)

2 to 4 sprigs fresh rosemary

Fleur de sel or Maldon salt

CONTINUED ON NEXT PAGE

1 **HEAT THE OVEN.** Position a rack in the center of the oven and heat to 400 degrees (375 degrees convection).

2 **HEAT THE SKILLET AND PREPARE THE POTATOES.** If the potatoes are much more than 1 inch in diameter, cut them in half or into large chunks. Once the oven is fully heated, set a 10- to 12-inch cast-iron skillet on the oven rack and heat for 15 minutes. Without removing the skillet from the oven, add the fat (using 2 tablespoons for 10-inch and 3 tablespoons for 12-inch) and let it heat for 5 minutes.

3 **ROAST.** Using sturdy oven mitts or pot holders, slide the oven rack out and add the potatoes and rosemary to the hot fat. Stir briefly with a long spoon and immediately slide the pan back into the oven. Shake the pan or stir the potatoes every 10 to 15 minutes to help the potatoes crisp up evenly. Continue roasting until the potatoes are crisp and golden on the outside and creamy inside, about 40 minutes.

4 **SERVE.** Immediately scoop up the potatoes with a slotted spoon or spatula, leaving the rosemary sprigs behind; transfer to a serving bowl and sprinkle with salt to taste. Serve immediately. These are best eaten soon after roasting, while still hot.

BRITISH ROAST POTATOES

Consult just about any British cookbook that includes recipes for a proper Sunday dinner—one that includes roast beef, potatoes, and gravy—and these are the potatoes you'll find: marvelously crisp and golden on the outside and fluffy and tender on the inside. The trick is to start by parboiling chunks of russet potatoes and then shaking them around in the pot vigorously to release some of their starches, making their edges soft and floury. This is what accounts for the wonderful brown and crisp exterior. Then the potatoes get dusted with a little semolina or flour (semolina makes them extra-crisp and a little sweet) and tipped into a roasting pan of preheated fat, where they roast until picture-perfect. The good news is that you don't have to wait until you plan a big roast beef dinner to serve these. They taste great alongside steak and roast chicken.

The tastier the fat you use, the tastier the potatoes. My preference is for goose or duck fat, but strained bacon drippings will add a wonderful salty, smoky edge to the potatoes. You can also use a neutral-tasting oil, such as peanut or grapeseed. Olive oil would detract from the flavor of the potatoes and is not advised.

SERVES 6
METHOD: Combination parboil and high heat
ROASTING TIME: About 1 hour (plus 3 to 4 minutes to parboil)

2 to 2½ pounds russet potatoes (or other starchy variety), peeled
Kosher salt

1 tablespoon semolina or all-purpose flour
2 to 3 tablespoons fat (see headnote)

1 **HEAT THE OVEN.** Position a rack in the center of the oven and heat to 400 degrees (375 degrees convection). Choose a soup pot that has a lid and two side handles (6-quart size works well) and fill it two-thirds full with cold water.

2 **PARBOIL THE POTATOES.** Cut the potatoes into large chunks (about 2 inches across) and drop them into the pot of water. If necessary, add enough water to cover the potatoes by 2 inches. Add a hefty pinch of salt and bring to a boil over medium-high heat. Adjust the heat to maintain a steady (but not violent) boil and boil for 3 to 4 minutes. Drain, shaking to get rid of any excess water, and return the potatoes to the pot. Put the lid on the pot and, grabbing the two handles and the lid, shake the

CONTINUED ON NEXT PAGE

potatoes around just enough so their edges fluff up and soften; don't shake so hard that you break the potatoes into smaller pieces. Sprinkle with the semolina or flour and stir or shake again to coat. *The potatoes can sit at room temperature like this for about 15 minutes if needed while you make sure the oven is preheated and dinner is on schedule.*

3 **ROAST AND SERVE.** Put the fat into a shallow-sided roasting pan (13 by 17 inches works well) and slide it into the preheated oven. Let the fat heat for 5 to 8 minutes. Slide the oven rack out (this is safer and easier than lifting out the roasting pan) and transfer the potatoes to the pan, being careful not to spatter yourself as you go. Spread the potatoes in an even layer and return to the oven to roast. After 30 minutes, turn the potatoes with tongs, and continue to roast until nicely browned and crisp, another 30 minutes. Serve immediately.

BRITISH ROAST
POTATOES

OVEN FRIES

The best French fries get fried twice. The first time cooks the potato through on the inside. The second time gives the potato its tasty brown exterior. I use the same principle when making oven fries, though there's no need for a big pot of oil. Instead I first parboil the fries and then roast them on a preheated pan at a high temperature (this is similar to the technique used for British Roast Potatoes, page 499). The result: fries that are deliciously crispy on the outside and light and fluffy inside.

Homemade fries, even these roasted ones, can't be considered "fast food." In addition to cutting the potatoes into fries and parboiling them, you have to turn the fries individually while they're roasting. Yet when you find yourself craving the crispy, salty goodness of French fries (without all the fat), these fries are definitely worth the effort. To make it easier on yourself, boil the potatoes an hour ahead; then all you need to do come dinnertime is pop them in the oven. You might notice that I don't suggest lining the baking sheet with parchment here. As much as I champion this method, the paper insulates the fries and defeats the purpose of preheating the baking sheet.

This recipe is easily multiplied, but you'll need a second baking sheet to give the fries the room they need to crisp up. Like all fries, these are good with ketchup, mayonnaise, vinegar, or flavored salt—or all three. See page 503 for a couple of my favorite accompaniments.

SERVES 3 TO 4
METHOD: Combination parboil and high heat
ROASTING TIME: About 30 minutes (plus 3 minutes to parboil)

2 large russet potatoes (about 1 ¾ pounds total), scrubbed

Kosher salt

2 tablespoons extra-virgin olive oil or neutral vegetable oil

1   **HEAT THE OVEN.** Position a rack in the center of the oven and heat to 450 degrees (425 degrees convection). Fill a large (4- to 5-quart) pot with cold water.

2   **CUT THE POTATOES.** Peel the potatoes and cut them lengthwise into ½-inch-thick by ½-inch-wide sticks (the lengths will depend on the length of the potatoes). Drop the sticks into the pot of water as you go. *You can do this up to 1 day ahead. Refrigerate the potatoes in the water if you plan to hold them for more than 2 hours.*

CONTINUED ON NEXT PAGE

3 **PARBOIL THE POTATOES.** Drain and rinse the potatoes (rinsing removes excess starch) and return them to the pot with enough cold water to cover by 2 inches. Add about a teaspoon of salt to the water. Partially cover the pot and bring to a boil over medium-high heat. Reduce the heat to medium and cook the potatoes until they begin show signs of tenderness, not more than 3 minutes. The best way to test is to pull out a fry with a pair of tongs and take a small bite; the fry should be beginning to soften but still firm.

Drain the potatoes by tilting the pot and letting them fall gently into a colander in the sink. (Dumping the potatoes all at once risks breaking the sticks.) Once drained, spread the potatoes out onto clean dish towels to dry. *The potatoes can sit for up to an hour before roasting.*

4 **ROAST AND SERVE.** Slide a heavy-duty rimmed baking sheet onto the middle oven rack to heat it. Transfer the potatoes to a platter, add the oil, and gently toss, using your hands to coat all the fries and being careful not to break the sticks. Remove the heated baking sheet from the oven, and transfer the potato sticks as quickly as you can to the heated sheet, leaving at least ½ inch between them—and without touching the hot baking sheet with your fingers. Return to the oven and roast, turning the fries with tongs and rotating the baking sheet once after 15 minutes and then after another 10 minutes, until the fries are crisp on the outside, tender inside, and lightly browned, about 30 minutes total. Roasted fries don't brown as deeply as fried fries; their crispy texture is a better measure, so taste one to see if it's to your liking. Sprinkle with salt, toss to distribute, and serve immediately.

OPTION 1: GARLIC-CHILE MAYONNAISE

Delicious as a dip for French fries, this is also marvelous on a grilled chicken sandwich or a burger.

MAKES ABOUT 1/2 CUP, ENOUGH FOR ONE BATCH OF OVEN FRIES

½ cup mayonnaise

2 tablespoons adobo sauce (from a can of chipotle peppers)

1 garlic clove, finely minced

1 tablespoon fresh lime juice

Kosher salt and freshly ground black pepper

IN A SMALL BOWL, stir together the mayonnaise, adobo sauce, garlic, and lime juice. Season to taste with salt and pepper.

OPTION 2: CORIANDER-FENNEL SALT

Sprinkle this salt over fries in place of regular salt and you have something really special. The seasoning is also wonderful with other roasted vegetables and popcorn.

MAKES ABOUT 1 TABLESPOON, ENOUGH FOR ONE BATCH OF OVEN FRIES

½ teaspoon coriander seeds

½ teaspoon fennel seeds

10 whole black peppercorns

¾ teaspoon finely grated lemon zest

1 teaspoon kosher salt

IN A DRY SKILLET over medium heat, cook the coriander seeds, fennel seeds, and peppercorns until fragrant, about 2 minutes. Transfer to a mortar or spice grinder and grind to a fine powder. Add the lemon zest and salt and stir to combine.

NUTTY ROASTED SUNCHOKES

I first served this to a group of friends visiting Vermont from Boston. It was autumn (they were up leaf-peeping, of course), and I'd invited them all by for drinks. I suppose I was showing off a little by putting out an embarrassment of local culinary riches—perfectly ripe farmstead cheeses, sausages from a nearby butcher, bread from my favorite baker, and a bowl of roasted locally grown sunchokes, also known as Jerusalem artichokes. My guests were gracious enough to ooh and ah over all the goodies, but they devoured the sunchokes. I even received a call weeks later asking for the recipe. So here it is.

If you're not familiar with sunchokes, this is a great starter recipe. If you already know (and, hopefully, love) these knobby little tubers, then here's a way to maximize their inherently sweet, nutty flavor. After roasting, toss the sunchokes with a little walnut oil and crunchy toasted nuts to offset their crisp-tender texture and mild flavor. Chop the walnuts finely enough so they stick to the chunks of sunchokes, and provide toothpicks for spearing. If you find you love sunchokes, as I do, consider serving them as a side dish, much like roasted potatoes, as well.

SERVES 6 AS AN APPETIZER
METHOD: Moderate heat
ROASTING TIME: 20 to 30 minutes

¾ to 1 pound sunchokes (see page 506)
Scant ¼ cup walnut halves or pieces
1 tablespoon unsalted butter, melted

Kosher salt and freshly ground black pepper
1 tablespoon roasted walnut oil (see page 505)

 HEAT THE OVEN. Position a rack in the center of the oven and heat to 375 degrees (350 degrees convection). If desired, line a heavy-duty rimmed baking sheet with parchment paper.

2 **PREPARE THE SUNCHOKES.** Rinse the sunchokes and scrub them vigorously with a vegetable brush, bring careful to get at any dirt that may be tucked into one of the knobby spots. It's fine if you actually scrub some of the skin off, but that's not your objective. Depending on the size of the sunchokes, leave them whole or cut them into largish bite-size pieces, about the size of a large olive. Spread the sunchokes on a towel to dry while you toast the nuts.

3 **TOAST THE WALNUTS.** Spread the walnuts on a baking sheet and toast until fragrant and beginning to brown, about 8 minutes. Set aside.

4 **SEASON AND ROAST THE SUNCHOKES.** Arrange the sunchokes on the baking sheet. Drizzle with the butter, season with salt and pepper, and toss to coat. Roast, turning once or twice with a metal spatula so they cook evenly and shaking to restore an even layer, until they are just tender, 20 to 30 minutes. Watch carefully toward the end, as sunchokes have the unique characteristic of going from tender to mushy in a matter of minutes. Test for doneness by piercing a piece with the tip of a paring knife; you want to feel just the slightest bit of resistance. If any are done before the others, remove them and cover lightly with foil to keep warm.

5 **SERVE.** Immediately drizzle the roasted sunchokes with walnut oil. Taste for salt and pepper and transfer to a serving platter. Finely chop the walnuts and scatter over the top. Serve with toothpicks for spearing.

CONTINUED ON NEXT PAGE

Roasted Walnut Oil

GOOD NUT OILS, LIKE GOOD OLIVE OIL, ARE NEVER INEXPENSIVE, AND WALNUT OIL IS NO EXCEPTION, BUT WHEN IT COMES TO FLAVOR, YOU'RE GETTING A lot for what you pay for. A small tin of roasted walnut oil packs a wallop of toasty, nutty complexity; a little goes a long way. When shopping for roasted walnut oil, avoid "refined" oil, which will be clear in color and bland in taste. Instead, the oil should be dark and redolent of the roasted nuts from which it's made. (Actually, the traditional method for making roasted walnut oil goes back to the ancient Greeks and involves pressing the nuts and then roasting the paste before extracting the oil.) Good brands to look for are Leblanc, Loriva, and La Tourangelle. Most are labeled *roasted*, but some use the term *toasted* to mean the same thing: The nuts are heated to give the oil its characteristic flavor. Once opened, keep the tin in the refrigerator for 6 to 8 months. Roasted walnut oil turns bitter if heated. Use it in salad dressings or as a quick drizzle for roasted or steamed vegetables.

OPTION: PLAIN ROASTED SUNCHOKES

SCRUB THE SUNCHOKES as directed in step 2, leaving them whole. Roast as directed in step 4. Depending on their size (larger ones will take longer), they may take slightly longer to roast, up to 45 minutes for golf-ball-sized ones. Skip the walnut oil and walnuts and serve hot. Makes enough for 3 to 4 as a side dish.

Shopping for and Handling Sunchokes

THE BEST TIME TO SHOP FOR SUNCHOKES (JERUSALEM ARTICHOKES) IS IN THE FALL THROUGH THE WINTER. THESE HARDY, PRODUCTIVE TUBERS THRIVE IN the Northeast (where I live), and so I find them readily at farmers' markets and food co-ops. (Elsewhere, look for them in the exotic produce section.) Sunchokes are so prolific, in fact, that many gardeners renounce them because of their spreading, tenacious growing habits. At the market, look for sunchokes with smooth, taut skin without any spots of green or signs of sprouting. They should be firm—give them a squeeze to check—with no soft spots and feel heavy and dense in your hand. Don't choose any that are dried out or shriveled. Choose sunchokes that are all about the same size so they will cook at about the same rate.

As with most vegetables, there are many varieties of sunchokes with subtle flavor distinctions, but I've not seen any market promote these finer points of pedigree. For now, simply look for them to be labeled *sunchokes*, *Jerusalem artichokes*, or *sunroot* (the Native American name). Fresh sunchokes can be kept in a plastic bag in the produce drawer of your refrigerator for up to a week.

It's worth noting that sunchokes are similar to cabbage and beans when it comes to digestion, and some people are more sensitive than others to their effects. For this reason, I recommend starting by offering them as an appetizer before you serve up a whole heaping side dish.

HERB-ROASTED ROOTS

Every fall, when the markets are overflowing with every manner of root vegetable, I often end up with a bin full of different root vegetables of various colors and shapes, and not enough of one to make a dish. Happily, a mix of roots roasts up beautifully as long as I apply a little kitchen sense when I cut them up. The trick is to cut the vegetables so they roast at an even rate—quick-cooking, higher-moisture roots such as carrots, turnips, parsnips, onions, and potatoes should be left larger, while dense, slow-cooking types like beets, celeriac, and rutabagas should be cut into smallish chunks.

The recipe here calls for carrots, turnips, onions, and beets, but you can easily substitute other seasonal finds, including celeriac, rutabaga, potatoes, and parsnips. I like to use red beets to paint everything a pretty pink hue, but golden beets are also nice, and they don't bleed onto the other vegetables. Whatever combination you use, keep in mind that you want 6 to 8 cups of raw vegetables (they will shrink down some in the oven).

This makes a fine side dish for roast chicken and pork. It can also be a vegetarian main course when combined with a whole grain, such as farro. For a special treat, toss the roasted vegetables with *dukkah*, an addictive Egyptian nut-and-spice blend (recipe follows).

SERVES 4 TO 6

METHOD: High heat

ROASTING TIME: 45 to 50 minutes

4 to 5 carrots (about ¾ pound), peeled, halved or quartered if fat, and cut into 1 ½-inch chunks

3 medium beets (about ¾ pound), peeled and cut into ¾-inch cubes

2 medium turnips (about ¾ pound), peeled and cut into 1-inch wedges

¾ pound small onions or shallots, peeled and cut through the root end into ¾-inch wedges

1 head garlic, broken into cloves, peeled and root ends trimmed

3 leafy sprigs fresh rosemary

3 leafy sprigs fresh thyme

3 small bay leaves, preferably fresh

2 tablespoons unsalted butter, melted

2 tablespoons extra-virgin olive oil

Kosher salt and freshly ground black pepper

CONTINUED ON NEXT PAGE

1 **HEAT THE OVEN.** Position a rack in the center of the oven and heat to 400 degrees (375 degrees convection). If desired, line a heavy-duty rimmed baking sheet with parchment paper.

2 **SEASON THE VEGETABLES.** Combine the vegetables and the garlic on the baking sheet. There should be enough room so the vegetables are not more than one layer deep. Toss in the herbs and drizzle on the butter and oil. Season with salt and pepper and toss to coat the vegetables evenly. Spread them evenly, tucking the herbs underneath to prevent them from burning.

3 **ROAST AND SERVE.** Roast, tossing with a spatula a few times and shaking to restore an even layer, until the vegetables are very tender and browned in spots, 45 to 50 minutes. Check by piercing each variety with a skewer or a fork. Remove the herb stems (most of the leaves will have fallen off) and the bay leaves and discard. Serve warm.

OPTION: HERB-ROASTED ROOTS WITH *DUKKAH* (HAZELNUT AND SESAME SPICE MIX)

I discovered *dukkah* on a visit to the World Spice Merchants shop just below Pike Place Market in Seattle. Entering the shop is a heady experience, and I could spend hours breathing in the exotic aromas and reading the labels on the countless jars of unfamiliar spices and blends. Anytime I am lucky enough to stop in, I come away with new spices to try at home, and *dukkah* was one of my more recent—and successful—finds. The mix originated in Egypt, where it is used as a dip for pita bread and as a table condiment. I quickly used up the few ounces I bought in Seattle, sprinkling it on everything from salads to roast vegetables, and soon tried to make my own, which I found even tastier for its freshness. Most every *dukkah* blend contains toasted coriander, cumin, sesame, and black pepper, along with either roasted chickpeas or hazelnuts. I use hazelnuts because they are easier to toast and give a richer flavor. The mix gets rounded out with a little dried mint or thyme, your choice (fresh herbs would add unwanted moisture to the mix). In addition to sprinkling it on roasted root vegetables (try it on the carrots on page 510 in place of the gremolata), I encourage you to try it as a dip for strips of pita, adding a few tablespoons of olive oil to moisten the *dukkah*. The recipe can easily be doubled or tripled.

MAKES ABOUT 6 TABLESPOONS SPICE MIX

¼ cup hazelnuts

2 teaspoons coriander seeds

1½ teaspoons cumin seeds

¼ teaspoon whole black peppercorns

1½ tablespoons white sesame seeds, hulled or unhulled

½ teaspoon dried mint or dried thyme

¼ teaspoon kosher salt

1 **TOAST THE NUTS.** If you are making this while the vegetables roast, spread the nuts in a pie tin and toast in the 400-degree (375-degree convection) oven until fragrant and lightly browned, 6 to 8 minutes. (If you're making the *dukkah* for another use and the oven is not on, toast the nuts in a small skillet over medium heat, shaking the pan frequently, until fragrant and lightly toasted, about 6 minutes.) Let the nuts cool. If they have skins, rub them with a clean dish towel to remove.

2 **TOAST THE SPICES.** Combine the coriander seeds, cumin seeds, and peppercorns in a small skillet over medium heat and toast, shaking frequently, until fragrant and beginning to darken, about 1 minute. Transfer to a small plate to cool completely.

3 **TOAST THE SESAME SEEDS.** Return the skillet to medium-low heat and add the sesame seeds. Toast briefly, stirring once or twice, until they are beginning to darken, about 30 seconds depending on the heat. Stay close by, as hulled sesame seeds burn quickly. (Unhulled seeds, if using, will take longer to toast, 2 to 3 minutes.) Set aside to cool completely.

4 **GRIND AND COMBINE THE NUTS AND SPICES.** In a medium-size mortar or a small food processor, grind the spices (coriander, cumin, and peppercorns) to a coarse powder. Transfer to a small bowl. Next combine the hazelnuts and sesame seeds in the mortar or food processor and grind until the hazelnuts are coarsely chopped; be careful not to overwork them, or they will become an oily paste. Add the ground nuts and seeds to the spices and stir in the mint and salt.

5 **SERVE.** Toss the dukkah onto the vegetables as they come out of the oven (after removing the herb stems) and serve warm. *Dukkah* will keep, tightly covered, in the refrigerator for a few weeks. For the best flavor, let it come to room temperature before using.

ORANGE-ROASTED CARROTS WITH GREMOLATA

I think I owe carrots an apology. For the longest time I thought of these reliable roots as a kitchen staple but rarely used them for anything more than the base for stews and braises (along with onions and celery, as a part of a classic *mirepoix*). Sure, I would occasionally munch away on a carrot stick to avoid grabbing a more indulgent snack, but I realized recently that I rarely reached for a bunch of carrots when dreaming up a vegetables side dish for dinner. That's all changed now that I've discovered how good carrots can be when sliced into thick rounds and roasted in a hot oven until tender and caramelized. To bring out their inherent sweetness, I drizzle a little reduced orange juice over them near the end of roasting and then shower them with a zingy gremolata made from orange zest, parsley, and shallots. (See page 168 for a photo of the finished dish.)

The recipe is written for those who like to multitask in the kitchen: You reduce the orange juice and make the gremolata as the carrots roast. If you prefer to get ahead or have other things that need your attention (homework or the main course, or both), by all means prepare the juice and gremolata in advance. They can keep for several hours at room temperature. Serve these with roast pork or beef, or make it part of a multidish vegetarian feast.

SERVES 4
METHOD: High heat
ROASTING TIME: 40 to 50 minutes

1½ pounds carrots, peeled and sliced diagonally into ½-inch-thick pieces
2 tablespoons extra-virgin olive oil
¼ teaspoon crushed red pepper flakes
Kosher salt and freshly ground black pepper

1 medium navel orange
2 tablespoons finely chopped fresh flat-leaf parsley
1 tablespoon minced shallots
1 scant teaspoon honey

1   **HEAT THE OVEN.** Position a rack in the center of the oven and heat to 400 degrees (375 degrees convection). If desired, line a heavy-duty rimmed baking sheet with parchment paper.

2 **ROAST.** Pile the carrots in a large bowl. Drizzle with oil, season with red pepper flakes, salt, and pepper, and toss to coat. Transfer to the baking sheet in a single layer and roast, stirring every 15 to 20 minutes and then shaking the pan to restore an even layer so they cook evenly, until tender and starting to brown, 30 to 40 minutes. (The fresher the carrots, the more quickly they will cook.)

3 **MEANWHILE, MAKE THE GREMOLATA AND GLAZE.** Zest enough of the orange (preferably with a microplane) to get 1 teaspoon orange zest. Put the zest in a small bowl and stir in the parsley and shallots. Season with a good pinch of salt. Set aside.

Squeeze the juice of the orange into a very small saucepan (you should have ⅓ to ½ cup). Add the honey and simmer over medium heat until reduced by about half, 6 to 10 minutes. Keep an eye on the juice so it doesn't scorch. Set aside.

4 **GLAZE AND SERVE.** When the carrots are tender and beginning to brown, pour the reduced orange-juice-and-honey mixture over them and toss to coat. Continue roasting until the carrots are deeply browned in spots (being careful not to scorch the orange glaze), another 5 to 10 minutes or so. Transfer to a serving dish and sprinkle the gremolata over the top. Serve immediately.

Why Baby Carrots Don't Roast Well

AMERICANS EAT A LOT MORE CARROTS THAN WE USED TO. INDUSTRY ESTIMATES CLAIM WE WENT FROM EATING ABOUT 6 POUNDS PER PERSON annually back in the 1960s to over 10 pounds today, and this increase can be attributed largely to the rise of baby carrots. In fact, baby carrots now make up about 70 percent of all the acreage of carrots grown in California (our largest carrot-growing region by far). Does this mean that most carrot farmers have switched over their fields to growing tiny little carrots? No, not at all. The uniformly stubby carrots sold in supermarkets everywhere as baby carrots are actually the 1986 invention of a California carrot farmer, Mike Yurosek. Frustrated by having to unload over two thirds of his crop because the carrots were too twisted, misshapen, or broken to sell whole, Yurosek came up with an idea that would radically change the American carrot industry. This ingenious farmer devised a plan to turn unwanted mature carrots into cute little crunchy "babies" by whittling them down to size with a potato peeler. (The proper name for these might be baby-cut carrots.) Today, carrot packing plants mechanically chop full-grown carrots into 2-inch sections, pump them through water-filled pipes and along into whirling cement-mixer-size peelers, and pare them down to the chubby little carrots that Americans munch by the bagful. This invention has led to higher fresh yields for carrot farmers. In fact, farmers growing carrots intended for the baby-cut market plant them close together so they stay slim and there will be less waste when the carrots are cut to size.

All in all, there is nothing inherently wrong with baby-cut carrots, but keep in mind that they tend to contain a large amount of water from being pumped through the processing system. When it comes to roasting, this added moisture results in inferior results. It's well worth taking the extra time to peel and trim full-size ones.

REAL ROASTED BEETS

When a recipe or a menu mentions roasted beets, it most likely refers to beets that have been wrapped in foil, whole, and cooked in the oven until tender. Truth is, beets cooked this way are steamed, not roasted (the foil traps their moisture during cooking, much as a covered pot would). Now, don't get me wrong, I love the sweet taste and tender texture of foil-cooked beets, but they lack the deeply concentrated flavor and delicious crisp edges of a properly roasted beet. To get real roasted beets, you need to peel the beets first, just as you would another hardy vegetable (such as winter squash or parsnips), and then cut them into chunks. Beyond their concentrated taste and jewel-like appearance, real roasted beets offer the advantages of cooking more quickly and being ready to go as soon as they are tender—no last-minute juggling of hot beets to slip off the peels. Granted, peeling raw beets can stain your hands; if this bothers you, wear a pair of plastic gloves, or shop for golden beets at the market.

To brighten the beets, strew a handful of fresh herbs (in particular dill, chives, and/or parsley) on top just before serving. Roasted beets also take well to being doused with a little vinaigrette, such as Cumin-Mint Vinaigrette (recipe follows). Or use them in salads, the way you would use any cooked beet.

SERVES 3 TO 4
METHOD: High heat
ROASTING TIME: About 40 minutes

1 pound beets, without greens, scrubbed	Kosher salt and freshly ground black pepper
2 tablespoons extra-virgin olive oil or a mix of olive oil and melted butter	1 tablespoon chopped fresh dill, chives, and/or flat-leaf parsley (optional)

1 **HEAT THE OVEN.** Position a rack in the center of the oven and heat to 400 degrees (375 degrees convection). If desired, line a heavy-duty rimmed baking sheet with parchment paper.

CONTINUED ON PAGE 515

REAL ROASTED BEETS (PAGE 513)
WITH CUMIN-MINT VINAIGRETTE

2 **PEEL AND SEASON THE BEETS.** Trim any stems from each beet and trim the root end. Using a vegetable peeler, peel off the outermost layer; you will see a difference in the texture, revealing the less fibrous inside. Cut the beets into ¾-inch cubes and place in a large bowl. Add the olive oil or oil-and-butter mix and season to taste with salt and pepper. Spread in an even layer on the baking sheet.

3 **ROAST AND SERVE.** Slide the beets into the oven and roast, stirring once or twice with a metal spatula and shaking to restore an even layer, until tender on the inside (check by piercing a cube with a paring knife) and browned on the outside, about 40 minutes. Sprinkle the herbs on top, if using (omit if you are making the vinaigrette), and serve hot or warm.

OPTION: CUMIN-MINT VINAIGRETTE

This dressing is both earthy (from the toasted cumin) and bright (from the mint), giving just the right lift to a bowl of roasted beets. You may notice that there's a little less olive oil than in a standard vinaigrette, to compensate for the oil used to coat the beets before roasting. For an alternative, substitute lime for the lemon and cilantro for the mint. You may also want to crumble a little feta or fresh goat cheese over the beets after tossing with the dressing.

MAKES ABOUT 1/4 CUP, ENOUGH FOR 1 POUND BEETS

1 tablespoon fresh lemon juice

1 teaspoon cumin seeds, toasted and lightly crushed

Kosher salt and freshly ground black pepper

2 tablespoons extra-virgin olive oil

¼ cup coarsely chopped fresh mint

IN A SMALL BOWL, combine the lemon juice and cumin. Add a pinch of salt and pepper. Whisk in the olive oil. Just before serving, stir in the mint. Pour over warm or room-temperature beets.

ROASTED PARSNIPS WITH BACON AND ROSEMARY

You know what they say about everything going better with bacon? Parsnips are no exception. Their mildly earthy, starchy-sweet character stands up wonderfully to the rich meatiness of bacon. In this recipe, I roast the bacon right along with the parsnips and rosemary; the bacon gets all crispy-crunchy while lending its savory, salty drippings to the dish. A little brown sugar and a splash of cider vinegar add sweet and tangy notes to create the perfect balance of flavors. This is an outstanding side dish for roast chicken and beef.

SERVES 4 TO 6
METHOD: Moderate heat
ROASTING TIME: 40 to 45 minutes

2 pounds parsnips, peeled

3 strips thick-cut bacon (about 4 ounces), cut crosswise into ½-inch lengths

1 tablespoon chopped fresh rosemary

1 tablespoon extra-virgin olive oil

Kosher salt and freshly ground black pepper

2 tablespoons brown sugar, light or dark

2 teaspoons cider vinegar

1   **HEAT THE OVEN.** Position a rack in the center of the oven and heat to 375 degrees (350 degrees convection). If desired, line a heavy-duty rimmed baking sheet with parchment paper.

2   **PREPARE THE PARSNIPS.** Using a sturdy knife, trim the stem end off the parsnips. Cut each parsnip into sticks that are 2 to 4 inches long and about ½-inch thick. As when cutting carrots, you may find that you leave the tapered bottom piece whole and need to halve or quarter the fatter top. Do your best to cut evenly sized sticks, but there's no need to haul out the ruler. Any extra-thin pieces will come out crisp and crunchy, while thicker pieces will be tender and sweet. As you cut, examine the parsnip core. If it stands out as deeper-colored and especially coarse and woody (you can poke it with the tip of a knife to see), cut it out with a paring knife.

3 **SEASON, ROAST, AND SERVE.** Combine the parsnips, bacon, rosemary, and olive oil in a large bowl. Season generously with salt and pepper and toss to coat. Transfer to the baking sheet, spreading everything in an even layer, and roast, stirring every 10 minutes, until the parsnips are almost tender and the bacon is beginning to crisp up, about 35 minutes. Sprinkle with the brown sugar and cider vinegar and roast for another 5 to 10 minutes, turning once or twice until the parsnips are browned and the bacon is crisp. Serve immediately.

Selecting and Handling Parsnips

LOOK FOR PARSNIPS FROM LATE FALL (THEIR SWEETNESS INTENSIFIES AFTER A GOOD HARD FROST) THROUGH SPRING. REAL PARSNIP ENTHUSIASTS LOVE to explain that spring-dug parsnips (those left to winter underground) are the sweetest of all. No matter when the parsnips were dug, they should be firm and not split or drying out. I prefer moderately sized roots, not too slender and not gargantuan, as they are easier to handle. At home, store the parsnips loosely in a ventilated plastic bag in the produce drawer. Like carrots, they are good keepers, lasting several weeks.

MAPLE-ROASTED BUTTERNUT SQUASH AND APPLES

This captures the essence of autumn in New England—squash, apples, and a touch of maple. You can almost imagine the vivid fall foliage out the window. It makes sense, then, that this comforting side dish is perfect for a potluck, as such gatherings remain a popular way to entertain in these parts. Not only does this serve a crowd, it is also easy to transport and dish up, and best of all, it's delicious either hot from the oven or at room temperature—anything but chilled. Roasting concentrates the sweetness of the squash and brings out the tart edge of the apples, creating a lovely balancing act. I prefer to keep the skin on the apples to provide a textural contrast with the velvety squash, but that's up to you. If the apples seem particularly thick-skinned (take a taste and you'll know), you may want to peel them before cutting. You can also make this with other winter squash varieties, such as buttercup, acorn, sweet dumpling, kabocha, and pumpkin. You'll need 2 baking sheets here so as not to crowd the squash and apples. Piling them all onto one sheet would leave you with something closer to a mash.

A sprinkling of nuts adds a welcome crunch, but the dish stands alone if you have people who don't eat nuts in the crowd. If there's room between the mashed potatoes and green bean casserole, consider adding this dish to your Thanksgiving table. It's also very good with roast pork.

SERVES 6 TO 8
METHOD: High heat
ROASTING TIME: About 40 minutes

1 butternut squash (about 2½ pounds), peeled, seeded, and cut into ¾-inch chunks (5 to 7 cups)

2 tart, crisp apples (about 1 pound), such as Granny Smith, Gravenstein, or Braeburn, quartered and cut into 1-inch chunks

2 tablespoons unsalted butter, melted

2 tablespoons extra-virgin olive oil

2 tablespoons pure maple syrup

2 teaspoons minced fresh marjoram (rosemary, thyme, or sage may be substituted)

Kosher salt and freshly ground black pepper

¼ cup pecans or walnuts, lightly toasted and chopped (optional)

1 **HEAT THE OVEN.** Position racks in the upper and lower thirds of the oven and heat to 400 degrees (375 degrees convection). If desired, line 2 heavy-duty rimmed baking sheets with parchment paper.

2 **SEASON THE SQUASH AND APPLES.** Combine the squash and apples in a large bowl and drizzle the butter, olive oil, and maple syrup over them. Season with the marjoram and salt and pepper and toss to coat. Transfer the mixture to the baking sheets, distributing it evenly and spreading it in a single layer.

3 **ROAST AND SERVE.** Slide the baking sheets into the oven and roast, turning the squash and apples with a metal spatula once or twice, until the squash is well caramelized on the outside and tender throughout and the apples are tender, about 40 minutes. Taste for salt and pepper, sprinkle with the nuts, if using, and serve hot or warm.

OPTION: ROASTED BUTTERNUT SQUASH AND GRAPES

This option comes from my sister, who loves grapes in any guise, and they are especially delicious roasted with chunks of winter squash. Simply substitute 2 to 3 cups of seedless red grapes (about 12 ounces) for the apples. Grapes are sweeter than apples, so eliminate the maple syrup. Sage is especially good here. The roasting time will be about the same.

Selecting and Handling Winter Squash

UNLIKE SUMMER SQUASH, WINTER SQUASH DOES NOT TAKE ITS NAME FROM THE SEASON IN WHICH IT'S HARVESTED. INSTEAD, NORTHERN FARMERS AND gardeners harvest winter squash in the autumn, before the hard frosts and snow come. The reason for its moniker is that winter squash develops a tough inedible rind as it matures that protects it for long storage, making it available throughout the winter.

At the market, select only varieties that appear fully grown with a thick rind. Squashes harvested before reaching their full maturity are less flavorful and have skins that are too thin to store well. The first indicator of top-quality winter squash is the stem. It should be dry and somewhat pinched or withered-looking, indicating that the squash was ripe enough nearly to fall off the vine at harvest time. Look for sturdy squashes that feel heavy and full.

CONTINUED ON NEXT PAGE

Lighter squashes tend to be stringy, with dried-out flesh. Choose ones with smooth, matte, dry skin. Avoid any with soft or spongy spots. A few blemishes or scars are fine as long as they are only skin-deep, without cracks or deep cuts, especially around the stem. Finally, the skin should be so thick that you can't easily gouge it with your thumbnail.

If planning to use winter squash within 2 to 3 weeks, leave it at room temperature in a well-ventilated bin. For longer storage, you need conditions similar to those in a root cellar: 50 to 55 degrees and slotted shelves or mesh to allow the air to circulate. If you don't have any such space (and few of us do), leave the longer-term storage to the growers and retailers and buy squash on an as-needed basis.

In terms of varieties, butternut squash is my first choice for roasting in chunks. The long, straight neck and smooth skin make it easier to handle than the more spherical varieties. Its dense, sweet flesh becomes creamy and intense in the heat of the oven. Other favorite varieties are buttercup and red kuri. Acorn squashes are among the most common; unfortunately, their texture can be slightly dry and their flavor a bit dull. The blue-gray, wart-covered Hubbard squashes have a wonderfully deep flavor, but the large size can make them unwieldy. Blue Ballet is a smaller version of Hubbard, but at 4 to 7 pounds it still feeds a crowd.

Of all the winter squash, butternut is the easiest to peel. Begin by dividing the squash into 2 pieces. Use a sturdy chef's knife to separate the straight neck portion from the more bulbous part that holds the seeds. Next, using a heavy-duty vegetable peeler or a sharp paring knife, remove the skin and fibrous greenish flesh right below. It may take several swipes with the peeler to remove all the greenish layer. Once the squash is peeled, cut the round portion in half and scoop out the seeds with a spoon. Chop the peeled squash into pieces as needed.

For other varieties, the best approach is first to cut the squash in halves, quarters, or other manageable pieces. With a spoon, scoop out the seeds and strings, and then peel away the rind with a heavy-duty vegetable peeler or a sharp paring knife.

MAPLE-ROASTED APPLES WITH CANDIED NUTS

We all know that we should eat more fruit for dessert, but sometimes we crave something just a little more decadent. Here's a way to transform apples into something bound to please even the sweetest tooth in the house: chunks of crisp tart apples, lightly sweetened with maple syrup, spiced with nutmeg and ginger, and roasted until tender and caramelized. To add some crunch, I make yummy candied nuts by tossing a handful of walnuts, cashews, almonds (whatever is on hand, really) with a little more maple syrup and butter and roasting them in the same hot oven as the fruit. Serve the fruit in shallow dessert bowls, sprinkled with nuts. Of course, you can always put a scoop of vanilla ice cream in the bowl first—I love the way the roasting juices mingle with the cold creaminess—but that's up to you.

SERVES 4 TO 5

METHOD: High heat

ROASTING TIME: 35 to 50 minutes

4 large tart, crisp apples (1½ to 2 pounds), such as Gravenstein, Cortland, Pink Lady, Braeburn, or Jazz

¼ cup plus 1 tablespoon pure maple syrup

4 tablespoons unsalted butter, melted

½ teaspoon nutmeg, preferably freshly grated

¼ teaspoon ground ginger

Pinch of kosher salt

¾ cup nuts (walnuts, hazelnuts, almonds, cashews, or any combination)

1 to 1½ pints high-quality vanilla ice cream (optional)

1   **HEAT THE OVEN.** Position racks in the top and lower thirds of the oven and heat to 400 degrees (375 degrees convection). Line a large heavy-duty rimmed baking sheet and a smaller pan (like a quarter sheet pan) with aluminum foil (or with reusable silicone mats if you have them).

CONTINUED ON PAGE 523

MAPLE-ROASTED APPLES WITH CANDIED NUTS
(PAGE 521) OVER VANILLA ICE CREAM

2   **PREPARE THE APPLES.** For most fresh apples, I like to leave the skin on because it helps the fruit hold its shape and provides texture. With some thick-skinned varieties, the skin is best removed. Take a taste of your apple and decide whether you need to peel it. Cut the apples (peeled or not) into quarters. Remove the seeds and cores and cut the quarters into ½-inch cubes. Pile the apples onto the larger baking sheet and toss with ¼ cup maple syrup, 3 tablespoons butter, and the nutmeg, ginger, and salt. Toss to combine and arrange the apples in a loose single layer on the sheet.

3   **ROAST THE APPLES.** Roast the apples on the bottom rack, tossing after 15 minutes and then after another 10 minutes so they roast evenly, until soft, slightly caramelized, yet not completely collapsed, 35 to 40 minutes. If they are not done after 35 minutes, toss them again and return them to the oven for another 5 to 10 minutes.

4   **MEANWHILE, PREPARE AND ROAST THE NUTS.** Spread the nuts out on the smaller baking sheet and drizzle with the remaining 1 tablespoon maple syrup, 1 tablespoon butter, and a pinch of salt. Toss to coat. Spread the nuts out in a single layer and roast on the rack above the apples, stirring once or twice, until the nuts are toasty and brown, about 10 minutes. Let the nuts cool for at least 10 minutes before serving.

5   **SERVE.** If the fruit has cooled to room temperature, slide it back into a moderate oven (350 degrees) for 10 minutes to warm slightly. Divide the ice cream, if using, among dessert bowls or sundae dishes. Spoon the warm fruit into bowls (on top of the ice cream, if using), and drizzle any juices from the pan over it. Top with candied nuts and serve.

ROASTED APPLESAUCE WITH THYME

The standard route to applesauce begins with simmering apples over low heat until they collapse into a tasty, if somewhat bland, puree. For a bolder sauce, try roasting the apples. Tossed with a little bit of butter and sugar, they sizzle and caramelize to create a sauce with a darker color and a deeper flavor. Making roasted applesauce is actually easier too, since you leave the apple peel on (the redder the skin, the rosier your sauce will be) and don't even need to seed or core the apples before roasting. The only work involved comes at the end of cooking, when you pass the cooked apples through a food mill. But this is perhaps my favorite part: I love standing over the food mill and inhaling the aroma of the cooked apples as I crank the handle. (If you don't have a food mill, you can still make the applesauce. Peel and core the apples before roasting, and then puree them in a food processor afterward.)

I prefer apples with a little tartness and spice for my applesauce and so tend to use such varieties as Empire, Cortland, Winesap, Idared, and Gravenstein. A mix of apples will give you even greater complexity of flavor. The addition of a little fresh thyme offers a change of pace from the usual applesauce flavoring triumvirate of cinnamon, nutmeg, and cloves. It also makes the sauce equally welcome with dinner or dessert. Serve it warm or chilled alongside roast meats, especially pork and chicken. Or, for a not-too-sweet dessert, top it with thick cream, plain Greek yogurt, or custard sauce. The recipe can easily be doubled; just use 2 pans so as not to overcrowd.

MAKES ABOUT 1 1/4 CUPS, ENOUGH TO SERVE 6 AS A CONDIMENT, 3 TO 4 AS DESSERT

METHOD: High heat

ROASTING TIME: 35 to 40 minutes

4 large apples (1 ½ to 2 pounds; see headnote above for varieties)

2 tablespoons unsalted butter, cut into small pieces

2 tablespoons Demerara sugar or light brown sugar

2 teaspoons fresh thyme leaves

1 ½ teaspoons cider vinegar

Pinch of kosher salt

1   **HEAT THE OVEN.** Position a rack in the center of the oven and heat to 425 degrees (400 degrees convection).

2   **PREPARE THE APPLES.** Cut the apples into quarters; don't peel, seed, or core them. Arrange the apples in a single layer in a 9-by-13-inch roasting pan or baking dish lined with parchment paper or a silicone mat. It's fine if the apples are crowded as long as they aren't stacked. Scatter the butter, sugar, thyme, vinegar, and salt over them and toss to coat.

3   **ROAST THE APPLES.** Slide the pan into the oven. After about 15 minutes, turn the apples over with a spatula. Continue roasting until the quarters begin to collapse, the cut surfaces caramelize in spots, and the flesh is very soft, 35 to 40 minutes.

4   **PUREE THE APPLES.** Work the apples through the medium disk of a food mill and into a bowl. Be sure to scrape the bottom of the roasting pan with a rubber spatula to capture every bit of juice.

5   **SERVE THE APPLESAUCE WARM OR CHILLED.** Applesauce keeps in an airtight container in the refrigerator for 4 to 5 days.

SLOW-ROASTED GRAPES

SLOW-ROASTED GRAPES

As the grapes slowly roast in a very low oven, they shrink and caramelize into concentrated little bites of sweet goodness. The little orbs lose their fresh juiciness and develop a sensuous, almost silky tenderness. I find all sorts of delightful uses for them, from sweet to savory, though because their flavor is so intense, I rarely serve them on their own. On the sweet side, I turn plain Greek-style yogurt into dessert by swirling a little honey into it and topping it with a handful of slow-roasted grapes. In fact, these grapes will complement any sort of custard or pudding (rice pudding is a favorite). In the realm of savory, they are wonderful in green salads—I especially like them with peppery arugula tossed with a simple vinaigrette. I also like to include them on a cheese plate—they taste amazing paired with soft-ripened cheese, such as Camembert and creamy blues—or as a component of an antipasto spread. They make a fine accompaniment to roast poultry, too, such as the roast goose on page 365. One suggestion: For savory uses, use olive oil for roasting; for sweet applications, go with the butter. The butter makes the grapes taste as though they've been cooked in a pastry crust—a grape tart with no tart shell!

MAKES ABOUT 1 CUP, ENOUGH FOR 4 SERVINGS
METHOD: Low heat
ROASTING TIME: 2 1/4 to 2 1/2 hours

¾ pound red grapes (2 heaping cups), preferably seedless, such as Red Globe, Crimson Seedless, or Red Flame; rinsed and stemmed

1 tablespoon extra-virgin olive oil or unsalted butter, melted

1 **HEAT THE OVEN.** Position a rack in the center of the oven and heat to 250 degrees (225 degrees convection). Line a heavy-duty rimmed baking sheet with parchment paper or a silicone mat.

2 **ROAST.** Arrange the grapes in a single layer on the baking sheet. Drizzle with the olive oil or butter and toss to coat. Roast, stirring with a spatula once or twice during cooking, until shriveled and lightly caramelized, 2 ¼ to 2 ½ hours. The grapes may be made ahead and kept refrigerated for several days. Return to room temperature before serving.

BROWN SUGAR-ROASTED PINEAPPLE

T alk about gilding the lily! Super-sweet pineapple slices are made sweeter still by sprinkling them with spiced brown sugar and then roasting them in a hot oven to caramelize and soften. I spike the sugar with a combination of cinnamon, cloves, and a pinch of ground star anise to provide a depth of flavor. A splash of orange liqueur adds a spiritous citrus note. Warm slices of roasted pineapple are delightful served over a bowl of creamy ice cream or slices of toasted pound cake.

SERVES 6
METHOD: High heat
ROASTING TIME: About 1 hour

1 small pineapple (about 3 pounds; see Shopping for Pineapple, page 530)
3 tablespoons unsalted butter, at room temperature
½ cup light brown sugar
¼ teaspoon ground cinnamon

⅛ teaspoon ground cloves
⅛ teaspoon ground star anise
Pinch of kosher salt
1 tablespoon orange liqueur, such as Grand Marnier or Cointreau

1   **HEAT THE OVEN.** Position a rack in the center of the oven and heat to 400 degrees (375 degrees convection).

2   **PEEL THE PINEAPPLE.** Lay the pineapple on its side on a cutting board. Using a large knife, cut off the top, slicing about ½ inch below the crown or stem (this is just below the point where the fruit widens at the "shoulders"). Next slice off the bottom, again removing about ½ inch. Now stand the fruit up on one cut end and remove the peel in wide strips, allowing your knife to follow the contours of the fruit as it bulges out in the middle and cutting only deeply enough to remove all of the peel and a minimum of flesh. As you cut you will notice a pattern of "eyes" (dark, bristly indentations). The most effective (and attractive) way to remove the eyes is to first recognize that they appear in spiral stripes around the contours of the pineapple. Make a shallow V-shaped diagonal cut on either side of a line of eyes to remove them. Continue mak-

ing shallow channels, removing a strip of eyes at a time. If there are still some eyes left when you've made your way around the entire fruit, go back over the pineapple with the tip of a paring knife or a vegetable peeler and dig them out (much the way you would remove the eyes from a potato).

3 **SLICE AND CORE THE PINEAPPLE.** Lay the pineapple back on its side and slice into ½-inch-thick rounds. Use a small, round cookie cutter or small paring knife to cut out and remove the fibrous core of each slice. Cut each round into 2 half-moons.

4 **SEASON THE PINEAPPLE.** Spread 1 tablespoon of butter on the bottom of a heavy-duty rimmed baking sheet. In a small bowl, combine the brown sugar, cinnamon, cloves, star anise, and salt. Sprinkle half the sugar mixture in the bottom of the baking sheet. Arrange the pineapple slices on top, overlapping slightly as necessary (the pineapple will shrink as it roasts). Sprinkle with the remaining sugar mixture. Dot the top with the remaining 2 tablespoons butter and sprinkle the orange liqueur over the slices.

5 **ROAST.** Slide the pineapple into the oven and roast, turning the slices every 20 minutes with tongs so that they are evenly coated with the sweet juices. Continue to roast until the pineapple and juices begin to caramelize, about 1 hour.

6 **SERVE.** The pineapple tastes best served warm. If made ahead, reheat in a warm oven for about 15 minutes. Spoon the caramelized juices over the fruit to serve.

OPTION: WHOLE ROASTED PINEAPPLE WITH CINNAMON

In the late 1990s, I worked on a gorgeous cookbook entitled *From My Château Kitchen*, written by my friend, long-time employer, and mentor, Anne Willan (founder of La Varenne Cooking School). Over the course of several weeks, while staying at the château of the title, we prepared the recipes for the photographs, and I'll never forget the fun we had making—and eating—a whole roasted pineapple studded with vanilla beans. At home, I swapped cinnamon sticks for the vanilla beans, because I liked the flavor combination—and because vanilla beans have become exorbitantly expensive.

If your market sells whole pineapples that are peeled and cored (but not sliced), that will save you some time and effort. Otherwise, peel a whole pineapple according to step 2 above. Next, remove the core using a long, thin-bladed knife or an apple corer (this is an awkward and somewhat dangerous process; simply do your best and be careful). Once it has been

CONTINUED ON NEXT PAGE

cored, stud the pineapple at intervals around the entire fruit with 5 to 6 cinnamon sticks, pushing them into the fruit so they won't fall out.

Next, make a sugar syrup in a small saucepan by combining ½ cup granulated sugar with ¾ cup water. Add the grated zest of 1 navel orange (1 heaping teaspoon) and squeeze the juice (about ½ cup) into the syrup. Add 1 teaspoon freshly grated ginger and 2 star anise pods. Bring to a simmer over medium-high heat and simmer for 3 minutes to dissolve the sugar and infuse the flavors.

Stand the pineapple upright in a 9-by-13-inch nonreactive baking dish (or 9-inch pie plate) and pour the syrup over the top. Roast in a 400-degree (375-degree convection) oven, basting every 20 minutes, until the pineapple is very fragrant and starting to brown and the syrup has begun to caramelize but remains liquid, about 40 minutes. Lay the pineapple on its side on a cutting board and cut into thick rings. Serve warm (leaving the cinnamon sticks in place or removing them if you prefer) and top with the juices. Serves 6.

Shopping for Pineapple

THE FIRST THING TO LOOK FOR IS A FRESH-LOOKING PINEAPPLE TOP, OR CROWN. THE PEEL OF THE FRUIT SHOULD ALSO APPEAR TIGHT AND SHINY. When you pick up the fruit, it should feel heavy for its size, and the flesh should yield slightly when pressed with your fingertip, but avoid any that have obvious soft or mushy spots. While you're holding the pineapple, turn it upside down and give the bottom a sniff. A ripe pineapple will have a sweet, light pineapple smell. If the fragrance is powerful and at all sour, the fruit may be overripe. The color of the peel will depend more on the variety than on ripeness. For instance, many of the newer super-sweet varieties, such as Golden Pineapple, are yellow all over, while some of the older varieties have a touch of green, especially at the base. In other words, judge ripeness by smell and feel, not by color.

Many markets sell already peeled and cored pineapple. As long as the containers smell fresh and have no signs of discoloration, they work well for Brown Sugar–Roasted Pineapple (page 528), saving you the trouble of peeling and coring. You will want a container that weighs about 2 pounds.

BUTTER-ROASTED PLUMS WITH VANILLA, GINGER, AND RUM

A few summers ago a new vendor showed up at my local farmers' market, calling herself the Plum Lady. A simple table holding fruit crates makes up her stand, and from late July on, she's there with a colorful array of fresh plums. Each week the Plum Lady's selection changes, according to what varieties are ripening in her orchard, and she always eagerly offers tastes of what she's brought to market. As the season progresses, I've tasted fruits that range from tart yellow bite-size plums with skin so thin it's almost translucent to big, fat-cheeked plums with deep purple juice that runs down your chin as you bite into them. Inevitably I bring home more than we will ever eat out of hand, and so I've come up with all sorts of way to use them—and quick roasting for an easy dessert is a favorite. To enhance their natural sweetness, I sprinkle the plums with a few teaspoons of sugar flecked with vanilla, fresh ginger, and lemon zest. A splash of rum makes this an elegant grown-up dessert, but you can skip the rum if making this for little ones. Bigger plums are best, but pretty much any firm-ripe variety will do. If they're tiny, reduce the cooking time by 6 to 8 minutes. Avoid plums that are too ripe or they will collapse during roasting.

The plums are best served hot or warm. I don't like to let them sit for more than an hour, as they will begin to sag and lose their bright flavor. These roasted plums make an adequate dessert on their own, but I would never discourage a dollop of lightly sweetened crème fraîche or a scoop of vanilla ice cream.

SERVES 4

METHOD: High heat

ROASTING TIME: 16 to 20 minutes

2 tablespoons unsalted butter, plus more
  for the pan

4 ripe but firm black or red plums (about 14
  ounces)

1 vanilla bean

1 tablespoon turbinado sugar

Kosher salt

1 teaspoon finely grated lemon zest

½ teaspoon grated fresh ginger

1 tablespoon fresh lemon juice

1 tablespoon rum, light or dark

CONTINUED ON NEXT PAGE

1 **HEAT THE OVEN.** Position a rack in the center of the oven and heat to 425 degrees (400 degrees convection). Generously butter a baking dish just large enough to hold the plums (8 by 8 inches works well). Cut the plums in half, discard the pits, and arrange them cut side up in the dish.

2 **SEASON THE PLUMS.** Split the vanilla bean and use the back of a small knife to scrape the seeds from the pod into a small bowl. Add the sugar and a pinch of salt and stir to combine. Stir in the lemon zest and ginger. Sprinkle the plums with the lemon juice and then the rum. Spoon the spiced sugar onto the plums. Divide the butter among the fruits, placing a little pat on each.

3 **ROAST.** Slide the plums into the oven and roast, basting a few times once the juices begin to flow, until the plums are just tender enough so the tip of a knife slides easily into the flesh, 16 to 20 minutes. Don't roast them for so long they fall apart.

4 **SERVE.** Let the plums cool for at least 5 minutes (and up to an hour) before serving. Spoon the juices over the top and serve hot or warm.

ORANGE-SCENTED HONEY-ROASTED FIGS WITH BLACK PEPPER

If I had to name the sexiest fruits, figs would top the list. I love everything from their velvety soft skin to the tender insides—and don't get me started on their ambrosial nectar. Now, imagine these same sexy fruits roasted in a hot oven with a drizzle of honey and a bit of orange juice, and you may be headed to an X rating. The black pepper will surprise some cooks, but don't let it scare you; it lends a unique counterpoint to all the sweetness. The orange juice helps prevent the caramelized juices from sticking to the pan and adds a nice hint of citrus. Roasted figs make a fine dessert, and you may want to dollop whipped cream or crème fraîche onto them just before serving. On the savory side, serve them in a cheese course, or with roast pork or poultry (they're excellent with duck and goose), or as an appetizer along with a few slices of cured ham or coppa.

SERVES 4 TO 6
METHOD: High heat
ROASTING TIME: About 14 minutes

12 fresh ripe figs, such as Black Mission, Brown Turkey, or Adriatic (green)

⅓ cup fresh orange juice

¼ cup honey

¼ teaspoon cracked black pepper

1 **HEAT THE OVEN.** Position a rack in the center of the oven and heat to 400 degrees (375 degrees convection).

2 **TRIM AND HALVE THE FIGS.** Cut the very tip of the stem from the figs. Only remove the tough outermost end; you want to preserve the full shape of the fig. With a sharp knife, cut each fig in half, cutting from stem to blossom end.

3 **ROAST AND SERVE.** Arrange the figs cut side up in a shallow baking dish that will hold them without too much extra room (9 by 13 or 9 by 9 inches works). Pour the orange juice into the pan, pouring it down the sides, not over the figs. Drizzle the cut sides of the figs with honey and sprinkle with pepper. Slide the dish into the oven and roast, spooning the orange juice over the figs once or twice, until the figs puff up a little and look juicy, about 14 minutes. Serve hot or warm.

ROASTED CHERRIES WITH CREAMY POLENTA

Roasting cherries in a moderate oven concentrates their sweetness without drying them out, so they come out juicy, tender, and caramelized, with a flavor made savory by the addition of shallots and thyme. When spooned on top of creamy polenta, the contrast of the dark juices makes a dramatic side dish that's especially wonderful with deeply flavored duck or game. I have also been known to enjoy this polenta on its own, eating it out of a thick pottery bowl on the couch—the ultimate cold-weather comfort supper.

SERVES 4 TO 6

METHOD: Moderate heat

ROASTING TIME: About 25 minutes

PLAN AHEAD: If you have only one oven and plan to serve this with the duck on page 362, you can roast the cherries ahead of time; keep them in a warm place until ready to serve.

¾ **pound fresh sweet cherries, halved and pitted**	**Kosher salt and freshly ground black pepper**
3 **tablespoons unsalted butter**	1 **cup coarse- or medium-grind polenta (cornmeal), preferably stone-ground and high-quality**
1 **tablespoon extra-virgin olive oil**	
1 **shallot, minced**	¼ **cup freshly grated Parmigiano-Reggiano cheese**
1 **teaspoon fresh thyme leaves**	

1 **HEAT THE OVEN.** Position a rack in the center of the oven and heat to 350 degrees (325 degrees convection). Line a heavy-duty rimmed baking sheet with parchment paper or a silicone mat.

2 **SEASON THE CHERRIES.** Toss the cherries on the baking sheet with 1 tablespoon butter, the olive oil, shallot, and thyme, and a pinch each of salt and pepper. Let the cherries sit at room temperature while you start the polenta.

3 **MAKE THE POLENTA.** In a heavy-duty 3- to 4-quart saucepan, heat 4 cups of water over medium-high heat. Season with a good pinch of salt, and before the water boils, add the polenta in a steady stream, whisking to prevent lumps. Let it boil briefly. Reduce the heat to medium-low and continue cooking, stirring frequently with a wooden spoon. (The whisk is helpful only for adding the cornmeal; after that a wooden spoon is your best tool.) As it cooks, the polenta should release slow, thick bubbles; just don't allow it to sputter violently. Continue simmering, stirring regularly, until very thick and creamy, 45 to 60 minutes. The longer it cooks, the more fully the grains will swell and soften and the creamier and better-tasting it will be. If the polenta gets too thick, add a few tablespoons more water.

4 **MEANWHILE, ROAST THE CHERRIES.** Put the baking sheet in the oven and roast, stirring every 10 minutes for even cooking, until the cherries are slightly shriveled and their juices have begun to caramelize, about 25 minutes. Set aside in a warm place if the polenta is not yet ready.

5 **FINISH THE POLENTA AND SERVE.** When the polenta is creamy and thick, with no trace of grittiness, stir in the cheese and the remaining 2 tablespoons butter and season to taste with salt and pepper. Spoon the polenta onto warm serving plates, into bowls, or onto a serving platter (a handsome wooden cutting board is traditional). Spoon the cherries and juices on top and serve immediately.

OPTION: BREAKFAST POLENTA WITH ROASTED CHERRIES

If you're a morning person and you want a comforting, filling breakfast, transform this dish from a savory side dish into a creamy porridge with a sweet cherry topping. Make the polenta with 3 cups whole milk plus 3 cups water in place of the 4 cups water (the higher proportion of liquid to grain gives you a softer porridge). Omit the cheese. Roast the cherries without the shallots, thyme, and black pepper and add a pinch of sugar when seasoning with salt. Toasted almonds add a welcome crunch. Also, I like to pass a pitcher of cream or a tub of plain yogurt to put on top.

ROASTED LEMON CHUTNEY

I've always been one to nibble on the lemon slice after I've finished my iced tea. And I do the same with the lemon twist left in the bottom of my martini glass. I just love the way the bitterness of the lemon peel becomes infused and tempered by the flavors of the drink. A similar alchemy happens in this recipe, in which slices of lemon, peel and all, get roasted until tender before joining up with some olive oil, red onion, and honey in the food processor. The result is a surprisingly creamy, sweet-tart condiment that works wonders on everything from grilled fish to roast chicken and pork. It also makes a unique, and unexpected, topping for bruschetta, especially when paired with some fresh ricotta or soft goat cheese.

Since you use whole lemons, peels and all, wash them first in warm soapy water. I also like to scrub the peel with a vegetable brush to remove any waxy residue; organic lemons don't seem to have that residue, so choose those if you can. The chutney will last for several days tightly covered and refrigerated. For the best flavor, let it come to room temperature before serving.

MAKES ABOUT 1 1/2 CUPS
METHOD: High heat
ROASTING TIME: 20 to 25 minutes

¼ cup finely chopped red onions or shallots

3 small lemons (4 to 5 ounces each), preferably organic, washed

¼ cup extra-virgin olive oil, plus more for brushing

1 tablespoon honey

Kosher salt and freshly ground black pepper

2 tablespoons chopped fresh mint, basil, or parsley

1   **HEAT THE OVEN.** Position a rack in the center of the oven and heat to 400 degrees (375 degrees convection). Line a heavy-duty rimmed baking sheet with aluminum foil or a silicone mat (use a smaller baking sheet if you have one, such as a 9-by-12-inch).

2   **SOAK THE ONIONS OR SHALLOTS.** Put the onions or shallots in a small bowl and fill with cold water. Set aside to soak; this reduces their pungency and prevents them from overpowering the chutney.

3   **TRIM THE LEMONS.** Set aside 1 lemon to use later. Slice about ¼ inch off both ends of the remaining 2 lemons and discard (because the ends are mostly pith, removing them helps prevent the chutney from being too bitter). Slice the 2 trimmed lemons into ½-inch-thick rounds and use the point of a knife to remove the seeds. Arrange the lemons on the baking sheet and brush them with a little olive oil. Turn and coat the second side with oil.

4   **ROAST.** Roast the lemons, turning every 10 minutes, until they are very tender with only a few spots of brown, 20 to 25 minutes. Don't let the lemons get at all crisp, and be careful, as they tend to brown on the bottom before the top. Set aside until cool enough to handle.

5   **MAKE THE CHUTNEY.** Transfer the lemons to a food processor fitted with the chopping blade. If there are any juices on the baking sheet, add these (frequently there are none; it depends on the lemons). Drain the onions or shallots, shaking off any excess water, and add to the processor. Add the honey and pulse several times until the lemons are coarsely chopped. Add the juice from half of the remaining lemon and the ¼ cup of olive oil. Continue pulsing until the chutney is fairly smooth and creamy, with just a few lemon chunks. Season to taste with salt and pepper and add more lemon juice to taste. Transfer to a small bowl. Let the chutney sit at room temperature for at least 2 hours to let the flavors meld. Just before serving, stir in the fresh herb.

MAPLE-ROASTED APPLES AND CANDIED NUTS
(PAGE 521)

SOURCES & RESOURCES

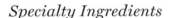

Specialty Ingredients

Cowgirl Creamery
www.cowgirlcreamery.com
866-433-7834
Producer and purveyor of American and European artisan cheeses.

Earthy Delights
www.Earthy.com
800-367-4709
Reliable source for wild mushrooms and other seasonal wild-harvested items, fresh specialty produce, cheeses, vinegars, and other hard-to-find ingredients.

Kalustyan's
www.Kalustyans.com
212-685-3451
Carries an enormous array of spices, herbs, and specialty ingredients from all over the world.

La Tienda
www.Tienda.com
800-710-4304
Importer of foods and other specialty items from Spain, including pimentón, olive oil, cured meats, and more.

More Than Gourmet
www.MoreThanGourmet.com
800-860-9385
Ohio-based company producing excellent reduced stocks (including *Demi-Glace Gold*).

Neuske's
www.Nueskes.com
800-392-2266
Wisconsin-based family-run business making top-quality applewood smoked bacon and hams since 1887.

Penzeys Spices
www.Penzeys.com
800-741-7787
National catalogue and retail company offering a wide selection of spices and seasonings.

Zingerman's Mail Order
www.Zingermans.com
888-636-8162
Offers an extraordinary selection of traditionally made foods, including Marash pepper, pimentón, harissa, fleur de sel, cheeses, and much more.

Meats and Poultry

D'Artagnan
www.Dartagnan.com
800-327-8246
Purveyor of naturally raised meats, poultry, and game, including duck, goose, and turkey.

Heritage Foods USA
www.HeritageFoodsUSA.com
718-389-0985
Source for heritage breeds of poultry and meat, specializing in products from small family farms and a "fully traceable" food supply.

Niman Ranch
www.NimanRanch.com
Sells humanely raised, antibiotic- and hormone-free meat (pork, beef, and lamb) from over 650 independent farmers and ranchers in the United States.

Preferred Meats
www.PreferredMeats.com
800-397-6328
Specializes in working directly with farmers to find top-quality, sustainable beef, pork, lamb, game birds, and game meat, including goat.

Sustainable Shopping Information

Blue Ocean Institute
www.BlueOcean.org/seafood/seafood-guide
On-line guide to ocean-friendly seafood choices; offers downloads for printable pocket guides as well as a mobile app.

Eat Well Guide
www.EatWellGuide.org
An on-line directory for family farms, restaurants, farmers' markets, grocery stores, Community Supported Agriculture (CSA) programs, and U-pick orchards in the United States and Canada.

Eatwild
www.Eatwild.com
State-by-state directory for finding pasture-raised meats and poultry, including listings for farms that will ship products.

LocalHarvest
www.LocalHarvest.org
On-line resource for finding farmers' markets, family farms, and other sources of sustainably grown food in your region. Includes sources for grass-fed meats, poul-

try, and many other locally grown foods in the United States.

Seafood Watch
www.MontereyBayAquarium.org/cr/
seafoodwatch.aspx
A trademarked program of the Monterey Bay Aquarium; offers information on making informed seafood choices. Also provides downloads for printable pocket guides and mobile apps.

Slow Food USA Ark of Taste
www.SlowFoodUSA.org/index.php/
programs/details/ark_of_taste
An international catalog of foods endangered by industrial agriculture and large-scale distribution. Reliable resource for information about heirloom and heritage varieties of plants and animals.

Equipment

Lodge Manufacturing Company
www.LodgeMfg.com
423-837-7181
Tennessee-based foundry making top-quality cast-iron cookware since 1896.

Sur la Table
www.SurLaTable.com
800-243-0852
Offers a good selection of roasting pans, gratin dishes, skillets, baking sheets, roasting racks, thermometers, and other cookware.

ThermoWorks
www.ThermoWorks.com
800-393-6434
Source for the Thermapen, a super-fast instant-read thermometer.

Williams-Sonoma
www.Williams-Sonoma.com
877-812-6235
Carries a good selection of roasting pans, gratin dishes, skillets, baking sheets, roasting racks, thermometers, and other cookware.

BIBLIOGRAPHY

Aidells, Bruce, and Denis Kelly. *The Complete Meat Cookbook*. Boston: Houghton Mifflin, 1998.

Aidells, Bruce, with Lisa Weiss. *Bruce Aidells's Complete Book of Pork*. New York: HarperCollins, 2004.

Allen, Darina. *Forgotten Skills of Cooking*. London: Kyle, 2010.

Bayless, Rick, with Deann Groen Bayless and JeanMarie Brownson. *Rick Bayless's Mexican Kitchen*. New York: Scribner, 1996.

Beard, James. *American Cookery*. Boston: Little, Brown, 1972.

Child, Julia. *The Way to Cook*. New York: Knopf, 1989.

The Cook's Illustrated Complete Book of Poultry. New York: Clarkson Potter, 1999.

Cost, Bruce. *Asian Ingredients*. New York: William Morrow, 2000.

David, Elizabeth. *Italian Food*. New York: Harper & Row, 1987.

Davidson, Alan. *The Oxford Companion to Food*. Oxford University Press, 1999.

Davis, Adelle. *Let's Cook It Right*. New York: Harcourt Brace, 1947.

Fearnley-Whittingstall, Hugh. *The River Cottage Meat Book*. Berkeley: Ten Speed, 2007.

_____. *The River Cottage Year*. London: Hodder and Stoughton, 2003.

Field, Michael. *Michael Field's Cooking School*. New York: M. Barrows, 1965.

Finamore, Roy. *Tasty*. Boston: Houghton Mifflin, 2006.

Goin, Suzanne, with Teri Gelber. *Sunday Suppers at Lucques*. New York: Knopf, 2005.

Goldstein, Joyce. *Italian Slow and Savory*. San Francisco: Chronicle, 2004.

Green, Aliza. *Field Guide to Produce*. Philadelphia: Quirk, 2004.

Greenberg, Paul. *Four Fish: The Future of the Last Wild Food*. New York: Penguin, 2010.

Gunst, Kathy. *Roasting*. New York: Wiley, 1995.

Hartley, Dorothy. *Food in England*. Guernsey: Guernsey Press, 1985.

Hazan, Marcella. *Essentials of Classic Italian Cooking*. New York: Macmillan, 1995.

Hemphill, Ian. *The Spice and Herb Bible*. Toronto: Robert Rose, 2006.

Henderson, Fergus. *The Whole Beast*. New York: Ecco, 2004.

Hopkinson, Simon, with Lindsey Bareham. *Roast Chicken and Other Stories*. New York: Hyperion, 1994.

Jenkins, Nancy Harmon. *The Essential Mediterranean*. New York: William Morrow, 2003.

Kafka, Barbara. *Roasting: A Simple Art*. New York: William Morrow, 1995.

Kamman, Madeleine. *The New Making of a Cook*. New York: William Morrow, 1997.

Krasner, Deborah. *Good Meat*. New York: Stewart, Tabori & Chang, 2010.

Larousse Gastronomique. Paris: Librarie Larousse, 1984 (Robert J. Courtine, editor; Prosper Montagné, author).

Link, Donald, with Paula Disbrowe. *Real Cajun*. New York: Clarkson Potter, 2009.

Madison, Deborah. *Vegetarian Cooking for Everyone*. New York: Broadway Books, 1997.

Malouf, Greg, and Lucy Malouf. *Artichoke to Za'atar*. Berkeley: University of California Press, 2008.

McGee, Harold. *On Food and Cooking*. New York: Scribner, 1984.

Moonen, Rick, and Roy Finamore. *Fish Without a Doubt*. Boston: Houghton Mifflin Harcourt, 2008.

Olney, Richard. *Lulu's Provençal Table*. New York: HarperCollins, 1994.

Olney, Richard, chief series consultant. *Beef & Veal*. The Good Cook. Alexandria, Va.: Time-Life, 1978.

_____ . *Lamb*. The Good Cook. Alexandria, Va.: Time-Life, 1981.

_____. *Pork*. The Good Cook. Alexandria, Va.: Time-Life, 1979.

_____. *Poultry*. The Good Cook. Alexandria, Va.: Time-Life, 1978.

Parsons, Russ. *How to Pick a Peach*. Boston, Houghton Mifflin Harcourt, 2007.

Peterson, James. *Cooking*. Berkeley: Ten Speed, 2007.

_____. *The Duck Cookbook*. New York: Stewart, Tabori & Chang, 2003.

_____. *Fish & Shellfish*. New York: William Morrow, 1996.

_____. *Meat*. Berkeley: Ten Speed, 2010.

_____. *Vegetables*. New York: William Morrow, 1998.

Rice, Bill. *Steak Lover's Cookbook*. New York: Workman, 1997.

Roden, Claudia. *The Good Food of Italy*. New York: Knopf, 1990.

Rodgers, Judy. *The Zuni Café Cookbook*. New York: W. W. Norton, 2002.

Rubel, William. *The Magic of Fire: Hearth Cooking*. Berkeley: Ten Speed, 2001.

Sahni, Julie. *Classic Indian Cooking*. New York: William Morrow, 1980.

Schlesinger, Christopher, and John Willoughby. *How to Cook Meat*. New York: William Morrow, 2000.

Schneider, Elizabeth. *Vegetables from Amaranth to Zucchini*. New York: William Morrow, 2001.

Steaks, Chops, Roasts and Ribs. Brookline, Mass: America's Test Kitchen, 2004.

Waters, Alice. *The Art of Simple Food*. New York: Clarkson Potter, 2007.

Weinzweig, Ari. *Zingerman's Guide to Good Eating*. Boston: Houghton Mifflin, 2003.

Willan, Anne. *La Varenne Pratique*. New York: Clarkson Potter, 1989.

_____. *Great Cooks and Their Recipes*. London: McGraw-Hill, 1977.

Wolfert, Paula. *Couscous and other Good Food from Morocco*. New York: Harper & Row, 1973.

ACKNOWLEDGMENTS

BEFORE I SALUTE THE GENEROUS AND TALENTED PEOPLE WHO DIRECTLY CONTRIBUTED TO THIS BOOK, I OFFER AN OPEN-ARMED "THANK YOU!" TO my amazing family and many wonderful friends. When it comes to naming names, there's not room to list the multitude who helped me to keep my head on straight and to remember what really matters, but their support and love run between the lines of every page of this book.

Much of my inspiration and determination came from colleagues, mentors, and friends whose composite knowledge and goodness is staggering. In particular, I extend a sincere note of gratitude to Jody Adams, Lex Alexander, Toni Allegra, Todd Coleman, Annie Copps, Kate Hays, Martha Holmberg, Susie Middleton, Maura O'Sullivan, Randall Price, Andrea Reusing, Gérard Rubaud, Robin Schempp, Heidi Swanson, Ari Weinzweig, Anne Willan, and Daphne Zepos. In addition, I owe special thanks to Fran McCullough for her editorial insights and contagious good cheer; Paula Wolfert for straightening me out on Marash pepper; and Leslie Zemsky for her gracious hospitality and indefatigable enthusiasm.

I hardly know where to begin to thank Roy Finamore. He's the first friend I call when I am completely flummoxed or frustrated in the kitchen or at the keyboard, and he's always there to talk me down, proffer smart advice, and get me back on track. His generosity and creativity are unmatched. The fact that Roy is both an exceptional cook *and* a brilliant editor means I lean on him more than is probably fair, but I'd be lost without him.

My heroes are the many accomplished authors whose works I rely on every day, and I like to think I am a better cook and writer for having read their books. The titles that have most influenced this book appear in the bibliography (page 542), but a few deserve distinction. I learned the gospel of presalting protein (along with other essential kitchen lessons) from Judy Rodgers—although she communicates it much more eloquently than I ever will. I turn to Bruce Aidells's books again and again for his expert take on all things meat, and I am constantly impressed and humbled by his depth of knowledge. And finally, I bow down to Hugh-Fearnley Whittingstall for his passion, commitment, and intelligence; his "Meat Manifesto" should be required reading for every meat-eater.

A cook can only be as good as her ingredients, and for that, I am hugely grateful to the farmers and producers here in Vermont and beyond who take pains to raise delicious and healthful foods for us to eat. And to the real butchers I know, including Shawn Badger, Franck Pace, Cole Ward, and Doug Wilson. I wish there were more like you.

I am indebted to the cadre of good (and careful) cooks who applied their talents and critical palates to testing my recipes. Your efforts allow me to sleep at night. They are Polly Alexander, Kate Hays, Allison Ehri Kreitler, Steven Lewis, Meg Suzuki, and Kate Thomas. An extra thanks to those good-humored testers who also kept me company in my kitchen: Kate Elderkin, Millissa Frost, and Sarah Mitchell Duddy.

Joanne Smart's editorial prowess and clear-sightedness helped guide me through the overwhelming process of wrangling my recipes and text into a manageable manuscript. Her ability to get what I was trying to say along with her genial optimism were a godsend. I also raise a glass to Tim Gaiser for his pitch-perfect wine and beer pairings.

Effusive thanks go to everyone involved in creating the gorgeous photographs. I can't imagine a more adept or more fun team than the one led by Quentin Bacon behind the camera, Michael Pedersen behind the stove, and Deb Donahue in charge of props. Thanks also to Tracy Keshani, Lauren Volo, Margaret Ward, and everyone at Good Light Studio. And to George Restrepo for pulling it all together into a beautifully designed book.

I remain deeply grateful to my agent, Doe Coover, who so skillfully navigated the side of publishing that I have yet to understand and who took such good care of me in the process. I count myself very fortunate to be published by W. W. Norton, and I remain in awe of the amount of attention they extended in shepherding this book from inception to the marketplace. In particular Louise Brockett, Sue Carlson, Julia Druskin, Ingsu Liu, Erin Lovett, Jeannie Luciano, Drake McFeely, Nancy Palmquist, Bill Rusin, Susan Sanfrey, and Melanie Tortoroli. Thanks go to Liz Duvall for her careful and humane copyediting. And I will be forever grateful to my editor, Maria Guarnaschelli, for throwing her heart, soul, and genius into the work. She was with me every step of the way, pushing when I needed a push, encouraging when I needed a boost, and never, ever giving up or taking the easy way out.

And lastly, my pillars. Elizabeth, for being my friend, my confidant, my cheerleader, and, most of all, just the best damn sister a girl could have. And Mark, again, for everything and for always.

INDEX

Note: Page numbers in **boldface** refer to recipes themselves; page numbers in *italics* refer to photographs.